RED SCARE

D1476310

Regin Schmidt

RED SCARE

FBI
and the Origins of Anticommunism
in the United States, 1919-1943

MUSEUM TUSCULANUM PRESS
UNIVERSITY OF COPENHAGEN
2000

Regin Schmidt: Red Scare
© Museum Tusculanum Press 2000
English revision by Joyce Kling
Composition by Ole Klitgaard
Cover design by Henrik Maribo Pedersen
Printed in Denmark by Narayana Press, Gylling

ISBN 87 7289 581 0

Supervisors:
Inga Floto and Niels Bjerre-Poulsen

Cover:
The official seal of the Federal Bureau of Investigation, and
Report by Special Agent C.W. Hughes on informant H-71's observations
of the activities of the syndicalistic Industrial Workers of the World
(Record Group 65, National Archives).

This book is published with the support of
The Danish Research Council for the Humanities
and
Unibank-fonden

Museum Tusculanum Press
University of Copenhagen
Njalsgade 92
DK-2300 Copenhagen S
Denmark
www.mtp.dk

Contents

Acknowledgements

Researching and writing this book was most of the time a lonely pursuit. Yet, the task was lightened by the kindness and support shown by numerous individuals and institutions. It is indeed a pleasure to remember and acknowledge the many who made this reconstruction of the evolution of the FBI's political role a possibility and a distinct pleasure.

I received generous financial assistance from several institutions. A graduate scholarship at the Department of History, University of Copenhagen, in 1992 to 1995 enabled me to complete my Ph.D. dissertation, on which this book is based. A grant from the Fulbright Society financed a position as Visiting Researcher at Georgetown University in 1992 to 1993, which enabled me to conduct research into the FBI records at the National Archives in Washington, DC. Assistance from the Knud Højgaard Fond made it possible to visit a number of other archives and universities throughout the United States. The publication of this book is financed by a grant from the Danish Research Council for the Humanities.

Visiting the United States, one is always struck by the helpfulness and aid given by the enthusiastic and efficient archivists and librarians everywhere. In particular, I would like to thank the following for assisting me during my visits to archives and libraries: John K. Vandereedt of the Civil Reference Branch, National Archives, Washington, DC; James H. Hutson of the Manuscript Division, Library of Congress, Washington, DC; the staff of the Research Unit, Office of Public Affairs, Federal Bureau of Investigation, Washington, DC; Phillip M. Runkel of the Marquette University Archives, Milwaukee, Wisconsin; Dwight Miller of the Herbert Hoover Library, West Branch, Iowa; Raymond Teichman of the Franklin D. Roosevelt Library, Hyde Park, New York; and Gregory A. Johnson of the Alderman Library, University of Virginia, Charlottesville, Virginia.

I would also like to thank the following archivists and librarians for answering my inquiries and for locating information: Louise T. Jones of The Historical Society of Pennsylvania, Philadelphia, Pennsylvania; Raymond W. Smock, Office of the Historian, U.S. House of Representatives, Washington, DC; Ellie Arguimbau, Montana Historical Society, Helena, Montana; Richard A. Shrader of the Manuscripts Department, University of North Carolina at Chapel Hill; Michael

Kohl of the University Libraries, Clemson University, Clemson, South Carolina; Ruth Anderson of the Minnesota Historical Society, St. Paul, Minnesota; Valerie Wingfield of the Rare Books and Manuscripts Division, The New York Public Library, New York; Gary Lundell of the Manuscripts and University Archives, University of Washington, Seattle, Washington; James D. Folts of the New York State Archives, Albany, New York; Karen S. Campbell of the Guy W. Bailey/ David W. Howe Library, The University of Vermont, Burlington, Vermont; Nancy Bartlett of Bentley Historical Library, University of Michigan, Ann Arbor, Michigan; and Dana Moffitt of the George E. Allen Library, Booneville, Mississippi.

In particular, I would like to thank Robert Self of Seattle, Washington, who not only researched the Poindexter papers at the University of Washington but also wrote a report on his findings.

Georgetown University, Washington, DC, provided the best possible surroundings and stimulating atmosphere during my nine months there as a Visiting Scholar, when I did the bulk of my archival research. I would like to thank Professor Ronald Johnson, College of Arts and Sciences, for making my stay so rewarding and for generously inviting me to his family's Thanksgiving dinner. The International Student House in Washington, DC, provided a roof over my head, meals on my table and many good friends. The Department of History, University of Copenhagen, provided an office, a computer and an inspiring intellectual forum.

Several individuals went above and beyond the call of duty in their assistance and support. Professor Inga Floto, Department of History, University of Copenhagen, initially stirred my interest in American history. She was always available for advice and encouraged me with her enthusiasm and support. Associate Professor Niels Thorsen, Department of English, University of Copenhagen, initially suggested the topic of FBI's political role and never failed to propose new avenues of inquiry. Associate Professor Niels Bjerre-Poulsen, Department of English at the Copenhagen Business School, generously agreed to read the manuscript and made several important comments, all of which helped to improve it. Joyce Kling of The Language Center, Copenhagen Business School, fought heroically to clean the text of grammatical errors. Mogens Pelt, Ph. D., recommended the manuscript to Museum Tusculanum Press, where Marianne Alenius and her merry crew guided the book toward publication with enthusiasm and professionalism. Finally, I want to thank Øyvind Søltoft for his friendship and for reminding me that there is a world outside the J. Edgar Hoover FBI Building.

Chapter 1

Introduction
The FBI and the Politics of Anticommunism

The subject of the following work is the development and institutionalization of the surveillance of political activities by the Federal Bureau
of Investigation during its formative years between 1919 and 1943.
Traditionally, historical research into modern American anticommunism, especially the era of McCarthyism in the 1950s, has tended to
explain the recurrent outbreaks of political intolerance and repression
as the result of an irrational and paranoid mass movement suffering
from "status anxiety," or as the product of partisan politics or the
activities of demagogues, most notably Senator Joseph McCarthy.
However, as a result of the revelations in the wake of the Watergate
scandals about the systematic abuses by the US intelligence community and because of the increased access to government files following
the strengthening of the Freedom of Information Act in 1974,
historians have become aware of the institutional and bureaucratic
factors behind the outbreaks of political intolerance.[1] Much of this
recent research has emphasized the decisive role played by the FBI in
the formulation of anticommunist politics. As one historian noted
when the FBI files began to become available to scholars as the result
of FOIA requests, "The political activities of FBI officials were
probably much more pervasive than is generally known and ...
historians still have a great deal to examine." He added that several
aspects of the recent anticommunist movement "need to be re-
written."[2]

---

[1]Richard M. Fried has noted that "this institutional or sectoral approach to McCarthyism
constitutes an important trend in recent scholarship" (Richard M. Fried, *Nightmare in Red. The
McCarthy Era in Perspective* (New York, 1990), 226). See also, M. J. Heale, *American Anti-
Communism. Combating the Enemy Within, 1830-1970* (Baltimore, 1990).
[2]Kenneth O'Reilly, *Hoover and the Un-Americans, The FBI, HUAC, and the Red Menace*
(Philadelphia, 1983), xi. Ellen Schrecker has suggested, based on recently opened FBI files
from the Cold War years, that McCarthyism should properly be renamed "Hooverism"
because of the pivotal role played by the Bureau in creating the anticommunist consensus:
"For the FBI was the bureaucratic heart of the McCarthy era" (Ellen Schrecker, *Many Are the
Crimes. McCarthyism in America* (Boston, 1998), 203).

Nevertheless, almost all of this research into the political activities of the FBI has taken its lead from the Senate Select Committee to Study Governmental Operations with Respect to Intelligence Activities, popularly known as the Church Committee, which during 1974-76 held hearings and published a number of reports on the federal intelligence agencies. However, the committee limited its inquiry to the period following 1936, when President Franklin D. Roosevelt secretly authorized the FBI to gather political intelligence on Fascist and Communist activities in the US.[3] Most accounts have relied heavily on the source material published by the committee and have accordingly focused on the post-1936 era and have generally explained the FBI's political surveillance as a result of the tensions brought on by the Cold War, the centralization of power in the "Imperial Presidency" and the establishment of the National Security State. For example, Athan Theoharis began his study of the FBI in 1936 "because FBI investigations of political activities were only authorized in August 1936 by Franklin Roosevelt's verbal order." He pointed to the powerful presidency, supported by both Democrats and Republicans, and the impact of the Cold War and McCarthyism as the decisive causes for the FBI's political role.[4]

Similarly, Morton Halperin's analysis of the federal intelligence agencies' political activities was primarily a popularization of the Church Committee's findings and he concluded that political surveillance was a function of international crises: "When confronted by the specter of war, the executive branch has called on the Bureau to conduct intelligence and counterintelligence operations in the United States. FBI intelligence has its roots in war and its authority to engage in intelligence activity derives not from statutes but from executive orders and instructions issued during wartime emergency."[5]

---

[3]US Congress, Senate, Select Committee to Study Governmental Operations with Respect to Intelligence Activities, 94th. Cong., 1st. Sess., *Hearings, Vol. 6, Federal Bureau of Investigation* (Washington, DC, 1976); ibid., 94th. Cong., 2nd. Sess., *Supplementary Detailed Staff Reports on Intelligence Activities and the Rights of Americans, Final Report, Books III and VI* (Washington, DC, 1976).

[4]Athan Theoharis, *Spying on Americans. Political Surveillance From Hoover to the Huston Plan* (Philadelphia, 1978), xi, 3-12, 229-234. For a similar emphasis on the Cold War, see, Athan Theoharis (ed.), *From the Secret Files of J. Edgar Hoover* (Chicago, 1991); Athan Theoharis (ed.), *Beyond the Hiss Case: The FBI, Congress, and the Cold War* (Philadelphia, 1982); Pat Watters & Stephen Gillers (eds.), *Investigating the FBI* (New York (1973), 1974).

[5]Morton Halperin (ed.), *The Lawless State. The Crimes of the U.S. Intelligence Agencies* (Harmondsworth, 1977), 93-94. For similar explanations, see, Natalie Robins, *Alien Ink. The FBI's War on the Freedom of Expression* (New York, 1992), 16-17; William W. Keller, *The Liberals and J. Edgar Hoover. Rise and Fall of a Domestic Intelligence State* (Princeton, N.J., 1989).

In line with this emphasis on the Cold War, a number of studies have analyzed various aspects of the FBI's political activities during this period, such as the use of aggressive methods against radicals, the Bureau's cooperation with the House Un-American Activities Committee, its targeting of the civil rights movement, and its involvement in various famous spy cases.[6]

A few studies have attempted to place the FBI's political role in a larger context and explained it in relation to the deeper beliefs and values of the American political culture. Frank Donner has argued that political surveillance must be understood as a reflection of "the depth and pervasiveness of the fear of communism" dominating the political culture to the extent of becoming "a mania that mobilizes the entire society in a comprehensive *kulturkampf*." According to Donner, this "American obsession with subversive conspiracies" betrays an underlying anxiety and insecurity about values and identities which is rooted in the American mobility and which leaves only economic wealth as a measure of status: "A resultant isolation and insecurity force a quest for selfhood in the national state, anxiety about an imperiled heritage, and aggression against those who reject or question it."[7] Similarily, David Garrow has characterized the FBI as a representative institution, reflecting such widely shared attitudes as nativism, xenophobia and ethnocentrism.[8] Both Donner and Garrow are clearly inspired by Richard Hofstadter's thesis about the "paranoid style," according to which irrational conspiracy theories are "deeply rooted" in the American society and they are not something the political leaders "can altogether create or manipulate, but something that they must cope with."[9] However, although both studies are focused on the post-World War II period, Donner, after a short introductory description of the development of federal political surveillance from World War I, follows the Church Committee and concentrates on the "intelligence upsurge" of the sixties, while Garrow's work is a detailed analysis of the FBI campaign against Martin Luther King, Jr. Thus, neither study throws

---

[6]For example, Kathy Perkus (ed.), *COINTELPRO. The FBI's Secret War on Political Freedom* (New York, 1976); O'Reilly, *Hoover and the Un-Americans;* Kenneth O'Reilly, *"Racial Matters". The FBI's Secret File on Black America 1960-72* (New York (1989), 1991); Allen Weinstein, *Perjury. The Hiss-Chambers Case* (New York (1978), 1979); Ronald Radosh and Joyce Milton, *The Rosenberg File. A Search for the Truth* (London, 1983).

[7]Frank Donner, *The Age of Surveillance. The Aims and Methods of America's Political Intelligence System* (New York, 1980), 9-10.

[8]David Garrow, *The FBI and Martin Luther King. From "Solo" to Memphis* (New York, 1981), 208-213.

[9]Richard Hofstadter, *The Paranoid Style in American Politics and Other Essays* (Chicago (1965), 1979), x; see also, David Brion Davis (ed.), *The Fear of Conspiracy. Images of Un-American Subversion From the Revolution to the Present* (Ithaca, N.Y., 1971), xviii-xxix, 1, 205, 208.

11

any new light on the specific reasons for the early establishment of the Bureau's political role.

Finally, recent scholarship has tended to personify and to a considerable extent explain the growth of the FBI's power in the person of J. Edgar Hoover, the Bureau's legendary director for 48 years (1924-72) and possibly the longest serving and most powerful non-elected government official in American history. It is significant that while no comprehensive history of the FBI has been written during the last decades, no less than four major biographies have been published. And while they have to some extent attempted to put Hoover into context with the larger social, economic, and political forces of his time, they nevertheless leave the general impression that the political power of the FBI was one man's work. Two of the biographies, both authored by journalists, contribute little to our understanding of the FBI's political role. Curt Gentry's *J. Edgar Hoover. The Man and the Secrets* is mainly a chronological account, based on secondary sources and a few published FBI documents. No serious attempt is made to find a deeper explanation of why Hoover and the Bureau became so politically powerful.[10] Anthony Summers' *Official and Confidential. The Secret Life of J. Edgar Hoover*, relies mainly on rumors, hearsay and witnesses of dubious reliability to advance the thesis that Hoover was blackmailed by the mafia to leave organized crime in peace.[11] Both of these accounts treat the FBI's political surveillance superficially and isolated from the larger political context. They concentrate on the more sensational and celebrated cases without offering a satisfying and thorough explanation. More important are the two other biographies by historians, Richard Gid Powers' *Secrecy and Power. The Life of J. Edgar Hoover* and Athan Theoharis and John Stuart Cox' *The Boss. J. Edgar Hoover and the Great American Inquisition*, which will be discussed in more detail below. Like the rest of the recent literature on the FBI, however, these two biographies also concentrate on the Cold War era.[12]

Despite their different emphases and differing explanations, most of the recent literature on the political activities of the FBI shares a

---

[10]Curt Gentry, *J. Edgar Hoover. The Man and the Secrets* (New York, 1991); for criticism, see Michael Wreszin, "'Gee But I'd Like to Be a G-Man'," *Reviews in American History*, Vol. 20, No. 2 (June 1992), 258-263; Richard Gid Powers, "Taking Hoover Out of Context," *The New Leader*, Vol. LXXV, No. 2 (February 10-24, 1992), 19-20.

[11]Anthony Summers, *Official and Confidential. The Secret Life of J. Edgar Hoover* (New York, 1993); for critique, see Stephen Ambrose, "The Case Against Hoover," *The Washington Post*, February 21, 1993; Peter Maas, "Setting the Record Straight," *Esquire*, May 1993, 56-58.

[12]Richard Gid Powers, *Secrecy and Power. The Life of J. Edgar Hoover* (New York, 1987); Athan Theoharis & John Stuart Cox, *The Boss. J. Edgar Hoover and the Great American Inquisition* (New York (1988), 1990).

common focus on the Cold War. Thereby, they ignore the possibility of continuity and give the impression that the activities were an aberration from the normal workings of the American political system.They indicate that, if the Bureau played a political role before the Cold War, it was somehow of limited consequences. In short, the implicit view of most recent research into the political role of the FBI or Hoover seems to be that the early Bureau of Investigation, before it became the famous crime-busting and Communist-hunting FBI of the 1930s, was a more or less obscure organization with limited political influence. As summed up by Kenneth O'Reilly, the Bureau's efforts to create an anticommunist opinion prior to the Cold War "were restrained and had limited success" and the Bureau itself was an "undisciplined, somewhat ineffectual, highly politicised" organization.[13]

However, there are several reasons for taking a closer look at the early political activities of the FBI. First of all, when the Cold War broke out in the latter half of the 1940s, the FBI's political surveillance was firmly institutionalized. Thus, if we intend to discover the deeper reasons for the Bureau's political role, it is necessary to analyze how this role developed and was established during its formative years before World War II. The Cold War, the Imperial Presidency and the National Security State, as well as the driving force of Hoover himself, undoubtedly added to and increased the Bureau's influence, but the Bureau was deeply involved in political activities as early as the Red Scare 1919-20, before Hoover became director. This indicates that the fundamental explanation must be found in the deeper and long-term political structures and institutions.

Secondly, most FBI files from 1922 until today are still classified and only made public in response to FOIA requests. This means that only a number of scattered case files are available for research and that substantial portions of this material concerning the identity of sources and informers, investigative techniques, personal information and national security are still withheld. The result is substantial lagoons in our knowledge, which makes it nearly impossible to piece together a comprehensive picture of the full extent of the FBI's political activities after 1922. In contrast, the entire Bureau archive from its founding in 1908 until 1922 has been declassified and turned over to the National Archives, presenting a unique opportunity to study without restrictions the development and growth of federal political surveillance, including the Bureau's role in the first nationwide Red Scare of 1919-20.

---

[13]O'Reilly, *Hoover and the Un-Americans*, 5, 17.

Theories on the Development of the FBI's Political Role

The literature, which deals with the development of the FBI's political surveillance before World War II, may be divided into three categories: Early political and journalistic polemics, studies focusing on the political and cultural environment, and a few studies from the 1970s and 1980s which focus on the FBI's bureaucratic interests and ambitions.

Max Lowenthal and Fred Cook's histories of the FBI were journalistic exposés and harshly critical treatments. They argued that the Bureau had violated the rights of suspected subversives during the Palmer raids, had conducted political espionage during the Harding administration, and that its heralded defense of civil rights and war on organized crime were much overrated.[14] However, both studies were based entirely on public sources, they read more like a prosecutor's brief against the FBI than as well-balanced treatments, and they never developed a deeper explanation of the Bureau's political role.

A number of historians have explained the evolving political role of the FBI as a result of popular hysteria, widespread political intolerance and a tradition of nativism. In the authorized history of the FBI, Don Whitehead described how the fledgling Bureau reacted during the Red Scare to a combination of public fear, anarchist bombings, and Communist activities.[15] Studies of the Red Scare have generally portrayed it as a period of popular anticommunist hysteria, which pushed a somewhat reluctant Department of Justice into arresting and deporting alien radicals.[16] Richard Gid Powers has argued that the political activities of the FBI have been an expression of "symbolic politics." He argued that the political leaders in times of crisis deployed the FBI as a symbolic gesture against the "public enemy" of the moment, such as gangsters, German spies or Communists, in order to prove their leadership and calm the public. Thus, the Bureau's political surveillance was a reaction to deeper public fears, the Red Scare was "a capitulation to public hysteria by the government," and the FBI's

---

[14]Max Lowenthal, *The Federal Bureau of Investigation* (New York, 1950); Fred Cook, *The FBI Nobody Knows* (New York, 1964).

[15]Don Whitehead, *The FBI Story. A Report to the People* (New York, 1956), quotes from pp. 13 and 15.

[16]Robert K. Murray, *Red Scare. A Study in National Hysteria, 1919-1920* (New York (1955), 1964); John Higham, *Strangers in the Land. Patterns of American Nativism 1860-1925* (New Brunswick, N.J., 1955); Stanley Coben, *A. Mitchell Palmer. Politician* (New York, 1963); John M. Blum, "Nativism, Anti-Radicalism and the Foreign Scare, 1917-1920," *The Midwest Journal*, Vol. III, No. 1 (Winter 1950-51), 46-53; Stanley Coben, "A Study in Nativism: The American Red Scare of 1919-20," *Political Science Quarterly*, Vol. LXXIX, No. 1 (March 1964), 52-75.

fundamental function was "to calm the public by fighting crime in whatever symbolic form the popular mind might imagine it."[17]

These "environmental" explanations beg a number of questions: Did a widespread and popular anticommunist hysteria exist after World War I? Did it pressure the FBI into suppressing radical activities? Did the Wilson administration and the federal security bureaucracies have their own, independent anticommunist interests and objectives? Did the federal authorities react to events or did they also try to influence the opinion? Did the FBI act before the outbreak of the alleged hysteria? And was the Bureau's political involvement more extensive than it has been assumed?

In contrast to the "environmental" interpretation, and in line with the general trend of recent anticommunism research, a few authors have focused more on the institutional and bureaucratic factors behind the development of the early FBI political surveillance. A fore-runner of this school was William Preston, Jr., who used the files of the Bureau of Immigration to trace the development of federal deportation policies and practices in the decades before the Palmer raids. According to Preston, the Red Scare was not a dramatic aberration in American politics, but rather the logical consequence of decades of growing federal intolerance against alien radicals. This intolerance had its roots in the American nativistic tradition and was promoted by local elites, business groups and patriots. However, many important decisions were made by increasingly powerful federal officials, who by the end of World War I had developed their own independent interest in internal security matters; according to Preston, "as public servants these officials felt duty-bound to promote just such a crusade," which eventually led to the Palmer raids.[18] Although Preston focused on the Immigration Bureau's attack on the Industrial Workers of the World and did not specifically deal with the FBI's operations, his study was groundbreaking in pointing to the importance and influence wielded by the federal security bureaucracy as early as the first Red Scare and to the wealth of information to be found in the files of federal agencies.

Michal R. Belknap also focused on "the extent to which bureaucratic considerations and personal ambition can influence the scope and

[17]Richard Gid Powers, *G-Men. Hoover's FBI in American Popular Culture* (Carbondale, Ill., 1983), 25-29, quotes from pp. 27 and 26; also, Powers, *Secrecy and Power*, esp chapter 5.
[18]William Preston, Jr., *Aliens and Dissenters. Federal Suppression of Radicals, 1903-1933* (New York (1963), 1966), 192-193.

intensity of government attacks upon dissent."[19] He explained the Bureau's evolving political activities between 1917 and 1925 as the result of the desire of ambitious bureaucrats to increase their appropriations and to justify the necessity of their operations; thus, "those who do the dirty work of repression are basically bureaucrats whose primary concerns are advancing their careers and promoting the interests of their agencies."[20] Although Belknap did not have access to the files of the early Bureau and based his interpretation on previous works and other secondary sources, he did in line with Preston point out the important role played by federal security agencies and aggressive federal officials in promoting an anti-radical agenda instead of simply reacting to outside pressures.

Several historians have developed this thesis about bureaucratic self-interest and have argued that the Bureau by the early 1920s was, in effect, out of political control. David Williams argued that the Bureau came to exercise surveillance authority as a result of the break-down of the political control exercised by all branches of government, which found "anti-crime and anti-radical sloganeering more attractive" than the protection of civil liberties. On a deeper level Williams attributed the FBI's political role to the need of corporate capitalism to stabilize industrial relations and limit popular participation in the democratic process: "Political and economic leaders used the Bureau in an attempt to undermine popular support of reform and radical movements."[21] However, this is the only time Williams mentions this thesis and he never further substantiates it and, thus, it is left as an undocumented assertion. Perhaps the most important claim made by Williams is that the Bureau violated Attorney General Harlan F. Stone's ban in 1924 against the investigation of lawful political activities and without the knowledge of its superiors continued to collect political intelligence. This indicates that the Bureau as early as 1924 was out of political control and had achieved a high degree of autonomy. Says Williams: "beneath the facade of cooperation and obedience, the FBI persisted in old ways."[22]

[19]Michal R. Belknap, "The Mechanics of Repression: J. Edgar Hoover, The Bureau of Investigation and the Radicals 1917-1925," *Crime and Social Justice*, Vol. 7 (Spring-Summer 1977), 49.

[20]Ibid., 56.

[21]David Williams, *"Without Understanding": The FBI and Political Surveillance, 1908-41* (unpubl. Ph.D. Dissertation, University of New Hampshire, 1981), 2-3; see also, David Williams, "The Bureau of Investigation and its Critics, 1919-1921. The Origins of Federal Political Surveillance," *The Journal of American History*, Vol. 68, No. 3 (December 1983), 560-579.

[22]Ibid., 259; in general, 253-287.

This thesis about an early Bureau autonomy has been further developed by Athan Theoharis and John Stuart Cox. They made a detailed analysis of internal FBI documents from the period around 1924 and found that "Hoover shrewdly contrived a way to circumvent Stone's explicit ban" and continued to receive "an unbroken stream of reports about radical activities."[23] According to Theoharis and Cox, Hoover continued to receive political intelligence from a network of agents, various private sources and police informers and evaded effective control by classifying the reports of the Bureau investigations as information from confidential sources and filing them in parallel files. Thereby he effectively concealed them from outside control.[24] However, Theoharis and Cox' own material does not support these conclusions. Rather it indicates that only a few investigations were conducted after 1924 and that most of the political surveillance did in fact cease after Stone's ban.[25] Moreover, the authors seem to underestimate the extent of the Justice Department's knowledge about the Bureau's activities and the White House's use of the Bureau's political resources from Harding to FDR.

The most recent treatment of the early FBI is Theodore Kornweibel, Jr.'s *"Seeing Red." Federal Campaigns Against Black Militancy, 1919-1925*, which describes federal intelligence agencies, including the Bureau of Investigation (BI), and their surveillance of black protest during the Red Scare. Kornweibel argues that the intelligence community was used by the government, reflecting the prevailing racial attitudes among the white population, to suppress black militancy and maintain the existing racial hierarchy. Kornweibel also argues that federal surveillance of the black community had become so entrenched by 1924 that it continued despite Store's ban.[26] Although based on exhaustive use of the early BI files, the account is limited to the surveillance of a few prominent black leaders, organizations and magazines, and it does not fully explain the role of the modern state in containing political oppositional movements.

---

[23]Theoharis & Cox, 105.
[24]Ibid., 105-110.
[25]Samuel Walker, "The Boss as Bureaucrat," *Reviews in American History*, Vol. 16, No. 3 (September 1988), 462. Theoharis has also argued that Hoover misused President Roosevelt's instructions from 1936 to investigate Fascist and Communist activities to secretly establish a permanent political surveillance program on a far larger scale than envisioned by FDR (Athan Theoharis, "The FBI's Stretching of Presidential Directives, 1936-1953," *Political Science Quarterly*, Vol. 91, No. 4 (Winter 1976-77), 649-672; however, he has apparently later modified this argument in the light of new information which indicated that FDR was aware of the extent of the FBI activity (see, Theoharis & Cox, 171-181, 191-198, 215-223).
[26]Theodore Kornweibel, Jr., *"Seeing Red." Federal Campaigns Against Black Militancy, 1919-1925* (Bloomington and Indianapolis, 1998).

Consequently, this "bureaucratic autonomy" thesis leaves several important questions unanswered: To what extent did the political surveillance continue following Stone's ban in 1924? How much did the Justice Department, Congress and the president know about the activities? In particular, how close was the Bureau's relationship to the White House?

Moreover, these studies suffer from several weaknesses. First of all, since most of these studies were published, several important primary sources have become available, in particular the early FBI files. Even the most recent works, such as the Hoover biographies, have not made use of these files, possibly because they antedate Hoover's directorship. David Williams uses only a few, selected files for his study, and Theodore Kornweibel, Jr. uses only the files concerning black activists.[27] The view that the Bureau was out of political control has tended to downplay the role of government policies and has obscured the part played by the Bureau's political surveillance in the centralization of power in the modern federal state during the Progressive Era. Finally, as noted above, there are reasons for reevaluating whether the Bureau was, in fact, free of political control after 1924 and to ascertain more fully the possible interests and motives of the administrations in the 1920s and 1930s for employing the Bureau in political activities.

The Theses

It is the intention of the following work to explain the origins and development of the FBI's political role during its formative years from 1919 to 1943. 1919 has been chosen as the beginning because the Bureau had no established political function before World War I and its activities during the war were on an ad hoc basis and limited to the wartime emergency. However, with the outbreak of the Red Scare in 1919, the Bureau commenced the systematic surveillance of political activities which became a permanent part of the American political system. In the words of historian Robert K. Murray, "Certainly, the hunt for radicals during the 1919-20 period 'made' the Bureau of Investigation and started it on the road to becoming the famous FBI of the present day."[28] 1943 has been chosen as the end of the study

---

[27]A few case studies of various aspects of the Red Scare, based on the early Bureau records, have hinted at their potential research value, see, Peter H. Irons, "'Fighting Fair': Zechariah Chafee, Jr., the Department of Justice, and the 'Trial at the Harvard Club'," *Harvard Law Review*, Vol. 94, No. 6 (April 1981), 1205-1236; Robert A. Hill, "'The Foremost Radical Among His Race': Marcus Garvey and the Black Scare, 1918-1921," *Prologue*, Vol. 16, No. 4 (Winter 1984), 215-231; Paul Avrich, *Sacco and Vanzetti. The Anarchist Background* (Princeton, N.J., 1991).

[28]Murray, *Red Scare*, 193.

because the FBI's political role was firmly institutionalized at the time of World War II and because 1943 marked the establishment of the FBI's involvement in the federal loyalty program.

The major part of the study is concentrated on the Bureau's role during the Red Scare, 1919 to 1920. There are several reasons for focusing on the Red Scare. Since it was here that the FBI entered the domestic political scene, an understanding of the causes might contribute to explain the FBI's political role in general. The Red Scare was the first serious outbreak of anticommunist or anti-radical intolerance and repression and an analysis of its causes might likewise aid in an understanding of anticommunism in American history. It may also help to put the phenomenon of McCarthyism in perspective. Moreover, the existing explanation that the Red Scare was caused by an irrational, mass-based hysteria has never been seriously challenged but, as it will be argued, there are a number of reasons for questioning its validity. Finally, although ideally the subjects of historical research should not be determined by the availability of the sources, the Red Scare presents a unique opportunity for analyzing the Bureau's political activities without restrictions, since the only part of the FBI files, which have been opened in their entirety, is from the period 1908-22.

The analysis of the Bureau's role during the Red Scare is inspired by recent scholarship, which views anticommunism as the product primarily of the political system and of institutional factors rather than of a popular mass movement, and it will focus on four main questions: the longer term interests and policies of the federal government; the more short-term policies and motives of the Wilson administration and Justice Department and Bureau of Investigation officials; the Bureau's relationship to what might be termed expressions of organized opinion such as interest groups, local authorities and Congress; and, finally, the nature of the Bureau's role in connection with the race riots, national strikes and the Palmer raids. A major question here is whether the Bureau's involvement was a reflection of outside pressure or internal interests.

In the final chapter, the FBI's continuing political activities after the Red Scare will be analyzed, albeit more briefly and summarily because they were not as extensive and intense as during the previous period. Also, the available source material is incomplete (only a limited number of FBI political files after 1922 have been declassified), and some aspects of the FBI's activities, such as its role during the Roosevelt administration, have been covered by a number of other works.[29] This part of the study is devoted to the question of whether the FBI was acting on its own initiative and free of effective political control after the Red Scare or whether the Bureau might be said to be an integrated part of the political system. In particular, its developing relationship to the White House will be examined and the motive and rationales of the administrations from Harding to Roosevelt for expanding the FBI's political role will be analyzed.

The following work has two main theses. First, in contrast to most recent scholarly research into the political activities of the FBI, it will be argued that the FBI's political role developed and was institutionalized long before the Cold War era, in fact, as early as the first Red Scare. The Bureau's political intelligence connection to the White House was not a product solely of the New Deal or the "Imperial Presidency" but began as early as 1921 and was used continually since by the executive in times of social unrest, domestic criticism or foreign crisis. Secondly, and more fundamentally, it will be argued that the basic explanation for the establishment of the Bureau's political role is not to be found in the demands of a public hysteria or an autonomous Bureau but in the centralization of power in the federal government. The role of the state from the Progressive Era was to support, stabilize and defend the emerging corporate order against "irresponsible" competition, economic waste and inefficiency as well as social unrest and threats against the status quo. Just as the mushrooming federal agencies, bureaus and commissions were employed to regulate the economy and ameliorate the most severe social consequences of industrialization, urbanization and immigration, the state during the first decades of the century increasingly used its resources to control, contain and, in times of crisis, to repress social unrest and political opposition. Thus, the institutionalization of the FBI's political activities from 1919 was at bottom a part of the federalization of social control in the form of political surveillance.

The Sources

The most important and valuable source of information concerning the early political activities of the Bureau, which in particular sheds new

---

[29]For example, Kenneth O'Reilly, "A New Deal for the FBI: The Roosevelt Administration, Crime Control and National Security," *The Journal of American History*, Vol. 69, No. 3 (December 1983), 638-658; O'Reilly, "The Roosevelt Administration and Black America: Federal Surveillance and Civil Rights During the New Deal and World War II Years," *Phylon*, Vol. XLVIII, No. 1 (March 1987), 12-25; O'Reilly, "The Roosevelt Administration and Legislative-Executive Conflict: The FBI vs. the Dies Committee," *Congress and the Presidency*, Vol. 10, No. 1 (Spring 1983), 79-83; Charles F. Croog, "FBI Political Surveillance and the Isolationist-Interventionist Debate, 1939-1941," *The Historian*, Vol. 54, No. 3 (Spring 1992), 441-458.

light on its role during the first Red Scare, consists of the investigative case files of the FBI from 1908 to 1922 in Record Group 65 in the National Archives. This collection, which has largely been ignored by historians since it was opened in 1977, comprises an estimated 3 million pages of memoranda, reports, telegrams, news clippings and so on, documenting the Bureau's various political activities during this period, and it has been characterized as "invaluable" for research into the evolution of federal intelligence or American radicalism.[30] However, it should be noted that research into these records entails a number of practical problems. The files were microfilmed in the early 1950s and the original files subsequently destroyed. The existing microfilm is of a very poor quality, often difficult to read, and especially some portions of the index and many carbon copies of outgoing letters are totally illegible. A number of files were clearly in disorder when microfilmed, making it a time-consuming if not impossible task to reconstruct the files; in a number of instances, the index contains erroneous references, and documents or files were missing in their entirety. Since the index contained references both to a main file on a subject and cross-references to other files, in which the subject is mentioned (so-called "see references"), a complete search regarding any subject proved to be an extremely slow process.

Apart from these practical problems, it is apparent that the collection does not contain the perhaps most sensitive political files. Some files, possibly because the investigation was still active, were transferred when the Bureau established a new filing system in late 1921 and are either part of Classification 61 (treason or misprision of treason), which can also be found in Record Group 65, or are still classified and maintained at the FBI today. Moreover, during a congressional investigation in 1924 it was revealed that the Bureau had maintained a confidential file, which contained the reports on sensitive political investigations, and when Hoover that same year became director he discovered "a so-called confidential file which was kept separate from the regular Bureau files."[31] The index contains a number of references to this confidential file, which has either been destroyed or merged with the existing FBI files.

---

[30]Lorin Lee Cary, "The Bureau of Investigation and Radicalism in Toledo, Ohio: 1918-1920," *Labor History*, Vol. 21, No. 3 (Summer 1980), 440; for the estimate, see Theodore Kornweibel, introduction to *Federal Surveillance of Afro-Americans 1917-25*, xxii (microfilm).
[31]J. Edgar Hoover, Memorandum for Mr. Martin, May 22, 1924, 62-1824-85, FBI/FOIA; US Congress, Senate, Select Committee on Investigation of the Attorney General, *Investigation of Hon. Harry M. Daugherty Formerly Attorney General of the United States, Hearings*, 66th. Cong., 1st. Sess. (Washington, DC, 1924), Vols. II, 1960, III, 2465-2467, 2540; also, Williams, *"Without Understanding,"* 16-17.

It should be stressed, then, in assessing the value of the early Bureau records that they are extremely difficult to work with and that they may not be complete. In addition it should be noted that many of the Bureau reports are often clearly prejudiced and tendentious in their findings about radical activities. However, while this makes them an unreliable source for such questions as to whether a particular organization had revolutionary designs or whether a strike or a riot was caused by subversive elements, it does make them a valuable source to the thinking and ideology of Bureau informers, agents and officials.[32]

In addition to the early Bureau records, which constitute the core of the following study, a number of FBI files, which have previously been released in response to FOIA requests and are available at the FBI headquarters in Washington, the Marquette University Archives in Milwaukee, Wisconsin, and have been published on microfilm editions, were consulted.[33] So were the files of other government agencies involved in the surveillance of political activities, such as the Department of Justice and the Military Intelligence Division.[34] A number of manuscript collections were also used to shed light on the political context in which the Bureau operated; for example, the papers of all the presidents and most of the Attorneys General as well as prominent administration officials and members of Congress were used.[35] A final major source concerning the Bureau's political activities consisted of various government publications, such as the transcripts of hearings, exhibits and reports of congressional investigations into the activities of the Department of Justice in 1920, 1921 and 1924 and of congressional anti-radical inquiries in 1919 and 1930-31 as well as the Bureau's annual appropriations hearings and the Attorney General's annual report to Congress on his Department's activities. Newspaper material was only used in a limited way, primarily to ascertain the

---

[32]For the problems connected with the use of FBI records, see, Steven Rosenwurm and Toni Gilpin, "The FBI and the Farm Equipment Workers: FBI Surveillance Records as a Source for CIO Union History," *Labor History*, Vol. 27, No. 4 (Fall 1986), 485-505; William C. Pratt, "Using FBI Records in Writing Regional Labor History," *Labor History*, Vol. 33, No. 4 (Fall 1992), 470-482.

[33]Since there was a backlog of some 9000 FOIA requests at the FBI and an estimated waiting period of 3 to 4 years in 1992, it was not considered practical to use the FOIA to obtain additional files; for the problems in connection with using the FOIA at the FBI, see Seth Rosenfeld, "Keeping Secrets," *Columbia Journalism Review*, Vol. 31 (March/April 1992), 14-15.

[34]Not all government records for the period are available for research. For example, the files of the Immigration Bureau are still classified and only accessible through the FOIA and a number of the Bureau's files concerning the Palmer raids have been lost (Williams, *"Without Understanding,"* 138, 156n47).

[35]Unfortunately, the papers of A. Mitchell Palmer, the Attorney General during the Red Scare were unavailable; according to his biographer, Palmer removed his most important records when he left the Justice Department in 1921 and they as well as his personal papers subsequently disappeared (Coben, *A. Mitchell Palmer*, xi).

extent of Bureau leaks or attempts to influence the opinion and most of this material was found in the Bureau files, in J. Edgar Hoover's scrapbooks which are deposited in the J. Edgar Hoover Memoriabilia Collection in Record Group 65 in the National Archives, or via *The New York Times Index.*

Chapter 2

The Origins of the Red Scare

1919: The Revolution That Never Was
The big Red Scare of 1919-20, a short-lived but intense period of political intolerance and repression of Communists, radicals and other non-conformists, was not an isolated incident but part of a larger American tradition. Alongside the celebrated tradition of political pluralism, diversity and civil liberties ran another, darker tradition of intolerance, enforced conformity and repression. As early as 1798, facing war with France and internal Jeffersonian opposition, the Federalists enacted and proceeded to use the Alien and Sedition Acts, which, among other things, enabled the government to deport treasonable aliens and to prosecute any anti-government activities and writings. In 1886 the nation experienced an anarchist scare following the Haymarket Square bomb, and during World War I pacifists, socialists and alleged German sympathizers were persecuted. All through the 19th century and until the New Deal in the 1930s, unions were regarded as criminal conspiracies by the courts and ruthlessly fought by the employers, while the black minority was oppressed and forced to live in a subjugated position in the South. Later, Japanese-Americans on the West coast were interned in concentration camps during World War II, suspected Communists were the targets of the McCarthy era and anti-war protesters harassed during the sixties and seventies.[1]

1919 was one of those dramatic years, like 1968, filled with unrest, protest and the clashing of social and political forces, when, for a short moment, the future of the nation seemed to hang in the balance.[2] The reasons for the unrest were many and complex. The almost instant reconversion from wartime production and government planning in November 1918 brought chaos to the economy. The rapid demobilization threw hundreds of thousand of veterans into the job market and

---

[1]For the intolerance in American history, see, John Higham, *Strangers in the Land. Patterns of American Nativism. 1860-1925* (New Brunswick, N.J., 1955); David H. Bennett, *The Party of Fear. The American Far Right from Nativism to the Militia Movement* (New York (1988), 1992); Seymour M. Lipset & Earl Raab, *The Politics of Unreason. Right-Wing Extremism in America, 1790-1970* (London (1970), 1971).
[2]The most comprehensive account is Murray, *Red Scare.*

led to growing unemployment. During 1919 and 1920 an average inflation of 15% ate into the salaries and savings of the middle and lower-middle classes. At the same time, groups which had subdued their narrow interests to the wartime national harmony now burst forward to claim their rewards. Organized labor, which had grown in strength under the government's recognition but had only obtained modest increases in wages, revolted and demanded that its right to collective bargaining be recognized in addition to higher wages and improved working conditions. The employers were determined to break the unions and reclaim complete control of the work place. As a result, a wave of strikes, more than 3,600 involving 4 million workers or a fourth of the work force, swept the country. Blacks had migrated in great numbers to the North during the war, gaining employment in the industry and serving in the army "to make the world safe for democracy." They began to demand equal rights and increasingly favored retaliation against injustices, while many whites were determined to beat back the blacks. Consequently, the summer of 1919 was marred by a wave of lynchings in the South and race riots in Northern cities. At the same time, the partisan political debate flared up with an aggressive Republican majority in Congress which insisted on weakening the Democratic President Woodrow Wilson and dismantling his domestic reforms, blocking the League of Nations and recapturing the White House in 1920.

Simultaneously with this unrest, radicalism was on the rise, seemingly threatening the existing order. The Bolshevik revolution in Russia in 1917 frightened many with its calls for the overthrow of established governments and the expropriation of private property, and the Brest-Litovsk peace accord with Germany seemed to make the Bolshevik regime a traitor to the Allied cause if not actually pro-German. Thus, anti-German passions of the war were therefore transferred to the Bolsheviks. In 1919 Communism threatened to spread to Western Europe with Red uprisings in Germany and Hungary, and in March the Third International was founded in Moscow to direct the worldwide revolution. In the US, radicals, already identified with disloyalty because of their opposition to the war, were vitalized by the apparent Bolshevik advances. During the spring and summer the Socialist Party split, and in September two Communist parties were established. The Communists were very active in their agitation and predicted optimistically the imminent overthrow of the capitalist classes and the government, followed by the establishment of Soviets. In fact, the would-be revolutionaries were few, numbering at most perhaps some 40,000, most were recent

European immigrants and already hopelessly isolated from American reality and traditions.

The Red Scare was, at bottom, an attack on these movements for social and political change and reform, particularly organized labor, blacks and radicals, by forces of the status quo. It might briefly be described as a breathtaking series of dramatic events, mainly between February 1919 and January 1920. On February 6, a general strike was called by the Seattle Central Labor Council in support of a shipyard strike. Although the strike was peaceful and had legitimate labor demands, it was branded a revolutionary uprising by employers and conservatives. Mayor Ole Hanson requested federal troops to break the strike, which lasted just five days. Immediately following the strike a Senate committee, the Overman Committee, which had originally been formed to investigate German propaganda in the US, shifted its focus and held public hearings on Bolshevik activities. It reveled in lurid accounts of Red atrocities and such topics as the alleged nationalization of women in Soviet Russia. Thus the Red menace was placed on the political agenda.

The spring of 1919 was marred by outbreaks of political violence. In late April, postal authorities intercepted 36 packages containing bombs addressed to prominent politicians, judges and other state officials. On the following May Day, radical demonstrations in several cities were attacked and broken up by mobs of patriotic soldiers and sailors. The violence culminated on June 2, when bombs exploded in eight cities, and among the intended victims was Attorney General A. Mitchell Palmer. In response, Palmer declared war on the radicals, warned of an imminent revolutionary uprising, and mobilized the Justice Department by establishing a special political section, the Radical Division, headed by a 24-year old ambitious bureaucrat, J. Edgar Hoover.

The social unrest, which had been building up since the Armistice, culminated during the summer and fall of 1919. During the summer, a number of particularly violent race riots engulfed cities throughout both the South and the North. 120 people were killed. The impact of the Red Scare became evident when Southern politicians and the authorities claimed that blacks had been influenced by radicals. In September the Boston police walked out, demanding that its union be recognized. The authorities and the press branded the strike as Bolshevistic influenced, Massachusetts Governor Calvin Coolidge declared that "there is no right to strike against the public safety by anybody, anywhere, any time" and proceeded to dismiss the whole police force. Later that same month some 365,000 steel workers went on strike, demanding the right to collective bargaining. The steel industry, led by the powerful Judge Gary of US Steel, was determined not to give in and used strikebreakers and company police to crush the walk out and claimed that the strike was a revolutionary plot. Undermined by the charges of radicalism, the strike ended in utter failure in January 1920. The national coal strike followed on November 1. It was effectively broken by the federal government with an injunction which forbade any strike activity on the part of labor leaders.

Meanwhile, the Justice Department had launched its dramatic all-out war against the radical movement. Its main weapon was the deportation provisions of the immigration laws, which enabled the government to expel aliens who advocated or who belonged to organizations which advocated the overthrow of the government with force or violence. On November 7, federal agents raided the headquarters of the anarchistic Union of Russian Workers and arrested some 1,200 members, most of whom were Russian immigrants. Following swift deportations proceedings, on December 21, 249 aliens were deported on the USS *Buford,* nicknamed the "Soviet Arc." Shortly after this success, on January 2, 1920, the Bureau of Investigation raided offices and homes belonging to Communists in 33 cities and arrested between 5,000 and 10,000 suspected subversives, often with great brutality and in many cases without warrants. At the same time, the Justice Department investigated the political activities of American citizens and lobbied for a peacetime sedition law, which would effectively put an end to revolutionary agitation.

Although the repressive measures of the federal government were by far the most dramatic and important, other agencies of authority and opinion leaders eagerly participated in the defense of the existing order. The courts generally interpreted civil liberties in a restricted sense, Congress expelled the socialist Victor Berger and debated proposals to restrict free speech, the states convicted 300 citizens for violating the criminal syndicalism laws, and the New York State Legislature expelled five socialist Assemblymen. Finally, the press played an important role in the Scare by exaggerating the radical threat and printing sensational accounts of revolutionary plottings, while patriotic societies attacked non-conformists and left-wingers within the educational system, the church and cultural life.

The Red Scare petered out in 1920 as suddenly as it had begun. The Labor Department, which had formal jurisdiction over deportation matters, regained control over the process, reinstated due process and refused to deport most of those arrested by the Justice Department.

Even conservatives opposed the exclusion of duly elected legislators, employers feared that the deportations might halt the flow of cheap, immigrant labor, while organized labor and the press feared they would become the targets of a sedition law. Finally, there was simply no longer such an urgent need for coercive measures as the racial and labor unrest died down and radicalism declined. However, while individual and private anti-radical activities faded away, institutional and bureaucratic anti-radicalism, once introduced and established in 1919, became a permanent feature. The Bureau of Investigation continued to collect political information and to keep the president informed, anti-radical congressional committees reappeared during the following decades and local police still monitored radicals.

An Apathetic Opinion
Historians have generally claimed that the Red Scare was the product of a public hysteria triggered by the patriotic fever remaining after the war, the social unrest, and the fear that Bolshevism would spread from Russia. Added to this were more profound anxieties caused by social and cultural changes brought about by the urbanization, industrialization and immigration of the previous decades. Thus, the Red Scare was more cultural than political in its origins and a part of a larger movement for 100% Americanism, religious fundamentalism and immigration restriction. According to most historians, these factors combined in 1919 to spark off a wave of public intolerance directed toward political minorities, particularly anarchists, Communists and others believed to be radicals or radical sympathizers. Robert K. Murray has described "how thoroughly the fear of domestic bolshevism permeated the body politics by late 1919" and that "the public mind was under the influence of a tremendous social delirium ... national insanity ruled...."[3] According to Murray, it was this "colossal fear" of the public,[4] which finally pressured the federal government, primarily the Department of Justice and the Bureau of Investigation, to take action. The government was actually rather reluctant to become involved, "most officials in Washington were less concerned about the radical menace than were their constituents" and the government "did not immediately show any inclination to undertake specific action against the red menace," but by the fall of 1919, "many government officials were also succumbing to rising hysteria...."[5] Thus, the Bureau

---

[3]Ibid., 166, 217, 239.
[4]Ibid., 209.
[5]Ibid., 190, 194, 191.

was forced to enter the political scene and to stage dramatic mass arrests and deportations of alien radicals in order "to satisfy mounting clamor for the government to act...."[6] Since public opinion and the popular hysteria have been seen as the initiators of the Red Scare, most historians have given scant attention to the government's interests or policies and have merely treated them as the almost automatic expressions of the public will.

First of all, we cannot establish with any degree of certainty the content or nature of the public opinion in this pre-opinion poll era; there simply exist no reliable figures or statements of what the minority or majority thought about a given subject. Most accounts of the Red Scare are based on Robert Murray's study, and its reconstruction of the public mood is primarily based on a reading of a large number of contemporary newspapers and periodicals.[7] However, he gives innumerable examples of how unreliable and sensational the papers were during this period and how they tried to whip up a hysteria by deliberately exaggerating the radical danger.[8] In another context, Melvin Small has criticized the use of the press to ascertain the mood of the public during the Progressive Era. He has pointed to the fact that comparative studies of editorials and presidential election returns have failed to find any meaningful correlations between the two: "In the last analysis, what have passed for studies of mass opinion, often have been elaborate examinations of newspaper and magazine editorials. Historians have continually confused editorial opinion with public opinion, despite the fact that social scientists several decades ago clarified the relationship."[9] Stanley Coben has tried to substantiate the thesis about the existence of a public pressure on the government by using letters from citizens to the Department of Justice, but it is apparent from his own text and his footnotes that most of the letters came from business

[6]Ibid., 192. For similar explanations see for example, Higham, 222-229; Stanley Coben, *A. Mitchell Palmer. Politician* (New York, 1963), 196-197, 218, 221, 229, 236, 244-245; Murray B. Levin, *Political Hysteria in America. The Democratic Capacity for Repression* (New York, 1971), 3, 52, 57-59, 61, 65, 72, 114, 156; Whitehead, 40, 47, 51; Ralph de Toledano, *J. Edgar Hoover. The Man in His Time* (New York (1973), 1974), 44, 48-51, 62; John M. Blum, "Nativism, Anti-Radicalism and the Foreign Scare, 1917-1920," *The Midwest Journal*, Vol. III, No. 1 (Winter 1950-51), 46-53; Paul L. Murphy, "Sources and Nature of Intolerance in the 1920s," *The Journal of American History*, Vol. LI, No. 1 (June 1964), 60-76; Stanley Coben, "A Study in Nativism: The American Red Scare of 1919-20," *Political Science Quarterly*, Vol. LXXIX, No. 1 (March 1964), 52-75.
[7]Murray, x-xi.
[8]For example, ibid., 34-36, 64-65, 71-72, 97-98, 113-114, 115-116, 125, 129, 134, 140, 156, 172, 186, 208-209.
[9]Melvin Small, "Historians Look at Public Opinion," 18, in, Melvin Small (ed.), *Public Opinion and Historians. Interdisciplinary Perspectives* (Detroit, 1970), 13-32. According to Small, the press can at best be used to ascertain what subjects people were thinking about but not what they were thinking about them (ibid., 21). On the difficulty in determining "public attitudes" of the past, see also, Murphy, 60.

and professional men. This is hardly proof of a widespread, popular hysteria.[10] It is highly questionable, therefore, whether the literature on the Red Scare has substantiated its thesis about the existence of a popular anti-radical movement.

Another, even more fundamental objection to the prevailing picture of the Red Scare is its deep dependency on the so-called "consensus" or "pluralist" school of thought among historians and political scientists. Practically all of the studies of the Red Scare date from the 1950s and early 1960s and are clearly inspired by the contemporary drama of McCarthyism. For example, Murray notes in his work, published just as McCarthyism was coming to an end in 1955, that "Since it would appear from the current trend of events that many of the same problems and fears which plagued the American public of 1919 still bother us today, it seemed of particular value to return to that almost forgotten scene."[11] In other words, Murray and other authors saw in the Red Scare a clear parallel to the contemporary scene and therefore transferred their view of the causes of McCarthyism to that earlier period. The prevailing view among historians and political scientists of that time was that McCarthyism was an irrational, mass-based populist movement, composed of social groups which for one reason or another suffered from "status anxiety," and which brought pressure on the more tolerant political elite to repress unpopular minorities. Thus, according to this view, political repression was the result of pressure from below and, consequently, there was implicit in this theory a distrust of "mass politics" and democracy itself.[12] This view of the democratic capacity for repression is most clearly expressed by Murray, who notes that "in a democracy what the general public thinks and does also in the long run vitally affects the government. Hysteria, therefore, is particularly dangerous to the democratic system .... ultimately it also destroys intelligent action by the government."[13]

---

[10]For example, Coben, *A. Mitchell Palmer*, 183, 306n7; also, 214, 317n66. An indication, albeit unrepresentative and of uncertain reliability, of the lack of public hysteria is a letter from former Secretary of the Treasury William G. McAdoo to President Wilson at the end of July 1919, at a time when the public supposedly had become excited about the danger of a revolutionary uprising because of a number of anarchist bombs in June. McAdoo reported that, "The two things which are concerning the average man and woman more than anything else are, first, the high cost of living and, second, taxation" (Link (ed.), *The Papers of Woodrow Wilson*, Vol. 62, 71).

[11]Murray, 281. Murray also writes that "the underlying hysterical spirit of American anti-bolshevism, which the Red Scare represented, lives on" (Ibid., 278).

[12]For examples of the "pluralist" view see, Daniel Bell, (ed.), *The Radical Right* (New York (1955), 1979); Lipset & Raab, *The Politics of Unreason*; Hofstadter, *The Paranoid Style in American Politics*.

[13]Murray, 190.

30

While acknowledging the existence of popular intolerance, most historians have abandoned the "status anxiety" theory. Later studies have rejected the notion about a populistic grass-roots movement in support of McCarthyism.[14] Instead, historians have pointed to "the Imperial Presidency," partisan rivalry, the National Security State, and elitist interest-groups as the causes of anticommunist policies during the Cold War.[15] In a study of political intolerance and repression during McCarthyism, the political scientist James L. Gibson found that in states where the elite was more intolerant, more repressive laws were enacted than in states where the mass opinion was more intolerant. This led him to conclude that "political repression occurred in states with relatively intolerant elites. Beyond the intolerance of elites, the preferences of the mass public seemed to matter little."[16] The absence of a mass-based public hysteria is further indicated by the fact that according to a 1954 poll, at a time when McCarthyism was at its height, only 1% of the public said that they were worried about the internal threat of Communism in the US.[17] Thus, according to this analysis, repressive government policies during the McCarthy era were initiated by the political elite, while the role of the public opinion and the political culture was more that of setting the limits to how far the repression could go. In a later study on the causes of state level political repression during the Vietnam war, Gibson even speculated that perhaps "one reason why we so often observe so much intolerance in the United States is that the American people have learned from their leaders that the appropriate response to threatening disruptions from unpopular political minorities is repression."[18] Thus, instead of the "pluralist" theory of the 1950s and 60s, which explained repressive

---

[14]Nelson W. Polsby, "Towards an Explanation of McCarthyism," *Political Studies*, Vol. VIII, No. 3 (1960), 250-271; Michael Paul Rogin, *The Intellectuals and McCarthy: The Radical Specter* (Cambridge, Mass. & London, 1967).

[15]Earl Latham, *The Communist Controversy in Washington. From the New Deal to McCarthyism* (Cambridge, Mass., 1966); Robert Griffith, *The Politics of Fear: Joseph R. McCarthy and the Senate* (Lexington, Ky., 1970); Robert Griffith and Athan Theoharis, eds., *The Specter. Original Essays on the Cold War and the Origins of McCarthyism* (New York, 1974); Athan Theoharis, *Seeds of Repression: Harry S. Truman and the Origins of McCarthyism* (Chicago, 1971); Fried, *Nightmare in Red* ; Heale, *American Anticommunism* ; Schrecker, *Many Are the Crimes*.

[16]James L. Gibson, "Political Intolerance and Political Repression During the McCarthy Red Scare," *American Political Science Review*, Vol. 82, No. 2 (June 1988), 518; also, 513-518.

[17]Ibid., 519.

[18]James L. Gibson, "The Policy Consequences of Political Intolerance: Political Repression During the Vietnam War Era," *Journal of Politics*, Vol. 51, No. 1, February 1989, 31; also, Gibson, "Political Intolerance and Political Repression," 520, 521-522. Even today, a significant number of Americans believe that the government would suppress various forms of opposition: For example, 79% of whites and 86% of blacks believe the government would not allow a nationwide strike and 40% of whites and 64% of blacks do not believe the government would allow public meetings in opposition to official policies (James L. Gibson, "The Political Consequences of Intolerance: Cultural Conformity and Political Freedom," *American Political Science Review*, Vol. 86, No. 2 (June 1992), 342).

government policies as caused by a hysterical opinion, more recent studies of the opinion poll data suggest that repressive McCarthy era legislation was initiated by an intolerant political elite and that the general opinion was to a large extent unconcerned about the issue of Communist subversion and played a somewhat peripheral and insignificant role.

The fundamental problem of the "pluralist" or "consensus" school, which dominated American historical thinking during the 1950s and early 1960s and which lies at the heart of the still generally accepted explanation of the Red Scare, is that it to some extent downplayed the significance of basic group differences and conflicts and instead assumed that public events and policies were supported by a consensus of Americans. American history was seen as fundamentally harmonious and larger crises were viewed as short aberrations from the normal state of affairs and were often explained as the result of socio-psychological difficulties.[19] If we instead accept that social conflicts existed and search for groups, which might have had an interest in an antiradical campaign and which were in a position to promote it, we find the business community and other organized economic and conservative groups.

The Business Offensive

There were several reasons for the militancy of the business community in 1919. During the war, as a result of the government's regulation of labor relations, organized labor's influence and prestige had increased significantly and the number of organized workers had doubled. With the end of the war, the American Federation of Labor was determined to capitalize on its gains and to win the right to collective bargaining, improved working conditions and higher wages to off-set the wartime increase of the cost of living. At the same time, there were proposals for maintaining or even extending the government's regulation of the economy after the war. To mention one example, the so-called Plumb plan proposed government ownership of the railroads and the United Mine Workers called for the nationalization of the coal mines. Business leaders and conservative spokesmen reacted strongly against such talk of "industrial democracy" and increased federal planning, and they were just as determined to

---

[19]William A. Muraskin, "The Social-Control Theory in American History: A Critique," *Journal of Social History*, Vol. 9, No. 4 (June 1976), 559-561; Samuel P. Hays, "The Social Analysis of American Political History, 1880-1920," *Political Science Quarterly*, Vol. LXXX, No. 3 (September 1965), 374-375, 393. For an example of an explanation of political repression as caused by the elite, see, Robert Justin Goldstein, *Political Repression in Modern America. From 1870 to the Present* (Cambridge/New York, 1978).

maintain their domination over industrial relations and to roll back the growth of state intervention to its pre-war position.[20]

The cornerstone of the employers' counter-attack was the open shop campaign, which rapidly grew from a local and spontaneous reaction by groups of employers to labor militancy and strikes to a well-organized and well-financed national campaign in 1919-20. The ostensible idea of the open shop was the non-discrimination of employees regardless of whether they were organized or not, in contrast to the closed shop which required union membership of all employees. In reality, the purpose of the campaign was to undermine the position of the unions by a policy of non-recognition and the denial of employment to and the discharge of union members. In order to win support for what was at bottom a union-breaking campaign, an extensive propaganda drive was organized by such powerful employer organizations as the National Founders Association, the National Metal Trades Association, the US Chamber of Commerce and the National Association of Manufacturers, which established a separate Open Shop Department and issued an *Open Shop Bulletin*. By 1920, the open shop campaign was active in 240 cities.[21]

The main goal of the propaganda was to discredit unions as subversive, Bolshevistic and alien to basic American values. While the open shop was named the "American Plan" and packaged as representing 100% Americanism, providing equal opportunity for all, the closed shop was called "sovietism in disguise" and "un-American," unionism was "nothing less than bolshevism" and the Plumb plan was branded "'Plumb' Bolshevistic." Unions, according to the most extreme anti-union publication, the *Open Shop Review*, were nothing less than "the greatest crime left in the world" and the conservative AFL, no less than the Bolsheviks, showed utter "disregard for the law."[22] Hammering away with its well-oiled machinery of speakers, publications and releases on the theme of Bolshevism within organized labor, the employers not only undermined the position of the unions, but also spread the suspicion of radicalism in general.

---

[20]Allen M. Wakstein, "The Origins of the Open-Shop Movement, 1919-1920," *The Journal of American History*, Vol. I.I, No. 3 (December 1964), 464-465; Hays, 391; Higham, 224-225; Murphy, 63-64. When Secretary of the Navy Josephus Daniels in May 1919 spoke with members of the Republican controlled House Military Affairs Committee, he noted afterwards that "Most of them opposed any extension of governmental control & deplored extension to socialistic measures" (E. David Cronon (ed.), *The Cabinet Diaries of Josephus Daniels 1913-1921* (Lincoln, Nebraska, 1963), 414).
[21]Wakstein, 460-475; Irving Bernstein, *The Lean Years. A History of the American Worker, 1920-1933* (Boston, 1960), 153-157.
[22]Bernstein, 147-148; Murray, 92-94, 117-119, 164-165, 267-269.

Simultaneously with this propaganda campaign a number of more direct, union-breaking techniques were put to systematic use by the employers. Corporations compiled and exchanged blacklists of union members and "agitators" who were fired or refused employment. New employees were required to sign a "yellow dog" contract, in which they pledged not to join a union. Employers appealed to the courts to issue labor injunctions to break strikes. Private detectives were employed to infiltrate, spy on and create internal dissension within unions – and in some cases to act as agents provocateur and provoke labor unrest, which would then be suppressed by the employers. Strikebreakers were hired, often with armed guards, and large steel, coal and metal mining corporations established their own private police system, such as the infamous Pennsylvania Coal and Iron Police, which was used as a private army against strikers. Finally, complete control of the labor force was introduced with company towns, which isolated workers from the outside and subjected them to constant surveillance.[23]

The employers' associations were not only the most effective private force behind the anti-radical propaganda in 1919, there are indications that at least some of the radical agitation and political violence during the Red Scare was a part of the anti-union campaign – and that the government had knowledge of the activities. The number and influence of the private detective agencies was quite extensive following the war. It has been estimated that by 1928 some 200,000 labor spies were at work and that the three largest detective agencies in total earned $65 million during the decade. Some observers suspected that the detectives deliberately exaggerated the revolutionary threat and radicalism within the unions in order to frighten the employers and, thereby, create a brisk business for themselves.[24] In the summer of 1919, at the beginning of the government's anti-radical campaign, Francis Fisher Kane, the US attorney in Philadelphia, wrote to Attorney General A. Mitchell Palmer and informed him that a number of the most extreme agitators, who had been kept under surveillance by the Bureau of Investigation, had turned out to be spies employed by private detective agencies who had "been actively stirring up trouble, formenting it by their activity, and even at times creating, as I believe, evils that did not exist." According to Kane, the purpose of the provocations was to increase business: "Of course, it is the meat they feed on, – they know on which side their bread is buttered." In

[23]Bernstein, 148-153; also, Murray, 135, 145-148.
[24]Frank Morn, "The Eye That Never Sleeps." A History of the Pinkerton National Detective Agency (Bloomington, Indiana, 1982), 159; William R. Hunt, Front-Page Detective: William J. Burns and the Detective Profession 1880-1930 (Bowling Green, Ohio, 1990), 104; Bernstein, 149-150.

Kane's opinion, much of the revolutionary activity may have been caused by these ambitious agencies: "If the Philadelphia situation is a sample of what exists in other large cities, it would certainly indicate that the danger from Bolshevism in America is not as great as the newspapers would have us believe it to be."[25] The BI files show that the Bureau suspected that at least some of the anarchist bombs in 1919 were caused by private detectives. For example, the Los Angeles field office reported that private detectives were the most likely perpetrators of a number of terrorist bomb attacks against Southern California oil fields in order to be employed to guard the installations: "I know that these things have happened before, and were done by unscrupulous detectives and agencies, and no doubt these 'frame-ups' will continue for some time."[26]

The Patriotic Right

The most active private participants in the Red Scare were perhaps the patriotic societies. There existed more than 30 such organizations in the years following the war, but they only had a combined membership of perhaps 25,000. They were in fact just "the mouthpieces of single leaders or small cabals," which were subsidized by corporations and businessmen to propagandize against organized labor; one such patriotic leader, Harry A. Jung of the American Vigilant Intelligence Federation, noted confidentially concerning its anti-radical propaganda, "That it has been a paying proposition for our organization goes without saying...."[27] In any case, the connections between the business community and the societies were close. The National Security League and the National Civic Federation were both financed by leading businessmen and corporations such as J. P. Morgan, John D. Rockefeller, T. Coleman DuPont, William K. Vanderbilt, US Steel, Carnegie Steel Company and Standard Oil. Other organizations were established by local and often ultraconservative economic interests. The American Constitutional Association was operated by the largest coal and utility companies in West Virginia, while the Better America Federation in California was run by a small group of extreme right-wing businessmen in Los Angeles.[28]

[25]Letter, Francis Fisher Kane to A. Mitchell Palmer, July 16, 1919, DJ 202600-39-2, Record Group 60, National Archives (microfilm).
[26]Report, S. A. Connell, November 22, 1919, OG 376413, RG65, NA.
[27]Murphy, 67; for the patriots in general, see, Norman Hapgood (ed.), *Professional Patriots. An Exposure of the Personalities, Methods and Objectives Involved in the Organized Effort to Exploit Patriotic Impulses in these United States During and After the Late War* (New York, 1927).
[28]Levin, 201-203; Murray, 84-87; Edwin Layton, "The Better America Federation: A Case Study of Superpatriotism," *Pacific Historical Review*, Vol. XXX, No. 2 (May 1961), 138-139.

The only exception to this pattern was the American Legion, established in 1919 to represent the interests of the veterans of the war and to fight radicalism within the US. Even though it claimed more than 840,000 members in 1920, it was hardly representative of the views of the veterans. 55% of its founding members were officers, and it was primarily an upper- and middle-class organization. Available figures from 1938 show that only 2% of its members were farmers and just 4% were unskilled workers,[29] and according to the latest study of the Legion, "there was considerable coincidence of interest and sentiment between the conservative small businessmen who made up the Legion's rank and file and other right-wing groups in America."[30]

These well-financed societies launched an elaborate propaganda campaign, primarily by issuing pamphlets and newsletters with such titles as "The Enemy within Our Gates" and "If Bolshevism Came to America," providing speakers for public meetings, lobbying state and federal legislatures and organizing such patriotic demonstrations as the Constitution Day. The primary objective was to promote the "American plan" and attack organized labor as subversive and Bolshevistic. Thus, the societies warned that a gigantic conspiracy threatened the US and that a revolutionary uprising was imminent, while the national steel strike in 1919 was labeled "an effort of anarchists ... to destroy the government" and the following coal strike was simply branded a "Bolshevik revolution."[31] The American Defense Society and the National Security League also demanded that the educational system and government be purged of radicals and that aliens be Americanized.[32] Some of the more extreme organizations, like the Better America Federation, went further and attacked all forms of government regulation, social legislation and public ownership for being seditious and un-American and even demanded that free speech and the right to vote should be restricted.[33]

The Sensationalistic Press
While the patriotic organisations functioned as the de facto propaganda departments of the employers in their open shop campaign, the

---

[29]William Pencak, *For God and Country. The American Legion, 1919-1941* (Boston, 1989), 49, 58-59, 81.

[30]Ibid., 104.

[31]Murray, 84-87, 150, 155; Levin, 198-201.

[32]J. G. Tucker, Special Report, Radical activities in Greater New York District, June 12, 1920, OG 208369, RG65, NA; letter, Ralph Easley to Francis P. Garvan, March 4, 1920, BS 202600-823, ibid.; John Carver Edwards, *Patriots in Pinstripe. Men of the National Security League* (Washington DC, 1982), 129-134.

[33]Layton, 140-147.

role of the press was more complicated and determined by both economic and ideological considerations. There were numerous examples during the Red Scare that the press presented isolated incidents of violence or unrest in sensational, screaming headlines and systematically exaggerated the radical danger.[34] Even S. A. Connell of the Bureau's Los Angeles field office noted that the local papers were making people "unduly alarmed" by giving too much publicity to the activities of the syndicalist union, the Industrial Workers of the World (IWW): "As for myself, I am not alarmed at the excitement which is now going on in Los Angeles over the activities of the IWW but I believe it has been 'scared up' considerably by the newspapers which relate every arrest and incident connected with the IWW movement by printing large scary headlines in their papers, and thus alarming the people to such an extent that they believe that the IWW's are liable to attack them."[35]

One reason for the sensationalism of the press was, undoubtedly, that it provided a substitute for the dramatic war news and ensured a steady circulation. As noted by John Morton Blum, "The negotiations at Versailles and the treaty fight did not provide the stuff of circulation. Bombs, strikes, and bolsheviks; red hunts, deportations, and injunctions did."[36] Another reason was that most of the larger and influental dailies, such as the *New York Times,* the *Washington Post* and the *Chicago Tribune,* reflected the conservative ideological preferences of their owners and followed a clear pro-business and anti-radical line, not only in their editorials but also in their news columns. Some papers were owned by powerful "press barons," who made no pretense of being objective but used their papers to spread right-wing political propaganda. For example, Norman Chandler's *Los Angeles Times* openly supported the Merchants and Manufacturers Association, the city's open shop organization,[37] and according to a later observer, "*The Times* sanitized and laundered the operations of a rich anti-labor establishment and its politicians; it repeatedly used Red Scares to crush any kind of social-welfare legislation."[38] Other papers were directly owned or dominated by corporations. The Anaconda Copper Mining Company in Montana owned the *Butte Daily Post* and the *Anaconda Standard* while the rest of the press in the state dutifully

---

[34]For example, Murray, 34-36, 64-65, 71-72, 76-77, 78, 97-98, 113-114, 115-116, 125, 126-127, 129, 134, 140, 146, 150, 156, 158-159, 208, 245.
[35]Report, S. A. Connell, November 22, 1919, OG 376413, RG65, NA.
[36]Blum, 52-53.
[37]Bernstein, 154-155.
[38]David Halberstam, *The Powers That Be* (New York, 1979), 116-117.

followed the company line because of their dependence on income from advertising and printing contracts: "The Anaconda Company utilized its vast political and economic power to pressure these newspapers to follow the company line."[39]

The States Crack Down

Finally, it has been claimed that repressive measures adopted during the Red Scare by local state legislatures are the clearest and most reliable indicators of the existence of a hysterical public opinion. It has been argued that since local politicians and authorities were closer to the public than the federal government, local state laws were the most genuine expression of the will of the people.[40] However, the question is how representative the state legislatures were. The 19th Amendment to the Constitution, granting women the right to vote, was not ratified until August 1920 and before that time women were only able to vote in a limited number of states. Furthermore, around the turn of the century blacks and poor whites were disfranchised in the South. For example, in Louisiana the number of registered voters declined from 294,000 in 1897 to 93,000 in 1904.[41] A large part of the population, then, did not have the opportunity to express their views in the political process. Moreover, state legislatures were often dominated by conservative minorities and business interests. As pointed out by Robert Wiebe, rural interests often had disproportionate influence in the legislatures and they became natural centers of opposition to progressivism as a reaction to the centralization of power in the cities and in Washington.[42] For example, the New York State Legislature, in possibly the most repressive state during the Red Scare, was controlled by rural, up-state conservative Republicans, who reacted strongly to radicalism in the cities. It was primarily this rural bloc which voted for the exclusion of five legally elected socialistic assembly men in 1920.[43] Despite decades of attempted reforms of the political system, other state legislatures were wholly dominated by local economic interests.[44] For example, in Texas the elected representatives were in the pocket

[39]Arnon Gutfeld, "The Ves Hall Case, Judge Bourquin, and the Sedition Act of 1918," *Pacific Historical Review*, Vol. XXXVII, No. 2 (May 1968), 163n2.
[40]For example, Murray, 231.
[41]C. Vann Woodward, *The Strange Career of Jim Crow* (3rd. rev. ed., New York (1955), 1974), 84-85; Gabriel Kolko, *Main Currents in Modern History* (New York, 1976), 307.
[42]Robert H. Wiebe, *The Search for Order 1877-1920* (New York, 1967), 176, 213-214.
[43]Lawrence H. Chamberlain, *Loyalty and Legislative Action. A Survey of Activity by the New York State Legislature 1919-1949* (Ithaca, New York, 1951), 2-5; Julian F. Jaffe, *Crusade Against Radicalism. New York During the Red Scare, 1914-1924* (Port Washington, New York, 1972), 163-164, 239-240.
[44]Kolko, 305.

of an alliance of "the interests," a combination of the railroads, oil corporations, banks, sulphur and natural gas companies.[45] Political life in California was to a large degree shaped and dominated by the powerful and ultraconservative Chandler empire; according to David Halberstam, "*The Times* was not an organ of the Republican Party of Southern California, it *was* the Republican Party."[46] This conservative political influence reached directly into local police forces. During the Progressive Era most of the police forces of the larger cities established so-called Anarchist Squads, Bomb Squads or Red Squads, which specialized in the investigation of anarchist activities and surveillance of radicals and unions. According to Frank Donner, these local political police forces often had close connections to the local business and political elite and were occasionally paid to act as strikebreakers.[47]

There were, of course, a number of reasons why the Red Scare subsided in 1920, such as the containment of Communism in Russia, the decline of social unrest and radical activities in the United States, and a heightened awareness of the importance of civil liberties. Nevertheless, an important contributing factor was the fact that when the anti-radical campaign in 1920 began to seriously threaten the employers' own economic interests, they consequently subdued their propaganda. In early 1920, when the national coal and steel strikes had been effectively broken and organized labor forced on the defensive, a number of industrialists began to fear that the anti-radical campaign might get out of hand, permanently stigmatize alien workers as radicals and lead to immigration restriction, thereby cutting off the flow of cheap labor. The Inter-Racial Council, which was backed by some of the largest employers and some of the most influental organizations behind the open shop campaign, such as the National Founders Association and the American Constitutional Association, defended the immigrant worker from the charge that he was the chief instigator of unrest and Bolshevism.[48] Led by the *New York Times* much of the press, fearing that the hysteria would result in a federal sedition law which might be used to restrict the freedom of the press, abandoned its warnings of an imminent revolutionary uprising and began to question the government's repressive policies.[49]

[45]Robert Caro, *The Years of Lyndon Johnson. The Path to Power* (New York (1982), 1983), 46-48, 79-83.
[46]Halberstam, 117; in general 107-121.
[47]Frank Donner, *Protectors of Privilege. Red Squads and Political Repression in Urban America* (Berkeley, Calif., 1990), 12-43.
[48]Higham, 232; also, Levin, 84-86.
[49]Murray, 245.

There are strong indications that what might be termed the public Red Scare, that is, the anti-radical campaign outside the federal government, was not an expression of a broad-based public hysteria caused by post-World War I dislocations, unrest and fear of Bolshevism. Instead, it was an integrated part of a reactionary political campaign, instigated by employers and their conservative allies in the employers' associations, patriotic societies, state legislatures and the press. Their basic aim was to break the power of organized labor, institutionalize the open shop in the American industry and halt or even roll back the growing government regulation of the economy. The widely publicized warnings of a Bolshevik threat to the US and the charges of subversion and treason levelled against unions and reform measures were all parts of this offensive by the conservative elite to regain its once uncontested and preeminent position of power. This, of course, does not mean that public opinion did not matter or that people were not concerned about radicalism. However, we simply have no reliable information about the state of the opinion, and the central point of the preceding discussion is that no matter how widespread the fear was, it was initiated from above by the elite. To use Gibson's interpretation of McCarthyism, the role of the political culture and public opinion consisted of determining the limits to the repression already set in motion from above. The Red Scare was not caused by popular nativism or political intolerance, but it might be argued that they made it possible for the elite to pursue such a repressive line for a time during 1919 and 1920. This, however, still leaves open the questions of which interests and policies did the government have in the Red Scare and what was the nature of its relationship to the conservative elite's campaign?

"The Search for Order"

Most accounts of the origins of the FBI's political surveillance suffer from a failure to put the Bureau's activities in proper perspective and to see them as an integrated part of the growth of the modern, centralized bureaucratic state and its increasing control and regulation of all aspects of society. Thus, the Bureau's political role must be understood basically as the product of long-term institutional and structural changes within the political system rather than as the result of short-term aberrations in the political culture brought about by the eruptions of irrational public hysteria.

It seems to be generally agreed by historians that the period from about 1890 to 1920, traditionally designated the Progressive Era, on a general level was characterized by a process of modernization.

During this period the society made a decisive break with the old order of largely decentralized, isolated and selfsufficient communities – the "nation of loosely connected islands" in the words of Robert Wiebe – and moved toward the development of the modern society. This society was characterized by centralization and formal organization and shaped by new bureaucratic values. According to Wiebe, this development was supported by the leading segments in public and private leadership by 1920: "A bureaucratic orientation now defined a basic part of the nation's discourse. The values of continuity and regularity, functionality and rationality, administration and management set the form of problems and outlined their alternative solutions."[50]

This general development toward organizational centralization affected the role of the federal government profoundly. While the progressive movement comprised a variety of different groups and interests, for example social reformers, muckrackers and urban and government reformers, it might be argued that it was at bottom influenced and often led by business interests and their political and intellectual allies. According to this view of progressivism as "corporate liberalism," the intention of much of the economic, social and political legislation was to accommodate the laws, customs and thinking of the society to the emerging corporate order. Thus, while the business community formerly had insisted on the principle of laissez-faire – and many small and medium sized businesses, such as those represented by the National Association of Manufacturers, continued to do so – the more sophisticated corporate leaders declared an end to wasteful and "irresponsible" competition and called on the state to play an active role in providing for the continuing economic expansion at home as well as abroad, adequate financing and regulation of the market. One direct consequence of this development was the acceptance and regulation of the large trusts rather than their destruction and the return to a former state of laissez-faire and individual competition. At the same time, in order to stabilize the system and avoid serious popular opposition, representatives of the more conservative unions and social reformers were recognized and given some influence within the political system and a number of social

---

[50]Wiebe, quotes from pp. 4 and 295; for similar organizational interpretations, see for example, Samuel P. Hays, *American Political History as Social Analysis* (Knoxville, Tenn., 1980), 244-263; Martin J. Sklar, *The United States as a Developing Country. Studies in US History in the Progressive Era and the 1920s* (Cambridge, 1992), 37-40; Joan Hoff-Wilson, *Ideology and Economics. US Relations with the Soviet Union, 1918-1933* (Columbia, 1974), vii-xii; Louis Galambos, "The Emerging Organizational Synthesis in Modern American History," *Business History Review*, Vol. XLIV, No. 3 (Autumn 1970), 279-290.

reforms were enacted with the support of the corporate leaders.[51] The dynamic role of the state in the new corporate order had two direct consequences, both of which led to the federalization of political surveillance in the Bureau of Investigation: the centralization of power in the federal bureaucracy and the drive to use this new and powerful machinery for social control on a national level.

This active and vigorous role of the federal government tended to increase the power of the president and the executive branch, which possessed the resources to identify the problems, define their solution and administer the many new laws and regulations. During the Progressive Era power shifted from the direct representatives of the people, the Congress, to the president, who was now expected to initiate and formulate legislative programs.[52] In other words, the shift from representative democracy to administrative leadership was the result of the search for efficiency in the political system. At the core of this new administrative system was the organization of industries and professions in voluntary and decentralized private trade associations and groups, which were coordinated, assisted and to some degree regulated by state agencies and commissions. Thus, during the early decades of the century the number and scope of federal agencies, commissions and bureaus, staffed by trained, professional experts, appointed on the basis of their professional skills and working objectively and impartially in accordance with established rules and regulations, experienced an almost mushroom growth. Following the establishment of the Interstate Commerce Commission in 1887 to regulate the railroad industry, an entire structure of regulatory agencies was formed: The Federal Reserve Board and the Federal Trade Commission were established in 1913, the Federal Power Commission in 1920 and the Federal Radio Commission in 1927. At the same time, numerous permanent bureaus were formed or strengthened, such as the Interior Department's Division of Forestry and the Commerce Department's Bureau of Corporations. After the expansion of the federal bureaucracy during the New Deal and World War II, the

---

[51]For the concept of "corporate liberalism" in general, see, Sklar, 102-142; James Weinstein, *The Corporate Ideal in the Liberal State: 1900-1918* (Boston, 1968), *passim*; Kolko, 8-23; Ellis W. Hawley, "The Discovery and Study of 'Corporate Liberalism'," *Business History Review*, Vol. LII, No. 3, (Autumn 1978), 309-320; for a critique of the concept, see, Alan L. Seltzer, "Woodrow Wilson as 'Corporate Liberal': Toward a Reconsideration of Left Revisionist Historiography," *The Western Political Quarterly*, Vol. XXX, No. 2 (June 1977), 183-212.

[52]Wiebe, 189, 193, 294-295; Barry Dean Karl, *Executive Reorganization and Reform in the New Deal. The Genesis of Administrative Management, 1900-1939* (Cambridge, Mass., 1963), 218. For Woodrow Wilson's thinking on the strong executive and the administrative state, see Niels Aage Thorsen, *The Political Thought of Woodrow Wilson 1875-1910* (Princeton, N.J., 1988), 41-67, 89-140.

number of departments and their regulatory bureaus and divisions had reached a staggering 2,133 by the early 1950s.[53]

The Bureau of Investigation and "the Administrative State"
It was in this context that the Bureau of Investigation was established in 1908 within the Department of Justice in response to the increasing demand for federal regulations. In 1907 Attorney General Charles Bonaparte drew the attention of Congress to the fact that the Department was woefully unequipped to deal with the increasing number and complexity of anti-trust, banking and land cases. He therefore requested that a permanent division of investigation be established, which would be be staffed by trained investigators and would therefore in progressive terms be more efficient, economical and reliable. When Congress instead responded by banning the Department's previous practice of borrowing investigators from the Treasury Department's Secret Service since it was a circumvention of the appropriation statutes, Bonaparte on July 1, 1908, hired a force of 9 Secret Service agents who were required to report to Chief Examiner Stanley W. Finch. On March 16, 1909, the incoming Attorney General, George Wickersham, formally designated Finch's force of some 20 special agents, 50 naturalization examiners, 7 land fraud investigators and 12 general examiners the Bureau of Investigation.[54]

Later historians have uncritically accepted the official FBI legend that when J. Edgar Hoover was appointed director in 1924 he purged the Bureau of incompetent and politically appointed agents and reformed and professionalized the Bureau: historians have thereby presented 1924 as a watershed in FBI history, as a clear break between the "old" and the "new" FBI, and have, in fact, obscured the Bureau's progressive roots. For example, the FBI's quasi-official historian, Don Whitehead, characterized the early Bureau as "a disorganized and loosely directed agency without character or discipline ... There were no fixed standards of training or personal conduct. Political endorse-

[53]Wiebe, 160, 185-188, 190-191; Eva Etzioni-Halevy, *Bureaucracy and Democracy. A Political Dilemma* (London (1983), 1985), 113.

[54]Williams, *"Without Understanding,"* 24-48. The circumstances surrounding the establishment of the BI have been the subject of a lively debate: According to later critics of the Bureau, Congress opposed any form of governmental detective bureau and Bonaparte acted against its express wishes in establishing the detective force (Lowenthal, 3-13; Vern Countryman, "The History of the FBI: Democracy's Development of a Secret Police," in, Pat Watters and Stephen Gillers, *Investigating the FBI* (New York (1973), 1974), 49-52). Later supporters of the Bureau have argued that a corrupt Congress opposed the creation of the Bureau, fearing that it would be used against them (Whitehead, 17-21; de Toledano, 10-11). However, in the most thoroughly documented analysis, Williams has argued pursuasively that Congress opposed the borrowing of Secret Service operatives but approved the establishment of the Bureau of Investigation within the Justice Department.

ments carried more weight than experience or character in the selection of agents." Thus, the Bureau was "totally unequipped" to deal with German sabotage and espionage in the US during World War I, and the excesses and injustices of the Palmer raids in 1919-20 were to a considerable extent a direct consequence of the agents' lack of experience and training.[55] This view has been echoed by later historians such as Kenneth O'Reilly, who described the pre-Hoover FBI as "an undisciplined, somewhat ineffectual, highly politicized organization...."[56] Actually, the Bureau was firmly rooted in progressivism and its organizational development and various administrative reforms from 1908 reflected the bureaucratic ideals of professionalization, rationality and efficiency.

The Bureau was organized in a tight hierarchial system in order to achieve clear and effective command and control of its operations. From the beginning the Bureau's personnel was detached to field offices (classified as supervising offices, supervised offices and independent offices) throughout the country, each of which was directed by a special agent in charge (SAC). The SAC reported to his division superintendent, who in turn reported to the Bureau headquarters in Washington, DC. The field force also cooperated with the local US district attorneys who were the Justice Department's highest ranking local representatives and who advised the special agents in such matters as the interpretation of the law and directives.[57] In Washington, DC, the head of the Bureau (Stanley W. Finch 1908-12, A. Bruce Bielaski 1912-19, William J. Flynn 1919-21, William J. Burns 1921-24 and J. Edgar Hoover 1924-72), was initially designated chief examiner, then chief and finally director. From 1908-19 and again from 1925 he reported directly to his political superior, the Attorney General, and during 1919-25 to an Assistant Attorney General.[58]

Except for a brief interlude with centralization during Director Burns' tenure in 1921-24, the Bureau tried to decentralize responsibilities and thereby increase its flexibility and efficiency. In 1920, following the explosive growth of the Bureau during the war and the Red

---

[55]Whitehead, 13-14. See also Watters and Gillers (eds.), 55.

[56]O'Reilly, *Hoover and the Un-Americans*, 17. See also, Robins, 33. On Hoover's reforms, see further, Powers, *Secrecy and Power*, 144-158; Alpheus Thomas Mason, *Harlan Fiske Stone. Pillar of the Law* (New York, 1956), 149-153; de Toledano, 71-78; Theoharis & Cox, 95-100, 116-120. The only authors who have noted the continuity in the Bureau's reforms are Lowenthal, 307-314, and Williams, 306-312, but even they have failed to see them as part of the larger organizational reforms of the Progressive Era.

[57]Ralph P. Miller, "Proposed Reorganization of the Field", n.d. (August 1920), OG 390982, RG65, NA.

[58]M. A. Jones, Memorandum, Supervision of Bureau by Other than Attorney General, July 3, 1956, O/C 30, FBI/FOIA.

Scare, an internal report on the Bureau's organization and administration stressed the need for decentralization: "On the face of it, it is ridiculous to believe that a man sitting at a desk in Washington can tell another man carrying on an investigation of John Doe in Little Rock, Arkansas, how to make his investigation." Instead, the Washington, DC, headquarters should concentrate on "the definition of policies and the proper formulation of general methods of work and a really adequate supervision of those comparatively few cases in which its supervision is necessary and can be adequately exercised," while the SAC "will be responsible for the conduct of his office ..."[59] In order to maintain control of the field force, the division superintendents as the director's "direct representative" were required to visit the field offices regularly "in order that the field employees may feel that they are a very important part of a very important Bureau of the Government ..."[60] William Burns attempted to centralize control by abolishing the position of division superintendent and introducing an elaborate system of weekly administrative reports, with the aim of enabling a "very careful supervision of the field forces in order that the highest degree of efficiency might be attained."[61] When J. Edgar Hoover in 1924 assumed the directorship, he again decentralized the Bureau, increased the responsibilities of the SACs, and inaugurated a system of inspection of the field offices.[62]

In order to achieve as competent and impartial results as possible, the Bureau strove from the beginning to professionalize its personnel and to avoid appointments on the basis of personal connections or political affiliations. Attorney General Bonaparte originally intended that the employees should be both fully trained and possess knowledge of the law,[63] but since the Bureau was not equipped during its early years to train the new special agents, applicants were selected on the basis of former law enforcement experience or a background in the

[59]Miller, "Proposed Reorganization of the Field", n.d. (August 1920), OG 390982, RG65, NA.

[60]Report of Committee on Field Organization, n.d. (August 1920), ibid.

[61]US Department of Justice, *Annual Report of the Attorney General of the United States, 1923* (Washington, DC, 1923), 68. See also, *AG Report 1922*, 67; US Congress, House, Subcommittee of House Committee on Appropriations, *Appropriations, Department of Justice, 1923. Hearing*, Pt. 2 (Washington, DC, 1922), 137; US Congress, House, Subcommittee of House Committee on Appropriations, *Appropriations, Department of Justice, 1924. Hearing*, Pt. 2 (Washington, DC, 1922), 69.

[62]*AG Reports 1924*, 60-61; *1925*, 106; *1930*, 79; US Congress, House, Subcommittee of House Committee on Appropriations, *Appropriations, Department of Justice, 1926. Hearings*, (Washington, DC, 1925), 57; letter, Harlan F. Stone to Felix Frankfurter, February 9, 1925, box 104, Felix Frankfurter Papers, Library of Congress; Mason, 151; Whitehead, 69.

[63]Williams, *"Without Understanding"*, 30.

law.[64] The Bureau worked continuously to improve the standard and quality of its personnel. In 1920 the Bureau required that special agents "have knowledge of the law, more particularly the Federal Law, have experience in investigating work, and as a general rule he should have at least a High School education or an education equivalent thereto."[65] In 1923 the Bureau experimented with selecting the best new law graduates for its anti-trust work.[66] When Hoover became director in 1924 the requirements for legal training were strengthened so that the share of special agents with a legal background increased from 30% in 1924 to 74% in 1933.[67]

At the same time, the Bureau began to train its agents. In 1920 an internal review noted that "In the past the Bureau has typically gone upon the theory that the way to teach a boy to swim is to throw him into deep water," an approach which had resulted in much "ineffectual and unsuccessful" work.[68] It was proposed to establish a short training course during which the newly appointed agent would be taught the rules and regulations governing the Bureau and the rudimentary essentials of investigatory work.[69] In 1921 two training schools located at the field offices in New York City and Chicago were opened,[70] and in 1928 they were merged into a central training school in Washington, DC.[71] Furthermore, in order to increase discipline and efficiency, strict codes of conduct were introduced[72] and promotions came to be based on "uniform performance appraisals" rather than seniority or political connections.[73]

The Bureau standardized its rules, regulations and procedures in order to achieve uniformity and predictability. Apparently the Bureau as early as 1913 used a "book of rules" for the instruction of its

---

[64]US Congress, Senate, Select Committee on Investigation of the Attorney General, *Investigation of Hon. Harry M. Daugherty Formerly Attorney General of the United States, Hearings*, 66th. Cong., 1st. Sess. (Washington, DC, 1924), Vol. III, 2452, 2464, 3156-3157; Research Unit, Office of Public Affairs, FBI, *Abridged History of the Federal Bureau of Investigation* (Washington, DC, n.d.), 2.

[65]Report of Committee on Selection, Training and Salaries, August 1920, OG 390982, RG65, NA.

[66]*Investigation of Daugherty*, Vol. III, 3156.

[67]Ibid., 3253-3256; letter, Stone to Frankfurter, February 9, 1925, box 104, Frankfurter Papers, LC; memorandum, United States Bureau of Investigation, March 17, 1933, box 10, OF-10b, Franklin D. Roosevelt Library.

[68]Miller, "Proposed Reorganization of the Field", n.d. (August 1920), OG 390982, RG65, NA.

[69]Report of Committee on Selection, Training and Salaries, August 1920, ibid.

[70]*AG Reports 1921*, 128-129; *1922*, 67; *1923*, 69; *Appropriations, Department of Justice, 1923*, Pt. 2, 136-137; *Appropriations, Department of Justice, 1924*, Pt. 2, 69.

[71]FBI, *Abridged History of the FBI*, 4; *AG Reports 1929*, 68; *1932*, 104.

[72]Whitehead, 70-71; Theoharis & Cox, 113-114, 117-118; Powers, 153-155.

[73]*AG Report 1924*, 61; FBI, *Abridged History of the FBI*, 4; Mason, 151; Whitehead, 69.

agents,[74] and in 1920 a committee of experienced Bureau officials were directed to compile "a manual of instructions for the field offices."[75] In 1928 the Bureau issued its *Manual of Rules and Regulations and Instructions* to guide the administrative and investigative work.[76] In 1920, the Bureau began a process of specializing by dividing its investigations into violations of federal criminal laws, enemy aliens, radical political activities and other general intelligence matters, and high cost of living.[77] At the same time, the Bureau also cut down on the amount of paper work by separating administrative and investigative functions and simplified its procedures by introducing a single uniform report form.[78] The Bureau also strove to develop a simple and effective filing system for the rapidly expanding mass of letters, reports and memoranda. During its early years, the Bureau's archives consisted of several separate files but after some failed attempts the Central Records System was established in 1921. It classified each document according to federal crime designation, case number and document number, and it enabled instant access to all records.[79]

In order to obtain as objective and rational results as possible, the Bureau introduced scientific methods. At the turn of the century, police forces began using fingerprints for identification purposes, and in 1921 Director Burns took the initiative to centralize the two existing national criminal fingerprint collections in the US, the Department of Justice collection at Leavenworth, Kansas, and the bureau run by the International Association of Chiefs of Police in Washington, DC.[80] After various delays, Congress in 1924 appropriated the necessary amount for the move and in 1930 approved the establishment of a permanent Division of Identification and Information within the Bureau.[81] The move toward "scientific law enforcement" continued

---

[74]Lowenthal, 332.

[75]Committee Assignments, n.d. (c. August 1920), OG 390982, RG65, NA.

[76]*AG Reports 1928*, 70; *1929*, 68; J. Edgar Hoover, Memorandum for the Attorney General, February 6, 1933, Taylor-Gates Collection, Herbert Hoover Library.

[77]*AG Report 1920*, 186.

[78]Miller, "Proposed Reorganization of the Field", n.d. (August 1920); Report of Committee on Reports, August 1920, OG 390982, RG65, NA; *AG Report 1924*, 61; *Appropriations, Department of Justice, 1926*, 58; Mason, 151.

[79]Gerald K. Haines & David A. Langbart, *Unlocking the Files of the FBI. A Guide to its Records and Classification System* (Wilmington, Delaware, 1993), xi-xii; *AG Report 1924*, 61.

[80]*AG Report 1921*, 129; *Appropriations, Department of Justice, 1923*, 132-133, 137; *Appropriations, Department of Justice, 1924*, 80-83. Apparently, President Harding opposed the centralization on the grounds that it would entail "a very marked increase in expenses" (letter, Warren Harding to Harry M. Daugherty, November 28, 1921, File 10-b, Series 4, Warren G. Harding Papers, LC).

[81]*AG Reports 1924*, 71-72; *1925*, 122-123; J. Edgar Hoover, Memorandum for the Attorney General, February 6, 1933, Taylor-Gates Collection, HHL; memorandum, United States Bureau of Investigation, March 17, 1933, box 10, OF 10-b, FDRL; Whitehead, 133-135.

with the creation of the Bureau Laboratory in 1932, which firmly established FBI scientists as the highest authorities in criminal cases.[82]

Finally, the Bureau continuously sought to streamline its organization and to cut away any unnecessary fat. In 1920, when the force of special agents numbered 579 located in 108 field offices, an internal review stressed the inefficiency and waste of the many small one- or two-men field offices: "The agent in charge, with little real administrative work to do, seems to enjoy spending time in his office listening to trivial complaints, with many of which we have no proper concern ... Particularly if he is located in one of the smaller cities, the agent in charge is likely to have a crowd of intimates and hangers-on who cost vastly more in the time they take than they will ever give. The whole tendency is toward making the Bureau a petty eaves-dropping detective agency." Consequently, it was recommended that the small field offices be closed down, the remaining field offices be situated near transport and communication junctions to make them as effective as possible, and the personnel reduced.[83] The rationalization plan was immediately put into effect and by the end of the decade the number of field offices had been reduced to 30 and the number of special agents to 356.[84] Beginning in 1928, the field offices were relocated to increase their effectiveness.[85] All the while, thanks to "careful supervision" and "scientific administrative systems," the Bureau was able to report better results and increased efficiency.[86] In its attempt to achieve a high level of professionalization, standardization, and objectivity, the Bureau of Investigation was a direct product of the search for order through rationality and efficiency during the Progressive Era. Its administration and procedures were, so to speak, the nuts and bolts of an increasingly effective machine which was an integrated part of the "emerging bureaucratic system" that came to dominate American society around World War I.[87]

---

[82]Whitehead, 145-149.

[83]Miller, "Proposed Reorganization of the Field", OG 390982, RG65, NA.

[84]J. Edgar Hoover, Memorandum for the Attorney General, February 2, 1933, Taylor-Gates Collection, HHL; memorandum, United States Bureau of Investigation, March 17, 1933, box 10, OF 10-b, FDRL; *AG Reports 1920*, 187; *1924*, 60-61; *1925*, 107.

[85]*AG Reports 1928*, 70; *1930*, 79; *1931*, 92.

[86]The quote is from *AG Report 1926*, 100. For the claims of increased efficiency, see for example, *AG Reports 1920*, 187; *1921*, 128-129; *1924*, 60, 72; *1925*, 107, 123-124; *1927*, 61, 67; *1928*, 70-71, 76-77; *1929*, 69; *1932*, 107; *Appropriations, Department of Justice, 1926*, 59, 74; memorandum, United States Bureau of Investigation, March 17, 1933, box 10, OF 10-b, FDRL. For criticism of the Bureau's claims and use of statistics, see, Joseph Bayliss, Memorandum re: J. Edgar Hoover, n.d. (1929), box 25, PP, HHL; Lowenthal, 340-346; Cook, 205-213.

[87]Wiebe, 293.

The expansion of the Bureau was a function of the increased federal intervention in society since 1900. By the end of progressivism in 1924 the Bureau had jurisdiction over 60 classifications of crime, of which the most important were antitrust, banking, bankruptcy, neutrality statutes, interstate theft of automobiles (Dyer Act), white slavery (Mann Act), illegal interstate shipment of liquors and obscene materials, impersonation, location of fugitives, crimes on Indian reservation and government property, the Chinese exclusion laws and federal internal revenue, land and customs regulations.[88] The Bureau was only given added responsibilities in five more areas in the period of governmental restraint 1925-32, among which, however, was the important Lindbergh Kidnapping Law of 1932, which for the first time brought the Bureau into the business of crime fighting. The era of government expansion during the New Deal 1933-39 brought another 29 crimes under the FBI's jurisdiction, among which were interstate transportation of stolen goods, unlawful flight across state lines, bank robberies and violations of the numerous New Deal laws and regulations. During World War II another 17 crimes were made federal.[89]

Consequently, the size of the Bureau's budget and personnel increased in parallel with the expansion of the federal bureaucracy. While total public expenditure grew from 7% of the BNP in 1890 to 24.6% in 1950 and the expenditure of the administrative federal budget increased from $659 millions in 1908 to $8,841 millions in 1939, with a high of $18,492 millions in 1919, the Bureau's budget increased from $485,000 in 1916 to $2,350,000 in 1919 and $6,025,000 in 1937. When the war broke out in 1941, the FBI's appropriations had increased to $14,543,800.[90] At the same time, while the number of federal civilian employees increased from 356,754 in 1908 to 794,271 in 1919 and 1,042,420 in 1940, the Bureau's initial small staff of 34 in 1909 increased to 1,127 in 1920, was then reduced to a low of 643 in 1929 and then expanded rapidly again to 7,420 in 1941. Two years into the war, the total number of FBI employees had grown to 13,317.[91]

---

[88]Williams, 49; Whitehead, 330n7. For the number of classifications, see Haines & Langbart, *passim.*

[89]Haines & Langbart, *passim.*

[90]Figures for total public expenditure are taken from Etzioni-Halevy, 113-115; the federal budget is from US Bureau of Census, Department of Commerce, *Historical Statistics of the United States from Colonial Times to Present* (Washington, DC, 1975), Vol. 2, 1104; the FBI budget is from *Sundry Civil Appropriation Bill 1920*, 307; *AG Reports 1919*, 298; *1937*, 204; *1941*, 285.

[91]Figures for the total number of federal employees are from *Historical Statistics of the United States*, Vol. 2, 1102; FBI figures are from FBI, *Abridged History of the FBI*, 2; Powers, 137; J. Edgar Hoover, Memorandum for the Attorney General, October 31, 1929, 67-561-35, FBI/FOIA; Whitehead, 185.

Recent historical research, inspired by the so-called "organizational synthesis" school, has shown that the newly established federal bureaucracies soon wielded tremendous political power and that ambitious, aggressive and highly ideologically motivated officials often initiated and shaped public policy as well as administered it. Since the regulatory agencies often were entrusted with broad discretionary powers and since they were "operating outside the process of democratic politics,"[92] they soon became, in the words of Eugene Lewis, "the most powerful instrument for social, political and economic change in the political universe" and "they inevitably reduce the significance of the traditional political system and thereby alter the face of democratic government and politics."[93] A number of case studies have described how officials in the State and Commerce Departments constituted perhaps the most important organized opposition to the recognition of Soviet Russia between 1917 and 1933, how State Department bureaucrats helped to shape American policy at the Washington Naval Conference in 1922, and how a few officials in the new and ambitious Commerce Department were the driving force behind the establishment of the US Chamber of Commerce in 1912, motivated both by an interest in US economic expansion abroad and a desire to create its own constituency to help lobby Congress in support of the Department's policies.[94] Thus, one major effect of the centralization of power in the federal government was the increasing power and influence of the often ambitious and aggressive bureaucrats. This was what Immigration Commissioner Frederic C. Howe termed "the administrative state," dominated by officials and bureaucrats who "have it in their power to shape politics, to control executive action, and to make the state a bureaucratic thing."[95]

The Federalization of Political Surveillance
The other major consequence of the more active role of the state was the desire and the preparedness of the economic and political elite to use this new centralized power for social control on a national level. Since "bureaucratic management lent itself equally to social control and to social release," the possibility always existed that the new,

[92]Christopher L. Tomlins, *The State and the Unions. Labor Relations, Law, and the Organized Labor Movement in America, 1880-1960* (Cambridge (1985), 1989), 75.
[93]Lewis, 238, 241.
[94]Hoff-Wilson, especially, vii-viii, 70, 121-123; Galambos, 285; Richard Hume Werking, "Bureaucrats, Businessmen, and Foreign Trade: The Origins of the United States Chamber of Commerce," *Business History Review*, Vol. LII, No. 3 (Autumn 1978), 321-341; Hawley, 319.
[95]Frederic C. Howe, *The Confessions of a Reformer* (New York (1925), 1967), 255-256.

efficient state apparatus might be used in times of crisis to regulate political behavior and activities.[96] The Progressive Era was a period of severe social dislocations and political threats to the existing order. For those in authority, the social problems in the wake of the rapid and often uncontrollable industrialization since the Civil War, the explosive urbanization with its attendant evils of slum dwellings and the new waves of immigrants from Southern and Eastern Europe all seemed to threaten the stability and cohesion of the status quo. While still relatively small and without influence, radical movements opposed to the capitalist system were on the rise and seemed a foreboding of what the future had in store. Such groups as the Socialist Party and the Industrial Workers of the World were appealing to and organizing an increasing number of the dispossessed. The socialist candidate for president, Eugene Debs, increased his share of the popular vote from 87,814 in 1900 to 900,672 in 1912, and at the same time the party elected 73 mayors, some 1,200 lesser officials and its first member of Congress, Victor Berger of Wisconsin. The IWW seemed particularly menacing to the propertied interests and the political leadership with its militant, syndicalist ideology and its stated goal of "One Big Union" for all workers. At the height of its power, before World War I, it numbered perhaps 300,000 members nationally, with its strongest support in the Midwest. The IWW led a series of violent strikes and free speech campaigns, most notably the successful textile strike in Lawrence, Massachusetts in 1912.[97] Organized radical opposition had probably never been stronger or struck as much terror in the hearts of the elite as during the Progressive Era.

With the growing radical opposition and threatening social upheavals, the elite and the state were faced with what has been called a major contradiction of the American political system: "How to protect the status quo while maintaining the forms of liberal political democracy."[98] To put it another way, the social inequalities and injustices of the corporate order in combination with the right to agitate and organize in opposition to the existing system threatened the stability of the system. The state needed to protect itself and the economic interests "against the consequences of its own liberalism."[99] As long as those in authority were neither willing to solve basic social

---

[96]Wiebe, 223.

[97]For the SP, see James Weinstein, *The Decline of Socialism in America 1912-1925* (New York, 1967), *passim*; for the IWW, Melvyn Dubofsky, *We Shall Be All. A History of the Industrial Workers of the World* (Chicago, 1969), *passim*.

[98]Donner, *The Age of Surveillance*, 3. For the liberal state's use of political repression, see also, Alan Wolfe, *The Seamy Side of Democracy. Repression in America* (New York, 1973).

[99]Keller, 5-6.

problems, such as racial discrimination and poverty, nor to impose authoritarian rule, the state was forced to play an active role in political socialization and social control.

The idea that it was the role of the government to impose "social efficiency" or social control through management and planning was inspired by Frederick W. Taylor's program of scientific management of the factory. According to spokesmen of the new order, it was the task of the new and powerful federal bureaucracy to provide for the efficient and rational functioning of society by bridging the inequalities and conflicts and enforcing a form of social harmony or solidarity and thereby protect the emerging corporate order. This notion of "social efficiency," the transferring of the regulation and streamlining of the shop floor to the political sphere, was believed to be best conducted by the strong executive and his administrative experts. In the words of Samuel Haber, the idea of "social efficiency" had "crystalized the sentiment for social control into a concept of planning" and enabled the elite, troubled by the idea of majority rule, to avoid "the levelling tendencies of the principle of equality."[100]

Thus, as pointed out by Samuel Walker, the creation of what has been called "the surveillance state," the attempt to systematically and permanently regulate political beliefs and activities, was an outgrowth of the penetration of society by government bureaucracies early in the century and might be viewed as a parallel to the effort to regulate the economy.[101] On a more general level, a shift took place from the informal social controls of the local and isolated communities of the 19th century to the more formal and intrusive social control of the modern centralized state.[102] In fact, the development of the Bureau's political role can be seen as part of a larger centralization and federalization of anti-radical and antiunion activities during the Progressive Era. One part of this development concerned what might be termed the organized anti-radical propaganda and exposure, which traditionally had been conducted by a number of patriotic groups, most of which were financed by the business community and conservative interests. With the notable exception of the American Legion, these private groups, which still played an important role in the Red Scare, declined during the 1920s and 1930s. Their functions were increas-

---

[100]Samuel Haber, *Efficiency and Uplift. Scientific Management in the Progressive Era 1890-1920* (Chicago, 1964), 167, 116; also, x-xii, 60, 99-107, 111-116, 143, 166-167; also, Weinstein, *The Corporate Ideal*, xiv-xv, 252-253; Kolko, 29-33; for a discussion of the use of the concept of social control in the Progressive Era, see Muraskin, 559-569.
[101]Walker, "The Boss as Bureaucrat," 464.
[102]Gary Marx, *Undercover. Police Surveillance in America* (Berkeley, Calif., 1990), 32-35.

ingly taken over by congressional investigating committees, beginning with the temporary Overman Committee in 1918-19 and culminating with the permanent House Un-American Activities Committee in 1945. The same general trend toward centralization, professionalization and bureaucratization of anti-radical propaganda efforts took place on the state level, with the temporary Lusk Committee of the New York State Legislature during the Red Scare and the permanent California Un-American Activities Committee from 1940.[103] Thus, anti-radical politics were transferred from more or less uncoordinated private interest groups to the permanent institutions of the state.

The other part of this development concerned what might be termed the surveillance and harassment of radical activities. Since the 1850s these functions had been the responsibilities of private detectives such as the Pinkerton National Detective Agency and the William J. Burns Detective Agency, which specialized in infiltrating unions and breaking strikes for the employers.[104] While the private detectives continued to spy on employees and fight unions well into the 1930s, it might be argued that their functions gradually were being taken over by state police agencies both on a local and a national level. During the Progressive Era, as previously mentioned, most larger cities established "Red Squads" to watch radical activities, often financed and used by the local business community against organized labor.[105] And, of course, on a national level the Bureau of Investigation was charged with the responsibility of watching and containing radical activities.

The drive to federalize political surveillance was basically a reflection of the wishes of corporate interests and their allies to make the control and regulation of political activities more efficient with the employment of the emerging government bureaucracy and its resources. As Paul Murphy has described the thinking among leaders of the Progressive Era, "The new bureaucratic structure should be called in to work on the dissent problem, the loyalty problem, or the Americanization problem. Possibly, it was time for the federal government to resort to techniques of surveillance and suppression in order to contain forces rapidly getting beyond the control of local or private

---

[103]For the decline of the patriotic societies, see Murphy, "Sources and Nature," 74-75; Edwards, *Patriots in Pinstripe*, *passim*; private red-hunters did not altogether disappear, however, see Donner, *The Age of Surveillance*, 414-451; for the congressional committees, see Walter Goodman, *The Committee. The Extraordinary Career of the House Committee on Un-American Activities* (New York, 1968); for the state committees, see Chamberlain, *Loyalty and Legislative Action;* M. J. Heale, "Red Scare Politics: California's Campaign Against Un-American Activities," *Journal of American Studies*, Vol. 20 (1986), 5-32.
[104]For the private detectives in general, see Morn, *"The Eye That Never Sleeps"*; Hunt, *Front-Page Detective*.
[105]Donner, *Protectors of Privilege*.

directing elites."[106] One of those calling for the federalization of surveillance and control was Robert A. Pinkerton of the Pinkerton National Detective Agency. In 1901, in response to the assassination of President McKinley by Leon Czolgosz, a self-proclaimed anarchist, Pinkerton advocated "the organization of a perfect system of police control" of anarchists and others advocating the violent overthrow of the government. Describing such a system in accordance with the bureaucratic values of the Progressive Era, Pinkerton argued that its staff should be appointed on the basis of experience, that the organization should be kept completely free of political influence and should function continuously and in a "clean-cut, businesslike manner" in order to be as effective as possible: "If the Government is to take an active hand in the suppression of Anarchism, I would advocate the forming of a special department for this purpose, whose whole attention could, at all times, be given to this very serious question." Pinkerton outlined a system of informers who were to infiltrate and report on the activities of the 'Reds': "These people should all be marked and kept under constant surveillance and on the slightest excuse be made harmless."[107] Later, during the Red Scare, William Pinkerton specifically called for the centralization of the surveillance of anarchists and Bolsheviks in the Bureau of Investigation.[108]

This federalization was personified by William J. Burns, the head of the Burns Detective Agency, famous for his sensational crime cases and notorious for his aggressive anti-union tactics. Burns became director of the Bureau of Investigation in 1921-24 in which capacity he simply continued his former activities in close cooperation with corporate interests. Thus, the growth and increasingly active role of the federal government produced a powerful bureaucracy and a willingness among the political and economic elite to use this new instrument for social control and political surveillance against threats to the new corporate order. The federal government's growing regulation of social and political activities can be seen in the development of its policies concerning immigration, organized labor, and the black minority. The government's policies in all three areas also show that the Bureau's activities during the Red Scare were not a sudden break or aberration from normal policies but rather the logical consequence of growing federal social control.

---

[106]Paul Murphy, *World War I and the Origins of Civil Liberties in the United States* (New York, 1979), 47-48.
[107]Robert A. Pinkerton, "Detective Surveillance of Anarchists," *The North American Review*, Vol. 173, No. 5 (November 1901), 609-617; quotes from pp. 609 and 617.
[108]Morn, 180-181.

Controlling the Aliens

In 1882 the federal government entered the field of immigration control when Congress passed a law which excluded such groups as convicts, lunatics, idiots and persons likely to become public charges from entering, and the Immigration Act of 1891 formally placed immigration under federal authority. It established administrative procedures for the exclusion process, extended the denial of admission to polygamists and other groups, and, for the first time, provided that aliens who had become public charges within the first year of entering should be deported. During the Progressive Era these restrictions were gradually strengthened: In the wake of the assassination of President McKinley, Congress passed the Immigration Act of 1903, which extended the time frame during which aliens who had become public charges could be deported, from one to three years, and, more importantly, provided for the exclusion and deportation of anarchists. It enabled the government, for the first time since the Alien and Sedition Acts of 1798, to deport solely on the grounds of opinions. Immediately after the enactment an English anarchist was deported by the federal authorities, an act which according to John Higham signalled "the small beginnings of a permanent and portentous federal policy."[109]

The legal basis for the political deportations of the Red Scare years was established by the Immigration Act of 1917, which had been prepared and debated since 1912 in response to the strikes and agitations carried out by the Industrial Workers of the World (IWW). The law extended the anarchist provision of the 1903 act by making any alien, regardless of how long time he had resided in the US, deportable on the grounds of "advocating or teaching the unlawful destruction of property, or advocating or teaching anarchy or the overthrow by force or violence of the Government of the United States or of all forms of law or the assassination of public officials...."[110] The law also restricted immigration by providing for a literacy test, increased the admission tax from $4 to $8 and excluded, among others, vagrants, chronic alcoholics and Hindu and East Indian immigrant

---

[109]Higham, 113; for the immigration legislation since 1882, see ibid., 44, 48-49, 99-100, 111-112; Nathaniel Honh, "The Origin of American Legislation to Exclude and Deport Aliens for Their Political Beliefs, and Its Initial Review by the Courts," *The Journal of Ethnic Studies*, Vol. 18, No. 2 (Summer 1990), 1-36. For the 1798 laws, see, James Morton Smith, *Freedom's Fetters. The Alien and Sedition Laws and American Civil Liberties* (Ithaca, N.Y., 1956). For the suppression and deportation of alien anarchists, see, Linda Cobb-Reiley, "Aliens and Alien Ideas: The Suppression of Anarchists and the Anarchist Press in America, 1901-1914," *Journalism History*, Vol. 15, Nos. 2-3 (Summer/Autumn 1988), 50-59; Robert J. Goldstein, "The Anarchist Scare of 1908. A Sign of Tensions In the Progressive Era," *American Studies*, Vol. XV, No. 2 (Fall 1974), 55-78.

[110]Preston, 83; for the background of the act, see ibid., 73-85.

laborers.[111] In October 1918 the Departments of Justice and Labor took advantage of the war emergency and pushed through Congress an immigration bill, which extended the deportation provisions to "aliens who are members of or affiliated with any organization that entertains a belief in, teaches, or advocates the overthrow by force or violence of the Government of the United States ... or that advocates or teaches the unlawful destruction of property...."[112] This was, in other words, a "guilt by membership" provision which meant that the authorities did not need to prove individual beliefs or actions but simply that the alien belonged to an anarchistic organization in order to arrest and deport him.

The immigration policy of the Progressive Era culminated with the Immigration Act of 1921, which attempted to reduce immigration by limiting it to a quota for each country of 3% of the number of the nationalities living in the US in 1910. This would restrict the new immigration from Southeastern Europe. The National Origins Act of 1924 tightened the quota system even further to 2% of the 1890 figures, something which brought the immigration from Southeastern Europe to an almost complete halt, excluded all Japanese immigration and limited the total immigration to 150,000 a year.[113] As a result of the increasingly restrictive immigration legislation, the numbers of aliens excluded from entering the US grew from 2,164 in 1892 to 33,041 in 1914, and 30,284 in 1924. At the same time, the number of aliens deported increased from 637 in 1892 to 4,610 in 1914, and 6,409 in 1924.[114]

Beginning around 1915, the federal government led by the Bureau of Naturalization in the Department of Labor and the Interior Department's Bureau of Education, joined during the war by the Committee on Public Information and the Council of National Defense, organized an extensive Americanization program aimed at speeding up the assimilation process and inoculating the new immigrants with traditional American values. According to one study, the federal program was "even more extensive than those of state, local, and private agencies."[115] Reflecting the progressive system of cooperation between

---

[111]Higham, 202-204.

[112]The act is reprinted in, US Congress, Senate, Committee on the Judiciary, *Charges of Illegal Practices of the Department of Justice,* 67th. Cong., 2nd. Sess. (Committee Print, n.d. (1922)), 3, box 107, George W. Norris Papers, LC; for the role of the departments, see, Higham, 221; Preston, 181-183.

[113]Higham, 311, 324.

[114]*Historical Statistics of the United States,* Pt. 1, 114.

[115]John F. McClymer, "The Federal Government and the Americanization Movement, 1915-24," *Prologue,* Vol. 10, No. 1 (June 1978), 24.

government regulatory agencies and voluntary, private groups, the Bureau of Education, for example, worked closely together with the business-dominated National Americanization Committee to fit immigrant workers into the industry and launched an extensive public relations campaign with the aim of "controlling the foreign-language press and shaping its influence along the lines of a better Americanism and in opposition to Bolshevism."[116]

The emerging federal control of immigrants was legalized by the U.S. Supreme Court. In 1893, the court held in *Fong Yue Ting v. United States* that the act of deportation did not constitute punishment in a legal sense but was simply an administrative process since, according to the court, "it is but a method of enforcing the return to his own country of an alien who has not complied with the conditions upon the performance of which the Government of the Nation, acting within its constitutional authority and through the proper departments, has determined that his continuing to reside here shall depend."[117] The defintion of deportation as an administrative action had the immediate consequence of eliminating the courts from the deportation process, since the courts traditionally were reluctant to interfere with administrative decisions. As long as the decision was based on "some" evidence, was in accordance with the law and not grossly unfair, the courts would not take up appeals from aliens.[118] Moreover, the Court held in its 1893 decision that since the deportation process was an administrative and not a criminal proceeding, "the provisions of the Constitution, securing the right of trial by jury and prohibiting unreasonable searches and seizures and cruel and unusual punishments, have no application."[119] In other words, the Supreme Court established as the law of the land that aliens who were arrested and held for deportation by the federal authorities had neither the right to appeal to the courts nor were they entitled to any constitutional rights; in the words of William Preston, "Due process in deportation was smashed on the rock of judicial decision in 1893, never to be put together again."[120] When Attorney General A. Mitchell Palmer claimed during the Red Scare that aliens had no right to constitutional protection

[116]Ibid., 34; in generel see, ibid., 29-37.

[117]The decision is reprinted in, *Charges of Illegal Practices of the Department of Justice*, 13-14, box 107, Norris Papers, LC.

[118]Letter, Anthony Caminetti to Francis P. Garvan, June 27, 1919, OG 341761, RG65, NA.

[119]*Charges of Illegal Practices of the Department of Justice*, 14, 26, box 107, Norris Papers, LC.

[120]Preston, 11. When Preston published his study in 1963, the 1893 decision had still not been reversed and, consequently, was still the basis for the deportation process (ibid., 273). By 1970, the machinery created during progressivism had become so effective that 16,893 aliens were deported and 303,348 were required to depart the US (*Historical Statistics of the United States*, Pt. 1, 114).

against arrests without warrants, unreasonable searches and seizures, self-incrimination, high bail and long detention,[121] he was merely expressing the logical consequence of the Court's position.

Congress had delegated the administration of the deportation process to the Department of Labor and its Bureau of Immigration. Since aliens had no constitutional rights and judicial intervention was rare, the treatment of aliens was determined exclusively by the department's rules and practices. The system was, in the words of W. Anthony Gengarelly, "arbitrary, void of legal checks, and subject to manipulation."[122] Moreover, the Bureau of Immigration seemed to be more interested in obtaining swift results, than protecting the aliens against injustices; according to Assistant Secretary of Labor Louis F. Post, "the whole spirit of the Immigration Bureau was the police spirit of keeping the alien out or putting him out without much regard to the facts."[123] As a result, during the first two decades of the 20th century the administration of the deportation process became increasingly more summary and effective as one rule after another was watered down. First, it was an initial requirement for making an arrest that the secretary of labor had issued a warrant of arrest based on "prima facie" evidence that the alien was deportable. But over the years it became customary in cases in which it was feared that the alien might escape before the warrant arrived from Washington, DC, to take the alien into custody without a warrant. Second, since 1908 it had become a widespread practice within the Bureau of Immigration to simply obtain warrants by telegraph, thereby in effect speeding up the process and avoiding the need for some evidence before the arrest. Third, in order to obtain a confession from the alien, it became the established practice over the years to conduct a "preliminary hearing" at the time of arrest and to restrict the alien's right to counsel at the formal hearing to "preferably at the beginning of the hearing ... or at any rate as soon as such hearing has proceeded sufficiently in the development of the facts to protect the Government's interests...."[124] Finally, following the

---

[121]US Congress, Senate, Subcommittee of the Committee on the Judiciary, *Charges of Illegal Practices of the Department of Justice. Hearings on "Report upon the Illegal Practices of the United States Department of Justice", Made by a Committee of Lawyers on Behalf of the National Popular Government League, and a Memorandum Describing the Personnel of the Committee. Referred "for such Action as the Committee on the Judiciary May Care to Take with Reference to the Same." January 19 to March 3, 1921*, 66th. Cong., 3rd. Sess. (Washington, DC, 1921), 31, 640-641.
[122]W. Anthony Gengarelly, "Secretary of Labor William B. Wilson and the Red Scare, 1919-1920," *Pennsylvania History*, Vol. XLVI, No. 4 (October 1980), 314.
[123]US Congress, House, Committee on Rules, *Investigation of Administration of Louis F. Post, Assistant Secretary of Labor, in the Matter of Deportation of Aliens. Hearings Before the Committee on Rules*, 66th. Cong., 2nd. Sess. (Washington, DC, 1920), 228-229; also, 64-65.
[124]*Charges of Illegal Practices of the Department of Justice*, 5, box 107, Norris Papers, LC; in general see also, Preston, 13-16

formal hearing the case was forwarded for review and decision by the secretary of labor, but through the years this process became more and more perfunctory and more in the nature of the secretary "rubber-stamping" the recommendations of the commissioner general of immigration.[125]

During the Progressive Era, this system, which in the words of Preston "was the natural growth of an administrative technique unrestrained by publicity or opposition,"[126] became so effective in realizing the ideals of the bureaucratic order that some 90% of those arrested were eventually deported.[127] Thus, it can be concluded, on the basis of the increasingly restrictive policies formulated by all branches of the federal government, that the Bureau of Investigation's execution of the Palmer raids and deportations was not a deviation from the established policies, but the Bureau "had simply carried traditional immigration practices to a logical conclusion...."[128]

The Betrayal of the Blacks

The tendency toward increased federal regulation and control was even more pronounced in the area of racial relations. The background to the development during the Progressive Era was the federal government's decision in "the Compromise of 1877" to withdraw its remaining occupation forces from the former Confederate states and thereby, in effect, abandon the blacks in the South. The federal government's withdrawal enabled the South to discriminate and subordinate the black minority by the disfranchisement and the introduction of segregation of most public facilities, working places and housing. In 1896, the Supreme Court upheld the constitutionality of the South's "Separate but Equal" doctrine. This movement toward discrimination was an integrated part of Southern progressivism. For example, the disfranchisement of the black voters was viewed by Southern progressives as an effective and rational way of reforming the often corrupt election processes.[129] According to C. Vann Woodward, "In fact, the

---

[125]*Charges of Illegal Practices*, 311-312; Preston, 17; Gengarelly, 314.
[126]Preston, 18.
[127]Ibid., 208-209, 332-333n105.
[128]Ibid., 220. Preston has also noted that the sensational character of the Palmer raids 1919-20 "obscured the fact that the road to these incidents had been charted many years before" (Ibid., 1).
[129]Rayford W. Logan, *The Betrayal of the Negro, from Rutherford B. Hayes to Woodrow Wilson* (New York, 1965), 23-124, 165-275, 354, 371-392; Kenneth O'Reilly, *Nixon's Piano. Presidents and Racial Politics from Washington to Clinton* (New York, 1995), 53-82; Arthur E. Ekirch Jr., *Progressivism in America. A Study of the Era from Theodore Roosevelt to Woodrow Wilson* (New York, 1974), 83-85; Woodward, 69-74, 83-92, 97-102.

typical progressive reformer rode to power in the South on a disfranchising or White-Supremacy movement."[130]

During the Progressive Era discrimination and segregation also reached into and soon permeated the federal bureaucracy. At the turn of the century, Washington, DC, was a sort of safe haven for blacks with opportunities unequalled anywhere else. 94,446 blacks lived in the capital, of whom 24,500 worked in the federal administration, to a large degree on equal terms with their white co-workers.[131] Although discrimination against black employees had always occurred sporadically, it gained momentum during the administration of Theodore Roosevelt, who decided that in order to win the Republican nomination in 1904 he had to ally himself with the Southern "lily white" wing of the party against the conservative leadership. The president gave up defending the cause of equal rights for blacks and segregation was introduced in several federal departments.[132] The Wilson administration expanded segregation to include those departments with the largest number of black employees, such as the Treasury and Post Office Departments, and began the practice of systematic discrimination against blacks from civil service positions.[133] Despite protests from black leaders and liberals, the segregation in the federal bureaucracy continued and was even expanded further during World War I and the Republican administrations in the 1920s; one of the affected departments was the Justice Department.[134] As noted by Kathleen Wolgemuth, when systematic segregation was introduced in the federal bureaucracy, government began actively to define social customs: "Federal segregation was by far the worst blow dealt the Negro race in its years of freedom, for it signified official approval of a practice against which Negroes were fighting by gradual or active means.... Now that the government was entering the arena of segregationist activities, such tendencies would increase and would operate with official sanction."[135]

---

[130]Woodward, 91.

[131]Kathleen Wolgemuth, "Woodrow Wilson and Federal Segregation," *The Journal of Negro History*, Vol. XLIV, No. 2 (April 1959), 159, 170.

[132]Seth M. Scheiner, "President Theodore Roosevelt and the Negro, 1901-1908," *The Journal of Negro History*, Vol. XLVII, No. 3 (July 1962), 169-182; August Meier & Elliot Rudwick, "The Rise of Segregation in the Federal Bureaucracy, 1900-1930," *Phylon*, Vol. XXVIII, No. 2 (Summer 1967), 180; Ekirch, 135-136, 230.

[133]Cronon (ed.), 32-33; Wolgemuth, 158-173; Ekirch, 229-233; Arthur S. Link, *Woodrow Wilson and the Progressive Era, 1910-1917* (New York (1954), 1963), 63-66; O'Reilly, *Nixon's Piano*, 82-90.

[134]Meier & Rudwick, 181-184.

[135]Wolgemuth, 170, 169.

What might be termed the federalization of segregation during the Progressive Era had two immediate consequences for the federal government's policy toward the black minority. On the one hand a reluctance to actively protect the civil rights of blacks when they were being violated by whites, and on the other hand an increasing willingness to use the federal bureaucracy to control and contain any black challenges to the existing racial order. Supported by several Supreme Court decisions, the Justice Department repeatedly refused to intervene against the wave of lynchings of blacks in the South during the first decade of the century, arguing that it had no jurisdiction to interfere in the internal affairs of the states.[136] In 1910, an internal Justice Department memorandum explained the government's position: "Under the decisions, there is no authority in the United States Government to protect citizens of African descent in the enjoyment of civil rights generally in the states from individual aggression. The right assailed must be one which the citizen, whether black or white, possesses by virtue of the Constitution and laws of the United States." According to the memorandum, the department only had jurisdiction to prosecute when a local state denied its citizens their civil rights (the so-called "color of state law") or in cases of involuntary servitude.[137] But even in these areas the federal government only became involved with some reluctance. For example, in the years before World War I, the Bureau of Investigation seems to have investigated a considerable number of allegations of peonage, but following the war the Bureau all but abandoned them because so few ended with a successful conviction.[138] Except for a single sensational case in 1922 in Louisiana, the Bureau also avoided interfering with the re-emerging Ku Klux Klan.[139]

In contrast to their reluctance against getting involved in the protection of civil rights, the federal authorities did not hesitate to use the Bureau of Investigation to control real or perceived threats by the

---

[136]Robert L. Zangrando, *The NAACP Crusade Against Lynching, 1909-1950* (Philadelphia, 1980), 15, 19-20.

[137]Memorandum as to the Authority of the United States to Protect Negroes in the States in the Enjoyment of Civil Rights, March 31, 1910, OG 3057, RG65, NA. See also, O'Reilly, *"Racial Matters"*, 9.

[138]Theodore Kornweibel Jr., *Introduction to Federal Surveillance of Afro-Americans (1917-1925)* (Microfilm: Frederick, Maryland, n.d.), x; William Cohen, "Riots, Racism, and Hysteria: The Response of Federal Investigative Officials to the Race Riots of 1919," *The Massachusetts Review*, Vol. XIII, No. 3 (Summer 1972), 380n17; O'Reilly, *"Racial Matters,"* 15-16.

[139]O'Reilly, 16. A case from 1920 helps to illustrate how the Bureau went about investigating the Klan. In December 1920, the NAACP asked the Bureau to investigate allegations of KKK intimidation of black voters in Florida during the recent elections. After having interviewed the local white leaders, the Bureau reported that it was unable to find any indications of election fraud and thereupon closed the case (Reports, Harry C. Leslie, December 30, 1920, with att. Report of Walter F. White, Ass. Sec., NAACP; A. V. French, December 7, 1920, BS 213410-2, RG65, NA).

black community to the racial status quo. It has often been claimed that the Bureau's interest in black activities began either during World War I or the Red Scare in 1919, and therefore might be explained as a response to either the patriotic or anti-Bolshevik hysteria.[140] It can actually be traced back to the beginning of the Great Migration, the movement of some 400,000 Southern blacks to the Northern ghettos during the period 1915-19. The Great Migration was caused by several economic and social factors. The Southern black population, 80% of which worked as agricultural laborers and sharecroppers, was severely affected by the increasing cost of living following the outbreak of the war in 1914, an agricultural depression in the South, and systematic discrimination and intimidation. The Southern blacks were attracted to the North because of the growing demand for cheap labor in the industry. Despite the fact that these social forces behind the migration were well-known and much publicized at the time,[141] the Wilson administration feared a political plot. Apparently suspecting that the black migrants might use their newly acquired voting rights in the North to support the Republicans, who had historically championed the cause of abolition and civil rights, and thereby adversely affect the outcome in several closely contested states in the Midwest in the 1916 presidential election, the Department of Justice warned of a conspiracy to transport blacks from the South to vote fraudently and ensure a Republican victory.[142]

The Bureau of Investigation was used by the administration to attempt to substantiate its conspiracy theory.[143] From September to November 1916 an extensive inquiry was conducted by the federal agents who interviewed officials from railroad and steamship companies, which had transported blacks to the North, and tracked down numerous black migrants.[144] Despite its efforts, the Bureau was unable

[140]O'Reilly, *"Racial Matters,"* 12, dates the beginning of the Bureau's racial investigations to the outbreak of World War I (see also, Lowenthal, 128), while Cohen, 383, Arthur Waskow, *From Race Riot to Sit-In. 1919 and the 1960s* (Garden City, New York (1966), 1967), 188, and William M. Tuttle Jr., *Race Riot. Chicago in the Red Summer of 1919* (New York, 1975), 227, date them to the summer of 1919; only Kornweibel, x, traces them to the Great Migration in 1916.

[141]Dewey H. Palmer, "Moving North: Migration of Negroes During World War I," *Phylon*, Vol. XXVIII, No. 1 (Spring 1967), 52-56; Nancy J. Weiss, *The National Urban League 1910-1940* (New York, 1974), 93-99.

[142]Charles Flint Kellogg, *NAACP. A History of the National Association for the Advancement of Colored People*, Vol. I, 1909-1920 (Baltimore, 1967), 224; Kornweibel, x; O'Reilly, *Nixon's Piano*, 91.

[143]For instructions to investigate allegations of fraudlent voting, see letters, A. Bruce Bielaski to H. C. Clabaugh, October 19, 1916, and to Thomas Cartwell, October 29, 1916, Misc. 10015, RG65, NA.

[144]Letters, Bielaski to F. B. Carbarino, October 26, 1916; to Billups Harris, October 21, 1916; to John Wilson, November 1, 1916; to William B. Matthews, October 23, 1916; to Calvin Weakley, October 24, 1916; to H. C. Clabaugh, October 28, 1916; Bielaski, Memorandum

to find any evidence of a Republican conspiracy to transport blacks to the North to ensure a Democratic defeat at the polls, and it concluded instead that it was a typical political rumor springing up in the heat of the campaign as a result of, as one agent noted, " ... each party having only a healthy, natural and perfectly proper suspicion of their opponents."[145] Not surprisingly, the agents found ample evidence that the main inducement for the migrants had been the large number of available jobs at a higher wage in the industry and that the knowledge of the opportunities in the North had spread through the black communities by letters sent back home.[146] However, the fact that the administration and the Bureau investigated unsubstantiated rumors that blacks were being used in a conspiracy against the government indicated that the federal government viewed the black minority with deep suspicion, a view that would guide the policy and attitude of the Bureau during the war.

Even before the US entered the war in April 1917, the South was full of rumors of German agents trying to recruit blacks to fight against the white population as a sort of fifth column.[147] The Arkansas State Council of Defense informed the quasi-official American Protective League about growing unrest among the blacks in Little Rock: "No doubt a good deal of this is due to the propaganda that has been very vigorously carried on by German influences in order to upset the racial situation, and to drive away the agricultural labor of the South ... Whether this is a part of the German propaganda or not, no more insidious and ingenius plan could be adopted for crippling the South and its resources, as well as necessitating very comprehensive steps to be taken for domestic defence."[148] Another worried Southerner asked the Justice Department to suppress the alleged German activity, claiming that " ... there has been a persistent campaign conducted by alien enemies among the darkies, with a view of inciting their hatred

---

for Mr. Graham, October 30, 1916, ibid. BI collected long lists of migrants, see, letter, Local White Slave Officer to Bielaski, November 8, 1916, with att. list; H. G. White to Leverett F. Eaglesby, November 4, 1916, with att. list; Clabaugh to Bielaski, October 27, 1916, with att. list; report, A. J. Devlin, October 24, 1916, with att. list, ibid.

[145]Report, Arthur Bagley, October 31, 1916; also, reports, J. J. McLaughlin, November 1, 1916; Arthur Bagley, November 1, 1916, Misc. 8024, ibid.; Billups Harris, November 4, 1916; Todd Daniel, November 6, 1916; letter, Local Officer, Baltimore, to Bielaski, n.d., Misc. 10015, ibid.

[146]Reports, Billups Harris, November 6, 1916; H. M. McClintock, October 30, 1916; L. N. Cantrall, November 1, 1916; Billups Harris, November 2, 1916, ibid.

[147]Theodore Kornweibel Jr., *No Crystal Stair. Black Life and the Messenger, 1917-1928* (Westport, Conn., 1975), 4-9.

[148]Letter, Durand Whipple to A. M. Briggs, July 3, 1917, OG 3057, RG65, NA.

against their own government."[149] According to the view among Southern whites, black discontent was not caused by the injustices of the segregation system but by outside influences.

The files of the Bureau of Investigation show that the Bureau began its investigation of black disloyalty before the outbreak of war, indicating that Bureau officials fully shared the South's anxieties. As early as March 29, 1917, a few days before President Wilson asked Congress to declare war against Germany, Bureau Chief A. Bruce Bielaski asked his agents to investigate "alleged German activities to prevent Negoes in enlisting for war, or to incite sedition among them...,"[150] and five days later he wrote to the field: "Quite a number of complaints have been received by this Department that attempts are being made by German agents to stir up sedition among the Negroes in this country. It is desired that you be on the look-out for anything of this nature which may come to your attention, with a view to determining the interests which are back of these alleged attempts."[151] During the next year and a half, the Bureau energetically pursued every rumor about German propaganda and subversion among blacks. No tale seemed too incredible or too wild to be investigated. For example, the agents were directed to look into the obviously fabricated story of German agents attempting to "stir up sedition among the Negroes in this country and to move them to German South America, where they are said to be educated and drilled, with a view to fighting the United States."[152] Despite its zeal, the Bureau was never able to substantiate this or any other rumor of German intrigue.[153]

---

[149]Letter, F. G. Aulebrook to Department of Justice, May 27, 1918; for similar requests, see, letters, Bielaski to John E. Boze, April 10, 1917; to J. W. McKee, November 6, 1917; to Henry B. Mitchell, April 26, 1917; to Rev. Will Jensen, April 28, 1917; Senator Morris Sheppard to Secretary of War Newton D. Baker, June 19, 1917, with att. letter, State Senator John Henderson to Morris Sheppard, June 16, 1917, ibid.

[150]Letter, A. Bruce Bielaski to C. S. Weakley, March 29, 1917, ibid.

[151]Letter, Bielaski to A. J. Devlin, April 3, 1917, ibid.

[152]Letter, Bielaski to R. H. Daughton, April 10, 1917, ibid. For the investigation of German propaganda among blacks, see, letters, Wm. M. Smith to Hon. R. E. Byrd, May 2, 1917; Bielaski to W. R. McElveen, May 3, 1917; Edward Lowe to Bielaski, March 5, 1917; Bielaski to Lowe, March 8, 1917; Bielaski to J. R. McKissick, April 9, 1917; Bielaski to Samuel W. Long, March 14, 1917; Bielaski to Billups Harris, March 28, 1917; reports, Ralph Daughton, April 30, 1917; J. L. Webb, April 1, 1917, ibid.; S. D. Bradley, March 19, 1919, OG 369936, ibid.

[153]The Bureau reported that it had been informed by a former US Attorney "that he is satisfied that there is no substantial basis for the rumors that pro-German propagandists have been or can operate with any success among the Negroes." (Letter, Special Agent to Lewis J. Baley, June 19, 1917, OG 3057, ibid.) The rumors were also denied by black ministers (letter, Director of Missions, Board for Colored Missions, to Attorney General Gregory, April 9, 1917, ibid.). Historians agree that even though there did exist some antiwar sentiment among the black population, there never were any indications of pro-German feelings (Kornweibel, *No Crystal Stair*, 9).

The Bureau's suspicion about black disloyalty was so great that it did not limit its probe to German activities. According to Bureau thinking, blacks were vulnerable to any form of subversive agitation. The Bureau investigated allegations that socialist agitators in Cleveland, Ohio, had been advising blacks that it was unnecessary for them to register for the draft.[154] In Waco, Texas, the agents looked into rumors that blacks were planning an uprising against the whites,[155] and in Washington, DC, it was feared that blacks would turn on the whites when the troops left the city.[156] In San Antonio, Texas, a black minister who was alleged to have spoken against conscription was investigated.[157] Elsewhere, the Bureau looked for evidence that white radicals had attempted to persuade blacks to strike or that Mexicans had tried to influence blacks.[158]

The Bureau was particularly alert to any kind of black protest which might be construed as opposition to the war. When the National Colored Soldiers Comfort Committee launched an appeal for aid to the families of 13 black soldiers who had been executed following the race riot in Houston in August 1917, the Bureau tried to have the organization's collection cards banned from the mail. This was done even though an investigation had found no indication of pro-German sentiments. Drawing the attention of the public to the plight of the relatives of the soldiers seemed reason enough to be suppressed.[159] The publication of an article entitled "Shall the Negro Fight?" prompted an investigation, and the local assistant US attorney informed Bielaski that he was confident "that this article is a veiled effort, originating from some alien enemy" and promised to take swift action: "... I am taking this matter up with the publisher of the paper, and hope to be able to prevent any further articles of like nature."[160]

The two most influential black publications during the war, the *Crisis* and the *Chicago Defender,* were singled out for particular close scrutiny by the Bureau. Despite the fact that the *Crisis* was moderate in tone

---

[154]Letter, Special Agent to Bielaski, June 2, 1917, OG 3057, RG65, NA.
[155]Report, B. C. Baldwin, September 13, 1917, ibid.
[156]Report, W. W. Grimes, September 11, 1917, ibid.
[157]Report, Manuel Sorola, September 7, 1917, ibid.
[158]Reports, T. S. Marshall, September 2, 1917; John E. Hawkins, April 16 and 17, 1917, ibid. See also, report, R. L. Barnes, September 4, 1917; letter, Div. Superint. to Bielaski, September 5, 1917; the Military Intelligence Division also passed on an "unconfirmed rumor" to the BI that "certain Hindu suspects" were agitating among the blacks against military service "and advising them to flee to Mexico" (Letter, Gen. M. Churchill to Bielaski, October 4, 1918, ibid.).
[159]Letter, US Attorney, Arkansas, to Bielaski, January 19, 1918; reports, J. E. Elliot, January 21 and 29, 1918, letter, Bielaski to William H. Lamar, January 26, 1918, OG 369936, ibid.
[160]Letter, Ass. US Attorney to Bielaski, April 25, 1917, with att. clipping; also, letter, Bielaski to J. M. Offley, April 30, 1917, OG 3057, ibid.

and refrained from openly criticizing America's participation in the war, Bureau officials suspected from the beginning that the paper was engaged in spreading German propaganda.[161] It took no action until the spring 1918, when it received several complaints from politicians and others to the effect that the paper was pro-German and attempting to stir up the blacks.[162] At the same time, a Bureau informant in Waco, Texas, reported that the *Crisis* appeared to be of "a very agitating nature" and thought that there might be a connection to the Houston riot.[163] The Atlanta, Georgia, field office also notified Washington that, "In reading over this magazine, there are articles therein which tend to excite the Negro race in this section against the white people, and the magazine is made up mostly of articles on lynching Negroes in the South and in agent's opinion should be suppressed."[164] The paper should be banned by the authorities, then, not because of any opposition to the war or disloyalty, but because its crusade against lynchings challenged the existing racial order in the South. In May 1918, Bielaski asked the Justice Department for a decision, but the department found no grounds on which to ban the paper and prosecute the editors.[165] The department did, however, authorize Bielaski to launch an investigation to ascertain whether the paper was financed by foreign sources or whether it was used unwittingly by the German propaganda, but in both instances the probe came to nothing.[166]

The *Chicago Defender* was likewise investigated for reasons other than opposition to the war. The paper was investigated as early as 1916 because of its enthusiastic encouragement of the Great Migration

---

[161]Reports, McElveen, April 30, 1917; Paul Hofhorr, May 26, 1917, OG 17011, ibid.; for *The Crisis* in general, see Kellogg, 271-274; for the investigation, see also, Kornweibel, *"Seeing Red,"* 54-55.

[162]Letters, Clifford L. Butler to Bureau of Investigation, April 28, 1918; Bielaski to Butler, May 10, 1918; Senator Ollie M. James, April 27, 1918; Bielaski to James, May 10, 1918; reports, Leverett F. Englesby, April 5, 1918; G. C. Drautzburg, December 16, 1917, OG 17011, RG65, NA.

[163]Letter, Special Employee to Bielaski, May 10, 1918, ibid.

[164]Report, Howell E. Jackson, May 10, 1918, ibid. The NAACP, which published *The Crisis*, was repeatedly investigated because of its anti-lynching agitation during the war (reports, W. L. Hawkins, October 31, 1918; In re: NAACP, July 8, 1918, ibid.; F. R. Cotton, January 16, 1918, OG 369936, ibid.; Report: Negro Agitation, November 12, 1918, OG 258421, ibid.).

[165]Bielaski, Memorandum for Mr. Bettman, May 10, 1918; Alfred Bettman, Memorandum for Mr. Bielaski, May 16, 1918; letter, Bielaski to A. R. Gere, May 21, 1918, OG 17011, ibid.

[166]Alfred Bettman, Memorandum for Mr. Bielaski, June 1, 1918; letters, Bielaski to Charles DeWoody, June 4, 1918; Bielaski to R. H. Daughton, June 4, 1918; Memorandum for Mr. Bielaski, June 5, 1918; report, Lieut. W. T. Carothers, June 13, 1918; Lieut. Carothers, Supplementary Report, July 24, 1918, ibid. The investigation was finally abandoned in the summer of 1918, when *The Crisis'* editor, W. E. B. Du Bois, was offered a post in the MID to help out with black grievances during the war (Alfred Bettman, Memorandum for Mr. Bielaski, July 9, 1918, ibid.).

and the Bureau had contemplated having it barred from the mails.[167] During the war the *Defender's* editor, Robert Abbott, was brought in for questioning,[168] but apparently the paper was saved from further suppression because the Bureau was unable to reach a consensus concerning the paper's loyalty. Whereas the Chicago field office was inclined to view the paper as "loyal to the core,"[169] agents in the South feared that the paper might intentionally create unrest and be part of a German plan "of creating a home problem to engage the attention of this country."[170] Other black publications were not so lucky. The editor of the *San Antonio Inquirer* was sent to prison for criticizing the executions of a number of black soldiers following the Houston riot,[171] and A. Philip Randolph and Chandler Owen, editors of the socialistic the *Messenger,* were arrested and the magazine denied second-class mailing permit by the Post Office until 1921.[172]

On July 2, 1917, a major race riot erupted in East St. Louis, Illinois, resulting in the deaths of at least 39 blacks and 8 whites. The riot was primarily caused by racial and social tensions brought on by the Great Migration. For some time the industry had tried to break the local unions by importing large numbers of unorganized black laborers from the South, and the animosity of the white population was further increased by sensational press accounts of black crime and rumors circulated by the Democratic party machine of Republican – and black – political corruption. Once started, the city officials were unable to control the riot and members of the local white militia even participated in the white mobs' assaults on blacks.[173] Despite the fact that the riot was perpetrated by gangs of whites who attacked and murdered defenseless blacks, and despite repeated demands for federal intervention,[174] the Wilson administration refused to intervene, arguing that "no facts have been presented to us which would justify federal action...."[175] Wilson also hesitated to meet with black leaders and con-

---

[167]Report, F. C. Pendleton, October 6, 1916; letter, Bielaski to H. C. Clabaugh, October 16, 1916, Misc. 9969, ibid.; Kornweibel, *"Seeing Red,"* 38-39.

[168]Reports, J. E. Hawkins, April 16, 1917; F. R. Hilliard, April 17, 1917, OG 5911, RG65, NA.

[169]Report, B. D. Adbit, December 22, 1917, ibid.

[170]Report, Edward S. Chastaln, April 24, 1917; also, report, E. J. Kerwin, May 2, 1918, ibid.

[171]Patrick S. Washburn, *A Question of Sedition. The Federal Government's Investigation of the Black Press During World War II* (New York, 1986), 21-22.

[172]For the arrest, see, report, Special Agent Sawken, August 10, 1918, OG 265716, RG65, NA; also, Kornweibel, *No Crystal Stair,* 3-4, 53; Daniel S. Davis, *Mr. Black Labor. The Story of A. Philip Randolph, Father of the Civil Rights Movement* (New York, 1972), 21-22; Kornweibel, *"Seeing Red,"* 76-79.

[173]Kellogg, 224; Zangrando, 36-37.

[174]Arthur S. Link (ed.), *The Papers of Woodrow Wilson*, Vol. 43, 103-104, 112, 116, 123, 222-223.

[175]Ibid., 300; also, 297-298.

demn publicly the attacks on blacks, apparently following the advice of his secretary, Joseph Tumulty, who feared that if Wilson took such an initiative "the fire will be re-kindled and that a greater impetus will be given to an agitation which is contagious in its effects."[176] When the president finally, a year later, issued a statement condemning mob violence and lynchings, he did so in general terms and did not specifically mention racially motivated violence or the fact that almost all mob violence was perpetrated by whites.[177]

In contrast to this reluctance to protect the civil rights of blacks and to provide leadership against racial violence, the federal authorities were quick to look for subversive influences behind the riot. On July 3, 1917, the day after the riot began, Bielaski telegraphed the Chicago field office, in whose district East St. Louis was located, and ordered an investigation to ascertain if German influences had caused the violence.[178] Even though the agents found no indications of German activity, they did succeed in blaming the disturbances on the black population. Agent J. J. McLaughlin reported that the riot was "the outgrowth of of (sic) trouble brewing for some time due to the Negroes taking the white men (sic) jobs and robberies on the part of the Negroes."[179] Bielaski seemed reluctant to give up the conspiracy theory and he inquired if the Chicago field office was "reasonably certain" that there were no foreign influences at work. Subsequently, he passed on information received from the military to the effect that the riot had been instigated by Dr. Le Roy Bundy, a local black leader and dentist, who was rumored to be a German agent.[180] When the following inquiry failed to unearth any concrete evidence of enemy activity in East St. Louis or any other violations of the federal law, but instead pointed to the local unions as the likely perpetrators, the investigation was quietly dropped.[181]

The Bureau was also used by the administration to investigate critics of its attitude toward the riot. Demands that Wilson should actively support federal legislation against lynchings and mob violence were

---

[176]Ibid., 139; also, 146, 342-343, 359, 412-413.

[177]Ibid., Vol. 49, 97-98.

[178]Telegram, Bielaski to Brennan, July 3, 1917, OG 28469, RG65, NA.

[179]Report, J. J. McLaughlin, July 5, 1917, ibid.; also, reports, W. C. Coss, July 5, 1917; E. J. Brennan, July 6, 1917, ibid.

[180]Telegrams, Bielaski to Brennan, July 21 and 25, 1917, with att. letter, Lee D. Appelwhite to the Surgeon General, July 4, 1917, ibid. The military also informed BI that the riot had been caused by the local unions as an attack on the imported black workers, see, letter, Div. Superint. to Bielaski, July 21, 1917, ibid.

[181]Reports, Brennan, July 25, 1917; Wm. Brashear, July 27 and 30, 1917, ibid.

referred by the White House to the Bureau,[182] an open letter by Kelly Miller of Howard University to Wilson, entitled "The Disgrace of Democracy", was noted by the Bureau,[183] and pamphlets dealing with the riot were investigated out of fear that they might cause unrest in the South.[184] When some ten thousand blacks took part in the "Negro Silent Protest Parade" to protest the killings, Washington instructed the Providence, Rhode Island, field office to ascertain "just what influences were behind this movement. Was it purely a local affair or is there any evidence that the movement was fostered by outside sources?"[185] After checking its sources, the field office was able to report back what was common knowledge, namely that the parade was organized by the civil rights organization the NAACP.[186]

The War Against Radical Labor
It might be argued that the role of the expanding federal government in relation to organized labor consisted on the one hand of undermining militant unions such as the syndicalist Industrial Workers of the World and breaking up national strikes which threatened the stability of the economic system while on the other hand recognizing and supporting the conservative unions led by the American Federation of Labor.[187] The first attempt of the federal government at intervening in a major strike was made in response to the Great Strike of 1877, when a national railroad walkout triggered a wave of sympathy strikes, effectively paralyzing much of the industry. Federal troops were introduced to restore law and order and following the strike the federal and state governments, aided by generous business contributions, reorganized the national guard to be used in future labor disturbances.[188] Since the executive branch before World War I played a limited role in controlling labor relations (for example, the Department of Labor, originally established to compile labor statistics, was not elevated to

---

[182]Letters, Mary Ogden ? to Woodrow Wilson, July 30, 1917; Jordan to Wilson, July 4, 1917, OG 28469, ibid.; William Holmes to Wilson, August 17, 1917, OG 3057, ibid.

[183]Report, Warren W. Grimes, February 20, 1918, OG 369936, ibid.

[184]Report, J. L. Webb, August 23, 1917; letter, Bielaski to T. W. Quinlen, September 1, 1917, OG 3057, ibid.

[185]Letter, Bielaski to Tom Howick, October 18, 1917, OG 67118, ibid.; also, letter, Howick to Bielaski, October 16, 1917, with att. handbill, ibid.

[186]Letter, Howick to Bielaski, October 27, 1917, ibid.; for the parade, see, Kellogg, 226; Zangrando, 37-38.

[187]For this general policy, see Weinstein, *The Corporate Ideal,* especially chapters 1, 2, 5, 7 and 8.

[188]Barton C. Hacker, "The United States Army as a National Police Force: The Federal Policing of Labor Disputes, 1877-1898," *Military Affairs,* Vol. XXXIII, No. 1 (April 1969), 255-264; Jerry M. Cooper, "The Army as Strikebreaker – The Railroad Strikes of 1877 and 1894," *Labor History,* Vol. 18, No. 2 (Spring 1977), 179-196.

cabinet level until 1913 and was primarily authorized to mediate in labor conflicts[189]), federal labor policies were instead formulated by the courts, which were traditionally staunchly anti-union. During the 19th century the courts had usually found labor associations to be criminal conspiracies, which interfered with free trade and bound its members to a set of rules, which were independent of the law. The Progressive Era Supreme Court was guided by the overriding view that unions were "an invasion of entrepreneurial rights and dismissing legislative attempts to endorse them as legitimate bargaining agencies."[190] In a series of decisions the courts held most union tactics to be illegal coercion of the employers, struck down union membership agreements, and, most significantly, the Supreme Court in 1908 decided that the Sherman Anti-Trust Act applied to unions and that consequently certain strikes were an illegal interference with interstate trade. At the same time, the courts proved more than willing to grant labor injuctions in the form of court orders to restrain strikers, thereby indicating the federal government's interest in maintaining an un-restrained and free trade.[191]

While the government had a long tradition for strikebreaking, the Wilson administration during World War I took steps to attack radical labor. Guided by an overriding concern for ensuring an uninterrupted supply of war materials, the administration began regulating industrial relations by creating the National War Labor Board which improved the position of organized labor by recognizing it as the representative of labor, accepted the right to collective bargaining and officially approved the eight hour day. Although the membership of the AFL doubled between 1916 and 1920, the price was the unconditional support of organized labor to the government and the war effort, which, in the words of one labor historian, reduced the AFL to the "de facto instrument of the Wilson administration."[192]

At the same time the federal authorities dealt harshly with the most important radical union, the syndicalist Industrial Workers of the World (IWW). For some time, Western business interests and politicians had lobbied the Wilson administration to intervene and sup-

---

[189]Harold W. Metz, *Labor Policy of the Federal Government* (Washington, DC, 1945), 7-9.
[190]Tomlins, 30.
[191]Ibid., 36-40, 46-50, 83-84; Metz, 26-27; William E. Forbath, "The Shaping of the American Labor Movement," *Harvard Law Review*, Vol. 102, No. 6 (April 1989), 1111-1256; David Brody, *Workers in Industrial America. Essays on the 20th Century Struggle* (New York, 1980), 25-26.
[192]Ibid., 42-44; see also, Metz, 27; Simeon Larson, *Labor and Foreign Policy. Gompers, the AFL, and the First World War, 1914-1918* (Rutherford & London, 1975); Frank L. Grubbs, Jr., *The Struggle for Labor Loyalty: Gompers, the A. F. of L., and the Pacifists, 1917-1920* (Durham, N.C., 1968).

press the union. In October 1915, the governors of California, Washington, Oregon and Utah called for a federal investigation into "abnormal disorder and incendiarism" and threats allegedly made by the IWW. As Attorney General Thomas Gregory informed Wilson, the Justice Department inquiry had only been able to establish that the IWW membership was mainly made up of "agitators, men without homes, mostly foreigners, the discontented and unemployed who are not anxious to work, and men of a very low order of intelligence and morals" but it had found no concrete evidence of violations of the federal law.[193] Again, on July 17, 1917, 8 Western governors complained that IWWs were burning wheat fields and instigating labor unrest. In order to prevent local vigilante activity, they presented a plan to the administration according to which all suspected members of the IWW should be interned by the federal government without trial and that all press accounts regarding the IWW should be suppressed. The plan, however, was vetoed by Wilson and came to nothing.[194]

It has been claimed that the later federal repression of the IWW was a response to this Western pressure.[195] However, as shown by Melvyn Dubofsky, the federal government had its own, independent interest in suppressing the IWW. According to Dubofsky, Washington was guided by an overriding determination to protect the production of war materials: "Unsure of what Wobblies in fact wanted, aware that the IWW's propaganda called for revolution, and fearful that the IWW, whatever its actual motives, might actually sabotage the war effort, federal officials honestly believed they had only one recourse – to restrain the Wobblies from interfering with national security."[196] This interpretation is supported by the fact that on July 11, six days before the governors' proposal was put forward, Attorney General Gregory made the decision to prosecute the IWW and that six days later the Justice Department authorized a nationwide investigation by the Bureau of Investigation to ascertain whether the IWW was financed by the Germans or whether its members had violated any of the wartime

---

[193]Link (ed.), *The Papers of Woodrow Wilson*, Vol. 36, 188-190.
[194]Ibid., Vol. 43, 157-158, 200, 203, 222, 280-281, 494-495; ibid., Vol. 47, 194-198; Cronon (ed.), 178, 180, 183, 199, 285. On the vigilante activity against the IWW, see, H. C. Peterson & Gilbert C. Fite, *Opponents of War, 1917-1918* (Madison, 1957), 49-60. Although President Wilson opposed the internment plan, he wholeheartedly supported the prosecution of the IWW: Wilson informed his Attorney General that the IWWs "certainly are worthy of being suppressed" and he noted at another time that he hoped the government had done enough to effectively put an end to the IWW's activities (Link (ed.), *The Papers of Woodrow Wilson*, Vol. 47, 232-233; Vol. 49, 538-539).
[195]Preston, 122, 124-127.
[196]Dubofsky, 401. According to Dubofsky, federal officials were especially worried about IWW interference with the Western spruce and copper production (ibid., 410).

laws.[197] That this action was undertaken independently of the Western governors is evident from a letter from Gregory to Wilson in which he reminded the president of "the intended action I have in mind with respect to the I.W.W.," adding that it was being executed "through the usual channels, and I have not considered it advisable to reveal my plans to any of these western governors...."[198]

Having determined that the IWW might constitute a potential threat against the war effort, the government's attack followed soon. On September 5, 1917, Bureau agents raided IWW offices and private homes in 33 cities across the nation and confiscated tons of material. Later the same month, 166 officers, organizers and secretaries of the IWW were indicted for having conspired to obstruct the production of war materials by strikes and sabotage and for having unlawfully aided young men not to register for the draft and having caused insubordination in the military forces.[199] Attorney General Gregory informed Wilson that "the evidence is sensational and very convincing, and to the effect that these people have been teaching sabotage in its most outrageous form, and have deliberately attempted to interfere with various Government endeavors immediately connected with the prosecution of the war."[200] In fact, it is clear that the authorities had no concrete evidence against any individual member or leader for having violated the law and that they simply based their case on the organization's extreme and often revolutionary propaganda. In August 1918, following a mass trial in Chicago, 99 defendants were found guilty on all counts and sentenced to prison terms of up to 20 years, thereby, in effect, destroying the IWW as an effective labor force.[201]

The Wilson Administration and the Red Scare
For several reasons the existing literature has down-played the importance of the Wilson administration's interests in general and the Bureau of Investigation's interests specifically in the anti-radical crusade. First and foremost, since most historians have agreed that the Scare was initiated from below, by the public hysteria, they have concentrated on explaining the deeper forces and processes which

---

[197]Ibid., 404-405.
[198]Link (ed.), *The Papers of Woodrow Wilson*, Vol. 44, 17.
[199]*AG Report 1918*, 53-54, 104; Peterson & Fite, 62-63, 237-238; Dubofsky, 406-407.
[200]Link (ed.), *The Papers of Woodrow Wilson*, Vol. 47, 604.
[201]Peterson & Fite, 237-241; Dubofsky, 433-437; National Civil Liberties Bureau, *The Truth About the I.W.W. Facts in Relation to the Trial at Chicago by Competent Industrial Investigators and Noted Economists* (New York, April 1918); Philip Taft, "The Federal Trials of the IWW," *Labor History*, Vol. 3, No. 1 (Winter 1962), 57-91; Philip S. Foner, "United States of America Vs. Wm. Haywood, et al.: The I.W.W. Indictment," *Labor History*, Vol. 11, No. 4 (Fall 1970), 500-530.

triggered this fear, while the government in general has been depicted as a reluctant agent, which simply reacted to the hysteria. One central theme has been that the Wilson administration, due to the president's preoccupation with the debate about the Versailles treaty, his subsequent breakdown and severe illness, and disagreements within the cabinet, was in effect leaderless during much of the Red Scare. According to Murray, "the ability of the government to withstand mounting public pressure rapidly weakened,"[202] thereby implying that stronger leadership would have meant a more tolerant course. Secondly, most of the studies of the Red Scare were made in the 1950s and 1960s when Justice Department and Bureau of Investigation records were still closed to researchers and little was known about the internal deliberations and policies of the government agencies most actively engaged in the Scare.[203]

It is difficult if not impossible to ascertain President Wilson's thinking on the Red Scare and whether he genuinely shared the fear of Bolshevism in the US. On the one hand, Wilson several times indicated that he opposed repression and favored a more permissive course. For example, in February 1919 Wilson rebuked Postmaster General Albert Burleson for his continuing censorship of radical publications, stressing that "I cannot believe that it would be wise to do any more suppressing. We must meet these poisons in some other way,"[204] and he supported a proposal for general amnesty of those who had been sentenced to long prison terms for opposing the war.[205] And, most significantly, on April 14, 1920, at the first cabinet meeting held since Wilson's break-down in September 1919, when the Palmer raids were discussed, the president reportedly admonished the Attorney General "not to let the country see red".[206]

On the other hand, at no time did Wilson take effective action to end the administration's repressive policies, and, in fact, as early as October 1918 reportedly expressed his fear in private to an officer of the Military Intelligence Division of the possibility of the spread of Bolshevism within the US.[207] Wilson also vehemently opposed the release of the socialist leader, Eugene Debs, who had been convicted

---

[202]Murray, 205; in general, see 200-205; for the view that the cabinet was somewhat more active, see Coben, *A. Mitchell Palmer*, 209-211.

[203]None of the earliest works from the 1950s had access to government files; Higham noted that he had been denied access to Justice Department papers for 1919-20 (Higham, 401), and he added that the account by Murray, who also was unable to utilize government records, "still leaves important questions about federal policies unanswered" (Higham, 409).

[204]Link (ed.), *The Papers of Woodrow Wilson*, Vol. 55, 327.

[205]Ibid., Vol. 62, 555-559.

[206]Cronon (ed.), 518.

[207]Link (ed.), Vol. 53, 20-21.

for his anti-war views.[208] Moreover, at a cabinet meeting on June 10, 1919, the president apparently did not make any objections when Palmer discussed the Department of Justice plans for rounding up and deporting radical aliens and presented his proposal for a peace-time sedition law intended "to reach radical socialists who did not resort to force...."[209] In his State of the Union message in December 1919, Wilson attacked revolutionary elements as "enemies of this country" and urged Congress to pass Palmer's sedition bill: "With the free expression of opinion and with the advocacy of orderly political change, however fundamental, there must be no interference, but towards passion and malevolence tending to incite crime and insurrection under guise of political evolution there should be no leniency."[210] At later cabinet meetings Wilson apparently approved a proposal that the administration should make public State Department information on Bolshevik propaganda activities in the US, and that the Labor Department should deport the unofficial Soviet ambassador to the US, Ludwig C. A. K. Martens.[211] Although the president did not direct or order the government's anti-radical crusade, and did in a few instances oppose repressive actions, he supported and approved such important steps as the deportation of radical aliens and a peace-time sedition law.

More importantly, however, Wilson actively participated in creating a fear of disloyalty and subversion during his campaign for the ratification of the Versailles treaty. During his final speaking tour to the West in September 1919, two themes ran through his speeches, apart from the general arguments in favor of the treaty. First, Wilson threw suspicion on the opponents of the treaty and indicated that they were, in fact, disloyal. Wilson claimed that pro-German interests were behind the opposition to the treaty and that "there is an organized propaganda against the League of Nations and against the treaty proceeding from exactly the same sources that the organized propaganda proceeded from which threatened this country here and there with disloyalty." He attacked those with divided loyalties as "un-American", arguing that "any man who carries a hyphen about him carries a dagger that he is ready to plunge into the vitals of this republic whenever he gets the chance ... My fellow citizens, it is only certain bodies of foreign sympathies, certain bodies of sympathy with foreign nations that are organized against this great document...."[212] From

[208]Ibid., Vol. 62, 58, 98.
[209]Cronon (ed.), 418.
[210]Link (ed.), Vol. 64, 111, 112.
[211]Cronon (ed.), 541-542, 574.
[212]Link (ed.), Vol. 63, 501; also 140, 199, 448.

there it was a small step to hint that even the senators who opposed the treaty were somehow aiding the cause of the enemy. Although he pointed out that he was not accusing the senators of being disloyal, he repeatedly noted that "what they are attempting to do is exactly what Germany desires,"[213] and he asked his "honorable and enlightened" opponents "to reflect upon this proposition that, by holding off from this League, they serve the purposes of Germany..."[214] On September 6, in Kansas City, Wilson went so far as to connect his opponents to Bolshevism, stressing that "Opposition is the speciality of those who are Bolshevistically inclined" and added that he was certainly not accusing his colleagues of being Bolshevistically inclined but was "merely pointing out that the Bolshevistic spirit lacks every element of constructive opposition." Wilson warned that "I hope there won't be any such thing growing up in our country as international Bolshevism, the Bolshevism that destroys the constructive work of men who have conscientiously tried to cement the good feeling of the great peoples of the world."[215]

A second theme which dominated Wilson's speeches was that the central purpose of the treaty and the League of Nations was to create a new world order and that without it disorder and unrest would spread. Wilson asked his listeners whether they honestly thought "that none of that poison has got in the veins of this free people" and he painted a chilling picture of how "the poison of disorder, the poison of revolt, the poison of chaos" was being spread through the modern means of communications from Europe to the US: "And quietly upon steamships, silently under the cover of the postal service, with the tongue of the wireless and the tongue of the telegraph, all the suggestions of disorder are spread through the world.... And men look you calmly in the face in America and say they are for that sort of revolution, when 'that sort of revolution' means government by terror, government by force, not government by vote."[216] According to Wilson, the US was already being infiltrated and only the ratification of the treaty and the League of Nation could stop the slide into political disorder and unrest: "Do you find everybody about you content with our present industrial order? Do you hear no intimations of radical change? Do you learn of no organizations the object of which is nothing less that to overturn the government itself?"[217] Regardless

[213]Ibid., 321.
[214]Ibid., 456; also, 334.
[215]Ibid., 73.
[216]Ibid., 77; also, 175.
[217]Ibid., 434; also, 95-96, 354, 454.

of his personal estimate of the Bolshevik menace within the US or his attitude toward repression, President Wilson added fuel to the flames in his attempt to gain public approval for the League of Nations.

A few members of the Wilson cabinet did not see any imminent revolutionary threat. For example, Secretary of the Interior Franklin Lane did worry about the rising class consciousness among American workers but he did not see any reason to fear a class war and he opposed political repression. He advised Congressman Herbert C. Pell Jr. that "I find that no good comes from calling names," and he agreed with Frank I. Cobb of the *New York World* that "repression ... promotes the growth of error. We are not going to destroy socialism, or prevent it from becoming strong by refusing to answer it."[218] Others, even though often sympathetic to the demands of labor, publicly warned of the dangers of Bolshevism and argued that the government should take steps to suppress it. Secretary of Labor William B. Wilson, a former union official of the United Mine Workers, in April 1919 told a conference of mayors that any alien who agitated for the overthrow of government was "an invading enemy" who should be "simply deported to the country from which he comes."[219] The Labor Department established a program in which "able and efficient men who were wage-workers themselves" were dispatched to the industrial centers to conduct counter-propaganda.[220] Secretary of the Navy Josephus Daniels, who as early as January 1919 received reports from the Office of Naval Intelligence concerning the possibilities of unrest,[221] during 1919 repeatedly warned of "the danger of bolshevism overturning Americanism."[222] When Postmaster General Albert Burleson was instructed by President Wilson to cease censoring the press following the Armistice, he simply scribbled across Wilson's letter, "Continued to suppress and courts sustained me every time."[223] Burleson opposed negotiations with organized labor concerning the impending coal strike in October 1919 because, as Daniels noted in his diary, he "Sees red & think country is full of bolshevists."[224]

Other members more actively promoted a clear anti-radical course and it is significant that none of them apparently did so because they

---

[218]Anne Wintermute Lane & Louise Herrick Wall (eds.), *The Letters of Franklin Lane. Personal and Political* (Boston, 1922), 311-312, 317, 320, 326; also, 384-387.
[219]Gengarelly, 318.
[220]Letter, William B. Wilson to James Duncan, April 22, 1920, Correspondance 1920, William B. Wilson Papers, Historical Society of Pennsylvania.
[221]Cronon (ed.), 364.
[222]Ibid., 469; also, 419-420.
[223]Link (ed.), Vol. 55, 327n1.
[224]Cronon (ed.), 453.

felt pressured by the public, such as it has been claimed by most historians. To the contrary, they did so because they genuinely feared that Bolshevism was becoming a serious threat within the US and they were concerned that the public and most politicians were not sufficiently aware and aroused by it. On June 4, 1919, two days after bomb explosions in eight cities, Joseph P. Tumulty, the president's secretary, wrote to Wilson in Paris that the attack was "a symptom of the terrible unrest that is stalking about the country," and he warned of "a movement that, if it is not checked, is bound to express itself in an attack upon everything that we hold dear."[225] Later that summer, Tumulty advised Wilson to "warn the country against Bolshevist propaganda."[226]

The strongest anti-Bolshevik voice within the cabinet was the Secretary of State, Robert Lansing. As early as January 1918, Lansing characterized a Soviet appeal to the workers of the allied countries as "a very real danger in view of the present social unrest throughout the world,"[227] and he predicted that such revolutionary forces "may have to be reckoned with even in this country."[228] The intensity of Lansing's anti-Bolshevik feelings is indicated by a private note, jotted down at the time of the Russian revolution, in which he noted that "Greed, lust, cruelty and hate are the foundation stone of that hideous and loathsome structure which the Bolsheviks are seeking to erect on the ruins of social order and civilized states."[229] Like President Wilson, Lansing feared that the Bolsheviks might take advantage of the turmoil and unrest brought on by the war if the peace negotiations were not speedily concluded. In April 1919, he noted impatiently that "Days pass, weeks pass, months pass, the eyes grown hopeless with waiting turn to the Red Demon who gives with lawless, bloody hand to his worshippers. Who can blame the starving ones for seeking his aid?"[230]

By the time he returned from the Paris Peace Conference in July 1919, Lansing had become thoroughly concerned about the spread of revolutionary sentiments within the US. He noted the atmosphere of "unrest and wide dissatisfaction at present conditions" and the growing "strong socialistic, if not Communistic, sentiment, which

[225]Link (ed.), Vol. 60, 153.
[226]Ibid., Vol. 62, 542.
[227]US Department of State, *Papers Relating to the Foreign Relations of the United States. Lansing Papers 1914-1920*, Vol. II (Washington, DC, 1940), 348.
[228]Ibid., 353. See also, Robert Lansing, Memorandum on Post-Bellum Conditions and Bolshevism, October 28, 1918, Private memoranda, Robert Lansing Papers, LC.
[229]Henry William Brands, Jr., "Unpremediated Lansing: His 'Scraps'," *Diplomatic History*, Vol. 9, No. 1 (Winter 1985), 31.
[230]Ibid.

directly menaces our democratic institutions even though it is not Bolshevism in the extreme form." As Lansing saw it, the danger lay in the increasing popularity of Bolshevik agitation against the capitalists, "a movement which appeals to the many," and the real threat it posed to the existing system and the whole American way of life: "The time has come when something ought to be done to stem the tide of this movement which threatens to inject Socialism into our political system, and through that agency to destroy Individualism on which our national institutions and industrial activities rest. It is the most sinister tendency of popular thought that this Republic has ever had to combat because it strikes not only at our national life but at the very roots of modern civilization." Lansing suggested that the reason why Bolshevistic ideas were becoming popular was the widespread and "vulgar belief," inspired by the war, that the government was able to cure all economic evils by legislation and regulation.[231] A month later, Lansing had become even more worried about the menace of Bolshevism, asking himself "I wonder how long we can tolerate the radical propaganda which is being carried on in this country and is teaching the laboring class to revolt against the present economic order. How long can we go on this way without a disaster? The peril seems to me very great." Should the Bolsheviks succeed in overthrowing the existing order, Lansing predicted "class-despotism with the attendant evils of brutality, license, misery and economic chaos."[232]

The secretary of state clearly felt that the public was too receptive to the radical ideas and he repeatedly proposed that the president should warn the people about the true nature and dangers of Bolshevism. On August 7, Lansing urged Wilson to publicly attack the Bolshevistic doctrines and he enclosed a memorandum by DeWitt C. Poole, Jr., former US chargé at Archangel, who argued that the Bolshevik movement intended to bring about a world revolution and that all democratic countries "are in a danger of being poisoned by a propaganda of violence and unreason which aims to subvert the Government of the United States and other non-Bolshevik governments."[233] When Wilson indicated his willingness to "warn the country against Bolshevism in some way that may attract attention,"[234] Lansing submitted a draft of a proposed statement composed by Poole to be issued by the president. Its purpose was "to warn people in general

[231]Lansing, The Spread of Bolshevism in the United States, July 26, 1919, Private memoranda, Lansing Papers, LC.
[232]Lansing, Tendency Toward Communistic Ideas, September 1, 1919, ibid.
[233]Link (ed.), Vol. 62, 202-205.
[234]Ibid., 281.

against the evil fatuity of Bolshevism," and it claimed that the Bolshevik revolution was part of a German plot, that the Bolsheviks were ruling "by a reign of terror" and that they were attempting by propaganda to undermine and destroy all governments.[235]

Lansing's State Department was, together with the Justice Department, the strongest force behind the Red Scare. It was dominated by the view that the Bolsheviks had destroyed all that was of value in Russian life and that they moreover represented a real and imminent threat to Western civilization. Therefore, the Department pursued an inflexible policy of non-recognition toward Soviet Russia.[236] In November 1918, the Department instructed the embassy in London "to follow closely all efforts at bolshevik propaganda both here and abroad,"[237] and the Department at an early date had an eye on Americans who might spread Bolshevik propaganda in the US. For example, State Department official Leland Harrison argued that the journalist and Communist John Reed should be denied reentry into the US upon his return from Russia in March 1918 "in view of the undoubted Bolsheviki propaganda which he will carry on upon his arrival in this country."[238]

There is no support for the contention that State Department officials felt pressured by a hysterical opinion, but, on the contrary, these officials, guided by their ideological hostility toward the Bolshevik system and their determination to oppose any attempt to recognize the new regime, sought to influence public opinion against Soviet Russia. In other words, the State Department's support for the Red Scare was a result of its own, foreign policy interests.[239] As a con

---

[235]Ibid., 323-324, 441-448; also, 456. Apparently, the statement was never made public.

[236]Frederic L. Propas, "Creating a Hard Line Toward Russia: The Training of State Department Soviet Experts, 1927-1937," *Diplomatic History*, Vol. 8, No. 3 (Summer 1984), 209-226; John Lewis Gaddis, *Russia, the Soviet Union and the United States. An Interpretive History* (2nd. ed., New York (1978), 1990), 105-113; David S. Fogelsong, *America's Secret War Against Bolshevism. U.S. Intervention in the Russian Civil War, 1917-1920* (Chapel Hill & London, 1995).

[237]US Department of State, *Papers Relating to the Foreign Relations of the United States. 1918. Russia*, Vol. I (Washington, DC, 1931), 726.

[238]Letter, Leland Harrison to A. Bruce Bielaski, March 11, 1918, OG 182787, RG65, NA. Also, letters, Harrison to Bielaski, February 26, 1918, and Bielaski to Harrison, March 19, 1918, ibid. The State Department continued to follow Reed, see for example, letters; Department of State to Bielaski, July 25, 1918; Bielaski to Charles DeWoody et al., August 22, 1918; W. L. Hurley to J. E. Hoover, September 2, 1920, ibid. The State Department also took an interest in Crystal Eastman, wife of socialist editor Max Eastman (letter, L. L. Winslow to Frank Burke, September 16, 1919, BS 202600-823, ibid.).

[239]For the State Department's Eastern European Division's later efforts to influence public opinion during the 1920s, see Propas, 212-213. According to Foster Rhea Dulles, the State Department's attempt to increase anti-Bolshevik feelings were at least to some degree tied up with the American intervention in Russia: "Governmental agencies made the most of these fears and kept up a barrage of anti-Bolshevik propaganda throughout 1919 which was at least partially inspired by the need to justify the policy of intervention in both Archangel and Siberia. . . . official spokesmen were thus intensifying fear and hatred of Bolshevism. . . . "

sequence, the State Department publicized a pamphlet with the title *The Photographic History of the Bolshevik Atrocities.* [240] It launched an inquiry into the authenticity of the so-called Sisson documents, which had been made public in 1918 by the Committee on Public Information and which supposedly proved that the Germans had engineered the Bolshevik revolution.[241] However, the State Department's main argument against the recognition of Soviet Russia was the existence of Bolshevik propaganda in the US. On November 1, 1919, Acting Secretary of State William Phillips declared that the Bolsheviks' goal was world revolution and they "have availed themselves of every opportunity to initiate in the United States a propaganda aimed to bring about the forcible overthrow of our present form of Government," and he claimed that these revolutionary activities were financed by Russian gold reserves.[242] On August 10, 1920, in a formal statement of US policy toward Russia, Secretary of State Bainbridge Colby reiterated that Russia was striving to bring about Bolshevistic revolutions in other countries, including the US, and that consequently "We cannot recognize, hold official relations with, or give friendly reception to the agents of a government which is determined and bound to conspire against our institutions...."[243] In 1924, the State Department's Red Scare campaign climaxed when the Department succeeded in thwarting a movement to recognize Soviet Russia by presenting a lenghty report on Bolshevik activities in the US, compiled by the Bureau of Investigation, which concluded that "the subversive and pernicious activities of the American Communist Party and the Workers' Party and their subordinate and allied organs in the United States are activities resulting from and flowing out of the program elaborated for them by the Moscow group."[244]

(Foster Rhea Dulles, *The Road to Teheran. The Story of Russia and America, 1781-1943* (New York, 1944), 144, 146).

[240]Letter, J. E. Hoover to W. L. Hurley, June 2, 1920, JD 209264-23, RG60, NA (microfilm).

[241]For the State Department and Bureau of Investigation cooperation in this inquiry, see letters, Alan J. Carter to J. E. Hoover, January 8, 1921; Hoover to Carter, January 29, 1921; Hoover, Memorandum for the Files, March 7, 1921; Carter to Hoover, May 25, 1921, with att.; Carter to Hoover, May 28, 1921; Hoover to Carter, May 28, 1921; William W. Smith to Secretary of State, June 7, 1921; George B. Snell to Hoover, July 18, 1921; Hoover to Snell, July 22, 1921; Snell to Hoover, July 25, 1921, with att., all in BS 202600-1998, RG65, NA. For the inquiry, see also, George F. Kennan, "The Sisson Documents," *The Journal of Modern History*, Vol. XXVIII, No. 2 (June 1956), 133.

[242]US Department of State, *Papers Relating to the Foreign Relations of the United States. 1919. Russia* (Washington, DC, 1937), 161.

[243]US Department of State, *Papers Relating to the Foreign Affairs of the United States. 1920*, Vol. III (Washington, DC, 1936), 468; also, 463-469.

[244]US Congress, Senate, Subcommittee of the Committee on Foreign Relations, *Recognition of Russia. Hearings. Letter from the Secretary of State Transmitting information relative to propaganda carried on in the United States, directed from the United States*, 68th. Cong., 2nd. Sess. (Washington, DC, 1924), Pt. 2, 530.

At the lower levels of the federal bureaucracy, ideological and institutional interests also determined policy in 1919 more than the public opinion. In particular the military intelligence community, which had barely existed before 1917 and which during the war had established a powerful position regarding internal security in the US, had strong bureaucratic interests in maintaining its influence. When America entered World War I in April 1917, the staff of the Military Intelligence Division (MID) consisted of just two officers and two clerks. At the time of the Armistice in November 1918 it had grown to an effective force of 282 officers, 29 noncommissioned officers and 948 civilian employees and was deeply involved in domestic intelligence gathering in the form of plant protection and surveillance of labor unrest and radical organizations. Similarily, the Office of Naval Intelligence (ONI) had grown during the war from an initial staff of 8 officers and 18 clerks to 306 reservists, 18 clerks and 40 naval attaches and assistant attaches and was involved in waterfront and plant protection.[245] MID, in particular, was aggressive in maintaining its internal security position in 1919. Unaffected by the end of hostilities, the agency continued to compile information on domestic activities and it even obtained an emergency appropriation of $400,000 from Congress to monitor radical activities. Influenced by the national steel strike in the fall of 1919, the MID feared that a general strike or even a revolution might break out. The intelligence officers prepared the so-called "War Plans White," which provided for the deployment of the US army against an expected force of 1.5 million armed revolutionaries. According to Joan Jensen, the MID did not act in response to an anti-radical hysteria but rather in accordance with its own ideology, "the United States Army was so removed from its own people that it identified with the authoritarian governments of Europe. The isolation of the army from the mass of American people was never as complete as it was during that winter of 1919."[246] With the assistance of 250,000 American Legion members in 23 states the MID continued to monitor unions, radicals, socialists, the IWW and blacks until 1922, when it was directed to cease its domestic activities due to the general lack of radical activities and in consideration of the reputation of the military.[247]

In summary, by 1919 the federal political leadership and bureaucracy on all levels had developed their own ideological and institu-

---

[245]Select Committee to Study Governmental Operations with Respect to Intelligence Activities, *Supplementary Reports on Intelligence Activities,* Book VI, 76-94, especially, 76, 85 and 91.
[246]Joan Jensen, *Army Surveillance in America, 1775-1980* (New Haven, 1991), 190-191.
[247]Ibid., 194, 197-199.

tional interests in an anti-radical crusade: President Wilson used scare tactics to promote the Versaille treaty and the League of Nations, several cabinet members genuinely feared that Bolshevism might threaten American institutions and tried to awaken the opinion, the State Department sought to foster a strong anti-Bolshevik opinion to gain support for its non-recognition policy toward Soviet Russia, and the intelligence services strove to maintain their internal security positions. In other words, it might be argued that the Bureau of Investigation's role and activities during the Red Scare, which institutionalized the Bureau's political surveillance, were not determined by an irrational opinion but by the various long-term and short-term interests and policies of the federal government.

Chapter 3

The Bureau and the Red Scare

The Bureau and the Drive for Bureaucratic Expansion

It might be argued that besides responding to the larger policies of the federal government, the Bureau of Investigation's course during the Red Scare was to a large degree influenced by its institutional interests and ideology.[1] Like the military intelligence agencies, the Bureau had experienced a dramatic growth during the war. For example, its budget had increased from a mere $485,000 in fiscal year 1916 to $1,100,000 in FY 1918 and $2,350,000 in FY 1919,[2] and at the same time the staff of special agents had increased from only 300 just before America's entrance into the war in 1917 to 579 in 1920.[3] With the Armistice, however, the Bureau not only faced a halt in this bureaucratic expansion but even a cut-back to pre-war levels. First of all, the legal basis for the Bureau's internal security investigations was made up of a number of wartime laws, such as the Espionage Acts of 1917 and 1918 and the Selective Service Act, and it was generally held, even by Justice Department officials and conservative politicians, that they were only temporary and would not be enforced with the end of hostilities.[4] Secondly, President Wilson had been determined to avoid the establishment of a permanent internal security apparatus during the war, and he therefore opposed military jurisdiction in espionage and sabotage cases and approved that the government utilize the services of volunteers, who would be discharged after the war. Conse-

---

[1]The only attempts to interpret the activities of BI as a result of its institutional interests are Murphy, 66, and Belknap, "The Mechanics of Repression," 49-58.

[2]FY1916 figures are from, US Congress, Senate, Subcommittee of the Committee on Appropriations, *Sundry Civil Appropriation Bill, 1920. Hearings,* 66th. Cong., 1st. Sess. (Washington, DC, 1919), 307; FY 1918 and 1919 from, *AG Reports, 1918 ,* 334, and *1919 ,* 298.

[3]The 1917 figures are from, US Congress, Senate, Subcommittee on the Committee on Appropriations, *General Deficiency Bill 1917. Hearings,* 65th. Cong., 1st. Sess. (Washington, DC, 1917), 37, and the 1920 figures from Powers, 137.

[4]For the wartime legislation, see *AG Reports 1917,* 73-76, and *1918,* 17-25, 47-48, 54; for the view of the Justice Department and Congress, see US Congress, Senate, *Investigation Activities of the Department of Justice. Letter from the Attorney General transmitting in response to a Senate resolution of October 17, 1919, a report on the activities of the Bureau of Investigation of the Department of Justice against persons advising anarchy, sedition, and the forcible overthrow of the government, November 17, 1919,* Senate Doc. No. 153, 66th. Cong., 1st. Sess (Washington, DC, 1919), 6; also, "Unpreparedness in the War against Radicalism," *The New York Times,* November 23, 1919.

quently, the government employed so-called "dollar-a-year-men" for war work and the Bureau cooperated with the patriotic organization the American Protective League to conduct investigations. With the end of the war, the Bureau no longer had any jurisdiction in domestic political intelligence matters, and it had no permanent division to handle such work. Furthermore, Attorney General Thomas Gregory on December 21, 1918, ordered the APL to disband, thereby depriving the Bureau of a large part of its investigative force.[5] Moreover, the Bureau had been strongly criticized by the press and by Congress for its conduct of so-called "slacker" raids in New York City during September 3 to 5, 1918. During the raids, 35 special agents, aided by 2,000 members of the APL, 1,350 soldiers, 1,000 sailors and hundreds of police officers, in their search for draft evaders stopped all men of conscription age on the streets and arrested an estimated 50,000 for not carrying their registration cards; in the end only some 5% were found to be slackers.[6] According to President Wilson's doctor, Cary Grayson, the controversy surrounding the raids "which were conducted with such a high-handed disregard for the law" made the Bureau a target for reorganization after the war.[7] Thus, when the Bureau chief since 1912, A. Bruce Bielaski, resigned shortly after the Armistice on December 21, 1918, he issued instructions that the Bureau be cut back to its pre-war level,[8] which would mean an 80% cut of the budget and almost 50% cut in personnel. In other words, it can be inferred that the Bureau had profound institutional interests in finding a new domestic enemy and thereby maintain its internal security role.

In fact, a similar example of how the Bureau whipped up a public scare in order to increase its jurisdiction and appropriations does exist. In 1910, Congress had passed the Mann Act, popularly known as the White Slavery Act, which was aimed at organized vice rings and made the interstate transportation of women "for immoral purposes" a federal crime. The newly formed Bureau quickly seized on the new assignment as an opportunity to expand. The following year a separate White Slavery branch was established with headquarters in Baltimore and in 1912 the then Bureau Chief Stanley W. Finch was named special commissioner for white slavery cases. The Bureau was already

[5]For Wilson's wartime policies and the APL, see Joan Jensen, *The Price of Vigilance* (Chicago, 1968), 41-43, 59-62, 120-122, 125-129, 246; *AG Report 1918*, 16. The APL tried to continue its activities in 1919 but was ordered to stop by the new Attorney General A. Mitchell Palmer in April 1919 (Jensen, 247-258, 262-265).
[6]Lowenthal, 24-35; Whitehead, 37-39; Peterson & Fite, 231-235; Jensen, *The Price of Vigilance*, 199-215.
[7]Link (ed.), *The Papers of Woodrow Wilson*, Vol. 60, 115.
[8]Jensen, *The Price of Vigilance*, 246.

spending the second largest amount of its resources, $31,449, on white slavery cases, which was only exceeded by anti-trust cases ($47,279). In 1913, white slavery became the most important category of investigative work for the Bureau in terms of resources spent ($59,639 as opposed to $28,700 for anti-trust cases). That same year Finch requested $200,000 alone for the white slavery investigations and tried to scare Congress to appropriate the funds by characterizing the methods used to entice women into prostitution as "hideous in the extreme" and portrayed organized vice as "one of the greatest dangers in this country": "In fact, it might almost be said that unless a girl was actually confined in a room and guarded – owing to the clever devices of these white slave traffickers – there was no girl, regardless of her station in life, who was altogether safe."[9] By applying a broad interpretation of the Mann Act and using it even in cases where men transported consenting women across interstate lines for the purpose of "fornication and adultery," the Bureau in effect became a "moral police," which could legally inquire into people's private lives.[10] Moreover, it increased the Bureau's workload tremendously and, thereby, its need for additional appropriations. During the period 1922-39 the Bureau investigated 54,780 white slave cases, which was the second largest category of federal crimes, and since 1910 to the present the FBI has investigated a total of 409,991 Mann Act cases.[11] Thus, by exaggerating the danger of organized vice, portraying it as a real menace to the American society, and by broadly interpreting the law, the Bureau in its formative years succeeded in expanding in size and jurisdiction from an obscure and subordinate government bureau, primarily engaged in examining bank frauds and anti-trust violations, to a growing and influental bureaucracy, engaged in sensational and headline-stealing cases.

It seems reasonable to conclude that the Bureau at the beginning of 1919 was highly motivated in promoting an anti-radical campaign in order to safeguard its bureaucratic interests, to avoid the drastic cutbacks which seemed unavoidable after the war, and perhaps to establish a more permanent position in the field of internal security. This much was indicated in 1921 by the lawyer Jackson Ralston during a Senate committee hearing on the activities of the Justice Department

---

[9]Williams, *"Without Understanding,"* 51; in general 49-53. Finch added that "There was need that every person be on his guard, because no one could tell when his daughter or his wife or his mother would be selected as a victim" (Lowenthal, 15; also, 14-21).
[10]Williams, *"Without Understanding,"* 52.
[11]1922-39 figures are from Countryman, "The History of the FBI," in Watters & Gillers (eds.), 53; the figures since 1910 are from Hines & Langbart, 29.

during the Red Scare, where Ralston explained the government repression of radicals with the requirements of the growing Bureau:
"That Department of Investigation had to justify its existence.... There
was a training up of the public mind in the first instance to expect red
outbreaks, and I think that training up was deliberate.... This Bureau
of Investigation which had to get appropriations of liberal size from
Congress."[12] Secretary of Labor Wilson likewise confided later to a
close friend that most of the clamor had been manufactured and was
due to the activities of the Justice Department: "The whole thing was
done with a hurrah that gave the country the impression that it was
honey-combed with anarchy and revolution."[13]

The Personification of Social Unrest

The Bureau might also be said to have been influenced by what might
be termed an institutional ideology, which tended to color both internal and external statements of Bureau officials. One reason why this
particular way of thinking became institutionalized was undoubtedly
that the Bureau was a police organization, whose aim was to identify
perpetrators of crimes; in other words, special agents and officials of
the Bureau were trained and worked according to the assumption that
violations of the law and other abnormalities, such as social unrest or
riots, were caused by individuals. Moreover, most Bureau and Justice
Department officials were either lawyers and thereby members of a
traditionally staunch conservative profession, or either came from or
went to important positions in the corporate world. Most officials were
personally committed to the economic and political status quo and
shared conservative ideas and values.[14]

---

[12]*Charges of Illegal Practices*, 273-274.
[13]Letter, Wilson to James Duncan, April 22, 1920, Correspondance 1920, Wilson Papers,
Historical Society of Pennsylvania.
[14]On the conservatism of the law profession, see Jerold S. Auerbach, *Unequal Justice* (New
York, 1976); for examples of connections to corporations: Francis P. Garvan, Assistant
Attorney General in charge of radical investigations 1919-21, later went to the Chemical
Foundation (letter, Garvan to Roosevelt, June 16, 1933, PPF, 1985, FDRL); John T.
Creighton, Special Assistant to the Attorney General in charge of the BI 1919-21 later became
an official at the National City Bank of New York and vicepresident of the City Bank Farmers
Trust Co.; John W. H. Crim, Assistant Attorney General 1921-23, came from a law practice
where he represented such clients as the N.H.&H. Railroad Co. (both from *Who Was Who in
America*, Vol. I, 1897-1942 (Chicago, 1968), 276); A. Bruce Bielaski, BI director 1912-18,
became assistant general manager of the National Buildings Fire Underwriters (ibid., Vol. IV,
1961-1968 (Chicago, 1968), 85); Mortimer J. Davis, BI official 1917-25, became assistant
director of Fraud Prevention Dept. of the National Association of Credit Management (*Garvey
Papers*, Vol. I, 412n4); George F. Ruch, BI official 1918-23, became an official in H. C. Frick
Coal Co. (Whitehead, 331n2); and William J. Burns, BI director 1921-24, came from a
position of director of the Burns Detectice Agency, which among other things operated as
strikebreaker for large corporations.

86

The ideology of the Bureau, as it primarily was expressed in public statements, might be characterized as an attempt to personify larger outbreaks of social unrest or organized opposition to the existing system and conditions. According to the Bureau's thinking, the social, economic and political system of America was basically sound and well-functioning since it provided enough opportunities for anyone willing to make an effort and provided the democratic institutions to which anyone could take his complaints or desires for improvements or reforms. Consequently, Americans in general were contented and loyal to the system. The Bureau at one point noted the almost ideal conditions in the US: "Good pay and happy homes do not revolt. The great mass of the people of the United States are well paid and in comfortable homes." It added that "In ordinary times it is not easy to find a body of American labor susceptible to revolutionary teaching."[15] As the Bureau saw it, most Americans recognized the advantages of the system even when they had complaints: "The American wageworker has many just complaints against conditions, but he is not complaining of his Government or the institutions which he has so constantly and loyally supported in the past."[16]

It followed naturally from this assumption that if most people were satisfied and loyal, then serious outbreaks of unrest or fundamental challenges to the existing system were not caused by social inequalities or injustices but must have been brought on by agitators, who had infiltrated and led astray the innocent majority. As noted in an internal report, "the Russian is very quiet and peacable until he is stirred up by the radical agitator."[17] This idea of the seduction of the people was used to explain away most of the social unrest following the Armistice. Thus, the strike among West Virginian coal miners in 1919 was instigated by anarchist agitators of the Union of Russian Workers who were "leading astray the earnest laborers...,"[18] and the national railroad strike was brought on by subversive elements from the IWW and the Communist Party while "the workers ... were for the most part innocent dupes in the business...."[19] A "systematic scheme of propaganda" among otherwise innocent Russian immigrants had resulted

[15]"The Revolution in Action" (Part II of a popular survey prepared by the Department of Justice), reprinted in, US Congress, House, Committee on the Rules, *Attorney General A. Mitchell Palmer on Charges Made Against Department of Justice by Louis F. Post and Others. Hearings,* 66th. Cong., 2nd. Sess. (Washington, DC, 1920), 234, 235.
[16]Ibid., 8.
[17]Letter, SAC Pittsburgh to Frank Burke, October 8, 1919, BS 202600-184, RG65, NA.
[18]J. E. Hoover, Memorandum upon the Work of the Radical Division, August 1, 1919 to March 15, 1920, OG 374217, ibid.
[19]*AG Palmer on Charges,* 32.

in "the raw material has been converted into anarchists-syndicalists, Communists, and terrorists...."[20] The unrest among the black population was caused by "the influence of the radical movement upon his emotional nature" and the fact that "the negro being widely informed and led by capable and, in some cases, unscrupulous leaders...."[21]

The most elaborate version of this idea was the so-called "boring-from-within" theory concerning organized labor. According to this theory, the radicalization of labor and the outbreak of strikes were not caused by genuine grievancies but by radicals, who had infiltrated conservative and loyal unions and used them to stir up trouble. According to the Bureau's observations, "there is a concerted effort upon the part of the anarchists, the Communists, and of anti-American elements to inject their insidious and pernicious propaganda into the rank and file of the American Federation of Labor," where these "crafty 'borers from within'" were "appealing to the vicious and to the ignorant, which are to be found in all organizations...." Thus, it should be understood "that this is no fight between capital and labor, as the ultraradical agitator insist, but that it is a fight between organized government and anarchy."[22] The Bureau even hinted that this "boring-from-within process" was not limited to unions but also took place in "the judiciary, and even in high Government offices."[23]

In order to discredit these evil agitators, the Bureau was not content to brand them merely as subversives and radicals but sought, to use a formulation by Murray B. Levin, to dehumanize the troublemakers.[24] Thus, the radical movement was "a dishonest and criminal one,"[25] the reds were "criminal aliens" of "misshapen caste of mind and indeciencies of character,"[26] and their American sympathizers were "criminals, mistaken idealists, social bigots, and many unfortunate men and

---

[20]Report, E. B. Speer, April 9, 1919, BS 202600-184, RG65, NA.
[21]Robert A. Bowen, The Radical Press in New York City, n.d., box 10, Robert A. Bowen Papers, Clemson University Libraries.
[22]Quotes from *AG Palmer on Charges*, 193, 191 and 28-29.
[23]Ibid., 193. The "boring-from-within" theory might be seen as a predecessor of the "Trojan horse" theory of the Cold War, by which the FBI tried to explain away the importance of the declining number of US Communists and argued that the few remaining members of the CPUSA had infiltrated otherwise patriotic organizations, especially unions, liberal groups, pacifists and civil rights organizations, and were using them to stir up trouble (see Donner, *The Age of Surveillance*, 105-107, 139-144).
[24]Levin, 152-157.
[25]Letter, A. Mitchell Palmer to Mr. Lyman Abott, January 27, 1920, JD 205492-338.5, RG60, NA (microfilm).
[26]A. Mitchell Palmer, "The Case Against the Reds," February 1920, reprinted in, David Brion Davis (ed.), *The Fear of Conspiracy. Images of Un-American Subversion From the Revolution to the Present* (Ithaca, N.Y., 1971), 227.

women suffering with varying forms of hyperaesthesia."[27] In 1920, Attorney General Palmer informed a congressional committee that most radicals in the US were not genuine Americans but aliens or foreign-born citizens and stressed that they were not motivated by legitimate political concerns or ideas. They were either "idealists with distorted minds," "many even insane," others were "professional agitators who are plainly self-seekers" and a large number were "potential or actual criminals whose baseness of character leads them to espouse the unrestrained and gross theories and tactics of these organizations." As proof of his description, Palmer invited anyone to examine the Justice Department's photographic collection of revolutionaries: "Out of the sly and crafty eyes of many of them leap cupidity, cruelty, insanity, and crime; from their lopsided faces, sloping brows, and misshapen features may be recognized the unmistakable criminal type."[28]

Since the radical movement was not a genuine reaction to social injustices or inequalities and since it was led by alien, criminal or insane agitators, it followed that the movement was not a legitimate political or social force. According to the Bureau, the "'Red' movement does not mean an attitude of protest against alleged defects in our present political and economic organization of society. It does not represent the radicalism of progress."[29] Similarly, the growing black radicalism "is not one of wholesome endeavour to alleviate and correct the wrongs under which the Negro labors" but it aimed at increasing "race antagonism."[30] The whole radical movement, Palmer informed Congress, was simply aiming at "the creation of misery and bankruptcy – the field ground for revolution": "That is why we have so much of the sabotizing of industry, the deftly engineered slowing down of production, the constant stalling of machinery, especially transportation industry, and the crippling effect of general strikes, otherwise 'political' strikes."[31] Often the Bureau did not stop at marginalizing radicalism but compared it to an uncleanness or illness which had infected society. Thus, the radical ideas were "poisonous theories" and "alien filth,"[32] which had badly "infected" the "body of labor" and

---

[27]Attorney General's New Year message, reprinted in "Palmer Pledges War on Radicals," *The New York Times*, January 1, 1920.
[28]*AG Palmer on Charges*, 26-27.
[29]"Palmer Pledges War on Radicals," *The New York Times*, January 1, 1920.
[30]Robert A. Bowen, Radicalism and Sedition Among the Negroes as Reflected in Their Publications, July 2, 1919, box 10, Bowen Papers, Clemson University.
[31]*AG Palmer on Charges*, 19.
[32]Palmer, "The Case Against the Reds," in Davis (ed.), 226-227.

behaved like "the presence of diseased tissue in the human body."[33] Palmer expressed his fears that "the continual inoculation of poison virus of social sedition, poisonous to every fiber and root, to every bone and sinew, to the very heart and soul" would result in "the revolutionary disease."[34] Seen in this way, the Bureau perceived its role as that of a surgeon or a cleaning service whose task it was to get rid of the dirt and disease of political life. According to the Bureau, it intended to "clean up the country," it was "sweeping the nation clean,"[35] and it was engaged in "social sanitation."[36]

The third element of the Bureau's counter-subversive thinking was the assumption that the agitators' primary weapons in influencing and leading astray people consisted of radical publications. According to a Justice Department report submitted to Congress, "One of the most potent and farreaching influences in stirring up discontent, race prejudice, and class hatred in this country is the large number of radical newspapers and other publications which are given wide circulation." The report pointed out that the radical press was used "as a means of propaganda to educate his fellow workman and inoculate him with the doctrine of anarchism, communism, and radical social-ism, and thus enlist his services in the revolution."[37] The Bureau claimed that it had shown conclusively that "in all the strikes in the United States this radical propaganda enters into the situation. These radicals, as we have found, take advantage of the ordinary strikes that occur throughout the country, intensify them, and create a great deal of trouble and disorder."[38] This idea that the radical press was a main cause of social unrest was widely shared by agents in the field. For example, E. B. Sisk of Globe, Arizona, reported that "highly inflam-matory and seditious papers" were creating a "revolutionary spirit" among the IWWs in Arizona.[39] Harold Nathan linked the circulation of the socialistic the *Liberator* near the shipyards in Newport News, Virginia, to labor unrest: "There has recently been strikes and walk-outs amongst the plumbers and ship yard workers here and it can readily be seen that the promulgation of IWW or Bolsheviki theories

---

[33]*AG Palmer on Charges*, 234.

[34]Ibid., 18-19.

[35]Palmer, "The Case Against the Reds," in Davis (ed.), 226-227.

[36]*AG Palmer on Charges*, 18-19.

[37]*Investigation Activities of the Department of Justice*, 11, 12. See also, Robert A. Bowen, The Radical Press in New York City, n.d., box 10, Bowen Papers, Clemson University. On the importance of the radical press in Bureau thinking, see also, Donner, 49-50.

[38]US Congress, House, Subcommittee of Committee on Appropriations, *Appropriations, Department of Justice, 1925. Hearings*, 68th. Cong., 1st. Sess. (Washington, DC, 1924), 91-92.

[39]Report, E. B. Sisk, May 3, 1919, BS 202600-282, RG65, NA.

in this vicinity at this time would be of the outmost detriment and danger to the government."[40]

Perhaps the justifications given by Bureau officials and agents for investigating or suppressing the radical press can give us an indication of how the Bureau defined what was objectionable. In 1919 and 1920, Robert A. Bowen, director of the Justice Department's Bureau of Translations and Radical Publications in New York, compiled three reports on the radical press.[41] Bowen did not analyze in details the publications but reprinted long extracts from a total of 131 articles he found to be particularly objectionable. If these articles are classified according to their contents, we find that Bowen objected to 83 articles because they expressed support for and advocated a Bolshevistic revolution and the violent overthrow of the existing order; 15 because of their criticism of the capitalistic state and its injustices; 10 because of their anarchistic opposition to all forms of organized society and state; 9 because of their calls for a revolutionary May 1 and the radicalization of strikes; 8 because of their syndicalistic agitation for the forcible confiscation of the means of production; and 6 because of their opposition to US foreign policy, especially their characterization of World War I and the Versailles treaty as imperialistic. In his brief comments to the extracts, Bowen made it clear that he primarily objected to the radical press' advocacy of violent revolution and its violent language. The Communist publications were in general "objectionable" and "vicious" because they argued for "the establishment of the rule of the proletariat" by employing "extreme utterance,"[42] and the rest of the radical press was criticized for the "violence in their own utterances" and for being "extreme in their denouncement of the present system."[43]

According to comments by special agents, they objected in particular to any form of fundamental opposition to the American political, economic and social system. E. B. Sisk was of the opinion that literature "which is steadfastly preaching, at least covertly, the overthrow of our government and the rule of this country by 'the masses' which is nothing but Bolshevist propaganda" should be suppressed.[44]

<hr>

[40]Report, H. Nathan, September 11, 1918, OG 136944, ibid.
[41]The three Bowen reports are: Report on Official Communist Organs Published in New York City, December 8, 1919; Report on the Radical Press of New York City, December 29, 1919; The Radical Press in New York City Since the January 1920 Raids, June 11, 1920, all in box 10, Bowen Papers, Clemson University.
[42]Bowen, Report on Official Communist Organs Published in New York City, December 8, 1919, ibid.
[43]Bowen, Report on the Radical Press of New York City, December 29, 1919, ibid.
[44]Letter, E. B. Sisk, to Hon. Thomas A. Flynn, September 3, 1919, BS 202600-282, RG65, NA.

Special Agent E. Kosterlitzky of the Los Angeles field office repeatedly recommended that radical papers be barred from circulation because of their "venomous radicalism," because they were filled with "disrespectful comments on the laws of this country and the administering authorities," and because the "cartoons are slurring and satirical in the extreme."[45] According to Special Agent F. F. Weiss, a paper which glorified the German revolution in 1918, opposed intervention in Russia and criticized capitalism was "most untimely and a propaganda of the most dangerous sort."[46] Other agents objected to publications because of their "tendencies looking toward social equality,"[47] "an open and scurrilous statement against the form of government,"[48] and simply because they were "vicious."[49]

The final element of the Bureau's anti-radical thinking was the so-called "parlor Bolsheviks" or "aristocratic reds," the well-educated and wealthy members of the upper-classes who were thought to give their moral and financial support to the radical movement. On the one hand, the Bureau seemed to view the "parlor Bolsheviks" as particularly sinister and dangerous, since they were influencing people while they were hiding behind their respectable facades and making sure not to come to the attention of the authorities. According to Robert Bowen, the "parlor Bolsheviks" were back of "the encouragement of the revolutionary idea in its more theoretic, academic form" and their propaganda was "far more insidious" than open calls for violent revolution, since they always made sure to stay on the right side of the law and therefore could not be legally suppressed.[50] On the other hand, Bureau officials often seemed to regard these wealthy intellectuals with contempt as ridiculous and starry-eyed dilettantes. Attorney General Palmer described them as "those educated men and women who, from the advantage or the pinch of their position of life, have been strenuously thinking with none too commendable logic about the incongruities and injustices of the times, and, catching the revolutionary thought, have turned to it both their feelings and interests. Among them are the 'parlor Bolsheviki', the Philistines of our social period, who, enveloped in cigarette smoke and airs of superiority, have lost the touch of just proportion in their measurements of 'the good and the

[45]Reports, E. Kosterlitzky, July 23, 1919, ibid.; February 19, 1920, OG 136944, ibid.
[46]Report, F. F. Weiss, November 20, 1918, ibid.
[47]Letter, J. V. Bell to Frank Burke, May 6, 1920, BS 202600-282, ibid.
[48]Report, James C. Tormey, December 2, 1919, OG 136944, ibid.
[49]Letter, Roy C. McHenry to J. T. Suter, July 14, 1919, ibid.
[50]Bowen, The Radical Press in New York City, n.d., box 10, Bowen Papers, Clemson University.

bad in modernism,' and lent themselves to writing and talk and financial contributions – these people seldom take the risk of doing anything – toward paddling along the revolutionary flood."[51] Behind this mixture of fear and ridicule seemed to lie an intense hostility reserved for those who, in the eyes of the Bureau officials, had betrayed their class.

The Bureau's exertions to identify and gather evidence against presumed "parlor Bolsheviks," despite the obvious lack of evidence in support of its theory, might give an indication of how deeply held this belief in the existence and dangerousness of these supposed wirepullers was. The Bureau started with an unsuccessful search for an authoritative list of prominent and wealthy sponsors of radical organizations. In November 1919, in a response to a request from Washington, M. J. Davis of the New York field office submitted two lists of "persons who are, or have been, active in furthering Bolshevist activities or connected with societies lending financial and moral aid to such propaganda," one taken from the pages of the socialist daily the *New York Call*, and the other from information culled from the Bureau files. Davis seemed to have difficulty in proving the presumed radical sympathies of those mentioned, however, and the list consisted of organizations and persons who had been known for their pacifist activities during the war. Davis explained that "it appears those persons and organizations which were pacifists, radical or anti-military during the war had among their membership and officers almost the same persons who are now supporting Bolshevism after the war."[52]

Special Assistant to the Attorney General in charge of the Radical Division J. Edgar Hoover kept looking for more concrete evidence. One month later, upon being informed by Robert Bowen that wealthy women were allegedly financing radical publications in New York, he told Bowen that he was "particularly interested" in "Parlor Bolsheviks" and therefore requested "a list of the names of all wealthy persons who are giving financial assistance" to the radical movement "in order that we may be able to know exactly, if possible, the source of income of

[51]*AG Palmer on Charges*, 25.

[52]Report, M. J. Davis, November 28, 1919; "List of names of prominent persons suspected of radical sympathies, published in the issues of 'The New York Call', August 18, 1919 to August 24, 1919," n.d., BS 202600-1451, RG65, NA. The *New York Call* list contained the names of 84 persons, among them the social reformer Jane Addams, historian Charles Beard, the Commissioner of Immigration Frederic C. Howe, liberal editor of the *Nation* Oswald G. Villard, President Wilson's son-in-law John N. Sayre, author Lincoln Steffens and so on. The Bureau's own list contained a number of pacifist organizations such as the League for the Amnesty of Political Prisoners, Women's International League, the American Union Against Militarism and the National Civil Liberties Union.

the radical element in the United States."[53] In his answer, Bowen admitted that his knowledge was based solely on "hear-say and rumor, though possible not althogether inaccurate at that" and referred Hoover to Postmaster Patten and Deputy State Attorney General Samuel Berger of New York as his sources.[54] Berger had publicly announced that he had compiled a list of "dilettante 'reds'," primarily prominent pacifists who contributed financially to the radical press, which he had reportedly turned over to the federal authorities.[55] Confronted by the Bureau both he and Patten admitted that they had neither any list nor any concrete information to back up their statements.[56] Again in 1921 the Bureau tried to identify the alleged rich and influental backers of radical organizations and publications.[57]

According to the Bureau's anti-radical thinking, both as it was expressed internally and in public, the American political, economic and social system was fundamentally just and sound and provided adequate opportunities and prosperity for most people. Serious social upheaval or opposition to the government was not caused by any basic dissatisfaction but by subversive agitators, aided and abetted by "parlor Bolsheviks," who sowed their seeds of discontent by their sinister use of propaganda. In this way the Bureau's ideology can be characterized as an expression of what has been termed "the paranoid style" or "conspiracy theory" of American politics. This *weltanschauung* explains historical events as the results of conspiracies, sees dark plots and manipulations behind outbreaks of social unrest and views political leaders and intellectuals with suspicion.[58] The solution to the social unrest of 1919, the wave of strikes, the race riots and radical politics, followed naturally from the Bureau's thinking: There was no need for fundamental and comprehensive social reforms such as "industrial democracy" or racial equality, but simply for the identification and neutralization of the radical agitators. With the troublemakers removed from the scene, calm and order would once again descend on the society.

---

[53]Letter, J. E. Hoover to Robert A. Bowen, December 24, 1919, JD 205492-8, RG60, NA (microfilm).
[54]Letter, Bowen to Hoover, January 2, 1919 (1920), BS 202600-1451, RG65, NA.
[55]"Says Rich Radicals Finance 'Red' Press," *The New York Times*, October 18, 1919.
[56]Letter, George F. Lamb to Frank Burke, January 22, 1920, BS 202600-1451, RG65, NA. For the BI's inquiries, see also, letters, Hoover to Lamb, January 6, 1919 (1920), ibid., and Burke to Lamb, January 13, 1920, BS 202600-823, ibid.
[57]Memorandum for Mr. Grimes, April 28, 1921, BS 202600-282, ibid.; reports, E. M. Blanford, May 31, 1921; Adrian L. Potter, May 26, 1921; letters, W. R. Bryce to Chief, May 24, 1921; Chief to T. M. Reddy, June 15, 1921, all in BS 202600-2126, ibid.
[58]Hofstadter, 29-40; Lipset & Raab, 14-17; Levin, 141-175.

The Bureau Network and Political Associationalism

It has often been claimed that one of the most important factors behind the Justice Department and the Bureau of Investigation's decision to become actively involved in the anti-radical campaign was the patriotic organizations, which conducted a highly effective lobbying campaign against the federal government; thus, the Bureau's political activities were to a large extent a product of the pluralistic, pressure group society.[59] However, the relationship between the Bureau and the patriotic organizations was somewhat more complex and reciprocal than previously believed. First of all, as previously mentioned, the federal authorities were not passive or reluctant in connection with the issue of domestic security in 1919 (and, thus, in need of pressure from the outside to become involved) but were continuing decades of growing federal regulation and control. By 1919, federal officials had their own, independent interests in the Red Scare, such as obtaining public support for the League of Nations and the policy of non-recognition of Soviet Russia, fear of growing domestic Bolshevism and the bureaucratic and ideological interests of the intelligence community.

In this connection, political scientists have for some time shown that political institutions do not simply function as neutral brokers which respond to outside pressures. In fact, bureaucrats have a great deal of discretion in the selection of which interest groups they will allow themselves to be pressured by, and, moreover, the bureaucrats regularly influence the interest groups and use them to gather support for their policies. Sometimes the officials even participate actively in the establishment of interest groups which then act as extensions of the state agencies. In other words, public officials often organize public pressure, which is then used to legitimize state policies which would have been implemented anyhow. In the words of one bureaucratic theorist, the relationship between bureaucratic agencies and interest groups can most fittingly be characterized as a "symbiotic" one in which "they not only serve those groups' interest but also use them to further their own."[60]

The relationship between the Bureau of Investigation and the patriotic organizations can be described as a parallel to the idea of what has been called the "associational order," which was a basic part of the state-corporate system established during the Progressive Era and which expanded during the 1920s. In the economic sphere the intention was that in order to avoid the inefficiency, social anarchy and

[59]For example, Murray, especially 84-94; Levin, 197-208; Jaffe, 227-233.
[60]Etzioni-Halevy, 147; also, 60, 146, 148; see also Lewis, 8, 20-21.

economic instability of cut-throat competition, each industry, trade or profession would organize in trade associations or professional societies and in a voluntary and decentralized manner cooperate on achieving rationality, efficiency and ethical behavior. The federal government, in the form of the "associative state," would closely cooperate with the associations and private groups and provide guidance and coordination in what was in effect an attempt at implementing national planning. In 1919, there existed 700 national associations and by 1929 they had increased to more than 2,000 together with a forest of state regulatory bureaus, committees and agencies. In general, the relationship between the two was one of mutual dependency: the associations lobbied and looked for services from the bureaus, while the bureaus influenced the private groups and used them to mobilize political support for their policies.[61] The advantage from the point of view of the federal bureaucracy was that by working through the private interest groups it expanded its power beyond the capabilities of its own limited resources and at the same time kept its involvement hidden.

The Bureau and the Patriotic Right

The Bureau of Investigation's particular version of this voluntary cooperation in the field of political ideas was established during World War I. One private organization with which the Bureau cooperated was the National Security League. In June 1917, its secretary, Captain Robert Morris, placed the services of the League at the Bureau's disposal. Morris pointed out that, of course, the League could not conduct investigations but he did note that the organisation was "engaged in noting any movements in the state which would be against the interests of this Government." Special Agent in Charge Todd Daniel was not disturbed by the vagueness of Morris' expression and informed Washington that "This report will be filed for further reference as it is possible that we will often be able to cooperate to advantage with Mr. Morris."[62] During the rest of the war, the League functioned as an intelligence network for the Bureau, informing the

---

[61]For the "associative state," see Wiebe, 297-299; Hays, "Social Analysis of Political History," 391-392; Wilson, *Ideology and Economics*, ix-xi; Joan Hoff Wilson, *Herbert Hoover. Forgotten Progressive* (Boston, 1975), 98-103; Ellis W. Hawley, "Herbert Hoover, the Commerce Secretariat, and the Vision of an 'Associative State', 1921-1928," *The Journal of American History*, Vol. LXI, No. 1 (June 1974), 116-140.

[62]Report, Todd Daniel, June 9, 1917, OG 24621, RG65, NA. The following analysis of the BI network is based on a systematic search of all references in the BI index to the four nationally most important patriotic societies during the Red Scare: The National Civic Federation, the American Defense Society, the National Security League and the American Legion.

government on all activities the League found to be suspicious. For example, in March 1918, the Elmhurst, New York, branch submitted "a list of names of persons who are designated as strong pro-German and very strong pro-Germans."[63] In return, the Bureau provided special agents as protection against potential pro-German troublemakers at the League's patriotic meetings,[64] and gave advice on how to treat German employees (Bielaski urged that loyal "alien enemies" not be discharged).[65]

Another cooperative partner during the war was the American Defense Society. It promised the authorities it would fight "the widespread campaign of treason, sedition, and disloyalty" being waged by "pro-Germans, socialists, pacifists, anti-militarists, conscientious objectors, anarchists, I.W.W.'s, so-called friends of Irish freedom and other organizations," and it had ambitious plans for surveillance: "We hope to have active workers in every city and town, and a patriotic listener in every block."[66] Initially, the Bureau sympathized completely with the Society's intentions, noting at one point that "the American Defense Society is a patriotic organization and bears an excellent reputation,"[67] and it accepted information from the Society on such subjects as suspicious people in Little Rock, Arkansas, conditions in Cuba and the political situation in Washington, DC.[68]

However, the relationship soon turned sour, apparently because of the Society's overzealousness in its pursuit of subversive elements. In January 1918, the assistant US attorney in Boston complained that the ADS had encouraged people to send any information on suspected German activities in the US to the Society instead of to the federal authorities.[69] The Society defended its behavior by accusing the assistent US attorney of not doing enough to combat German in-

---

[63]Letter, Henry L. West to A. Bruce Bielaski, March 26, 1918; also letters, Bielaski to West, March 30, 1918; Bielaski to DeWoody, March 30, 1918, OG 24621, ibid. For other examples of information from the NSL, see letters, West to Hon. Thomas W. Gregory, February 26, 1918; West to Bielaski, April 22, 1918, ibid.

[64]Reports, J. L. Worden, January 22, 1918; O. A. Bowen, May 11, 1918, ibid.

[65]Letters, West to Bielaski, with att., November 15, 1917; Bielaski to West, n.d., ibid. Apparently, Mrs. S. Stanwood Menken, wife of the NSL president, was investigated by the Bureau for her views; according to a BI report, "With this woman's decided pro-German, anti-British, anti-Wilson feelings, the agent believes her to be a questionable person to be the 'guiding star' of a League possessing the possibilities of the National Security League" (Report, W. G. Springer, March 29, 1918, OG 106741, ibid.).

[66]Letter, Richard M. Hurt to Mr. J. W. Works, December 5, 1917, OG 93248, ibid.

[67]Letter, Wm. M. Offley to Dr. C. N. Dolan, November 23, 1917, ibid.

[68]Letters, Offley to Bielaski, January 25, 1918; Henry M. Earle, April 22, 1918; H. D. Craig, n.d., with att. report: Washington, DC, October 10, 1918; for other examples, letters, Offley to Miss. Anna E. McAuliffe, November 19, 1917; Offley to Rev. V. A. M. Mortensen, November 19, 1917, all in ibid.

[69]Letter, US Att. to Henry M. Earle, January 5, 1918, ibid.

fluences.[70] The Bureau reacted on the one hand by criticizing the Society, pointing out that "We do look, however, with some doubt on the activities of the American Defense Society and its methods and I know that some of our officers feel that so far as they know of the activities of the Society that they are detrimental rather than helpful."[71] The Justice Department denied that it had any connection with the ADS,[72] and the Bureau even launched an investigation of the Society for possible violation of the Espionage Act.[73] On the other hand, however, the Bureau continued to accept information from the ADS. Bureau Chief Bielaski noted in an internal letter that for the time being it was the policy of the Bureau that "it would be well to overlook the aggravating circumstances in the situation, and without calling on that organization for aid in investigating work, accept any information they place at your disposal."[74]

The most notorious example of public-private cooperation in the area of internal security during the war was the relationship between the Bureau and the American Protective League. In March 1917, a Chicago businessman, Albert M. Briggs, proposed the establishment of an organization, consisting of the leaders of the business community and a network of informants, which would keep the Bureau informed about disloyalty, industrial disturbances, and activities "likely to injure or embarrass" the government. The APL was not, as often claimed, an expression of a grassroots hysteria but was, in effect, an instrument used by the business elite to impose conformity under the guise of the war and suppress radical unions and other opponents. According to the historian of the League, Joan Jensen, the leaders of the APL "were a cross-section of the ruling business elite of the Progressive Era, captains of industry or rubber barons, depending on how one viewed them,"[75] and most of its rank-and-file were from the upper or middle classes and "accepted the American political and social system as sacrosanct; indeed, their place within it would be threatened by change."[76] Before the end of the war, the APL had grown to an effective national force of 250,000 members, distributed on some

[70]Letter, Earle to Bielaski, January 9, 1918, ibid.
[71]Letter, Bielaski, January 19, 1918; also, Bielaski to Hon. Thomas J. Reilly, n.d., ibid.
[72]Letter, Special Assistant to the Attorney General to R. P. Lamborn, March 9, 1918, ibid.
[73]Reports, American Protective League, August 28, 1918; F. C. Pendleton, September 14, 1918; J. M. Tolivar, September 18, 1918, ibid.
[74]Letter, Bielaski to Frank R. Stone, January 16, 1918, ibid.
[75]Jensen, *The Price of Vigilance*, 140; also, 17-25, 28.
[76]Ibid., 144. See also, Peterson & Fite, 19.

12,000 branches; its expenses of some \$2-3 millions were paid by a group of employers and corporations.[77]

For several reasons, such as the Bureau's lack of resources, the Wilson administration's opposition to a permanent security structure, and its intention of avoiding any form of vigilante activity, the APL was brought under the close control of the Bureau. It was given a quasi-official status as the investigatory arm of the Bureau, first designated as "Cooperating with the United States Department of Justice" and from May 1918 as "Auxilliary to the Justice Department."[78] The members of the APL assisted the Bureau in its investigations of the IWW, monitored alien enemies, compiled information on pacifists and critics of US participation in the war, conducted loyalty checks of government employees and investigations in connection with passport applications, and aided the Bureau in its slacker raids. In total, the APL conducted 3 million investigations for the Bureau (and another 3 million for the military) or some 80% of the Bureau's domestic security work.[79] According to the Justice Department, the APL had proven to be invaluable and "constitutes a most important auxiliary and reserve force for the Bureau of Investigation" and added: "It is safe to say that never in its history has this country been so thoroughly policed as at the present time."[80] Thus, an internal security structure was established, in which the Bureau controlled and used private organizations, financed and staffed by the business community and conservative groups, thereby increasing its influence throughout society.[81] Another precedent for official and private cooperation was created during the war. FBI apologists later claimed that the many instances of illegal activities and injustices perpetrated by the APL were expressions of the popular wartime hysteria and committed by overzealous APL members who acted independently of the Bureau.[82] In fact, the Bureau kept the APL under tight control and in its eagerness for as much information as possible encouraged the private sleuths to perform such questionable operations as gaining access to the bank accounts of suspects, intercepting and opening letters, breaking in and obtaining private papers, tapping telephones and using

[77]Jensen, *The Price of Vigilance*, 145-148, 156.

[78]Ibid., 17-19, 41-43, 52-53, 89, 102, 120-122, 125-129.

[79]Ibid., 57-81, 155-156, 158-217.

[80]*AG Reports 1917*, 83, and *1918*, 15.

[81]As Bureau Chief Bielaski assured Congress, "volunteer citizens' associations ... pay their own expenses. We do not have to pay the expense of citizens' associations, or anything of that sort" (US Congress, Senate, Subcommittee of the Committee on Appropriations, *General Deficiency Bill, 1917. Hearings on H.R. 12*, 65th. Cong., 1st. Sess. (Washington, DC, 1917), 37-38).

[82]For example, Whitehead, 34-39; de Toledano, 48.

dictaphones to listening in on conversations. According to Joan Jensen, "The Bureau of Investigation had strayed so far from its primary function, the investigation of violations of federal law, that it was difficult now to draw the line."[83]

During the Red Scare this cooperation between the Bureau and its private allies, which might be termed as "political associationalism," played an essential role in the Bureau's ability to mobilize public support and influence the political debate. Thus, patriotic organizations lobbied the Justice Department and the Bureau to suppress radical and Bolshevik activities more vigorously, and, when the authorities did intervene, support their initiatives publicly. In particular, as the largest organized anti-radical force, the American Legion was especially active in lobbying the federal government.[84]

The Bureau's interest in the patriotic organizations is indicated by the fact that it kept a close watch on their activities and compiled a special list of "anti-Bolshevik organizations."[85] For example, the Bureau noted with interest that the American Defense Society in collaboration with New York mayors had organized a counter-demonstration on May 1, 1920, called "America Day."[86] It also noted that the National Security League called for the disbarment of the socialist Morris Hillquit, worked for the defeat of socialist candidates in New York elections, and planned a membership campaign with the ambitious goal of one million members.[87] The Bureau also filed reports on a wide range of the American Legion's activities, such as its calls for the boycott of Japanese businesses in Los Angeles, for the employment of the 600,000-700,000 unemployed veterans, the release of Eugene Debs and its attempts to stop the import of German movies;[88] Bureau

---

[83]Jensen, *The Price of Vigilance*, 223; also, 148-154, 299. The Supreme Court held in 1921 that it was not in violation of the Constitution when the government used private citizens to gather information by illegal methods such as breaking-in and stealing (ibid., 153).

[84]For example, letters, John T. Creighton to Chester A. Lewis, September 12, 1919; A. Mitchell Palmer to C. H. Longman, November 26, 1919; Palmer to Hon. W. R. Green, November 26, 1919; Palmer to Harry G. Cramer, November 25, 1919; Palmer to Roscoe J. McGee, January 9, 1920, all in OG 371688, RG65, NA. For an example of local AL pressure of the BI, see reports, S.A.Connell, November 21 and 22, 1919, OG 376413, ibid.

[85]List, "Anti-Bolshevik Organizations," n.d., OG 367403, ibid.

[86]Unidentified, May 1, 1920, OG 208369, ibid.; see also, letter, Frank Burke to C. L. Kemp, July 17, 1919, OG 93248, ibid. The BI also investigated whether an ADS pamphlet, according to which people pledged "myself anew as an American patriot to fight anarchy and Bolshevism" by sending $1 to the ADS, was part of a fraud (report, Holman Cook, April 23, 1919, with att. pamphlet, "True Americans This Way," and note, Offley, May 5, 1919, ibid.).

[87]J. G. Tucker, Special Report, Radical Activities in Greater New York District, March 6, 1920; Tucker, ibid., June 5, 1920; John L. Haas, ibid., July 31, 1920, OG 208369, ibid.

[88]Reports, E. Kosterlitzky, July 20, 1920, OG 371688, ibid.; J. T. Flourney, General Intelligence Report no. 43, for week ending September 24, 1921, BS 202600-9-41X, ibid.; W. J. Buchanan, Radical Activities in the Buffalo District, June 6, 1921, BS 202600-1613-11, ibid.; letter, Matthew C. Smith to L. J. Baley, May 5, 1921, BS 216034-1, ibid. For similar examples, see, reports, S. A. Connell, January 20, 1920, OG 371688, ibid.; M. J. Davis,

agents even monitored Legion meetings when they suspected that the Justice Department's policies would be criticized.[89] In some instances, the Bureau used the information from its surveillance of patriotic activities in its anti-radical campaign. For example, when the Bureau discovered that the Legion had taken legal action against a professor in Montana, Arthur Fisker, for having been a conscientious objector during the war, the Bureau promptly began an investigation of him.[90]

The reason for the Bureau's interest in the activities of the patriotic organizations was that they could be of assistance to it, particularly as a way of collecting information for the Bureau. Thus, the National Civic Federation provided the Bureau with information on such topics as alleged radical infiltration of the church, especially the Presbyterian, Episcopalian, Methodistic and Catholic Churches, and Communist infiltration of organized labor.[91] The ADS often informed the federal authorities about pacifistic activities, and, for example, kept the Women's International League for Peace and Freedom under close surveillance. When people asked the Bureau for its opinion about the WILPF, Director Burns directed their attention to pamphlets issued by the ADS which accused the organization of being subversive.[92] The Bureau's use of the American Legion to gather information is indicated by a letter from Legion official Arthur Wood to Hoover: "Your letter of February 3 has been received and I am taking it right up with the people who ought to know, asking them to send me whatever information they have about this organization, so that I can forward it to you."[93] This network of private intelligence would prove especially valuable when the Bureau was forced to curtail most of its political surveillance functions in 1924; even without active investigations, the

---

Special Report, Monthly Report on Radical Press for Period June 16th. to July 15th., 1921, BS 202600-33-285, ibid.; W. L. Buchanan, Radical Activities in the Buffalo District, September 5, 1921, BS 202600-1613-29, ibid.; J. M. Tolivar, July 25, 1921, BS 202600-1693-10, ibid.; P-134, August 15, 1921, BS 202600-1943-8, ibid.

[89]Report, Geo. T. Holman, November 22, 1919, OG 371688, ibid. In this instance, however, the agent was able to inform Washington that the assembled legionnaires had pledged their support to the authorities and that "On the whole, agent believes that this meeting was rather helpful to the Department of Justice than otherwise. . . . " (ibid.).

[90]Reports, D. Dickason, July 15, August 8 and September 24, 1921, BS 202600-2334-1/2/3, ibid.

[91]Report, J. G. Tucker, Special Report, Radical Activities in Greater New York District, February 19, 1921, BS 202600-51-3, ibid.; letters, Ralph Easley to Hon. Harry M. Daugherty, May 1, 1922 and William Burns to Easley, May 8, 1922, 61-714-24, box 4, Series 10, FBI Records, Marquette University Archives.

[92]J. E. Hoover, Memo for Mr. Baughman, March 26, 1923 with att. report, 61-1538-17, box 1, series 7, ibid.; Hoover, Memo for Mr. Baughman, March 30, 1923, 61-1538-20, ibid.; letters, Amy Woods, July 11, 1924, and Harlan F. Stone to Woods, July 17, 1924, 61-1538-62, ibid.

[93]Letter, Arthur Wood to J. E. Hoover, February 4, 1920, OG 371688, RG65, NA.

Bureau was assured a steady stream of political intelligence from patriotic groups.

The Bureau also leaked otherwise confidential information to the patriotic societies for their use, thereby, in effect, turning them into propaganda outlets of the federal government. When the NCF requested a statement from the Attorney General about his opinion about Soviet Russia, Frederick Latimer of the Bureau's Radical Publications Division was told that "This organization is a strongly anti-radical body and I believe it would be very desirable to make a strong reply to them for their use."[94] Using the NCF as a middleman, the Bureau also provided material for anticommunist articles in the *Christian Herald*, which resulted in a thank-you note to the effect that "As a matter of course we are emphasizing the irreligious attitude of the Communists. Your offer of quotations from 'Red' literature with references to the state, law, industry, marriage, the family, etc., is one well welcomed. When you have them in hand I will be very glad to have copies of anything in our office."[95] At a meeting in 1921 between Hoover and a representative from the American Legion, Robert Adams, Hoover was reported to have assured Adams "that they were very glad to have our cooperation and promised to furnish us with anything he thought would be of value."[96] Years later, Charles W. Taylor, Deputy Commander of the Legion, recalled how he had received "direct from the office of Mr. Burns" a large number of "genuine Communistic propaganda pamphlets which were being distributed in this country by the Communists"; according to Taylor, "These pamphlets were very valuable ... as a basis for addresses and parts of addresses which were continually given in public."[97] Thus, the Bureau provided some of the ammunition for the patriots' anti-radical crusade.

The Bridgman Affair
The best documented example of the Bureau's sophisticated use of private interest groups to further its anti-radical policies by spreading anti-radical propaganda and obtaining private funds at the same time

---

[94]Memorandum for Mr. Latimer, May 15, 1920, OG 388447, ibid.

[95]Letter, Rae D. Henkle to Frederick P. Latimer, February 13, 1920, ibid.; also, Henkle to Francis P. Garvan, February 13, 1920; Herbert Barry to Latimer, March 16 and 24, 1920, ibid.

[96]Pencak, 312-313. According to Pencak, who searched the files of the American Legion, information on the AL-FBI cooperation is either "unavailable or nonexistent." (Ibid.)

[97]Letter, Charles W. Taylor to Hon. Robert G. Simmons, March 24, 1932, att. to J. E. Hoover, Memorandum for Assistant Attorney General Dodds, April 4, 1932, JD 202600-16, RG60, NA (microfilm).

was the so-called Bridgman affair. On August 22, 1922, Bureau agents, acting on a tip from a confidential informant within the Communist Party and assisted by the local sheriff and twenty deputies, raided the secret national convention of the Communist Party, held in some cottages in the woods near the small village of Bridgman at Lake Michigan. During the raid the Bureau captured a large number of internal party documents and literature and took into custody 16 party leaders, who were turned over to the local authorities for prosecution according to the Michigan criminal syndicalism law.[98] However, since the local authorities were reluctant to spend the necessary funds for the trial, the Bureau set out in conjunction with its network of patriotic organizations to influence the public opinion and obtain funds for the case.

First, Richard M. Whitney of the ADS was given access to photostatic copies of the documents captured during the raid and was provided with additional confidential information from the Bureau files by Director Burns, Hoover and Hoover's assistant in the Radical Division, George F. Ruch, Jr. Whitney used this material as the basis for a series of articles on the radical danger in the *Boston Transcript*, later published as *Reds in America*. Whitney did not make any secret of his collaboration with the Bureau. He admitted the Bureau's assistance during the Bridgman trial and his book was presented as an account of "The present status of the revolutionary movement in the United States based on documents seized by the authorities in the raid upon the convention of the Communist Party at Bridgman, Michigan, August 22, 1922...."[99] Some time later, a former Special Agent, Franklin L. Dodge, recalled how Whitney was "given a room and desk space in Mr. Hoover's office in the Dept. of Justice building and for months the Dept. of Justice files were turned over to Mr. Whitney with no one else in this room."[100] This is supported by the draft of a letter, prepared by Hoover but never sent, according to which Whitney "was accorded access to the official files of this Department in gathering the

[98]For accounts of the Bridgman affair, see, Whitehead, 53; Belknap, 52-54; Theodore Draper, *The Roots of American Communism* (New York, 1957), 363-372.

[99]For Whitney's trial deposition, see "Says Michigan Reds Seek Class Hatred," *The New York Times*, January 31, 1923, clipping in box 1, J. Edgar Hoover Memoriabilia Collection, RG65, NA; the complete title of the book was *Reds in America: The Present Status of the Revolutionary Movement in the United States Based on Documents Seized by the Authorities in the Raid Upon the Convention of the Communist Party at Bridgman, Michigan, August 22, 1922, Together with Descriptions of Numerous Connections and Associations of the Communists Among the Radicals, Progressives, and Pinks* (New York, 1924).

[100]Memorandum, Facts furnished by Franklin L. Dodge formerly connected with the Department of Justice, January 21, 1927, box 278, Thomas J. Walsh Papers, LC.

material for these articles."[101] Apparently, Joseph T. Cashman of the NSL was also aided in the preparation of his book *America Asleep: The Menace of Radicalism.*[102]

Next, the Bureau used these publications and its patriotic network to obtain funds for the trial. On October 9, 1922, Ralph M. Easley of the National Civic Federation sent the Whitney articles to Howard E. Coffin of the Hudson Motor Car Company in Detroit and described the problem of financing the trial since the local authorities had no money and the federal government was prohibited by law from spending anything on state affairs. Easley confided to Coffin that his organization "have been asked to look into the matter of raising a fund to meet this exigency. An official from Washington is going to meet with some of our people at luncheon on Friday to see what, if anything, can be done," and he asked Coffin to look into the possibilities of obtaining private funds.[103] At the meeting with the unidentified "party from Washington" it was decided to keep the NCF's role in the matter secret "as that would do more harm than good, neither would it be advisable to raise funds in 'Wall Street'." Instead, it was proposed to approach the Michigan authorities and have them issue a public call for funds. It was also suggested that Alexander I. Rorke, known for his prosecutions of criminal anarchy cases in New York, and Archibald Stevenson, counsel for the red hunting New York Lusk Committee, should assist the local authorities with the case: "The Washington representative is very anxious that this should be done."[104] It seems clear that the Bureau through the NCF was organizing the trial against the Communist leaders and securing private sponsors; when Coffin went to Washington he was told by Easley to confer with Bureau Director Burns and he arranged for the hiring of Rorke to assist with the prosecution.[105] Thus, the cooperative network enabled the Bureau to use one patriotic organization, the ADS, to publicize the Commu-

---

[101]Letter, Director to Hon. Frank L. Greene, July 18, 1923, 61-4216-unrecorded, RG65, NA. In the final version, the letter simply noted that Whitney's articles were "taken from the files of the Department of Justice" (Letter, William J. Burns to Greene, July 20, 1923, 61-4216-1, ibid.).

[102]Murphy, 71.

[103]Letter, Ralph M. Easley to Howard E. Coffin, October 9, 1922, box 23, National Civic Federation Papers, New York Public Library. For the BI-NCF cooperation in funding the trial, see also, Marguerite Green, *The National Civic Federation and the American Labor Movement 1900-1925* (Washington, DC, 1956), 421-422.

[104]Letter, Easley to Coffin, October 19, 1922; also, unidentified to Easley, October 21, 1922; telegram, Easley to Coffin, October 23, 1922, all in box 23, NCF Papers, New York Public Library.

[105]Telegrams, Coffin to Easley, November 1, 1922; Easley to Coffin, November 2, 1922; letters, Easley to Coffin, November 2, 1922; Coffin to Easley, November 23, 1922; telegrams, Coffin to Easley, November 26, 1922; Easley to Coffin, November 27, 1922, ibid.

nist danger and another, the NCF, to help arrange and finance the trial.

The Centralia Massacre

The Bureau also protected the largest patriotic group, the American Legion. The Legion was founded by 20 officers in Paris on February 15, 1919, and its first caucus was attended by 450 members a month later; by 1920 it had grown to 843,013 primarily upper- and middle-class members.[106] The Legion immediately became the leading anti-Bolshevik organization. At its caucus in St. Louis in April 1919 a strong anti-radical resolution was passed, calling for the deportation of alien Bolsheviks and IWWs. At its first national convention in November it pledged its support to the authorities in maintaining law and order and suppressing the activities of the "Un-Americans". The Legion's most effective method by which to maintain "order" was mob violence, which was used on numerous occasions to break up public meetings, interrupt speakers, destroy offices and run radical agitators out of town. According to William Pencak, without the American Legion, "the Red Scare of 1919-20 might not have so effectively stopped American radicalism dead in its tracks."[107]

While the Bureau was eager to suppress left-wing organizations and persons on the basis of their utterances and opinions alone, the Bureau seemed reluctant or even unwilling to take any action against the Legion's actual use of political violence. It is noteworthy that except for a number of anarchist bombs in June 1919, almost all political violence was perpetrated by right wing or patriotic groups, yet the authorities concentrated on repressing the victims. In a revealing incident in Los Angeles in November 1919, members of the American Legion invaded a meeting at the local IWW headquarters, severely whipped a number of those present and completely wrecked the offices. Instead of pursuing the Legionnaires, the Bureau immediately launched an investigation of the IWW members and noted with sympathy that "These young men of the American Legion are no doubt in earnest and intend to stop all further radical meetings, and I may say that I believe that the authorities agree with them."[108] At the same time the Bureau was informed by the MID that the Legion was preparing

---

[106]Pencak, 49, 53-59, 81.

[107]Ibid., 320; also, 146-157.

[108]Report, S. A. Connell, November 21, 1919; also, report., November 22, 1919, OG 376413, RG65, NA. It should be noted in connection with the representativity of these examples that a complete search of the BI files in RG65, NA, for all references to the American Legion was made, but that a number of files apparently were missing (OG 381167/209264/387413 & BS 202600-35-209/202600-39-111/207236-21/213059-20).

an attack on a radical book shop in Chicago, but there is no record as to whether the Bureau intervened or not.[109] When one Howard Werntz complained to the Justice Department about the "lawless and pernicious activities" of the Legion and demanded to know why the Wilson administration did not intervene, he was told by Assistant Director and Chief Frank Burke that "You have failed, however, to state any definite acts taken by the American Legion which you term to be lawless and pernicious" and referred any complaints to the US attorney in Pittsburgh for "proper attention."[110] Only a few examples of Bureau investigations of violence initiated by the Legion exist and none of them apparently lead to prosecutions.[111]

The double standard employed by the Bureau toward the Legion concerning political violence became evident in its investigation of the most dramatic example of mob violence during the Red Scare, the Centralia massacre. On November 11, 1919, an American Legion Armistice parade in the small lumber town of Centralia, Washington, was fired upon by members of the IWW hiding inside its local headquarters under circumstances that have never been fully solved. During the ensuing melée, four Legionnaires were killed, the IWW hall stormed, a number of IWWs captured and one, Wesley Everest, lynched by the enraged Legionnaires.[112] Special Agents F. D. Simmons and F. W. McIntosh of the Seattle field office were immediately dispatched to Centralia. The initial instructions from Washington to "Investigate situation at Centralia completely" and "Ascertain if any of the subjects are alien" were clearly based on the assumption that the violence had been started by the IWW and that the incident could be used to deport alien members.[113] Upon arriving just five hours after the shooting, the agents found that there was considerable talk of hanging the jailed IWWs, in the words of McIntosh, "Rumors were as plentiful as falling

[109]Telegram, Burke to Brennan, November 28, 1919, OG 371688, ibid.

[110]Letter, Frank Burke to Howard M. Werntz, December 2, 1919; also, Werntz to Department of Justice, November 24, 1919; Werntz to Bureau of Investigation, December 6, 1919, all in OG 371688, ibid.

[111]See, reports, Wm. M. Doyas, November 24, 1919, and Earle C. Farriah, November 25, 1919, OG 21746, ibid.

[112]For accounts of the massacre, see, Walker C. Smith, *Was It Murder? The Truth About Centralia* (Seattle, 1922); Federal Council of the Churches of Christ in America, et al, *The Centralia Case. A Joint Report on the Armistice Day Tragedy at Centralia, Washington, November 11, 1919* (New York, 1930); Robert K. Murray, "Centralia: An Unfinished American Tragedy," *Northwest Review*, Vol. 6, No. 2 (Spring 1963), 7-18; John M. McClelland, Jr., "Terror on Tower Avenue," *Pacific Northwest Quarterly*, Vol. 57 (April 1966), 65-72; Robert L. Tyler, *Rebels of the Woods: The I.W.W. in the Pacific Northwest* (Eugene, Oregon, 1967), 155-184; Tom Copeland, *The Centralia Tragedy of 1919. Elmer Smith and the Wobblies* (Seattle & London, 1991); John McClelland, Jr., *Wobbly War. The Centralia Story* (Tacoma, Washington, 1987); Pencak, 149-153. There exists no study, as far as can be established, of the federal role in the affair.

[113]Telegram, Frank Burke to Simmons, November 12, 1919, OG 376413, RG65, NA.

leaves in autumn, and of all varities." The agents spent the rest of the day trying to prevent any vigilante action by spreading the false rumor that troops were on their way to restore order; they were unable, however, to prevent the lynching of Everest during the following night.[114]

It soon became apparent that the county prosecutor had made up his mind about the case even before he began his investigation. According to agent McIntosh, the prosecutor was determined to put all of the blame on the IWW by arguing that the shooting of the paraders was, in effect, an ambush, a premeditated and unprovoked act, and he ignored all evidence to the contrary.[115] At first, the agents seemed to share this view and they wired Washington the following day that the IWWs had fired on the Legionnaires "without provocation."[116] However, having analyzed the prosecutor's case, gone over the scene of the crime and interviewed the witnesses, the agents came to another conclusion. One George Brown and his daughter, Miss Mabel Brown, who had been standing on the curb directly across the IWW hall, told McIntosh that before the shooting began, a soldier had stepped out of the ranks, walked to the door of the IWW hall and had tried to open the door. When this failed, he had turned in the direction of the parade and called, "Come on, boys." Several Legionnaires had thereupon left the parade and it was at that moment, when they were proceeding toward the IWW hall and the first soldier succeeded in opening the door, that the firing from within the hall and from across the street had commenced and the soldier at the door had fallen mortally wounded. Another witness, Mrs. R. V. Elmendorf, corroborated the fact that the column of soldiers had halted before the shooting.[117]

This information convinced the agents that the cause of the tragedy was not the revolutionary plotting of the IWW but instead the extreme agitation against the IWW, which had been conducted in Centralia during the preceding six months. The agents neglected to say by whom but it seems reasonable to assume that it had been organized by the Centralia Citizens Protective Association, a group of local businessmen opposed to the IWW and led by Warren O. Grimm, commander of the local American Legion post and one of those killed during the

[114]Report, F. W. McIntosh, November 16, 1919, ibid.; see also, letter, F. D. Simmons to Burke, November 20, 1919, ibid.
[115]Report, F. W. McIntosh, November 20, 1919, ibid.
[116]Telegram, McIntosh to Burke, November 12, 1919, ibid.
[117]Reports, F. W. McIntosh, November 16, 1919, and February 20, 1920, ibid.

shooting:[118] Fearing that they would be raided during the parade, as they had been in 1918 during a previous parade when their furniture and equipment were burned, the IWWs this time had armed themselves. When they saw a group of Legionnaires leave the parade and approach the hall, they thought that the attack was under way and opened fire in self-defense. According to McIntosh, "There is not a shred of evidence, nor a logical theory" to support the contention that the IWW had planned the ambush, nor that the Legionnaires should have planned a raid in advance. The clash was the culmination of the anti-IWW campaign and both parties acted impulsively: "What was done by the ex-soldiers appears to have been done on the spur of the moment, on impulse; and the previous feeling existing generally between the two factions made the first move a signal for rather concerted action by those within available reach."[119]

The Bureau had reliable information to the effect that the Legionnaires had made the first move and had tried to enter the IWW hall and that the IWWs had not planned to ambush the soldiers but had acted in self-defense. These facts were ignored by the county prosecutor and had not been disclosed in the papers.[120] If made public, the information would free the IWWs from the charge of premeditated murder and, perhaps, change the general public's perception of the IWW as a terrorist group, which deliberately shot at unarmed and peaceful veterans celebrating the Armistice. Yet the Bureau chose to keep silent about its knowledge. As Simmons informed Washington, the Bureau's investigation "throws new light on matter and should be kept absolutely confidential by Department at this time as I believe County Prosecutor will resent publication as an interference with his case."[121] Thus, in order not to antagonize the local prosecutor and, incidentally, avoid criticizing the American Legion or the local business elite, the results of the Bureau investigation of the Centralia massacre were quietly filed away.

Despite its knowledge, the Bureau assisted the local prosecutor in his attempt to get the 11 arrested IWWs convicted of first-degree murder. Agents even advised him how to refute the statements of the Browns and Mrs. Elmendorf – whom the agents previously had found to be of such vital importance in solving the case – "if vigorously

---

[118]For the Centralia Citizens Protective Association, see, McClelland, *Wobbly Wars*, 59-62; Copeland, 45-46.
[119]Report, F. W. McIntosh, November 20, 1919, OG 376413, RG65, NA.
[120]Ibid.
[121]Telegram, Simmons to Burke, November 15, 1919, ibid.

cross-examined."[122] During the trial in Montesano, special agents reported on the activities inside as well as outside the court room. Despite the fact that most of the mob violence in 1919 had been instigated by Legionnaires, the agents were clearly more concerned about possible IWW violence and saw the Legion as a force for maintaining order. Special Agent M. J. Fraser concluded a report on the possibility of violence by noting that "The Legion as a body are watching during the day and night so that nothing may start and that no trouble may occur."[123] The double standard employed by the Bureau is also indicated by the fact that anybody who contributed to the IWW's Centralia General Defense Fund was indexed in the Bureau files and the field offices were notified of the names so that the contributors could be put under surveillance.[124]

The Bureau never revealed its findings in the Centralia case and on March 12, 1920, two of the remaining 10 defendants were acquitted, one declared insane, and seven found guilty of second-degree murder and sentenced to 25 to 40 years in jail. The following June, in a report to Congress, the Bureau used the incident as proof of the IWW's campaign of "sabotage and lawlessness" and stated: "The Centralia, Wash., outrage was an evidence of the I.W.W. agitation."[125] The Centralia case illustrates how the Bureau, for political reasons, exonerated the activities of the local business community and the American Legion and blamed the IWW for the outbreak of political violence. Thus, it assisted in portraying the Legionnaires as innocent victims and the IWWs as murderous terrorists and dangerous revolutionaries.

The Destruction of the World War Veterans
As previously noted, bureaucracies might actively assist and support certain interest groups in order to create its own constituency. The Bureau's investigation of the World War Veterans might be seen as such an example. It was by no means a foregone conclusion in 1919 that the American Legion would become the leading spokesman for the veterans and become such an influental, conservative force in national and local politics. The most serious competitor was the now almost

---

[122]Report, F. W. McIntosh, February 20, 1920; for the cooperation, also, telegram, Carbarino to Burke, January 2, 1920; letter, Frank Carbarino to Burke, January 9, 1920, ibid.

[123]Report, M. J. Fraser, March 4, 1920; also, report, Roy A. Darling, March 8, 1920, ibid.

[124]See, telegrams from Frank Burke, June 29, 1920, ibid. While the Bureau ignored the activities of the Legion, agents were instructed to obtain copies of the court's charge to the jury or any other evidence indicating "that I.W.W. is unlawful organization" (Telegram, Suter to Carbarino, February 27, 1920, ibid.).

[125]*AG Palmer on Charges*, 182.

forgotten World War Veterans (WWV), which in March 1919 had endorsed a frankly radical program calling for jobs, a $500 bonus and for government distribution of surplus land and private property to the veterans. The WWV openly challenged the Legion, calling it an instrument of "monopoly and privilege," and was soon, according to its own estimate, of equal size with some 700,000 members.[126]

As far as can be determined, the Bureau's investigation began in January 1921 when it received information on the activities of the WWV from the MID, another federal bureaucracy with an interest in veterans' interest groups, to the effect "that the World War Veterans, a radical organization opposed to the American Legion, are seeking the assistance of organized labor in their membership campaign."[127] The Bureau was soon lobbied by the Legion to launch an investigation of its competitor. The national Legion headquarters in Indianapolis submitted an internal WWV letter to the Bureau, requesting that "you keep us advised of any developments in connection with this."[128] In March 1921, a Legion official met with Calvin S. Weakley of the Indianapolis field office to perfect arrangements whereby he might confidentially turn over information on the WWV to the Bureau. According to Weakley, it was arranged with "Mr. Bowles whereby at any time he secures any information on this or matters of a similar nature, he would communicate immediately with the Indianapolis office" and Bowles further told Weakley that "personally he believed this was an organization which would warrant a thorough investigation...."[129] The Legion subsequently submitted a report on the WWV to the Bureau, which denied that it was a legitimate veterans' organization and called it "an effort on the part of the radical elements of the labor movement to organize such service men as are in sympathy with them."[130] The Legion post in Bridgeport, Connecticut, informed federal agents that the WWV "is being fostered at this time by the I.W.W. and that the organizers are camouflaged under the cloak of the

[126]Pencak, 51. The WWV claimed to have 22 state organizations and 400,000 members in 1921 (Reports, James J. Lee, May 22, 1921, BS 207238-22; August H. Loula, June 1, 1921, BS 207238-23, both in RG65, NA).

[127]Letter, Mathew C. Smith to L. J. Baley, January 26, 1921, BS 207238-8, ibid.; also, Smith to Baley, February 8, 1921, BS 207238-9X, ibid. It is impossible to reconstruct completely the beginning of the investigation since the initial reports, numbered BS 207238-1 to -6, are missing.

[128]Letter, Lemuel Bowles to J. E. Hoover, February 18, 1920, with att. letter, BS 207238-9X, ibid.

[129]Letter, Calvin S. Weakley to Chief, Bureau of Investigation, March 5, 1921, BS 207238-12, ibid.

[130]Letter, Harrison Fuller to Frank B. O'Connell, March 15, 1921, BS 207238-unrecorded, ibid.

American Federation of Labor."[131] The business community, too, was interested in suppressing the WWV. The Bureau received from unidentified "manufacturing interests" a report from an informer, who had infiltrated the organization and was able to report that the WWV membership consisted of "either Red Socialists, I.W.W. Bolshevists or Communists" and that "The information, the type of men and the murderous thought toward the annihilation of our Government has astounded me. I am surprised that our Government has apparently taken no steps toward curbing this dangerous organization."[132]

As previously mentioned, bureaucracies tend to a large extent to decide themselves by which groups they will be pressured, and while the Bureau seemed reluctant to investigate or criticize the American Legion's vigilante activity despite protests from the public, it was more than willing to join the crusade against the WWV. In the course of its investigation, the Bureau shared information with the MID,[133] and informants infiltrated the organization and reported on its internal meetings.[134] The WWV's recruitment of new members and its agitation for government aid to veterans, the right to collective bargaining and the nationalization of the railroads and public utilities were closely followed by the Bureau,[135] and its convention and public meetings were monitored by the federal agents.[136] When Senator William Borah in 1923 addressed a mass meeting in New York, organized by the WWV, in support of amnesty for the remaining political prisoners from the war, agents were on hand to report the senator's speech to Washington.[137]

Despite its extensive surveillance, the Bureau never quite seemed able to make up its mind on how to evaluate the WWV, though it was convinced that it somehow functioned as a sort of front organization

[131]Report, James J. Lee, May 22, 1921, BS 207238-22, ibid.

[132]Report, W. H. Newberry, April 4, 1921, BS 207238-16, ibid.

[133]For information from MID, see, letters, Mathew C. Smith to L. J. Baley, April 9, 1921, BS 207238-17, ibid.; Smith to Baley, May 5, 1921, BS 207238-19, ibid.; William J. Burns to Lieut. Col. Stuart Heintzelman, September 7, 1921, BS 207238-41, ibid.; for BI information to MID, see, letters, Burns to Heintzelman, July 19 and 31, August 5 and 7, and September 18, 1922, all in 10110-2283 (US Military Intelligence Reports: Surveillance of Radicals 1917-41 (microfilm)).

[134]Reports, P-134, September 20 and 24, 1921, BS 207238-unrecorded, RG65, NA; P-134, September 19, 1921, BS 207238-42, ibid.; P-132, September 19, 1921, BS 207238-44, ibid.

[135]Reports, James J. Lee, July 26, 1921, BS 207238-34, ibid.; D. H. Dickason, August 8, 1921, BS 207238-35, ibid.; James J. Lee, August 15, 1921, BS 207238-36, ibid.; James J. Lee, August 31, 1921, BS 207238-40, ibid.

[136]Reports, J. E. Winkle, June 27, 1921, BS 207238-31, ibid.; D. H. Dickason, August 20, 1921, BS 207238-38, ibid., and August 27, 1921, BS 207238-39, ibid.

[137]Report, name deleted, March 12, 1923, 62-5097-61, box 1, Series 10, FBI Records, MU; also, letter, Edward J. Brennan to Burns, February 28, 1923, 62-5097-56, ibid.; reports, name deleted, February 28, 1923, 62-5097-56, ibid.; name deleted, March 1, 1923, 62-5097-56, ibid.

for subversive forces. In March 1921, J. Edgar Hoover summarized the information in the files of the Bureau, MID and the State Department on the WWV. He referred to its radical program and its opposition to the Legion and regarded it as a particularly "objectionable feature" that it was possible to become a member of a WWV auxiliary even without a military record, "the sole qualification being sympathy with the aims and objects of the WWV." According to Hoover, this auxiliary was being used by "the I.W.W. and other groups of like character to gain control of the ex-soldiers" and he quoted uncritically from a Bureau report according to which it was the organization's ultimate aim "to be the securing of complete political control of the country" by uniting all radical groups and parties in the US. This undocumented allegation led the Radical Division chief to the conclusion that it was "the first expression of a truly radical program and the first public advocacy of union with some of the admittedly radical movements."[138]

However, by June the Bureau's official view was that the WWV was composed by "'liberal' ex-service men" and it had met with considerable success in uniting with radical veterans groups, but it was "not affiliated with the I.W.W. and there is no probability of such an affiliation."[139] Perhaps the explanation for the conflicting views is that the Bureau had no concrete proof of subversive activities on the part of the WWV and simply objected to its radical policies. Especially its outspoken hostility to the open shop and the American Legion posed a threat to the Legion, whose membership was declining during the early 1920s because of its opposition to the veterans' bonus. Thus, one Bureau report illustrated the WWV's alleged radicalism by pointing out that it was "taking a part in organizing against the open shop as well as offering themselves and members in different localities for the purpose of propaganda against the open shop."[140] A report on its national convention in 1921 emphasized its close connections to organized labor and recounted that the convention went on record to show that the WWV "were the opposite of the American Legion and pointed out particularly, that its members will never act as strikebreak-

---

[138]J. E. Hoover, Memorandum for the Files, March 19, 1921, with att., memo, World War Veterans, March 10, 1921, BS 207238-14X, RG65, NA.

[139]Letter, Chief to William P. Hazen, June 2, 1921, BS 207238-unrecorded, ibid.

[140]Report, Gerald P. Murphy, June 9, 1921, BS 207238-25, ibid. Because of disagreements on its attitude toward the question of veterans' bonus, the American Legion lost some 240,000 members between 1920 and 1925, which might explain its eagerness to get rid of the WWV (Penzak, 83).

ers";[141] for this reason it was believed "a good policy to watch this organization."[142]

A few examples indicating that the Bureau sought actively to undermine the position of the WWV exist. For example, Special Agent James J. Lee noted that the WWV was growing in Bridgeport due to the Legion's opposition to the bonus. When he discovered that a number of black veterans had organized their own veterans group instead of joining the Legion out of fear of the white Legionnaires' antagonism, Lee advised the Legion to establish a separate black post.[143] Furthermore, the Bureau in some cases searched for minor violations of the law in order to put an end to WWV activities. During 1922 and 1923, the Bureau investigated WWV national President Jack Bradon who was alleged to be a Communist and suspected of turning the WWV into a Communist front organization with the aim of disseminating propaganda within the Army.[144] The Bureau first tried to verify whether his marriage was legitimate with a view toward prosecuting him according to the Mann Act and the War Insurance Act, but when this turned out to lead nowhere, the Bureau investigated whether his citation for "exceptional gallantry" during the war was a fraud.[145] When the agents discovered that Bradon was a genuine war hero, the Bureau got in contact with the Veterans Bureau "in order that the Bureau may be advised of Bradon's activities" but found that he did not receive any disability compensation from the government.[146] Although the Bureau apparently was never able to discover any concrete violation by Bradon and to put an end to his activities, the Bureau did leak confidential information on his political activities to

---

[141]Report, August H. Loula, July 7, 1921, BS 207238-33, RG65, NA.

[142]Report, Re: Convention of World War Veterans Held at Chicago, July First to Fourth, 1921, July 6, 1921, BS 207238-unrecorded, ibid.

[143]Reports, James J. Lee, June 14, 1921, BS 207238-26, and June 25, 1921, BS 207238-30, ibid. Another example of BI influence on the policies of the American Legion took place in 1920 during the Bureau's fight against Assistant Secretary of Labor Louis F. Post over the deportation of alien radicals. In October 1920 BI agents who were member of the Legion were encouraged to attend its national convention in Cleveland so that they could influence the Legion to take a stand against Post (Dominic Candeloro, "Louis F. Post and the Red Scare of 1920," *Prologue*, Vol. 11, No. 1 (Spring 1979), 53n45).

[144]Letters, William J. Burns to Lt.Col. Stuart Heintzelman, August 7, 1922, 61-1078-6; Edward J. Brennan to Director, August 8, 1922, 61-1078-7; Thomas F. Baughman, Memorandum in re: Jack Bradon, March 2, 1923, 61-1078-13, RG65, NA.

[145]Reports, C. E. Argabright, February 6, 1922, 61-1078-2; Argabright, February 13, 1922, 61-1078-1; letter, Burns to R. O. Samson, February 20, 1922, 61-1078-3; reports, H. D. Knickerbocker, February 18, 1922, 61-1078-4; J. H. Noonan, February 23, 1922, 61-1078-5, ibid.

[146]T. F. Baughman, Memorandum for Mr. Hoover, March 10, 1923, 61-1078-10; Burns, Memorandum for Mr. Bohner, March 14, 1923, 61-1078-10; report, J. T. Flourney, March 21, 1923, 61-1078-11; letter, Burns to Brennan, April 10, 1923, 61-1078-11, ibid.

Congressman Walter H. Newton and continued its surveillance of the WWV president.[147]

It has often been claimed that the Bureau as a responsible and professional government agency was determined to keep the Legion under control in order to avoid a recurrence of the vigilantism of the war,[148] but the Bureau's own files show that agents did encourage and assist the American Legion in its violent attacks on radicals. When the Veterans Non Partisan League, a WWV affiliate and alleged Communist group, tried to organize in Springfield, Mass., it was "broken up" by members of the Veterans of Foreign Wars, the American Legion and the United Spanish War Veterans, who, according to the Springfield field office, were "confidentially co-operating with this office of the Bureau."[149] In March 1923, when the WWV attempted to organize a branch of the Association of Disabled Veterans of the World War, they were immediately investigated by the Bureau. When it became clear that there was no legal way to prosecute the radical veterans, Special Agent Adrian L. Potter subsequently informed Washington that he had "imparted this information to commanders of various veteran organizations of recognized and patriotic standing, in an effort to prevent carrying out of work planned by subjects."[150] There are no records showing that Washington objected to this form of cooperation between public and private anti-radical forces and it is impossible to know if these examples were execptions to the rule or whether there were others that possibly did not leave a paper trail.

It is difficult to establish with any degree of certainty the impact of the Bureau's activities on the position of the WWV. According to William Pencak, the WWV, which had been a serious contender to the Legion in 1919, was moribund by the beginning of the 1920s, partly done in by the declining unemployment among the veterans and partly

---

[147]Letter, Walter H. Newton to Burns, October 10, 1922, 61-1078-9; Baughman, Memorandum in re: Jack Bradon, October 16, 1922, 61-1078-8; letter, Burns to Newton, October 18, 1922, 61-1078-9, ibid. For the continued surveillance, see, letter, Burns to Brennan, April 21, 1923, 61-1078-12; report, T. F. Weiss, October 16, 1923, 61-4545-1; Burns, Memorandum for Mr. Bohner, October 22, 1923, 61-4545-2; report, J. T. Flourney, October 26, 1923, 61-4545-3, ibid.

[148]According to the official history of the FBI, the Bureau was determined after World War I that "vigilantism and amateur sleuths have no place in law enforcement" and that one of Hoover's reasons for cooperating with (and controlling) the Legion during World War II was his desire to "avoid the growth of a vigilante movement" (Whitehead, 39 and 209). According to Powers, "Keeping the Legion at bay was a concern of Hoover's throughout his career; his worries about its capacity for vigilantism may have been as much caused by the example of the *Freikorps* as by the Centralia lynching" (Powers, *Secrecy and Power*, 502n5).

[149]Report, Adrian L. Potter, March 3, 1923, 61-3516-1, RG65, NA.

[150]Ibid.; also reports, E. J. Connelley, March 22, 1923, 61-3516-2, ibid.; E. B. Hazlett, April 13, 1923, 61-3516-3, ibid.

114

by the Red Scare.[151] Thus, the Bureau at least aided in undermining and containing the threat from the WWV and, thereby, helped to establish the American Legion as the dominating representative of the veterans and as the most enthusiastic supporter of the Bureau. In other words, the Bureau as an activist bureaucracy sought to create its own constituency. For example, in 1934 the Bureau suggested to the American Legion that it should lobby Congress for "adequate funds and power" so that the Bureau could "deal with this scandalous situation" of growing radicalism during the depression.[152] What seemed to be the expressions of an organized public opinion, demanding increased power to the Bureau, were, in fact, inspired and influenced by the Bureau.

Following the Federal Lead: The Bureau and the States
During the Red Scare, a majority of the states enacted legislation which sought to outlaw radical agitation. 35 states passed some form of sedition, criminal anarchy or criminal syndicalism laws, which usually punished the advocacy in speech or writing of the overthrow of government or the existing industrial or social system with force or violence or by any unlawful means, or the advocacy of organized resistance to the government, or the use of abusive language against public officials or the government, with a maximum fine of $5,000 or up to 10 years in prison. 32 states passed so-called Red flag legislation, which prohibited the display of the Red flag in public assemblies or parades. It has been estimated that a total of 1,400 people were arrested and some 300 convicted according to these laws.[153] This has usually been seen as an indication of the fact that the states were more repressive than the federal government and were reacting directly to popular demand. In the words of Murray, "the states far surpassed the federal government in the actual suppression, or threats of suppression ... and illustrated more clearly than the federal government the extent of hysteria in the nation in late 1919 and early 1920."[154]

First of all, it should be noted that in a number of instances local authorities repressed radical activities so effectively that the Bureau's services were not needed. As mentioned previously, the local officials in Centralia were determined to crack down on the IWW and, as will

---

[151]Pencak, 51.
[152]Ibid., 312-313.
[153]Eldridge Foster Dowell, *A History of Criminal Syndicalism Legislation in the United States* (Baltimore, 1939); Robert C. Sims, "Idaho's Criminal Syndicalism Act: One State's Response to Radical Labor," *Labor History*, Vol. 15, No. 4 (Fall 1974), 511-527.
[154]Murray, 231.

be described later, the Bureau's limited role in the Seattle general strike and the Boston police strike was a result of the effective and vigorous intervention of the local authorities. Various conspiracy theories notwithstanding, the Bureau played no active role in the most famous political case of the era, the trial against the Italian anarchists Nicola Sacco and Bartolomeo Vanzetti for having murdered a paymaster in Braintree, Massachusetts, in 1920.[155]

However, as previously pointed out, it is questionable to what extent the state legislatures were reflecting the public opinion since a substantial part of the populace was denied participation in the political process, in particular in the South, and at least a number of state legislatures were dominated by local business interests. Moreover, the states, at least to some degree, were heavily influenced by and followed the lead of the federal government in the area of political repression. As pointed out by Lawrence H. Chamberlain in his study of the New York State Legislature's Red hunting activities, it is striking that its investigations of un-American practices have "followed closely upon the heels" of similar initiatives by the federal authorities. The legislature's investigative committee, the so-called Lusk Committee, was established on March 20, 1919, ten days after the Overman Committee of the US Senate had ended a month-long hearing into Bolshevik propaganda activities in the US. The Lusk Committee's two major raids against radicals, on November 8, 1919 and January 3, 1920, took place the day after the Bureau's nationwide Palmer raids. The New York State Legislature's exclusion of five socialist assemblymen followed ten days after the US House of Representative's exclusion of Victor Berger, the socialist congressman from Wisconsin.[156] It seems reasonably to assume that at least some state legislatures were inspired by the federal initiatives.

In fact, during the Red Scare, Attorney General A. Mitchell Palmer toured the country to win support for his anti-radical crusade and spoke before several state legislatures, urging them to enact strong sedition and syndicalism laws to suppress radical activities; a number of the assemblies quickly followed his suggestions.[157] The Justice Department's interest in state laws stemmed from the fact that whereas the federal criminal code prohibited actual attempts at overthrowing

---

[155]For the theory that the Bureau helped to convict Sacco and Vanzetti for political reasons, see William Young and David E. Kaiser, *Postmortem. New Evidence in the Case of Sacco and Vanzetti* (Amherst, 1985), 124-133; for the argument that the Bureau played no role, see, Francis Russell, *Sacco and Vanzetti. The Case Resolved* (New York, 1986), 173-182; the Bureau's Sacco & Vanzetti file is 61-126, FBI/FOIA.

[156]Chamberlain, 10, 16-17, 49n56.

[157]Murray, 232; also, Lowenthal, 277.

116

the government or the actual use of violence against the government, there existed no federal sedition or syndicalist laws which could be used to punish the advocacy of revolution or use of violence. The government had the authority to deport radical aliens, but it had no legal means to reach citizens preaching anarchistic or Bolshevistic doctrines. Thus, to get around this legal obstacle, it was the policy of the Justice Department to turn over any information on radical activities of American citizens to local authorities for prosecution according to state sedition or syndicalist laws.[158] Although Hoover noted that many of the otherwise "excellent syndicalist and anti-anarchist laws" were "exceedingly broad and may even go too far in the direction of the abridging of free speech," he notified the Department that the Bureau was directed to investigate all cases of American citizens who were involved in radical activities and that "this office likewise prepares a summary of the information at hand and transmits same to the local authorities for such use as they may care to make."[159] According to the Bureau, this cooperation with the states "resulted in the purging from those communities of the obnoxious elements...."[160]

The Bureau files reveal that it exercised considerable influence both in drafting the state sedition and syndicalist laws and in intiating prosecutions. Perhaps this partly explains, besides the fact that the states might have borrowed from one another, why so much of this kind of legislation passed during the Red Scare was so strikingly similar in both contents and language. In at least one instance, the Bureau actually drafted a state sedition bill. In March 1919, Special Agent A. V. Levensaler, a graduate of Harvard Law School, wrote an anti-Bolshevik bill for New Hampshire Attorney General Oscar L. Young. It prohibited the teaching, advocating or practicing of "Bolshevist" doctrines and was passed by the legislature the same month.[161]

Bureau agents also assisted state legislators in the drafting of bills. In California, during the debate on a criminal syndicalist bill in 1919, agents of the Sacramento field office "kept in touch with members of the California legislature and furnished them with copies of laws passed in other states and with suggestions concerning the advantages of a conspiracy clause in such law." As a result of the agents' advice, a conspiracy law was passed in July 1919 which made it a crime for

---

[158]Earl J. Davis, Memorandum for Assistant Attorney General Holland, January 22, 1924, JD 202600-2734-4, RG60, NA (microfilm); *AG Report 1921*, 131.
[159]J. E. Hoover, Memorandum Upon Work of Radical Division, August 1, 1919, to October 15, 1919, October 18, 1919, OG 374217, RG65, NA.
[160]*AG Palmer on Charges*, 190.
[161]Williams, *"Without Understanding,"* 124-125.

two or more persons to conspire to commit a crime, a statute which proved particularly effective in prosecuting members of the IWW.[162] When the authorities in Utah contemplated amending the existing syndicalist and sabotage law, the Bureau provided the legislators with copies of the criminal syndicalist laws of California, Washington, Idaho, Kansas, Colorado, Nebraska and Illinois so that parts of these could be incorporated to make "a good, strong, workable syndicalist and sabotage law."[163] In 1921, the Bureau began systematically to collect information on all state laws, so that it would be in a position to assist more effectively local legislators in framing bills and local prosecutors in using the laws.[164]

Once passed the Bureau also assisted in defending state sedition laws against attempts to weaken or repeal them. When the California legislature in April 1923 discussed proposals to repeal or amend the criminal syndicalist law, Special Agent in Charge Frederick L. Esola of the San Fransisco field office "unofficially" assisted supporters of the law, lobbied members of the Legislative Committee and "data was furnished to the interested parties opposing said bill (to repeal) as to the radical situation in California and the apparent need of criminal syndicalist restrictions"; as a result, the two proposals to repeal and amend the law were defeated.[165] Opponents of state sedition laws were also investigated. For example, the Bureau collected and indexed a list of 14,239 names of people who had signed a petition for the recall of the Washington state criminal syndicalist law, noting that the signers "present a representative directory of who's who in the radical circles in the state of Washington."[166] In Los Angeles, protest meetings against the criminal syndicalist law were monitored and resolutions

[162]Report, F. W. Kelly, October 7, 1919; also, letter, Frank Burke to E. M. Blanford, November 1, 1919, OG 345429, RG65, NA. It should be noted that the BI index and files were searched systematically for all references to criminal anarchy, criminal syndicalist and sedition laws, but that apparently only a portion of such subjects was indexed under these headings.

[163]Report, E. S. Kimball, May 2, 1923, 61-147-50, ibid.

[164]Letters, C. E. Breniman to Chief, May 11, 1921, with att., BS 202600-2105-1X; Edward J. Brennan to Chief, May 12, 1921, with att., BS 202600-2105-6; F. X. O'Donnell to Chief, May 12, 1921, with att, BS 202600-2105-8; C. E. Breniman to Chief, May 18, 1921, BS 202600-2105-10; F. W. Kelly to W. R. Bryon, May 19, 1921, BS 202600-2105-11; Billups Harris to Chief, May 21, 1921, with att., BS 202600-2105-12; Harris to Chief, May 26, 1921, with att., BS 202600-2105-13; Harris to Chief, May 31, 1921, with att., BS 202600-2105-15; Harris to Chief, June 24, 1921, with att., BS 202600-2105-17; N. H. Castle to W. R. Bryon, May 11, 1921, with att., BS 202600-2105-unrecorded; Fred A. Watt to W. R. Bryon, May 17, 1921, with att., BS 202600-2105-unrecorded; G. O. Holdridge to T. M. Reddy, April 30, 1921, BS 202600-2105-unrecorded; report, Mortimer Davis, July 7, 1921, BS 202600-2105-21, ibid.

[165]Report, Frederick L. Esola, April 5, 1923, 61-3741-1, ibid.; see also, report, D. F. Costello, March 21, 1925, 61-3741-2, ibid.

[166]Letter, F. W. Kelly to Chief, August 2, 1921, BS 202600-2105-22, ibid.

favoring its repeal reported to Washington.[167] When a man from Lincoln, New Hampshire, protested to the speaker of the state legislature that the state law was a restriction of free speech, he was promptly investigated by the Bureau.[168]

The Bureau also played an influential role in initiating prosecutions under the state laws. Often the Bureau would refer information concerning radical publications to state authorities; thus, copies of the black socialistic paper the *Messenger* were turned over to the San Francisco police with the intention of having it banned according to the California criminal syndicalist law,[169] and the California authorities were encouraged to prosecute the socialistic the *Liberator*.[170] It was likewise suggested that the New York authorities should employ that state's criminal anarchy law against the Communistic the *Revolutionary Age*.[171] Sometimes Bureau agents would advise local prosecutors on how to employ state laws against radical activists. Agents explained the provisions in the criminal anarchy, syndicalism and conspiracy statutes to various county and district attorneys in California and taught them how to apply them to specific cases.[172]

It is significant, in view to the prevailing explanation of the Red Scare as a grass-roots movement, that the Bureau sometimes had to put considerable pressure on local officials, who seemed either not interested or lukewarm in using the state laws. Special Agent George H. Hudson reported that he was making efforts to get the Bureau involved in a California case against an IWW activist, "owing to the fact that the District Attorney at Stockton has not been connected with any of the cases apportaining to the IWW activities, and the evidence in this case being entirely of a foreign nature to him." As far as Hudson was concerned, "I don't see how he can very well proceed in this prosecution" without the assistance of the Bureau.[173] The case was only prosecuted because the Bureau agents conducted the investigation and assisted the inexperienced DA.[174] The Bureau also took the lead when the Bingham, Utah, police in May 1923 arrested two IWW organizers and asked the Salt Lake City field office what to do with

[167]Reports, A. A. Hopkins, February 18, 1924, 61-3675-4, and February 27, 1924, 61-3675-5, ibid.

[168]Williams, *"Without Understanding,"* 125-126.

[169]Report, N. H. Castle, July 9, 1919, OG 258421, RG65, NA.

[170]Report, E. Kosterlitzky, February 19, 1920, OG 136944, ibid.

[171]Report, Roy C. McHenry, July 22, 1919, ibid.

[172]Reports, SA MacCormack, February 15, 1919; F. W. Kelly, October 7, 1919, OG 345429, ibid.

[173]Report, Geo. H. Hudson, August 14, 1919, ibid.

[174]Reports, F. W. Kelly, July 21 and October 21, 1919, ibid.

them. Special Agent E. S. Kimball immediately got in contact with a number of local law enforcement officials and received their assurances that they would employ the Utah syndicalist and sabotage against the IWWs: "They each expressed their desire to test out this law, stating that they would be pleased to accept the Government's cooperation." Apparently, Kimball was not completely convinced that the local officials possessed the proper anti-radical attitude since he informed Washington that the case would go to court "Unless the local authorities of Salt Lake City and County get cold feet ...."[175]

In fact, the Bureau in some instances was forced to abandon efforts to employ state laws to radical activities because of local resistance. In 1922, a Bureau informant suggested that IWW advances in the Southern California oil fields should be halted by initiating prosecutions under the criminal syndicalism law, but this idea had to be dropped because of "considerable friction" between the local authorities and the oil companies.[176] One of the strongholds of the IWW was Butte, Montana, and in 1920 the Bureau contemplated using the criminal syndicalism law against its leading members. The county attorney reviewed the Bureau's case and agreed to prosecute, but the problem was that both the district judge and the state Attorney General were unsympathetic to the government's plans. According to the Butte field office, they were in fact radicals themselves; as agent J. L. Webb disappointedly told Washington, "Thus we are brought face to face with the realization of the impossibility of Government Agents to accomplish anything in Butte and of the uselessness of their sojourning in any great numbers in this section."[177]

Because of the reluctance exhibited by a number of state authorities to prosecute radicals, it seems likely to assume that the Bureau was, in effect, the initiator of and driving force behind a number of those state syndicalist cases, which have been seen as evidence of popular hysteria. The perhaps most spectacular state prosecution of the period, the previously mentioned Bridgman, Michigan, case against the leadership of the Communist Party was, despite the Bureau's later claims that it

[175]Report, E. S. Kimball, May 2, 1923, 61-147-50, ibid.
[176]Reports, A. A. Hopkins, August 15, 1922, 61-997-12, and March 1, 1923, 61-997-16, ibid.
[177]Report, J. L. Webb, May 11, 1920, 61-01, box 1, investigative reports, ibid. The Bureau's antagonism toward Butte officials is also indicated by a comment regarding George Bourquin, son of US District Judge George M. Bourquin, who was characterized in a BI report: "He is yellow, has no back-bone and, like his father, inclined toward radicalism...." (Report, D. F. Costello, October 24, 1920, ibid.). The Bureau in particular blamed Judge Bourquin and his alleged sympathy for the radicals for the "serious" situation in Butte (for BI criticism of Bourquin and its attempts to remove him, see, David Williams, "The Bureau of Investigation and its Critics, 1919-1921: The Origins of Federal Political Surveillance," *The Journal of American History,* Vol. 68, No. 3 (December 1983), 564-565).

was "entirely a state case" in which it had played the wholly subservant role of assisting the state authorities and provided them with information, from beginning to end a Bureau case directed from Washington.[178] It was a Bureau informant within the Communist Party, Francis A. Morrow, codenamed K-97, who had alerted the Bureau to the fact that a secret Communist convention would take place in the vicinity of St. Joseph, Michigan, and it was agents from the Chicago office, acting under instructions from Washington and led by Special Agent Jacob Spolansky, who located the convention at Bridgman. They organized and conducted the raid on August 22, assisted by the local sheriff and twenty deputies; the state police, however, refused to participate. Following the arrests of 17 top Communists, it was K-97 who led the agents to a cache of hidden party records in the woods, and Bureau agents who guarded and interrogated the prisoners. It was the Bureau who persuaded the reluctant local authorities to prosecute under the Michigan state syndicalism law, unused since its enactment in 1919, by promising to raise funds to cover the expenses, and the Justice Department provided a lawyer to assist with the case. At the trial in 1923, Communist Party Secretary Charles Ruthenberg was sentenced to five years in prison but died before his appeal was decided, and the later CPUSA leader, William Z. Foster, was freed by a hung jury.[179]

Another important state prosecution initiated by the Bureau took place in Pittsburgh, Pennsylvania. In April and May 1923, the Bureau conducted a series of raids against members of the Workers' Party (the legal Communist party) in cooperation with city and county police. A total of 27 Communists were arrested and a mass of office equipment, party records and literature was confiscated. Bureau Division Superintendent E. B. Spencer pledged the Bureau's assistance to the local district attorney in the prosecution of the cases under the state syndicalism law.[180] When the Allegheny County assistant district attorney asked Washington for information, the Bureau was directed "to give some concrete assistance" by the Justice Department, and the local prosecutor was provided with information on the connection of

---

[178]For the Bureau and the Justice Department's denials during an argument with the ACLU, see, letters, Mabel Willebrandt to Norman Thomas, September 19, 1922, JD 202600-2721-1; John W. H. Crim to American Civil Liberties Union, October 31, 1922, JD 202600-2721-4; Ass. AG to J. Barnard Walton, January 23, 1923, JD 202600-2730-2, RG60, NA (microfilm); *Appropriations, Department of Justice, 1924*, 75-77; *Appropriations, Department of Justice, 1925*, 92-93; Belknap, 53-54; Williams, *"Without Understanding,"* 230-231.
[179]Draper, 366-372; Belknap, 52-53. Some of the Communist records captured during the raid were published by the Bureau in *Recognition of Russia. Hearings*, Pt. 2, 286-292, 300-302
[180]Williams, *"Without Understanding,"* 232-233.

the Workers' Party with the Comintern and the activities of a number of party leaders.[181]

According to a status report by the Bureau, it had furnished information about the radical activities of American citizens to state authorities and "it is to be noted that convictions have been obtained in all cases under the various state laws."[182] According to official figures, during fiscal year 1921-22 alone the Bureau secured 115 convictions under state syndicalism laws.[183] Since it has been estimated that a total of 300 were convicted under state syndicalism laws, it is likely, if these figures are accurate, that at least a substantial part of these cases were conducted on the initiative of the Bureau. In other words, the number of state prosecutions during the Red Scare might not reflect a broadly based grass-roots hysteria but rather indicate the determination of the federal government to use state laws in order to reach and suppress the political activities of American citizens.

The Bureau also established an informal network with city and state investigative bodies. The reason for this was the small number of special agents and the fact that they were not empowered to make arrests or carry weapons until 1934. In order to execute large scale operations on a national basis, such as simultaneous raids across the nation, it was necessary to obtain the cooperation of local police forces. As pointed out by Frank Donner, the creation during the Red Scare of specialized "Red Squads" by a number of big city police departments was influenced by "the need for an operating arm for the repressive federal campaign against radicals."[184] The Bureau files confirm that the Bureau in a number of instances used local police forces to collect information and execute raids against radicals. For example, during the national coal miners strike in the fall of 1919, agents were directed to establish close contacts with local chiefs of police, sheriffs and state constabularies and a number of raids were made against radical strikers. Local police forces also assisted during the Palmer raids against alien anarchists and Communists in 1919 and 1920.[185]

---

[181]J. E. Hoover, Memorandum for Mr. Ridgely, June 4, 1925, JD 202600-2728; H. S. Ridgely, Memorandum for the Bureau of Investigation, June 8, 1925, ibid.; letter, H. S. Ridgely to Ralph H. Smith, June 11, 1925, JD 202600-2728-6, RG60, NA (microfilm).

[182]J. E. Hoover, Memorandum Upon Activities of the Radical Division, Department of Justice, May 1, 1920, OG 374217, RG65, NA.

[183]*Appropriations, Department of Justice, 1924*, Pt. 2, 70, 76.

[184]Frank Donner, *Protectors of Privilege*, 41; in general, 37-43.

[185]For the BI's general policy of cooperation with local police forces, see Report of Committee on Cooperation, August 17, 1920, OG 390982, RG65, NA; for cooperation during the miners' strike, see Edgar B. Speer, Special Report to Frank Burke, October 31, 1919, and report, Ernest W. Lambeth, December 23, 1919, OG 303770, ibid.; for cooperation during the steel

The most reckless and powerful of the local investigative bodies was the Joint Legislative Committee Investigating Seditious Activities of the New York legislature, popularly known as the Lusk Committee after its chairman, Republican state Senator Clayton Lusk. Although the committee was a legislative investigating agency, charged with inquiring into seditious activities in the State of New York and to report its findings to the legislature, the committee soon abandoned the usual procedure of conducting public and executive hearings. Instead it relied on search warrants to execute raids against radical centers and offices throughout the state, whereby a number of radical leaders were taken into custody and charged with violating the criminal anarchy statute, and a mass of records and literature was confiscated and presented at public hearings as evidence of the radical danger. At the hearings and press conferences sensational but unfounded accusations were made, liberal and other reform organizations were discredited as subversives, and lists of suspected radicals or sympathizers were made public. The committee had its own staff of investigators and translators and it cooperated closely with other state agencies, such as the state attorney general's office and the New York Bomb Squad.[186]

The Bureau established close ties with the Lusk Committee through its chief investigator, Rayme W. Finch, who until the spring of 1919 had been a Bureau agent in the New York field office. The cooperation between the two agencies apparently began when the Bureau in July 1919 allowed an informant, who had infiltrated and taken notes at meetings at the Rand School of Social Science, an educational branch of the Socialist Party, to testify before the Lusk Committee in its attempt to revoke its charter.[187] The pivotal role played by Finch became clear when New York Special Deputy Attorney General John B. Trevor, who was attached to the committee, requested that the

---

strike 1919, see reports, H. F. Blackmon, September 26, 1919, and V. P. Creighton, October 1, 1919, ibid.; for the Bureau's use of local Red Squads during the Palmer raids, see reports, E. Anderson, November 21, 1919; J. L. Haas, November 19, 1919; C. J. Scully, November 11, 1919; J. A. Brann, November 8, 1919, H. C. Leslie, November 11, 1919, BS 202600-184, ibid.; for cooperation during the Sacco & Vanzetti case, see, letters, William J. Burns to A. S. Mahone et al, October 29, 1921, 61-126-66, FBI/FOIA.

[186]On the Lusk Committee in general, see Chamberlain, 9-52; Jaffe, 119-142. The committee has described its activities in, New York Senate, Joint Legislative Committee Investigating Seditious Activities, *Revolutionary Radicalism. Its History, Purpose and Tactics with an Exposition and Discussion of the Steps Being Taken and Required to Curb It. Report*, Part I, Vol. I (Albany, N.Y., 1920), especially, 20-28. For a particular aspect of the committee's activity, its surveillance of black radicalism in New York, see, J. M. Pawa, "Black Radicals and White Spies: Harlem, 1919," *Negro History Bulletin*, Vol. 35, No. 2 (October 1972), 129-133.

[187]Letters, Charles D. Newton to William M. Offley, July 12, 1919; Offley to William J. Flynn, July 16, 1919; Frank Burke to Offley, July 23, 1919, OG 147169, RG65, NA.

Lusk Committee be allowed access to the Bureau's files on the black socialist A. Philip Randolph "for study, and possible for development into a case."[188] When the New York office discovered that its two reports on Randolph, dated April 3 and June 12, 1919, had been misplaced, it was arranged for Finch to come to the office "in an endeavour to locate the afore-mentioned papers."[189] Later, arrangements were perfected whereby the committee might obtain information from the Bureau files directly from Washington. On October 7, the Lusk Committee was advised to get in contact with J. Edgar Hoover "and I have no doubt that such information and cooperation as you desire, concerning subject matter, can be obtained through him."[190]

In return for this assistance, the Lusk Committee functioned as a sort of intelligence network for the Bureau. Thus, Finch turned over information on radical activities in New York and Cleveland and on the black leader Marcus Garvey. He also arranged for the assistance of the Bureau in the committee's interrogation of the Soviet trade representative to the US, Ludwig C. A. K. Martens, in exchange for providing the Bureau with the results of the inquiry.[191] The Bureau also worked through the committee's Associate Counsel Archibald Stevenson. When Special Agent Frank Faulhaber requested permission to obtain access to material confiscated by the committee and the New York Bomb Squad during their raid on the headquarters of the alleged anarchistic organization, the Union of Russian Workers, Stevenson answered "that the federal Bureau could have any and all information in his possession...."[192] In connection with the Bureau's deportation of URW members in late 1919, it was agreed that the New York office "will in the future be enabled to secure all information regarding this organization which might be in the possession of the Lusk Committee."[193] The Bureau also received an 11 page list of radicals in New

[188]Letter, John B. Trevor to Frank Burke, August 11, 1919, with att. letter, Trevor to William Offley, August 7, 1919, OG 265716, ibid. Finch's close ties with the Bureau are indicated by the fact that he is classified in the BI index as "informant", but all references on the card have been deleted, indicating that BI files on Finch have been removed or destroyed (BI general index 1908-22, RG65, NA).

[189]Report, C. J. Scully, August 20, 1919, OG 265716, ibid.

[190]Letter, R. M. Doyas to Joint State Legislative Committee, October 7, 1919; also, letter, Doyas to J. E. Hoover, October 7, 1919, BS 202600-184, ibid.

[191]Letters, R. W. Finch to William J. Flynn, August 12, 1919; Frank Burke to Finch, August 14, 1919; Burke to J. A. Baker, August 14, 1919, OG 350625, ibid.; Wm. Offley to Burke, September 2, 1919, OG 185161, ibid.; G. F. Lamb to Burke, September 22, 1919; Burke to Lamb, September 25, 1919, OG 350625, ibid.

[192]Report, Frank B. Faulhaber, September 12, 1919; also, ibid., September 22, 1919, BS 202600-184, ibid.

[193]Letter, Lamb to Burke, November 13, 1919, with att. "List of members, taken from the finance book of the Union of Russian Workers, City of New York," n.d.; also, report, Victor Valjevec, November 24, 1919, ibid.

York, which had been compiled by the committee, and in January 1920, Special Agent Frank J. Seib spent several days combing the committee files for information on the IWW.[194]

Thus, it can be concluded that the Bureau actively cooperated with and in some instances even initiated some of the red hunting activities on the local level, which have normally been viewed as expressions of the grass-roots hysteria that was the real basis for the Red Scare. The reason for this was the lack of a federal peacetime sedition law which forced the Justice Department to use state laws to punish US citizens for their radical activities. Thus, the Bureau in several instances assisted state legislators in drafting strong criminal syndicalism and sedition bills, lobbied them against repealing existing laws and investigated opponents of the laws. Moreover, the Bureau initiated a number, perhaps a majority, of the state prosecutions by submitting information on political activities to local authorities and by subsequently providing expert advice to state prosecutors, who in several cases seemed inexperienced in conducting political trials; in some cases, the Bureau even had to put pressure on rather uninterested or even reluctant local authorities to bring the cases to trial. At the same time, the Red Squads and the Lusk Committee functioned as the Bureau's operating arm on a local level, conducting raids, arresting a number of radical leaders and confiscating organizational records and literature. Seen in this way, it can be argued that the Bureau did not just react to local demands but, as in the case of the interest groups, excercised a considerable influence on the national anti-radical community.

---

[194]Letter, Lamb to Burke, January 31, 1920; report, Frank J. Seib, February 4, 1920, OG 208369, ibid.

Chapter 4

Constructing the Red Scare

Assessing the Revolutionary Danger: The Seattle General Strike

In most of the existing literature on the Red Scare, the Bureau of Investigation is not mentioned until the federal government in response to the anarchist bombs in June 1919 organized the Radical Division and charged it with the preparation of deportation cases against radical aliens. The general impression is that the Bureau took no active part in the hunt for radicals during the first half of 1919 and that it remained passive during the series of dramatic political events that spring, such as the Seattle general strike in February, the sensational Senate hearings on the Bolshevik danger during February and March, the investigation by the Lusk Committee, the anarchist bombs in April and June, and the May Day riots. In other words, the Bureau – and the federal government – only entered the scene when the popular anti-radical opinion had been formed.[1] However, the Bureau files show that the federal agents participated actively from the very beginning of the Red Scare, namely in the Seattle general strike.

The Bureau had been watching political activities on the West Coast since 1915. In November of that year the Bureau dispatched Special Agent Frank Carbarino to monitor the activities of IWWs and socialists, and he alerted Washington to the danger that the IWW was preparing a "direct action." He added that "Conditions in Seattle are ripe for agitation, as there seems to be an army of unemployed, and the IWW seems to cater to this class," whom Carbarino described as "those who never work, and never will, no matter how renumerative the position, as a laborer."[2] During the war, the radicalization of local unions and the increasing popularity of the IWW had led to waves of illegal arrests of radicals, committed both by patriotic groups, local authorities and federal agencies. In order to impose some order on the city, the Justice Department dispatched Clarence L. Reames, special assistant for war-related cases, who proceeded to centralize the anti-

---

[1] See for example, Murray, 3-81; Coben, *A. Mitchell Palmer,* 196-207; Higham, 222-230; Levin, 28-34; Powers, *Secrecy and Power,* 56-63.

[2] Report, Agent Carbarino, November 29, 1915; also, report., November 28, 1915, OG 91928, RG65, NA.

radical campaign by prohibiting arbitrary arrests. At the same time, he began to implement a plan in conjunction with the Immigration Bureau and the local business community for the detention of 3,000 to 5,000 suspected alien members of the IWW in internment camps for later deportation. However, the secretary of labor vetoed this ambitious scheme, but not until some 150 aliens had been arrested.[3]

At the end of the war in November 1918, there was growing unrest and dissatisfaction among the shipyards workers with the basic national wage of $6.40 per day set by the Macy Shipyard Adjustment Board.[4] Reames called the attention of the Justice Department to what he called the growing Bolshevik or revolutionary propaganda in Seattle and he requested that a force of federal agents be dispatched to ascertain if the situation was developing into a seditious conspiracy. Special Assistant to the Attorney General Alfred Bettman recommended to Bureau Chief Bielaski to investigate but he did caution him to avoid "unlawful, arbitrary and undemocratic suppression of meetings or seizure of papers or the like or anything giving these people the feeling that they are subjected to unlawful government suppression."[5] Before transmitting these instructions to Special Agent in Charge in Seattle F. D. Simmons, Bielaski referred to a report from the Office of Naval Intelligence on IWW and Bolshevik activities in Seattle and noted that "I should like to keep up with these activities as well as possible and am sure you are covering same."[6] The Bureau, then, initiated its surveillance of radical activities immediately following the war and well in advance of any popular demand.

The Bureau's surveillance operation in Seattle illustrates the unreliability of its network of informants. The Bureau received most of its information from informants employed by the American Protective League, the Minute Men and the Pinkerton Detective Agency, who had infiltrated the Seattle Central Labor Council, the Soldiers', Sailors', and Workmen's Councils, the shipyards and the IWW. The

---

[3]For the federal anti-IWW crusade in Seattle during WWI, see Preston, 152-172; for the Bureau's wartime surveillance of Bolsheviks, anarchists and the Russian consulate in Seattle, see, for example, reports, S. E. Webb, August 12 and 22, 1918; Agent Petrovitsky, August 10, 1918, OG 91928, RG65, NA.

[4]For the Seattle general strike in general, see, Robert L. Friedheim, *The Seattle General Strike* (Seattle, 1964); Robert L. & Robin Friedheim, "The Seattle Labor Movement," *Pacific Northwest Quarterly*, Vol. 55, No. 4 (October 1964), 146-156; Robert L. Friedheim, "Prologue to a General Strike: The Seattle Shipyard Strike of 1919," *Labor History*, Vol. 6, No. 2 (Spring 1965), 121-142; Terje I. Leiren, "Ole and the Reds: The 'Americanism' of Seattle Mayor Ole Hanson," *Norweigan-American Studies*, Vol. 30 (1985), 75-95; report, Spl. Empl. McIntosh, November 30, 1918, OG 91928, RG65, NA.

[5]Alfred Bettman, Memorandum for Mr. Bielaski, November 22, 1918, ibid.

[6]Letter, A. Bruce Bielaski to F. D. Simmons, November 30, 1918; also, letter, Bielaski to Simmons, December 18, 1918, ibid.

set-up of this network ensured that the Bureau would receive biased information since the Pinkerton Agency was hired by the employers to watch the radicals and to break strikes, and the APL and the Minute Men were both patriotic societies, financed and used by the business community to gather information on radical activities.[7] The informants' reports contained alarming assessments of radical influence within the Seattle labor movement. On the basis of several such reports, the APL in late November 1918 estimated that more than 50% of all shipyard workers were either revolutionaries or Bolsheviks, and an APL informant, who had infiltrated the work force at the Skinner & Eddy Shipyard and gained the radicals' trust, suggested that some 70% of the workers were either Bolsheviks or sympathized with the revolution.[8] Other informants claimed that 40% of the union members were pronounced Bolsheviks and that they were, in fact, in control of the unions, and that 50% of the truckers in the International Longshoremen's Association were avowed Bolsheviks.[9] One APL informant summed up the alarming number of revolutionaries: "It is safe to say that there is 20,000 avowed Bolshevists in Seattle and suburbs today. 20,000 today but heaven only knows how many in six months from now, for they are growing by leaps and bounds."[10]

The informants reflected the view that unrest and radicalism were caused by the cunning agitators who were leading the contented workers astray with their misleading and inflammatory literature; according to one excited informant, "The yards are honeycombed with agitators who tell the men they are earning forty to fifty dollars per day net, that they will get $50 if they will join the Bolshevists, to prove their arguments dozens of inflammable sheets are being sold and thousands of Bolsheviki booklets, the ignorant worker is so filled with this inflammable stuff that he falls an easy victim to the Bolshevists

---

[7]Preston, 155-156. On the Minute Men, which had some 12,000 members in Seattle and which conducted some 1,000 arrests of suspected disloyal elements in 1918, see Jensen, *Price of Vigilance*, 125-129. The close cooperation between the Minute Men and the Justice Department is indicated by the letterhead of the organization, which contained the statement that it was "Organized with the Approval and Co-operating with the Federal Officials." The organization also stated that it had been the objective of the Minute Men during the general strike "to discredit the principal actors of the Bolsheviki element, who were endeavoring to capture organized labor" and that they had furnished information to that effect to the federal authorities (letter, S. J. Lombard to Hon. Miles Poindexter, February 17, 1919, box 385, Miles Poindexter Papers, University of Washington Libraries). The dependency of the Seattle field office on information from the patriotic organization is indicated by a report from November 1919 which mentioned that the office had received "considerable information" on the radical movement from the Minute Men, but that it was not so well informed now since the organization had ceased to operate in October 1919 (F. D. Simmons, Radical Activities in the Seattle District, November 2, 1919, OG 91928, RG65, NA).
[8]Reports, Walter R. Thayer, November 26 and December 10, 1918, ibid.
[9]Reports, Walter R. Thayer, January 13, 1919; Chas. H. Heighton, January 14, 1919, ibid.
[10]Report, Walter R. Thayer, December 12, 1918, ibid.

because there is no counter education, no restraint on the agitator, no restraint on the tons of damnable literature they are selling openly on the streets of Seattle."[11] As a result of this subversive activity, according to the informants, a number of former conservative labor leaders had joined the ranks of the radicals.[12]

The informants' uncritical acceptance of the radicals' optimistic predictions and exaggerated rhetoric imparted a hysterical tone to their reports. In late November 1918, Operative #109 of the Pinkerton Detective Agency, who had infiltrated the Ames Shipyard, reported that all metal trade unions intended to join together in one big industrial union with the aim of calling a national shipyards strike.[13] In the beginning of December, an APL informant reported that IWW leaders were threatening to take over the industry during the next big strike. He predicted that unless the government intervened by banning the circulation of radical literature and deporting alien agitators, the Bolsheviks would shortly control the entire Northeast "root and branch."[14] One APL informant, who had infiltrated the Seattle Central Labor Council, was of the opinion that the radical leaders were planning to use a strike to trigger off a revolution.[15] Yet another APL informant predicted that a shipyard strike would lead to the imposition of martial law "and martial law would be the beginning of the end of permanent peace in this country for there are thousands of Bolsheviki sympathizers in the United States," and he conjured up a nightmare vision where "the Bolshevist spirit will control industry in the United States in a few years as certain as sunrise."[16]

As it became clear that a shipyard strike in Seattle was unavoidable, the reports from the informant network to the Bureau became even more hysterical and apocalyptic in their prophecies. The strike was now beyond a shadow of a doubt a dress rehearsal for the coming revolution. Pinkerton Operative #109 warned that a strike now would pose a direct threat to the government.[17] An APL informant, who had infiltrated the IWW, reported that leading socialists, Bolsheviks and IWWs had agreed upon launching a gigantic propaganda campaign throughout all the large industrial centers of the Northeast with the purpose of recruiting millions of unskilled workers and taking over the

---

[11]Report, Walter R. Thayer, December 12, 1918, ibid.
[12]Reports, Walter R. Thayer, December 6, 1918, and January 21, 1919, ibid.
[13]Report, Chas. H. Heighton, November 29, 1918, ibid.
[14]Report, Walter R. Thayer, December 6, 1918, ibid.
[15]Report, Walter R. Thayer, December 10, 1918, ibid.
[16]Report, Walter R. Thayer, December 12, 1918, ibid.
[17]Report, Chas. H. Heighton, December 17, 1918, ibid.

control of the AFL with the ultimate aim of overthrowing the present system: "There is no question but that labor all over the country is being hypnotized by Bolshevik propaganda, and if that propaganda is allowed to spread, unmolested, and the Bolshevists are allowed to carry out their Eastern campaign I solemnly assure you that within the next two years the United States will be under Soviet rule," he claimed.[18] A no less scary report was received from Minute Men Informant No. 9, who on January 21, the day the shipyard strike began, predicted that the radicals planned to take control of the industry and then launch the world revolution: "They are to establish councils of this order all over the North American continent and in time throughout the whole world, accomplishing this by a series of general strikes including labor of every description. They hope that the government will see the necessity of allowing this to be done without police interference but if not then force is to be used."[19]

In addition to the informants of the patriotic societies and the detective agencies, the Bureau also received information from the conservative unions, which were interested in purging the labor movement of undesirable radicals. On January 23, representatives of Local No. 40 of the Engineers' Union met with W. A. Blackwood of the Minute Men and it was agreed that the Minute Men should keep the union informed of radical activities during the strike. In a report to the union, the patriotic society at length reviewed the information in its files which allegedly proved that the strike was Bolshevistic-IWW controlled and it was suggested that the union should get rid of all radical agitators.[20] Consequently, Paul Scharenberg, secretary of the California State Federation of Labor, submitted the names of a number of particular radical IWWs active in Seattle to the Bureau and even proposed to turn over their entire personal records to the federal agents and thereby "giving men of this character their just deserts."[21]

It is significant that despite receiving this mass of alarming information, the Seattle field office did not seem convinced that the strike was the first step in a Bolshevik revolution in the US. On January 21, 1919, 25,000 to 30,000 shipyard workers went on strike in protest against the national basis wage set by the Macy Shipyard Adjustment

[18]Report, Walter R. Thayer, January 10, 1919; also, report., January 13, 1919, ibid.
[19]Report, Walter R. Thayer, February 7, 1919, ibid.
[20]Report, Walter R. Thayer, February 5, 1919, ibid. According to the Minute Men, "we have been supported by certain of the International Officers of Labor, who have conferred with us and we have furnished them, and will furnish the Government" with information on the radical strike leaders (letter, S. J. Lombard to Hon. Miles Poindexter, February 17, 1919, box 385, Poindexter Papers, UWL).
[21]Report, G. W. Crossen, February 10, 1919, OG 91928, RG65, NA.

Board. The situation was investigated by Special Agent Petrovitsky, who in several reports expressed the view that the fear of a revolutionary uprising was much exaggerated. Just before the outbreak of the strike, Petrovitsky noted that "The situation needs and deserves careful study but this agent's observations are that the disloyalty toward the Government may be exaggerated."[22] According to Petrovitsky, the anti-radical atmosphere was primarily caused by Seattle Chief of Police Joel Warren's repeated and unfounded warnings against a threatening Red reign of terror and rumors that radicals were buying and stockpiling weapons. Clashes between demonstrators and the police were provoked by the authorities, "no doubt for political capital of the mayor and Chief of Police."[23] Shortly before the outbreak of the general strike, Petrovitsky remarked with reference to Mayor Ole Hanson and Warren's stated determination to suppress any attempt at rebellion, that "It would disappoint many if the strike did not come to pass."[24]

Petrovitsky, then, did not really believe that Seattle was on the brink of revolution but was of the opinion that the anti-radical campaign was promoted for political reasons; why, then, did the special agent and the Bureau not inform the public of the true state of affairs but instead, subsequently, take action to repress the radicals? The answer seems to lie in the values and ideology which dominated the thinking of Bureau officials and agents alike and which tended to color their assessments in the direction of personalizing outbreaks of social unrest. According to Petrovitsky, the shipyard workers were lazy and spoiled, the "majority loaf about their work" and they had been attracted to the work because of the possibility of drawing "high wages and hide from real work."[25] The reason for the unrest, then, was not low wages or unsatisfactory working conditions, but outside agitators in the form of IWW activists from Montana. They constituted "a rough element

[22]Report, Petrovitsky, January 16, 1919, ibid. For the outbreak of the strike see, report, Petrovitsky, January 25, 1919, ibid.; Leiren, 85. One exception to this calm attitude by the BI took place when the Bureau got hold of a letter from a radical union leader, in which he referred to the radicals' intentions of breaking with the AFL; consequently, SAC Simmons informed Washington that "If this break becomes effective, there is no doubt but that the labor organizations in the West would be influenced largely, and almost controlled, by a very radical element" (Letter, F. D. Simmons to W. E. Allen, January 4, 1919; also, report, Walter R. Thayer, December 28, 1918, OG 91928, RG65, NA).
[23]Reports, Petrovitsky, January 16 and February 3, 1919, ibid.
[24]Report, Petrovitsky, February 3, 1919, ibid. A further indication that the BI did not perceive the strike to be revolutionary was the BI's attitude toward arrested IWWs. When the police took into custody 11 IWWs for distributing a IWW paper, the BI agent, who had been alerted, found the paper "is probably not seditious" and proceeded to free all of the IWWs, with the exception of two aliens who were handed over to the immigration authorities for possible deportation (report, Chas. H. Heighton, December 21, 1918, ibid.).
[25]Reports, Petrovitsky, January 28 and 31, 1919, ibid.

attracted to the coast on account of the high wages paid,"[26] and the agent found them to be "men without families who have no interest in society and property except to stir up trouble" and who had purely subversive aims for instigating the strike: "They are a class that is challenging the supremacy of the Government – they are striking against the Government – rather than against the bosses." And to underline the basic illegitimacy of the strike, Petrovitsky claimed that the agitators had one further purpose, to lay their hands on the union funds.[27] The shipyard workers who, according to Petrovitsky, had no reason to complain, lazy and high-paid as they were, were being led astray by subversive outside agitators, who were using the strike for their own political and pecuniary purposes. Moreover, the Bureau's chief investigator of the strike fully shared and supported the open shop campaign of the business community and conservative forces. According to Petrovitsky, the closed shop was "vicious" and a tool of the radicals to control the labor movement, and he optimistically predicted that the strike "will result in much good in that it will result in open shop in Seattle."[28] He noted approvingly that if broken effectively, the strike would mean the "weeding out undesirable workers and open shop in many instances."[29]

The Seattle field office, then, did not see the strike as a revolutionary attempt to overthrow the government but it did put the blame for the widespread dissatisfaction on radical agitators. This view also prevailed when 70,000 members of the 110 unions represented in the Seattle Central Labor Council on February 6 went on strike in sympathy with the striking shipyard workers, thereby touching off the first general strike in American history.[30] While Mayor Hanson justified the deployment of federal troops with the imminent revolutionary danger and US Attorney Robert Saunders informed Washington that "Intention of strike is revolution led by extreme element openly advocating overthrow of Government,"[31] Special Agent in Charge Simmons was confident that although the "radical element"

---

[26]Report, Petrovitsky, January 16, 1919; also, ibid., January 28, 1919, ibid.
[27]Report, Petrovitsky, January 30, 1919, ibid. It is interesting that before the strike Petrovitsky acknowledged that there were social causes for the unrest: "There is a congestion here. Prices are high. Houses to live in hard to find and rents high" (Report, Petrovitsky, January 16, 1919, ibid.). Once the strike broke out, these social causes disappeared completely from his reports (for example, report, Petrovitsky, January 25, 1919, ibid.).
[28]Reports, Petrovitsky, February 1 and January 28, 1919, ibid.
[29]Report, Petrovitsky, February 8, 1919, ibid. For a similar view of the causes of the strike by a conservative Seattle attorney, see letter, Dudley G. Wooten to Hon. Miles Poindexter, January 25, 1919, box 426, Miles Poindexter Papers, UWL.
[30]Telegram, Simmons to Allen, February 7, 1919, OG 91928, RG65, NA; Leiren, 75, 85-86.
[31]Preston, 198; Murray, 62-64.

was "aiming toward rebellion ... when majority of laboring men learn that radical element are aiming at rebellion sentiment will change."[32]

It was in consequence of this view that the Bureau made preparations for the identification and neutralization of the radical agitators so that normal conditions could be restored and the open shop established. During the strike, the Bureau compiled lists of the names of active union members and agitators and opened files on all leading radicals.[33] One such file was opened on James Duncan, secretary of the Seattle Central Labor Council and a leading spokesman for the general strike. The file consisted mainly of reports from APL informants on Duncan's union activities, which contained long quotes from meetings and speeches and characterized him as "the Bolshevist leader of Seattle." They also noted that "Duncan has caused more trouble to the employers of Seattle than any other union leader, and since he has become an open advocate of Bolshevism he will unquestionably prove equally dangerous in the future."[34] Once the file had been opened, the Bureau continued to monitor Duncan's union activities after the strike and to add reports to the file. In 1920, the Bureau prepared a memorandum on him, indicating his dangerousness in the eyes of Washington, in which he was called "the greatest agitator on the Pacific coast."[35]

Special Agent Petrovitsky had for some time contemplated taking alien agitators into custody and keeping them interned until they could be deported by the Immigration Bureau, thereby disrupting the strike.[36] When it became clear that the general strike would be broken by the local authorities, he argued that such an action "would be unwise on the part of the Department of Justice at such a time as the present," thereby implying that it could be done after the strike had ended.[37] At a long conference of federal officials in Seattle on February 9, two days before the strike was finally called off, attended by Special Assistant to the Attorney General Reames, Commissioner General of Immigration Henry M. White, Thomas Foster of the Secret Service and Special Agent in Charge Simmons, the consensus of opinion was that "owing to rapid change of events," that is, the imminent failure of the strike, it was inadvisable to arrest the leading agitators "as this

---

[32]Telegram, Simmons to Allen, February 7, 1919, OG 91928, RG65, NA.

[33]Reports, Petrovitsky, February 4 and 13, 1919, ibid.

[34]Report, Petrovitsky, February 19, 1919; also, report, Walter R. Thayer, December 6, 1918, OG 339091, ibid.

[35]George F. Ruch, memorandum, In Re: James Duncan, June 17, 1920, ibid. For surveillance reports in the file, see, reports, Petrovitsky, June 26, 1919; #836, July 11, 1919; F. D. Simmons, July 23, 1919, ibid. For Duncan in general, see Murray, 59-60; Weinstein, *Decline of Socialism in America,* 227.

[36]Reports, Petrovitsky, January 16 and 30, 1919, OG 91928, RG65, NA.

[37]Report, Petrovitsky, February 7, 1919, ibid.

might cause unions to take firmer stand." The federal officials predicted that as a result of the failure, the AFL and conservative union men would purge the unions of the radical agitators: "There will be no union opposition then in case of arrests."[38] In other words, the apparent restraint of the Bureau in suppressing the strike was purely tactical. The Bureau had first contemplated arresting the strike leaders during the strike, but when it became clear that it would be broken and end in failure anyway, it was thought that dramatic federal arrests would only provoke the strikers. Therefore, the federal authorities decided to wait until things had calmed down and, in the meantime, compiled lists of suspected subversive elements.

At 12 o'clock on February 11, 1919, the strike was called off, having succumbed to a combination of local unpopularity, the opposition of the local authorities, and internal disagreement between the conservative and radical factions of the labor movement. This demonstrated the weakness of the radicals and the gulf between their optimistic rhetoric and the real world; according to one federal agent, "The strike as far as union labor is concerned is lost and amounted to nothing, simply inconveniencing people for two or three days."[39] Immediately, the Bureau swung into action. On the same day that the strike was terminated, Special Agents Robert P. Collins and Walter H. Thayer, assisted by police officer A. H. Petri, raided the IWW Propaganda Committee and confiscated two large boxes of IWW literature together with the organization's letters, minute books and other records and brought the acting secretary, James J. Exstel, in for questioning.[40] On the following day, the two federal agents accompanied by members of the Sheriff's office raided the IWW Defense Committee on Pacific Block and took into custody 26 IWW members. Aliens were turned over to the immigration authorities with a view toward initiating deportation proceedings while American citizens were turned over to the local authorities for prosecution under the Washington criminal anarchy law.[41] Thus, the Bureau broke up the activities of the IWW and sent a warning to radicals and union leaders alike.

---

[38]Telegram, Simmons to Allen, February 9, 1919, ibid.

[39]Report, D. W. Edwards, February 11, 1919, ibid.; for the end of the strike, see Murray, 61-64; Leiren, 87; Preston, 199.

[40]Reports, Robert P. Collins February 12, 1919; Walter H. Thayer, February 12, 1919, OG 91928, RG65, NA.

[41]Report, Walter H. Thayer, February 14, 1919, ibid. For the subsequent state prosecution against 30 leading IWWs or radicals, see report, S. O. Samson, March 20, 1919, ibid. The Bureau's repressive activity was well-known to its conservative allies; thus, the Minute Men in Seattle looked "for numerous other arrests of more prominent individuals in the near future, and various actions on the part of the Federal Government, having in view the cancelation of naturalization papers, and deportation of those troublesome leaders" (Letter, S. J. Lombard to Hon. Miles Poindexter, February 17, 1919, box 385, Poindexter Papers, UWL).

Other federal officials were genuinely concerned about the general strike. The State Department called Seattle for "one of the hotbeds of Russian anarchists,"[42] and the Secret Service seriously believed that the strike "was intended to be the starter of a revolution to overthrow the Government of the United States" and that the IWW was now laying concrete plans for the revolution to take place on May 1: "It being the idea to establish a Soviet Government with Philadelphia for the headquarters for the Eastern states; Chicago for the Middle states and Seattle the Western states."[43] Special Assistant to the Attorney General in Seattle Reames was also of the opinion that radical leaders had plotted to use the general strike to win over the soldiers, overthrow the government and establish a Soviet rule, and he requested the Justice Department in early March to dispatch a force of twenty agents to conduct an exhaustive investigation into the attempted rebellion. Before initiating the inquiry, Acting Bureau Chief William E. Allen directed two seasoned agents, R. O. Samson of Denver and F. W. Byrn, Jr., of Butte, Montana, to proceed to Seattle and evaluate the situation.[44] After having conferred with Reames and Simmons, read the Seattle office files and surveyed the situation, Samson and Byrn concluded that the strike had been a "purely local labor trouble." It had been caused by "radical and IWW element" who had taken advantage of the widespread dissatisfaction with the wages to distribute radical propaganda and to attempt to take control of the unions. The agents found no evidence to support the theory of a revolutionary plot: "That there seems no reason believe Seattle strike different character from any other insofar as affecting Government," they wired Washington. They advised against launching a widely publicized federal inquiry as it would only be perceived as an attack on organized labor in general and might revitalize the radicals.[45] As a result, the Bureau and the Justice Department took no further steps in the matter.[46]

---

[42]Letter, L. Winslow to W. E. Allen, April 4, 1919, OG 91928, RG65, NA..

[43]Report to US Secret Service Chief W. H. Moran, April 9, 1919, ibid. Before the general strike, Thomas Foster of the local Secret Service office informed Senator Miles Poindexter of Washington in a "Personal and Confidential" letter that the situation appeared "pretty serious" since the returning soldiers and sailors were joining the IWW and that "I fear greatly that conditions here are tending toward a revolutionary aspect" (Letter, Thomas Foster to Hon. Miles Poindexter, January 24, 1919, box 427, Poindexter Papers, UWL).

[44]For Reams' views, see report, R. O. Samson, March 20, 1919, OG 91928, RG65, NA; see also, reports, S. O. Samson, March 8, 1919; F. W. Byrn, Jr., March 8, 1919, ibid.

[45]Report, R. O. Samson, March 20, 1919, ibid.

[46]W. E. Allen, Memorandum for Mr. O'Brian, March 17, 1919, ibid.

Publicizing the Revolutionary Danger: The Overman Committee

In September 1918 the Senate Committee on the Judiciary had appointed a subcommittee headed by Senator Lee Slater Overman, Democrat of North Carolina, to investigate charges made by, among others, A. Mitchell Palmer, then alien property custodian and Attorney General from March 1919, against the United States Brewers' Association and the liquor industry for harboring pro-German sentiments and for attempting to influence politicians and the public opinion by bribes and by controlling the press. The Overman Committee interpreted its mandate broadly and launched a wide probe into both the activities of the brewing and liquor interests and "pro-German propaganda and activities" in general, thereby initiating, for the first time in US history, a congressional investigation of political activities and opinions.[47]

It has generally been assumed that when the Senate in February 1919 extended and broadened the committee's mandate to include the investigation into Bolshevik propaganda in the US, the senators responded to and reflected the growing anti-radical opinion in America, heightened by the imminent Seattle general strike.[48] There are, however, several indications that agencies and individuals connected with the federal government played an important role in channeling the anti-German hatred, whipped up by the government during the war to gain popular support for the intervention in Europe, into an anti-Bolshevik hysteria. Thereby, the committee was provided with its new raison d'être and the government with a means through which it could publicize the radical threat. In other words, instead of explaining the Overman Committee as a product of the public opinion, there are reasons for viewing it as an instrument by which the opinion was influenced and shaped.

One argument in favor of this interpretation is the fact that federal officials during late 1918 and early 1919 deliberately tried to foster an anti-Bolshevik opinion by carefully disseminating authoritative information on the Red menace. The first step was the publication of

---

[47]US Congress, Senate, Subcommittee on the Judiciary, *Brewing and Liquor Interests and German and Bolshevik Propaganda. Report and Hearings Submitted Pursuant to S. Res. 307 and 439*, 66th. Cong., 1st. Sess, Senate Document No. 62 (Washington, DC, 1919), Vol. I, III-V. The Overman Committee is only briefly mentioned in the literature and there is no comprehensive study, based on the primary sources, on this early forerunner of the HUAC (see, for example, Goodman, 5; O'Reilly, *Hoover and the Un-Americans*, 14; Murray, 94-98; the most thorough account by Lowenthal, 36-66, is based on the committee's public hearings).
[48]For the view that the Overman Committee was "a direct result of the patriotic and antiunion sentiment" in 1919 and that its "subsequent findings reflected that sentiment" because its members "succumbed to the emotionalism of the time," see Murray, 94; for the view that this and other investigations "contributed to the sense of crisis to which Hoover and Palmer responded in 1919," see Powers, *Secrecy and Power*, 62.

The German-Bolshevik Conspiracy in October 1918 by the federal wartime propaganda agency, George Creel's Committee on Public Information. The publication consisted of a number of purportedly genuine official Russian documents, smuggled out by the CPI's representative in Russia, Edgar Sisson, which allegedly proved that Lenin and Trotsky were German agents and that the Bolshevik revolution was a German conspiracy to dominate Russia. According to the publication, the documents showed "that the Bolshevik revolution was arranged for by the German Great General Staff, and financed by the German Imperial Bank and other German financial institutions... They show, in short that the present Bolshevik government is not a Russian government at all, but a German government acting solely in the interests of Germany and betraying the Russian people...."[49] Even on the surface this theory was highly implausible and a number of American and British officials seriously doubted the authenticity of the documents. Later studies by George Kennan have confirmed that the Sisson documents were in fact forgeries and that the CPI had put considerable pressure on some consulting experts to confirm the authenticity of the documents, according to one of the experts, in order to "help to promote that emotional upsurge necessary for the mobilization of all our resources to be thrown into the struggle."[50] By publicizing the Sisson documents, the CPI put an official stamp of approval on the documents and launched the thesis that the Bolshevik revolution was financed and controlled by Germany, thereby enabling the wartime passions against the Germans to be transferred into an anti-Bolshevik opinion following the Armistice.

During January 1919, federal officals began publicizing the danger of Bolshevik propaganda in the US. On January 6, the New York office of the Justice Department announced that secret agents had recently arrived from Russia carrying $500,000 to finance Bolshevik propaganda activities. However, the federal officials reassured the public that the government was adequately prepared: The Justice Department was watching Bolshevik meetings "with interest", the postal authorities were scanning a number of left-wing publications, and the Secret Service had "the Reds in this country card indexed and that activities

---

[49]US Committee on Public Information, *The German-Bolshevik Conspiracy* (Washington, DC, October 1918), 3, copy in BS 202600-1998-2, RG65, NA. See also, US Department of State, Confidential. Memorandum on Relations Between the Bolsheviks and the Imperial German Government in the Spring of 1918, n.d., BS 202600-1998-3, ibid. See further, Stephen L. Vaughn, *Holding Fast the Inner Lines. Democracy, Nationalism, and the Committee on Public Information* (Chapel Hill, N.C., 1980), 77.
[50]George F. Kennan, "The Sissons Documents," *The Journal of Modern History,* Vol. XXVIII, No. 2 (June 1956), 132; in general, see 130-154; George F. Kennan, *Soviet-American Relations, 1917-1920* , Vol. I (London, 1956), 412-420, 441-457.

in the interest of Bolshevism could be summarily ended by deportation, because most of its supporters are aliens."[51] On January 19, The *New York Times* quoted an unnamed "Government official," only identified as one "whose duties have to do with the German, Bolshevist, I.W.W., and certain phases of Socialistic propaganda in the United States," who noted that radical agitation had been on the rise since the Armistice and that for the first time since the US entered the war, "these papers are openly advocating class war in the United States and the setting up of a form of Bolshevist Government." The paper had apparently been given access to official reports on the radical press and to translations of the foreign-language papers, as these were quoted at length. According to the article, "a great mass of documents dealing with this propaganda" had been turned over by the government to the Overman Committee with the intention of initiating a congressional investigation.[52] Clearly, federal officials were both trying to influence the public opinion and Congress and convince them of the Bolshevik danger in the US.

Another driving force behind the creation of the anti-Bolshevik scare in early 1919 was the mysterious figure of Archibald E. Stevenson, a zealous anti-Communist and New York lawyer with extensive intelligence connections. During the war Stevenson had chaired the Committee on Aliens, a branch of the New York Mayor's Committee on National Defense.[53] During the Overman Committee hearings Stevenson was introduced as a member of the Military Intelligence Division. This was promptly denied by Secretary of War Newton D. Baker, but according to the New York branch of the MID, Stevenson had indeed been associated with its "propaganda section" although his exact position remained obscure.[54] It has also been claimed that Stevenson worked for the Bureau of Investigation but it has proved

[51]"Bolshevist Fund Here," *The New York Times*, January 7, 1919. The Comintern archive has since confirmed that Comintern agents during 1919 and 1920 smuggled 2,728,000 rubles into the U.S. (Harvey Klehr, John Earl Haynes & Fridrikh Igorevich Firsov, *The Secret World of American Communism* (New Haven & London, 1995), 21-25). It is unclear on what evidence, if any, the Justice Department based its claims.

[52]"Senate Inquiry Directed at Reds," *The New York Times*, January 19, 1919. The unnamed federal official was most likely either Solicitor General William H. Lamar of the Post Office Department, who later gave evidence to the Overman Committee on the radical press, or Robert A. Bowen, director of the Justice Department's Bureau of Translations and Radical Publications (for Lamar's evidence, see *Brewing and Liquor Interests and German and Bolshevik Propaganda*, Vol. III, 1110-1124; for Bowen, see, Robert A. Bowen, "Bureau of Translations and Radical Publications," n.d. (1961); Bowen, memorandum, n.d. (1919?), box 10, Robert A. Bowen Papers, Clemson University).

[53]Jaffe, 119.

[54]For Stevenson at the Overman Committee hearings, see "IWW Gaining Here, Senators Are Told," *The New York Times*, January 23, 1919; "Lists Americans as Pacifists," *The New York Times*, January 25, 1919; Donner, *The Age of Surveillance*, 291n; for Newton's denial and the MID's confirmation, see Link (ed.), *The Papers of Woodrow Wilson*, Vol. 54, 398-399n1.

impossible to verify this allegation since several Bureau files on Stevenson are missing from the National Archives.[55] What is known for certain is that Stevenson went on to become chief counsel to the Lusk Committee, in which position he cooperated with the Bureau. Later in 1921, he became a free-lance Red hunter, all the time keeping the Bureau informed about his activities and discoveries.[56]

In early January, Stevenson was appointed by the Union League Club, one of the most exclusive and influental clubs in New York City whose rich members had worked for the Justice Department during the war as so-called one-dollar-a-year men fighting disloyalty, to head a committee to study Bolshevism and propose remedies for combating it.[57] As a result of this probe, Stevenson, on January 22 and 23, testified before the Overman Committee and deftly elaborated on the theme that the Bolsheviks were in the employ of the Germans. He thereby, simultaneously, mobilized the existing anti-German feelings against the radicals and gave the committee, which had been established to inquire into pro-German propaganda, a reason for going after the Bolsheviks. He argued that all pacifists, who had continued their agitation after the US had entered the war in April 1917, had aided and abetted Germany and could therefore properly be characterized as disloyal or pro-German. Stevenson submitted a list of alleged disloyal persons, containing the names of 62 prominent persons, supposedly taken from the government's files.[58]

He linked up these disloyal and pro-German pacifists with the post-war radical movement by claiming that many of the individuals and organizations, who had opposed US participation in the war, were now to be found in the radical movement. Stevenson argued that since revolutionary socialism had its origins in Germany and in Marx' works, it then logically followed that the "Bolsheviki movement is a branch of the revolutionary socialism of Germany."[59] He added that Bolshevism constitued "the gravest menace to the country to-day," since all kinds of radicals, Bolsheviks, socialists, IWWs, anarchists and "parlor Bolsheviks" were uniting under its red flag and their propa-

---

[55]The claims are made in Lowenthal, 49; Jaffe, 119. The missing files are BS 212293-3 and BS 61-441, RG65, NA.

[56]Letter, T. M. Reddy to William J. Flynn, February 1, 1921, BS 202653-2, ibid.

[57]"Union League to Study Bolshevist Movement," *The New York Times*, January 10, 1919; for the Union League Club during WWI, see "'They Never Stopped Watching Us.' A Conversation Between Roger Baldwin and Alan F. Westin," *The Civil Liberties Review*, November/December 1977, 19-20.

[58]*Brewing and Liquor Interests and German and Bolshevik Propaganda*, Vol. II, 2704-2715; the list can be found on pp. 2782-2785; the list was reprinted in, "Lists Americans as Pacifists," *The New York Times*, January 25, 1919, I:4.

[59]*Brewing and Liquor Interests and German and Bolshevik Propaganda*, Vol. III, 14, 16.

ganda campaign was amply financed by the Russian coffers.[60] Stevenson demanded that Bolshevism should be rooted out at once by the deportation of all alien agitators, the exclusion of seditious literature from the US, the enactment of a peacetime sedition law to punish radical citizens, the introduction of a comprehensive campaign of counter-propaganda beginning in the schools and US intervention in Russia to topple Lenin's government.[61]

It can be argued, then, that the Overman Committee's investigation of Bolshevik propaganda was influenced to a greater degree by government announcements and Stevenson's "revelations" than by a frightened public opinion. On February 4, shortly after Stevenson had finished his testimony, the Senate adopted resolution No. 436, introduced by Senator Thomas J. Walsh, which authorized the committee to inquire into "any efforts being made to propagate in this country the principles of any party exercising or claiming to exercise authority in Russia" and "any effort to incite the overthrow of the Government of this country or all government by force, or by the destruction of life or property, or the general cessation of industry."[62] The immediate justification for initiating the investigation was given by Senator William E. Borah during the debate on the resolution, when he referred to a public meeting held two days before at the Poli Theatre in Washington, DC, in support of the Bolshevik government.[63]

No attempt has previously been made to establish the relationship between the first congressional investigation of political activities and opinions and the Bureau of Investigation; one historian has even claimed that the Overman Committee received no assistance from the Justice Department.[64] However, the Bureau files reveal that the committee and the Bureau cooperated closely during the inquiry and that it might be argued that the federal agents used this friendly forum to influence the public opinion and publicize the radical danger. The fact that the Bureau was willing to assist Senator Overman is not surprising; the senator was indexed in the Bureau files as "Overman, Lee S. – Senator – Informant" and he submitted information on a number of political and potential disloyal activities during the war and

---

[60]Ibid., 19-29, 34-36.
[61]Ibid., 36.
[62]Ibid., Vol. I, XXIX.
[63]"Senate Orders Reds Here Investigated," *The New York Times*, February 5, 1919; Murray, 94-95.
[64]Jensen, *The Price of Vigilance*, 266-267.

the Red Scare.[65] Even before the establishment of the committee in 1918, Overman turned over a clearly antisemitic letter to the Bureau alleging that Jewish organizations in the US were controlled by the Germans and rumors concerning disloyal activities by "The Textile/Machine Works."[66] During the Red Scare, Overman notified the Bureau about unsubstantiated rumors to the effect that German and Austrian owned ammunitions factories in the US were supplying the radicals with weapons and about the identity of the perpetrators behind the anarchist bombs on June 2, 1919.[67] The senator turned over to the Bureau an anonymous letter which accused Assistant Secretary of Labor Louis F. Post of being a "philosophical socialistic anarchist" and for sabotaging the swift deportation of alien anarchists. Overman noted that "As a rule I consign all anonymous letters to the waste paper basket, but as this letter mentions the names of one or more high officials in the Government service who are avowed sympathizers with the Bolsheviki movement, I am sending it to you for such consideration as you think it deserves." Acting Bureau Chief William E. Allen assured Overman that the rumor about Post's political views was "receiving careful consideration."[68] Another member of the committee, Senator Knute Nelson, also informed the Bureau about political activities. When Annie Riley Hale of the pacifist organization Women's League for Peace and Freedom asked Nelson about his positions on the League of Nations and the blocade against Soviet Russia, Nelson immediately notified the Justice Department that she might be a Bolshevik agent and asked that she be investigated.[69] Apparently, the Justice Department had also used

---

[65]Lee S. Overman entry in the BI general index, BI files 1908-22, RG65, NA. The Overman Papers in the University of North Carolina at Chapel Hill apparently contain no information on his relationship with the Bureau (information provided by Lynn Roundtree).

[66]Letters, George F. G. Morgan to Overman, n.d.; Overman to A. Bruce Bielaski, April 9, 1918; Bielaski to Overman, April 11, 1918, OG 175392, RG65, NA.; J. C. Barton to Overman, July 19, 1918, OG 108999, ibid. The Bureau's answer to the last letter was, "I thank you for your information and will say to you confidentially that the parties mentioned are now being very carefully investigated by this Department" (Letter, Bielaski to Overman, July 25, 1918, ibid.). For further information from Overman to the BI, see, letters, Bielaski to Overman, June 5, 1918, OG 201641, ibid. Apparently, the Bureau refused to inform Overman whether some corporations were pro-German, see letters, Overman to Bielaski, December 8, 1917, with att. letter, J. W. Seaver to Overman, December 5, 1917; Bielaski to Overman, December 21, 1917, OG 115940, ibid.

[67]Letters, Overman to A. Mitchell Palmer, November 3, 1919, with att. letter; Frank Burke to Overman, November 6, 1919, OG 94701, ibid.; F. C. McDowell to Overman, June 5, 1919; Overman to Chief, BI, June 6, 1919; W. A. Allen to Overman, June 12, 1919, OG 363726, ibid.

[68]Letters, anonymous to Overman, June 5, 1919; Overman to Chief, Division of Investigation, June 6, 1919; W. H. Allen to Overman, June 11, 1919, OG 115940, ibid.

[69]Letters, Knute Nelson to A. Mitchell Palmer, June 20, 1919; Palmer to Nelson, June 25, 1919; Geo. W. Lillard to W. E. Allen, June 19, 1919; Allen to Wm. M. Offley, June 25, 1919, OG 82811, ibid.

Overman during the war to increase the public's fear of enemy subversion. In early 1917, the senator referred to "creditable reports from Secret Service men," supplied by the Justice Department, and warned of an army of 100,000 foreign spies in the US.[70]

The formal cooperation between the Bureau and the committee began during its investigation of German propaganda activities. Attorney General Thomas Gregory granted the committee access "to the files of this Department in all cases in which there is not some special reason why it should not be done" and designated Special Agent William R. Benham to assist the committee in its inquiry.[71] While on loan, Benham conducted a number of investigations of German and Bolshevik activities for the committee, monitored radical meetings, analyzed IWW, socialist, anarchist and Bolshevik literature, looked into the background of and examined witnesses, and collected government information and statistics on conditions in the US and Russia, all the while keeping the Bureau informed about his activities.[72] The extent of the cooperation is indicated by the fact that Benham spent several days following the inquiry engaged in separating the files of the Bureau and the committee.[73]

In return for this valuable assistance, the committee turned over to the Bureau information from outside sources regarding radical activities. Thus, the Bureau received various information on IWW and Bolshevik activities,[74] claims that Germany was behind Bolshevik activities,[75] that the movie industry was "in league and hearty sympathy and accord with the Bolshevik propaganda"[76] and that "the respect-

[70]McClymer, "The Federal Government and the Americanization Movement, 1915-24," 25-26n5. For Overman's views on the unrest and the threat of radicalism in 1919, see, Lee S. Overman, "Reactionary Policies of Our Social Revolution," *The Forum*, Vol. LXII, No. 1 (July 1919), 41-47.

[71]Letters, Major E. Lowry Humes to Thomas Gregory, November 4, 1918; Gregory to Overman, November 16, 1918, OG 341494, RG65, NA.

[72]For Benham's investigations for the committee, see reports, Wm. R. Benham, January 14, 21 and May 21, 1919; Memorandum for Major Humes, January 20, 1919; for the surveillance of meetings, see report, Benham, February 3, 1919; for the analyzis of literature, see reports, Benham, February 5 and 10, 1919; for the examination of witnesses and their testimonies, see reports, Benham, January 6, February 19, April 3 and 4, 1919; for the collection of various information, see reports, Benham, March 20, 21, 22, 24, 25, 26, April 14 and 16, 1919; for Benham's assistance to the committee, see in general, reports, Benham, January 14, 21, 27, 31, February 4, 11, 13, 14, 15, 19, 25, March 1, 3, 7 and 12, 1919, all in ibid. For an example of the Bureau investigating witnesses before the committee, see telegram, Offley to Allen, March 3, 1919, ibid.

[73]Reports, Wm. R. Benham, May 22 and 23, 1919; see also, reports, Benham, May 24, 26, 27, 28, 29 and 31, 1919, ibid.

[74]Letters, Wm. E. Farr, February 5, 1919; Florence Harper to Captain Lester, February 18, 1919; Miles Poindexter to Overman, February 28, 1919; Harry New to Overman, March 4, 1919, ibid.

[75]"The Evidence," n.d., ibid.

[76]Letter, George Demming to Overman, February 5, 1919, ibid.

able, parlor-socialist editors" of such liberal publications as the *New Republic*, the *Dial* and the *Nation* deserved a closer look.[77] Among the letters to the committee which ended up in the Bureau's growing political files was one from W. A. Blackwood of the Minute Men, who called the Seattle general strike "a revolution instigated and brought about by IWW's having joined hands with the bolsjeviki and all forms of radicals and having all become bed-fellows" and who expressed the hope that "they are candidates for the penitentiary on the grounds of treason."[78] Another came from a former Bureau agent who informed the senators that the radical movement on the West coast was "well-financed and surprisingly well organized" and suggested that the committee get in contact with the Bureau: "I want to state that I know the poisonness doctrine of political radicalism has a big hold out here. I am convinced our country is heading for much trouble and useless expense if immediate action to curb the extreme radicals is not definitely taken."[79]

More importantly, the committee hearings provided a platform for federal officials and anticommunists to educate the public on the Bolshevik terror in Russia and its dangers to America. The Bureau's former chief, A. Bruce Bielaski, added to the atmosphere of suspicion by telling the committee that although German-Americans had behaved remarkably loyal to the US during the war, the various anticonscription and antimilitary organizations had consisted of a "bunch of pacifists, conscientious objectors, and pro-German people" who had actively and subversively opposed the successful conduct of the war. He claimed that the Hearst press had followed a pro-German line by espousing anti-British and anti-Japanese views. To prove his point, Bielaski presented a list, which had been found on a German representative in the US, containing the names of a number of prominent American professors and editors, who by implication were thought to be sympathizers with the enemy.[80] To further mobilize the opinion, a memorandum prepared by James A. Horton of the Post Office Department was read into the record which claimed that an analysis of the radical press published since the Armistice showed that every radical group, IWWs, socialists, radical socialists and anarchists, for the first time were uniting under the banner of Bolshevism. Their

---

[77]Letter, William S. Davis to Knute Nelson, February 8, 1919, ibid.

[78]Letter, W. A. Blackwood to Miles Poindexter, February 8, 1919, att. to letter, Poindexter to Overman, February 27, 1919, ibid.

[79]Letter, Killick to Overman, February 5, 1919, ibid.

[80]*Brewing and Liquor Interests and German and Bolshevik Propaganda*, Vol. II, 1399-1401, 1586-1597, 2246-2257.

aim was "the overthrow of the Government of the United States by means of a bloody revolution and the establishment of a Bolshevist republic," and extracts from a large number of wild and optimistic radical publications, predicting the imminent world revolution, were made public.[81] According to alarming figures disclosed by the government at the hearings, the radicals in total had no less than 15,000 unions and "recruiting agencies" nationwide which were utilized to spread Bolshevik propaganda.[82]

It seems reasonable to assume that the Overman Committee's hearings into Bolshevik propaganda, held from February 11 to March 10, played a decisive role in constructing the image of a radical threat to America in 1919. The senators gave a sympathetic listening to and accepted at face value the often undocumented rumors and allegations made by a long line of witnesses, most of whom had visited Soviet Russia during or after the revolution in an official or private capacity and almost all of whom were openly hostile to the Bolsheviks. Several themes ran through the various testimonies. It was taken for granted on the basis of the Sisson documents, Lenin's journey through Germany in 1917, the Brest-Litovsk treaty, rumors of German economic influence in Russia, and the presence of German officers in the Red Army, that the Bolsheviks were controlled by the Germans. Another common theme was that Russian Bolshevism was heavily influenced by Jews, some of whom came from New York's Lower East Side. Moreover, much time was taken up by describing in lurid details the Red terror, the Tjekka's random arrests and executions, the forced labor and hunger, the confiscation of private property and the widespread looting, without mentioning the circumstances of the civil war or the White terror. Accounts of the alleged socialization of women, the practice of free love, the nationalization of children, and the luxurious living of the Bolshevik leaders went unopposed into the public record.

Having thus presented the inhuman and destructive character of Russian Bolshevism, the witnesses went on to argue that its sympathizers in the US were subversives since they were financed and backed by the Russians. Bolshevism was viewed as a potential threat because radicals of all stripes, IWWs, socialists, parlor-Bolsheviks and anarchists, were uniting under its banner; as summed up by one witness, "Bolshevism is a greater menace to the world, gentlemen, even than

---

[81]Ibid., Vol. III, 1110; in general see ibid., 1110-1125; see also, "Extremists Here Plan a Revolt to Seize Power," *The New York Times*, March 11, 1919.

[82]"IWW Propaganda Is Country-Wide," *The New York Times*, March 12, 1919.

was German militarism...."[83] Consequently, the witnesses proposed that the radical agitation in America be met with counterpropaganda, the outlawing of seditious literature, and that Bolshevism be contained by a policy of non-recognition and blocade of Russia. Some, like the former ambassador to Russia, David Francis, even advocated allied intervention to overthrow Lenin.[84] In contrast, witnesses who showed sympathy for the Bolsheviks or who opposed US intervention, such as John Reed, Louise Bryant and Albert Rhys Williams, were treated as hostile witnesses and submitted to aggressive and searching cross-examination about their political opinions and ideas.[85] Thus, instead of presenting a balanced and factual picture of the Bolshevik system in Russia and the weak position of the domestic radical movement, the committee, in effect, functioned as a summary court against left-wing activities and opinions.

The Bureau exercised considerable influence on the Overman Committee's publicizing of the Communist menace. It gathered much of the information for the committee, examinined the witnesses, and assisted with the preparation of the committee's final report. From the end of March to the middle of May, Special Agent Benham worked full-time together with the committee's chief investigator, Major E. Lowry Humes, on preparing the draft of the report, and it was Benham who on May 19 delivered the initial draft to Senator Overman.[86] Benham's central role in the preparation of the report is indicated by the fact that he took part in the committee's internal deliberations on its findings and subsequently participated in the final rewriting of the draft.[87]

The final report by the Overman Committee was based on the stated assumption that if properly informed about the aims and methods of the Bolsheviks no sound-minded person would champion such an ideology. Thus, the report went on to describe the Communist system in Russia as "a reign of terror unparalleled in the history of modern civilization," which was characterized by widespread misery and hunger, the confiscation and nationalization of all private property, and the taking of hostages. The report also described the systematic disfranchisement of whole classes of the population, the inauguration

---

[83]*Brewing and Liquor Interest and German and Bolshevik Propaganda,* Vol. III, 303; for the hearings in general, see ibid., passim.
[84]For Francis' testimony, see ibid., 935-985.
[85]See ibid., 465-561 (Louise Bryant); 561-601 (John Reed); 603-691 (Albert Rhys Williams); 693-723 (Bessie Beatty); 723-762 (Frank Keddie); 763-896, 1008-1024 (Raymond Robins).
[86]Reports, Wm. R. Benham, March 18, 29, 31, April 1, 5, 7, 8, 9, 11, 16, 22, 23, May 16 and 19, 1919, OG 341494, RG65, NA.
[87]Reports, Wm. R. Benham, May 20, June 6 and 12, 1919, ibid.

of "a program of terror, fear, extermination, and destruction," the suppression of the church and the press and the establishment of "a state of free love." The committee openly condemned the radical movement in America for promoting such a system by appealing to "the hatred and the lowest instincts of the more ignorant elements of the population, reinforced by the criminally inclined" and aiming at "the overthrow of existing governmental institutions and the complete demoralization of modern society." The report ended by conjuring up a nightmare vision of the United States following a Bolshevik take-over, in which criminals and aliens would terrorize the defenseless population, and the dictatorship would seize all farms, land, industrial plants, private dwellings, newspapers, and banks and repress all religious practice. Radical sympathizers were accused of being "champions of discontent and disorder, offering no practical and acceptable ideal...."[88] Finally, the committee recommended government control and regulation of the foreign-language press, a peacetime sedition law, the registration of all private organizations and a federal law against the use of bombs.[89] These proposals would all increase the authority and political role of the Bureau considerably.

Keeping the Files Up to Date

The Bureau files show that the Bureau continued, despite the end of hostilities and the expiration of the Espionage Act, to keep radical groups under close observation. One such group consisted of prominent sympathizers of the Bolshevik cause, such as John Reed and Max Eastman, whose speeches on conditions in Russia and criticism of the Allied intervention were closely monitored and filed for later use.[90] One experienced agent, Feri F. Weiss of the Boston office, was deeply concerned about the growing support for Bolshevism in the US since the Armistice and of the ability of such speakers as Reed to whip up a revolutionary enthusiasm among an audience. He suggested a policy of "crushing with an iron hand the Bolshevik agitators, who seem to be springing up like mushrooms all around us" and predicted that "it

[88]*Brewing and Liquor Interests and German and Bolshevik Propaganda*, Vol. III, XXIX-XLV.
[89]Ibid., XLV-L. For an apparent early draft of the recommendations, see note, n.d., in OG 341494, RG65, NA.
[90]For the surveillance of John Reed, see reports, Geo. S. Forbes, December 12, 1918; Feri F. Weiss, December 30, 1918; R. W. Finch, March 19, 1919; George W. Williams, March 25, 1919; Case of John Silas Reed, Compiled by Julian W. Bowes, Secret Service, 3 reports, n.d.; Julian W. Bowes, Daily Reports on John Reed, May 14, 15, 16, 23, 31, 1919, OG 182787, ibid.; for the surveillance of Max Eastman, see letter, SAC to E. S. Wertz, December 12, 1918; Alfred Bettman, Memorandum to Mr. Allen, January 3, 1919; reports, T. E. Campbell, February 11, 1919; A. F. Kearney, February 13, 1919; W. A. Weymouth, March 4, 1919; A. H. Loula, March 20, 1919; Wm. M. Doyas, March 25, 1919, OG 9814, ibid.

is only common sense to suspect that they will try a coup-d'etat as soon as they feel sure of their ground...."[91] Another group consisted of left wing socialist papers, like the *Revolutionary Age* and the *Liberator,* both of which were collected and carefully analyzed by Bureau agents.[92] Revealingly, while the Bureau had no legal justification for investigating and no possibility of prosecuting, the Bureau justified its surveillance with the view that the "contemplated legislation by Congress will amply cover this situation."[93] A third group, which was monitored by the Bureau during the early part of 1919, was the movement in support of general amnesty of those who had been convicted for opposing the war. Organizations such as the American Freedom Congress, the National League for Release of Political Prisoners, the League for the Amnesty of Political Prisoners, the American Freedom Convention, the Workers Amnesty League and the Political Amnesty League were all investigated, meetings covered, letters opened, members interviewed and activities followed.[94] Apparently, the Bureau feared that this movement might be used to unite all the different radical groups into a truly revolutionary organization.[95] Again the federal agents justified the surveillance with a possible, later use: On January 31, Acting Bureau Chief William E. Allen directed the New York office the "keep up pretty closely" with the League for the Amnesty of Political Prisoners, noting that "This is a subject which may be of particular interest to the Department later."[96] One month later he observed that the organization was being watched: "There seems to be nothing else that we can do."[97] Clearly, the Bureau was worried about the apparent increasing popularity of Bolshevism and therefore continued to monitor the radical movement during the winter and spring of 1919, anticipating and preparing for a later crackdown.

---

[91]Report, F. F. Weiss, December 8, 1918, OG 182787, ibid.

[92]For *The Revolutionary Age,* see, W. E. Allen, Memorandum for Mr. Bettman, January 20, 1919; Alfred Bettman, Memorandum to Mr. Allen, February 6, 1919; letter, Allen to George Kelleher, February 24, 1919; reports, John B. Hanrahan, April 23, 1919; Roy McHenry, April 29, May 19 and 25, 1919, OG 136944, ibid.; for *The Liberator,* see report, W. W. Grimes, March 13, 1919; letters, acting agent in charge to Allen, April 25, 1919; L. Winslow to Allen, May 14, 1919, ibid.

[93]Letter, W. E. Allen to Roy C. McHenry, May 28, 1919, ibid.

[94]Reports, A. H. Loula, April 9, 1919; R. W. Finch, April 4, 1919; Agent Howler, March 31, 1919; E. B. Oulashin, March 3, 1919; C. H. Oldfield, February 20, 1919; Agent Howick, February 11, 1919; R. W. Finch, March 4, 1919; A. H. Loula, May 31, 1919; Agent Farley, February 14, 1919; F. M. Sturgis, May 30, 1919; Agent Howick, February 17 and April 21, 1919; S. Apelman, March 5, 1919; letter, W. E. Allen to P. J. Barry, May 23, 1919, OG 180980, ibid.

[95]Report, R. W. Finch, March 13, 1919, ibid.

[96]Letter, Allen to Wm. M. Offley, January 31, 1919, ibid.

[97]Letter, Allen to C. H. Oldfield, March 1, 1919, ibid.

"The Anarchist Fighters": The Bombscare of 1919

Between April 28 and 30, 1919, 30 identical packages containing homemade bombs either arrived at or were intercepted on their way to their intended victims who all, in the words of the Bureau, "represented State authority or counter-radical activities of some nature." They included members of the Wilson administration, federal law enforcement officials, members of Congress, judges, mayors, governors, local police officials and prominent capitalists. Only one person, the maid of former Senator Thomas Hardwick of Georgia, was seriously injured.[98] On the night of June 2, nine bombs went off almost simultaneously in seven different cities and except for an attack on the Church of Our Lady of Victory in Philadelphia, all of the intended victims were state or federal officials and judges involved in the prosecution of radicals. The most sensational of the bombings occurred in Washington, DC, where the front of Attorney General Palmer's house was totally demolished and the assassin himself was blown to bits when the bomb accidentally detonated prematurely. The fact that all of these explosions were the result of an organized conspiracy was indicated by the discovery in the close vicinity of all the bomb sites of identical leaflets, entitled *Plain Words* and signed "The Anarchist Fighters," which vowed to destroy the capitalist oppressors.[99]

Although these bombings were never officially solved, the leading historian of American anarchism, Paul Avrich, has convincingly argued that they were part of a campaign against the government hatched by a group of Italian anarchists, followers of the foremost Italian anarchist leader in America and fiery advocate of direct action, Luigi Galleani, in retaliation for the repression of anarchists during the war. According to Avrich's estimates, at most some fifty to sixty anarchists took part in the planning and actual carrying out of the plot.[100] There are strong indications that the Bureau knew that the bombings were the work of a small group of anarchists. Since February 1918, Bureau agents had linked the Galleanists to previous unsolved bomb explosions and the group was one of a few prime suspects from the very start of the investigation. As early as July 1919 the Bureau thought it had identified the dead bomber as one of Galleani's active disciples. On October 10, Hoover informed his superiors in the Justice Department that the "Galleani Group and the Pro Prensa Society seem to be the centers of suspicion and the investigation at the present time is being

[98]*AG Palmer on Charges*, 158; Paul Avrich, *Sacco and Vanzetti. The Anarchist Background* (Princeton, N.J., 1991), 140-144; Murray, 69-71.
[99]Avrich, 149-156; Murray, 78-80; Whitehead, 39-40.
[100]Avrich, especially 102-107, 138-140, 146-147, 156-159.

conducted to ascertain if there is not some inner group composed of members of each of these organizations which have directed the various bomb outrages."[101] By early 1920, the federal agents were confident that the bombing conspiracy had originated with members of the Galleani group.[102] Apparently, the limited scope of the conspiracy was well known among high officials of the Wilson administration from the very beginning. When President Wilson received the reports on the bombings in Paris on June 4, his personal doctor Cary T. Grayson noted in his diary that the bombings "are apparently being carried on in an effort to force the Government to stop its prosecution of the anarchistic leaders and the I.W.W., who have tried to terrorize the country."[103]

Despite their internal assumptions that the bombings were carried out by a small conspiracy of one or two groups of anarchists as reprisals for government repression, Justice Department and Bureau officials nevertheless presented them as part of a nationwide attempt by radical forces to overthrow the government by force. In early April, before the assassination attempts, the Justice Department announced that a conspiracy by anarchists in Pittsburgh to seize the government arsenal and use the explosives to "lay the city in ruins" had been uncovered and eleven anarchists arrested. However, no corroborating evidence was presented and nothing more was heard of this dramatic plot.[104] Following the discovery of the mail bombs in late April, Justice Department officials expressed the view that the conspiracy was of Bolshevist and IWW origin and had been intended to ignite a May Day reign of terror. Possibly as a result of these and similar announcements, May 1, 1919, was marred by a number of riots in Boston, New York City and Cleveland, where peaceful paraders were attacked by mobs of patriotic activists and soldiers. Although almost all of the violence was perpetrated by right-wing forces, Attorney General Palmer stated that the Justice Department was analyzing May Day speeches to find any proof of calls for the use of revolutionary force.[105]

---

[101]J. Edgar Hoover, Confidential Report of Radical Division For Week Ending October 10, 1919, October 10, 1919, OG 374217, RG65, NA; Avrich, 122-128, 168-171.

[102]*AG Palmer on Charges*, 159-163; Avrich, 172-173. In 1922, Special Agent William J. West of the Boston office finally identified the dead would-be assassin of Attorney General Palmer as Carlo Valdinoci, a member of the Galleani inner group (reports, W. J. West, January 28, 1922, 61-1003-1; W. J. West, November 9, 1922, 61-1003-5, RG65, NA. The inquiry was finally closed in 1924, see letters, Nelson Boyd to Hoover, August 19, 1924, and Hoover to Boyd, August 26, 1924, 61-1003-7, ibid.; however, a later report on the case is still classified, see withdrawal sheet for report, November 25, 1927, FBI 5/12/89, ibid.).

[103]Link (ed.), *The Papers of Woodrow Wilson*, Vol. 60, 114.

[104]Murray, 69.

[105]Coben, *A. Mitchell Palmer*, 204; *The New York Times Index 1919* (New York, 1920), 50; for the May Day riots, see Murray, 73-77; Jaffe, 89-93.

Following the June 2 bombings, the official announcements became even more specific in characterizing the explosions as part of a nationwide plot by radicals to overthrow the government and they warned that further, more spectacular, attacks were expected. On June 3 one official declared that a campaign had been launched to start "a reign of terror in the United States,"[106] and Attorney General Palmer followed up on June 13 by calling the bombings "a combined and joint effort of the lawless classes of the population to injure, if not destroy, the Government."[107] Playing on the officially sanctioned theory of a German-Bolshevik conspiracy, recently appointed Bureau Director William J. Flynn declared after a month's investigation that those involved in the bombings were "connected with Russian Bolshevism, aided by Hun money," although he provided no proof for this allegation.[108] Some officials even hinted at a specific date when the revolution would break out. Flynn referred to radical agitation calling for a general strike in support of the jailed labor activist Thomas Mooney, who had been convicted of a 1916 bombing in San Francisco, and he warned that a general radical uprising against the government might take place on July 4, although he later denied having made such a statement.[109] However, on June 24, Assistant Attorney General Francis P. Garvan noted that it was difficult to predict what the radicals might do: "It all depends on what breaks out in the country. Suppose a July Fourth celebration broke out throughout the country. It all depends. You can not tell from day to day... There is a great deal of talk to that effect."[110] Despite strong suspicions that the bombings were the work of a small group of anarchists who were retaliating against government policies, Justice Department and Bureau officials sought to portray the attacks as the first step in a nationwide radical uprising.

There is another indication that the explosions were used to dramatize plans already under way in the Justice Department. Immediately following the June 2 bombings, Attorney General Palmer announced a thorough departmental reorganization in order to improve its anti-radical capabilities. Francis P. Garvan, a former assistant district attorney in New York and chief investigator of the alien property custodian, who according to Palmer was "without a superior in the

---

[106]Avrich, 165.
[107]US Congress, House, Subcommittee of Committee on Appropriations, *Sundry Civil Bill, 1920. Second Hearing,* 66th. Cong., 1st. Sess. (Washington, DC, 1919), 304.
[108]Coben, *A. Mitchell Palmer,* 208.
[109]Lowenthal, 77; *The New York Times Index 1919,* 49; for the Mooney general strike, which never materialized, see Murray, 114-117.
[110]US Congress, Senate, Subcommittee of the Committee on Appropriations, *Sundry Civil Appropriation Bill, 1920. Hearing,* 66th. Cong., 1st. Sess. (Washington, DC, 1919), 8.

business of the detection of crime.... He knows the criminal classes and they know him, and they have the most holy and healthy respect for his powers," was appointed Assistant Attorney General in charge of investigations.[111] At the same time, the Bureau of Investigation was placed under the supervision of Assistant Attorney General in charge of Miscellaneous Matters John T. Creighton.[112] William J. Flynn, former head of the Secret Service and described by Palmer as "an anarchist chaser," "the great anarchist expert in the United States" who knew all of the anarchists and "can pretty nearly call them by name," was named as the new Bureau director.[113] As his assistant director and chief, Palmer appointed Frank Burke, former manager of the New York office of the Secret Service.[114]

This dramatic mobilization of the Justice Department for the war against radicalism has usually been viewed as a spontaneous response to the bombings and the public demands for action;[115] however, these initiatives seem to have been in preparation for several months. Following the end of the war, Attorney General Gregory, the special assistants in charge of wartime prosecutions, John Lord O`Brian and Alfred Bettman, and Bureau Chief Bielaski together with most of his administrative force had all resigned from the Justice Department, necessitating a larger organizational reshuffle.[116] According to Palmer's subsequent statements to a congressional committee, both Garvan and Flynn had been picked for their positions as the leaders of the government's anti-radical campaign some time before the bombings: "I have been working on these plans for two months. It is not an easy job to reorganize an institution like this. I had the acceptance of Mr. Garvan, and two days before this bomb explosion, on June 2, I had Mr. Flynn's acceptance, so I knew what our plans were and that they were going to be put through...."[117] It seems entirely plausible that the Justice Department deliberately exaggerated the radical threat in the summer of 1919 to obtain public support and the necessary appropriations from Congress for an expansion of the government's anti-radical efforts.

---

[111]*Sundry Civil Bill, 1920,* 305.

[112]*AG Report 1919,* 12; M. A. Jones, Supervision of Bureau by Other than Attorney General, July 3, 1956, O/C 30, FBI/FOIA.

[113]*Sundry Civil Bill , 1920,* 306.

[114]*AG Report 1919,* 12.

[115]For example, Whitehead, 40-41; de Toledano, 51; Murray, 80; Coben, *A. Mitchell Palmer,* 207; Avrich, 166; Donner, *Age of Surveillance,* 33; Powers, *Secrecy and Power,* 63.

[116]See *AG Report 1919,* 12, 16-17; Coben, *A. Mitchell Palmer,* 207.

[117]*Sundry Civil Bill, 1920,* 306.

Later, when Attorney General Palmer became the target of much criticism because of the excesses and injustices of the campaign, he defended himself by claiming that he had only acted in accordance with the wishes of the general public and Congress. According to Palmer, "the public demand for prompt counteraction on the part of the Government was reflected in the action of the Congress in making generous appropriation to the Department of Justice to support the thorough reorganization of our Bureau of Investigation, which was then inaugurated, and to proceed with all diligence and thoroughness to cope with the apparent evil."[118] However, at the time the Wilson administration did not seem to feel pressured by a hysterical Congress; two days after the bombings, on June 4, the presidential secretary, Joseph P. Tumulty, informed the president that "Very few people, and especially the gentlemen on the Hill, realize the absolute seriousness of the whole situation."[119] A closer analysis of the congressional appropriations hearings during this period shows that the Justice Department needed to put considerable pressure on the committees in order to obtain the funding necessary for the campaign. Even then, Congress in several instances appropriated less than asked for, indicating that the people's representatives were somewhat reluctant to finance the Red Scare.

On June 13, Attorney General Palmer asked the Subcommittee of the House Committee on Appropriations for an additional $500,000 to finance the investigation of "ultraradicals or Bolshevists or class-war agitators." This would mean a total appropriation for the Bureau of $2,000,000. In order to justify his request, Palmer claimed to have confidential information on the imminent outbreak of the revolution: "We have received so many notices and gotten so much information that it has almost come to be accepted as a fact that on a certain day in the future, which we have been advised of, there will be another serious and probably much larger effort of the same character which the wild fellows of this movement describe as revolution, a proposition to rise up and destroy the Government at one fell swoop."[120] Palmer added that the supplementary appropriation was necessary to make up

---

[118]*AG Palmer on Charges*, 7; see also, *Charges of Illegal Practices*, 581. This has been repeated by, among others, de Toledano, according to whom, "In June 1919, the Congress had responded to public clamor and press attack ... by ordering the Attorney General of the United States, A. Mitchell Palmer, to put an end to the violence and radical activity which was shaking the country" (de Toledano, 51).

[119]Link (ed.), *The Papers of Woodrow Wilson*, Vol. 60, 153.

[120]*Sundry Civil Bill, 1920*, 304.

for the reduction of the military intelligence services and that a large sum in itself would have a deterrent effect on the criminal elements.[121]

Apparently, the congressmen were not convinced of the seriousness of the radical threat despite Palmer's urgent warnings, and on June 24, Garvan appeared before the Senate Subcommittee of the Committee on Appropriations to put additional pressure on its members. Again it was argued that the extra $500,000 were needed for the reorganization of the Bureau, to make up for the loss of the other intelligence agencies, and the "quite serious" conditions throughout the country regarding "anarchism and Bolshevism." According to Garvan, the Russians were pouring money into the US to finance the radical agitation at the rate of $2 million a month, and the growing radicalism was shown by the fact that since the Armistice the number of radical papers had increased by 150 to a total of 450. When asked if there was "an organized effort to destroy the Government in this country," Garvan, without hesitating, answered "Certainly." However, some senators expressed reluctance to subsidize an expansion of the Bureau's political operations. For example, Senator Reed Smoot noted ironically, when Garvan argued that "there is a certain psychological value in having ample support," which would deter the radicals from attacking, that "there is no psychological question that enters into the spending of the appropriation. If we give you $2,000,000, every dollar of it will be expended." He openly mocked Garvan with reference to the many Justice Department press releases on the progress made by the Bureau in the search for the illusive bombers: "Do you think if we increased this to $2,000,000 you could get one single bomb thrower? I do not mean in the papers; I mean actually get him?"[122] As a result of the apparent scepticism of Congress and, possibly, the reluctance of the Republicans (who controlled the committee and who thought it a bad idea to build up the Democratic administration as the savior of the nation against the Communists), a total of $1,600,000 was appropriated to the Bureau. This was $400,000 less than requested by Palmer and Garvan.[123]

Thus, to finance the Red Scare, Palmer was forced to go back to Congress and once again request an additional appropriation. On

[121]Ibid., 306-309.
[122]*Sundry Civil Appropriation Bill, 1920*, 7-8.
[123]US Congress, House, Subcommittee of Committee on Appropriations, *First Deficiency Appropriation Bill, Fiscal Year 1920*, 66th. Cong., 1st. Sess. (Washington, DC, 1919), 457. Apparently, no previous analysis has noticed this initial cut in the Justice Department's request; for example, Belknap simply notes the final increase in the budget (Belknap, 50), and according to Donner, "In the latter part of June 1919 Palmer persuaded Congress to appropriate $500,000 supplementary to the $1,5 million already appropriated for fiscal year 1920. . . . " (Donner, *The Age of Surveillance*, 33).

August 28, the Attorney General appeared before the House Subcommittee of the Appropriations Committee and asked for no less than $1,000,000 to cover an expected deficiency during fiscal year 1919 (July 1919 to June 1920), which would give the Bureau a total budget of $2,600,000. Palmer referred to the need for comprehensive investigations into "the ultraradical class war movement" and again based his request on confidential information on future attacks: "We have intimations that there will be general outbreaks of a similar character at some dates in the future which have been given to us. It is necessary for us to follow those intimations out and watch these people with great care."[124] This time Palmer succeeded in getting his money, giving the Bureau a final budget of $2,725,000 for the detection and prosecution of crimes. Despite the coming of peace, it was an increase of $375,000 over its wartime budget for fiscal year 1919,[125] but it only happened after repeated requests and the use of scare tactics. In other words, the pressure to finance the Bureau's anti-radical campaign came from the Justice Department, and the process hardly seems to reflect a popular mandate for the government's policies.

On March 18, 1920, following the dramatic raids and initial deportations of alien radicals, Palmer once again appeared before the Subcommittee of the House Committee on Appropriations seeking $2,500,000 for the Bureau's operations in fiscal year 1921; according to the Attorney General's estimates, some 40% of this amount would go to the investigation of radicals.[126] Once again, Palmer justified the request with his confidential information, and he claimed that the raids had prevented a plan fomented by Communist agents, financed by Soviet Russia, to develop the widespread labor unrest into a revolutionary strike with the aim of capturing the government: "I will not put in the record the evidence we have, but our files are filled with proof that that is what they were after."[127] Despite the success of the Bureau in foiling the plotters and the apparent calm in the country, Palmer warned against letting the guards down. The radicals had conceived a devious way by which to carry on their subversive activities, namely by turning over the work to American citizens, who could not be deported or prosecuted: "I think it highly important that those people should be watched."[128] The committee, however, apparently disagreed and only

[124]*First Deficiency Appropriation Bill, Fiscal Year 1920,* 458.
[125]US Congress, House, Subcommittee of Committee on Appropriations, *Sundry Civil Appropriation Bill, 1921,* 66th. Cong., 2nd. Sess. (Washington, DC, 1920), Pt. 2, 1588; *AG Reports 1919,* 298, and *1920,* 466.
[126]*Sundry Civil Appropriation Bill, 1921,* Pt. 2, 1588, 1605.
[127]Ibid., 1590.
[128]Ibid., 1604-1605.

appropriated $2,000,000 or $500,000 less than requested. As Palmer later bitterly informed the congressmen, he had already cut $1,000,000 from his request before presenting it to the committee: "I thought you would accept that in the spirit in which it was offered, but you went me one better and reduced me $500,000, which taught me a lesson that I shall not soon forget."[129] One possible explanation for the committee's attitude was that the Republican majority wanted to embarrass the Democratic administration by playing on the conflict between the Justice and Labor Departments about the administration of the deportation laws. According to subcommittee chairman James W. Good "we did not believe it was a wise expenditure to make, that is, to have the Department of Justice arrest a man who was guilty and after he was proven guilty have another department turn him loose, which had a tendency to make him more of an anarchist than he was before."[130] Thus, the fight over appropriations was very much part of a partisan struggle in an election year.

As a consequence, the Attorney General in December 1920 informed Congress of an estimated deficiency of $500,000 for fiscal year 1921 and at the same time requested $2,650,000 for fiscal year 1922.[131] However, the Justice Department clearly had problems in justifying the expenditure of such amounts, since the recent nationwide investigations and raids had uncovered no concrete plans for an uprising or coup, no hidden caches of arms or secret funds had been found and, in fact, the federal agents had only been able to come up with a handful of pistols and guns.[132] In the absence of any evidence of revolutionary activity, the Justice Department instead used the existence of radical propaganda as proof of the growth of the radical menace. In November 1919, Congress had been informed that the federal agents had counted a total of 471 different radical publications, which was an increase of 50 since the Armistice and the best indication

---

[129]US Congress, House, Subcommittee of Committee on Appropriations, *Sundry Civil Appropriation Bill, 1922*, 66th. Cong., 3rd. Sess. (Washington, DC, 1920), Pt. 2, 1146. Donner, apparently unaware of the cut, writes that "Palmer appeared in March 1920 for an equally generous renewal for the following fiscal year" (Donner, *The Age of Surveillance*, 44).

[130]*Sundry Civil Appropriation Bill, 1922*, 1148-1149.

[131]Ibid., 1146.

[132]As Assistant Secretary of Labor Louis F. Post informed Congress, "With all these sweeping raids all over the country, there have been three pistols; I think it is, brought to our attention in the scores of cases that have come to us. Three pistols, two of them .22 caliber. . . . Now, there are the dangerous weapons – nothing found to show they were criminals or undertaking to manufacture anything dangerous. . . . " (US Congress, House, Committee on Rules, *Investigation of Administration of Louis F. Post, Assistant Secretary of Labor, in the Matter of Deportation of Aliens. Hearings on H. Res. 522*, 66th. Cong., 2nd. Sess. (Washington, DC, 1920), 71). Palmer was forced to admit that only a few weapons had been found by the Bureau but argued that "that is immaterial. The number of revolvers can in no sense be an element in a determination of the potential danger of these aliens" (*AG Palmer on Charges*, 48).

of the "wave of radicalism" that had swept the nation.[133] At the hearing on December 4, 1920, Palmer claimed that the foreign subsidized propaganda "is on the increase, and we would fall short of our duty if we did not continue to keep a very close watch on all their activities."[134] At the same time the Justice Department released its annual report which showed that there now were no less than 625 radical papers in the US and that this agitation had "been growing constantly" since the spring of 1920.[135] It is unclear how reliable an index these figures were of the extent of radicalism; for example, no list of the papers classified as radical was ever made public and no attempt was ever made to ascertain the circulation of the papers or to distinguish between the large number of short-lived papers with a limited circulation and the fewer, larger and more permanent papers.[136] The committee, apparently, was not convinced by the arguments. Because of the deficiency, the Bureau received an additional $400,000 for fiscal year 1921, giving it a total budget of $2,400,000, but at the same time the committee appropriated only $2,000,000 for fiscal year 1922, or $650,000 less than requested.[137] The general impression of the Justice Department's attempts to finance the Bureau's political operations during the Red Scare 1919-20 is that it had to put considerable pressure, in the form of almost apocalyptic warnings of an impending uprising, on a reluctant Congress. This, in turn, either because of the usual partisanship or because it simply did not see the need for the expenditures, repeatedly reduced the Attorney General's urgent requests.

This pattern repeated itself when the Bureau tried to keep the Red Scare alive during the early 1920s. Once again, the absence of any clear revolutionary threat to the government and an apparent public apathy forced the Bureau to resort to scare tactics to obtain the necessary funds from Congress. The recurring theme of Bureau Director William J. Burns was that one should not be deceived by the lack of radical activities for below the calm surface the radicals were

---

[133]*Investigation Activities of Department of Justice*, 12.
[134]*Sundry Civil Appropriation Bill, 1922*, Pt. 2, 1150.
[135]*AG Report 1920*, 177, 179.
[136]One agent, who was instructed to list the radical papers published in his district, complained that it was a difficult term to define, "What I might think is disloyal might not meet with approval" (Letter, W. R. Bryce to William J. Flynn, May 24, 1921, BS 202600-2126-X, RG65, NA). According to Robert A. Bowen, director of the Bureau of Translations and Radical Publications, "the numerical circulation of most of these publications is not definitely established.... " (Robert A. Bowen, The Radical Press in New York City, n.d., box 10, Bowen Papers, Clemson University).
[137]For the FY 1921 budget, see *AG Report 1921*, 415; for the FY 1922 appropriation, see *AG Report 1922*, 295.

redoubling their efforts at overthrowing the government and using more subtle and dangerous methods. In other words, the subversive forces had gone underground and the domestic peace was in itself evidence of the growing danger. In March 1922, Burns requested $2,425,000 for fiscal year 1923, an increase of $425,000 over the previous year's budget, and he justified it with the fact that "the radical activities have increased wonderfully." Burns informed Congress that the radicals had abandoned their previous strategy of openly attacking the government with bombs and were instead conducting an underground propaganda campaign, "and very little is ever said in the newspapers about it, but we are in very close touch with it, and it is stronger now than it ever was ... it is all underground work, and a great deal of it is going on."[138] Despite Burns' earnest plea that "I can not impress upon you too much how dangerous they are at the present moment,"[139] Congress only appropriated $2,250,000 which, despite being an increase of $250,000 over the previous year, were $175,000 less than requested.[140]

Following a somewhat subdued appearance before Congress in November 1922, during which Burns simply noted that radicalism still was on the rise, something which he based on the continued Moscow-directed underground propaganda and the alleged increase of radical papers by 358 since 1921 to a total of 611,[141] he once again tried to breathe some life into the dying Red Scare in March 1924. Burns informed the congressmen that "Radicalism is becoming stronger every day in this country. They are going about it in a very subtle manner." According to the director, the Bureau had "documentary proof" that the Soviet government was subsidizing a propaganda campaign and urging the overthrow of the United States government by force. This was being conducted through 567 papers and in schools, colleges and even churches across the nation and it was responsible for much of the labor unrest. Burns was unable to contain his anxiety, warning that "I dare say that unless the country becomes thoroughly aroused concerning the danger of this radical element in this country we will have a very serious situation."[142] Possibly, these warnings helped to

---

[138]US Congress, House, Subcommittee of Committee on Appropriations, *Appropriations, Department of Justice, 1923*, 67th. Cong., 2nd. Sess. (Washington, DC, 1922), Pt. 2, 131; for the request, see ibid., 123.

[139]Ibid., 145.

[140]*AG Report 1923*, 302.

[141]US Congress, House, Subcommittee of Committee on Appropriations, *Appropriations, Department of Justice, 1924*, 67th. Cong., 4th. Sess. (Washington, DC, 1922), Pt. 2, 70, 76.

[142]US Congress, House, Subcommittee of Committee on Appropriations, *Appropriations, Department of Justice, 1925*, 68th. Cong., 1st. Sess. (Washington, DC, 1924), 93; also, 91-94.

avoid a reduction of the Bureau's budget despite the decline in radical activities. The Bureau was appropriated $2,242,240 for its operations in fiscal year 1924 and $2,392,794 for fiscal year 1925.[143]

It seems, then, that the Justice Department had to overcome considerable obstacles in convincing Congress to fund the Bureau's political operations. In the summer of 1919, Congress initially reduced the supplementary appropriation by $400,000 and only later granted a deficiency appropriation of $1 million after repeated requests. The March 1920 request from Palmer was initially reduced by $500,000 and only later was the Bureau granted a $400,000 deficiency appropriation. In December 1920 Palmer's request was reduced by $650,000, and Burns' request in March 1922 was likewise cut back by $175,000. It seems reasonable to assume that the Justice Department only overcame Congress' apparent reluctance by warning in 1919 against an imminent attempt at overthrowing the government and later by claiming that radical propaganda was on the increase.

Organizing the Red Scare

What were the specific reasons for the Bureau's central role and influence during the Red Scare? We can identify three such sources of power: an efficient bureaucratic organization, its monopoly of information, and the Bureau's image of objectivity and nonpolitical expertise. On August 1, 1919, even before the Justice Department had persuaded Congress to appropriate the necessary money, a Radical Division was established within the Bureau as the command post for the administration's anti-radical crusade. As its director, Palmer appointed J. Edgar Hoover, who had been engaged in the registration and internment of alien enemies during the war and recently promoted to the rank of special assistant to the Attorney General.[144] Hoover's closest assistants were George F. Ruch, who assisted in the drafting of the Division's briefs against the Communist parties, which provided the legal basis for the infamous Palmer raids, and who, judging from the Bureau files, specialized in the investigation of radical activities

---

[143]*AG Reports 1924,* 302, and *1925,* 319. Another contributing reason for the continuing large appropriation may have been Burns' willingness to use the Bureau for patronage appointments. For example, in May 1922 Burns directed J. Edgar Hoover, then assistant director, to hire a Colonel George R. Shanton, who had been recommended by Representative James W. Husted, chairman of the Subcommittee of the House Appropriations Committee which held the Bureau's purse strings (letter, Burns to Hoover, May 5, 1922, 67-561-unrecorded, FBI/FOIA).

[144]For the establishment of the Radical Division, see *AG Report 1919,* 15-16; for Hoover's background, see Powers, 38-55; Theoharis & Cox, 19-56.

among blacks, and Thomas F. Baughman, who played an important part in the actual execution of the Palmer raids.[145]

The Radical Division played a decisive role in shaping the Red Scare by establishing a huge archive on radical activists and organizations, collecting and analyzing thousands of radical publications, investigating a number of major strikes and riots, preparing thousands of deportation cases and cases against American citizens for state prosecution, executing the nationwide Palmer raids and publicizing the radical danger through a carefully conducted propaganda campaign. Yet the Division was surprisingly small; the staff at the Bureau headquarters in Washington, DC, consisted in 1919-20 of only 31 persons (3 assistants, 5 stenographers, 17 clerks, 4 typists and 2 messengers), or a third of the total Bureau headquarters staff. Moreover, the actual investigations in the field were made by a force of only 61 special agents, who worked full-time on radical activities, and some 35 confidential informants. Although the field force was assisted from time to time by other agents, the federal anti-radical campaign was run by a full-time staff of only 127 employees.[146]

One reason why this small force was able to wield such power and achieve so many results seems to be the establishment of an extremely efficient and hierarchial organizational structure in accordance with the Weberian ideals of the Progressive Era. In order to be able to digest and act on the mass of information coming into the Division, a "reviewing system" was organized, according to which all Bureau reports from the field dealing with radical matters were marked "Attention Mr. Hoover" and transmitted directly to Hoover's office. Following an initial examination, the reports were routed to the editorial room where abstract cards were made on all radical persons, periodicals, organizations, movements, states and cities. This enabled the staff to obtain with a moment's notice all of the important information without having to consult the files themselves. The reports were then transmitted to the official in charge of the case and any further instructions to the field were sent out via Hoover's office. Finally, all reports and correspondance were indexed and filed.[147] This procedure seems to have functioned extremely efficiently: At the height

---

[145]For Ruch, see Whitehead, 331n2, and Theoharis & Cox, 111; for Baughman, see Whitehead, 337n6; Powers, 91-92, 104; Theoharis & Cox, 82-83.

[146]Memorandum Upon the Work of the Radical Division, August 1, 1919 to March 15, 1920, n.d., OG 374217, RG65, NA; *Sundry Civil Appropriation Bill, 1921*, Pt. 2, 1589. The staff at the Bureau HQ in 1922 numbered 96 employees (*Appropriations, Department of Justice, 1925*, 86).

[147]The reviewing system is described in an undated and unidentified memorandum in OG 374217, RG65, NA.

of the Red Scare, from August 15, 1919, to March 13, 1920, according to internal Division figures, Hoover's small staff received and handled 17,526 reports, 7,328 letters, 3,166 publications and 1,407 telegrams (this was an average of 98 reports, 41 letters, 18 publications and 8 telegrams handled per working day).[148]

Another reason why the Radical Division was able to exercise an influence beyond its limited resources was its network of other government agencies, with which the Division cooperated and from which it received an extensive amount of information. For example, between August 20, 1919, and November 3, 1920, the Division received a copy of the Military Intelligence Division's "Weekly Situation Survey," which contained information on such topics as general radical activities, labor unrest, subversion among blacks, troop morale, conditions in foreign countries, nationalistic groups in the US, the Jewish population, Communist and IWW activities, and so on.[149] During the nationwide coal miners' strike in late 1919, the MID also transmitted copies of its weekly "Industrial Situation Map" to the Division.[150] The Radical Division also received reports on various radical activities in the US from the Office of Naval Intelligence and the Secret Service and on American radicals abroad from the State Department, while the Post Office Department submitted information on radical papers.[151] As previously noted, on a local level the Bureau received information from state authorities and investigating committees and used the red squads as its operational arm. Thus, the Radical Division was able to take advantage of the combined state and federal

---

[148]Memorandum Upon the Work of the Radical Division, August 1, 1919 to March 15, 1920, ibid.

[149]Letter, Wrisley Brown to Frank Burke, October 8, 1919; Confidential. Weekly Situation Survey for Week Ending December 3, 1919. Military Intelligence Division, General Staff. Section M.I.4.; ibid., December 10, 17, 24, 31, 1919, January 7, 14, 21, 28, February 4, 11, 18, 25, March 10, 17, 24, 31, April 7, 14, 21, 28, May 5, 12, 19, 26, June 2, 9, 16, 23, 30, July 7, 14, 21, 28, August 4, 25, September 1, 15, October 6, 27 and November 3, 1920, OG 377098, ibid.

[150]Letters, Lieut. Col. Wrisley Brown to Frank Burke, December 6, 1919; Burke to Brown, December 6, 1919, OG 303770, ibid.

[151]For information from ONI, see for example, letters, George W. Williams to William E. Allen, May 14, 1919, with att. report, OG 17011, ibid.; Williams to Allen, March 8 and 29, 1919 with att. reports, OG 91928, ibid.; Memorandum, ONI to JD, October 14, 1919, OG 352037, ibid.; for Secret Service, see reports, Julian W. Bowes, n.d. and May 14, 15, 16, 23, 31, 1919, OG 182787, ibid.; Report to Chief W. H. Moran, April 9, 1919, OG 91928, ibid.; for the State Department, see letters, W. L. Hurley to Frank Burke, April 27, 1920; Robert T. Snow to Burke, April 30, 1920; Chargé d'Affaire to Sec. of State, June 15 and July 2, 1920; Hurley to Hoover, September 2, 1920, OG 182787, ibid.; Hurley to Hoover, October 23, 1920, OG 384378, ibid.; Hurley to Hoover, April 22, 1921, BS 202600-591-2, ibid.; Hurley to William J. Burns, May 18, 1922, 61-783-9, and June 20, 1922, 61-783-10, and August 24, 1922, 61-783-11, ibid.; Dept. of State to Hoover, October 16, 1924, 61-1092-3, ibid.; for the Post Office Department, see reports, L. E. Bates, April 5, 1921, BS 202600-8-5, ibid.; M. J. Davis, August 29, 1919, OG 387162, ibid.; W. H. Lamar to Allen, May 29, 1919, OG 182249, ibid.

law enforcement and intelligence agencies to cast a fine-meshed net over the nation in its hunt for subversive elements.

Apart from a highly efficient organization and network, two other conditions enabled the Radical Division to effectively dominate the Red Scare from the summer of 1919. It is a well-known fact from bureaucratic theory that one important source of the political power of public organizations is their often near monopoly over vital information which enables them to describe problems and define their solution. Whereas the press, interest groups and politicians may each hold some pieces of the puzzle, only the public bureaucracy has the capabilities to collect and analyze most or all of the sources.[152] Although the Radical Division, because of the state of the existing legislation, was originally established with the primary purpose of preparing deportation cases against alien radicals, Hoover informed his superiors in the Justice Department after two and a half months of investigation, "the trend of the work of the Division so shaped itself that only a portion of the time could be given to the deportation cases."[153] Instead of simply collecting evidence for deportation cases, the Division sought to become the leading authority on all matters concerning the radical movement. It undertook the research and ana- lysis of the deeper social end economic conditions, the theoretical and historical background of the various organizations, their connections with the international movements, and, despite the lack of any federal sedition law, of the radical activities of American citizens.[154] In July 1920, the Radical Division was reorganized and renamed the General Intelligence Division (GID). In addition to radical activities it was put in charge of "all matters referring to general intelligence," including such areas as Japanese activities within the US and abroad, the Mexican situation, international espionage and border controversies, with a view toward specializing "on the broader phases of international relations."[155]

---

[152]See, Lewis, especially, 6, 238; Etzioni-Halevy, 33, 58, 90.

[153]J. E. Hoover, Memorandum Upon Work of Radical Division, August 1, 1919, to October 15, 1919, October 18, 1919, OG 374217, RG65, NA.

[154]Memorandum, op.cit., August 1, 1919 to March 15, 1920, ibid.; for the Division's research in general, see also, J. E. Hoover, Memorandum Upon Activities of the Radical Division, Department of Justice, May 1, 1920, ibid.; *AG Reports 1919*, 15-16; *1920*, 178; *1921*, 129, 131.

[155]J. Edgar Hoover, Memorandum for Mr. Burke, July 26, 1920, OG 374217, RG65, NA. For a complete listing of the GID's responsibilities, see *Appropriations, Department of Justice, 1924*, Pt. 2, 69-71; see also, *Appropriations, Department of Justice, 1923*, Pt. 2, 127; *AG Reports 1922*, 68-69; *1923*, 69-71.

The Radical Division was organized and presented as the best informed authority on the radical movement. According to the Justice Department, the Division's work was "cumulative in nature" and it enabled the government "to study the situation from a more intelligent and broader viewpoint."[156] The Department claimed that the Division had "probably accumulated a greater mass of data upon this subject than is anywhere else available,"[157] and Attorney General Palmer prided himself on the "remarkable record of facts, available for future use at the hands of the Government."[158] At the core of the Division's data base on the radical movement were the Bureau's extensive investigative files. This archive consisted of several series of which the "Miscellaneous File" contained the records of 42,975 cases from the period 1909 to 1922, the so-called "Old German" series, which contained records of German enemy aliens, anti-war protesters and radical activities until 1920, consisted of 391,901 cases, and the "Bureau Section" series contained more than 307,231 cases from the period 1920-21; in all some 700,000 cases, many of which contained information on legal political activities.[159]

In order to be able to use this mass of information efficiently, an "Editorial Card Index" was established which contained the most important information on five categories. First, individuals who had been "reported to the Bureau of Investigation as being in any way involved or connected with the radical movement" which included not only "the extreme anarchist but also the more moderate radical."[160] Since no attempt at verifying the information was apparently made, this meant that any person who had been mentioned in Bureau reports, whether on the basis of rumors, by informers, as a participant in a public meeting, or as a subscriber to a radical paper, was carefully indexed. Each entry contained the name, address, file number, nationality, citizenship and a short summary of the person's political activities, and the staff in charge of the preparation of the index was instructed that "any particular radical remarks or articles should be immediately called to Mr. Hoover's attention."[161] Second, all organizations, societies and clubs were indexed together with information on their membership and a summary of their meetings and activities.

[156]*AG Report 1920,* 179-180; also, *AG Report 1919,* 15.
[157]Ibid., 13.
[158]*Sundry Civil Appropriation Bill, 1922,* Pt. 2, 1150.
[159]The files are described in, US National Archives, *Investigative Case Files of the Bureau of Investigation 1908-1922* (Washington, DC, 1983), 2-3; Haines & Langbart, xi-xii.
[160]Memorandum, op.cit., August 1, 1919 to March 15, 1920, OG 374217, RG65, NA.
[161]Unidentified memorandum, n.d., ibid.

Third, all publications "which are particularly called to the attention of the Radical Division" were indexed together with information on the publishers, editors, their circulation and their general content. Fourth, cards were prepared on each state, city and foreign country, noting the radical situation and the active individuals and organizations in each locality. Finally, separate index cards were prepared on particular important movements or events, such as the bomb plot of June 2, 1919, the steel strike in Pittsburgh, negro agitation, or the labor situation in Washington. This index enabled the staff of the Division to retrieve instantly the essential information dealing with radical persons, organizations, publications, and so on and thereby more efficiently control the investigations in the field.[162] Because of the automatic indexing of all information in the Bureau reports, the Editorial Card Index grew explosively from 80,000 cards in March 1920 to 100,000 in May 1920, 200,000 in December 1920 and 450,000 index cards by December 1921.[163]

The Division also prepared more detailed memoranda on individual radicals. So-called "Abstracts" were compiled on alien radicals, whom the Division desired to get deported, containing information on the alien's background and activities and important quotes from speeches and articles. It is unclear how many "Abstracts" were compiled, but it is known that the Division prepared 6,396 deportation cases during its first eight months of investigation and that an additional 750 cases were completed in 1921-22.[164] "Biographies" on all authors, publishers and editors with any connection to "an ultraradical body or movement" and legal memoranda on the leading agitators were likewise drawn up, containing stenographic reports of speeches and relevant extracts of articles. By the end of 1919, some 60,000 such personal files had been prepared.[165]

A major source of the Division's analysis of the radical movement consisted of the radicals' own literary outpourings. All kinds of radical books, magazines, papers, and pamphlets and every constitution, program and platform of radical organizations were systematically collected, either through purchase or confiscation during the numerous

[162]Unidentified memorandum, n.d., ibid.; Hoover, memorandum op.cit., October 18, 1919, ibid.; memorandum, op.cit., August 1, 1919 to March 15, 1920, ibid.

[163]Memorandum, op.cit., August 1, 1919 to March 15, 1920, ibid.; Hoover, memorandum op.cit., May 1, 1920, ibid.; *AG Reports 1920*, 173, 179; *1921*, 129.

[164]For the "Abstracts," see unidentified memorandum, n.d., OG 374217, RG65, NA; for the number of deportation cases, see *Sundry Civil Appropriation Bill, 1921*, Pt. 2, 1589; *Appropriation, Department of Justice, 1924*, 70.

[165]For the "Biographies," see *AG Report 1920*, 178; Lowenthal, 91; for the legal memos, see, Hoover, memorandum op.cit., May 1, 1920, OG 374217, RG65, NA.

raids, and incorporated into the Division's Radical Library.[166] By the fall of 1920, this collection had become so large that it could no longer be housed in the Division offices, and Hoover was compelled to request the Library of Congress to take possession of it.[167] The radical papers were analyzed by two sections. In New York, the Bureau of Translations and Radical Publications under the direction of Robert A. Bowen, consisting of a staff of some 45 translators and analysts, read and translated all foreign language and English language radical publications in that city, while the Radical Publications Section under the command of William F. Keohan systematically kept track of and indexed all radical papers in the US. In 1920, these two sections were reading 625 papers of which 236 were in 25 different foreign languages.[168]

Besides its efficient organization and virtual monopoly over information, a third source of the Radical Division's influence during the Red Scare consisted of what Eugene Lewis has termed "the creation of an apolitical shield." Whereas politicians, interest groups and the press are commonly understood to pursue their own, narrow self-interests, public bureaucracies usually claim to be neutral, free of partisanship and serving the broader public interest, thereby concealing and legitimizing what might otherwise be perceived as political acts and decisions.[169] Attorney General Palmer presented a Bureau report on the radical movement to Congress by noting that "Authoritative information is infinitely more impressive than the fabrications of the propagandists or the necessary imperfect reports of the press."[170] The Justice Department described the Radical Division staff as objective and nonpolitical experts, "with no social or economic theories to exploit, but with the simple desire to work intelligently and effectively."[171] They were men "who have no other motive than the performance of their duty, who have no other desire than to execute the orders

[166]For the collection of radical materials, see, letters, R. N. Butterworth to Lewis J. Baley, October 13, 1920; Bliss Morton to Lewis J. Baley, October 13, 1920; Robert Boren to J. E. Hoover, October 11, 1920; W. M. Lamar to Hoover, September 20, 1920, BS 202600-282, ibid.; for the Radical Library, see *AG Reports 1920*, 178; *1921*, 129.

[167]Letter, Hoover to Herbert Putnam, Librarian of Congress, September 15, 1920, BS 202600-282, RG65, NA.

[168]The Bureau of Translations and Radical Publications is described in, Robert A. Bowen, "Bureau of Translations and Radical Publications," n.d. (1961), box 10, Bowen Papers, Clemson University; for the Radical Publications Section, see *Investigation Activities of the Department of Justice*, 12; the 1920 figures are from *AG Report 1920*, 179. These sections were reorganized and reduced in 1920, see, Hoover, Memorandum for Mr. Scott, October 2, 1920, OG 374217, RG65, NA.

[169]Lewis, 17-19, 230-233.

[170]*AG Palmer on Charges*, 14.

[171]*AG Report 1919*, 15-16.

of the Department of Justice in the enforcement of the law..."[172] The Justice Department repeatedly based this claim of dispassionate objectivity on the professionalization of its employees. "These splendid men, these real Americans," as Palmer called them, were selected in a totally non-political manner and solely on the basis of their professional qualifications, many had university degrees and most were trained lawyers. Thus, according to Palmer, "it is harder to get into the Bureau of Investigation than it is into any Government service in Washington."[173]

The Radical Division was able to dominate the Red Scare because of its resources, knowledge and expertise. However, although the Division derived much of its influence and power qua its bureaucratic position, this should not lead to the conclusion that it was autonomous and acted independently of the political leadership. In fact, the Division was under close supervision of the Justice Department and the federal government was well-informed of its activities. As previously noted, the Bureau was supervised by John T. Creighton and the Radical Division by Assistant Attorney General Garvan and they both kept in close contact with the Division's activities. Garvan was continuously kept informed of the Division's investigations and all deportation cases were transmitted through Creighton for further action.[174] The Division's political surveillance activities were also widely known within the federal administration. Beginning in January 1920, the Division began distributing a biweekly "Bulletin of Radical Activities," later renamed "General Intelligence Bulletin" and published weekly, to all government officials "as by the nature of their duties are entitled to the information." It summarized the information gathered by the Bureau on a wide range of radical activities, from strikes to the activities of unions, radical leaders, organizations, the press, blacks and the Sinn Fein, thus providing "a bird's eye view of all situations at home or abroad which will keep the officials properly informed."[175] The Division also distributed a monthly "Report on the

---

[172]*AG Palmer on Charges*, 75; also 104 and 106.
[173]Ibid., 74-75; also, *Sundry Civil Appropriation Bill, 1922*, Pt. 2, 1148.
[174]Unidentified memorandum, n.d., OG 374217, RG65, NA.
[175]*AG Report 1920*, 173-174. For the Bulletins, see US Department of Justice, Bulletin of Radical Activities, No. 1, January 1st. to 17th., 1920, MID 10110-1683-1, to General Intelligence Bulletin, No. 72, Week Ending October 1, 1921, MID 10110-1683-241 (MID Reports: Surveillance of Radicals 1917-41, microfilm). This Bulletin was based on weekly reports from the field offices, see for example those for Detroit District (BS 202600-1689, RG65, NA), Pittsburgh District (BS 202600-1768, ibid.), Greater New York District (OG 208369/BS 202600-1628/BS 202600-33, ibid.), Philadelphia District (BS 202600-1617, ibid.), Washington, DC, (BS 202600-9, ibid.), Boston (BS 202600-22, ibid.), and Buffalo District (BS 202600-1613, ibid.). See also, letters, Frank Burke to Frank L. Carbarino, January 17, 1920; Hoover to Carbarino, January 17, 1920; Chas. E. Breniman to Burke, April 27, 1920;

Radical Press" to a number of federal agencies.[176] To use a formulation by Max Weber, the Division functioned as the "precision instrument" of the political leadership.[177] In other words, to find the deeper explanation for the policies and activities of the Division and the Bureau, we should look at the government's overall policies and decisions.

Acting Chief to J. P. Huddleston, September 16, 1920, OG 374217, ibid.

[176]Letters, J. Edgar Hoover to Major Mark Brooke, October 16, 1923, with att. report; Hoover to the Director, MID, June 4, 1925, with att. report; Hoover to the Director, MID, November 19, 1925, with att. report; Hoover to the Director, MID, January 18, 1926, with att. report, all in MID 10110-2513 (MID Reports: Surveillance of Radicals 1917-41, microfilm).

[177]Etzioni-Halevy, 33.

Chapter 5

1919: Containing the Social Unrest

While Bureau officials had their own ideological and bureaucratic interests in an anti-radical campaign, the Bureau's primary function in 1919 was to contain and undermine social unrest and political movements, which might threaten the existing social, economic and political order. In particular, the Bureau was called on by the federal government in its response to the race riots, the national strikes and the anarchist and Communist movements.

"The Government Is Watching"
Political surveillance is usually perceived as a passive and concealed act, whereby information is collected clandestinely to keep the government informed, as a basis for the political decision-making process and to prevent political violence by extremist groups. However, in the following it will be argued that the Bureau's activity had an additional and perhaps even more important purpose, namely to make the radicals aware that the government was watching and thereby to intimidate them into passivity. It should at the beginning be emphasized that, of course, the Bureau's primary objective was to collect information on the activities of the radical movement. For this purpose the Bureau employed a number of different methods. In order to identify radicals, lists of subscribers to radical papers were collected; for example, the Bureau indexed 282 subscribers to radical papers in Oklahoma, 300 recipients of IWW literature in Milwaukee, 459 subscribers to various IWW publications across the nation, and 130 distributors of the *Revolutionary Age* nationwide.[1] The Bureau also copied various lists being circulated on prominent radicals,[2] licence

---

[1] Reports, T. F. Weiss, March 16, 1920, BS 202600-282; Chas. L. Harris, March 25, 1920, 61-01; letter, Edward J. Brennan to Frank Burke, July 28, 1920, with att. list, BS 202600-282; report, John Hanrahan, May 19, 1919, OG 136944, all in RG65, NA. See also, reports, Geo. W. Berg, October 8, 1919, BS 202600-282; letter, Acting Chief to Wm. P. Hazen, August 25, 1919, and report, Wm. P. Hazen, August 26, 1919, OG 27151; report, E. B. Sisk, September 10, 1919, BS 202600-282, ibid.

[2] Report, J. S. Apelman, August 16, 1920, BS 202600-282, ibid. It was noted about one such list that many of those listed "are well-known radicals, but the list also contains a great many so-called 'liberals', 'intellectuals', or 'parlor Bolshevists'" (Letter, M. J. Davis to Frank Burke, November 28, 1919, with "List of names of prominent persons suspected of radical sympathies, published in the issues of 'The New York Call', August 18, 1919 to August 24,

numbers of cars parked outside radical meetings were noted and the owners identified,[3] and signers of resolutions or protests to the government were likewise indexed by the Bureau.[4] Apart from the routine surveillance of speeches, meetings and conventions and the reading of the radical press, the Bureau kept abreast of radical activities by employing more covert and intrusive methods. In some cases, prominent radicals were shadowed, letters and telegrams were intercepted, offices were broken into and searched without warrants, meetings were bugged with dictaphones, and bank accounts were monitored.[5]

The most important – and controversial – intelligence source was the informer or informant in the Bureau's terminology. The Bureau distinguished between two types of informants, "Informants" who either casually or regularly submitted information to the local field office, and the "Special Informant" who was working directly for the headquarters in Washington, DC (a special agent working undercover was known as an "Undercover Man"). During the 1919-20 period the Radical Division used a force of 35 informers to report on political activities.[6] Since it was a precondition for a successful operation that the informers were able to mix with their surroundings without arousing suspicion, the Bureau used specialized informants for particular situations. Black informants such as William A. Bailey (code-

1919," OG 27151, ibid.).

[3]Report, N. J. Donnelly, June 7, 1920, OG 180980, ibid.

[4]Letters, Robert M. Carswell to Frank Burke, May 27, 1920, with att. resolution, OG 82811, ibid.; Burke to Chas. P. Tighe, December 22, 1919; Burke to George F. Lamb, December 11 and 31, 1919; Burke to Wm. P. Hazen, December 31, 1919; Burke to Geo. E. Kelleher, June 19, 1920; Burke to H. B. Pierce, June 10, 1920; Burke to E. M. Blanford, June 10, 1920; Burke to A. T. Bagley, June 10, 1920; Ass. AG to Charles Leino, September 27, 1920; Ass. AG to Phil Hogan, September 25, 1920; A. E. Briggs to Woodrow Wilson, May 30, 1920; Parry Walton to Woodrow Wilson, June 2, 1920, OG 180980, ibid.

[5]For examples of intensive shadowing, see memo, telephone calls, November 1, 1919; reports, V. P. Creighton, November 2, 5, 7, 10, 13, 1919, OG 303770, ibid.; for mail interception see, reports, V. P. Creighton, November 2, 4, 6, 10, 15, 1919; report, Wm. Sausele, December 17, 1919, OG 303770, ibid.; for surreptitious entries, see report, Feri F. Weiss, December 12, 1918, OG 136944, ibid.; Williams, *"Without Understanding,"* 130-131; for buggings and eavesdropping, see Reports, J. F. Kropidlowski, September 14, 1917; W. T. Sanders, Jr., September 14, 1917, BS 202600-823, RG65, NA; Wm. M. Doyas, November 3, 1919, OG 303770, ibid.; for the monitoring of bank accounts, see reports, M. J. Davis, October 31, 1921, 100-375204-X5 (Federal Surveillance of African-Americans: Microfilm); V. P. Creighton, November 5, 1919; Joseph Polen, November 28, 1919; Oscar Schmitz, December 8, 1919, OG 303770, RG65, NA. The frequency of these methods is not known for this period; the only reliable figures derive from a Senate investigation in the mid-1970s, according to which informants were used in 83% of the cases, police sources in 74%, institutional sources in 50%, interviews in 40%, interviews with the subject in 20%, physical surveillance in 18%, electronic surveillance in 5% and surreptitious entry or mail openings in 1% of the cases (Select Committee to Study Governmental Operations with Respect to Intelligence Activities of the United States, *Hearings, Vol. 6*, 367).

[6]R. B. Spencer, Frank R. Stone and Chas. P. Tighe, Report of Committee on Informants, Under-Cover Men and Blue Slips, August 1920, OG 390982, RG65, NA.

named WW), James W. Jones (800) and Herbert S. Boulin (P-138) were used to infiltrate radical black groups,[7] female informants such as Marion Barling and Amoretta Fitch won the confidence of Emma Goldman and the Women's Peace Party,[8] and members of the United Mine Workers were employed as informers during the national coal strike in late 1919.[9]

The Radical Division was convinced of the value and importance of its informers. According to Hoover, the informers in general were reliable, of "an extremely high type," and without them the Division would "be completely at sea when it comes to the handling of Radical work."[10] It was Hoover's position that the informers were the only effective means by which the Division could be kept fully advised on the activities and plans of the often secretive extremist groups and that their presence could prevent acts of violence. In support of this last contention, Hoover claimed that no acts of violence by radicals had been committed since the bombings during the summer of 1919.[11] Apart from the dubious value of this claim – there are no indications that the Division actually prevented any planned acts of terrorism and despite its informers it was unable to prevent the worst terror bombing of the period, the Wall Street explosion on September 16, 1920, – some informers, apparently, achieved considerable success in infiltrating radical groups. Francis A. Morrow (K-97), a shipfitter and socialist, joined the Camden, New Jersey, branch of the Communist Party in 1920 and rose to become secretary of the district committee and a delegate to the party's secret convention in 1922.[12] Eugenio Ravarini (D-5), an Italian immigrant and a former carabinier, succeeded between September 1919 and March 1920 in penetrating some of the most secretive anarchist groups on the East coast, among them the Gruppo L'Era Nuova in Paterson, New Jersey, and learned some of the secrets about the June 2, 1919 bombings.[13] According to

---

[7]For these three black informants, see Robert A. Hill (ed.), *The Marcus Garvey and Universal Negro Improvement Papers*, Vol. II (Berkeley, Calif., 1984), 170n1, 203n4, 541n1; Kornweibel, *"Seeing Red,"* 26-27, 62-63, 92-93, 110-115, 120-127, 136-137, 145-147.

[8]For Barling, see report on meeting at the Hotel Brevoort, October 27, 1919, OG 15446, RG65, NA; for Mrs. Fitch, see reports, John S. Menefee, February 3, 10, 24, 28 and March 3, 1919, OG 82811, ibid.

[9]Report, Edgar B. Speer, October 31, 1919, OG 303770, ibid.

[10]Hoover, Memoranda for Mr. Burke, February 10, 1920, OG 391465, ibid., and March 16, 1920, OG 374217, ibid.

[11]Hoover, memorandum op.cit., October 18, 1919, ibid. Compare this with the FBI's stated policy on the use of informants in the internal security field in the 1970s: "Informants provide one of the best and most complete forms of coverage to the law enforcement officer. Sometimes they are the only means of penetrating subversive or extremist organizations" (*Hearings, Vol. 6, Federal Bureau of Investigation*, 444).

[12]Draper, 366-369; Belknap, 52.

[13]Avrich, 178-180.

Hoover, the most valuable political informer in the employ of the Bureau was #836, who, as far as can be ascertained, entered the stage in May 1918 when he reported on John Reed.[14] During the Red Scare #836 infiltrated the American Civil Liberties Union, was in contact with the staff of the *Liberator,* and reported on the deliberations of the central strike committee of the national steel strike.[15]

However, it is obvious that since the informers were paid for their services and these were only needed by the government in case of unrest or troubles, the informers would tend to exaggerate the amount of radical activity in order to hold on to their jobs. As an internal Bureau policy document noted, "there is a marked tendency among a great majority of informants to endeavor to perpetuate their jobs, and for the person who employs them to have an exaggerated idea of their importance to the service."[16] One example of this was informant H-71, who began submitting reports on radical activities to the Salt Lake City office when he lost his regular job. Despite sending long and tedious reports of little value on the internal fights of the few IWWs and Communists in Utah, he was highly recommended by his Bureau handlers. Only after 10 months, when he could no longer keep alive the illusion of a radical danger in the Mormon state, was H-71 discharged from the service.[17] Perhaps the best example of a systematic exaggeration of the radical danger on the part of informers occurred during the Seattle general strike, when, as previously described, informers from the Pinkerton Detective Agency, the APL and the Minute Men claimed that a major part of the strikers were Bolsheviks and that the strike was the first step of a worldwide revolution.

It is only common sense to assume that in order to function effectively, the surveillance must be conducted in absolute secrecy and its methods not revealed in order not to alert the radicals to take precautions against the spies and go underground. It is therefore a striking aspect of the Bureau's political surveillance in this period that it was often conducted so openly, and on occasions even aggressively, that the intention seems to have been to intimidate radicals and

[14]Report, #836, May 27, 1918, OG 182787, RG65, NA; For Hoover on #836, see Hoover, Memorandum for Mr. Burke, February 10, 1920, OG 391465, ibid.

[15]Reports, #836, March 30, 1920, BS 202600-823, ibid.; #836, March 24, 1920, OG 136944, ibid.;#836, February 18, 25, March 4, 17, 23, May 26, September 10, 18, 25, October 13, 1919, OG 352037, ibid.

[16]Spencer, Stone and Tighe, Report of Committee on Informants, Under-Cover Men, and Blue Slips, August 1920, OG 390982, ibid.

[17]Letter, C. W. Hughes to William J. Burns, October 22, 1922, with att. report, C. W. Hughes, October 22, 1921, 61-147-1; reports, C. W. Hughes, December 20, 1921, 61-147-6; Hughes, December 29, 1921, 61-147-7; Hughes, January 3, 1922, 61-147-8; E. S. Kimball, March 15, 1922, 61-147-15; H. W. Hess, May 4, 1922, 61-147-21; Kimball, May 31, 1922, 61-147-26; Kimball, July 17, 1922, 61-147-39, ibid.

frighten potential sympathizers away from joining. That this was a deliberate strategy is supported by several statements by Justice Department officials. When Attorney General Palmer in June 1919 requested Congress to finance the anti-radical campaign, he stressed its preventive effect by arguing that "we must let these people know that we mean business," a large appropriation "will show these men that we are going to go the limit," and the message must be conveyed to the radicals that "the best men in the country are going to be on their trail everywhere."[18] Assistant Attorney General Garvan also informed Congress that "every detail of what we have against each one of these people is known to every one of them."[19] Palmer argued that the most important result of the Bureau's surveillance, apart from the collection of information, was "the knowledge that it imparts to these persons of revolutionary design that the Government is watching them very closely, because no secret service of this character can engage in this kind of investigative work without the persons aimed at being very fully aware of our activities."[20] Clearly the purpose of publicizing the activities of the Bureau was to intimidate the radicals. Accordingly, the Justice Department made sure to inform Congress in details about the ongoing surveillance, stating publicly that the Radical Division was conducting "a systematic and thorough supervision" of the radicals and was "carefully observing and following the trend of the ultra-radical movement in the United States...."[21] During a congressional hearing Palmer showed the representatives a handful of papers, explaining that "I have here mailing lists of these radical papers showing who is reading this stuff mostly," and he added innocently, "I simply state that the Department of Justice has it and it is at the disposal of any proper agency of the Government."[22] Thereby, he served notice that the authorities were watching people's reading habits.

The existence of the Bureau files makes it possible to sketch in some detail how this supposedly passive and covert surveillance made itself visible and felt. Surveillance reports of agents show that in several instances it was assumed by the radicals that as a matter of course they were being watched by the government. One speaker at a black radical meeting began by stating "that he was sure Department of Justice men were in the audience, and, if so, he would invite them down into the

---

[18]*Sundry Civil Bill, 1920,* 307.
[19]*Sundry Civil Appropriation Bill, 1920,* 7.
[20]*Sundry Civil Appropriation Bill, 1922,* Pt. 2, 1150.
[21]Quotes from *AG Reports 1920,* 172, and *1921,* 130.
[22]*AG Palmer on Charges,* 195.

front seats so that they would not miss anything,"[23] while a speaker at a political amnesty meeting said that "he knew the Department of Justice agents were there and dared them to come on the stage and contradict what he said."[24] Sometimes, however, the agents made no great effort at concealing their presence. Special Agent T. C. Wilcox reported how he had been pointed out by the speaker at a political amnesty meeting, who had told the agent: "I hope that you hireling go over this meeting and report to your capitalist masters every word I have said."[25] Agent Feri F. Weiss apparently did not see the irony of the situation when he was detected during a speech by John Reed and invited to sit on the platform beside the speaker: "It certainly speaks well for American Democracy, when the leader of the Boston radical element invites the representative of the Department of Justice on the platform as a guest of honor...."[26] That the radicals were well aware that their public meetings were being monitored is also indicated by Emma Goldman's later remembrance that during her lecture tour across the nation in the fall of 1919 "our every movements (were) watched by local and federal agents, every utterance noted down and attempts made to silence us."[27]

Another more direct way to make their presence felt was to seek out radical activists and interview them, thereby imparting the knowledge that they were under investigation. Thus, signers of petitions for political amnesty were interviewed, radical members of the United Mine Workers were questioned about their activities during the coal strike, radical news-dealers were grilled about their political sympathies and their subscribers, pacifist organizations were visited by federal agents who inquired about their membership, background and finances, and agents turned up at civil liberties groups to collect copies of their literature.[28] Moreover, sometimes the zealous agents used the occasion to warn against taking part in radical activities. For example, the secretary of the New York branch of the Women's Peace Party, Mrs. Margaret Lane, was cautioned against distributing literature "that

[23]Report, M. A. Joyce, January 22, 1920, OG 369936, RG65, NA.

[24]Report, Billups Harris, July 20, 1919, OG 180980, ibid.

[25]Report, T. C. Wilcox, January 20, 1920, ibid.

[26]Report, Feri F. Weiss, August 15, 1918, OG 182787, ibid.

[27]Emma Goldman, *Living My Life* (New York (1931), 1970), Vol. II, 709.

[28]For signers of political amnesty petitions, see report, James C. O'Neill, June 23, 1920, OG 180980, RG65, NA; for the UMW members, see report, J. R. Burger, November 22, 1919, OG 303770, ibid.; for the news-dealers, see reports, Ed Portley, October 17, 1919, OG 96283, ibid.; Agent Cooney, September 6 and 19, 1919, OG 27151, ibid.; for the pacifists, see reports, H. Poling, October 21, 1918, OG 82811, ibid.; Clinton P. Sinks, June 30, 1919, ibid.; for the civil libertarians, see reports, W. B. Matthews, April 1, 6 and 8, 1918, BS 202600-823, ibid.

might tend to embarrass the present policies of the Government,"[29] while a black editor received a strong reprimand from a Bureau agent for publishing an article entitled "Stop Going With Hat in Hand Asking for What You Want, But Go With Gun in Hand and Demand What You Want."[30] No act seemed too small to be pointed out as objectionable by the Bureau. When a Russian immigrant named Shiplacoff predicted a revolution in the US, he was immediately warned by Special Agent L. S. Perkins that it was a risky thing to do, which acoording to the agent had the desired effect: "Shiplacoff was evidently frightened, and said to some one present to tell his wife not to get scared; that he would come out of it all right, but his manner was uneasy."[31] When the Los Angeles office was notified by an informant that a citizen had been observed reading the liberal the *Nation*, the man was interrogated and, according to the agent's report, "was warned by agent against social propaganda, and subject assured agent that he is 100 percent (sic) American and, being innocent of any wrong doing or wrong intent, would heed the warning."[32]

The Bureau repeatedly made sure that it was widely known that it was investigating. During the steel strike in the fall of 1919 information that federal agents had been dispatched to suppress any activities of the radicals, IWWs or Bolsheviks was systematically leaked to the press. That such leaks had the intended effect is indicated by a number of Bureau reports on the railroad strike in 1920. For example, the failure of the strike in Arizona was attributed to reports that federal agents were enroute to investigate and press accounts of government activity, "as expressions were heard on the streets indicating that many of the men did not care to 'buck' the Government."[33]

Surprisingly, the Bureau made no secret of some of its most sensitive surveillance methods. When a Washington lawyer named James Stanislaus Easby-Smith complained to Bureau Chief Bielaski that his telephone had been tapped by federal agents, this was denied but, as Easby-Smith subsequently informed President Wilson, Bielaski "at the same time admitted and boasted that he had tapped the telephones of other lawyers, that he did this without the knowledge or consent of the Telephone Company, and that he had experts with instruments by

[29]Report, W. B. Matthews, January 11, 1918, OG 82811, ibid.
[30]Letter, Jno. H. Paulus to Frank Burke, October 18, 1919, and report, Jno. H. Paulus, October 19, 1919, OG 267600, ibid.
[31]Report, L. S. Perkins, May 20, 1918, OG 182787, ibid.
[32]Report, E. Kosterlitzky, May 29, 1919, OG 386663, ibid.
[33]Report, Ralph H. Colvin, April 22, 1920, OG 370556, ibid.; also, letter, A. R. Gere to J. L. Cooper, April 22, 1920, ibid.

which this was easily done."[34] The leader of the ACLU, Roger Baldwin, had the same experience with Special Agent R. W. Finch of the New York field office, when he was brought in to arrange the ACLU records which had been confiscated by the Bureau: "With great pride, he showed me his telephone-tapping equipment and asked if I wanted to listen in on any conversation; he'd put on anyone I named." When Baldwin declined and told the agents of his disgust, "they laughed me off as naive."[35]

The Justice Department was also relatively frank about its use of informers. Attorney General Palmer told Congress that "there are employed in the Bureau of Investigation confidential employees whose duty it is to obtain information upon the activities of the radicals in this country and in pursuit of that duty they have joined organizations ... for the purpose of obtaining such information."[36] Director Burns specifically requested funds for the employment of informants, noting that "We need them badly just now...."[37] It can be argued that even though it was the overriding concern of the Bureau to keep the informers in place and their real identity concealed, that there was a positive side effect to the occasional uncovering of informers, since such incidents tended to create an atmosphere of suspicion and even paranoia among radicals, thereby disrupting their political activities. For example, in 1920 Eugenio Ravarini (D-5) was uncovered by the anarchist Carlo Tresca and was forced to flee for fear of reprisals.[38] At the same time, James Wormley Jones (#800), who had won the confidence of the black nationalist leader Marcus Garvey and worked in his office, was recognized by a physician of the public health service who was aware of his Justice Department connections.[39] In 1923 the Communist Party was shaken when first District Secretary Francis A. Morrow (K-97) surfaced as a government witness at the Bridgman trial against the party leaders and then #854, who had infiltrated the party's national office in New York, was exposed as an informer.[40]

The public acknowledgement of the existence of an extensive network of informers and their occasional exposure undoubtedly had

[34]Link (ed.), *The Papers of Woodrow Wilson*, Vol. 40, 467.
[35]"They Never Stopped Watching Us," 20. The Bureau had used the tapping of telephones extensively since 1908 (see, Jensen, *Price of Vigilance*, 150-151). For an example of the tapping of the telephone of a labor leader during the Red Scare, see report, Wm. M. Doyas, November 3, 1919, OG 303770, RG65, NA.
[36]*AG Palmer on Charges*, 49.
[37]*Appropriations, Department of Justice, 1923*, 135.
[38]Avrich, 179-180.
[39]Hill (ed.), *The Marcus Garvey and UNIA Papers*, Vol. II, 429-430.
[40]For Morrow, see Draper, 371-372; for #854, see letter, Edward J. Brennan to William J. Burns, April 14, 1923, 61-783-unrecorded, RG65, NA.

the effect of creating internal mistrust and fear among radical groups. The members of the Communist Party were dominated by a feeling of paranoia, and much of their time and energies were taken up with mutual accusations of being informers. For example, Louis C. Fraina, the international secretary of the party, was forced to defend himself at an internal party trial against accusations of being a spy for the Justice Department.[41] Informant D.D., who had infiltrated the suspected anarchist group the Union of Russian Workers in New York, described the members' fear of being watched. According to one report, "Berezovsky told us to keep away from two men whom they suspected to be informers,"[42] and a few days later, "Kraskovsky was not inclined to talk much this morning, he said that there is someone among the members of the Union of Russian Workers in this city who keeps the Department of Justice posted as to what is actually going on."[43] The fear that there might be informers in other groups scared the Union from communicating with other radicals, thereby undermining their work: "They fear that there might be some informer among the radicals of the city, and he might spoil their plans, so they will lay low for awhile and then will start to organize."[44]

The Bureau on occasions even engaged in the direct suppression of radical activities, and the use of three methods in particular appear with some frequency in the files: the denial of passport applications, the confiscation of radical publications and raids. In 1918 a passport law had been passed, requiring that all American citizens leaving the US should be issued with a passport. Since the Bureau was given the responsibility of investigating the passport applications for the State Department, this gave it a tremendous influence. In fiscal year 1920 alone, the Bureau conducted some 292,000 name checks in its index and 10,000 field investigations of visa applications.[45] That political opinions and activities were one of the subjects investigated is indicated by the Chicago field office's instructions regarding the

---

[41]Draper, 226-232; Weinstein, *The Decline of Socialism in America*, 230-233. The extent to which the fear of informers disrupted the Communists' activities is indicated by a Bureau surveillance report on a meeting of the Communist controlled Trade Union Education League: "They decided that they will not hold any big meetings as there are too many stool piegons (sic) around but that the regular committee will give instructions to the active members by word of mouth" (Report, A. A. Hopkins, June 26, 1923, 61-714-105, box 4, Series 10, FBI Records, MU).

[42]Report, D.D., December 2, 1919, BS 202600-184, RG65, NA.

[43]Report, D.D., December 13, 1919, ibid.

[44]Report, D.D., January 14, 1920, ibid.

[45]*AG Reports 1918*, 19, and *1920*, 168. Investigations of passport applications of American citizens ceased with the peace resolution of March 3, 1921, but the Bureau was still charged with investigating aliens' passport and visa applications; 20,002 such inquiries were made in FY 1922 and 19,590 in FY 1923 (*AG Reports 1921*, 133; *1922*, 68; *1923*, 69).

investigation of visa applications. According to this, as part of the background inquiry of the applicant, the radical and IWW files in the office should be checked for any references and the neighborhood investigation should determine, among other things, "is he of radical tendencies or a member of any radical society."[46] There are a number of examples which indicate that the Bureau recommended that passport applications be denied for political reasons. When the liberal journalist Amos Pinchot applied for a passport, the Bureau directed the attention of the State Department to his membership of the pacifist American Union Against Militarism and the National Civil Liberties Bureau and recommended that "Before a passport is issued to Mr. Pinchot I think careful consideration should be given to his connection with this organization."[47] In connection with the application of one Martin M. Johnson, the State Department was informed that, according to the Bureau's files, he had been a socialist candidate for mayor in Des Moines, Iowa, and had opposed the war: "In view of these facts it is recommended that the application of this subject for passport be denied."[48] When two officials of the Universal Negro Improvement Association, the organization established by the black nationalist leader Marcus Garvey, sought to visit Africa, the Bureau told the State Department that Garvey "is the cause of the greater portion of the negro agitation in this country" and that in the opinion of the Bureau, "it would be simply furthering the operations of this organization should these passports be granted, and it is therefore requested that same be declined."[49] Thus, the Bureau was able to block the travels of people with objectionable opinions.

A second and even more effective method to suppress radical activities consisted of the silencing of the radical press. Following the expiration of the wartime Espionage Act, which had authorized the government to declare papers which were thought to interfere with the war effort, nonmailable and withdraw their second-class mailing privileges and, in flagrant cases, prosecute their editors,[50] the Bureau was without legal means to directly suppress radical propaganda. Initially, Bureau officials contemplated prohibiting private express

---

[46]Instructions, Edward J. Brennan, att. to letter, Brennan to William J. Flynn, August 3, 1920, 61-01, RG65, NA.
[47]Letter, A. Bruce Bielaski to R. W. Flourney, October 21, 1918, BS 202600-823, ibid.
[48]Letter, J. Edgar Hoover to Chas. B. Welsh, May 6, 1920, JD 202600-16-13 (DJ Invest. Files II).
[49]Hill (ed.), *The Marcus Garvey Papers*, Vol. II, 336.
[50]*AG Report 1918*, 47-54; Peterson & Fite, 92-101; Weinstein, 90-91, 144; Robert A. Bowen, untitled memorandum, n.d. (1919?), box 10, Bowen Papers, Clemson University. The most famous wartime trial against an oppositional paper was the trial against *The Masses* ; for this case see OG 9814, RG65, NA.

companies, which were used by a number of publishers to distribute their papers and avoid government control, from carrying radical publications but this had to be abandoned as long as the papers themselves were legal.[51] Consequently, Attorney General Palmer proposed that a peacetime sedition law be enacted, the intention of which, Hoover made clear in an internal memorandum, was to prevent "the actual printing and sale" of radical publications;[52] in other words, permanent state censorship. While the bill was pending, it was the expressed policy of the Justice Department that it had no legal authority to seize radical publications or otherwise ban them from circulation. In March 1920, Hoover noted that "there is no statute which would give the department authority to hold such literature and because of adverse comment which might arise in connection with the retention of this literature I deem it advisable that we keep copies of same and allow delivery to addresses."[53]

Nevertheless, despite the clear illegality of such acts, the Bureau across the nation took the law into its own hands and suppressed free speech. In Pittsburgh, agents prevented the showing of a radical movie, *The Contrast*.[54] On numerous occasions, shipments of radical literature, including the *Revolutionary Age* and the *Liberator,* were confiscated.[55] One agent, E. B. Sisk of Globe, Arizona, explained the procedure: "I have followed the custom of seizing these papers on search warrant issued on my affidavit that they are believed to contain matters 'seditious and treasonable and intended to be used in the violation of a penal statute of the United States'." This seems to be a somewhat farfetched claim since there was no federal law against radical papers or propaganda, but he argued that he found it entirely proper that literature "which is steadfastly preaching, at least covertly, the overthrow of our Government and the rule of this country by 'the masses' which is nothing but Bolshevist propaganda, should be seized and destroyed...."[56] In San Francisco the Bureau cooperated with the local police in enforcing the California criminal syndicalist law and

---

[51]Claude R. Porter, Memo to Chief, BI, n.d., BS 202600-282, ibid.

[52]J. E. Hoover, memorandum op.cit., October 18, 1919, OG 374217, ibid. For the sedition bill, *Investigation Activities of the Department of Justice,* 14-15.

[53]Letter, J. E. Hoover to Frank H. Stone, March 16, 1920, BS 202600-282, RG65, NA; also, letters, Wm. P. Hazen to Frank Burke, August 21, 1919; Burke to Hazen, August 25, 1919, OG 27151, ibid.

[54]Report, H. J. Lenon, March 10, 1923, 61-792-36, ibid.

[55]See for example, reports, N. H. Castle, August 23 and September 9, 1919; E. Kosterlitzky, February 19, 1920, OG 136944, ibid.; Geo. W. Berg, October 11 and 16, 1919; A. A. Hopkins, May 10, May 29 and June 5, 1920; E. Kosterlitzky, December 9, 1919; letters, Chas. E. Breniman to Frank Burke, October 7 and 16, 1919, BS 202600-282, ibid.

[56]Letter, E. B. Sisk to Thomas A. Flynn, September 3, 1919, ibid.

cracking down on radical newsstands, and it boasted to Washington about the results of its campaign to enforce conformity in the city: "Agent also desires to report that as a result of advice and cooperation on the part of this department, the open circulation and sale of all radical publications in San Francisco is being effectually suppressed by the police in the enforcement of this enactment."[57]

The third and arguably the most effective repressive method was the raid which had the advantage of disrupting the workings of radical organizations by taking into custody their leaders and the most active members and by confiscating their records and literature. This method was perhaps used more frequently during this period than previously believed. As previously noted, the Bureau conducted raids against IWW offices following the Seattle general strike, but the best known operations were the nationwide Palmer raids in November 1919 and January 1920 against alien members of the Union of Russian Workers, the Communist Labor Party and the Communist Party, during which an estimated 10,000 were arrested. Apart from the immediate aim of deporting those detained, the raids undoubtedly had the added effect of intimating other radical aliens; following the arrests of 56 aliens among the striking mine workers in West Virginia, one agent reported that "The arrests of the radicals had had a wonderful effect throughout the district and the foreigners were the first to show signs of willing-ness to return to work."[58] Raids and arrests were also employed to break the nationwide railroad strikes in 1920 and 1922, and during the last one alone some 1,200 striking workers were taken into custody by the Bureau.[59] The frequency of these operations meant that sometimes the mere threat of arrest and deportation was enough to curb radical activities and strikes.[60]

It can be concluded, then, that the Bureau assumed a more ag-gressive position than previously believed, and that the Bureau did not limit its role to the collection of information but attempted to in-timidate radical activists and thereby create an atmosphere of con-formity.

[57]Report, F. W. Kelly, June 23, 1919, OG 359940, ibid.
[58]Report, Ernest W. Lambeth, December 26, 1919, OG 303770, ibid.
[59]A. H. Loula, Weekly Summary of Radical Activities, April 16, 1920, OG 370556, ibid.; *AG Report 1923*, 70. For other examples of the use of raids to break up organizations, see reports, A. A. Hopkins, August 8, 1922, 61-997-11, and September 20, 1922, 61-997-14, RG65, NA.
[60]See for example, report, H. J. Lenon, September 4, 1924, 61-4326-2, ibid. The Bureau also lobbied the immigration authorities and the courts to deny citizenship to radical aliens, see report, Ed Portley, November 23, 1919, OG 303770, ibid.

Defending the Racial order

It has previously been assumed that the Bureau's investigation into black radicalism during the Red Scare did not begin until the summer of 1919 and only after pressure from anxious Southern politicians in the wake of a series of particularly violent race riots.[61] However, there are several arguments which support the contention that the Bureau investigation of black radicalism had been in progress before the summer of 1919 and that it was not initiated as a result of outside pressure. First of all, as previously shown, the Bureau's investigation of black political activities went as far back as the Great Migration in 1916 and had accelerated during the war. In both instances it was assumed by federal officials that black dissatisfaction or unrest was caused by outside agitators, in 1916 by Republican officials and during the war by German agents. It seemed to be an institutionalized attitude among federal officials to suspect that the black population was potentially disloyal to the government.

Moreover, while the Wilson administration was reluctant to condemn lynchings and the assaults of whites against blacks, it seemed prejudiced against the black population, instinctively blaming it for any acts of violence and suspecting it of disloyalty. As previously noted, the Wilson cabinet, half of which was of Southern origins, had since 1913 extended the segregation of blacks throughout the federal administration. The extent to which racial prejudices dominated the Wilson administration is indicated by its response to the race riots during the summer of 1919, which were in all instances triggered by the attacks of white mobs on blacks in an attempt to keep them in a subjugated position.[62] For example, despite the fact that the Washington, DC, riot in July was instigated by white soldiers and sailors, Secretary of the Navy Josephus Daniels apparently took no initiative to restrain the Navy personnel despite requests to do so and privately blamed the riot on the attacks of blacks on white women.[63] Secretary

---

[61]William Cohen, "Riots, Racism, and Hysteria: The Response of Federal Investigative Officials to the Race Riots of 1919," *The Massachusetts Review*, Vol. XIII, No. 3 (Summer 1972), 383; William M. Tuttle, *Race Riot. Chicago in the Red Summer of 1919* (New York, 1975), 227; Coben, *A. Mitchell Palmer*, 213, 316n61; Arthur I. Waskow, *From Race Riot to Sit-In. 1919 and the 1960s* (Garden City, N.Y. (1966), 1967), 188; Mark Ellis, "J. Edgar Hoover and the 'Red Summer' of 1919," *Journal of American Studies*, Vol. 28, No. 1 (April 1994), 39-59. The most detailed study of federal surveillance of black radicals during the Red Scare is Kornweibel's *"Seeing Red."* It describes primarily the intelligence agencies' investigations of the most prominent black leaders and only in passing mentions the inquiries into the race riots. In contrast, the following analysis is concentrated on the BI's investigations into the riots of 1919 and the light they throw on the Bureau's racial attitudes. Although Kornweibel based his account on an exhaustive use of the federal records, he did not use all available primary sources such as the important Robert Bowen papers.

[62]See, Waskow, 12-174; Cohen, 376.

[63]Cronon (ed.), 427; also, Waskow, 24.

179

of the Interior Franklin K. Lane noted in a private letter that "The Negro is a danger that you do not have. Turn him loose and he is a wild man. Every Southerner fears him."[64] When President Wilson was urged by black leaders to make a public statement condemning the attacks and lynchings of blacks, he hesitated until September and then only expressed his "shame as an American citizen at the race riots" in general terms. Since he did not specifically criticize the whites for instigating the violence, he in effect did not distinguish between the white attackers and the black defenders.[65]

In line with this prejudiced attitude toward the blacks, the president was quick to suspect them of disloyalty toward the government. On March 10, 1919, Wilson was reported by his personal physician, Dr. Cary Grayson, of being worried that "the American negro returning from abroad would be our greatest medium in conveying Bolshevism to America." He referred to instances where blacks had demanded higher wages and to the experiences of the black soldiers in France, where they had been treated on equal terms with the whites, something which Wilson thought had gone to their heads.[66] In other words, the Wilson administration needed no outside pressure to suspect blacks of disloyalty.

It is apparent that the Bureau had been investigating black radicalism in the strictest secrecy for some time before the riots. On July 29, Governor W. P. Hobby of Texas requested the Attorney General to ascertain "if there is not an ulterior or Bolsheviki influence at work in an organized way to incite race trouble in the South."[67] Bureau Assistant Director and Chief Frank Burke instructed the San Antonio field office to cooperate fully with the Texas authorities and to receive any information they might possess, but he added that the Bureau had been investigating black radical activities for some time: "This work, however, is highly confidential and the fact that the Bureau is making such an investigation should not be given publicity in any way."[68]

In fact, the Bureau had been investigating black political activities ever since the Armistice. One reason was the administration's concern

---

[64]Lane and Lane (eds.), 313.

[65]Link (ed.), *The Papers of Woodrow Wilson*, Vol. 61, 576; Vol. 62, 233-234, 260, 313; Vol. 63, 196.

[66]Ibid., Vol. 55, 471.

[67]Letters, W. P. Hobby to A. Mitchell Palmer, July 29, 1919; Hobby to C. E. Breniman, July 29, 1919; Breniman to Frank Burke, July 31, 1919, OG 369955, RG65, NA.

[68]Personal and Confidential letter, Burke to Breniman, August 4, 1919, ibid. For the ensuing Bureau investigation into IWW and Bolshevik propaganda among blacks in Texas, see, letters, J. V. Bell to Breniman, January 20, 1920; Bell to E. A. Hegan, January 15, 1920, ibid.; report, F. M. Spencer, November 4, 1919; letter, Breniman, November 8, 1919, OG 382422, ibid.; report, W. W. Green, September 17, 1919, OG 382476, ibid.

180

that black leaders, who intended to participate in the Pan African Congress in Paris, would lobby the Peace Conference on behalf of the world's black population and possibly embarrass the administration by criticizing the racial conditions in the US.[69] In December 1918, the Bureau received the alarming news from an informant that the National Equal Rights League led by the prominent civil rights activist William Monroe Trotter intended to send delegates to lobby at the Peace Conference, and in April 1919 it turned over its extensive file on the organization to the State Department.[70] The Bureau's main worry was that W. E. B. Du Bois, editor of the *Crisis* and a leading figure of the NAACP, might turn up in Paris and disturb the proceedings. Special Agent J. G. C. Carraway reported that Du Bois was a "'rock-the-boat' type," accused him of harboring both German and socialistic sympathies and warned that he might try to "introduce Socialistic tendencies at the Peace Conference." Carraway recommended that Du Bois be kept under constant surveillance while in Paris and he was highly suspicious of the black delegates who were going to Paris: "The question is – who is behind the peace delegates, and the finances?.... It is very important that this be thoroughly investigated, and an attempt made to establish *who* is behind the whole affair. It is hard to tell what effect this propaganda will have at the peace table."[71] The Bureau, then, at an early stage was investigating black activities because of the government's foreign policy interests.

The Bureau was also closely watching black radical activities during the early part of 1919. For example, as early as March the speeches of the black socialists A. Philip Randolph and Chandler Owen were monitored and the circulation of their paper, the *Messenger,* was investigated.[72] Bureau officials were also eager to resume the surveillance of the most prominent civil rights organization, the NAACP, which had been halted during the war. In late November 1918, Bureau Chief Bielaski directed the attention of the Justice Department to the NAACP because he felt that it had intentionally misquoted President

---

[69]For the State Department's opposition to the Pan African Congress, see, Link (ed.), *The Papers of Woodrow Wilson*, Vol. 54, 126; for the Congress, see, Kellogg, 277-284.

[70]Report, J. G. C. Corcoran, December 23, 1918, OG 369936, RG65, NA. The Bureau informed the State Department that the National Equal Rights League "has been the subject of considerable investigation on our part in the past" (Letter, W. E. Allen to L. L. Winslow, April 5, 1919, ibid.).

[71]J. G. C. Carraway, Memorandum for Mr. Benham, December 3, 1918, OG 17011, ibid. Possibly the Bureau informed the State Department about Du Bois; in May 1919 the Bureau acting chief noted that "the files of this office contain ... voluminous reports on the activities of its (i.e. *The Crisis'*) editor ..." (Letter, W. E. Allen to Wm. Offley, May 23, 1919, ibid.).

[72]Reports, R. W. Finch, March 10, 1919; A. H. Loula, July 7, 1919; M. J. Davis, July 31, 1919, OG 258421, ibid.; H. A. Lewis, May 8, 1919, OG 265716, ibid.

Wilson, but the Department saw no reason for reopening the case.[73] However, in May 1919, when the Bureau received information from the Office of Naval Intelligence to the effect that articles in the recent issues of the NAACP paper the *Crisis* "would tend to inflame the Negro race," Washington directed the New York office to collect copies of the paper and to "keep in touch with this paper and report when it contains any articles of a doubtful character."[74] The Louisville, Kentucky, office launched an investigation of the NAACP's agitation against lynchings and discrimination, explaining that "such literature naturally has not a healthy effect upon the colored people ..." In other words, in the opinion of the Bureau the fundamental racial problem was not the repression of the black population but its attempts to fight back, – and the agents betrayed their prejudice when they noted that the fact that several well-educated blacks had refused to cooperate with the Bureau proved that "education makes a Negro somewhat irresponsible."[75]

On July 2, 1919, Robert A. Bowen, director of the Justice Department's Bureau of Translations and Radical Publications in New York, compiled a report, entitled "Radicalism and Sedition Among the Negroes as Reflected in Their Publications." This was some three weeks before the outbreak of the first of the major race riots, in Washington, DC, and almost two months before Southern congressmen made their demands for a federal investigation. The tone of the report indicates that leading federal officials had been concerned about black radicalism for some time.

According to the report, "dangerous influences" were at work among the blacks and there existed a "concerted effort, abetted by certain prominent white publicists, to arouse in the negro a well-defined class-consciousness, sympathetic only with the most malign radical movements." In the opinion of Bowen, "the negro masses" might become a dangerous power in the hands of the ablest black editors and writers, whom Bowen accused of preaching violence in retaliation for lynchings and of advocating the cause of the IWW and Bolshevism. Bowen

---

[73]A. Bruce Bielaski, Memorandum for Mr. Bettman, November 22, 1918; Alfred Bettman, Memorandum for Mr. Bielaski, January 9, 1919, OG 306451, ibid.
[74]Letters, Geo. M. Williams to W. E. Allen, May 14, 1919, with att. report; W. E. Allen to W. M. Offley, May 23, 1919; W. M. Offley to W. E. Allen, June 10, 1919; report, A. W. Willet, July 3, 1919, OG 17011, ibid.
[75]Report, N. B. Brennan, July 14, 1919, BS 198940, ibid.; also, reports, N. B. Brennan, June 24, 26, 28, July 2, 21, 1919, ibid. The Bureau failed in its attempt to prosecute the NAACP and to have its literature barred from the mails (Letters, SAC to William J. Flynn, August 31, 1919; Frank Burke to William H. Lamar, September 15, 1919, with. att. telegrams; Lamar to Burke, September 23, 1919, OG 17011, ibid.). Another black organization which was investigated in early 1919 was The League of Colored People (report, R. W. Finch, March 10, 1919, OG 258421, ibid.).

traced the radicalization of the black population to their participation in the war and noted that the radicalism of the black press had "become remarkably accelerated" during the first half of 1919. He characterized the *Negro World* as "an avowedly radical sheet," and accused the *Messenger* of "negro sedition and flagrant disloyalty." Although it was Bowen's main argument that blacks were becoming radicalized, and he noted that an attempt was being made to establish an "organized alignment with the most destructive forces of our political life today" and to indoctrinate blacks to become "strongly race conscious and class conscious," he mentioned no other specific political demands by blacks. What he characterized and criticized as black radicalism was, in fact, the increasing determination of blacks in 1919 to defend and even retaliate against lynchings and other injustices. Bowen was particularly worried about "a sense of resentment and race antagonism," "the tone of menace and the threat of violent resistance," "a dangerous sense of racial antagonism," "increasing defiance" and "he is encouraged to become increasingly more insolently scornful." In other words, at bottom Bowen was concerned about the black community's increasing unwillingness to accept its place in the existing racial hierarchy and he tended to personify the unrest as caused by radical agitators. As Bowen concluded his report, "It is not, in my opinion, an attitude that the government can safely ignore."[76] The Bureau's approach to the black community even before the outbreaks of the riots was characterized by an attempt to uphold the racial order.

The Red Summer of 1919

The assumption that the Bureau was pressured into investigating black radicalism is primarily based on a chain of public statements. On July 30, following the Washington, DC, riot and immediately after the outbreak of the Chicago riot, Attorney General Palmer stated that the riots "were due solely to local conditions and were not inspired by Bolshevik or other radical propaganda" despite the fact that the Bolsheviks had spent a large amount of money and distributed a large quantity of literature in the South but apparently to no avail.[77] Palmer's statement has been explained with the supposition that he

---

[76]Robert A. Bowen, Radicalism and Sedition Among the Negroes as Reflected in Their Publications, July 2, 1919, box 10, Bowen Papers, Clemson University Libraries. Bowen himself was from Charleston, South Carolina, where he had grown up on plantations in the decades following the Civil War and he vehemently shared the racial attitudes of the white South (for Bowen, see Register to the Robert Adger Bowen Papers, ibid.).
[77]"No Bolshevism in Riots," *The New York Times*, July 31, 1919.

was either unaware of the Bureau's activities or later opportunistically changed his mind to take advantage of the Red Scare.[78] On August 25, Representative James F. Byrnes of South Carolina in a speech in Congress blamed radical black leaders of having instigated the recent riots. Byrnes wondered whether it was more than a coincidence that a number of cities so widely separated had simultaneously been engulfed in racial conflicts and he quoted long passages from the *Crisis* and the *Messenger,* claiming that "They show that the negro leaders had deliberately planned a campaign of violence." Byrnes also pointed out that the *Messenger* must have been financed by outside sources, since the publication was printed on expensive, fine-quality paper and carried only a few advertisements: "It is evident that the IWW is financing it in an effort to have the negro of America join it in their revolutionary plans." Byrnes ended by calling on the government to keep the black press under surveillance and to use the wartime Espionage Act to prosecute black leaders.[79] The following day the *New York Times* reported that unidentified "officials" of the Justice Department agreed with Byrnes' accusations, characterized them as "well founded" and pointed out that radical papers "were springing up over the country." The article ended by noting: "Agents of the Department of Justice are investigating. Facts thus far developed lead officials to believe that IWW and Soviet influence were at the bottom of the recent race riots in Washington and Chicago."[80] There was a clear contradiction between Palmer's earlier denial of Bolshevik complicity and the Justice Department's support of Byrnes, and the change of opinion has been explained as a spontaneous reaction to Byrnes' speech. According to William M. Tuttle, Jr., "Partly as a consequence of Byrnes' accusation, the Justice Department initiated an investigation of radicalism and sedition among black people."[81] However, an analysis of the Bureau files on the investigation into the riots suggests a somewhat different explanation for the Bureau's behavior, namely that the federal authorities began the inquiry on their own initiative, and that the progress of this internal investigation accounts for the Justice Department's shifting positions.

The wave of race riots, which swept the nation in what has been called the "Red Summer" of 1919, numbering some 25 major riots

---

[78]For the claim that he was unaware of the ongoing inquiry, see, Kornweibel, *No Crystal Stair,* 101n16; for the claim that Palmer changed his mind, see Tuttle, 228; Coben, *A. Mitchell Palmer,* 213, 316n61.

[79]"Blames Race Riot on Negro Leaders," *The New York Times,* August 26, 1919; Kornweibel, *No Crystal Stair,* 85-87.

[80]"Russian Reds and IWW Blamed for Race Riots," *The New York Times,* August 27, 1919.

[81]Tuttle, 227.

that left more than 120 dead, was primarily caused by the Great Migration. An estimated 450,000 blacks had left the oppression in the South in search of freedom and opportunities in the industrial cities in the North. On the one hand, the blacks were met by an increasing white hostility because black laborers were often used as low-paid strike breakers, white opposition to integrated neighborhoods, and white determination to preserve the social and racial status quo. This white backlash manifested itself in a record number of 78 lynchings in 1919 and in the bombings of several black residents in white neighborhoods. On the other hand, the experiences of the 400,000 black soldiers who had participated in the war to make the world safe for democracy had dramatically changed the attitude of the black community. "The New Negro," as the new generation of proud and self-assured blacks were known, was militantly determined to defend himself and even to retaliate against any injustices and assaults.[82] Bureau officials had for a long time been suspicious of black loyalty and, as indicated by Bowen's report, feared that the black population was being aroused to challenge the racial order. It reacted promptly to the riots, and as Frank Burke informed the MID in early August, while the Bureau had only paid limited attention to radical propaganda among blacks at first, later developments, meaning the riots, had caused them to step up their surveillance.[83] The Bureau did not need any outside pressure and was already involved when the first demands for federal investigations were made by Southern politicians. In line with the racial thinking of Bureau officials since at least 1916, Bureau officials and agents' instinctive reaction to black discontent was to personify it; in 1916 and 1917 the troublemakers were thought to be Republicans and Germans, now radical agitators were believed to the the instigators.

On July 19, following several racial clashes in, among other places, Charleston, North Carolina, and Longview, Texas, rumors of attempted assaults by blacks on white women in Washington, DC, exaggerated by an irresponsible and senationalist press, led to attacks and attempted lynchings of blacks by mobs of white soldiers and sailors. When groups of blacks decided to fight back, the events escalated into a four day riot with 6 dead and about 100 injured.[84] In line with its long-time policy, the Bureau ignored the issue of civil

---

[82]La Feber & Polenberg, 117-119; Tuttle, 21-31, 74-92, 101-226, 262; Waskow, 38-40; Kornweibel, *No Crystal Stair*, 88-94; Cohen, 376-379.

[83]Henry G. Sebastian, Memorandum for Colonel A. B. Coxe, August 9, 1919, MID 10218-361-3, Glasser file (Federal Surveillance of Afro-Americans, 1917-25: Microfilm).

[84]Waskow, 21-33.

rights violations and immediately launched an investigation into possible radical activity. Although the Bureau found no evidence of radical complicity, it did to a certain degree succeed in blaming the blacks for the riot instead of the whites who had actually initiated the violence. Though some agents did find that the blacks had only defended themselves,[85] one agent reported after having interviewed white witnesses that the riot was brought on by "an infuriated populace made so by the open and frequent assaults of negroes on white women in this city."[86] Another agent also rejected that radical propaganda had played any role but at the same time concluded that the racial tension was due to a mixture of the black population's distrust of the police, the "mixing of the races" and assaults by blacks on whites.[87] The overall impression created by the Bureau reports was that even if the violence had been started by the whites, it was a justifiable reaction to the presence of blacks in the city and their assaults on white women. In other words, the Bureau supported the white community's attempt at defending the existing racial hierarchy with violent means. At the same time, these reports may explain the background for Attorney General Palmer's statement on July 30, in which he rejected the view that the recent unrest had been caused by radical influences. Since the results of the Washington, DC, investigation was the only information available to the Justice Department (no reports on the Chicago riot had yet been received), this was most likely the basis for Palmer's opinion. The reason why the Justice Department later changed its position is to be found in the development of the Bureau's next investigation.

Just five days after the Washington, DC, riot had subsided, a clash between blacks and whites on a Chicago beach turned into the most serious riot of 1919. Due to violent gangs, a sensational press and completely unprepared local authorities, it lasted for five days, resulted in 38 dead and some 500 injured, and was quelled at last with the employment of the state militia.[88] It has previously been assumed that the Bureau only played a minor role in the official response to the

---

[85]Reports, W. W. Wright, July 22, 1919; M. E. Tucker, July 22, 1919; P. M. Kamon, July 31, 1919, OG 369936, RG65, NA.

[86]Report, F. C. Baggarly, July 23, 1919, ibid.

[87]Report, M. A. Joyce, July 30, 1919, ibid. In contrast to the Bureau, the MID seemed to believe that a secret black society, the "Boule," had organized the riot and submitted a report containing such an allegation which had been received from MI4, the British Military Intelligence (Report on Washington Riot, n.d., ibid.; see also, Cohen, 390-396; for the "Boule," see Hill (ed.), *Garvey Papers*, Vol. II, 24n3).

[88]Tuttle, 3-10, 32-66; Waskow, 38, 41-44.

Chicago riot,[89] but just two days after the outbreak of the riot, Assistant Director and Chief Frank Burke instructed the Chicago field office to ascertain if radical propaganda among the blacks had caused the riot.[90] At the same time, news of the investigation was apparently leaked to the press. The same day the *New York Tribune* was able to disclose that the Justice Department and the Lusk Committee were looking into the theory that the IWW, financed by Soviet Russia, had plotted the recent riots.[91] The Bureau, then, reacted instinctively and began searching among the blacks for subversive influences, a reaction which reflected the Bureau's underlying prejudices and tendency to personify social unrest.

The Chicago office invested a considerable amount of time and energy in its search for evidence of radical involvement in the riot. Agents interviewed and received information from local authorities, union officials, packers, realtors, workers and black leaders, but they all denied that radicalism had played any part in the unrest and instead they pointed to the social, economic and racial dislocations and conflicts in the wake of the great influx of blacks before and during the war.[92] Nevertheless, the tone of several reports indicated the agents' prejudiced attitude toward the black population. For example, one agent noted that an employer who was opposed to social equality and favored segregation "seems to know and understand the race problem in Chicago better than any man whom agent has interviewed."[93] Whereas interviews with whites apparently were reported impartially and without personal comments, Mrs. Ida Wells-Barnett, a founding member of the NAACP, was called a "notorious race agitator." She was condescendingly referred to as one who was looked upon by the black community as "a sort of super-woman, who does big things for the negro race," and the agent summarized her remarks in the following way: "Her statements was the old, old story about the maltreatment of the colored people in the South."[94]

---

[89]According to Waskow, the Bureau's only contribution was an investigation of some fires during the riot: "The federal government made no other official entrance into the Chicago riot" (Waskow, 45). Kornweibel, *"Seeing Red,"* 42-43, 84-85, 165, briefly mentions the BI investigation.

[90]Telegram, Frank Burke to Brennan, July 29, 1919, OG 369914, RG65, NA.

[91]"Reds Accused of Stirring up Negro Rioters," *The New York Tribune,* July 29, 1919, clipping in OG 3057, ibid.

[92]Reports, A. H. Loula, July 30 and 31, 1919; J. Spolansky, August 1, 1919; Mills Kitchin, August 2 and 7, 1919; J. P. Folsom, August 4 and 7, 1919; T. F. Muller, August 7, 1919, OG 369914, ibid.

[93]Report, Mills Kitchin, August 7, 1919, ibid.

[94]Report, Mills Kitchin, August 2, 1919, ibid.

Despite the overwhelming mass of evidence pointing toward the underlying social, racial and economic conditions as the causes of the riot, the Bureau nevertheless ended up by concluding that radical propaganda after all had played a role. The most likely explanation of how this was possible is that the Bureau officials were following their instinctive mistrust of the loyalty of blacks. One report, after having noted all the evidence pointing toward the Great Migration and the following conflicts as the basic reason for the riot, added that one of the "contributing causes" was the radical black press. The agent singled out the *Defender,* which was accused of waging "a campaign of hate against the white race." The report concluded by naming one Frank A. Dennison, a black Colonel, as "the chief individual agitator," and by accusing the *Chicago Tribune* of fomenting unrest by "continually setting up false standards of social equality," aided by Mrs. Wells-Barnett and the *Messenger,* which was described "as incendiary as the Tribune is inaccurate."[95] Another report on the radical press in Chicago stressed its demands that blacks should defend themselves and fight for their rights and its attempt to "create class feeling."[96] The Bureau officials in Washington ignored the evidence pointing toward the underlying causes and instead chose to focus on the Chicago agents' allegations. On August 13, twelve days before Byrnes' accusations against the IWW and the Bolsheviks and his calls for government intervention, Frank Burke directed that an "immediate and vigorous investigation" be made of the black press in Chicago: "I am particularly anxious to determine whether or not the IWW organization or other radical elements are sending funds to the encouragement of the negro agitation."[97] Clearly, according to the thinking of Bureau officials, the black population had to be responsible for the riots and they in turn had to have been led astray by subversive elements.

Thus, when Justice Department officials confirmed Byrnes' allegations on August 26, they merely made public what they were trying to prove internally, namely that the IWW or some other radical organization had financed the radical black press and thereby instigated the unrest which led to the riot. Motivated by its political and racial ideology and assumptions, and in direct contrast with the

---

[95]Ibid.

[96]Report, A. H. Loula, August 2, 1919, ibid.

[97]Letter, Frank Burke to Edward Brennan, August 13, 1919, ibid. The investigation found evidence of increasing IWW propaganda following the riot but it never seemed able to find any firm proof that the IWW had financed the black press or instigated the riot (report, J. Spolansky, August 29, 1919; letter, Burke to Brennan, June 21, 1920, ibid.).

overwhelming mass of evidence at hand, the Bureau independently had reached the same conclusions as Byrnes and other Southern politicians. In fact, the similarities between the Bureau's internal deliberations of August 13 and Byrnes' speech of August 25 (both focused on the theme of possible IWW funding of the black radical press and both singled out the *Messenger* as particularly objectionable) leave open the possibility that Justice Department or Bureau officials had provided Byrnes with his extracts from the black press. Although this is only conjecture and no evidence to support it can be found in the primary sources,[98] it would be in keeping with Bureau practice of leaking information to the public which it was then in a position to authoritively confirm.

On October 1, a deputy sheriff and a railroad special agent were shot outside a black church in Hoop Spurr, near Elaine in Philips County, Arkansas, which sparked off violent clashes between the races. The area was not pacified until federal troops were deployed on the following day. Local whites claimed that the blacks in the church had been planning an armed insurrection and eventually 122 blacks were indicted of whom 12 were found guilty of first-degree murder and sentenced to death while a large number of blacks were given long prison terms. However, later studies have established that a number of black sharecroppers led by the black farmer Robert L. Hill had organized the Progressive Farmers and Household Union of America in order to bargain collectively with the white planters about the price of their cotton. Determined to break up the union, a group of whites had opened fire on the church and, when the black sharecroppers and farmers tried to defend themselves, had hunted them down. Whereas only five whites were killed, an estimated 50 to 60 blacks died.[99]

The Little Rock field office was immediately instructed to investigate and it dispatched Special Agent W. R. McElveen to the trouble spot. On the one hand, McElveen found no evidence to support the view that the blacks had planned a massacre on the whites, and in particular he found that the rumors concerning a cache of arms and ammunition were based on a misunderstanding since it had no relation to the riot.[100] On the other hand, the Bureau reports presented a view of the

---

[98]As far as can be determined, the Bureau files in RG65, NA, contain no information on any cooperation with Byrnes, and the Byrnes Papers in Clemson University Libraries likewise have no information concerning his August 25, 1919 speech (letter from Michael Kohl, Head, Special Collections, Clemson University Libraries, January 20, 1995).

[99]Waskow, 121-140.

[100]Telegram, Frank Burke to McElveen, October 2, 1919; memorandum, McElveen, October 3, 1919; telegram, Burke to McElveen, October 4, 1919; report, McElveen, October 5, 1919; telegrams, Murray to Burke, October 6, 1919; Burke to McElveen, October 7, 1919; report, McElveen, October 8, 1919; telegram, McElveen, to Burke, October 9, 1919; report,

black farmers and the riot which was very much in accordance with the racial attitude of the Bureau. According to the Bureau, the black farmers were an ignorant lot, easily led astray by the unscrupulous agitator, Robert Hill. One report noted in connection with Hill's propaganda: "This of course would deceive only the ignorant, but the negroes were mostly of that kind."[101] According to McElveen, there was no question about who was to blame for the outbreak of the violence. Hill and another union leader, V. S. Powell, were "the real instigators of the whole matter,"[102] who had stirred up the blacks in the church to start firing on the whites without provocation. McElveen also repeated an unfounded local rumor that the black insurrectionists had received outside assistance when he noted that "some indication white man advising."[103]

The prejudiced attitude of the Bureau agents and their inclination to side with the whites was most clearly reflected in the agents' close cooperation with the local white elite and their almost uncritical acceptance of its views. The agents' conclusions were to a large extent based on information furnished by the local authorities.[104] One agent, E. J. Kerwin, even went so far as to share the fruits of the Bureau's investigation with the white planters, explaining his clear abandonment of any pretense of neutrality with the comment: "The planters here and plantation owners who were working large number of negro families were very much interested in what had been going on and I took the time and trouble to inform them what we had found and showed the the (sic) constitution and by laws of the negro union also cards used." Kerwin made it his business to tell the worried planters about the black sharecroppers' demands and advised them to put informants among the blacks, and he was able to report that the planters felt reassured by the Bureau's intervention: "They all seemed to rest easier however with the knowledge that the government thru this department had simply let it be known that investigations were being made, as they informed me the good results would over come all that the negroes had already done, because they were afraid of the government and did not want any trouble in that way or from that

McElveen, October 9, 1919, OG 373159, RG65, NA.
[101]Report, C. M. Walser and C. H. Maxey, October 10, 1919, ibid.
[102]Memorandum, McElveen, December 30, 1919, ibid.
[103]Report, McElveen, October 4, 1919; telegram, McElveen to Burke, October 6, 1919, ibid. Local whites accused a white attorney, O. S. Bratton, of being a co-conspirator since he had been hired by the union to represent it in the dispute with the planters (Waskow, 123, 126-128).
[104]Report, McElveen, October 4, 1919, OG 373159, RG65, NA.

source."[105] Thus, the Bureau was already investigating and, in effect, lending its support to the local white elite in its efforts to break the black union, when the *New York Times* on October 8 hinted that the IWW might have instigated the riot and called on the Attorney General to investigate "at once."[106] Although the Bureau was unable to find any evidence of a radical conspiracy behind the unrest, the Bureau in its final report on the Elaine riot again put the blame for the violence squarely on the shoulders of the black community by characterizing the conflict as a "negro insurrection" and a black "uprising."[107]

The Bureau's main problem, however, was that its investigations had failed to turn up any direct links between radical activities and the riots. The Bureau's attempt to get around the unfortunate lack of evidence was first presented in an internal memorandum by J. Edgar Hoover in the middle of October in what was to become the Bureau's and the Justice Department's official version of the events. According to the Radical Division chief, the Bureau's inquiry had found that "the direct cause" of each riot "was purely local," but that "it is no doubt quite true that a secondary cause of the trouble was due to propaganda of a radical nature." Hoover did not present any evidence to support his theory although he did mention that the *Messenger* contained "the most notorious instances of radical propaganda...."[108] Thus, while admitting that the riots had been caused by local problems, Hoover still managed, without any proof whatsoever, to implicate radical propaganda in the riots. Hoover followed up when he, in a response to a request from Assistant Attorney General Francis Garvan, directed William Keohan of the Radical Publications Section to prepare a summary "in connection with the negro activities and in particular the activities of the 'Messenger'...."[109]

The Justice Department also began shaping the public opinion by selected leaks which emphasized the extent and influence of radical agitation among blacks. On October 19, the *New York Times* informed its readers that "Evidence is in the possession of the Government of the efforts of agitators of the IWW, Bolshevists, and radical Socialist groups to stir up discontent among the negroes ..." According to

---

[105]Memorandum, E. J. Kerwin to McElveen, November 4, 1919, ibid.

[106]"Plotters Behind the Plot," *The New York Times*, October 8, 1919.

[107]George F. Ruch, Memorandum for Mr. Hoover. Negro Insurrection at Hoot Spur and Elaine, in Philips County, Arkansas, January 3, 1920, OG 373159, RG65, NA. Ruch apparently based his report on a report by McElveen, December 30, 1919, ibid., which also called the riot an "uprising."

[108]J. E. Hoover, Memorandum Upon Work of Radical Division, August 1, 1919, to October 15, 1919, October 18, 1919, OG 374217, RG65, NA.

[109]Hoover, Report of Radical Section for Week Ending October 10, 1919, ibid.

unnamed "Federal officials," "the doctrines of Lenin and Trotzky are being circulated among negroes in all parts of the country" by means of newspapers, magazines and black organizations. The article concluded by hinting at sinister influences: "This propaganda among negroes is well financed and it is understood that the authorities know the source of the funds."[110] In early November, the *Chicago Daily News,* which apparently had been granted access by Garvan, was able to quote from the Justice Department's forthcoming report on the radical attitudes of the black press, thereby creating a public demand that the report be made public.[111]

The Justice Department made public two reports on the cause of the riots. The first, entitled "Radicalism and Sedition Among the Negroes as Reflected in Their Publications," was compiled by Robert A. Bowen as a follow-up to his first report of July 2 and published as a part of the Attorney General's report of November 17 to the Congress on the department's investigation of radicalism. The second, entitled "Agitation Among the Negroes," was prepared by George Ruch of the Radical Division and submitted to Congress on June 1, 1920, as part of the Department's report on the activities of the Radical Division.[112] Despite differences, they agreed that radical agitation and activities had not been the immediate cause of the riots but that the radicals instead had taken advantage of the conflicts to spread their ideas and, thereby, aggravate the disturbances. Bowen's report dealt primarily with the contents of the black press and did not deal with the riots specifically, but he did note that the radical black leaders had "been quick to avail themselves of the situation as cause for the utterance of inflammatory sentiment ...";[113] in other words, the radicals reacted to the riots but did not directly cause them. Ruch was more explicit when he stated that the Bureau had not found "any concerted movement on the part of negroes to cause a general uprising throughout the country" and the cause of each riot "was purely local." However, with the exception of Chicago, Ruch ignored the fact that the riots had begun with attacks by whites on the blacks and that these had only defended

---

[110]"Reds Are Working Among Negroes," *The New York Times,* October 19, 1919.
[111]Waskow, 77-78, 188.
[112]The Bowen report can be found in *Investigation Activities of the Department of Justice,* 161-187, and the Ruch report in *AG Palmer on Charges,* 189-190. The Bowen report was published without identifying the author, giving rise to speculation that Hoover was the author (see, Waskow, 189; Cohen, 382n21). The Bureau's copy of the report is unsigned (report, October 29, 1919, OG 3057, RG65, NA), but the original draft, dated October 28, 1919, and signed by Bowen can be found in box 10, Bowen Papers, Clemson University Libraries. Ruch's authorship of the second report is indicated by his initials GFR on the draft in the Bureau files (report, Negro Agitation, May 14, 1920, OG 3057, RG65, NA).
[113]*Investigation Activities of the Department of Justice,* 162.

themselves and in some cases retaliated, and he put all of the blame on the black community. According to Ruch, the riot in Washington, DC, and a clash in Omaha, Nebraska, were at least to a certain degree caused by assaults by blacks on white women, and the violence at Elaine originated with the black union.[114]

Nevertheless, neither report thought that radical propaganda was immaterial. Ruch elaborated on Hoover's earlier theory and argued that the agitation undoubtedly constituted "a secondary cause" of the riots, since "there has always appeared the stirring up of the racial hatred upon the part of radical publications." Ruch went on to note the activity of the Communist Party, the IWW and Marcus Garvey's Universal Negro Improvement Association and quoted from, among others, the *Messenger,* which according to Ruch "had been able to effectively fan the flames of discontent." However, the only direct link, which Ruch was able to bring to light, was a single "very vicious leaflet" which had been distributed during the Washington, DC, riot.[115] Bowen more explicitly advanced the thesis that radical black leaders, financed by unknown sources, subverted the loyalty of the black community. According to Bowen, the agitation of the black press in support of "open defiance and ... counsel of retaliation" reflected "a well-concerted movement among a certain class of Negro leaders of thought and action to constitute themselves a determined and persistent source of a radical opposition to the Government, and to the established rule of law and order." Bowen noted that these radical editors were mostly "men of education," at least one of whom had a Harvard degree, and their magazines were of such a high quality that they must be in "the possession of ample funds." According to Bowen, they were attempting "to induce" their readers to "'seeing red'". Again, then, the image of the cunning agitators leading the otherwise contented blacks astray.

An analysis of Bowen's reasons for criticizing the radical black press adds support to the argument that Bureau officials were more worried about the growing black opposition and challenge to the existing racial hierarchy than about black political radicalism. He did mention "the identification of the Negro with such radical organizations as the IWW and an outspoken advocacy of the Bolsheviki or Soviet doctrines" and "the political stand assumed toward the present Federal administration, the South in general, and incidentally, toward the peace treaty and the League of Nations" as attitudes of the black press which

---

[114]*AG Palmer on Charges,* 190.
[115]Ibid., 189-190.

constituted a serious threat to the government. However, it is clear from the context that he was primarily worried that the black press propagandized the message of "race consciousness," which according to Bowen was "always antagonistic of the white race and openly, defiantly assertive of its own equality and even superiority." He reserved the major part of his criticism for such expressions of black opposition to the racial order as "the ill-governed reaction toward race rioting," meaning the determination of blacks to defend themselves, "the threat of retaliatory measures in connection with lynching," and "the more openly expressed demand for social equality, in which demand the sex problem is not infrequently included," meaning the white tabu, interracial relationship or marriages.[116] In other words, Bowen equated blacks defending themselves against lynchings and aspiring to gain social equality as a threat to the system of racial subordination and thus to law and order. This attitude was underlined by the report's extensive quotations from the black press, primarily the *Messenger,* where the themes of black self-consciousness, the need for blacks to organize and to protect themselves against lynchings and other injustices were mentioned more frequently as examples of "the dangerous spirit of defiance and venegeance" than the themes of political radicalism or Bolshevism.[117] The Bureau, then, was primarily disturbed, not by the alleged political radicalization of blacks, but by their increasing racial consciousness. As one contemporary critic of the report noted, the report did not prove the existence of a seditious conspiracy among the black population, "it simply shows that the negro has just grounds for complaint at his treatment in this country, and has sense enough to know it and sense enough to say it in a clear, intelligent and forcible way. Indeed, it seems that this latter is what shocks the writer of the report more than anything else."[118]

Although the Bureau acknowledged that the causes of the riots in 1919 were purely local and that they were not part of a radical conspiracy, the introduction of the theory that radical propaganda had constituted a secondary cause and the publication of Bowen's report on the black radical press shortly after the riots both tended to obscure the Bureau's conclusion and instead left the general impression that radical agitation, after all, had somehow influenced the blacks and been responsible for the riots. The Bureau thereby helped to divert

---

[116]*Investigation Activities of the Department of Justice,* 162.
[117]Ibid., 163-187; quotation from p. 187.
[118]James Weldon Johnson, "Views and Reviews. Report of the Department of Justice on Sedition Among Negroes," *The New York Age,* December 20, 1919, clipping in box 10, Bowen Papers, Clemson University Libraries.

attention away from the underlying social, racial and economic factors behind the unrest. There are indications that the Bureau's arguments had considerable impact on the ensuing political debate on how to prevent future racial clashes. The Bowen report was given extensive publicity; for example, extracts were printed in the *New York Times,* and the *New York World* reprinted portions of it verbatim, calling it "a most exhaustive study" and claiming that "some startling revelations concerning the activities toward radicalism among the negroes are made."[119] The Justice Department also distributed the report to various opinion leaders.[120] When Congress debated a resolution introduced by Senator Charles Curtis of Kansas, calling on the Senate Judiciary Committee to investigate riots and lynchings with an aim toward passing a federal anti-lynching law, the Justice Department helped to derail the debate by informing Congress that it was investigating radical involvement in the riots. Attorney General Palmer told the Judiciary Committee about the numerous "appeals to racial hatred" made by radicals on behalf of the blacks.[121] Black leaders were forced on the defensive and compelled to show that their calls for equal rights and for resistance against attacks and lynchings were not un-American or Bolshevistic propaganda.[122] It might be argued that the federal government cooperated with the Southern white establishment in using the Red Scare to contain the black population at the bottom of the racial hierarchy.

The Surveillance of Black Radicals

During the Red Scare between 1919 and 1924, the Justice Department repeatedly claimed to have uncovered evidence of Communist or radical influence behind black political activities. In November 1919, Attorney General Palmer informed Congress that the radical movement looked upon the black population "as particularly fertile ground" for spreading their propaganda, in effect questioning the loyalty of all blacks: "These radical organizations have endeavored to enlist Negroes

---

[119]"Radicalism Among Negroes Growing, U.S. Record Shows," *The New York World,* November 17, 1919, clipping in box 10, Bowen Papers, Clemson University Libraries.

[120]Letters, J. Edgar Hoover to Colonel John A. Dapray, November 25, 1919; Francis P. Garvan to H. C. Lyman, January 8, 1920; Garvan to Emmett J. Scott, December 4, 1919, OG 3057, RG65, NA.

[121]The Bureau provided Senator Curtis with a copy of the Bowen report, see letters, Charles Curtis to Chief of the Bureau of Investigation, October 27, 1919; Frank Burke to Curtis, November 18, 1919, ibid.; for the resolution, see Waskow, 193-194, 205-206.

[122]"Colored Editors' Statement" and "Negroes Deny Radicalism," unidentified clippings in box 10, Bowen Papers, Clemson University; "Radicals", *The Crisis,* December 1919, clipping in ibid.

on their side, and in many respects have been successful."[123] A year later the Justice Department repeated his assertion that "one of the favorite fields" for the Communist propaganda was among the blacks "who have been appealed to directly ... for support in the movement to overthrow the Government of the United States."[124] Director Burns, in his appearances before the House Appropriations Committee, continued to single out the black minority as one of the main targets of the Communists' subversive activity.[125] However, there are strong indications that these accusations were without any foundation and that radical political activities were not the Bureau's primary concern. First of all, there never was much evidence of Communist or other kinds of organized radical interest in the black community during this period. According to Theodore Draper, the early Communist movement had no support among blacks, in fact "Negroes counted least of all in the early Communist movement," and not a single black delegate attended any of the founding conventions in 1919.[126] A recent study, based in part on newly released federal intelligence files from this period, found no Communist interest in blacks before 1921. Even after that, the Workers Party, as the Communists then called themselves, was only able to recruit a few black members, owing to "the prejudice and paternalism displayed toward blacks who attended Communist meetings and in part as a result of the party's near-exclusive stress on the issue of class over that of race."[127]

The apparent lack of any Communist influence does not, of course, exclude the possibility that Bureau officials genuinely believed that radicals were subverting the loyalty of the blacks. However, it is striking, in contrast to its public statements, how relatively seldom the Bureau internally justified its surveillance of black activities with radical or Bolshevik infiltration. In fact, if we look at the Bureau's four most important black investigations during the Red Scare, only one organization, the African Blood Brotherhood, was watched because of its Communist sympathies. The NAACP was kept under observation because of its prestige and influence, Randolph and Owen's the *Messenger* primarily because of its demands for social equality and the right to interracial marriage, and Marcus Garvey because he was the

---

[123]*Investigation Activities of the Department of Justice*, 13.
[124]*AG Report 1920*, 178.
[125]*Appropriations, Department of Justice, 1923*, Pt. 2, 127; *Appropriations, Department of Justice, 1924*, Pt. 2, 70.
[126]Draper, 192.
[127]Michael W. Fitzgerald, Michael Furmanovsky & Robert A. Hill, "The Comintern and American Blacks," in Hill (ed.), *The Marcus Garvey Papers*, Vol. V, 841-854; quote from p. 842.

most prominent black leader. With the exception of the ABB, these black organizations, publications and individuals were all investigated because, at bottom, they were believed to pose a threat to the existing racial order.

It is true that the Bureau in the course of its surveillance of the NAACP, the most respectable and influental civil rights organization of its time, received information to the effect that it was radically inclined. For example, it was informed by private sources that the NAACP was "the principal organization now engaged in creating discontent among the negroes" and that their expressed willingness to fight for their rights merely proved "that they were a bunch of Socialists and pacifists."[128] Assistant Attorney General Perry Herron also told the Bureau that the NAACP "has done more to create race friction in this country than any other agency I know" and that the latest issue of its paper, the *Crisis*, was "Bolshevistic."[129] The Bureau was particularly interested in its editor, W.E.B. Du Bois, who was suspected of harboring strong radical sympathies and being in favor of the IWW.[130] On the other hand, one Bureau official called the NAACP "a bona fide" organization and added that the Attorney General was said to be a supporter, while the Washington, DC, field office was of the opinion that the organization was "operated along conservative and peaceful lines for the betterment of race conditions and has always been in opposition to the colored radical organizations" and that the *Crisis* was not radically inclined.[131] The best explanation for this apparent inconsistency is probably, as suggested by Theodore Kornweibel, that the federal authorities were disturbed by the NAACP and the *Crisis'* prestigious positions and their considerable influence among the black population, in particular their extensive anti-lynching campaign, and that they wanted to discredit them as subversive but simply failed to find any concrete evidence to support their accusation.[132]

---

[128]Letter, W. A. Blackwood to William J. Flynn, July 3, 1919, OG 3057, RG65, NA; K-500, Report of Law and Order Group, For July 30, 31 and August 1, 1919, OG 370678, ibid.
[129]Perry Herron, Memorandum for the Hon. William J. Burns, February 3, 1923, 61-826 (Federal Surveillance of African-Americans, 1917-25: Microfilm).
[130]Especially, reports, L. Herman, February 23, 1920, OG 383474, RG65, NA; H. J. Lenon, September 19, 1921, BS 202600-1768-24, ibid. Some files on Du Bois are missing, such as OG 372168 and BS 158260-1; there is also a reference in the index to a "Confidential File," which has apparently been removed or destroyed since it is neither in the early Bureau files in RG65, NA, nor in the Du Bois file maintained at the FBI today (file 100-99729, FBI/FOIA).
[131]Memorandum to Frank Burke, in re: Radical Negro Activities, October 28, 1919, OG 258421, RG65, NA; report, J. T. Flourney, November 7, 1921, 61-308-1, ibid.
[132]Kornweibel, *No Crystal Stair,* 74; Kornweibel, *"Seeing Red,"* 54-75. For the NAACP's anti-lynching campaign, see Kellogg, 209-246, who concludes on the NAACP's influence in the black community: "Negroes had responded to the tension of the war years and their aftermath by aligning themselves with the NAACP and by subscribing to *The Crisis* as never before in the history of the organization" (Ibid., 246). For an example of NAACP enquiries to the Bureau

It would seem logical to assume that A. Philip Randolph and Chandler Owen's avowedly socialistic and even pro-Bolshevistic the *Messenger* was investigated because of its political views. On August 12, 1919, Hoover noted that the paper was believed to be "the Russian organ of the Bolsheviki in the United States, and to be the headquarters of revolutionary thought," and he directed that an inquiry be made into the citizenship and political connections of all the members of the editorial staff and the funding of the magazine.[133] An intensive investigation followed, Randolph and Owen were put under surveillance, their speeches covered and the circulation and financing of the *Messenger* were carefully scrutinized.[134] There are strong indications, however, that there was another and more fundamental reason why the Bureau was concerned about the publication. The Bureau clearly worried about the *Messenger's* influence among blacks. According to Bureau officials, the paper was "beyond doubt exciting the negro elements in this country to riot and to the committing of outrages of all sorts," it was "by long odds the most able and the most dangerous of all the Negro publications" and it was "the exponent of open defiance and sedition." Its two editors were called "two notorious negro agitators."[135] Apparently, however, it was not so much the possibility of propaganda in support of IWW or Bolshevik ideas that worried the officials, as Randolph's and Owen's repeated demands for social equality, including the right to interracial marriages. For example, at the beginning of its investigation, the Bureau was warned that the *Messenger* was "doing the most damage" because of its insistent demands for social equality: "Should the negro become fairly well organized and demand social equality, there is no doubt but that serious trouble would ensue throughout the entire Southern belt of the United States."[136] The agents who investigated the paper also seemed to give more attention to its demands for social equality than to its political views. While Bowen in his report on the radical black press criticized the *Messenger* for supporting the IWW and the Soviet

---

concerning lynchings, see report, James E. Amos, August 22, 1923, 61-3176-1, FBI/FOIA.

[133]Hill (ed.), *The Marcus Garvey Papers*, Vol. I, 479-480.

[134]The information on the investigation is extensive and can be found in OG 258421/369936/259364/265716/258694 & BS 202600-1717/1628/1754/1771, RG65, NA. It should be noted that several files were missing (BS 202600-228-10/1617-25/1784-X) and others did not contain any information despite references in the index (OG 86163/136944/17969/340162/345429).

[135]The quotes from, Patrick S. Washburn, *A Question of Sedition. The Federal Government's Investigation of the Black Press During World War II* (New York, 1986), 30; *Investigation Activities of the Department of Justice*, 172; letter, Frank Burke to Patrick J. Ahorn, January 20, 1920, OG 369936, RG65, NA.

[136]Letter, W. A. Blackwood to William J. Flynn, July 3, 1919, OG 3057, ibid.

government and for calling on blacks to organize and defend themselves against lynchings, he in particular stressed that the October 1919 issue of the paper was "the first time a Negro publication comes out openly for sex equality." He added that it was "the habit of most of the Negro publications to deny that they advocate social equality. The Messenger claims it and furthermore, with it, sex equality." According to Bowen, this demand for social equality was characterized by a spirit of "insolent bravado."[137] Thus, the Bureau seemed more concerned and preoccupied with the fact that the *Messenger,* with its demands for social equality, had mentioned and questioned a fundamental white tabu, interracial relationship, than with the fact that the editors also trumpeted the cause of socialism and Bolshevism.

The perhaps clearest example that the Bureau was reacting against real or perceived threats to the existing racial order, was the case against Marcus Garvey, the most powerful black leader of the immediate postwar era. Garvey, who was born in Jamaica, in 1917 founded the Universal Negro Improvement Association to gain support for his ideas of black nationalism and Pan-Africanism. Later, in 1919 he started the Black Star Line as a company owned and run by blacks. It was Garvey's goal to establish parallel and independent black institutions and he used a militant rhetoric in order to create a black consciousness and pride in the black race and identity. Kornweibel has called the UNIA "the largest, most powerful black mass organization ever formed in America," and it has been estimated that its membership at its peak consisted of between four and six million blacks.[138]

It is apparent from an analysis of the Bureau's internal justifications for investigating Garvey that the Bureau's main motivation was his position as the most influental black leader and his potential for mobilizing and unifying the black population in one single black nationalist movement. The surveillance began in earnest on July 10, 1919, when Special Agent M. J. Davis of New York reported that Garvey was "probably the most prominent Negro radical agitator in New York," that he was "an exceptionally fine orator" and that he was rapidly gaining in popularity among blacks: "It is surprising to note the excitement which Garvey is causing among the negro element in New

---

[137]*Investigating Activities of the Department of Justice,* 181; also 183. For the Bowen report's focus on *The Messenger* and the theme of social equality, see also, Kornweibel, *No Crystal Stair,* 91-92; Kornweibel, *"Seeing Red,"* 76-99.

[138]Kornweibel, *No Crystal Stair,* 135; for the membership figure, see, Robert A. Hill, "'The Foremost Radical Among His Race:' Marcus Garvey and the Black Scare, 1918-1921," *Prologue,* Vol. 16, No. 4 (Winter 1984), 223. For Garvey in general see Judith Stein, *The World of Marcus Garvey. Race and Class in Modern Society* (Baton Rouge, La., 1986), 3-6, 63-152. For the federal campaign against Garvey see also, Kornweibel, *"Seeing Red,"* 100-131.

York thru this steamship proposition."[139] Clearly concerned, Washington instructed the New York and Chicago field offices to begin collecting information on Garvey and the Bureau of Immigration was contacted with a view toward preparing a deportation case against the black leader.[140] When J. Edgar Hoover in October 1919 in an internal memorandum explained why Garvey should "be proceeded against," he repeated the main points from Davis' report and only at the end noted that Garvey's paper, the *Negro World*, upheld "Soviet Russian rule" and "there is open advocation of Bolshevism."[141] The way in which this claim was added to the last paragraph, following the details of why Garvey was influental, indicates that Hoover's prime concern was Garvey's position as a black leader and that the accusation of Bolshevism was thrown in to further discredit Garvey in the eyes of the Justice Department.

When the Bureau in May 1921 prepared a memorandum for the immigration authorities on why Garvey should not be allowed to return to the United States from a tour of the Caribbean, it too was noteworthy for the absence of any accusations of political radicalism. In directing that the memorandum be prepared, Hoover again made it clear that it was Garvey's power which was of concern, noting that Garvey was "the notorious negro agitator who has for many months been a cause of disturbance in this country." The final memorandum, in effect, argued that Garvey should be denied reentry because of his racial agitation, and it consisted mainly of quotations from Garvey's speeches and articles on such subjects as the possibility of a future race war, the call for blacks worldwide to organize, demands that blacks should defend themselves against lynchings and praise for the spirit of the "New Negro." The only instance in which Bolshevism was mentioned at all was in connection with a quotation of a letter by the poet Claude McKay, which had been published in the *Negro World*, and which championed the cause of Bolshevism.[142] Finally, in 1922 the

---

[139]Hill (ed.), *The Marcus Garvey Papers*, Vol. I, 454; see also, ibid., 388-389, 406-407, 411-412. Robert Hill has explained the opening of the case against Garvey with the fact that federal officials were concerned about radical propaganda among blacks following the riots in Washington, DC, on July 20 and 21 and in Chicago on July 27 (Hill, "'The Foremost Radical'," 220-221); but the investigation was in fact begun on the basis of Davis' report of July 10, indicating that the Bureau was concerned about Garvey's increasingly powerful position. In fact, the Bureau had initially noted Garvey's militant rhetoric in September 1918 (Kornweibel, *"Seeing Red,"* 101).

[140]Hill (ed.), *The Marcus Garvey Papers*, Vol. I, 458-459, 481-482, 485-486.

[141]Ibid., Vol. II, 72; the memorandum is printed in facsimile in Hill, "'The Foremost Radical'," 217. That the Bureau was not so much concerned about Garvey's political radicalism as his potential for uniting blacks and become a truly mass leader is also argued by Judith Stein, who noted that Garvey was persecuted "not because of what he did but because of what he might inspire" (Stein, 88).

[142]Hill (ed.), *The Marcus Garvey Papers*, Vol. III, 235, 398-415.

Bureau was able to charge Garvey with conspiring to use the mail to defraud, and in lobbying for a speedy trial Bureau officials revealed their concern about his continued racial activities. For example, Director Burns argued that Garvey "is the most prominent Negro agitator in the world today," and Hoover warned against "the renewed activities" of Garvey, whom he described as "a notorious negro agitator, affectionately referred to by his own race as the 'Negro Moses'." Hoover urged the Justice Department to speed up the prosecution "in order that he may be once and for all put where he can peruse his past activities behind the four walls in the Atlanta clime."[143] Clearly, what worried federal officials were not so much any possible Bolshevistic or radical political ideas or sympathies that Garvey might harbor, but his popularity in the black community and his potential for becoming a black nationalistic leader.

Apparently, the only black organization which was investigated explicitly because of its political radicalism was the small and rather insignificant African Blood Brotherhood. The group was brought to the Bureau's attention by the postal authorities, which in August 1919 forwarded complaints from the colonial authorities in British Guiana that the *Crusader* constituted an incendiary influence. In the course of the following investigation the Bureau was informed by Robert Bowen that the *Crusader*, edited by the ABB's leader, Cyril Briggs, was "entirely sympathetic with Bolshevism, Sinn Fein, Jewish agitation." According to Bowen it had in the past "been quite bad" though recent issues had been "comparatively moderate." In his November report on the black press Bowen noted as examples of "significant material" articles that opposed conservative blacks, lauded black superiority, and opposed lynchings and US intervention in Mexico.[144] The ensuing investigation of the *Crusader* led the agents to the ABB, which was infiltrated by two black informers. The Brotherhood's utopian goal, it was discovered, was the liberation of Africa "from the caucassions (sic) and restoring it to its rightful owners."[145] Nothing further happened until the summer of 1921 when confidential informants P-138, P-134 and #800 were instructed to monitor the group, apparently because the *Crusader* had been banned by the British in the Caribbean and was

---

[143]Ibid., Vol. IV, 579, 841. Garvey was sentenced to five years in prison in June 1923 and deported to Jamaica in November 1927 (Hill, "'The Foremost Radical'," 231).
[144]Report, M. J. Davis, August 29, 1919, OG 387162, RG65, NA; *Investigation Activities of the Department of Justice*, 166-168; Kornweibel, *"Seeing Red,"* 134; for the surveillance of the ABB in general, see ibid., 132-154.
[145]Report, W. W. Grimes, January 24, 1920, OG 387162, RG65, NA; also, letter, George F. Lamb to William J. Flynn, April 1, 1920, ibid.; reports, WW, February 28 and March 1, 1920, OG 185161, ibid.; J. G. Tucker, March 13, 1920, OG 208369, ibid.

accused of fomenting the race riot in Tulsa, Oklahoma. Two of the black informers, P-138 and #800, infiltrated the ABB and their reports left no doubt that the group had close connections with the Communist Party, mainly through contacts with one of the most famous of the early American Communists, Rose Pastor Stokes.[146]

The Bureau's suspicions about the ABB's links to the Communists were further strengthened when the Bureau was informed by the State Department that the black poet, Claude McKay, who was a member of the ABB, in November 1922 had participated in the Comintern's Fourth World Congress in Moscow. Here it had been decided, according to a confidential source of the American Legation in Riga, Latvia, "to begin an energetic propaganda campaign among the negroes in America in order to attract them to Communist organizations."[147] Suspecting that McKay might act as a courier for the Comintern, the Bureau and the State Department kept track of his travels across Europe and alerted its field offices in several ports and directed that "a very careful examination" be made upon his return.[148] Prompted by reports of Brigg's increasingly close connections with the Communists, a black special agent, Earl E. Titus, in August 1923 infiltrated the ABB and gained the confidence of its leader. Eventually, he became chairman of its meetings and worked in the *Crusader's* office, where he had access to the group's account books. The active surveillance ended at the end of 1923, when the ABB finally confirmed the Bureau's long-standing suspicions by merging with the recently established legal Communist party, the Workers Party.[149]

The Bureau, then, was not caught up in an anticommunist hysteria which induced it to hunt for subversives among the black population. Rather, the Bureau reacted to the growing black demands for equal

[146]Reports, P-138, June 6, 14, 22, July 13, August 6, 10, 22, 26, 31, 1921, BS 202600-2031, ibid.; P-134, August 29 and 30, 1921, ibid.; letter, William Burns to Edward J. Brennan, October 13, 1921, BS 202600-2674, ibid.; reports, P-134, October 20, 1921, 61-44-4 (Federal Surveillance of African-Americans. Microfilm); P-134, January 4, 1922, 61-50-24, ibid.; letters, #800 to Geo. F. Ruch, August 10, October 18 and December 24, 1921, 61-826, ibid.; Kornweibel, *"Seeing Red,"* 140-145.

[147]Report, Third International and the Negroes, December 4, 1922, att. to letter, Wm. Hurley to William J. Burns, January 11, 1923, 61-23 (Federal Surveillance of African-Americans. Microfilm); also, letter, Burns to Hurley, December 12, 1922; memorandum, in re: Claude McKay, February 3, 1923, 61-3497, ibid. For earlier investigation of McKay, see, letters, Hurley to Hoover, March 30, 1921; Lewis J. Baley to T. M. Reddy, April 11, 1921, both in BS 202600-1545, RG65, NA. For McKay's activities in Moscow, see Draper, 387; Fitzgerald, Furmanovsky & Hill, 843; Wayne F. Cooper, *Claude McKay. Rebel Sojourner in the Harlem Renaissance* (Baton Rouge, La., 1987), 171-192.

[148]See the extensive correspondance re McKay in files 61-23/50/3497, all in Federal Surveillance of African-Americans (Microfilm). McKay did not return until 1934, see Cooper, 289-291.

[149]For Titus' surveillance reports, see file 61-50 in Federal Surveillance of African-Americans (Microfilm). On the merging of the ABB and the Workers Party, see also, Fitzgerald, Furmanovsky & Hill, 842-843, 845.

rights and used the accusations about subversive agitators to contain the unrest. The Bureau's first priority was to protect the existing racial hierarchy. This argument is supported by the fact that other minorities, such as the Japanese-Americans, were also investigated en bloc for alleged subversive and pro-Japanese activities in 1920.[150]

It might be argued that the response of the federal government to the racial unrest in 1919 had two important consequences: First, the influence and importance of the Bureau were increased considerably by the institutionalization of its surveillance of the black community. From 1919 until the mid-1970s, with a ten year interruption between the mid-1920s to the mid-1930s, one of the main tasks of the Bureau's political responsibilities was to keep the government informed about the whole range of black activities, from race riots and political activities to civil rights movements.[151] Secondly, the effect of the Bureau investigation into the riots and the black press in 1919, because of the repeated accusations of radical or Communist complicity, had, all things considered, a strong influence on the public opinion and the creation of a public perception of an omnipresent radical subversion and agitation. In other words, the federal government's reaction to the racial unrest resulted in a more influental and powerful Bureau and an increase in the Red Scare.

---

[150]A cost-of-living investigation of the Japanese business community on the Pacific Coast in 1920 soon developed into a major inquiry into Japanese activities throughout the West and South; at no time was the issue of radicalism or Communism mentioned and it is clear that the Japanese population was put under surveillance merely because they were Japanese and, thus, like the blacks, of doubtful loyalty. In some areas, such as Galveston, Texas, all Japanese residents were indexed in the Bureau files (report, J. V. Bell, July 7, 1920, 65-1X, Investigative Reports, Box 1, RG65, NA); in Fresno, California, agents collected information on all Japanese engaged in businesses and on their prices (report, Geo. H. Hudson, July 16, 1920, ibid.); and in Seattle, Washington, the Bureau prepared a 28 page report on all Japanese landowners (report, M. V. Fahey, July 19, 1920, ibid.). All kinds of Japanese activities were looked upon with suspicion; for example, the Bureau investigated Japanese schools in California (report, E. Kosterlitzky, August 19, 1920, ibid.), Japanese who bought cameras in New Orleans (report, J. M. Tolivar, January 26, 1920, ibid.), and, especially, Japanese fishermen off the Pacific Coast who were believed to be, in fact, Japanese spies (reports, A. A. Hopkins, August 16 and 23, 1920; A. P. Harris, April 15, 1920, ibid.). One agent believed that the Japanese were trying to buy up as much land in California as possible and therefore constituted "a real menace to the American people unless this Government makes strict legislation governing them" (Report, W. A. Weymouth, March 26, 1920, ibid.). The special agent in charge in San Antonio concluded that "an organized effort is being made by Japanese to obtain agricultural lands in the Rio Grande territory for the purpose of colonizing them with Japanese from California" (Letter, Louis DeNette to Wm. J. Neale, September 16, 1920, ibid.). One of the responsibilities of the General Intelligence Division from 1920 was to keep an eye on Japanese activities in the US (J. E. Hoover, Memorandum for Mr, Burke, July 28, 1920, OG 374214, ibid.).

[151]For an overview of the Bureau's later surveillance of black activities, see O'Reilly, *"Racial Matters"*; Garrow, *The FBI and Martin Luther King, Jr.*; O'Reilly, "The Roosevelt Administration and Black America," 12-25; Washburn, *A Question of Sedition*; Joseph Boskin, "The Rite of Purification: The FBI and the Black Historical Possibility," *Reviews in American History*, Vol. 11, No. 3 (September 1983), 472-478.

Strikebreaking

It has often been assumed that the federal government's intervention in the labor conflicts in 1919 was caused by a hysterical public, who feared a revolutionary uprising among the workers. One argument has been that the government apparently only became active at a late stage. For example, according to Stanley Coben, Attorney General Palmer "hesitated to commit himself to antilabor policies" and, in fact, "did not intervene in the series of violent strikes between February and November 1919."[152] Specifically, the Justice Department "remained on the sidelines" during the steel strike, which broke out in September 1919, while the business community, the press, the military and a Senate committee tried to smear the strike as a radical plot. Not until 1920 did the Department accuse radicals of having taken part in the disturbances, but it "did not make these moves until months after the strike ended." Thus, according to this account, the Red Scare was promoted by groups outside the government; and it was only in late October, faced with an imminent national coal strike on November 1 and pressured by a public "fear of revolution or economic disaster," combined with the Senate's demand that he crack down on radical aliens, that Palmer decided to act:[153] "Not until others had proven the political potency of anti-labor activity, and criticism of Palmer's inactivity became so intense that it endangered his career, did he take the field against strikers."[154]

The other argument is based on assumptions about the government's motives for intervening against the coal strike. According to Murray, "There can be little doubt that the radical factor played some part in prompting government action," a deduction which is based exclusively on a meeting between President Wilson and Palmer at the White House on October 30, about which there are no sources as to what transpired. Murray, nevertheless, claims that "we can guess what happened" and he goes on to hypothesize that Palmer talked the stricken president into approving the application for an injunction, thereby outlawing the strike, by stressing the need for coal and the strike's "radical overtones."[155] Clearly, this reconstruction is influenced by the overall thesis that the administration was forced into action by an anti-radical hysteria.

Whereas the Justice Department vigorously investigated all kinds of radicals and dissenters and repeatedly exaggerated the revolutionary

---

[152]Coben, *A. Mitchell Palmer*, 173.
[153]Ibid., 176; also, 188.
[154]Ibid., 173.
[155]Murray, 156-157; also, 162.

204

danger, federal law enforcement officers behaved with much more restraint toward the business community. Under Palmer, the Department followed a cautious antitrust line intended not to antagonize big business and characterized by low-key prosecutions, sometimes by settlements out of courts which were favorable to the corporations, and often by dropping cases. Thus, while radicals and organized labor were harassed, cases against the business community were put on the back burner.[156] When US Attorney in Pennsylvania Francis Fisher Kane resigned his post in January 1920 in protest against the Palmer raids, he accused the Department of ignoring the munitions manufacturers, fraudulent contractors and other war profiteers in its anti-radical witchhunt: "I believe that by this policy we are playing directly into the hands of the capitalists and the large employers of the country."[157] Another administration critic, Immigration Commissioner Frederic C. Howe, noted that the Justice Department in 1919 had become "frankly an agency of employing and business interests" which had profiteered by the war: "Discussion of war profiteers was not to be permitted. The Department of Justice lent itself to the suppression of those who felt that war should involve equal sacrifice."[158]

Bureau officials repeatedly argued that they were neutral and not at all interested in ordinary labor conflicts. Hoover noted in an internal memorandum that "Legitimate strikes called by the American Federation of Labor, of course, are not to be investigated or inquired into unless it appears that there is some radical agitator involved who is engaged in the 'boring from within' process," and he stressed that under no circumstances were any confidential information to be given to employers.[159] In its instructions to the field, Washington cautioned its agents not to take sides in labor conflicts, pointing out that it was "extremely important that agents and employees should at all times avoid any statement or action which could be construed as a desire on the part of this Department to interfere for or against the orderly existence and activities of legitimate labor organizations."[160]

Nevertheless, the nature of the Bureau's work compelled the field force to cooperate more closely with the employers than with organized labor. The Bureau's internal rules specifically mentioned business

---

[156]Coben, *A. Mitchell Palmer,* 188-195.

[157]Letter, Francis Fisher Kane to A. Mitchell Palmer, January 12, 1920, printed in, *Charges of Illegal Practices,* 348-349.

[158]Howe, 276-277.

[159]J. E. Hoover, Memorandum for Mr. Davis, February 11, 1920, OG 374217, RG65, NA. Also, M. J. Davis, Memorandum for Mr. Hoover, February 7, 1920, ibid.

[160]Letters, Acting Chief to Frank R. Stone et al, February 17, 1920, OG 290720, ibid.; also, letter, Acting Chief to Bliss Morton, March 3, 1920, OG 374217, ibid.

interests as a force "considered important to maintain friendly relations with,"[161] and it is apparent from a number of reports that the agents had closer contacts and received much more information from the business community than from the unions.[162] For example, the Bureau received information on radical activities from such employer organizations as the US Chamber of Commerce and the National Metal Trades Association.[163] One agent in Cincinnati described in some detail how this cooperation functioned on a local level: "Agent interviewed Mr. J. M. Manley, Secretary of the Cincinnati Metal Trades Association, who has operatives covering the American Federation of Labor convention at the Armory Blgd., this city, and he has agreed to furnish this office with complete copies of the reports of each of his operatives covering the entire convention ..."[164] Clearly, the Bureau's contacts with the employers were used to gather information, in addition to radical activities, on such "legitimate" activities as AFL conventions.

The Bureau also received a steady stream of information on both radical and labor activities during the steel and coal strikes in late 1919. The Bureau field office in Gary, Indiana, dismissed complaints that its agents had aided the steel industry in intimidating the strikers, but it did report confidentially that it had accepted reports from the corporations on "alien radicals, Bolsheviks, IWWs or socalled 'reds'."[165] Bliss Morton, the special agent in charge in Cleveland, Ohio, informed Washington that his office had cooperated closely with a local employer: "This gentleman is connected with the steel industry in Youngstown and has a force of confidential operatives reporting to him daily. A large volume of information has been furnished this office concerning the activities of the radicals in Youngstown through this gentleman.... I might state that the confidential operative holds a very important position among the radicals in Youngstown."[166] During the coal strike the Bureau received an extensive amount of information on the striking miners from a number of large employer associations and

---

[161]Report of Committee on Cooperation, August 17, 1920, OG 390982, ibid.
[162]For example, letters, James J. McLaughlin to J. T. Suter, January 24, 1920, OG 290720, ibid.; Wm. P. Hazen to Frank Burke, February 19, 1920, ibid.; also, M. J. Davis, Memorandum for Mr. Hoover, February 7, 1920, OG 374217, ibid.
[163]For the US Chamber of Commerce, see for example, report, F. C. Baggarly, July 4, 1919, BS 202600-823, ibid.; for the National Metal Trades Association, see for example, letters, Edward Brennan to William J. Burns, December 8, 1921, 61-557-1, ibid.; Brennan to Burns, February 17, 1922, 61-1092-1, ibid.
[164]Report, deleted, June 22, 1922, 61-126-619, FBI/FOIA.
[165]Letter, Edward Brennan to Frank Burke, October 18, 1919, OG 352037, RG65, NA; also, telegram, Burke to Brennan, October 10, 1919; report, J. Spolansky, October 18, 1919, ibid.
[166]Letter, Bliss Morton to Frank Burke, April 5, 1920, OG 180980, ibid.

corporations, among those the Northern West Virginia Coal Operator's Association and the Consolidated Coal Co. of Jenkins, Kentucky.[167]

This close cooperation apparently led some employers to believe that the government agents were their allies against organized labor and in some instances requested the aid of the Bureau to repress active union members.[168] For example, a coal company in West Virginia requested the Bureau to put an end to the activities of a local UMW leader on the ground that he had been criticizing the president.[169] In Pittsburgh, the United Collieries Company submitted to the local field office a list of names of a number of UMW members who allegedly were involved in disseminating Communist propaganda. The Bureau soon dropped the case when the ensuing inquiry showed that the management had no concrete evidence and that the accusation had been made up by the company in an effort to break a legitimate strike concerning wages and working conditions. The investigation was not stopped, however, until the agents had intercepted the miners' mail and threatened those who were aliens with deportation if they did not cease their union activities.[170] In January 1922, J. G. C. Corcoran, a former Bureau agent and now an official of the Pierce Oil Corporation, informed George Ruch of the IWW's ongoing campaign to organize the workers in the company's oil fields and requested that the Bureau take "the necessary action to prevent the program of this organization going through."[171] The request led to an extensive investigation of the IWW affiliated union the Oil Workers Industrial Union throughout Oklahoma and California and the union was effectively prevented from organizing the oil workers in Southern California by the use of the state criminal syndicalist law.[172] The Bureau, then, despite its claims of neutrality, was willing to participate in the employers' union busting activities.

Because of their somewhat shady reputation as labor spies and strike breakers, the Bureau's relationship with the private detective agencies was always a sensitive subject. The Bureau strongly rejected accusations that it had employed the Pinkerton Detective Agency to conduct

---

[167]Letter, Calvin Weakly to Frank Burke, November 8, 1919, with att.; report, Ernest W. Lambeth, December 13, 1919; Memorandum for Mr. Hoover, December 10, 1919, OG 303770, ibid. For the Bureau's acceptance of reports from employer informers during the steel strike, see also, *Charges of Illegal Practices*, 226-228, 648.

[168]M. J. Davis, Memorandum for Mr. Hoover, February 7, 1920, OG 374217, RG65, NA.

[169]Memorandum, n.d., OG 303770, ibid.

[170]Reports, M. F. O'Brien, August 25, 1923, 61-4326-1, ibid.; H. J. Lenon, September 4, 1923, 61-4326-2, ibid.; M. F. O'Brien, October 9, 1923, 61-4326-3, ibid.

[171]Letter, J. G. C. Corcoran to George Ruch, January 19, 1922, with att., 61-997-1, ibid.

[172]Letter, William J. Burns to Jas. C. Findlay, February 2, 1922, 61-997-1, ibid.; reports, A. A. Hopkins, August 8, 1922, 61-997-11, ibid.; August 15, 61-997-12, ibid.; September 20, 1922, 61-997-14, ibid.; March 1, 1923, 61-997-16, ibid.; May 7, 1923, 61-997-19, ibid.

investigations in connection with the Sacco and Venzetti case. It claimed that it "has never employed or solicited the assistance of any private organization in the performance of its duties" and that the Justice Department had never utilized the services of any private detective agency: "The regular force of special agents of the Bureau of Investigation is fully adequate and competent to perform its own investigations without the assistance of private individuals."[173] That it was a touchy subject for the Bureau is indicated by the fact that the Bureau paid close attention to public criticism of the relationship. Thus, the Bureau closely followed a series of articles in the *New Republic* dealing with its cooperation with private detectives during strikes. It also seemed to take a particular interest in a resolution proposed by Senator Burton K. Wheeler in 1927, which proposed that the Senate conduct an investigation of the role of private detectives in labor conflicts.[174]

The internal Bureau rules cautioned the agents against cooperating too closely with private detectives and emphasized that "In no instance should we exchange information with private detective agencies except on authority of the division superintendent."[175] However, it is apparent that the Bureau received an extensive amount of information on labor activities and radicals during the Red Scare. Some of it was received from the corporations which had employed the detectives to spy on their employees. This was the case of the New Haven, Connecticut, corporation which submitted "copies of their reports received from the Pinkerton Agency which has been employed by them in connection with plant protection and which reports contain evidence against the most active agitators in the Naugatuck Valley."[176] The Bureau files confirm the suspicion of contemporary critics that it did receive information on a regular basis from a number of private detective agencies, in particular the Sherman Detective Agency, the Pinkerton Detective Agency and the Burns Detective Agency.[177] There is even an

---

[173]Letter, SAC to the Editor, Brockton Enterprise, June 5, 1922, 61-126-unrecorded, FBI/FOIA.

[174]Letter, John B. Hanrahan to William J. Flynn, March 30, 1921, BS 202600-964-3, RG65, NA; Senator Burton K. Wheeler file, 62-16195, box 1, Series 4, FBI Records, MU.

[175]Report of Committee on Informants, Under-Cover Men, and Blue Slips, August 1920, OG 390982, RG65, NA.

[176]Report, Warren W. Grimes, July 17, 1919, OG 341761, ibid.

[177]For the Sherman Detective Agency, see, report, Feri F. Weiss, December 30, 1918, OG 182787, ibid.; letter, F. O. Pendleton to Robert G. Slocumb, January 19, 1920, OG 384817, ibid.; report, A. A. Hopkins, March 26, 1923, 61-3675-1, ibid.; for the Pinkerton Detective Agency, see, reports, Chas. H. Heighton, November 29, December 17 and 28, 1918, OG 91928; for the Burns Detective Agency, see, letter, R. B. Spencer to William J. Burns, March 14, 1924, 61-5113-1, ibid.; reports, T. C. Wilcox, March 31, 1924, 61-5113-3, ibid.; Max F. Burger, April 15, 1924, 61-5113-4, ibid.

example of the Bureau sharing an informant with private detectives. The Sherman Services in New York, working on behalf of large employers, infiltrated the Union of Russian Workers with informant no. "40" and transmitted copies of his reports to the Bureau. When the informer was no longer of use to the detectives, "40" was hired by the Bureau as a special confidential employee at $5 per diem.[178]

In accordance with the government's overall policies, the Bureau also cooperated with organized labor at the same time as the employers were trying to break it with its open shop campaign and while the Bureau itself investigated strikes and other legitimate union activities. The American Federation of Labor under the leadership of Samuel Gompers was a conservative union, which accepted the capitalist system and fought to improve its position within its framework. It stayed out of politics, was organized according to crafts and was traditionally hostile toward unskilled workers in general and aliens in particular, since they were perceived as strikebreakers and sweaters. The AFL was opposed to radicals and Communists to such an extent that, according to Irving Bernstein, Gompers "regarded the AFL as the principal bulwark of American capitalism and democracy against Communism."[179] Thus, when the employers began their open shop campaign in 1919 and tried to discredit organized labor as being radical, pro-Bolshevik and un-American, the AFL defended itself by launching its own anti-radical campaign. It strongly denounced such radical methods as the general strike and the Communistic ideology, and it publicly warned against the danger of "boring-from-within" or radical infiltration of the unions. Although the AFL argued that it was unaffected by the activities of the radicals, its whole anti-radical rhetoric had the opposite effect of what was intended by indirectly conveying the impression that the radical danger was real and imminent. As noted by Robert Murray, in its zeal to take the wind out of the employers' sails by following a clear anti-Bolshevik line, "organized labor cooperated with them in digging its own grave."[180]

The unions often on their own initiative submitted information on radical labor activists to the Bureau. Hoover noted in an internal memorandum that the AFL "has from time to time called the attention of this office to certain instances wherein radical activities were

---

[178]Reports, C. J. Scully, September 2, 15, October 20, 1919; M. J. Davis, September 24, 1919, BS 202600-184, ibid.
[179]Bernstein, 94; also, 90-94; Brody, *Workers in Industrial America*, 21-24, 27; Tomlins, 76-77.
[180]Murray, 108. For the AFL's interest in combating radicalism, see also, Marguerite Green, *The National Civic Federation and the American Labor Movement 1900-1925* (Washington, DC, 1956), 421-422.

suspected," but he found it advisable to keep these contacts confidential since they "would be misconstrued by certain elements in the country and might also not be entirely desired from the viewpoint of the American Federation of Labor."[181] One such instance took place in the wake of the coal strike in December 1919. Even though the Justice Department had just broken the strike with the injunction, Frank Farrington, UMW official in Illinois, informed the Attorney General of the activities of radical agitators in a number of mine camps and emphasized his own anti-radicalism: "I most earnestly urge that this matter have your prompt attention as I assure you the officers of the Illinois Miners' Union are law abiding 100% American citizens and very anxious to clean out those who would destroy our American institutions and while I ask that you keep the source of this information confidential, I assure you we shall be very glad to do anything in our power to aid your Department in curbing these destructive influences."[182] Other union officials informed the Bureau about such radical activities as the "Open Forum," an organization of radical union members, the "American Freedom Convention," which campaigned for a general amnesty for political prisoners, and William Z. Foster's attempts to infiltrate the unions, and requested that the government investigate.[183]

In their eagerness to combat the radicals the unions even had their own force of informers, whose reports on the activities of their membership were submitted to the Bureau. Patrick O'Meara, president of the Connecticut Federation of Labor, promised to transmit any information about socialists or radicals from his informers, whom he had employed because "he considered the present radical movement as prejudicial to the labor situation and is obliged to keep informed of their movements...."[184] The close cooperation between the Bureau and the unions is evident from a request from Earl Hauck, a former special agent who was an attorney for the UMW, who requested that the Bureau keep an UMW convention under surveillance: "He states that the U. M. of A. will have some undercover men reporting to him and

---

[181]J. E. Hoover, Memorandum for Mr. Creighton, February 13, 1920, JD 202600-10 (DJ Invest. Files II). Ralph de Toledano has noted of this cooperation: "In fact, there was more than casual cooperation between the GID and the AFL, which began keeping files of its own on radicalism" (de Toledano, 55).
[182]Letter, Frank Farrington to Hon. A. Mitchell Palmer, December 30, 1919, OG 303770, RG65, NA. The letter led to a Bureau investigation of the conditions in the Illinois mining camps, see, letter, Frank Burke to J. J. McLaughlin, January 7, 1920, ibid.
[183]Williams, *Without Understanding,* 128-129; letter, C. L. van Dorn to W. B. Wilson, April 27, 1919, OG 180980, RG65, NA; report, Max F. Burger, November 27, 1922, 61-714-74, box 4, Series 10, FBI Records, MU.
[184]Report, Robert G. Jordan, April 9, 1920, OG 180980, RG65, NA.

he requests that his group and the Bureau agents exchange information concerning the movements and activities of the Communists."[185] The unions, then, were quite willing to inform on the political activities of their own membership and to assist the government in carrying out its anti-radical campaign.

A fairly well-documented example of how effectively the Bureau was able to use the AFL against the radicals comes from California. In the spring of 1923, the Labor Department's federal conciliator in the state, C. T. Connell, arranged a meeting between J. B. Dale, general organizer of the AFL, and Special Agent A. A. Hopkins. Hopkins found Dale to be "a man of considerable ability, conservative, and with good judgement and patriotic." He particularly noted that he was "uncompromisingly opposed to radicals, particularly the Communists and the IWW and expressed himself as ready to use all his efforts against the action of such revolutionary organizations." Following a series of meetings between the three officials, Dale proved his usefulness by breaking a general strike among the oil workers organized by the IWW by letting members of the AFL act as strikebreakers. As Hopkins reported, Dale "has at all time kept in constant touch with the federal mediator and this agent in reference to the situation."[186] Dale's motive, apart from his genuine desire to destroy the radical labor groups, was undoubtedly to obtain the government's acceptance and support against the employers by presenting the AFL as a determined enemy of radicalism. Dale and John Horn, secretary of the Los Angeles Central Labor Council, told Hopkins that if the employers were to be successful in their campaign to break organized labor, they would instead be faced with a revolutionary labor movement. Since the AFL was fighting "in the first line of trenches" against the reds, the union should "be supported both by the Government thru its departments, and by the employers of labor as well."[187]

The AFL's strategy enabled the Bureau to step up its crack down on radical activities. For example, with the aid of the AFL and the Los Angeles Central Labor Council an attempt by the IWW to organize a boycott of California products and to organize another general strike in the state was defeated, according to the Bureau to a large extent

---

[185]Letter, J. E. Bayliss to J. Edgar Hoover, January 10, 1927, 61-6128-3, box 4, Series 10, FBI Records, MU. However, the request was denied, see, letter, Hoover to Bayliss, January 18, 1927, ibid. The request was part of the UMW campaign to purge itself of radicals and Communists, see Dubofsky & van Tine, 128-130.

[186]Report, A. A. Hopkins, May 7, 1923, 61-997-19, RG65, NA.

[187]Report, A. A. Hopkins, June 26, 1923, 61-714-105, box 4, Series 10, FBI Records, MU.

thanks to the efforts of organized labor.[188] The close contacts between the union leaders and the Bureau also contributed to a moderation of California's trade union press, which had formerly been extremely radical in its views, and to end its attacks on the government and on the Bureau. This was a development that L. C. Wheeler, the special agent in charge in Los Angeles, attributed to, among other things, "the personal and confidential relations of several (labor) leaders with this Bureau and gratitude for assistance in their fight against the W. Z. Foster movement."[189] Thus, under attack from the employers, the AFL sought to ally itself with the government, in the process assisting the Bureau with purging the unions of radical activists and muffling its own press. The result was a freer reign for the Bureau to investigate the labor movement and a more conservative AFL.

Protecting the National Economy
The Wilson administration reacted to the strikes in 1919, especially the coal strike, more out of concern that they might threaten the stability of the economic system than because of a fear of any revolutionary uprising. The cabinet and administration officials did not seem to have lost their balance because of an anti-radical fear and, in fact, the issue of radicalism is only mentioned in a few, isolated instances. For example, Secretary of Interior Franklin Lane worried that a continuation of the steel strike would give an impetus to the radical movement and raise "a cynical smile on the lip of every red revolutionist the world round."[190] Postmaster General Albert Burleson opposed any negotiation with the striking coal miners; as Secretary of the Navy Daniels noted in his diary, Burleson "Sees red & thinks country is full of Bolshevists."[191] These were the exceptions, however, and even a leading spokesman for government intervention within the cabinet such as Secretary of State Lansing justified his position with a consideration for the employer's right to do as he pleased with his property.[192]

In fact, the administration had good reasons for being concerned about the economic stability. 1919 was in fact the most turbulent year

[188]Reports, A. A. Hopkins, January 18, 1924, 61-3675-3, RG65, NA; A. A. Hopkins, May 7, 1923, 61-997-19, ibid.
[189]Letter, L. C. Wheeler to William J. Burns, January 30, 1924, 61-1241-69, box 2, Series 10, FBI Records, MU. The AFL has traditionally cooperated with government intelligence agencies when its position has been threatened from the left; during the 1940s, when the AFL was challenged by the CIO, the AFL cooperated with local red squads (Donner, *Protectors of Privilege*, 51).
[190]Link (ed.), *The Papers of Woodrow Wilson*, Vol. 63, 583.
[191]Cronon (ed.), 453.
[192]Ibid., 449.

of the labor market in US history with 3,630 recorded strikes and lock-outs, participated in by a record number of 4,160,000 workers or 22.5% of the total work force.[193] The reason for the unrest was not political radicalism but a combination of several factors, such as the clash between organized labor's attempt at consolidating and extending its gains from the war and the firm determination of the employers to resist these demands and to introduce the "open shop," as well as the dramatic rise in the cost-of-living during 1919. Consequently, most strikes were supported by the American Federation of Labor and in most cases the demands dealt with the right to organize and bargain collectively, higher wages and shorter hours.[194]

An analysis of the Wilson administration's response to the three most significant strikes during the fall of 1919, the Boston police strike, the national steel strike, and the national coal strike, shows that the administration was primarily concerned about law and order and the stability of the national economy. Although the administration did not play an active role in the Boston police strike, which broke out on September 9, President Wilson did publicly condemn the action. Two day later, on September 11, Wilson, who was on his Western speaking tour to win public support for the League of Nations, called the strike "a crime against civilization" because it had left the city "at the mercy of an army of thugs." He stressed that police officers had a duty as public servants to put the public safety above their selfish interests.[195] That public safety was Wilson's main concern is confirmed by his congratulation to Governor Calvin Coolidge, who had steadfastly refused the strikers' demands and who was overwhelmingly reelected in November. Wilson hailed Coolidge's election as "a victory for law and order": "When that is the issue all Americans stand together."[196]

The administration took more decisive steps to prevent the nation-wide strike in the steel industry, which broke out on September 22. An estimated 250,000 to 365,000 workers walked out and thereby threatened to paralyze the key industry of the American economy.[197] The conflict was basically the result of the unions' demands for the right to bargain collectively, higher wages and better working conditions, and the steel industry's refusal, led by the powerful chairman of US Steel, Judge Elbert H. Gary, to meet with the union representa-

[193]David Montgomery, *Workers' Control in America* (Cambridge, 1979), 97.
[194]David Brody, *Workers in Industrial America*, 42-46; also, Murray, 111-112.
[195]Link (ed.), *The Papers of Woodrow Wilson*, Vol. 63, 196.
[196]Ibid., Vol. 64, 615.
[197]For the estimates, see David Brody, *Labor in Crisis. The Steel Strike of 1919* (Philadelphia & New York, 1965), 113, and Murray, 140.

tives. At the beginning, the administration seemed sympathetic toward organized labor. During the early part of September, Wilson tried in vain to prevail upon Gary to sit down and negotiate with the unions, and when the stubborn chairman refused, the president publicly criticized his obstinacy.[198] When Wilson failed to win over the employers, the administration instead put pressure on the unions to call off the strike or at least postpone it until after the President's Industrial Conference, which opened in Washington, DC, on October 6.[199] The administration's overriding concern was to avoid labor unrest and any interruption of the industrial production. Presidential statements to the Industrial Conference urged it to find ways and means to maintain "peace and harmony" throughout the industrial sector because "the nation's interests are paramount at all times." Wilson proposed that the conference adopt a plan "which will advance further the productive capacity of America through the establishment of a surer and heartier co-operation between all the elements engaged in industry."[200] However, the administration's attempt at conciliation collapsed when the employers refused to accept collective bargaining and the union representatives left the conference.[201]

The most drastic step taken by the administration to prevent a strike in the fall of 1919 was in the case of the coal strike. The United Mine Workers demanded a 60% increase in the wages, a six hour working day and a five day week. When their demands were rejected, the union called a strike on November 1. From the outset the administration seemed determined to prevent the strike from taking place because an interruption of the fuel supply would bring the economy to a halt and bring hardship to the population in the winter. In early September, when negotiations between the two parties were still underway, Secretary of Labor William B. Wilson advised the president to await the result of the discussions. Only if they should break down and threaten the supply of coal, should the administration "take such steps as the situation at that time would warrant."[202] With the president incapacitated by his stroke, the crucial decision to break the impending strike was made by his cabinet and other administration officials. On October 24, Presidential Secretary Joseph Tumulty issued a statement in which he declared it "a cruel neglect of our high duty to humanity" to allow a cessation of the production of coal, and he called on the

[198]Link (ed.), *The Papers of Woodrow Wilson*, Vol. 63, 29-31, 52-53, 65-66.
[199]Ibid., 149, 163.
[200]Ibid., 554, 585.
[201]Murray, 149.
[202]Link (ed.), Vol. 63, 55.

parties to refer their dispute to a board of arbitration while keeping the mines in operation.[203] The following day, the cabinet and the president approved a strongly worded statement prepared by Tumulty and Director-General of Railroads Walker Downer Hines. It called the impending strike "one of the gravest steps ever proposed in this country affecting the economic welfare and the domestic comfort and health of the people" and "a grave moral and legal wrong against the Government and the people of the United States." The statement listed four main arguments for disallowing the strike: it was a violation of the wage agreement made with the sanction of the US Fuel Administration during the war and in effect until April 1, 1920, it would increase the cost of living, it would create a disastrous fuel famine, and it would cut off the aid to the allies. The statement ended by stressing that "the well-being, the comfort and the very life of all the people" were of paramount concern above any selfish interests, and it promised that "the law will be enforced and the means will be found to protect the interests of the nation in any emergency that may arise out of this unhappy business."[204]

The administration, then, acted out of a desire to keep the coal supply running and prevent a cessation of the industry with its unpredictable consequences for the society. It employed the Lever Food and Fuel Control Act of 1917, which forbade anyone from interfering with the production of necessaries, to prevent the strike. Although a wartime law, it was still technically in effect since a peace treaty had not been signed. Following a meeting attended by, among others, Attorney General Palmer, Secretary of Labor Wilson and Assistant Attorney General Garvan, at which the administration's final plans were made, Palmer announced that "Every resource of the Government will be brought to bear to prevent a national disaster which would inevitably result from the cessation of mining operations."[205] On October 30, Palmer conferred with the president and apparently obtained his consent to the steps taken.[206] The following day, the Justice Department applied for and was granted a sweeping temporary restraining order by Judge Albert B. Anderson of the

---

[203]Ibid., 593-594.

[204]Ibid., 599-601. For the cabinet meeting on October 25, see, Cronon (ed.), 452-453.

[205]Coben, *A. Mitchell Palmer,* 179.

[206]Link (ed.), *The Papers of Woodrow Wilson,* Vol. 63, 608n1. Murray claims that Palmer acted on his own in persuading Wilson and obtaining the injunction (Murray, 156-157, 310-311n11), but he ignores that the cabinet discussed the situation on October 28 (Cronon (ed.), 453) and the meeting between Palmer, Secretary of Labor Wilson and others on October 29. For Secretary of Labor Wilson's opposition to the injunction, see letter, William Wilson to Woodrow Wilson, December 12, 1919 (not sent), Corresp. 1919, Wilson Papers, Historical Society of Pennsylvania.

Federal District Court in Indianapolis. It forbade the leaders of the United Mine Workers to issue any strike orders, to take any part in the strike, to publicly support the strike, or to distribute any strike pay, and it directed the UMW leadership to recall the strike order.[207] In the words of Dubofsky and van Tine, "Suddenly an economic struggle between workers and employers had been transformed into a political conflict between labor and the state; a private battle, in which compromise was ordinarily the rule had become a public crisis in which the rule of the law had to prevail."[208] It must be concluded that there is little support for the contention that the Wilson administration was influenced by an anti-radical fear to crack down on the coal strike. If the administration had been so motivated, we would expect this fear to have been more clearly reflected in the cabinet's deliberations and public pronouncements. In fact, the decision to contain the labor unrest was not a dramatic departure from previous policies. It fitted well with the government's overall position during the Progressive Era of stabilizing and protecting the corporate order by containing serious strikes and supporting conservative unions against radical labor.

The Boston Police Strike

The Bureau of Investigation was charged with two responsibilities during the wave of strikes in 1919: to keep the government informed on the strike situation in general and to investigate radical activities. The general intelligence function was motivated by "a desire to have the Department constantly supplied with first hand information of matters relating to the social and economic conditions of the country as a whole."[209] During the most turbulent period, between November 1, when the coal strike broke out, and the end of January 1920, when the unrest had subsided, the field offices wired Washington every Wednesday about the number of strikes in progress in each district, the

---

[207]In the District Court of the US, District of Indiana, In Equity, United States of America, Plaintiff, v. Frank J. Hayes et al (October 31, 1919), OG 303770, RG65, NA; letter, Charles P. Tighe to Frank Burke, November 1, 1919, ibid. This injunction was made permanent on November 8 (Link (ed.), *The Papers of Woodrow Wilson*, Vol. 63, 613n1). For the administration's later efforts to reach a negotiated settlement of the strike, see, William B. Wilson, Memorandum of the Secretary of Labor relative to his Position on the Coal Strike, n.d., Corresp. 1920, Wilson Papers, Historical Society of Pennsylvania; Robert Lansing, Dr. Garfield's Resignation as Fuel Administrator, December 12, 1919, Lansing Private memoranda, Lansing Papers, LC.
[208]Melvyn Dubofsky and Warren van Tine, *John L. Lewis. A Biography* (New York, 1977), 54-55.
[209]Letter, Acting Chief to Frank R. Stone et al, February 17, 1920, OG 290720, RG65, NA.

number of workers involved, and about the number of strikes commenced and ended during the week.[210]

The Bureau played only a limited role in the first of the important strikes during the fall of 1919, the Boston police strike. On September 9, 1,117 of the 1,554 police officers of the Boston police force walked out in protest against Police Commisioner Edwin Curtis' refusal to permit the police officers' organisation, The Boston Social Club, to affiliate with the AFL. He stated that that "a police officer cannot consistently belong to a union and perform his sworn duty."[211] Three days later, the Boston field office was directed by Washington to ascertain the extent of radical activity: "Make thorough investigation in police strike situation and ascertain whether radical elements or I.W.W.'s are in any way responsible for situation. Wire Department any information of particular interest that arises in local situation."[212] Clearly, the Bureau was reacting to the strike by personalizing it as the work of subversive agitators.

Although the strikers made no open radical demands and, in fact, their goal was to affiliate with the conservative AFL, the Bureau agents faithfully tried to prove the existence of a radical conspiracy. One agent was of the opinion that the fact that the Communist paper the *New England Worker* supported the strikers and that it was being distributed among them, "is the first step by the Communists and I.W.W.'s to stir up trouble." The agent expressed the opinion that "this is the first step on the part of the radicals to participate in the strike and make the most of a muddled situation, by fishing in troubled waters." Although the striking police officers had voted unanimously to return to work the previous day, the agent reported that if "the expressions agent heard from the policemen, and their faces indicate anything, they seemed determined to fight the strike to a finish."[213] Another agent mingled with the strikers and reported that he heard "considerable radical talk" while at the strike headquarters. Special Agent Harold M. Zorian, who had infiltrated the local branch of the Socialist Party, thought it highly suspicious that the socialists always

[210]Frank Burke, Circular letter to all Division Superintendents and Agents-in-Charge, October 29, 1919, quoted in, report, E. W. Byrn, Jr., November 1, 1919, ibid. For examples of the Bureau's weekly strike reports submitted to the MID, see, letters, Frank Burke to Brig. Gen. M. Churchill, November 4, 6, 13, 20, 26, December 11, 18, 26, 1919, January 2 and 8, 1920, ibid. For the instruction to end the special strike reports and instead include the information in the Weekley Report on Radical Activities, see, telegram, Burke to Atlanta, Ga., field office, et al, January 27, 1920, OG 303770, ibid.
[211]Murray, 123; in general 122-134.
[212]Telegram, Burke to Kelleher, September 12, 1919, OG 372926, RG65, NA; also, Memorandum in re: Strike of the Boston policemen, n.d. (September 13, 1919), ibid.
[213]Report, Feri F. Weiss, September 13, 1919, ibid.

seemed to have advance knowledge of future strikes, which led him to the conclusion that "the radical Socialist Party of America is connected by some means with the A.F. of L."[214]

It was all very vague, however, and despite their efforts most agents found no signs of radical activity in the strike, or, as rumored, that a general strike was planned in support of the police officers.[215] The strike collapsed completely when all the striking police officers were dismissed, and Governor Coolidge on September 14 rejected Samuel Gomper's offer to mediate with the comment that "There is no right to strike against the public safety by anybody, anywhere, any time." Nevertheless, the Bureau, as in the case of the Seattle general strike, continued its surveillance of alleged radical agitators. Union members, who had supported the strikers financially, were investigated, the Bureau tried to identify those who had allegedly expressed support for the idea of a general strike, and the agents for some time kept the situation in Boston under surveillance.[216] However, the Bureau's role and activities in the strike were rather limited and it apparently never attempted to influence the public opinion or discredit the strike as radically inspired. There were probably two reasons for this limited effort, namely that there was too little radical activity to make an accusation of subversion credible (police officers were probably the last group to be suspected of socialistic sympathies), and that the vigorous intervention by the local authorities quickly broke the strike and thereby rendered further federal initiatives unnecessary.

The Steel Strike

On September 22, one week after the police strike, the steel workers walked out. It has often been argued that the Justice Department remained passive while other groups endeavoured to whip up the Red Scare during the steel strike. However, the Bureau files show that the federal agents kept the strike leaders under close surveillance for months before the strike. The strike was directed by the National Committee for Organizing Iron and Steel Workers, which consisted of 24 unions. It had been formed by the AFL on August 1, 1918, with

[214]Reports, Dan F. O'Connell, September 16, 1919; Harold M. Zorian, September 12 and 13, 1919, ibid.
[215]See for example, reports, Daniel F. O'Connell, September 25, 1919; William J. West, September 23, 1919; John B. Hanrahan, September 30, 1919, ibid.; for the general strike, see for example, reports, M. L. McGrath, October 1, 1919; John B. Hanrahan, September 16, 1919; Dan F. O'Connell, September 16, 1919, ibid.
[216]Reports, Louis P. Nolan, September 26, 1919, ibid.; Charles M. Robinton, September 23 and 24, 1919, OG 290720, ibid.; John B. Hanrahan, November 8, 1919, ibid.

John Fitzpatrick as chairman and William Z. Foster as secretary-treasurer with the aim of initiating an organizing drive in the vital steel industry.[217] It has been known for some time that the steel employers had succeeded in infiltrating the committee,[218] but the Bureau also had its own informer, who kept the government informed about the strike leaders' deliberations.

It is unclear when confidential informant #101 began infiltrating the unions. The first reports from him in the files, which dealt with meetings of the Iron and Steel Workers of the AFL on the progress of the organizing campaign in Pennsylvania, are from as early as February 1919, which contradicts the assumption that the Bureau took no action until forced by a hysterical opinion late in 1919.[219] The informer at some point also infiltrated the National Committee and was by the end of May in a position to report the names of all the union leaders taking part in the planning of the organizing campaign, as well as their contemplated demands and methods. He reported that it was Foster's intention to organize all workers into "One Big Union" and to pressure the AFL into becoming more radical: "Regardless, however, of the outcome, a foundation for an industrial organization has been laid in the steel industry, and unless this organization is handled in a careful and astute manner, it will offer a fertile field for the IWW agitators, should they care to start a campaign."[220] Significantly, this was the only direct reference to the possibility of radical activities in #101's reports; his reports, in other words, confirmed that it was a legitimate union campaign without radical influences.

The informer kept the Bureau closely informed about the strike leaders' plans for the strike. He reported on the union officials' reaction to Judge Gary's rejection of their demands and on the discussions within the National Committee at the beginning of September on whether it should call a strike. When the committee at a meeting on September 9 to 11 decided to call the strike for September 22, the informer quoted Foster as predicting that 80% of the workers would support the walk-out and that it would last for three months: "Foster was very highly elated when the date was set for calling the strike. He acted like a child who had been promised a new

---

[217]Brody, *Labor in Crisis*, 61-65, 69-74.

[218]Ibid., 160; Murray, 146. The only previous account of the BI's surveillance of the steel workers is Charles H. McCormick, *Seeing Red: Federal Surveillance of Radicals in the Pittsburgh Mill District, 1917-1921* (Pittsburgh, 1997). However, McCormick's account is limited to the Pittsburgh area and to the surveillance of the Socialist Party, the IWW and the Communists, and neglects organized labor and the 1919 steel strike.

[219]Reports, #836, February 18, 25, March 4, 17 and 23, 1919, OG 352037, RG65, NA.

[220]Report, #836, May 26, 1919, ibid.

toy and had received it."[221] The informer was also able to keep the Bureau up to date on the National Committee's final preparations, on the funding of the strike and on the overall strategy of standing by the original 12 demands and not to make any separate agreements with individual corporations.[222]

Thanks to #101's reports, the Bureau knew immediately about every move and decision by the National Committee. Two days after the outbreak of the strike, #101 reported that according to Foster 340,000 steel workers were on strike and 80% of the industry was affected, but also that the strikers were subjected to brutality by local police forces and that the media in general followed a pro-employer line.[223] The mood among the strike leaders was still one of optimism in the following days, when Foster continued to report about a high number of strikers and, according to the informer, "In his opinion, we had them beat now." The unions continued to receive new applications for membership, which made John Fitzpatrick exclaim that "Labor had won the greatest battle of its life at this time, in as much as they had the steel trust licked if they would only hold as fast as they had been doing the last ten days."[224] #101 also passed on the information to the government that the AFL was determined to win the strike at any cost and that the leaders were convinced that the public opinion was behind them.[225]

Officials in Washington were thus in a position to follow how the strike began to fall apart in the beginning of October. The informer told his superiors that a number of local union leaders dissociated themselves from the National Committee and, in fact, seemed to support the employers. Moreover the committee was running out of money to pay for the bail for the large number of imprisoned strikers, and soon #101 reported to the Bureau that "Foster, himself looked very much depressed and care worn today. In fact, he looked as though he were all in."[226] The informer, in particular, identified Foster as the decisive figure on the committee. Three weeks into the strike, #101 noted that there was "considerable dissension and friction with the members of the National Committee at the present time" and that a great deal of the dissatisfaction was aimed at Foster, who, according to one committee member, "is getting so much publicity that his head

---

[221]Report, #836, September 15, 1919, ibid.; also, report, #836, September 18, 1919, ibid.
[222]Reports, #836, September 18 and 19, 1919, ibid.
[223]Report, #836, September 24, 1919, ibid.
[224]Reports, #836, September 25 and October 13, 1919, ibid.
[225]Report, #836, October 13, 1919, ibid.
[226]Report, #836, October 13, 1919, ibid.

is swelled and that whatever credit is coming for organizing the steel workers is not coming to Foster." According to #101, Foster was particularly vulnerable because many local union officials were hostile toward him. Several National Committee members expressed the opinion that the last hope for organized labor was if the Wilson administration were to intervene and mediate between the parties during the President's Industrial Conference in Washington.[227] As will be shown later, there are strong indications that the Bureau used its knowledge about Foster's precarious position to help discredit and undermine the strike.

The Bureau from the outset of the strike searched for possible radical activities. An internal memorandum by Radical Division chief Hoover noted that all agents located in the near vicinity of steel plants were advised to keep the situation under surveillance, and Bureau Director William J. Flynn personally inspected the forces.[228] When the Bethlehem Steel Company was hit by the strike on September 29, the Bureau dispatched agents to look for signs of "radical tendencies"; federal agents investigated alleged IWW agitation among the strikers in Lackawann, New York; a major inquiry was made into the extent of radical activity in Ohio; and the Bureau tried to ascertain whether radical elements were back of the continuing strike and demonstrations in November.[229]

The most spectacular attempt at suppressing radical activities during the strike has usually been described as an operation run entirely by the military. On October 4, as a reaction to the industry's use of black strikebreakers, riots broke out among the strikers and several plants were stormed in Gary, Indiana. Two days later the city was placed under martial law and the unrest was quelled by federal troops under General Leonard Wood. Wood soon made sensational headlines by claiming that radical elements had tried to use the strike as a revolutionary uprising and that the perpetrators of several of the recent bombings had instigated the violence at Gary. In a dramatic use of force on October 15, the military conducted a series of 80 raids against alleged radical strongholds, arresting 120 suspected revolutionaries and confiscating an extensive amount of radical propaganda liter-

---

[227]Report, #57, October 12, 1919, ibid.

[228]J. E. Hoover, Memorandum Upon Work of Radical Division, August 1, 1919, to October 15, 1919, October 18, 1919, OG 374217, ibid.

[229]Reports, E. B. Speer, October 8, 1919; H. H. Bowling, October 14, 1919; V. P. Creighton, October 1, 1919; H. F. Blackmon, September 26, 1919; Geo. H. Bragdon, September 24 and 25, 1919; Frank Burke, Memorandum for Mr. Hoover, November 17, 1919; letter, Burke to Ellis Morton, November 8, 1919; Francis P. Garvan, Memorandum for Mr. Burke, November 6, 1919, all in OG 352037, ibid.; report, Joseph Polen, November 14, 1919, OG 290720, ibid.

ature.[230] Since the Bureau took no apparent part in the raids and even refused to corroborate the Army's charges of a Bolshevik plot, it has been assumed that the Bureau was not involved and perhaps even reluctant to participate in the red hunt.[231]

It is true that the Bureau did not participate in the raids themselves and that it did not think much of the military's accusations. Special Agent in Charge Edward Brennan of the Chicago office, which had Gary under its supervision, confidentially informed Washington that "in passing (I) will say that it is my opinion that most all that has been said in the press alleging to have emanated from the military authorities and the Military Intelligence is 'bunkum'."[232] Hoover similarily informed the Justice Department that the dramatic disclosures apparently "were more fiction than truth."[233] On the other hand it is apparent from the files that the Bureau did play an important behind-the-scenes role in Gary. Even before the outbreak of the national strike, Special Agent Jacob Spolansky of the Chicago office directed confidential informant #115 to infiltrate the IWW and to pose as a radical agitator among the steel workers in Gary.[234] At the same time, agents were instructed to investigate radical activities and the Chicago office received numerous reports on "alien radicals, Bolsheviks, I.W.W.'s or socalled 'reds'" from outside sources such as steel corporations, municipal and state authorities, and the MID.[235] Sometime before October 13, the agents compiled a list of "various alleged radicals" who were staying in Gary, which was then submitted to the MID. Since this took place just before the raids, the Bureau list might actually have formed the basis for the military's subsequent raids.[236] This did not end the Bureau's involvement. Following the raids, Bureau agents interrogated the 120 "alleged alien radicals," who had been taken into custody, and started deportation proceedings against 7 of them.[237] Thus, the Bureau played an important role in the

---

[230]Murray, 146-148; Brody, *Labor in Crisis*, 134-136. For an example of Wood's claims, see "Wood Blames Reds for Gary Disorders," *The New York Times*, October 19, 1919. Brody has noted in regard to the value of the military's accusations: "No evidence ever revealed Bolshevik control of the strike in Gary" (Brody, *Labor in Crisis*, 136).

[231]Coben, *A. Mitchell Palmer*, 174, 176.

[232]Letter, Edward Brennan to Frank Burke, October 18, 1919, OG 352037, RG65, NA.

[233]Hoover, memorandum op cit., October 18, 1919, OG 374217, ibid.

[234]Report, J. Spolansky, September 17, 1919, OG 352037, ibid.

[235]Letter, Brennan to Burke, October 18, 1919, ibid.; also report, Jacob Spolansky, October 18, 1919, ibid.

[236]Report, H. S. Hibbard, October 13, 1919, ibid. This was apparently done on the Chicago office's own initiative and without the knowledge of Washington, for upon the receipt of the report, Assistant Director and Chief Frank Burke inquired of Chicago on whose authority this had been done (telegram, Burke to Brennan, October 17, 1919, ibid.).

[237]Letter, Brennan to Burke, October 18, 1919, ibid.

intervention in Gary by compiling information on radicals, providing the military with the names of radical activists, which were likely used during the raids, and by subsequently questioning and opening deportation cases against those arrested.

Most historians agree that radical influences played little if any role in the steel strike. In the words of labor historian David Brody, the strike was the result of a "rank and file" movement in which the workers, dissatisfied with the traditional seven days weeks and twelve hours days, falling real wages, and growing unemployment after the war, forced the National Committee to call the strike even though it was not yet strong enough to win the strike. Significantly, 98% of the union members who took part in the referendum supported the strike. The National Committee made no political demands but limited its demands to such issues as the right to collective bargaining, an eight hour day, higher wages and the abolition of the company unions.[238] The radicals' influence on the strike was minimal. The recently formed Communist parties had little contact with organized labor and were ideologically opposed to strikes unless they developed into a revolutionary situation. The steel strike, in fact, "failed to rouse any enthusiasm among the Communists."[239] The IWW, even if it had wanted to, was too weakened by the wartime persecutions to make any impact on the strike.[240]

Although no concrete evidence or signs of radical activities during the steel strike have been found in the Bureau files, the federal agents did not remain passive but tried actively to discredit and undermine the strike in several ways. First, it is normally assumed that an effective investigation must be conducted in secret so that the suspects do not go in hiding or cover up their tracks. However, the Justice Department carefully leaked news of its surveillance activities to the press, thereby putting the strikers and their sympathizers on notice that they would be watched by the government. During the early days of the conflict, papers were able to report that the Bureau had entered the strike and was searching for radical agitators. The day following the outbreak of the strike, the *Chicago Herald* reported on "US Agents in Strike Zone," two days later the paper carried the headline that "US is Watching Actions of Reds in Steel Strike," while the *Chicago Post* exclaimed that

[238]Brody, *Labor in Crisis*, 78-81, 95-100, 113-115.
[239]Draper, 198.
[240]Dubofsky, 453.

"Federal Agents Comb Zone of Strike for Reds."[241] On September 26, the *New York Times* revealed that Bureau Director William J. Flynn had arrived at Pittsburgh, the center of the steel industry, "to investigate the steel strike." Its source was US Attorney E. Lowry Humes, with whom the Bureau had cooperated closely when he was chief counsel for the Overman Committee.[242] The following day, again with Humes as the source, the paper reported about Flynn's visit and added ominously that "it is understood Mr. Flynn is co-operating to the fullest extent with the local offices of the Department of Justice and there are hints that important developments may take place."[243] The *Washington Times* was also able to bring the story about the federal investigation in Pittsburgh under the headline "Chief Flynn and Secret Agents Busy in Pittsburgh."[244] Clearly, the effect of this publicity, at least some of which was based on information provided by Justice Department officials like Humes, was to brand the strike in the public mind as a criminal or subversive affair, and to warn off workers and political activists from participating in it.

The most important effort to undermine the strike, however, was the Bureau's campaign against the secretary-treasurer of the National Committee and the leading spirit behind the organizing drive, William Z. Foster. Foster was clearly the weak link in the strike leadership and he had made plenty of extreme statements in the past, which could be used to smear his person and thereby discredit the strike as a revolutionary plot. Foster, who grew up in the slums of Philadelphia and had held a variety of jobs, was a former member of the Socialist Party, from which he had been excluded in 1909 because of his participation in a left wing faction. He had also been a member of the IWW, which he had left in 1912 in a dispute about the correct union strategy. The IWW had traditionally positioned itself as the radical alternative to the conservative AFL and had agitated for the organizing of all workers in "One Big Union." Following a visit to Europe in 1910 to 1911, Foster became a spokesman for the "boring-from-within" strategy, which he defined as "the policy of militant workers penetrating conservative unions, rather than trying to construct new, ideal industrial unions on

[241]"US Agents in Strike Zone," *The Chicago Herald*, September 23, 1919; "US is Watching Actions of Reds in Steel Strike," *The Chicago Herald*, September 25, 1919; "Federal Agents Comb Zone of Strike for Reds," *The Chicago Post*, October 9, 1919, all clippings in OG 352037, RG65, NA.
[242]"Both Sides Claim Gains," *The New York Times*, September 26, 1919.
[243]"Break in Strike Expected Monday," *The New York Times*, September 27, 1919.
[244]"Chief Flynn and Secret Agents Busy in Pittsburgh," *The Washington Times*, September 25, 1919, clipping in OG 352037, RG65, NA.

the outside."[245] In this period, Foster wrote a number of articles in the IWW paper *Solidarity,* and published a pamphlet entitled *Syndicalism,* in which he in a militant language argued for the necessity of a revolution in the US, and in which he stated that "The syndicalist ... recognizes no rights of the capitalists to their property, and is going to strip them of it, law or no law."[246] After having been active in a number of small syndicalist groups, Foster took charge of the AFL organizing campaign among the packing-house workers in Chicago in 1917.

According to previous accounts, the original source behind the circulation of the information about Foster's past political activities was a local journalist in Pittsburgh and the information was then taken up by the steel industry and conservative politicians.[247] However, according to internal Bureau documents, it was the Bureau which "unearthed" the facts about Foster's background, and "Foster's record as revealed by the Department of Justice showed that he had been previously an I.W.W. and a syndicalist and that he had failed to make any change in his fundamental principles after he became a power in the American Federation of Labor."[248] Most likely, the information came from the extensive Bureau files on Foster.[249] As Hoover informed his superiors in the Justice Department, a detailed memorandum upon Foster's past and present activities, "showing him to be an anarchist and syndicalist," had been prepared and "This information has been submitted informally to the senate committee investigating the steel strike."[250]

The Senate Committee on Education and Labor had begun an investigation into the steel strike, and although it is impossible to ascertain to what degree the Bureau's disclosures influenced the course

---

[245]Dubofsky, 222; for Foster's background in general, see, ibid., 221-226; Draper, 311-312; Edward P. Johanningsmeier, *Forging American Communism. The Life of William Z. Foster* (Princeton, N.J., 1994), 10-87.

[246]Brody, *Labor in Crisis,* 138.

[247]Ibid., 136-139; Murray, 143-144.

[248]Memorandum Upon the Work of the Radical Division, August 1, 1919 to March 15, 1919, OG 374217, RG65, NA.

[249]The central index to the early Bureau files 1908-22 (in RG65, NA) contains 74 references to Foster, some of which date back to the period before World War I (OG 2326/18198/32437/18789).

[250]J. E. Hoover, Memorandum Upon Work of Radical Division, August 1, 1919, to October 15, 1919, October 18, 1919, RG65, NA. Although no copy of the memorandum to the Senate committee was found when the Bureau files in RG65, NA, were searched, and it might be argued that Hoover had an interest in exaggerating the accomplishments of the Radical Division before his superiors and to claim credit for the failure of the strike, there is no reason to doubt that the Radical Division did submit information on Foster's background to the Senate committee. Justice Department officials could easily have verified the accuracy of the claim, and the Division would hardly have referred to its role in a report to Congress in 1920 unless it was true (for the report, see *AG Palmer on Charges,* 170-171).

of the inquiry – the steel industry and parts of the press were at the same time using Foster's articles to present the strike as a Bolshevik conspiracy – the senators soon zeroed in on Foster. On October 3, in the second week of the strike, Foster was questioned at a committee hearing about his political opinions, and when he refused to completely dissociate himself from his previous syndicalist statements, the strike was effectively discredited as a radical enterprise; in the words of David Brody, "The last piece had been fitted in place to complete the picture of the steel strike as a dangerous radical movement."[251] In its final report on the strike, published while the steel workers were still out, the committee emphasized Foster's role and concluded: "Behind this strike there is massed a considerable element of IWWs, anarchists, revolutionists, and Russian Soviets, and ... some radical men not in harmony with the conservative elements of the American Federation of Labor are attempting to use the strike as a means of elevating themselves to power within the ranks of organized labor."[252]

The Bureau followed up by reporting to Congress that the entire conflict had, in fact, been engineered and manipulated by Foster and the IWW. The Bureau's explanation of the conflict was a perfect example of its tendency to personify complex social and economic dislocations, ignore the underlying causes and blame the individual agitator for the unrest. The Bureau also ignored the fact that it was unable to prove any radical activities on Foster's part during the strike. The surveillance of the National Committee showed that he had concentrated his efforts on the organizing campaign while leaving the revolutionary propaganda to others, and he was, in fact, perceived by the Communists as "a renegade and traitor" for working for the conservative AFL.[253] The Bureau told Congress that the strike "was really the culmination of the efforts of its leader, W. Z. Foster, ... to organize the steel workers ostensibly for the American Federation of Labor, but in reality for effecting his 'boring from within' methods." His intention of triggering the strike was no less than the purging of the AFL of its conservative leadership and to "form the greatest revolutionary labor movement the world has ever seen." According to the Bureau, Foster worked closely with the IWW behind the scenes, IWW agitators "wormed their way" into the ranks of the steel workers and spread dissatisfaction, and "with the assistance of various radical

---

[251]Brody, *Labor in Crisis*, 143-144; for the hearing in general, ibid., 141-142; Draper, 444-445n15; Johanningsmeier, 142-143. For the steel industry's campaign against Foster, see Levin, 43-45; Murray, 143-144.

[252]Quoted in, Coben, *A. Mitchell Palmer*, 175.

[253]Draper, 313; also, Brody, *Labor in Crisis*, 139.

organizations Foster was successful in bringing about a general strike of the steel workers...."[254]

The Bureau, then, did not remain on the sidelines during the steel strike in September and October of 1919, such as has previously been believed, but participated actively in the smearing of the strike as a radical conspiracy. According to all accounts, this smear campaign was immensely effective. It created dissension and suspicion within the National Committee and labor's own ranks (the AFL began putting Foster under surveillance), eroded popular support for the strikers and enabled the employers to stand firm in their rejection of all demands. The remaining strikers resumed work in January 1920 without a single of their original twelve demands having been met.[255] As Hoover noted internally, the Bureau's disclosures "have quite apparently had a very salutary effect upon the failure of the radical elements in the steel strike."[256] Congress was informed by the Attorney General that thanks to the Justice Department's action "in exposing the plan of W. Z. Foster," the strike had ended with the failure of the radical "borers from within" and "a complete victory for the American Federation of Labor."[257] Although these statements must be taken for what they were, attempts to take the credit for undermining the strike, they nevertheless point to the fact that the Bureau played a vital role in painting the picture of the strike as an imminent radical uprising.

The Coal Strike
The Bureau also played a hereto largely unknown but vital role in the breaking of the coal strike and in the discrediting of the conflict as a radical uprising. As in the case of the steel strike, the Bureau succeeded in infiltrating the strike leadership sometime before the strike became effective on November 1 and was thereby able to keep the Justice Department continuously advised on the union officials' deliberations and planning. On October 29, Assistant Director and Chief Frank Burke advised Assistant Attorney General Garvan that the Executive Board of the United Mine Workers was meeting in Indianapolis to make a final decision as to whether they should stand by their demands and let the strike go forward. He added that the meeting was taking place behind closed doors but that "my informant assures me that he can obtain minute reports and has Lewis' promise of

---

[254]*AG Palmer on Charges*, 170-171.
[255]Brody, *Labor in Crisis*, 143-145, 174; Murray, 152.
[256]Hoover, memo op cit., October 18, 1919, OG 374217, RG65, NA.
[257]*AG Palmer on Charges*, 171.

admission."[258] Via the Indianapolis office the informer kept the Bureau up to date on the attitudes among the UMW leadership: their dissatisfaction with President Wilson's condemnation of the strike, their unanimous support for the strike and their hope for government mediation: "... Lewis and other officials do not wish to stand responsible and are in receptive mood for governmental suggestions and help." However, the informer was of the opinion that the strike could not be avoided due to the tremendous pressure excercised by the members upon the leaders.[259] Two days before the date set for the strike, the informer advised the Bureau that the UMW had decided to stand by its demands and to let the strike notice stand despite the imminent government injunction.[260]

The injunction, handed down by Judge Anderson on October 31, which forbade the UMW leaders to take any part in the strike, provided the administration with a legal basis for deploying the full force of the Bureau to find any signs of active UMW involvement. When the injunction was issued, an internal Bureau memorandum noted, "Anticipate they will violate the injunction. Will have to look out for contempt court proceedings."[261] Attorney General Palmer simultaneously advised US attorneys to cooperate with US marshalls and Bureau agents to look for violations of the court decree. Bureau agents were instructed to keep the movements and speeches of the labor leaders under close surveillance and to keep Washington informed of all developments.[262]

The Bureau in particular concentrated its surveillance operation on UMW President John L. Lewis, although Bureau officials did not have high expectations of catching the cunning labor leader in violating the injunction. The Indianapolis office notified Washington that the UMW leadership would behave extremely carefully: "They are not going to send telegrams, letters, etc. but are going to pass the word along. They will not have an office but will keep their office in their hats. We have some men here who are pretty good but not good enough to shadow these men. Green and Lewis have evaporated and have gone probably to Washington, Springfield or Chicago."[263] The Bureau's loss of Lewis

---

[258]Frank Burke, Memorandum for Mr. Garvan, October 29, 1919, OG 303770, RG65, NA.
[259]Telegrams, Tighe to Burke, n.d. and October 29, 1919; Burke, Memorandum for Mr. Garvan, October 29, 1919, ibid.
[260]Telegram, Tighe to Burke, October 30, 1919, ibid.
[261]Memorandum, Indianapolis Situation, October 31, 1919, ibid.
[262]Letter, Allan K. Smith to Palmer, November 3, 1919; telegram, Breniman to A. R. Gere, November 3, 1919, ibid.
[263]Memorandum, Telephone Call, November 2, 1919, ibid.; also, memorandum, Telephone Calls, November 1, 1919, ibid. William Green was the UMW secretary-treasurer.

prompted a major search in Indianapolis and Washington until he was finally relocated at the UMW headquarters. The local field office was able to reassure Washington that "Lewis is now under constant surveillance and is spending his time at the U.M.W. of A. office and at the English Hotel where he takes his meals and sleeps."[264] Although the surveillance continued well into December even after the strike had been called off, the Bureau never discovered any concrete evidence that the UMW leader had violated the injunction. This was not surprising since Lewis had made all his preparations before the strike and took no part in the strike.[265]

The Bureau used all available means to obtain evidence against the UMW leaders. Special Agent V. P. Creighton made arrangements with the Postal Telegraph Company in Indianapolis so that the Bureau was given access to all telegrams to and from Lewis.[266] In this way the Bureau was able to read the telegrams between Lewis and Representative Everrett Sanders and all of the communication between the UMW headquarters and the local branches and officials.[267] In order to ascertain whether the UMW was paying strike benefits in violation of the injunction, the Bureau informally and in the strictest confidence was given access to the UMW accounts in the Indiana National Bank. The Bureau closely monitored how much was withdrawn each day and established that the union at no time had more than $5,000 in its strike fund but no less than $215,925.43 in its checking account. Creighton added that "This information was secured through absolute confidential source and while it is correct, if it is desired to officially confirm these figures, it will be necessary that a subpoena duces tecum be served on the Indiana National Bank."[268] Thanks to its close contacts to the banking community, the Bureau obtained the same informal access to the accounts of local UMW branches around the nation.[269] The Bureau also tapped the phones of the UMW leaders,

---

[264]Report, V. P. Creighton, November 5, 1919, OG 303770, RG65, NA. For the search, see, reports, M. A. Joyce, November 5, 1919; H. P. Alden, November 15, 1919; M. E. Tucker, In re: Confidential Investigation. John L. Lewis. Acting President of the United Mine Workers of America, November 21, 1919, ibid.

[265]For the results of the surveillance, see for example, reports, V. P. Creighton, November 6, 10, 15, 1919; F. M. Sturgis, November 11, 1919; Wm. Sausele, December 17, 1919; note, n.d.; Memorandum to Frank Burke, November 7, 1919, ibid. For Lewis' preparations and inactivity during the strike, see Dubofsky & van Tine, 56.

[266]Reports, V. P. Creighton, November 2, 4, 5, 6, 7, 10, 13, 1919, OG 303770, RG65, NA.

[267]Telegram, Tighe to Burke, November 6, 1919; report, Roy Samson, November 7, 1919, ibid.

[268]Report, V. P. Creighton, November 5, 1919, ibid.; also, reports, Creighton, November 2, 1919; Joseph Polen, November 28, 1919, ibid.

[269]For example, reports, Oscar Schmitz, December 8, 1919; M. L. Babbitt, December 3, 1919, ibid.

apparently without any warrants. Special Agent in Charge William M. Doyas of the Baltimore office reported that initially he had contemplated leasing a room in The Franklin Building, in which the offices of the Maryland Federation of Labor were located, in order to bug them with a dictaphone. This plan had to be abandoned since the room had already been taken. Instead, the agents put a tap on the telephone of the local AFL president, John H. Ferguson.[270]

This extensive surveillance operation provided the government with plenty of evidence about the UMW leaders' criticism and bitterness against the administration's attempt to break the strike but no concrete proof of any violations of the injunction.[271] However, the Bureau possibly had another and more important aim with the surveillance. As in the case of the steel strike, news of the activities of the federal agents was leaked to the press, most likely to frighten the labor leaders into calling off the strike. A transcript of a telephone conversation between AFL President Gompers and Lewis on November 7 confirms that the existence of the surveillance was common knowledge: "Now, I may say this, John: No matter how you may be beset by detectives and the wires and telephones tapped, we asked the Attorney General and received his assurance that whatever you may say to me over the phone will not at any time be used against you or others in any attempted proceedings or in any other way, so that you can talk freely upon the subject."[272] Clearly, the Bureau acted as the government's instrument in undermining and breaking the coal strike by intimidating the UMW leadership.

At the same time, the Bureau launched a major search for radical activities. In Pittsburgh, Division Superintendent Todd Daniel surveyed the coal mines in Western Pennsylvania and dispatched a force of special agents and undercover men. They were all miners and some were UMW members. They were charged with identifying all radical agitators, ascertaining their place of birth, citizenship and political affiliations, and being on the alert for the distribution of radical literature.[273] In Philadelphia lists of "reds" were compiled. In Baltimore the force of confidential informants was instructed to cover all meetings, report all "essential remarks," obtain the names and addresses of all agitators and union leaders, ascertain any kind of

[270]Report, Wm. M. Doyas, November 3, 1919, ibid.
[271]See reports, V. M. Simmons, November 4 and 10, 1919; F. W. Byrn, Jr., November 26, 1919; memorandum, Telephone Call, November 10, 1919, ibid.
[272]Quoted in Dubofsky & van Tine, 55-56.
[273]Edgar B. Speer, Special Report to Frank Burke, October 31, 1919; letters, Todd Daniel to Frank Burke, October 28, 1919, with att. letters, and October 30, 1919, OG 303770, RG65, NA.

support given to the strikers, including financial support and the establishment of co-operative stores, collect copies of all circulars and literature distributed by the strikers, and report all instances of picketing or threats against strikebreakers.[274] As a result, agents often cast a wide net looking for radicals. Special Agent John C. Rider reported that he was investigating "the advocation of radicalism by labor organizers or others affiliated with the Socialist, IWW, Syndicalist, Communist or Anarchist organizations",[275] while D. E. Tator was watching "the activities of the radical organizers, IWW's etc ... should they attempt to inoculate the striking mine workers with the idea that the present unrest is in fact a social revolution."[276]

A few times the agents did come upon, or so they thought, signs of radical activity. For example, an agent reported that 50% of the miners in Terre Haute, Indiana, were radical aliens who dominated the local branch of the UMW, and he recommended that in case the strike was prolonged that the authorities should prevent any trouble by intervening "quickly and perhaps harshly."[277] In West Virginia, the Bureau looked into an ominous but, as it eventually turned out, baseless allegation that Russian miners had taken charge of the strike and were threatening to march against Washington. In addition, the MID submitted a list of 148 alleged radicals who were agitating among the strikers in West Virginia.[278] However, these were scattered exceptions and in most instances the agents found no radical activity at all. For example, the inquiry into the situation in Williamson County in Illinois led to the conclusion that "there are not any Bolshevists among the men here, and that they have no use for the foreign agitators. At this time there are no indications of trouble here whatever."[279] In Linton, Indiana, the agents arrived at the conclusion that "the men are not actively engaged in breaches of the injunction, neither are they permitting outside radicals to enter...."[280] Special Agent Trevor B. Mathews, who had infiltrated the ranks of the strikers in Philadelphia, summed up the situation: "Everybody seems to be talking 'strike' but as yet I have failed to hear any mention of 'reds' – 'revolution' – or

[274]Report, J. F. McDevitt, October 29, 1919; letter, William M. Doyas to all Confidential Informants, November 3, 1919; report, Oscar Schmitz, November 16, 1919, ibid.
[275]Report, John C. Rider, November 1, 1919, ibid. For similar expressions, see, reports, V. F. Sawken, November 4, 1919; B. H. Burgess, December 5. 1919, ibid.
[276]Report, D. E. Tator, November 4, 1919, ibid.
[277]Report, V. S. Bachman, November 8, 1919, ibid.
[278]Telegram, Chief to Wilson, November 13, 1919; letter, Lieut. Col. Wrisley Brown to Frank Burke, November 26, 1919, with att.: Radicals identified in the coal field of West Virginia, n.d., ibid.
[279]Report, Chas. W. Fisher, November 4, 1919, ibid.
[280]Report, Wm. C. Sausele, November 23, 1919, ibid.

'radicalism'.... I talked to a few of the miners and they claim that there have not as yet been any radical speakers in this section. The miners to whom I spoke seem to know very little of radical activities. There is an undercurrent of Socialism in some of the remarks the miners make but this is prevalent in all labor disturbances; some of the miners look upon the coming strike as a sort of vacation."[281] After another week of investigating, Mathews reported that "Radicalism has not as yet made its appearances in this section among the miners."[282] A status report confirmed that these reports were representative of the general findings of the Bureau's investigation. Four days into the strike, after having been in contact with the field, a Bureau memorandum concluded: "Our under cover informants find no radicalism at all among any element."[283]

If the nationwide Bureau investigation did not provide any basis for the charge that the coal strike was radically inspired or led, it did provide the government with a much more complex picture of the conflict. Three themes run through the surveillance reports. First, agents and informers who infiltrated the ranks of the strikers reported that there was a widespread dissatisfaction with the working conditions and bitterness against the injunction.[284] Second, the federal agents at the same time found considerable discontent with the strike itself and that many miners were of the opinion that the demands put forward by the UMW leaders were too ambitious and unrealistic. But most strikers were reluctant to return to work, either because of loyalty to their union or fear of intimidation.[285] Third, the Bureau discovered that it was apparently a widespread phenomenon – and a contributory cause to the prolongation of the strike – that a number of employers refused to rehire the striking miners who returned to work in order to purge their companies of union members.[286] Thus, the Bureau's internal information contained little evidence of radical activities and,

[281]Report, Trevor B. Mathews, October 31, 1919, ibid.
[282]Report, Trevor B. Mathews, November 6, 1919, ibid.
[283]Memorandum, Telephone Call, November 4, 1919, ibid.
[284]For example, reports, E. Nagele, November 5, 1919; J. W. Hopper, November 7, 1919, ibid. The Bureau summarized its information on the strike, see Brief #3, November 3, 1919, and Brief #4, November 4, 1919, ibid. There are numerous reports from agents in the field relating to the general situation in the mining areas, the effectiveness of the strike, the mood among the miners and investigations of radical activities and violations of the injunction by the UMW leaders in OG 303770, ibid.
[285]For example, reports, V. M. Simmons, November 4, 1919; C. S. Weakley, November 5, 1919; C. E. Carpenter, November 8, 1919; Fred S. Dunn, December 19, 1919; T. F. Mullen, December 8, 1919; J. Shipper, November 8, 1919; B. H. Burgess, December 3 and 8, 1919, ibid.
[286]For example, reports, James W. Melrose, November 22, 1919; F. D. Jones, November 10 and 15, 1919; Lee Craft, December 8, 1919, ibid.

in particular, no concrete proof that the coal strike was part of a revolutionary movement.

Despite the confidential information to the contrary, the Bureau sought to portray the strike as radically inspired. In its final report on the coal strike, prepared by George F. Ruch of the Radical Division, which was presented to Congress in 1920, the strike was described as "a contest in the American Federation of Labor and between the patriotic elements therein and the radical forces." According to the Bureau, the strike was an attempt by the radicals to gain control over the union and the miners, but it was only able to come up with two pieces of evidence in support of its contention. First, it was argued that the "red element" had influenced the miners by distributing quantities of inflammatory literature, and this was based on three leaflets issued by the Communist Party and the Socialist Labor Party which had been found during the strike. Second, Ruch claimed that agitators from the Communist Party and the Union of Russian Workers had "continued to influence the miners," particularly in West Virginia and Pennsylvania, and were therefore "directly responsible for the unrest existing in those sections of the country."[287] In its annual report to Congress, the Justice Department claimed that as always, "the ultraradical element took advantage of an industrial disturbance arising from other causes, to make headway for their own cause." The Communist Party, in particular, had been active in "urging the workers to rise up against the Government of the United States."[288] Most likely, the charge of radical subversion of the strike, made in clear contradiction of the Bureau's internal evidence, was not so much the result of the federal officials being influenced by and even captured by a wave of public hysteria. Rather, the accusation was used to justify the government's intervention in and breaking of the strike; as the Justice Department pointed out, the injunction "brought the strike to an end and with it the activities of such ultraradicals as had sought to take advantage of the strike for their own purposes."[289] Thus, the Red Scare was used and promoted as part of the federal authorities' campaign to end the coal strike and thus to ensure the supply of fuel to the industry and the population in the face of the winter.

---

[287]George F. Ruch, report: Coal Strike, n.d., ibid.; for the report to Congress, see *AG Palmer on Charges*, 172-173.
[288]*AG Report 1920*, 175.
[289]Ibid.

The Surveillance of Organized Labor

The Bureau's intervention in the strikes during 1919 institutionalized its role of keeping unions and strikes under surveillance. For example, the federal agents continued to keep a close watch on the chief organizer of the steel strike, William Z. Foster, who in November 1920 established the Communist affiliated Trade Union Educational League and in 1923 finally declared himself to be a Communist.[290] During the early part of the 1920s, the Bureau subjected the organization to intense scrutiny: it was infiltrated, its meetings monitored, its finances and members investigated, and its literature systematically collected and analyzed.[291] Although it was obvious that the TUEL was an insignificant and marginal union – James Weinstein has characterized the TUEL as "an isolated and almost rootless organization, and Foster himself was cut off from the mainstream of the labor movement, as well as from the socialists and the IWW"[292] – the federal authorities exaggerated its importance in order to claim that the Communists made inroads into organized labor. For example, the Bureau claimed that the TUEL constituted "a definite, serious factor in the labor movement of this country,"[293] and the Justice Department stated that it was "meeting with marked success."[294]

The Bureau also continued the surveillance of the United Mine Workers. During 1920, coal strikes in Scranton, Pennsylvania, and Birmingham, Alabama, were investigated,[295] and the federal agents also monitored the violent strikes in Logan and Mingo Counties in West Virginia in 1921.[296] The Bureau was particularly interested in radical activities within the UMW; thus, in 1921 a convention held by the radical wing of the UMW as well as the regular UMW convention was investigated. In 1924 a major inquiry into the Progressive International Committee of the UMW, which consisted of Communist and other radical union members, was launched. The strength of the radicals within the various UMW locals was ascertained, their activities at the national UMW convention in early 1924 were closely followed and a number of delegates classified as "reds" by the federal detectives.[297]

---

[290]Draper, 314, 321-322; Jonanningsmeier, 150-207.

[291]See the numerous reports in file 61-714, box 4, Series 10, FBI Records, MU.

[292]Weinstein, *The Decline of Socialism,* 266.

[293]Report, Jacob Spolansky, March 31, 1922, 61-714-13, box 4, Series 10, FBI Records, MU.

[294]*AG Report 1921,* 130.

[295]For the Scranton strike, see the reports in BS 205194-66, RG65, NA; for the Birmingham inquiry, see the reports in BS 202600-113, ibid.

[296]See the reports in BS 205194-50, ibid., and the letters in file #400 and 934, Series 4, Warren G. Harding Papers, LC.

[297]The course of these inquiries into the UMW can be followed in files BS 202600-113, RG65, NA, and 61-1241, box 2, Series 10, FBI Records, MU.

Although few concrete signs of actual radical activities within the UMW were unearthed, the Bureau publicly intimated that the union was somehow influenced by subversive forces. Director Burns stated during a congressional hearing that the Bureau had investigated the national coal strike in 1922 and discovered that the Third International in Moscow had issued instructions to its representatives in the US "that they were to do everything possible to arouse the striking miners to the point of armed insurrection."[298] Thus, by ignoring the deeper causes of the strike and the de facto limited radical influence, Burns was able to portray a legitimate labor conflict as not only foreign directed but even as an attempted uprising against the government. The same was true about Burns' general explanation for strikes and labor unrest during the early 1920s, when he noted that "in my opinion the Soviet government is responsible for most of it, and the employment situation adds to it. There is no question about that."[299] He thereby identified subversive influences as the primary cause and the social conditions as only a contributing cause. In other words, as was the case in 1919, the workers' use of the strike weapon to win the right to organize, improved working conditions, shorter hours and better pay was portrayed as illegitimate and subversive acts which should be undermined and defeated in order to restore the existing order.

[298]*Appropriations, Department of Justice, 1925,* 93.
[299]*Appropriation, Department of Justice, 1923,* Pt. 2, 131.

Chapter 6

The Palmer Raids: Deporting Political Ideas

The dramatic mass arrests and deportations in late 1919 and early 1920 of up to an estimated 10,000 suspected alien anarchists and Communists, popularly known as the Palmer raids, marked the climax of the Red Scare. The description of the raids also constitutes the main part of most accounts of the Bureau's role during the Red Scare. It might be argued, however, that the discussion of the Bureau's role in the raids was derailed from the beginning by focusing on the issue of whether the federal agents used illegal methods. This tradition might be said to have started with a report prepared by the liberal National Popular Government League in May 1920 and signed by twelve prominent lawyers, among others Felix Frankfurter, Zechariah Chafee and Roscoe Pound, which was entitled *To the American People. Report Upon the Illegal Practices of the United States Department of Justice.* It accused the Department of violating the aliens' constitutional rights by making arrests and conducting searches and seizures without warrants, denying counsel to the detainees, keeping them imprisoned indefinitely on excessive high bail, and by mistreating them.[1] Two congressional hearings followed in 1920 and 1921, and both focused on the Bureau's alleged illegal methods.[2]

This debate about the use of illegal methods has left the impression that the Bureau's conduct was an aberration from normal, legal practices. It has provided support for the view that the raids were spontaneous and zealous operations, brought about by the demands of a hysterical opinion; according to this view, government officials were simply too frightened to observe the rights of the radical aliens. However, as demonstrated by William Preston, Jr., the Bureau's methods during the raids were not a dramatic break with previous policies. They were, in fact, simply the continuation of the practices and procedures developed by the immigration authorities during the previous two to three decades. Furthermore, they were technically

---

[1] National Popular Government League, *To the American People. Report Upon the Illegal Practices of the United States Department of Justice* (Washington, DC, 1920), especially, 3-9.

[2] *AG Palmer on Charges* and *Charges of Illegal Practices.* For example, Murray used much of his two chapters on the raids on a discussion of the Bureau's methods and Lowenthal spent some 120 pages of his history of the FBI to document the charges.

236

legal since the Supreme Court had held the deportation process to be an administrative and not criminal procedure and, consequently, aliens held for deportation had no constitutional rights. According to Preston, the Bureau "had simply carried traditional immigration practices to a logical conclusion...."[3] In other words, the federal government did not need outside pressure in order to treat the aliens harshly.

The Poindexter Resolution

The perception that the raids were spontaneous enterprises has led most historians to adopt the view that they were caused by the demands of a hysterical population. John Higham has described how "a supernationalist public opinion urged the federal government along the path of coercion,"[4] and Robert Murray has pointed out that "the ability of the government to withstand mounting public pressure rapidly weakened. Nowhere was this fact more apparent than in the matter of alien deportations."[5] According to these accounts, the decisive event which triggered the raids was the so-called Poindexter resolution. On October 14, 1919, Senator Miles Poindexter, Republican of Washington, told the Senate "that the increasing number of strikes is based on a desire to overthrow our Government, destroy all authority, and establish Communism." He warned that "There is grave danger that a Government will be overthrown when it ceases to defend itself. This is no time for sensitiveness on the part of public officials."[6] Poindexter introduced a resolution which was adopted by the Senate three days later. It requested the Attorney General to inform the Senate whether he had taken any "legal proceedings, and if not, why not, and if so, to what extent, for the arrest and punishment" of persons who "have attempted to bring about the forcible overthrow of the Government" and "have preached anarchy and sedition." Palmer was also requested to report if he had taken any "legal proceedings for the arrest and deportation of aliens" engaged in seditious activities.[7] The conventional explanations of the raids might be said to consist of two contentions: that the Poindexter resolution was the expression of a broadly based, grass roots hysteria and that the resolution pushed a somewhat reluctant and passive federal government into repressing the activities of radical aliens.

---

[3]Preston, 220; in general, also, 1-21.
[4]Higham, 228.
[5]Murray, 205; also, 191, 200, 206. For similar explanations of the causes of the raids, see, Murphy, "Sources and Nature," 65-66; Coben, "A Study in Nativism," 72-73.
[6]"Expose IWW Plot to Seize Power," *The New York Times*, October 15, 1919.
[7]*Investigation Activities of Department of Justice*, 5. Also, see, "Senate Asks Palmer for Data on Radicals," *The New York Times*, October 18, 1919.

Most historians have tended to ignore the political context of the Poindexter resolution. In fact, the resolution must be seen, not as the expression of the national mind, but as a continuation of the highly effective attack by the Republican Party against the Wilson administration during the midterm elections in 1918. The GOP's strategy was formulated primarily by former President Theodore Roosevelt, Senator Henry Cabot Lodge and Will H. Hays, chairman of the Republican National Committee. It consisted basically of questioning the patriotism of the Democrats by hinting that the administration was using the wartime emergency to introduce state planning of the economy and by accusing it of betraying the Allied cause with a negotiated peace settlement with Germany. A recurring theme of much of the Republican rhetoric was that the administration was sympathetic to and even infiltrated by socialists and Bolsheviks. Senator Lodge accused Wilson of being influenced by "the socialists and Bolsheviks among his advisers," while Hays claimed that "the socialistic tendencies of the present government" posed a threat to the system of free enterprise. He added that it was Wilson's intention following the war to reconstruct the economy "in unimpeded conformity with whatever socialistic doctrines ... may happen to possess him at the time." Parts of the press soon followed suit. The *New York Times* claimed that a "certain socialistic coterie" was exercising undue influence over the president and the *Rocky Mountain News* called for "a curb on the Bolsheviks in the Democratic party...." The business community and conservatives, frustrated with high taxes, government regulations and the growth of organized labor, responded, in the words of Samuel Hays, with "a massive rebellion" against the Wilson administration, giving the Republicans control of both houses of Congress.[8]

Poindexter's use of the anti-radical issue was a result partly of his political aspirations and partly of his long-held opinions. Since the summer of 1917, when the IWW led a large strike among the lumber and timber workers in his homestate of Washington, which virtually crippled the state's principal industry, forestry, Poindexter had been a spokesman for the swift suppression of the radical union. He called it "this seditious and anarchistic organization" and supported the idea

---

[8]For the 1918 campaign in general, see Thomas J. Knock, *To End All Wars. Woodrow Wilson and the Quest for a New World Order* (New York, 1992), 167-169, 176-181, 184-189; for "a massive rebellion," see Hays, "The Social Analysis of American Political History, 1880-1920," 391; for an account of the GOP leaders' determination in 1918 to destroy Wilson, see Link (ed.), *The Papers of Woodrow Wilson*, Vol. 67, 297-299; for an analysis of the 1918 election results, see, ibid., Vol. 51, 627-633, 646-648; for the opposition of the Republican Congress to "governmental control & ... extension to socialistic measures," see Cronon (ed.), 414.

of using the military against the IWW as "an excellent suggestion."[9] Poindexter was of the opinion that "every revolutionist, anarchist, and advocate of lawless force should be dealt with in the most severe and drastic manner." He added that there was no justification for violence or revolution: "These Bolshevists and so-called Industrial Workers of the World propose what they call a working man's government, eliminating all science, art, and every advance of civilization. Their ideas are foolish in the extreme and if carried out would bring about a reversion to savagery and mean the end of all civilization. If there is anything worth fighting for every resource at our command ought to be exerted to suppress this revolutionary movement."[10]

Senator Poindexter had also been one of the more outspoken Republican critics of the administration's alleged softness during the war. Thus, he argued that a peace based upon Wilson's Fourteen Points was tantamount to surrender and suggested that the president should be impeached if he entered into negotiations before Germany had capitulated unconditionally.[11] Poindexter also criticized the administration for not vigorously prosecuting disloyal elements and traitors, using its wartime powers to suppress legitimate criticism of the president and to construct a Democratic propaganda apparatus.[12]

Poindexter was a candidate for the presidency in 1919. He was backed primarily by the business community in his home state, and his main campaign theme was an elaboration on the Republican charges in 1918 that the Wilson administration was "soft on Bolshevism." Thus, in early 1919 Poindexter claimed that the IWW had been "catered to by the Administration ... and to that I think is due their activity." He explicitly blamed the Seattle general strike on the administration's "espousing the cause," and he criticized Wilson for having praised the Russian Bolsheviks in his Fourteen Point speech in January 1918, claiming that it was "of great benefit to the Communist movement."[13]

Poindexter's introduction of his resolution on October 14, criticizing the Justice Department for inactivity against seditious elements, must be seen as an integrated part of his campaign strategy against the

---

[9]Letter, Miles Poindexter to F. W. Henshaw, September 6, 1917, box 426, Miles Poindexter Papers, University of Washington Libraries; also, letter, Poindexter to G. W. Draham, December 21, 1917, ibid.

[10]Letter, Poindexter to Hon. Charles D. Haines, March 1, 1918, ibid.

[11]Knock, 170, 171, 176.

[12]Letters, Miles Poindexter to F. W. Henshaw, September 6, 1917 and John Lord O'Brian to Poindexter, February 9, 1918, box 426, Miles Poindexter Papers, UWL; Miles Poindexter, "Your Right to Speak Freely," *The Forum*, undated clipping in box 384, ibid.

[13]Howard W. Allen, *Poindexter of Washington. A Study in Progressive Politics* (Carbondale and Edwardsville, Ill., 1981), 206-210.

Democrats. The Democrats, who apparently were swayed by their own anti-radicalism and feared that they themselves might be perceived as "soft on radicalism," voted in support of the resolution. Significantly, having presented himself as the main opponent of the administration, Poindexter two weeks later announced his candidacy for the Republican nomination for president. In his first campaign speech he focused on the radical menace, contended that the wave of strikes was part of an anarchistic plot, accused the administration of aiding the Bolsheviks, and supported the open shop.[14] According to Poindexter, the revolutionary movement had received "powerful encouragement" from the administration and "Many of its advocates have occupied high place in the government." He therefore demanded that these unnamed disloyal officials be dismissed from government service.[15] The senator claimed that the president personally as well as "other Administration officials" on a number of occasions, such as in the famous case against the California labor leader Tom Mooney, had joined in the radicals' defense and had attacked the prosecution instead of enforcing the law: "It is scarcely to be expected that I.W.W. can be suppressed when the government espouses the cause of the most murderous of them."[16] As far as Poindexter was concerned, the situation was one of "affiliation existing between the Administration and sedition...."[17]

However, Poindexter's most important argument was the alleged failure of the Attorney General to take vigorous action to repress the revolutionaries. This contention was based on the assumption that the government had adequate means at its disposal to reach the activities of both aliens and citizens; failure to use these means fully indicated bad faith on Palmer's part. Thus, in addition to the introduction of the resolution, Poindexter repeatedly pointed out that the Justice Department had been given large, additional appropriations and that most of the agitation came from aliens, who were subject to deportation. He pointed out that while additional sedition legislation might be necessary in some cases, the existing criminal statutes could be used to

---

[14]Ibid., 218-219.

[15]"Announcement by United States Senator Miles Poindexter of His Candidacy for the Republican Nomination for the Presidency in 1920 – His attitude upon vital questions of the day," n.d., box 384, Poindexter Papers, UWL. On the copy of this announcement in the Poindexter papers an unidentified Democrat (he merely identified himself as "advice to Republicans by a Democrat") has scribbled the advice to Poindexter that "Your new Espionage bill will kill you" and, concerning the radical menace, "Will die of itself if let alone ... " (ibid.).

[16]Letter, Poindexter to Edson Johnson, November 19, 1919, ibid.

[17]Letter, Poindexter to Arthur W. Large, February 28, 1920, ibid.

prosecute the leaders of radical organizations.[18] Clearly, in his effort to portray the administration as derelict in its duty, or even treacherous in its laxity, Poindexter deliberately underestimated the importance of the Justice Department's initiatives and overestimated its options. Poindexter was unaware of or ignored the Department's previous anti-radical activities and failed to take into account the fact that the courts had found that the existing sedition statutes were inapplicable to the mere advocacy of the overthrow of the government by force or violence.[19]

Having campaigned against the Democrats for more than a year, accusing them of being in sympathy with the radicals, the Republicans, unaware of the Justice Department's preparations for a deportation crusade, were in a position to claim credit for the first wave of Palmer raids in early November 1919. In fact, the idea that the raids were triggered by the Poindexter resolution might be termed a myth constructed by the Republicans. Following the raids, the Republican Publicity Association described how the administration for a long time had taken no steps to curb the spread of radicalism and how the "country felt that once more it had been a victim of that watchful-waiting policy so characteristic of the Wilson administration." Finally, the Democratic Justice Department was forced to act because of the Poindexter resolution. The Republicans prided themselves on the "awakening of the Department" and announced that for "the present activity of the Department, the Country is evidently indebted to the virile Senator from the virile State of Washington."[20] Poindexter, too, congratulated himself on the "increased activity by the Department of Justice in enforcing the laws against anarchists" as a consequence of his resolution.[21] Clearly, the Poindexter resolution must be seen, not as the result of a bipartisan congressional consensus, but as an integrated part of Poindexter's presidential campaign. Its strategy was rooted in the successful Republican election campaign in 1918 and it primarily consisted of smearing the Wilson administration in general

---

[18]Letters, Poindexter to North Bend Lumber Company, November 18, 1919; Poindexter to J. C. H. Reynolds, December 8, 1919; Poindexter to W. L. Nossaman, December 13, 1919; Poindexter to Arthur W. Large, February 28, 1920, ibid. For Poindexter's arguments, see also "Unpreparedness in the War Against Radicalism," *The New York Times*, November 23, 1919.

[19]For the courts' decisions, see *Investigation Activities of the Department of Justice*, 6-8.

[20]Press release, the Republican Publicity Association, "Poindexter Resolution Brings Action, Sleeping Department of Justice Awakes," n.d. (c. November 1919), box 385, Poindexter Papers, UWL.

[21]Allen, *Poindexter of Washington*, 211. Another example of how the Republicans used the anti-radical issue for partisan purposes: On January 1, 1920, in an attempt to steal the limelight from the Democratic administration's raids against Communists the following day, the Republican District Attorney in Chicago staged raids and arrests against that city's radicals, thereby in effect warning the radicals against the coming repression (Draper, 204).

and Palmer, a possible Democratic candidate in 1920, in particular as radically inclined.

Moreover, Poindexter apparently did not represent a broad-based popular hysteria in his home state. First of all, there are no indications that the senator's strong anti-radical views won him much popular support, either in the state of Washington or nationally. Poindexter made no headway in the Republican primaries in 1920 and a public opinion poll before the Republican national convention ranked him only thirteenth among the candidates. More significantly, his record since 1917, which in addition to his crusade against radicals and unions also included opposition to federal aid for farmers, alienated many progressives, workers and farmers in Washington. He was soundly defeated by his progressive opponent in his effort to win reelection to the Senate in 1922. Despite the fact that Poindexter according to later historians was supposed to ride on a popular anti-radical current, his campaign, in the words of Poindexter's biographer, "had obviously failed to attract massive support." [22]

Judging from Poindexter's correspondance, the Republican senator was primarily supported by an alliance consisting of the business community, patriotic organizations, conservative attorneys and state and federal security officials. For example, at the time of the Seattle general strike, Poindexter was informed by the local office of the Secret Service that the situation appeared to be "pretty serious" and that "conditions here are tending toward a revolutionary aspect."[23] The Minute Men, the patriotic organization in the Northwest, characterized the strike as a "revolutionary uprising" and "an attempted revolution, or a fight between organized labor and the Bolsheviki."[24] No less alarming was a letter from a clearly upset Seattle attorney who called the strike "the most outrageous and unwarranted exhibitions of lawless violence in the history of the country." He pointed his finger at the Seattle Central Labor Council which was "a nest of anarchy and radicalism" that had been promulgating "disloyalty and sedition" for years. He concluded by blaming the disorder on the "cowardly policy" of the Wilson administration, which was aiming with the assistance of all the "socialistic sects and schisms" in the country "to perpetuate his rulership over the country."[25] Poindexter apparently agreed with his

---

[22]Allen, *Poindexter of Washington,* 221; *Dictionary of American Biography,* Suppl. 4 (New York, 1974), 670.

[23]Letter, Thomas B. Foster to Miles Poindexter, January 24, 1919, box 427, Poindexter Papers, UWL.

[24]Letter, S. J. Lombard to Poindexter, February 17, 1919, box 385, ibid.

[25]Letter, Dudley G. Wooten to Poindexter, January 25, 1919, box 426, ibid.

correspondents and he was clearly aligning himself with business groups, conservatives and anti-union interests with a view to the coming election. He told Alex Polson of the Polson Logging Company that the strike was a part of the international Communist conspiracy. He supported the open shop, and he called on the leading open shop advocate, the National Association of Manufacturers, to take some part "in shaping public opinion" against the radical menace.[26]

Apparently, his constituents in Washington made few demands upon Poindexter to start an anti-radical crusade in the months before he introduced his resolution in October. One of the few letters on radical activities to Poindexter before his introduction of the resolution was from the Holt Manufacturing Company in Spokane. It blamed the present labor unrest on the activities of radical agitators and called on Poindexter to start a counter-propaganda movement for the "moulding of public opinion." It noted that the 90% of the population "can be let in the right direction as easily as the wrong if you will do your duty by them, yourself and your country." Otherwise, the business executive warned, the Bolsheviks were poised to take over the country.[27] In fact, the loudest cry from his homestate for the suppression of radicals was voiced after Poindexter had introduced his resolution and was provoked by the clash in Centralia on November 11 between the American Legion and the IWW, which left four Legionnaires dead. Judging from Poindexter's correspondance, three groups in Washington demanded swift repression and deportation of IWW members. The first group consisted of the business community, led by the lumber industry, which for years had been endeavoring to break the IWW. For example, the Bloedel Donovan Lumber Mills, the Hibbard-Stewart Co., the Brace & Hergert Mill Company, the North Bend Lumber Company, the Employers Association of the Inland Empire, and the Tacoma Real Estate Association demanded that the IWW be immediately suppressed and that Congress enact a law prohibiting membership in the radical union.[28] Another group which advocated federal intervention against the IWW consisted, not surprisingly, of the American Legion, whose spokesmen were often prominent members of the business community too. E. S. Gill of the Noble Post No. 1 of

[26]Allen, *Poindexter of Washington*, 208; also, 216-217.
[27]Letter, The Holt Manufacturing Company to Poindexter, August 18, 1919, box 385, Poindexter Papers, UWL.
[28]Letters, J. J. Donovan to Poindexter, November 12, 1919, box 384, ibid.; H. C. Hibbard to Poindexter, November 12, 1919, box 385, ibid.; B. W. Sawyer to Poindexter, November 17, 1919, ibid.; R. W. Vinnedge to Poindexter, November 24, 1919, box 384, ibid.; J. C. H. Reynolds to Poindexter, December 2, 1919, ibid.; W. A. Barnes to Poindexter, December 20, 1919, ibid.

Seattle, who criticized the "utter incapacity" of the administration to prosecute the radicals, was also an executive of the Associated Industries of Seattle, while S. Warren Reid of the Legion post in Wenatchee represented the manufacturing company Wells & Wade.[29] Finally, State Attorney General L. L. Thompson supported the demands for a crack-down against the IWW.[30]

The Origins of the Deportation Campaign

The second main question regarding the resolution concerns its effects on the federal government. Since the first wave of federal raids against radicals followed some three weeks later, on November 7, this has often led to the explanation that they were caused by the resolution. According to Murray, the resolution "together with mounting public clamor, served as the immediate reason for Palmer's turning from less talk to more action."[31] Coben has argued that following the passage of the Poindexter resolution "Palmer decided that the 'very liberal' provisions of the Bill of Rights were expendable" and that Palmer "did not act against alien radicals ... until Congress demanded in unequivocal terms that he take immediate action."[32] Similarly, Powers has speculated that it was "likely" that the Attorney General after the adoption of the resolution "began pressing Hoover for results after all the poking and probing into the radical movement."[33] These accounts, then, have presupposed – as Poindexter and the Republicans did – that the Justice Department had taken few if any concrete steps against the alien radicals before the middle of October and have seen the resolution as the trigger of the subsequent repressive policies followed by the state.

On one level the resolution might be said to have influenced Palmer. Since it represented a partisan attack on the Attorney General, who was a possible Democratic candidate for president in 1920, he was clearly forced to defend himself and justify his policies. Thus, in a lengthy article published in February 1920, he did not hesitate to take

---

[29]Letters, E. S. Gill to Poindexter, November 25, 1919; S. Warren Reid to Poindexter, December 19, 1919; American Legion, Hoquiam Post No. 16 to Poindexter, December 19, 1919, ibid.

[30]Letter, L. L. Thompson to Poindexter, December 2, 1919, ibid.

[31]Murray, 196.

[32]Coben, *A. Mitchell Palmer*, 215-216, 245.

[33]Powers, *Secrecy and Power*, 77. de Toledano, 62, erroneously separates the first and second Palmer raids and claims that the second raid in January 1920 was directly caused by the Poindexter resolution and the Wall St. bomb. However, the resolution, as noted, was passed well before the first round of raids and the Wall St. bomb exploded on September 16, 1920, long after the raids. de Toledano clearly rearranged the chronology in order to be able to excuse the raids as the justifiable reaction to anarchistic terror. See also, Whitehead, 46-47; Cook, 96.

all the credit for saving the nation from the radical menace, pointing out that he had done so even though "I have been materially delayed because the present sweeping process of arrests and deportation of seditious aliens should have been vigorously pushed by Congress last spring." Palmer in particular criticized Congress and accused it of "ignoring the seriousness of these vast organizations that were plotting to overthrow the Government," and he claimed that he had found that "it was obviously hopeless to expect the hearty co-operation of Congress" in cleaning out the nation.[34] However, when Palmer later came under attack because of the Justice Department's high-handed treatment of the suspected alien radicals, he contended that he had only initiated the raids "in response to this resolution" and that "I was pursuing a policy which I submit the people called upon me to pursue, which the Senate called upon me to pursue, and which the Congress called upon me to pursue...."[35] In other words, when the Republicans criticized him for passivity he struck back by depicting himself as the lone savior of the nation despite an apathetic Congress; when he came under attack for his actions, not surprisingly, he tried to run away from his responsibility by portraying himself as the victim of a hysterical nation.

On the bureaucratic level, it is even less apparent that the administration's anti-radical policies were influenced to any greater extent by the resolution. Surprisingly, not only has it proved impossible to find any kind of explicit evidence in the Bureau files indicating that the Poindexter resolution pushed the federal agents into executing the raids,[36] but the files instead reveal that the Bureau's deportation

[34]A. Mitchell Palmer, "The Case Against the Reds," *Forum*, February 1920, reprinted in Davis (ed.), 226.

[35]*Charges of Illegal Practices*, 581; for a similar statement, see for example, *Sundry Civil Appropriation Bill 1921*, Pt. 2, 1604. This argument received support from Palmer's congressional allies, who held that "the public was much aroused" in the fall of 1919: "There was considerable impatience because of the apparent inactivity of the Department of Justice, and this was to some extent reflected in the unanimous adoption of a Senate resolution introduced by Senator Poindexter...." (US Congress, Senate, Committee on the Judiciary, *Charges of Illegal Practices of the Department of Justice*, 67th. Cong., 2nd. Sess. (committee print, n.d.), 10, box 107, George W. Norris Papers, LC).

[36]The Bureau files contain a comprehensive 34 page memorandum by Hoover on the results achieved by the Radical Division since its establishment and it is dated October 18, 1919, or four days after the introduction of the Poindexter resolution; this was possibly prepared for the Justice Department as a response to the resolution, though it might also have been part of Hoover's routine progress reports to the Department (J. E. Hoover, Memorandum Upon Work of Radical Division, August 1, 1919, to October 15, 1919, October 18, 1919, OG 374217, RG65, NA). The Bureau files also contain various statistics compiled by Hoover for Assistant Attorney General Garvan on the status of the deportation campaign in late October, and these were possibly also a result of the Senate inquiry (Hoover, Memorandum for Mr. Garvan, October 24, 1919, with att. list: Statistics on number of aliens deported from April 6th. 1917 to October 23, 1919, OG 341761, ibid.; Hoover, Memorandum for Mr. Garvan, October 31, 1919, ibid.). However, no instructions or memoranda from the Justice Department to the Bureau or Hoover's office, pressing them for immediate results or

campaign began much earlier than has previously been assumed and was well under way when the Senate passed the Poindexter resolution. In other words, it seems that the federal authorities anticipated and acted independently of the public opinion and, thus, that the initiative to the raids came from within the government rather than from the outside.

The best known political deportees of 1919 were the anarchists Emma Goldman and Alexander Berkman. Goldman was born in Kovno, Lithuania, in 1869 and had emigrated with her family to America in 1886. Following a short, failed marriage at the age of 17 to a fellow Russian immigrant, she was inspired by the Haymarket affair in Chicago in 1886, which ended in the trial and hanging of 7 anarchists for a bomb attack against the police, to dedicate her life to the cause of anarchism. Criss-crossing the nation on lecture-tours and writing in her journal *Mother Earth,* she agitated for individual freedom, including free love and birth control, and against the institutions of the capitalist system, including religion and imperialism. Her meetings were often broken up by the authorities and she was arrested countless times. Berkman originally came from St. Petersburg and achieved notoriety in 1892 when he shot and wounded Henry Frick of the Carnegie Steel Company during the violent Homestead strike for which he served a sentence of 14 years in prison. With their public images of amorality and violence, they symbolized everything that members of the upper classes and officials of the state feared about anarchism.[37]

Goldman and Berkman have usually been seen as casualties of the Red Scare, an impression which has been strengthened by the erroneous belief that they were caught up in the Palmer raids on November 7.[38] Their deportation has also been described as having been accomplished almost single-handedly by J. Edgar Hoover, who supposedly for moral and emotional reasons of his own was especially disgusted by Goldman's activities. In the most detailed account until now, Richard Gid Powers has described how Hoover picked the two anarchists for deportation, prepared and presented their cases and eventually convinced the immigration authorities to deport. According to Powers' thesis, Hoover deliberately used the two anarchists as

initiatives, have been found.

[37]Marian J. Morton, *"Nowhere at Home." Emma Goldman and the American Left* (New York, 1992), 1-80; Alix Shulman, *To the Barricades. The Anarchist Life of Emma Goldman* (New York, 1971), 1-173.

[38]This view of their arrests seems to have originated in Whitehead, 48, and is repeated in de Toledano, 60, and Theoharis & Cox, 69.

"celebrity radicals" to personify the Red Menace.[39] Powers based his account primarily on the files of the Justice Department, which only included a small portion of the Bureau papers. The complete Bureau file on Goldman and Berkman, which has not been used before, suggests a somewhat different interpretation: the deportation of the two anarchists in 1919 was, in fact, a foregone conclusion, the result of a long bureaucratic process which began as early as 1917 and which was only carried through to its logical conclusion in 1919.

The Bureau's main file on the two anarchists was opened in 1916, when the Bureau of Immigration in San Francisco requested an investigation of Berkman's anarchist journal the *Blast,* but the ensuing inquiry revealed nothing "of a character tending to incite arson, murder, or assassination."[40] Following the entry of the United States into the war, Goldman and Berkman embarked on a crusade against conscription and they were immediately put under intense surveillance by the Bureau. Agents took notes of Goldman's speeches, their journals and pamphlets were carefully scrutinized, their "No Conscription League" was infiltrated and all males liable for military service who attended their public meetings were approached by the Bureau and asked to show their draft cards.[41] On June 15, 1917, Special Agents McGee and Matthews arrested the two anarchists and charged them with urging men to refuse to register for the draft in violation of the Selective Service Act of May 1917. Following a swift trial on June 27, they were found guilty and given the maximum sentence of two years in prison and a $10,000 fine.[42]

It was Federal Judge Julius Mayer who began turning the wheels of the deportation machinery when he pronounced the sentences and requested Assistant US Attorney Harold Content to call the case to the attention of the immigration authorities so that the anarchists might be deported immediately upon completing their prison terms in 1919.[43] On July 12, Content wrote to Immigration Commissioner Frederic Howe, informing him of the trial and calling his attention to the fact

---

[39]Powers, *Secrecy and Power,* 80-81, 91; on Hoover's role, also, Theoharis & Cox, 66-67, 68-69; Summers, 37-38.

[40]Report, Don Rathbun, May 24, 1916, OG 15446, RG65, NA. For the early inquiry, also, note, Office of Naval Intelligence, April 7, 1917; letters, A. Bruce Bielaski to Rathbun, April 15, 1917; Bielaski to Comm. Edward W. McCauley Jr., April 17, 1917, ibid.

[41]The reports are numerous, see for example, reports, Emma Jentzer, May 26, 1917; J. Gassel, June 2, 1917; H. W. Grunewald, June 12, 1917; letter, Bielaski to Wm. M. Offley, June 2, 1917; telegram, DeWoody to Bielaski, June 2, 1917; reports, W. I. Wright, June 4, 1917; H. W. Grunewald, September 13, 1917, ibid.

[42]Letter, Offley to Bielaski, June 17, 1917; reports, William B. Matthews, June 21, 1917; J. C. Tucker, July 11, 1917, ibid. See also, Morton, 85-89.

[43]Report, P. Pignivolo, July 10, 1917, OG 15446, RG65, NA.

that whereas it was beyond dispute that Berkman was an alien, Goldman had on different occasions given conflicting accounts of her citizenship status. At the trial she claimed that she had been born in Russia and had automatically acquired US citizenship when her father was naturalized. But at a previous hearing, held when she had re-entered the country in 1907, Goldman had stated that she originally came from Königsberg in Prussia and derived her US citizenship through her earlier marriage. Content, however, was convinced that "Emma Goldman is really an alien" and stressed the importance of ensuring their deportation since they were "in fact the archanarchists of this country" and "exceedingly dangerous to the peace and stability of the United States." Content ended by requesting the Bureau of Immigration to initiate the deportation proceedings against Goldman and Berkman.[44] In March 1918, when the two anarchists had finally exhausted all appeal avenues and commenced serving their sentences, Commissioner General Anthony Caminetti of the Bureau of Immigration notified A. Bruce Bielaski that deportation proceedings had been initiated against Berkman while the case against Goldman was awaiting a decision concerning her citizenship status.[45] These actions by the federal authorities during the war almost made sure that the two anarchists would be deported upon their release in the early fall of 1919. It was certainly inevitable that Berkman, who was an alien and had committed actual violent acts, would be deported almost automatically pursuant to the Immigration Act of 1917, whereas Goldman's fate depended on a formal ruling on her citizenship status. In view of the determination of the federal officials to banish her from the country there seems no reason to believe that the eventual outcome would have differed materially if there had been no Red Scare.

The main target of the first round of raids on November 7, 1919, three weeks after the Poindexter resolution, the Union of Russian Workers, had likewise attracted the attention of the federal authorities at least since the war. The Bureau had for some time before the Red Scare contemplated deporting its members. The URW had been founded by exiled Russian anarchists in New York in 1907 and according to most sources had a membership of some 4,000, almost all of whom were Russian immigrants. It was, in fact, one of the reasons why the Justice and Labor Departments pressed Congress to strengthen the existing deportation statutes by enacting the Immigration Act of 1918, which made the membership of an anarchistic

---

[44]Letter, Harold S. Content to Hon. Frederick C. Howe, July 12, 1917, ibid.
[45]Letter, A. Caminetti to Bielaski, March 26, 1918, ibid.

organization a deportable offense. Although the secretary of labor never formally ruled that the URW was an anarchistic organization, Labor Department officials simply proceeded on the assumption that it was. At a conference in early July 1918, three months before the enactment of the new law, Labor Department and immigration officials discussed how to ensure the deportation of alien anarchists, among them members of the URW.[46] As early as mid-1918, then, the immigration authorities were contemplating the arrest and deportation of aliens proven to be members of the URW.

The Bureau of Investigation was contemplating the nationwide raids much earlier than has previously been believed. It is unclear exactly when the Bureau began its investigation of the URW, but by February 1919 the New York office had infiltrated the organization. The Bureau had succeeded in getting its hands on a copy of the URW's *Red Membership Book* from the local branch in Maspeth, Long Island. It turned out to include the organization's "Fundamental Principles," a statement which among other things called on the workers to "recognize their true interests and by means of a Socialistic revolution by force, gain control of all the wealth of the world." It added that "having destroyed at the same time all institutions of Government and power," they should "proclaim a society of free producers...." Based on these quotations, Special Agent L. B. Perkins concluded that "It would seem that, as this booklet advocates the overthrow of Government by force, those aliens who subscribe to its principles are subject to deportation, under the provisions of the Act of October 16, 1918."[47] The New York office continued its investigation and later that same month Division Superintendent Wm. M. Offley suggested that the Bureau should get in touch with the immigration authorities concerning the deportation of alien members of the URW, and he specifically proposed that the Bureau conduct a nationwide round-up.[48] The Bureau contacted the Immigration Bureau, which provided it with a confidential circular, setting forth its policy of enforcing the deportation statutes and which was to be followed in the proceedings against

---

[46]For the Immigration Act of 1918 and the July 1918 conference, see Avrich, 131-134; see also, Coben, *A. Mitchell Palmer,* 219. Murray, 206, erroneously claims that the decision by the Labor Department that URW membership was a deportable offense was not taken until November 1919 and was a result of the public hysteria. According to Constantine Panunzio, who made a contemporary study of the deportation cases, "no ruling was deemed necessary" by the immigration officials as the URW "has been considered frankly anarchistic" (*Charges of Illegal Practices,* 325).

[47]Report, L. B. Perkins, February 19, 1919, BS 202600-184, RG65, NA. The "Fundamental Principles" are printed in *Investigation Activities of Department of Justice,* 161. For the early infiltration of the URW, see also, report, N-100, February 28, 1919, BS 202600-184, RG65, NA.

[48]Letter, Wm. M. Offley to W. E. Allen, February 28, 1919, ibid.

the URW and similar organizations.[49] The Bureau also cooperated with the New York police and when their Bomb Squad in March raided the national offices of the URW, the Bureau was given access to the confiscated papers and records.[50] On April 9, Special Agent E. B. Speer of the Pittsburgh office prepared a comprehensive report on the history and activities of the URW, which would provide the basis for much of the Bureau's knowledge about the organization in the subsequent operation.[51] On May 20, the Bureau of Immigration confirmed that it had found the URW to be an anarchistic organization although it was pointed out that in order to deport an alien member additional proof of individual anarchistic activities was required.[52]

If the Bureau acted independently of the public opinion, how then do we explain its interest in the URW? Partly, the Bureau needed domestic enemies to justify its surveillance mission and large appropriations and partly it seems to have been motivated by its own anti-radical ideology. According to Speer's report, the URW was a dangerous, subversive group which "as it exists today is an aggregation of individuals to deny the power of Government and who have declared themselves for the annihilation of all institutions of Government and state."[53] In reality, the URW posed no danger to the state in 1919. A contemporary study found that after its anarchistic founders had returned to Russia in 1917 following the revolution, the branches of the organization became almost autonomous. Most members were, in fact, newly arrived Russian immigrants who were ignorant of the URW's original anarchistic doctrines and who had joined the organization for social reasons, either to meet other Russians or to take advantage of the educational courses in English and driving.[54] The Bureau, however, based its appraisal of the URW primarily on a literal reading of the "Fundamental Principles" and other literature of the organization which contained exaggerated and starry-eyed predictions of the coming revolution. A Bureau memorandum on the "Fundamental Principles" found "that it is the object and purpose of this organization to annihilate all the institutions of Government and state."[55]

---

[49]Letters, Allen to H. McClelland, March 1, 1919; Ass. Commissioner General to Allen, March 20, 1919, ibid.; Allen to Offley, March 22, 1919, with att. letter, John W. Abercrombie to All Commissioners of Immigration and Inspectors in Charge, March 14, 1919, OG 341761, ibid.

[50]Reports, unidentified, March 19 and April 8, 1919, BS 202600-184, ibid.

[51]Report, E. B. Speer, April 9, 1919, ibid.

[52]Memorandum for Chief of Bureau, July 16, 1919, ibid.

[53]Report, E. B. Speer, April 9, 1919, ibid.

[54]Coben, *A. Mitchell Palmer,* 219; Powers, *Secrecy and Power,* 76; Theoharis & Cox, 66.

[55]Memorandum for Chief of Bureau, July 16, 1919, BS 202600-184, RG65, NA.

After the execution of the raids, Hoover referred to a URW pamphlet entitled *Manifesto of Anarchists* as "one dealing with the overthrow of organized Government and the destruction of private property and adherence to all forms of violent anarchistic doctrines."[56]

Bureau officials interpreted the organization's social activities in context with their overall view of the URW so that instead of being indications of its harmless nature, they were perceived as proof of its devious activities. Hoover countered claims that the URW was mainly an educational society by noting that the contents of its literature "leaves no doubt in one's mind as to the kind of education which this organization is engaged in." Similarly, the URW's driving school was called "a camouflage for the Union of Russian Workers."[57] Thus, Bureau officials were determined to see the URW as a "front" organization, behind which dangerous anarchists were plotting the overthrow of the government. In a larger sense this view of the URW can be seen as a result of the Bureau's tendency to personify outbreaks of unrest and opposition to the existing order and explain them as caused by a few agitators leading astray the otherwise contented masses. One agent informed Washington that "the Russian is very quiet and peacable until he is stirred up by the radical agitator," and another added that behind its respectable facade the URW had conducted "a systematic scheme of propaganda" among the innocent Russian immigrants with the result that "the raw material has been converted into Anarchist-Syndicalists, Communists, and Terrorists...."[58] Motivated by its institutional interests and ideology the Bureau well in advance of any public fear during the summer and fall of 1919 had identified the URW as a subversive force in the US and together with the immigration authorities had embarked on the road to a national round-up and deportation of its alien members. In other words, the initiative behind this case as well as the Goldman/Berkman case must be said to have come originally from the federal authorities.

"A Vigorous and Comprehensive Investigation"

It has been claimed by several historians that the Justice and Labor Departments did not formally agree to cooperate on the deportation of alien radicals until sometime in the early fall of 1919. First of all,

---

[56]Letter, Frank Burke (intitials JEH) to E. J. Brennan et al, November 10, 1919, ibid. The manifesto was made public by the Bureau in *Investigation Activities of the Department of Justice*, 144-161.

[57]Letter, Burke to to Brennan, November 10, 1919, BS 202600-184, RG65, NA; *AG Palmer on Charges*, 75.

[58]Letter, SAC, Pittsburgh, to Burke, October 8, 1919; report, E. B. Speer, April 9, 1919, BS 202600-184, RG65, NA.

there is no basis for such a late date and the authors seem simply to have chosen it to fit their overall thesis of a public hysteria as the initiator.[59] In fact, it is possible on the basis of the Bureau files, which have not been used before, to trace the agreement between the departments to cooperate to June 1919 and to reconstruct the planning of the campaign, indicating that it was well prepared and anything but a spontaneous reaction.

With the end of the war, the Justice Department had abandoned prosecuting disloyal utterances, because it was the prevailing legal opinion that the Espionage Act of 1917 and the Sedition Act of 1918 were strictly wartime legislation. This left the Bureau without any legal weapon with which to silence radical activists.[60] The sedition provisions of the Federal Penal Code, Section 4, which provided penalties for anyone "who incites, sets on foot, assists, or engages in any rebellion or insurrection against the authority of the United States," and Section 6, which made it a felony to "conspire to overthrow, put down, or to destroy by force the Government of the United States," proved impossible to use to prosecute radicals on the basis of their activities and beliefs alone. In July 1919, a case against the members of the anarchistic El Ariete Society of Buffalo, New York, who were charged with having violated Section 6 by circulating a manifesto calling for the destruction of government by force and the establishment of a state of anarchism, was dismissed by the court. It held that Section 6 was a Civil War statute aimed at putting down an actual rebellion and not "the overthrowing of the Government ... by the use of propaganda...."[61] Commented Palmer, "this practically destroys its usefulness in dealing with the present radical situation."[62] A later Justice Department memorandum concluded that it had been impossi-

---

[59]Coben, *A. Mitchell Palmer,* 218, dates the agreement to "in the fall of 1919," although he cites as his sources a number of newspapers from June 1919 (ibid., 317n4); Gengarelly, 318, without giving any source, claims that it took place on the initiative of Palmer in "late October" and mentions the Poindexter resolution as basis for the contention that "Palmer was, at this time, also under popular and congressional pressure. ... "; and Theoharis & Cox, 65, also without giving any source, argue that the departments began cooperating sometime "in September." Possibly, these accounts were inspired by Palmer's later statement at a congressional hearing to the effect that the two departments did not agree to cooperate until December 1919 as a response to the violence and public anxiety at the time (see, *Charges of Illegal Practices,* 7).

[60]On the wartime use of the Espionage Act, see, *AG Reports 1917,* 74-76, and *1918,* 20-22, 47-48; Peterson & Fite, 15-17, 210-221; for the abandonment of the act, see, *Investigation Activities of the Department of Justice,* 6.

[61]Ibid., 6-7; for the sedition statutes, see *AG Palmer on Charges,* 29; *Charges of Illegal Practices,* 187; *Congressional Record,* April 14, 1920, 6106, clipping in Scrapbook: Impeachment Attempt, box 9, Louis F. Post Papers, LC. The status of the law is also discussed in, J. E. Hoover, Memorandum Upon Work of Radical Division, August 1, 1919, to October 15, 1919, October 18, 1919, OG 374217, RG65, NA.

[62]*Investigation Activities of the Department of Justice,* 6.

ble to bring radicals to trial despite their open calls for revolution: "The missing element is a specific and definitive agreement, fortified by at least some detail, to overthrow the Government."[63]

It was the absence of a peacetime sedition law, then, which forced the Justice Department to base its anti-radical campaign on the deportation statutes and, thus, to concentrate on radical aliens. The first part of the Immigration Act of 1918 made aliens who were found to be anarchists or "who believe in or advocate ... the overthrow by force or violence of the Government of the United States ... or ... who advocate or teach the unlawful destruction of property" subject to deportation; the act did not require actual acts of violence but only proof of belief in anarchistic doctrines. The second part of the act stipulated that "aliens who are members of or affiliated with any organization that entertains a belief in, teaches, or advocates the overthrow by force or violence of the Government of the United States ... or that advocates or teaches the unlawful destruction of property" were subject to deportation.[64] This was the "guilt by membership" provision which enabled the government to deport aliens merely on the basis of their membership in an organization, which had been declared by the authorities to be anarchistic.

Another reason for concentrating on aliens was the simple fact that a major part of the radical movement in 1919 did indeed consist of non-naturalized immigrants. The anarchist movement was apparently almost exclusively non-native. The largest group, the URW, was almost entirely composed of Russians, while smaller groups, such as the L'Era Nuova Group and the El Ariete Society, were made up of Italians and Spaniards, respectively. During the war, the percentage of aliens in the Socialist Party, which at that time was the strongest radical force in American politics, increased from 35% in 1917 to 53% in 1919. When it split in the summer of 1919, the newly formed Communist Party and Communist Labor Party were dominated by aliens, who made up 90% of their combined membership.[65] It was therefore well-founded when Palmer informed Congress that the recent anarchist bombings were perpetrated by "a lawless element amongst

---

[63]Ass. Att. Gen. Earl J. Davis, Memorandum for the Attorney General, June 10, 1924, JD 202600-2734 (DJ Invest. Files II).

[64]The text of the relevant sections of the 1918 Immigration Act is reprinted in, US Congress, Senate, Committee on the Judiciary, *Charges of Illegal Practices of the Department of Justice,* 67th. Cong., 2nd. Sess. (Committee Print, n.d.), 3, box 107, Norris Papers, LC.

[65]For the anarchists, see, *AG Palmer on Charges,* 166; J. E. Hoover, Memorandum Upon Activities of the Radical Division, May 1, 1920, OG 374217, RG65, NA; for the Communist parties, see Draper, 190.

the foreign-born persons,"[66] and the Radical Division estimated that "fully 90 percent of the Communist and anarchist agitation is traceable to aliens."[67] Seen in this perspective, the emphasis on deportation as the weapon to break the back of the radical movement appears to be not so much a spontaneous reaction to a nativist hysteria as a carefully prepared plan which took into account both the available means and the nature of the intended victims.

The chronology of the decision-making process further underlines the deliberate nature of the campaign. It has previously been the prevailing view among historians that following the bombings in June and the creation of the Radical Division on August 1, the Justice Department hesitated until the introduction of the Poindexter resolution in October to finally embark on the deportation campaign. According to Murray, "Prior to the late fall of 1919, the federal government had moved rather slowly against the domestic Bolshevik menace," and even following the creation of the Radical Division "the Justice Department did not immediately show any inclination to undertake specific action against the Red menace."[68] Coben has argued that during the summer and early fall the Department shied away from making any mass arrests or deportations: "Still the Attorney General took no action against radicals and seemed to have none planned."[69]

In fact, the campaign, which was already moving against Goldman/Berkman and the URW, might be said to have begun in earnest on June 10, when Palmer informed the cabinet about his plans.[70] That same day Secretary of Labor William B. Wilson wrote to Palmer, reminding him that the Labor Department and the Immigration Bureau had jurisdiction over deportation matters and that the Justice Department's only role consisted of furnishing relevant information. He proposed a conference between representatives of the two departments to work out a plan of cooperation.[71] During a series of conferences in June between officials of the two departments, headed by Assistant Attorney General Garvan, Acting Labor Secretary John W. Abercrombie and Commissioner General of Immigration Caminetti, "the closest cooperation and harmony in operations" was established between the Bureaus of Investigation and Immigration.[72] According to

[66] *Sundry Civil Bill, 1920,* 307.
[67] *AG Report 1920,* 177.
[68] Murray, 190, 194.
[69] Coben, 213.
[70] Cronon (ed.), 418.
[71] Letter, W. B. Wilson to Hon. A. Mitchell Palmer, June 10, 1919, OG 341761, RG65, NA.
[72] Memorandum Upon the Work of the Radical Division, August 1, 1919 to March 15, 1920, n.d., OG 374217, ibid.

the plan of cooperation agreed to between the departments, the Justice Department would investigate radical aliens, the Labor Department would issue warrants of arrest against those found to belong to anarchistc organizations, and the Justice Department would conduct the arrests and turn over the aliens to the immigration authorities for the formal deportation hearing and final decision. As a result of the conferences, it was also decided to concentrate the government attack on the URW. The Labor Department had found that membership in the other promising target, the Industrial Workers of the World, was not a deportable offense in itself, and it had further been found that there simply did not exist any other larger organization of anarchists. It was also decided that in order not to expose the identity of Bureau informers, such confidential information would be kept out of the official deportation records. Instead, an effort would be made to extract confessions from the aliens regarding their activities and membership of anarchistic organizations. As Caminetti told Garvan in a lengthy memorandum, such an arrangement would ensure that "the ends of good administration and the enforcement of the law were being furthered": "I believe that, in view of the situation confronting us, this is the best kind of an arrangement which we can make."[73]

The Bureau of Investigation did not wait until the Poindexter resolution to put the plan into effect. On July 12, Washington issued instructions to the field offices to compile lists of all alien radical leaders with a view to initiating deportation proceedings and the agents were impressed with the importance of obtaining evidence concerning their citizenship status and any radical statements.[74] On August 2, the Radical Division had finished 8 deportation cases against radical aliens, four days later the number had increased to 25 cases, and by August 12, Hoover's office had already compiled a list of the names of 83 aliens being considered for deportation.[75] That same day the field was again instructed that the "Bureau requires a vigorous and comprehensive investigation of Anarchistic and similar classes, Bolshevism, and kindred agitations advocating change in the present form of Government by force and violence, the promotion of sedition and revolution, bomb throwing, and similar activities." It was stressed that the inquiry should be "particularly directed to persons not citizens

[73]Letter, A. Caminetti to Francis P. Garvan, June 27, 1919, OG 341761, ibid.

[74]The instructions are mentioned in reports, A. H. Loula, July 17, 1919, and Frank O. Pelto, July 25, 1919, ibid.; for an example of a list of radical aliens, see report, W. W. Grimes, July 28, 1919, ibid.

[75]J. E. Hoover, Report of Radical Section for Week Ending August 2, 1919, August 2, 1919, ibid.; Hoover, Memorandum for Mr. Burke, August 6, 1919, ibid.; Geo. F. Ruch, Memorandum for Mr. Hoover, August 12, 1919, ibid.

of the United States, with a view of obtaining deportation." Noting that the "fullest cooperation exists" between the Labor and Justice Departments and in order to avoid confusion by centralizing the operation, the field force was directed to transmit their evidence directly to Washington instead of passing them on to the local immigration inspectors. The instructions also carefully defined the nature of the evidence required in deportation cases. It would first be necessary to prove the ideology and principles of the organization under investigation by analyzing its "charter, by-laws, or declaration of principles, official publications, and possibly by membership cards." Having established the anarchistic nature of the organization, "a general ground-work for deportation is furnished, affording in all instances deportable cases upon proof of alienship and membership in, or affiliation with, the organization." Such membership could be proven by membership cards, the confession of the alien, or any other evidence showing he had attended meetings or acted as an officer of the organization.[76] Clearly, the Bureau was prepared to use the "guilt by membership" provisions of the Immigration Act of 1918 and to conduct mass arrests of alien radicals. That this was no spontaneous idea caused by outside pressure is indicated by the results of a conference held on August 25 at the Labor Department between Caminetti and Peters of the Immigration Bureau, Creighton of the Justice Department and Hoover of the Radical Division. During the meeting the cooperation between the two departments was discussed and it was agreed to finish the cases against an initial 50 aliens and arrest them in a simultaneous round-up.[77]

Thus, it must be concluded that the federal government, motivated by its own institutional interests and anti-radical ideology, initiated the deportation campaign months before the public hysteria supposedly crystalized itself in the Poindexter resolution in October 1919. And the Labor and Justice Departments did not require any outside pressure to coordinate their efforts and plan for a nationwide round-up of alien radicals. As William Preston found in his study of the Immigration Bureau, in 1919 the federal government had developed an independent interest in the problem of internal security and had seized the initiative in the fight against radicalism. No one had to urge such officials as,

---

[76]William J. Flynn, Letter of Instructions to all Special Agents and Employees, August 12, 1919: The draft of this letter is dated July 26, 1919 and can be found in OG 341761, ibid. A copy of the final letter can also be found in file 10110-1194-332 (MID Reports: Surveillance of Radicals 1917-41 (Microfilm)). The instructions were based on a letter, Caminetti to Garvan, June 27, 1919, OG 341761, RG65, NA.

[77]J. E. Hoover, Memorandum of Conference with Bureau of Immigration Officials, August 25, 1919, August 26, 1919, ibid.

among others, Garvan of the Justice Department, Hoover of the Radical Division and Caminetti of the Immigration Bureau, to purge the country of the radical menace: "As public servants these officials felt duty-bound to promote just such a crusade."[78]

The Bureau Crusade: Banishing Emma Goldman and Alexander Berkman
The deeper explanation of why the deportation campaign achieved such momentum and reached such proportions during the fall of 1919 is to be found in the fact that the Bureau of Investigation and the Justice Department were able gradually to capture control of the entire deportation process. According to the immigration laws, the jurisdiction concerning the administration of the deportation process lay within the Labor Department and its Bureau of Immigration, and during the war the Bureau of Investigation's role had been limited to turning over any information it might possess about alien radical activities to the local immigration inspectors.[79] The reason why the Bureau was able to dominate the deportation process during the Red Scare was that the immigration authorities did not have sufficient resources. The Bureau of Immigration had only been appropriated $36,000 for deportation proceedings in 1919, and a request for an increase was denied by the House Appropriations Committee in August, indicating the Congress' reluctance to finance the campaign.[80] Thereby a bureaucratic vacuum was created which the Bureau with its greatly expanded force and its newly established Radical Division quickly moved in to take control of.

It should be noted that the Justice Department and the Bureau were acting without any legal basis whatsoever. The Bureau's annual appropriation was given for "the detection and prosecution of crimes." The deportation statutes were not criminal statutes and were placed under the administration of the Labor Department; according to a carefully worded Treasury Department memorandum, "there may be some doubt as to the propriety of the use of the appropriation for

[78]Preston, 192-193.

[79]A. Bruce Bielaski, Circular letter to all Special Agents and Employees, November 2, 1918, OG 341761, RG65, NA.

[80]*Sundry Civil Appropriation Bill, 1920,* 9; Hoover, Memorandum of Conference with Bureau of Immigration Officials, August 25, 1919, August 26, 1919, OG 341761, RG65, NA; Preston, 211. There are indications that the Labor Department did not approve of the Bureau's actions; later, when the Labor and Justice Departments split over the Palmer raids, the Labor Department refused to reimburse the Justice Department for the expenses it had occurred, claiming that it had acted "without request or authority" of the Labor Department (Letter, W. W. Warwick to Thomas J. Walsh, April 27, 1921, box 278, Thomas J. Walsh Papers, LC). For the view that the Secretary of Labor, William B. Wilson, was unaware of the Justice Department's use of the deportation process in 1919, see Gengarelly, 318.

detection and prosecution of crimes for expenses of this need."[81] Hoover frankly admitted in an internal memorandum that there was "no authority under the law permitting this department to take any action in deportation proceedings relative to radical activities."[82]

How the initiative for the deportation campaign was taken by Justice Department and Bureau officials, and to what extent they were motivated by their own internal security considerations can be illustrated with the case against Emma Goldman and Alexander Berkman. The Justice Department claimed publicly that its role in the case had been limited to merely furnishing information to the immigration authorities.[83] In reality, the case was handled almost solely from beginning to end by the Bureau while the Labor Department was relegated to a position at the sidelines, more or less rubber-stamping the decisions made by Bureau officials. The Bureau had for some time prepared for the deportation proceedings against the two anarchists, keeping an eye on them during their incarceration in 1918-19 and reading their mail for "our general information and investigations."[84] On August 23, with their release imminent, Hoover was informed by Immigration Bureau officials that Assistant Secretary of Labor Louis F. Post had refused to sign a warrant for deportation for Emma Goldman, apparently because of the uncertainty of her citizenship status. Hoover therefore asked for the Immigration Bureau's files on Goldman and advised the Justice Department that Goldman and Berkman were "beyond doubt, two of the most dangerous anarchists in this country and if permitted to return to the community will result in undue harm."[85] It did not take long for the Bureau to get the result it desired. A few days later, Assistant Director and Chief Frank Burke formally asked Caminetti to report on the status of the two cases and on September 5, the Labor Department issued warrants of arrest for Goldman and Berkman upon their release and agreed to fix their bail at $15,000 each.[86]

---

[81]Memorandum, W. W. Warwick, June 26, 1920, box 278, Walsh Papers, LC.

[82]Quoted in Preston, 210.

[83]For example, letter, A. Mitchell Palmer to Victor D. Robertson, November 24, 1919, OG 15446, RG65, NA.

[84]Letter, Wm. M. Offley to W. E. Allen, April 24, 1919, ibid. For examples of intercepted mail, see letters, A. Bruce Bielaski to Arthur T. Begley, March 25, 1918; Allen to Offley, March 17, 1919, with att. letters; Lewis J. Baley to Bielaski, March 12, 1918, with att. letters; Allen to Offley, March 24, 1919; Bielaski to Charles DeWoody, August 30, 1918; Bielaski to DeWoody, December 9, 1918; Acting Chief to Offley, June 21 and July 14, 1919, ibid.

[85]Hoover, Memorandum for Mr. Creighton, August 23, 1919, ibid. Also, reports, J. G. Tucker, August 19 and 21, 1919, ibid.

[86]Letters, Frank Burke to Anthony Caminetti, August 25, 1919; A. Mitchell Palmer to Warden, Missouri State Prison, and to Warden, Atlanta Penitentiary, September 8, 1919; Memorandum for Mr. Keohan, September 18, 1919, ibid.

The case against Berkman was fairly straightforward and quickly disposed of. At a deportation hearing at the Atlanta penitentiary on September 20, Berkman refused to answer any questions on the grounds that no one had the right to meddle in his "attitude of mind." The immigration inspector therefore invited the Justice Department to present its evidence against Berkman and on September 26 Hoover was at hand to present the Department's brief against Berkman. Since it was an uncontested fact that Berkman was an alien, the brief concentrated on proving his anarchistic actions and appeals, something which was not difficult since he had published a book entitled *Prison Memoirs of an Anarchist* and numerous articles. The main accusation against Berkman was his failed assassination attempt against the industrialist Henry Frick in 1892, which he had frankly admitted and sought to justify as an attempt to remove a tyrant, claiming that "To remove a tyrant is an act of liberation, the giving of life and opportunity to an oppressed people." The author of the brief was clearly outraged and described how Berkman "shot him down in cold blood and attempted to do so without giving him a chance to fight for his life." The brief also analyzed Berkman's articles and pointed out that one "breathes with the most radical revolutionary sentiments" in its opposition to the government, another was "an attack upon the conservative and sane policy of the American Federation of Labor," while a third was particularly unpatriotic since it "refers to the American flag as a 'striped rag'."[87] Following Hoover's presentation, according to a Bureau memo, Berkman who previously had repeated his refusal to answer any questions "became a most willing witness and for five hours endeavored to explain away the over-whelming evidence introduced by the government with no success whatsoever."[88] The case was submitted to the Immigration Bureau for final decision and two months later Berkman was ordered by the Labor Department to surrender himself to the authorities on Ellis Island on December 5 for deportation to Russia.

[87]The brief is printed in *Investigation Activities of the Department of Justice*, 137-144; for drafts of the brief see, memoranda, Alexander Berkman, September 22, 1919, and, Re: Alexander Berkman. Deportation Matter, September 24, 1919, OG 15446, RG65, NA. Since both contain the initials EMR they were apparently not written by Hoover, such as has been generally believed (see Powers, *Secrecy and Power*, 86-87). For the deportation process against Berkman in general, see letter, Edward S. Chastain to Frank Burke, September 20, 1919; memorandum, Resume of Deportation Proceedings Instituted against Alexander Berkman, n.d., OG 15446, RG65, NA. For the Bureau's investigation of Berkman, see memorandum, Re Alexander Berkman, Deportation Matter, September 24, 1919, and report, K. K. McClure, September 25, 1919, ibid.
[88]Memorandum, Resume of Deportation Proceedings Instituted against Alexander Berkman, n.d., ibid.

The deportation of Emma Goldman proved somewhat more difficult to accomplish. When she was released from the Missouri State Prison in Jefferson City in late September, she was immediately taken into custody by the Immigration Bureau and served the warrant of arrest. In order that her lawyer could be present, the hearing was moved to New York and postponed for a month, while she was set free on bail of $15,000. In the meantime, the Bureau kept a close watch on her activities and Marion Barling, a female Bureau informer, wormed her way into Goldman's confidence and worked as her stenographer, all the time keeping the Bureau posted on Goldman's plans for a lecture tour.[89] The Bureau also systematically collected all of Goldman's writings and speeches, combing them for anarchistic views, and dispatched agents around the country to find evidence that she was not an American citizen. The officials in charge of the case were determined from the start to banish Goldman from the US; in late August, Hoover stated: "I believe that Emma Goldman's claim to citizenship can not be substantiated and every effort should be made to establish this fact." On October 17, even before the formal deportation hearing, immigration officials agreed that the Justice Department's evidence was sufficient to deport the female anarchist.[90]

The Bureau's case against Emma Goldman, presented by Hoover at her deportation hearing on Ellis Island on October 27 and at a supplemental hearing two weeks later, was based on the arguments that she was an alien and that she had repeatedly advocated the use of violence and opposition to the law. First, Hoover refuted Goldman's claim that she had acquired her citizenship through her father's and her husband's naturalizations. He argued that at the age of 24 years she had legally been too old to have been naturalized automatically when her father obtained his citizenship in 1894. She had subsequently lost her citizenship, which she had obtained through her marriage to Jacob A. Kersner, when his naturalization was cancelled by the immigration authorities in 1909 on the grounds that it had been obtained fraudulently. Second, Hoover contended that Goldman on various occasions had supported the use of violence by anarchists, such as the 1914 New York bomb explosion, which killed three anarchists and whom she publicly hailed as martyrs. The most important accusation

---

[89]For the deportation proceedings in general, see reports, Louis Loebl, September 18 and 19, 1919; memorandum, Resume of Deportation Proceedings Instituted against Emma Goldman, ibid.; For Barling, see Report on the meeting at the Hotel Brevoort, October 27, 1919, ibid.; see also, letter, Fred Hampton to Frank Burke, October 13, 1919, ibid.
[90]For the quote, letter, Frank Burke (initials JEH) to Bliss Morton, August 27, 1919, ibid.; for the October 17 agreement, see Hoover, Memorandum Upon Work of Radical Division, August 1, 1919, to October 15, 1919, October 18, 1919, OG 374217, ibid.

against her was the claim that her fiery speeches and articles, especially one in which she had defended the idea of tyrannicide, had influenced Leon Czolgosz to assassinate President McKinley in 1901. Hoover conceded that even though Goldman was not directly involved in the murder, nevertheless "she was instrumental in helping to form the unnatural ideas which Czolgosz held toward government and authority." Finally, her conviction in 1917 for obstructing the draft was used to prove her advocation of opposition to the law. For good measure Hoover introduced the most "flagrant parts" of 25 objectionable articles from Goldman's hand on such subjects as syndicalism, patriotism and atheism.[91] Both of the briefs against Berkman and Goldman were clearly based on the underlying theory that social unrest or political violence was caused not by fundamental economic or social problems but by individual agitators and that the order would be reestablished with their banishment.

It is apparent that the pressure for deporting the two anarchists came from the Bureau and that the motive was not so much to satisfy the opinion by serving the heads of two "celebrity radicals" on a charger, as it were, but by a genuine desire to put an end to their renewed political activities. While the Labor Department was considering their fate, Goldman and Berkman went on a lecture tour across the nation, closely followed by Bureau agents who opened their mail and took notes of their speeches. They sent back disturbing reports to Washington such as this one: "Particular attention is directed to the speech of subject Goldman, who stated, in the course of her remarks, that she was proud to state she was an anarchist; that she always had been an anarchist, and irrespective of whatever the United States Government might do to her she would always remain an anarchist."[92] Concerned about their activities, Hoover put pressure on the immigration authorities and repeatedly demanded that they be deported forth-

---

[91] The brief against Goldman is reprinted in *Investigation Activities of the Department of Justice*, 36-47; pp. 47-137 contain the exhibits. Emma Goldman claimed that the reason why Kersner had been denaturalized was to make it possible to deport her and that the action moreover was illegal since Kersner was already dead in 1909 (Goldman, *Living My Life*, Vol. II, 703, 712). However, the Bureau convincingly proved that Kersner died in January 1919, see memorandum, Resume of Deportation Proceedings Instituted against Emma Goldman, n.d., and Hoover, Memorandum for Mr. Stewart, October 8, 1919, OG 15446, RG65, NA. For the Bureau's investigation into Goldman's alleged connection to Czolgosz, see, reports, M. F. Blackmon, October 8, 1919; Peter P. Mindak, October 4, 1919; F. M. Sturgis, October 11, 1919, ibid. See also, Sidney Fine, "Anarchism and the Assassination of McKinley," *The American Historical Review*, Vol. LX, No. 4 (July 1955), 777-799.

[92] Report, Thomas C. Wilcox, November 28, 1919, OG 15446, RG65, NA. On the surveillance, see also, telegram, Burke to Brennan, November 25, 1919; report, John A. Dowd, November 26, 1919; letters, Ed. J. Brennan to A. L. Barkey and to George Lamb, November 28, 1919; report, A. H. Loula, December 1, 1919; telegram, Burke to Brennan, December 2, 1919, ibid. See also, Goldman, Vol. II, 708-709.

with. On October 30, he noted that five weeks had elapsed since Berkman's hearing and asked Caminetti to make a decision. On November 2, he called the attention of Caminetti to the upcoming lecture tour and warned him that it was his belief that it was the intention of the attorney of the two anarchists to drag out the deportation proceedings in order that they might continue their radical propaganda.[93] Five days later Hoover again pressed Caminetti for a decision, and by late November the Radical Division chief had lost his patience and reminded the immigration commissioner about the two anarchists' dangerous agitation: "It occurs to me that in view of the fact that these persons are now engaged upon a speaking tour throughout the country that the decisions in their cases should be expedited so that this department will know definitely whether they will be permitted to continue their present activities."[94] A letter from Attorney General Palmer to Secretary of Labor Wilson also showed that the Justice Department was primarily motivated by a desire to stop the agitation. Palmer requested that Berkman should not be allowed additional time in America to settle his affairs and argued "that this subject has been so actively engaged in anarchistic activities in this country and has so little regard for the laws and institutions of this country...."[95] As a direct result of this persistent pressure, the immigration authorities soon fell into line with the Justice Department and the Bureau. Goldman was ordered to surrender herself together with Berkman on December 5. Following a short legal battle and an abandoned appeal to the Supreme Court, the way was cleared for their deportation and, in Hoover's words, the return of "these two notorious characters back to the colder climate of Russia where their 'Red' activities may add an element of heat to that somewhat unsettled country."[96]

Rounding Up the Usual Suspects: The URW Raids
At least since the summer of 1918, immigration officials had regarded the Union of Russian Workers as an anarchistic organization, whose alien members were subject to deportation, and the Bureau had been

[93]Letters, Hoover to Caminetti, October 30 and November 2, 1919, OG 15446, RG65, NA.
[94]Quotation from, letter, Hoover to Caminetti, November 25, 1919, ibid.; also, Hoover to Caminetti, November 7, 1919, ibid.
[95]Letter, A. Mitchell Palmer to William B. Wilson, November 24, 1919, ibid.
[96]Letter, Hoover to Col. A. B. Cox, January 2, 1920, ibid. For the final legal battle, see memorandum, Resume of Deportation Proceedings Instituted against Emma Goldman, n.d.; Press Release, For Immediate Publication, n.d.; letters, Hoover to Francis G. Caffey, December 4 and 5, 1919, ibid.; "Court Fight Lost by Berkman and Goldman Woman," clipping from unidentified New York paper, December 9, 1919, box 1, J. Edgar Hoover Memoriabilia Collection, RG65, NA.

investigating the organization at least since February 1919. For some time officials had quietly made preparations for mass arrests and deportations of alien anarchists. The question is, why were these planned mass arrests not carried out until November 7, after the introduction of the Poindexter resolution? The answer is that it was a complicated and time-consuming process to prove definitively the anarchistic nature of the URW and to obtain evidence against a substantial number of its members. In short, what seemed from the outside as the apparent inertia of the Bureau was in fact a result of its determination to mount an operation on such a large scale that it would once and for all destroy the URW, intimidate radicals in general and influence the public opinion.

The first precondition for launching an impressive operation against the URW was to prove definitively the anarchistic nature of the organization. As Hoover explained to Wm. M. Offley of the New York office: "While it is known to us all that the principles of this organization are based upon the principles of anarchy, yet, in order to successfully obtain the deportation of an individual member of this organization it is necessary that the anarchistic nature of this organization can be fully established in a court of law should Habeas Corpus proceedings be instituted." Hoover therefore instructed Offley to interrogate and obtain an affidavit from an URW leader, stating that the "Fundamental Principles" were, in fact, the organization's official constitution.[97] Immediately the Bureau encountered complications. When an URW member was questioned in New York in late July, he admitted that the "Fundamental Principles" were indeed those adopted as the organization's constitution. However, he claimed that the *Red Membership Book,* which contained the principles, had subsequently been withdrawn and substituted by a harmless dues book, possibly because the URW had become suspicious when the federal agents started making inquiries about it.[98] When Peter Bianki, the secretary of the URW, was interrogated, he too admitted that the "Fundamental Principles" was the organization's constitution. But he also claimed that it had only been accepted by the local URW branches with reservation, thereby implying that the locals were not bound by the constitution.[99] Bureau officials tried to refute these statements; Hoover, for example, argued that "the constitution of the Union of Russian Workers in which the set of principles appeared has not been

[97]Letter, Frank Burke (initials JEH) to Wm. M. Offley, July 21, 1919, BS 202600-184, ibid; also, letter, Hoover to Caminetti, August 7, 1919, ibid.
[98]Letter, Burke to Offley, July 25, 1919; report, M. J. Davis, July 29, 1919, ibid.
[99]Report, Frank B. Faulhaber, August 31, 1919, ibid.

changed to date and consequently the principles are still binding upon the members of the federation."[100] Special Agent Frank Faulhaber noted that although "it appears that while the Unions throughout the country have not adopted or accepted the constitution and by-laws without reservation, at the same time all new members are shown the copy of the same document in our possession as being the constitution and by-laws ..."[101]

It was these weaknesses in the Bureau's evidence against the URW which slowed down the progress of the investigation and prevented an early crack down on the organization. At the same time, the necessity of proving the ideology of the organization helped to determine the nature of the subsequent raids. On August 15, some two months before the introduction of the Poindexter resolution, Hoover suggested to Frank Burke that it might be necessary to raid the national offices of the URW in New York City and obtain its papers and records in order to be able to prove the organization's anarchistic aims. Just prior to the raids, the New York office was instructed to ascertain where the books and records of the URW were kept as they had been hidden for fear of a federal raid.[102] In the instructions issued to the field concerning the execution of the raids, the agents were directed that "every effort should be made by you to obtain documentary evidence sustaining Anarchistic charge" and to search in particular for "papers and records of organization."[103] Thus, the extensive use of search and seizure during the raids was not a spontaneous undertaking but part of a carefully planned operation to get hold of the organization's internal records.

In order to be able to initiate the operation the Bureau needed to establish the identity of aliens connected with the organization and to prove their membership. The Bureau had been contemplating a nation-wide round-up ever since February 1919 and had received the Immigration Bureau's consent late in August. On September 15, Hoover suggested that the New York office should obtain the names of the most active members of the URW and that upon "securing this information, the individuals actively connected with this organization could be located and a simultaneous raid made throughout the United

---

[100]Letter, Burke (initials JEH) to E. J. Brennan, et al, November 10, 1919, ibid.; also, letter, Hoover to Caminetti, August 20, 1919, ibid.

[101]Report, Frank B. Faulhaber, August 31, 1919, ibid.

[102]Hoover, Memorandum for Mr. Burke, August 15, 1919; letter, Burke to George F. Lamb, October 25, 1919; also, letter, Wm. M. Offley to Burke, August 7, 1919, ibid.

[103]Telegram, Burke, re URW, November 5, 1919, ibid.

States."[104] The reason why the raids had still not been carried out when Senator Poindexter criticized the Justice Department for inactivity on October 14 was due to the scope of the contemplated operation. Hoover explained in a later memorandum: "While individual members of this organization could have been apprehended at ease, yet in view of the results to be obtained by a thorough round-up of these anarchists, it was thought better to wait until fully two to three hundred of its members could be taken into custody."[105] Thus, the raids against the URW had been under preparation for months and were delayed until November 7 simply because an operation on such a scale required painstaking preparations.

As in the case of the search for the organization's records, another feature of the raids, the forced confessions, was a product of the Bureau's need for evidence rather than the result of an atmosphere of hysteria. The Bureau obtained the names of the leaders of the URW, such as secretaries and delegates to URW conventions, from a perusal of radical publications, but the most important source for identifying members was the informers. Several of these, like "D.D." and "40," infiltrated the organization in New York and on the night of the raids were positioned in a building opposite the national offices of the URW from where they pointed out members to the Bureau agents.[106] The Bureau's use of informers to identify URW members posed an important problem, however, since the Bureau was determined not to introduce them as witnesses at the formal deportation hearing, since this would disclose their identity and destroy their usefulness in the future. The Bureau reminded its agents to "constantly keep in mind the necessity of protecting the cover of our confidential informants and, in no case shall they rely upon the testimony of such undercover informants during deportation proceedings."[107] Since the immigration

---

[104]Hoover, Memorandum for Mr. Burke, September 15, 1919, ibid. That the planning of the raids was well under way before the introduction of the Poindexter resolution is furthermore supported by a Hoover report prepared four days prior to the senator's speech, in which he informed the Justice Department that his office was in the process of identifying and locating the members and records of the URW "so that at the time set these persons and records may be taken into custody" (Hoover, Confidential Report of Radical Section, October 10, 1919, OG 374217, ibid.).

[105]Memorandum Upon the Work of the Radical Division, August 1, 1919 to March 15, 1920, ibid.

[106]For the identification of the URW leaders, see reports, J. G. Tucker, September 12 and 17, 1919; V. J. Valjavec, September 19, 29 and October 17, 1919; unidentified, n.d., BS 202600-184, ibid.; for "D.D.," see reports, D.D., October 26, 28 and 29, 1919; H. C. Leslie, November 11, 1919; C. J. Scully, November 11, 1919, ibid.; for "40," see reports, R. W. Finch, May 12, 1919; M. J. Davis, July 29 and September 24, 1919; C. J. Scully, September 2, 15 and October 20, 1919, ibid.

[107]William J. Flynn, Letter of Instructions, August 12, 1919, OG 341761, ibid. For a similar statement, letter, special agent (Newark) to Chief, October 26, 1919, BS 202600-184, ibid.

authorities were legally unable to deport aliens on the basis of secret testimony of informers but were bound to base the decision, in the words of Caminetti, on at least "a scintilla of evidence,"[108] the solution was to force the aliens to admit their membership. This was emphasized by the Bureau in its written instructions to its agents concerning the execution of the raids, in which it was pointed out: "Subjects should be thoroughly examined by you and none of the subjects taken into custody should be permitted to communicate with each other or with outside persons until examination by you has been completed." This meant that the aliens were to be interrogated at a preliminary examination before being turned over to the immigration authorities and that they would be held incommunicado and denied access to counsel. The importance of obtaining confessions was repeated in the instruction, and the agents were impressed that they should make "every effort to obtain from subjects statements that they are members of organization and believe in its anarchistic tendencies. This of outmost importance."[109] The decision to keep the aliens incommunicado and interrogate them without access to counsel, then, resulted from the Bureau's policy of protecting the confidentiality of its informers. The repeated orders to "make every effort" to obtain confessions from the aliens that they were members clearly put pressure on the agents to get quick results. These instructions must be judged to have been directly responsible for the widespread use of violence testified to by aliens after the raids.

Although the Labor Department had been one of the architects of the Immigration Act of 1918 it followed a moderate line in administering the "guilt by membership" provisions. In its guidelines to the immigration officials issued on March 14, 1919, it was stated that it was the policy of the Department "to avoid technicality or literalness in the enforcement of the law." According to the directive, no radical would be arrested or deported merely on the basis of his membership in an anarchistic organization but that additional evidence of individual activities was required.[110] In May, the Immigration Bureau informed the Justice Department that "mere membership" in the URW did not constitute sufficient ground for deportation but that "the alien must be an active Worker in order to be subject for deportation." This

[108]Letter, Anthony Caminetti to Francis P. Garvan, June 27, 1919, OG 341761, ibid.; also, Preston, 214.
[109]Telegram, Burke, re URW, November 5, 1919, BS 202600-184, RG65, NA. This instruction to obtain a confession was repeated in the final directive concerning the raids, see telegram, Burke to Lamb et al., November 6, 1919, ibid.
[110]John W. Abercrombie, Confidential letter to all Commissioners of Immigration and Inspectors in Charge, March 14, 1919, OG 341761, ibid.

meant that the Bureau would have to prove that each and every individual, in the words of Hoover, "were active propagandists or had become a menace in the community in which they reside," a lengthy process which threatened the Bureau's plans for a nation-wide round-up.[111] However, the extent of the Bureau's influence on the deportation process is indicated by the fact that during the late summer and fall it succeeded in forcing through a literal interpretation of the "guilt by membership" provision. In August, the New York office, which was handling the major part of the URW investigation, noted that "it will be recalled that the understanding of agents of this division is to the effect that mere membership in this organization is a sufficient ground for deportation, provided the subject is an alien."[112] By the time of the raids Washington pointed out to the field that since the URW had been found to be an anarchistic organization, "membership in the same is sufficient to warrant immediate deportation."[113] There are no indications to the effect that the Labor Department at any time formally changed its policy. It seems that the Bureau, because of the immigration authorities' lack of resources, simply moved in and gradually dominated the process.

The initiative behind the implementation of the raids also came exclusively from the Bureau. Having identified a sufficient number of the more active members of the URW, Hoover informed Caminetti on October 30 that "due to the increased activities of this organization" the Bureau was preparing the arrest of its alien leaders. The Bureau would furnish the Immigration Bureau with affidavits signed by agents (based on the information received from the confidential informers) stating that the aliens named were members of the URW and actively engaged in the organization's propaganda activities. Hoover requested that the Immigration Bureau issue warrants of arrest so that the Bureau could take the URW members into custody and turn them over to the immigration authorities.[114] The Immigration Bureau, then, was simply relegated to signing warrants of arrest on the basis of the words of informers and with no accompanying evidence. It was the expectation that they would subsequently deport the aliens primarily on the basis of forced confessions obtained during the preliminary examinations. On November 3, Hoover submitted the initial 34 affidavits, again

---

[111]Memorandum for Chief of Bureau, July 16, 1919, BS 202600-184, ibid.; Hoover, memorandum, July 17, 1919, ibid.
[112]Letter, Wm. M. Offley, August 7, 1919, ibid.
[113]Letter, Frank Burke to E. J. Brennan et al., November 10, 1919, ibid.
[114]Letter, Hoover to Caminetti, October 30, 1919, ibid. For the instruction to the field offices to submit the affidavits, see letter, Frank Burke to Wm. M. Doyas, October 29, 1919, ibid.

requesting the cooperation of the immigration authorities "in order that actual results may be accomplished in purging the communities of these undesirable elements." On November 7, the day planned for the raids, Hoover pressed for the issuance of the warrants to the local immigration inspectors.[115] Clearly, the Bureau was the driving force behind the raids.

The Bureau's domination of the deportation process determined the nature of the raids. First of all, previous accounts have claimed that the raids against the URW were quite limited, taking place simultaneously in 12 cities and netting an estimated 250 to 450 suspected radical aliens.[116] In fact, however, the raids may have taken place in as many as 18 industrial centers in the Northeast and according to a confidential list compiled by the Radical Division, a total of 1,182 suspected members of the URW were taken into custody on November 7.[117] These figures also show that only 500 warrants of arrest had been issued by the immigration authorities and that only 400 were actually served, indicating that the Bureau made 782 arrests without warrants. For example, in New York only 59 warrants had been issued but the agents nevertheless took 360 into custody, of whom only 52 were eventually held following the preliminary examination. In Detroit only 70 warrants had been issued but 350 arrests were made and all but 58 were soon released, and in Cleveland the agents were given only 56 warrants, but they took into custody 100 of whom only 66 were held. In total, of the 1,182 arrested nationally, the Bureau had sufficient evidence to hold only 439 for the formal deportation hearing.

The high number of detainees was a direct consequence of the fact that the Bureau executed the raids without the assistance of the immigration authorities. Instead of having the immigration inspectors, to whom the warrants had been issued by the Labor Department, serve the warrants during the raids, the Bureau agents indiscriminately rounded up everybody found at the URW meeting halls or offices. Not until they arrived at the Bureau offices were the detainees connected with the warrants; according to one New York agent, all those taken

---

[115]Letters, Hoover to Caminetti, November 3 and 7, 1919, ibid.

[116]The Justice Department itself claimed that 300 (*AG Report 1920*, 174) or 350 (*Sundry Civil Appropriation Bill 1921*, Pt. 2, 1590) were arrested; for figures between 250 and 450, see, Whitehead, 48; William E. Leuchtenburg, *The Perils of Prosperity, 1914-32* (Chicago, 1958), 77; Preston, 216; Murray, 196; Donner, *The Age of Surveillance*, 36; Summers, 37; Higham, 230. The only exception to these figures is Powers, *Secrecy and Power*, 78, who speculates from some local figures that a total of "several thousands" might have been arrested.

[117]The figure of 18 cities is mentioned in, Department of Justice, Press Release, For Publication in Daily Papers, November 8, 1919, BS 202600-184, RG65, NA; the figure of 1,182 detainees is found in, List, Union of Russian Workers (Raid of Nov. 7, 1919), n.d., att. to Hoover, Memorandum for Mr. Burke, January 22, 1920, ibid.

into custody were taken to the Bureau offices and following the preliminary examination, "those for whom warrants were not issued were released."[118] It was also a consequence of the Bureau's use of the raids as a fishing expedition; according to the New York office, all those found on the premises of the URW were taken into custody and "it is believed that among the records seized, the majority of these will be proven to be connected with the Union of Russian Workers."[119] In other words, the Bureau regarded the mere presence at the URW halls as a strong reason for suspecting that those found were members and that evidence could subsequently be found in the organization's records. Bureau officials seemed more concerned about the effectiveness of the raids than with the possibility that innocents were arrested or that the legal principle of making arrests only on the basis of probable cause was undermined. In a summary of the results achieved during the operation, Hoover praised the agents for having "established an enviable record for themselves" because the immigration authorities had only discharged 35 of the 439 cases submitted by the Bureau. While he indicated no concern for the large number of persons who had been arrested without warrants, he demanded "at once" an explanation by the field offices of "why all of the persons for whom warrants were issued in your territory have not been taken into custody."[120]

The other direct consequence of the Bureau's domination of the process was that there was no one to prevent that those taken into custody were intimidated and in some instances even mistreated. Determined to protect the confidentiality of its informers, from whom the Bureau had most of its information regarding the alien members, Bureau agents were under intense pressure to obtain confessions of membership during the preliminary examinations before the aliens were turned over to the immigration authorities. Not surprisingly, the official record is filled with affidavits by aliens, relating how they were mistreated during the raids and interrogations and forced to confess their radical activities.[121] How important it was for the Bureau to

---

[118]Report, H. C. Leslie, November 11, 1919, ibid.; for the use of this procedure during the January 1920 raids, see *NPGL Report*, 46.

[119]Report, C. J. Scully, November 11, 1919, BS 202600-184, RG65, NA; for the Justice Department's policy of regarding the presence at a URW meeting place as a clear sign of their membership, see *AG Palmer on Charges*, 76. According to an agreement between Hoover and Caminetti, agents could apply by telegraph for warrants after the arrests (letter, Caminetti to Hoover, November 11, 1919, BS 202600-184, RG65, NA).

[120]Hoover, Memorandum for Mr. Burke, January 22, 1920, ibid.; letter, Hoover to M. F. Blackmon et at., November 29, 1919, ibid.

[121]For these charges, *NPGL Report*, 11-20; *AG Palmer on Charges*, 75-84, 100-106; *Charges of Illegal Practices*, 93-94, 315, 335-336. Several newspaper reports, all of which supported the raids, confirmed the widespread use of violence against the aliens, see "Department of Justice

extract confessions is indicated by some figures from the New York office. After the raid against the Russian People's House, the URW national offices, 39 were held. The Bureau had no evidence against 10 of these who had simply been found on the premises, 8 were held because their names had been found on URW member lists, 4 because of their previous political activities, 1 was wanted by the Newark office, 1 was an American citizen who was turned over to the local authorities, and the largest group, 15, were held solely on their confessions that they were present or former members of the URW.[122] If these figures were representative of the general situation, then half of those the Bureau had any kind of evidence against were held solely on the basis of their confessions made during the interrogation by Bureau agents immediately following the raids.

The Bureau kept up its pressure on the immigration authorities to get quick results after those aliens suspected of or proved to be members of the URW were turned over for the formal deportation hearing. Despite the lack of any legal authority whatsoever, Bureau agents were allowed to present evidence at the hearings and, in effect, appear as prosecutors. Hoover also succeeded in convincing Caminetti of the necessity of fixing the amount of bail at $10,000, thereby ensuring the aliens' certain imprisonment until the final decision of their case, in some instances months away.[123] The motive for this was not so much a concern that the aliens might disappear before their deportation but a desire to put an end to their political activities; Hoover complained about several aliens who had been released on a $1,000 bail and "have renewed their activities subsequent to their release," and he requested that their bail be increased.[124] In the beginning of December, eager to dispose of the URW cases, Hoover telegraphed agents to "impress diplomatically importance upon local immigration inspectors" of closing the hearings and "Render any assistance necessary to complete work this week."[125] The Bureau clearly continued to dominate the proceedings even after the cases had

Men Seize Radicals on Second Anniversary of Soviet Rule," *The New York Herald*, November 8, 1919; "Arrests are Made Here in Round-up for Red Plotting," *The Washington Star*, November 8, 1919, clippings in BS 202600-184, RG65, NA; "200 Reds Caught Here," *The New York Times*, November 8, 1919; "Quick Deportation for Raided Reds," *The New York Times*, November 9, 1919.

[122]Report, C. J. Scully, November 11, 1919, BS 202600-184, RG65, NA.

[123]For the deportation hearings, see letters, Caminetti to Hoover, November 11, 1919; Frank Burke to E. J. Brennan et al, November 10, 1919; telegram, Burke to Akron et al, November 24, 1919, ibid.; for the bail, see telegram, Burke to Hartford, Conn., et al, November 10, 1919, ibid.; Hoover, Memorandum Upon Work of Radical Division, August 1, 1919, to October 15, 1919, October 18, 1919, OG 374217, ibid.

[124]Letter, Hoover to Caminetti, November 17, 1919, BS 202600-184, ibid.

[125]Telegram, Burke (initials JEH) to Detroit et al, December 4, 1919, ibid.

been transferred for final decision by the immigration authorities; in short, the immigration officials did little more than assist and rubber-stamp the Bureau's crusade.

Publicizing the Radical Menace

While the immediate objective was to deport as many active members of the URW as possible and thereby cause the destruction of the organization, the Bureau had deeper and more far-ranging intentions, namely those of intimidating all other radicals in general and influencing the public opinion by publicizing the red menace.

First of all, if the Bureau intended to spread fear among radicals by mounting raids on such a large scale, the raids must be said to have been very effective. One informer reported on the mood among the remaining URW members following the raids: "These people appear to be afraid of everything now. Their general view is that they must be prepared for unexpected raids and assaults because the Government has decided to persecute without rest, all radicals in general."[126] Another informer noted that several URW members "warned me to be careful because the Government are contemplating more deportations and arrests" and that they were so frightened that they themselves destroyed whatever remained of their literature after the agents' rampage.[127] The raids also had the effect of scarying people away from the radicals, thereby undermining their political activities. A Bureau agent noted that when a printer, who was about to print a leaflet entitled "Hands off Soviet Russia," "read the papers on Saturday morning referring to the raids made by Government agents he immediately took the forms off the press, would not print any more and remelted the matter contained in the attached circular."[128] In some instances the raids had more serious consequences for those arrested, even when the Bureau had no evidence against them and released them. Some were blacklisted as suspected Bolsheviks by the employers and were thereafter unable to find employment, while others lost their businesses during their confinement.[129] Clearly the raids served as an unmistakable warning not to get mixed up in radical politics.

Although it is nowhere stated explicitly in the internal Bureau papers, it is possible that the raids were intended to have an effect on the striking miners. First of all, the coal strike, which the government was determined to break, began on November 1 and the raids took

---

[126]Report, G.G., November 20, 1919, ibid.
[127]Reports, D.D., January 5, 1920 and December 1, 1919, ibid.
[128]Report, John A. Connolly, November 11, 1919, ibid.
[129]*NPGL Report*, 13, 16.

place seven days later. Secondly, the Justice Department later claimed that especially agitators of the URW had been active in influencing the miners in West Virginia, accusing them of "leading astray the earnest laborers" and thereby being "directly responsible for the unrest existing in those sections of the country."[130] Thirdly, when Hoover informed the Immigration Bureau about his intention to implement the raids, he referred to "the increased activities of this organization."[131] And finally, even if it was not the expressed intention of the Bureau officials to intimidate the strikers, it is apparent that that was one of the effects of the raids. In the period between November 14 and December 2, 56 alleged alien radicals, of whom at least 48 were members of the URW, were arrested by the Bureau in cooperation with the local sheriff in the mine fields of Northern District in West Virginia. Subsequently, 36 aliens were held by the immigration authorities for final disposition of their cases. As Special Agent Ernest W. Lambeth reported to Washington, "The arrests of the radicals had had a wonderful effect throughout the district and the foreigners were the first to show signs of willingness to return to work."[132]

Simultaneously with the raids, the Bureau launched a carefully orchestrated publicity campaign. Contrary to the view that the federal government was under popular and political pressure, Justice Department officials argued that it was necessary to educate politicians and journalists on the danger of radicalism. Hoover noted that it was only when he showed radical propaganda material to senators, congressmen and journalists "that they begin to realize the extent to which the propaganda of the pernicious forces in this country has gone." He added that as a result of his office's educational efforts, "Many of them have been surprised to learn of the organized propaganda existing and wonder at the extent to which the same has gone."[133] In late October, the Justice Department began preparing the public and the politicians for the necessity of the deportation campaign. An unidentified "Federal official" informed the *New York Times* that "at least 50,000 aliens in the United States ... were openly or secretly working for a Bolshevist form of government for this country" and that they were supported by "many of the 3,000 newspapers published in foreign languages." He produced a number of extreme and hair-raising

---

[130]Memorandum Upon the Work of the Radical Division, August 1, 1919 to March 15, 1920, n.d., OG 374217, RG65, NA; *AG Palmer on Charges*, 173.

[131]Letter, Hoover to Caminetti, October 30, 1919, BS 202600-184, RG65, NA.

[132]Reports, Ernest W, Lambeth, December 23 and 26, 1919, OG 303770, ibid.

[133]Letter, J. E. Hoover to Frank R. Stone, January 23, 1920, JD 205492-296, RG60, NA (microfilm).

extracts in the form of "official translations" from the radical press to support his contention. Having thus presented the enemy, the official hinted at the government's intentions: "The evidence of the activities of these foreigners is now in the possession of the Federal authorities, and there is reason for stating that a strict enforcement of the deportation laws against these alien trouble makers is among the possibilities of the near future."[134]

Of course, the sheer size of the raids themselves with more than a thousand simultaneous arrests in a dozen cities and the confiscation of tons of radical literature and records in itself must have had a profound impact on the public opinion and confirmed how widespread and dangerous the radical movement had become. In order to make sure that the public understood how dangerous an organization the URW was, the Justice Department in a press release on the night of November 7 described it as "even more radical than the Bolsheviki." It further claimed that the agents during their searches had found a bomb factory, "a complete counterfeiting plant" and "red flags, guns, revolvers, and thousands of pieces of literature...."[135] A comparison with several press reports on the raids show that a number of influental papers, among them the *Washington Star,* the *Washington Times* and the *New York Times,* based their accounts on the press release and often reprinted it verbatim without making any efforts to independently verify the official claims.[136] Others uncritically took their lead from information leaked by federal officials, no matter how preposterous and unfounded the allegations might seem. For example, the *New York Herald* reported that federal agents "believe" that they had prevented nothing less than "a nationwide uprising of Bolshevists" on the second anniversary of the Russian revolution; commented the paper, tongue in cheek, "The bombs were to be used to wreck stores, hotels and residences, and thereby to spread a reign of terror over the city, if possible. It was to be a revolution in America."[137]

Two days after the raids, on November 9, Assistant Attorney General Garvan released to the press a translation of the Manifesto of

---

[134]"50,000 Aliens Here Spread Radicalism," *The New York Times,* October 17, 1919. The unnamed official behind the leak might have been Robert A. Bowen, director of the Justice Department's Bureau of Radical Publications and Translations; a copy of the article was located in box 10, Bowen Papers, Clemson University.

[135]Department of Justice, Press Release, For Publication in the Daily Papers of Saturday, November 8, 1919, BS 202600-184, RG65, NA.

[136]See, "Arrests Are Made Here in Round-up for Red Plotting," *The Washington Star,* November 8, 1919, and "More Capital Arrests This Afternoon, Say Justice Dept. Agents," *The Washington Times,* November 8, 1919, clippings in ibid.; "Will Deport Reds As Alien Plotters," *The New York Times,* November 9, 1919.

[137]"Department of Justice Men Seize Radicals on Second Anniversary of Soviet Rule," *The New York Herald,* November 8, 1919, clipping in BS 202600-184, RG65, NA.

the URW, which had been found during the search of the URW offices. This too was often printed in toto and under such hair-raising headlines as the one in the *Washington Post*, which proclaimed "Kill Officials, Open Jails and Loot Homes of People, Manifesto of Reds in U.S." Across the frontpage of the *New York Times* the headline screamed: "Plan for Red Terror Here – Program of Organized 'Russian Workers' for Revolution Revealed – General Strike First Step – Then Armed Revolt and Seizure of all Means of Production and Articles of Consumption – Criminals to be Freed – Blowing up of Barracks, Shooting of Police, End of Religion, Parts of the Program."[138] The information handed out by the authorities was simply treated as authoritative and no paper seems to have pointed out the obvious difference between the exaggerated rhetoric of a pamphlet written by a group of Russian anarchists back in 1905 and the sedate nature of the URW in 1919. No one reading the information emanating from the Justice Department had any reason to doubt that the federal agents had nipped an actual revolt in the bud.

The final step in the Bureau's public relations campaign was to portray the URW as an actual terrorist organization. On November 25, the Bureau announced that it had discovered an actual bomb factory in the Russian People's House, which somehow had been overlooked during the previous raid, and the following day the papers ran headlines such as "Red Bomb Laboratory Found" and "Find Reds' Bomb Shop."[139] It is unclear just what the agents found; according to an internal report, the find consisted of "a full assortment of different acids believed to be used for making bombs, also testing tubes, scales and mixer."[140] Presumably, the agents had been carried away by their imagination; anyway, the supposed bombs soon disappeared and nothing further was heard of the matter.[141] However, by now the public image of the URW, which had been carefully shaped by the federal authorities, was that of a revolutionary, subversive and terrorist group, perhaps in some way implicated in the still unresolved June 2 bombings. The Bureau also tried to depict the URW as an agent for the Soviets. Even though the URW had been effectively broken up by the raids and subsequent deportations, Hoover later attempted to keep the Red Scare alive by claiming that the organization had revived and that members were "operating under the immediate direction of Nicolai Lenin" and that this proved that "the Soviet Government is actively

[138]*The Washington Post*, November 10, 1919, ibid.; *The New York Times*, November 10, 1919.
[139]Murray, 206.
[140]Report, E. Anderson, November 26, 1919, BS 202600-184, RG65, NA.
[141]Powers, *Secrecy and Power*, 80.

continuing its work in this country." [142] An internal Bureau report from about the same time noted that the few remaining URW members were expected shortly to return voluntarily to Russia and "consequently the breaking up of this organization is expected." [143]

The actual deportation of the aliens swept up in the first wave of Palmer raids must also be seen as a carefully orchestrated event, intended to increase the public anxiety just before the second wave of raids. On December 21, 1919, the only mass deportation of political dissidents in US history took place when the USS *Buford* left New York Harbor for Hango, Finland, carrying 249 aliens. 184 were members of the URW, 51, among them Goldman and Berkman, were individual anarchists, and the remaining 14 aliens were deported for having violated the immigration laws for other reasons. Bureau Director William J. Flynn announced that the 249 deportees represented "the brains of the ultra-radical movement." The aliens were described for the press as being well-heeled, carrying much luggage and large sums of money, implying that they had gotten rich by denouncing the capitalistic system. The departure early in the morning and the presence of a guard of 200 armed soldiers on board the *Buford* contributed to constructing a public image of the aliens as dangerous revolutionaries. [144] At the same time, the Bureau's briefs against Goldman and Berkman were released to the press. The *Washington Post,* for example, used the information to claim that Goldman had been "mentor of Czolgosz" and that "she has been involved directly or indirectly in nearly a score of killings and assassinations in the United States," while Berkman was portrayed as having "violated nearly every law and custom of this country." [145] Clearly, the whole operation was exploited to whip up public and political support for the Justice Department's anti-radical drive. The *New York Herald* was informed by officials that the action was "the beginning of an extremely rigorous policy against radicals. Another shipload is going out, perhaps this week, and a drive to cut down the Department of Justice's list of 60,000 radicals in the nation already has been started." An optimistic

[142]"US Holds 2 Russian Spies," clipping from unidentified paper, box 1, J. Edgar Hoover Memoriabilia Collection, RG65, NA.

[143]Report, unidentified, April 19, 1921, BS 202600-184-59, ibid.

[144]"249 Reds Sail, Exiled to Soviet Russia; Berkman Threatens to Come Back; Second Shipload May Leave This Week," *The New York Herald,* December 22, 1919; "Anarchist Leaders Fought to Last Legal Ditch to Escape Deportation," *The New York Tribune,* December 22, 1919; *Congressional Record,* January 5, 1920, all clippings in box 1, J. Edgar Hoover Memoriabilia Collection, ibid.

[145]"Emma Goldman Mentor of Czolgosz, McKinley's Slayer, Declare U.S. Investigators," *The Washington Post,* December 22, 1919, ibid.; see also, "Radical Writings of Emma Goldman Are Made Public," *The Washington Star,* December 22, 1919, ibid.

Hoover was quoted as stating: "The Department of Justice is not through yet, by any means. Other 'Soviet Arks' will sail for Europe just as often as it is necessary to rid the country of dangerous radicals."[146] It seems that contrary to the common assumption that the deportations were a response to the public hysteria, the deportations of Goldman, Berkman and the URW members, which had been under preparation since 1917 by the federal government, were used deliberately by an aggressive and ambitious Justice Department and Bureau of Investigation to shape the public opinion and enhance the Red Scare.

The Sedition Bill

It is possible to speculate on the federal security officials' underlying motive for participating actively in the fostering of the public's fear. During the war, the Bureau's internal security functions had expanded considerably and its appropriations had likewise increased on the basis of the Draconian Espionage Act of 1917, which was intended to suppress seditious and disloyal utterances. But the act had expired with the end of hostilities, leaving the Bureau without a legal weapon with which to silence radical citizens.[147] Thus, all through 1919 the Justice Department and the Bureau argued for the necessity of a peacetime sedition law, and, in fact, their interest in fostering the Red Scare might to a large extent be explained as a result of the desire to mobilize political support for such a law. The first attempt was made when the Overman Committee, aided by the Bureau, in the spring of 1919 publicized the Bolshevik menace and proposed a sedition law along the lines of the Espionage Act with the aim of "adequately protecting our national sovereignty and our established institutions."[148] The ambitious Bureau could not even wait until the enactment of the proposal before initiating its investigations; for example, in late May agents were instructed to collect information on the circulation of the

---

[146]*The New York Herald*, December 22, 1919 and *The New York Tribune*, December 22, 1919, ibid. The Bureau continued to keep Emma Goldman under surveillance even after her deportation. The Bureau intercepted and read all mail from the *Buford*, confiscating letters that were particularly "objectionable" (George F. Ruch, Memorandum for Mr. Hoover, February 16, 1920, OG 15446, ibid.; letter, Hoover to Caminetti, March 11, 1920, OG 341761, ibid.), and it continued to monitor her activities in Russia and recorded her growing disillusionment with the Soviet system (letters, Frank Burke to Geo. F. Lamb, June 22, 1920; report, A. H. Loula, July 10, 1920; letter, W. L. Hurley to Hoover, September 9, 1920, OG 15446, ibid.; reports, Reedy, January 21, 1921, BS 202600-746-2, ibid.; H. C. Leslie, January 20, 1921, BS 202600-532-9, ibid.; W. J. West, March 12, 1921, BS 186701-170-8, ibid.; J. G. Tucker, October 15, 1921, BS 202600-1628-184, ibid.).

[147]For the Espionage Act of 1917, as amended in 1918, see *AG Reports 1917*, 74-76, and *1918*, 20-22, 47-48; Peterson & Fite, 15-17, 210-221; for the cessation of Espionage Act prosecutions, see *Investigation Activities of the Department of Justice*, 6; Hoover, Memorandum Upon Work of the Radical Division, August 1, 1919, to October 15, 1919, October 18, 1919, OG 374217, RG65, NA.

[148]*Brewing and Liquor Interests and German and Bolshevik Propaganda*, Vol. 1, XLVII-XLVIII.

Revolutionary Age with the justification that the "contemplated legislation by Congress will amply cover this situation."[149] The investigations of the political activities of American citizens continued even though the Overman proposals were never passed by Congress.

On June 14, following his initial request to Congress to finance his anti-radical campaign, Attorney General Palmer appeared before the Senate Judiciary Committee and urged that legislation be passed which would make sedition, seditious utterances and the publication of seditious literature a federal crime. Inspired by the Attorney General's plea, some 70 sedition bills were subsequently introduced in both the Senate and the House. However, in line with Congress' reluctance against appropriating the necessary funds for the Bureau's activities, none of these bills were passed.[150] This, however, did not deter the Bureau from proceeding with its inquiries. In the instructions to the field on the preparation of deportation cases on August 12, the agents were directed also to collect information on the political activities of American citizens, either with a view of prosecuting under existing state laws or federal criminal laws or "under legislation of that nature which may hereinafter be enacted." Hoover noted that his Division had been indexing and filing information on citizens which was "awaiting use as soon as adequate legislation is passed which will reach the activities af American citizens who fail to appreciate the benefits accorded by their Government."[151] However, the Bureau still lacked a legal justification for its political surveillance of radical citizens.

Thus, on November 15, carefully taking advantage of the excitement created by the raids eight days before and the public relations campaign, Palmer submitted to Congress his proposal for a peacetime sedition law. It would make it a federal crime for citizens and aliens to advocate in any form, or commit any act, or to be a member of an organization advocating or inciting sedition. This was broadly defined as the intention "to cause the change, overthrow, or destruction of the Government or of any of the laws or authority thereof, or to cause the overthrow or destruction of all forms of law or organized government, or to oppose, prevent, hinder, or delay the execution of any law of the United States ... or threatens to commit any act of force against any person or any property...." The bill provided for a maximum sentence of twenty years in prison for citizens, the denaturalization and

---

[149]Letter, Acting Chief to Roy C. McHenry, May 28, 1919, OG 136944, RG65, NA.
[150]*Investigation Activities of the Department of Justice*, 8.
[151]William J. Flynn, Letter of Instructions to All Special Agents and Employees, August 12, 1919, OG 341761, RG65, NA; Memorandum Upon the Work of the Radical Division, August 1, 1919 to March 15, 1920, n.d., OG 374217, ibid.

deportation of naturalized citizens, and the deportation of aliens.[152] In his annual State of the Union message to Congress on December 2, President Wilson called attention to "the widespread condition of political restlessness in our body politic." He urged Congress to pass Palmer's sedition bill in order to "arm the Federal Government with power to deal in its criminal courts with those persons who by violent methods would abrogate our time-tested institutions." The president added: "With the free expression of opinion and with the advocacy of orderly political change, however fundamental, there must be no interference, but toward passion and malevolence tending to incite crime and insurrection under guise of political evolution there should be no leniency."[153]

"To Protect the Government's Interests"

The Bureau's deportation crusade culminated on January 2, 1920, in a series of simultaneous raids in 31 cities across the nation against meeting places, halls, editorial offices and headquarters of the newly formed Communist Party (CP) and Communist Labor Party (CLP). Several thousand suspected alien members were taken into custody and much of the parties' records and literature was confiscated. This operation was by far the largest of the Palmer raids and it has usually been seen as a direct result of the climactic public hysteria. For example, Murray claimed that "burdened by its collosal fear, the public now demanded new forays and more action," while Coben portrayed the Attorney General as being unable to "resist the demands of a hysterical public," and Murphy simply called the raids "a product of and response to excessive public hysteria...."[154] According to these accounts, the atmosphere of fear or, in the words of Murray, the "tremendous social delirium," which dominated the nation and which had pressured the reluctant federal government to initiate the first wave of raids in November, had finally spread to and captured control of the Justice Department and its Bureau of Investigation. The result was the excessive and irrational repression of the Communists; according to Murray, "The Palmer raids ... represented the most spectacular manifestation of government hysteria in 1919-20...."[155]

In the following it will be argued that the bureaucratic momentum of the Bureau's deportation campaign was the single most important

---

[152]The bill is printed in *Investigation Activities of the Department of Justice*, 14-15.
[153]Link (ed.), *The Papers of Woodrow Wilson*, Vol. 64, 110-111. See also, Murray, 201-202.
[154]Quotes from, Murray, 209; Coben, *A. Mitchell Palmer*, 244; Murphy, "Sources and Nature," 65-66. See also, Coben, "A Study in Nativism," 72-73.
[155]Murray, 217, 223.

factor behind the final Palmer raids against the Communist parties. Its almost complete capture of the control of the deportation process might be divided up into eight initiatives: First, the Bureau conducted the investigations on its own initiative. Second, it made the de facto decision on whom to arrest. Third, it avoided a formal ruling by the Labor Department on whether both parties were illegal according to the Immigration Act of 1918. Fourth, it executed the raids. Fifth, it conducted the preliminary examinations. Sixth, it caused a change in the alien's right to counsel. Seventh, it participated actively in the hearings. Eight, it pressured the immigration authorities to fix the amount of bail so high as to keep the aliens in custody indefinitely. Again, Justice Department and Bureau officials were moved by their own objectives, namely an ideological desire to destroy Communism in America and an institutional interest in mobilizing popular and political support for the sedition bill, rather than out of consideration for a hysterical opinion.

The January 1920 raids were the direct result of the Justice Department and the Bureau's determination to nip the Communist movement in the bud and prevent it from ever developing a mass following. The competing Communist Labor Party and Communist Party were established in Chicago on August 31 and September 1, 1919, after the revolutionary Left Wing had been expelled by the old guard of the Socialist Party. Both parties claimed exaggerated high membership figures but the most reliable estimate suggests that the parties had 10,000 and 27,000 members respectively. Both were dominated by radical aliens, mostly Russian and Eastern European immigrants, who made up 90% of the combined membership, a fact which made the early Communist parties extremely vulnerable to the government's deportation campaign.[156]

In reality, the Communist movement did not pose such a severe security risk to America in 1919-20 that it justified such drastic methods as mass arrests and deportations. As previously mentioned, the Communists were isolated from the social unrest after the war and played no role during the strikes and riots. The Communist parties did warrant surveillance, however. We now know that claims that Moscow smuggled substantial sums into the United States during the Red Scare were true. In 1919 and 1920, four Comintern couriers, including John Reed, carried a total of 2,728,000 rubles, the equivalent of several

---

[156]For the early CP and CLP in general, see, Draper, 66-72, 97-113, 131-134, 137-138, 148-161, 166-169, 176-184, 188-190; Weinstein, *Decline of Socialism*, 182-187, 192-205, 212-221.

million dollars, to the American Communists.[157] The American Communists also submitted to the directives from the Soviet Union. They promised obedience to the Comintern, and they followed orders to unite the competing parties and to abandon the IWW and to work within the AFL.[158] The Bureau was justified in keeping an eye on the infant Communist movement, but it exaggerated its revolutionary potential.

Nevertheless, the Justice Department on its own initiative from the very beginning prepared for a crack-down. Bureau agents infiltrated the founding conventions of the Communist parties in Chicago. Two and a half month later Hoover informed his superiors that he intended to obtain a decision by Caminetti as to whether alien members of the CP were deportable and thereby enable "the elimination of certain undesirable aliens...."[159]

According to the immigration laws, it was the responsibility of the secretary of labor to decide whether an organization advocated the overthrow of the government with force or violence and consequently whether its alien members were subjects for deportation. On December 15, Hoover transmitted to Caminetti the Radical Division's brief on the CP, requesting a ruling on whether or not the party fell within the provisions of the Immigration Act of 1918. Since the Justice Department was planning to round up the Communists just after New Year, this only gave the immigration authorities some 14 days to analyze Hoover's material and make a decision on the legal status of the CP. The main proposition of the brief was that "the Communist Party is an organization advocating and teaching the overthrow by force and violence of the Government of the United States and members thereof believe in and advocate and teach the overthrow by force or violence of the Government of the United States." This proposition was based on an analysis of the CP's connection with the Third International, quotations from the party's numerous millitant calls to conquer and destroy the state with force and violence in the form of mass action and to establish the dictatorship of the proletariat. Despite the fact that its own investigations had uncovered few signs of Communist involvement in the recent unrest, the brief claimed that the Communists had been influental in the riots and strikes. It was stated

[157]Harvey Klehr, John Earl Haynes & Fridrikh Igorevich Firsov, *The Secret World of American Communism* (New Haven & London, 1995), 21-24.
[158]Harvey Klehr, John Earl Haynes & Kyrill M. Anderson, *The Soviet World of American Communism* (New Haven & London, 1998), 16, 49.
[159]J. E. Hoover, Memorandum Upon Work of Radical Division, August 1, 1919, to October 15, 1919, October 18, 1919, OG 374217, RG65, NA; Memorandum Upon the Work of the Radical Division, August 1, 1919 to March 15, 1920, n.d., ibid.; Draper, 182.

definitively that the CP propaganda was "the cause of much of the racial trouble in the United States at the present time." As proof of "the responsibility of individual members" the brief quoted from the membership application, in which the applicant "after having read the constitution and program of the Communist Party, declares his adherence to the principles and tactics of that party and the Communist International; agrees to submit to the discipline of the party as stated in its constitution; and pledges himself to engage actively in its work."[160] Thus, the Bureau's case against the CP was based upon a literal reading of the party's program and propaganda literature and an exaggeration of its actual activities and influence.

In order to put maximum pressure on the immigration authorities, Hoover did not wait for a formal ruling by the secretary of labor on the CP brief. On December 22 he transmitted to Caminetti the names of 1,554 alleged alien members of the CP. According to Hoover, the list was based "upon careful and thorough investigations," but since the Bureau's knowledge about the aliens was based on information received from its confidential informers, who could not be exposed, the enclosed affidavits were simply sworn to by special agents and contained no supporting evidence. The Labor Department was not only unable to evaluate the Bureau's evidence, but Hoover furthermore stressed that "the interests of the country and the investigations made by this office demand immediate attention." He therefore requested that warrants of arrest be issued no later than December 27, in effect giving the immigration officials just five days to rubber-stamp the Bureau's list.[161] During the following days, Hoover continued to request warrants for arrest of the alleged alien Communists and by the end of the month the total number had reached 3,000.[162] By following this procedure the Bureau simply ignored the requirement of the deportation process that applications for warrants of arrest should be accompanied by at least "some substantial supporting evidence."[163] It

---

[160]The brief is reprinted in, *AG Palmer on Charges*, 321-331. The briefs on the CP and the CLP have usually been attributed to Hoover, who based his later status as an authority on communism on his alleged authorship, which he claimed was the result of his extensive study of the Communist movement in 1919 (J. Edgar Hoover, *Masters of Deceit. The Story of Communism in America and How to Fight It* (New York, 1958), v-vi; de Toledano, 52-58; Powers, *Secrecy and Power*, 96-101; Theoharis & Cox, 68-70; Donner, 40-41). However, according to Whitehead, 331n2, Hoover's "principal assistant" in the study was George F. Ruch, and a comparison with other Ruch memoranda in the files indicates that Ruch might actually have been the author.

[161]Letter, Hoover to Caminetti, December 22, 1919, JD 205492-6, RG60, NA (microfilm).

[162]Letters, Hoover to Caminetti, December 24, 27 and 31, 1919 and January 2, 1920, in JD 205492, ibid.; William B. Wilson to A. Mitchell Palmer, December 30, 1919, JD 205492-275, ibid.

[163]The Labor Department's rules for the administration of the deportation process are reprinted in, *Charges of Illegal Practices*, 5, box 107, Norris Papers, LC.

made sure that the immigration officials had neither the time nor the opportunity to review all of the applications. In effect, the Bureau had taken over the vital responsibility of deciding whom to arrest and had reduced the Immigration Bureau to simply rubber-stamping the Bureau's plans. This relentless pressure on the immigration authorities bore fruit on December 24, when Caminetti informed Hoover that a conference attended by Secretary of Labor Wilson, Acting Secretary John W. Abercrombie and Caminetti had agreed in a test case that members of the CP and the URW "aim to teach the same objective only by different methods." Consequently, all aliens held because of their membership in the CP were deportable; the decision was to be kept secret for the time being.[164] Wilson also agreed to issue the 3,000 warrants of arrest.[165]

There are strong indications that the Bureau officials were so confident at this stage of their domination of the deportation process that they pulled off a coup against the Labor Department by including the members of the smaller of the Communist parties, the Communist Labor Party, in the January raids.[166] On December 24, probably following the receipt of Caminetti's message that the Labor Department had found alien CP members to be deportable, Hoover transmitted a brief on the CLP to the Immigration Bureau. He stressed in his covering letter that the two Communist parties were "exactly similar" since both were "pledged to the principles and tactics of the 3rd. International; the only difference, as pointed out exists only in leadership." In contrast to the case of the CP, Hoover this time did not request a formal ruling by the Labor Department but in passing just informed Caminetti: "It is therefore the intention of this office to treat the members of the Communist Labor Party in the same category as those of the Communist Party."[167] The enclosed brief on the CLP was much shorter than the previously submitted CP brief, it referred to the CP brief for further details several times, and it repeatedly emphasized the point that the two parties were similar. Thus, it was pointed out that the "purposes and principles of the Communist Labor

---

[164]Letter, Caminetti to Hoover, December 24, 1919, JD 205492-15, RG60, NA (microfilm). As the solicitor of the Labor Department Abercrombie had close connections to the Justice Department, see Preston, 217-218; Gengarelly, 318.

[165]Letter, Wilson to Palmer, December 30, 1919, JD 205492-275, RG60, NA (microfilm).

[166]This issue has been the subject of some disagreement among historians: According to Stanley Coben, Hoover did perform a coup by "rashly" deciding not to ask the Labor Department for a formal ruling on the CLP (Coben, *A. Mitchell Palmer*, 224), while Richard Gid Powers has argued that it is "likely" that Hoover only proceeded with his plans for the arrests "only after learning both briefs had been approved by Wilson ... " (Powers, *Secrecy and Power*, 510n22).

[167]Letter, Hoover to Caminetti, December 24, 1919, JD 205492-10, RG60, NA (microfilm).

Party and the Communist Party are practically the same in each instance," and the brief went on to analyze the CLP's adherence to the Third International and its calls for the capture of the state power by means of the action of the masses. It concluded that the program of the CLP "conforms entirely" to the CP program, and it pointed out that the membership application of the CLP was "almost exactly similar to the membership pledge of the Communist Party."[168] It seems clear from the wording of the letter and the brief that it was the intention of the Bureau, once the CP had been found to be illegal according to the immigration law, to avoid a time consuming formal ruling and instead simply have the immigration officials accept the CLP as "similar" to the CP.

That this was in fact what happened and that the CLP brief was never brought to the attention of Secretary Wilson is supported by a letter of instructions issued by Caminetti on December 29 to all immigration inspectors concerning the raids. The commissioner general distinguished between the CP, which "the Department holds ... to be an organization mere membership in which brings an alien within the purview of the Act of October 18, 1918," and the CLP, which he simply described as being "in all essential particulars in so far as the act of October 18, 1918, is concerned, identical" with the CP.[169] Only the CP, it seems, had been formally designated as an illegal organization by the secretary of labor while the CLP was only considered as being identical. This interpretation is further supported by a letter, dated December 30, in which Secretary Wilson mentioned that he had been requested by Hoover to issue warrants of arrest only against alien members of the CP.[170] If Wilson had made a ruling on the CLP as well as the CP, it was to be expected that Caminetti and Wilson would have mentioned the two parties together. Instead the inference is that Hoover transmitted the CLP brief to Caminetti following the announcement of the CP ruling on December 24 and that the immigration officials adopted the view that no further rulings were necessary as the CLP was identical to the CP; they therefore never presented the CLP brief to the secretary. Finally, it should be mentioned that no reference to a ruling on the CLP has been found in the relevant Justice Department and Bureau files. In addition, whereas Secretary Wilson following the raids in early 1920 upheld the decision that alien members of the CP were deportable, he ruled that the CLP

---

[168]The CLP brief is reprinted in, *AG Palmer on Charges*, 375-377.
[169]The letter of instructions is reprinted in, *Charges of Illegal Practices*, 51.
[170]Letter, Wilson to Palmer, December 30, 1919, JD 205492-275, RG60, NA (microfilm).

was, in fact, not similar in purposes with the CP and did not come within the scope of the immigration law. Thus, he indicated that he had never previously made a ruling concerning the CLP.[171]

The Bureau's take-over of the deportation process triggered a protest from Secretary Wilson to Palmer on December 30. Wilson confirmed that he would issue the 3,000 arrest warrants although he expressed grave doubts "whether affidavits based upon information that cannot be revealed at the hearings establish the constitutional requirement of 'probable cause' for arrest ..." In other words, he opposed the Bureau practice of arresting on the basis of information supplied by unidentified confidential informers. Wilson also warned Palmer that the simultaneous arrests of 3,000 aliens would tax the Immigration Bureau's meager facilities, already overburdened by the URW raids which had resulted in a considerable backlog of other deportation cases, and cause long delays. He added: "We cannot, however, assume the responsibility for injury to innocent parties which would probably result from a hasty and imperfect examination of these cases through any attempt to pass upon them without giving full consideration to the law and all facts in each case." However, Wilson did not take the logical consequence of his views such as vetoing the proposed raids. Possibly due to his distaste of radicals and his ignorance of the details of the Bureau's crusade, he merely suggested that the Justice Department instead of carrying out the "nation-wide raid" should bring the cases one-by-one as they were being developed to the attention of the immigration authorities.[172]

The Bureau files confirm that, having moved in and captured control of the deportation process, the nature of the raids was determined by the Bureau's own priorities and determination to get results. The Bureau's fundamental problem during the preparations for the raids was caused by its reliance on its corps of informers within the Communist parties. As Hoover informed Caminetti: "As the activities of aliens who are radically inclined are always most secretive in character, it quite often is next to impossible to prove actual member-ship with the organization alleged to be anarchistic." However, the Bureau had been able to establish the identity of the radical aliens with the aid of its informers, but, as Hoover pointed out: "You of course

---

[171]Wilson's decisions in 1920 are reprinted in, *Investigation of Post*, 150-155.
[172]Letter, Wilson to Palmer, December 30, 1919, JD 205492-275, RG60, NA (microfilm); for Palmer's reply, see letter, Palmer to Wilson, January 2, 1920, JD 205492-243, ibid.; for Wilson's opposition to the raids, see also, letter, Wilson to James Duncan, April 22, 1920, Corresp. 1920, Wilson Papers, Historical Society of Pennsylvania; for a discussion of Wilson's motives for not vetoing the raids, see Gengarelly, 317-320.

will appreciate the inadvisability of calling such confidential informants as witnesses in the deportation hearings, for their usefulness as such informants would immediately be curtailed."[173] This dilemma had become abundantly clear during the hearings against members of the URW in November. For example, Todd Daniel, the special agent in charge of the Philadelphia office, informed Washington about a case which was based entirely on the statement by an informer to the effect that the alien had distributed anarchistic literature and was a member of the URW: "I took particular care not to mention this transaction in my communication with the immigrant inspector for the reason that if the alien were confronted with the facts they might suggest to him the identity of our informant, whose identity we cannot too scrupulously conceal."[174] Thus, as in the previous URW raids, the Bureau's determination to maintain the confidentiality of its informers, led it to rely on two other sources to prove the membership of the aliens, namely the membership books and records of the Communist parties and the confessions of the aliens.

Palmer pointed out in his answer to Wilson's protest that the basic reason for the use of simultaneous raids was that they would enable the federal agents to seize the internal records of the parties, whereas individual arrests would merely warn the Communists and enable them to destroy the material.[175] On December 27, Assistant Director and Chief Frank Burke reminded the agents of the importance of obtaining documentary evidence of the aliens' membership. He pointed out that the residences of Communist Party officials "should be searched in every instance for literature, membership cards, records and correspondance" and that the parties' offices and meeting halls should also be "thoroughly searched" for papers and records: "All literature, books, papers and anything hanging on the walls should be gathered up; the ceilings and partitions should be sounded for hiding places." Simultaneously, all aliens found on the premises should be put under arrest and searched for their membership books.[176] In some instances, these instructions led the zealous agents to seize, according to an

---

[173]Letter, Hoover to Caminetti, November 19, 1919, BS 202600-184, RG65, NA.
[174]Letter, Todd Daniel to Frank Burke, November 28, 1919, OG 341761, ibid. A contemporary study of the Immigration Bureau's files showed that in many instances the special agents at the hearings refused to reveal their sources, stating only that they were confidential and that their exposure would be detrimental to the interests of the government (see, *Charges of Illegal Practices*, 321, 323-324).
[175]Letter, Palmer to Wilson, January 2, 1920, JD 205492-243, RG60, NA (microfilm).
[176]Burke's instructions of December 27, 1919, are reprinted in, *NPGL Report*, 38-39, and *Charges of Illegal Practices*, 12-14 and 49-51.

internal Bureau memo, such items as "curtains, clothes, secular books, bibles, medicines, etc...."[177]

More importantly, in their eagerness for results the agents simply conducted most of the searches and seizures without warrants. Bureau officials proceeded on the basis of the decisions and policies of the federal courts and immigration authorities during the previous decades, according to which aliens in the deportation process were not protected by any constitutional guarantees. As Frank Stone, special agent in charge in Newark and a former immigration inspector who often advised Hoover in deportation matters, informed Washington, "evidence found at the time of his arrest on his possession or among his personal effects can be used against him, as these are administrative and not criminal proceedings...."[178] Consequently, Burke's instructions to the field left it "entirely to your discretion as to the methods by which you should gain access" and recommended that search warrants be procured from the local authorities only if it was deemed "absolutely necessary" "due to the local conditions in your territory."[179] Only if the local authorities insisted on due process should the Bureau agents observe the Fourth Amendment to the Constitution, forbidding search and seizure without warrant.

In order to obtain confessions of membership or political activities and beliefs, the Bureau employed three methods: the preliminary examination, the denial of counsel and indefinite confinement. In the instructions to the field, the agents were impressed with the importance of obtaining confessions at the preliminary examinations conducted immediately following the arrests and before the aliens were turned over to the Immigration Bureau. According to Burke's instructions, "every effort" should be made to prove the aliens' membership and "you should endeavor to obtain from them, if possible, admissions that they are members of either of these parties, together with any statement concerning their citizenship status." The agents were told that they only had until seven a.m. the following morning to complete their examinations.[180] In the final instructions before the

---

[177]W. W. Grimes, Memorandum for Mr. Hoover, August 27, 1920, OG 341761, RG65, NA; see also, Hoover, Memorandum for Assistant Attorney General Stewart, October 12, 1920, and Hoover, Memorandum for Mr. Grimes, October 19, 1920, ibid.

[178]Letter, Frank R. Stone to Hoover, February 12, 1920, ibid.; for similar views of the Justice Department that aliens in the deportation process had no constitutional rights, see also, letters, Hoover to Caminetti, March 20, 1920, and Hoover to Arthur B. O'Keefe, May 20, 1920, ibid.; *AG Palmer on Charges*, 71-73; *Charges of Illegal Practices*, 31, 640-642.

[179]*NPGL Report*, 38, 40. The Justice Department later claimed that the instructions referred to the search of private homes or to cases where aliens did not consent to searches (*AG Palmer on Charges*, 70, and *Charges of Illegal Practices*, 17-18), but the formulation "due to the local conditions in your territory" clearly refers to the more broader political situation in the states.

[180]*NPGL Report*, 38, 40.

raids, it was repeated that the aliens should be "thoroughly examined," that it was of "utmost importance" to prove their membership, and that in case the aliens refused to confess, "detailed examination should be made to bring out Communistic views of subject...."[181] Thus, strong pressure was brought to bear on the agents to obtain confessions by the aliens before the next morning. Not surprisingly, this resulted in numerous complaints by aliens that they had been mistreated and subjected to third degree interrogations while in Bureau custody.[182]

In order to make the whole process more effective and obtain more confessions, the Bureau sought to deny the aliens' right to counsel during the formal deportation hearing. According to subdivision 5 (b) of Rule 22, the Labor Department's guidelines for the administration of the deportation process, the alien at "the beginning of the hearing ... shall be apprised that he may be represented by counsel."[183] The Bureau experiences during the hearings against alleged members of the URW had shown that if a counsel were present at the hearing, he would advise the alien to remain silent and not answer any questions regarding citizenship status and party affiliation. According to Frank Stone, 90% of the aliens had refused to speak at the hearings, making it almost impossible for the Bureau to prove its cases.[184]

When the change of Rule 22 just prior to the execution of the January raids, depriving the aliens of their right to counsel, became a matter of some controversy during a congressional hearing in 1921, Hoover heatedly denied having taken any part in the decision and claimed that it had been done on the Labor Department's own initiative.[185] However, the Bureau files confirm that he did put con-

---

[181]Frank Burke's instructions of December 31, 1919, are reprinted in *Charges of Illegal Practices*, 19.

[182]Several historians have claimed that most acts of violence were committed by local police forces and vigilantes who assisted in the raids, thereby arguing that the excesses were the results of the local "grassroots" hysteria swelling up from below (see for example, de Toledano, 63; Coben, *A. Mitchell Palmer*, 228-229; Powers, *Secrecy and Power*, 103-104). These authors ignore the fact that a number of aliens specifically accused Bureau agents of having used force during the preliminary examinations in an attempt to extract confessions (see for example, *NPGL Report*, 31-36, 55; *Charges of Illegal Practices*, 58-59, 79, 334-335, 340; it should be mentioned that the Justice Department denied all accusations and submitted statements from all agents named by aliens, denying any wrong-doing, see for example, *AG Palmer on Charges*, 58-59, 107-115; *Charges of Illegal Practices*, 134-155, 426-431, 447-448, 459, 468-469, 573). It seems, then, if the aliens' accounts are to be believed, that the violence perpetrated during the raids was not the result of a local, popular hysteria but of the Bureau agents' eagerness to comply with Washington's instructions and obtain as many confessions as possible while the aliens were still in Bureau custody.

[183]*Charges of Illegal Practices of the Department of Justice*, 20-21, box 106, George W. Norris Papers, LC.

[184]*Charges of Illegal Practices*, 562, 564-565; for the strategy of "talk strike," see Preston, 214-216.

[185]*Charges of Illegal Practices*, 649; supported by de Toledano, 58-59; for the view that Hoover, while intending to pressure the immigration officials, never directly requested a change, see Powers, *Secrecy and Power*, 510n21.

siderable pressure on the immigration officials to change the rule. On November 19, Hoover informed Caminetti about the recent difficulties experienced by the Bureau in proving the aliens' membership at the hearings since "the attorneys who principally indulge in the practice of defending these anarchists before your inspectors have apparently advised them to the effect that they should under no condition make any statement concerning their affiliations or their connections or activities." Hoover therefore requested information on whether Rule 22 had been adopted by Congress or whether it was an internal Labor Department rule.[186] Even though Hoover did not explicitly request a change of the rule, the intention of the letter was clearly to pressure the immigration officials. Six days later, Hoover directed the attention of Caminetti to the problem caused by a "talk strike" among the alleged URW members held on Ellis Island.[187] On December 17, Hoover reminded the commissioner general of his previous enquiry regarding Rule 22, stressing that in view of the difficulties experienced in proving the cases against the URW members, which were "due to the arbitrary tactics of persons employed by such members," Hoover pressed for "an early reply" concerning the status of Rule 22 "in order that the same condition may not arise when future arrests are made of undesirable aliens."[188] The following day, Hoover kept the heat on Caminetti by pointing out the difficulties posed by the aliens' right to counsel.[189] Finally, on December 30, just three days prior to the raids against the Communists, the Labor Department gave in and Acting Secretary Abercrombie, on the recommendation of Caminetti, authorized that Rule 22 should be changed to read that the alien should be apprised of his right to counsel preferably at the beginning of the hearing "or at any rate as soon as such hearing has proceeded sufficiently in the development of the facts to protect the Government's interests...."[190] Thus, the Bureau in its pursuit of results succeeded in causing a change of the immigration authorities' rules from protecting the rights of the alien to protecting the interests of the federal government.

If the Bureau were unable to extract the necessary confession from the aliens during the vigorous preliminary examinations and hearings at which counsels were denied access, the federal agents had one final

---

[186]Letter, Hoover to Caminetti, November 19, 1919, BS 202600-184, RG65, NA.
[187]Letter, Hoover to Caminetti, November 25, 1919, ibid.; for this incident, see also, George Ruch, Memorandum for Mr. Hoover, November 25, 1919, OG 341761, ibid.
[188]Letter, Hoover to Caminetti, December 17, 1919, JD 203557-38, RG60, NA (microfilm).
[189]Letter, Hoover to Caminetti, December 18, 1919, OG 341761, RG65, NA.
[190]Reprinted in *Charges of Illegal Practices of Department of Justice*, 21, box 106, Norris Papers, LC.

means at their disposal to soften up the aliens, namely to keep them in custody indefinitely by the imposition of high bail. The official policy of the Labor Department was that bail in the amount of $10,000 would be "prohibitive" and in violation of the Eight Amendment, which bars "excessive" bail. The bail for the detained radical aliens had therefore been fixed at $1,000. Nevertheless, the Bureau in a number of cases urged the immigration officials to increase the bail to $10,000 with the argument that the aliens were mostly "young men and single and have admitted membership in the Communist Party."[191] The official justification for requesting such a high amount was that the authorities wanted to make sure that the aliens would show up at the hearing and that the amount was not excessive since the Communists had a considerable "slush fund" for just such a situation.[192] However, the Bureau files reveal that this was simply an excuse cooked up for the occasion. When the imposition of high bail was publicly criticized in the spring of 1920, Washington requested the field offices to submit information concerning aliens whose bail had been reduced and subsequently had disappeared. It was added that the "purpose is to show the reason for this Department asking large bond in case of alien anarchists and Communists." Unfortunately, the field offices were unable to find any examples of aliens, who had been released on bail, and who had failed to appear at the deportation hearings.[193]

In fact, the Bureau seems to have had two motives for the use of high bail. First, by keeping the alien in custody it was hoped that he might be more amendable to confess at the hearing, and according to Hoover, to release him before the hearing "virtually defeats the ends of justice and prolongs the hearings an unreasonable length of time."[194] The Bureau, again, was more concerned about getting results, that is, confessions, than about the aliens' rights. Secondly, it was clearly the intention of the Justice Department to use the high bail to prevent the aliens from pursuing their political activities. As Palmer explained to Secretary Wilson, the release of suspected alien Communists "is

---

[191]Letter, Caminetti to Hoover, February 13, 1920, att. to letter, Assistant Commissioner General to Acting Commissioner of Immigration, Ellis Island, February 13, 1920, OG 341761, RG65, NA; also, George Ruch, Memorandum for Mr. Hoover, January 19, 1920, ibid. Hoover later claimed that there were "very few" examples of bail over $500 (*Charges of Illegal Practices*, 94; also, 540), but a contemporary study of the files of the Immigration Bureau found that 20.5% of a sample of 200 cases were in the amount of $1,500 to $10,000 (ibid., 337-338).
[192]*AG Palmer on Charges*, 37-46; supported by de Toledano, 59; see also, *Charges of Illegal Practices*, 94-95, 539-540.
[193]Telegram, Burke to 33 field offices, May 12, 1920, OG 341761, RG65, NA; for examples of negative responses from the field, see telegrams, Lamb to Burke, May 13, 1920; Pierce to Burke, May 13, 1920; McLaughlin to Burke, May 13, 1920, ibid. For the controversy about high bail, see Lowenthal, 223-236.
[194]Letter, Hoover to Caminetti, January 22, 1920, OG 341761, RG65, NA.

particularly detrimental to the public welfare and will lead to a renewal of the insidious propaganda upon which members of these organizations have been engaged for the last four months."[195] From another perspective, Assistant Secretary of Labor Louis F. Post noted that the object of "this exorbiant bail" was to keep the alien "locked up whether he is innocent or guilty."[196] Thus, the particular characteristics of the raids, the warrantless searches and seizures, the vigorous preliminary interrogations, the denial of counsel, and the imposition of high bail, can all be traced to the internal priorities and decision-making process of the Bureau, rather than to the existence of a popular hysteria engulfing the government.

Destroying Communism in America: The January 1920 Raids
The mass quality of the raids was also a result of the Bureau officials' determination to mount as impressive and effective an operation as possible. First, according to the procedure agreed to by the Bureau and the immigration authorities, the Labor Department would transmit the warrants of arrest to the local immigration inspectors, who in turn would get in contact with the local Bureau offices. However, when it became clear on January 2, the date for the raids, that not all warrants would be issued in time to be served, it was decided that instead of postponing the whole operation the field force should proceed with the arrests and hold the aliens until the warrants were received. Thus, many aliens were taken into custody and held before the agents even knew the names of whom to arrest.[197] Secondly, it was the policy of the Bureau to regard the mere presence of an alien on the CP or CLP premises as prima facie evidence of affiliation with the parties and thus cause for arrest and interrogation. In other words, the raids functioned as a fishing operation and it was hoped that it would be possible afterwards, with either confessions or the membership records, to prove the membership of the aliens swept up in the raids.[198]

It is not known precisely how many were taken into custody during the night of January 2 as a result of these Bureau decisions. Following

---

[195]Letter, Palmer to Wilson, January 2, 1920, JD 205492-243, RG60, NA (microfilm).
[196]*Investigation of Post*, 189.
[197]For examples of such instructions, see telegrams, Burke to Samson, January 2, 1920; Burke to Laird, January 2, 1920; Burke to Kelleher, January 3, 1920, OG 341761, RG65, NA.
[198]*AG Palmer on Charges*, 69-70; *NPGL Report*, 48-49. According to the arrangement worked out between the Bureau and the immigration authorities, following the arrests the Bureau would apply for warrants against those arrested without warrants, see letters, Caminetti to Hoover, November 24, 1919, with att. telegram, Caminetti to Immigration Service, Ellis Island et al, November 24, 1919; letter, F. P. Pendleton to Frank Burke, December 8, 1919, OG 341761, RG65, NA; Hoover to Caminetti, January 3 and 6, 1920, and Caminetti to Hoover, January 8, 1920, JD 205492, RG60, NA (microfilm).

the preliminary examinations, a total of 2,435 suspected alien Communists (2,289 alleged members of the CP and 146 affiliated with the CLP) were turned over to the immigration authorities. But according to some local figures from New England, Buffalo and Detroit, between one quarter and two-thirds of those rounded up in the raids were released shortly for lack of evidence. If these figures are representative, it would mean that between 3,200 and 7,300 suspected alien Communists were taken into custody by the Bureau.[199]

Attorney General Palmer later claimed that the Justice Department had played only a secondary role in the planning of the raids and that the Bureau had only assisted in carrying out the arrests "acting under and for and by direction of the inspectors of immigration."[200] There are, however, several indications that the Bureau had now captured almost complete control of the deportation process so that the Communist raids were, in effect, exclusively a Bureau operation, with the immigration authorities relegated to the sidelines. For example, in the Bureau instructions to the field it was emphasized that "the arrests made are being made under the direction and supervision of the Department of Justice," and the Immigration Bureau likewise notified the immigration inspectors that under no circumstances were they to make the arrests on their own initiative: "To do so would be to invite disaster."[201] Besides conducting the preliminary examinations immediately following the raids, the Bureau agents also took an active part in the formal deportation hearings, which according to the Labor Department rules were supposed to be held by the immigration inspectors. Informed by Washington of the "utmost necessity" that the cases be completed "at the earliest possible moment" and directed to "render any and all reasonable assistance" to the immigration inspectors, the Bureau not only provided assistance in the form of guards and stenographers but in several instances the agents presented the government's case at the hearings and simultaneously acted as interpreter and counsel for the accused.[202] And despite the Justice Department's denials that its agents had participated actively in the hearings and questioned the aliens, the Bureau files confirm that the agents of at least four field offices acted as prosecutors in the hearings; for example, the Springfield office reported that its agents "attended

---

[199]For the number of those turned over to the Immigration Bureau, see *Investigation of Post*, 72-73; for the local figures of those released, see *Charges of Illegal Practices*, 55-56, 472-475, 566, 720-721.

[200]*Charges of Illegal Practices*, 22, 635-636.

[201]The instructions are reprinted in, *NPGL Report*, 39, and *Charges of Illegal Practices*, 52.

[202]For the instruction, see *NPGL Report*, 40; for examples of Bureau involvement, see *Charges of Illegal Practices*, 319-320, 340, 467-468.

hearings when notified by Boston office and cross examine aliens charged in Springfield cases."[203] Thus, the Bureau dominated the whole process to such a degree that its personnel acted as guards, stenographers, interpreters, prosecuting attorneys and counsels at the hearings. Federal Judge George W. Anderson, who presided over a number of habeas corpus cases against the government, concluded that the Justice Department had assumed control of the proceedings to the point of "relegating the Department of Labor to the function, almost purely formal, of making records of cases, in effect predetermined by the Department of Justice." Senator Thomas Walsh likewise found that the Bureau agents "were all moved by a common professional pride to hold as many of the prisoners as possible."[204]

It should be noted that the Bureau's eagerness in mounting as impressive and effective an operation as possible had dire consequences for many aliens as well as American citizens. A substantial number of those aliens arrested and held for deportation were not active Communists at all but were former members of the Socialist Party (SP) who had been enrolled automatically in the Communist Party when the foreign language federations of the SP transferred their membership en bloc to the newly formed CP in 1919. The aliens were often unaware of the transfer or its implications, and other aliens had simply joined the Communist parties for social or nationalistic reasons.[205] Although the Bureau had no legal authority to arrest American citizens because of their political activities, a number of citizens were swept up in the dragnet and turned over to the local authorities for prosecution according to state criminal syndicalist laws.[206] Because adequate preparations had not been made for the housing and feeding of several thousand of detainees, the aliens were

[203]Telegram, Butterworth to Neale, August 18, 1920, OG 341761, RG65, NA; also, Thomas F. Baughman, Memorandum for Mr. Hoover, August 20, 1920; report, Wm. P. Hall, August 18, 1920, ibid.; *NPGL Report*, 44-45; *Charges of Illegal Practices*, 60, 81. For the denials, see letter, Hoover to John Thomas Taylor, September 4, 1920, OG 341761, RG65, NA; *AG Palmer on Charges*, 38.

[204]*Charges of Illegal Practices*, 53; US Congress, Senate, Committee on the Judiciary, *Charges of Illegal Practices Against the Department of Justice*, 67th. Cong., 2nd. Sess. (committee print, n.d.), 21, box 106, Norris Papers, LC.

[205]According to a contemporary study of the deportation cases, 37% of those held for deportation might be termed "automatic members," while only 28% could be described as fully "conscious" members of the CP or the CLP (*Charges of Illegal Practices*, 326-327). For the term "automatic members," see also *Investigation of Post*, 75-78; *Charges of Illegal Practices*, 63, 77; for views that many of those taken into custody were hard-working and harmless immigrants, see ibid., 63, 312-314, 330-331, 342-343, 719; *Investigation of Post*, 76, 78-79, 259, 262; for the split of the SP and the automatic transfer of members to the new Communist parties, see Draper, 188-190; Weinstein, *The Decline of American Socialism*, 213n94.

[206]For instructions to turn over American Communists to the local authorities, see *NPGL Report*, 39; telegram, A. Mitchell Palmer to Moon, US Attorney, January 12, 1920, JD 205492-166, RG60, NA (microfilm).

kept in Bureau offices, police stations and makeshift prisons, which soon became overcrowded and insanitary. In the worst example, 800 aliens were held for days in a windowless corridor without ventilation and only one toilet in the Federal Building in Detroit.[207] Finally, numerous poor immigrant families, totally dependent on the weekly paycheck, suffered when their breadwinners were imprisoned often for months. Not until a public outcry demanded that the suffering be alleviated did the Bureau investigate and referred the cases to local charity organizations.[208]

It might be argued that the Bureau had two objectives in mind by making the raids as large and impressive as possible and by putting so much effort into proving so many cases as possible: the immediate one of breaking up the Communist parties and thereby eliminate them as a serious force in American politics, and a more important one of shaping the public opinion to support the Justice Department's further anti-radical agenda. As far as can be established, this frontal attack on the Communist parties, just four months after their establishment, was a stunning succes. According to Theodore Draper's figures, the number of dues-paying members of the Communist Party, by far the largest of the parties, declined abruptly from 23,624 in December 1919 to just 1,714 in January 1920. The raids not only scared away most of the members who had managed to avoid arrest, but the parties' activities were wrecked when most of their records and papers were confiscated and the party presses suppressed. Moreover, even though the Communist parties by no means were mass parties, were compromised by their close links to the Third International and were fraught with internal factionalism, the Palmer raids did hasten their decline. They were forced underground until 1923, which gave them a permanent image of conspiracy and subversion, and isolated them totally from the legitimate political debate.[209]

The Justice Department's public relations campaign began just prior to the raids with a New Year's message from the Attorney General to

---

[207]For Hoover's internal admission that the situation had resulted in "unsanitary conditions and much congestion," see letter, Hoover to Caminetti, January 6, 1920, JD 205492, ibid.; for the situation in Detroit, see *NPGL Report*, 22-23; *Charges of Illegal Practices*, 336, 706-723; for the Justice Department's public denials, see ibid., 458-464; *AG Palmer on Charges*, 60-63, 85-87. An internal Labor Department investigation of the situation in Detroit found that "the conditions could not have been worse ... " (letter, Ethelbert Stewart to Louis F. Post, April 5, 1920, Series 19/24, Wilson Papers, Historical Society of Pennsylvania).

[208]For the fact that the Bureau only intervened because of public criticism, see telegrams, Burke to Field Offices, January 8 and 9, 1920, OG 341761, RG65, NA; also, telegram, Burke to Blackmon, January 12, 1920; letters, T. E. Campbell to Frank Burke, March 29, 1920; Burke to Campbell, April 23, 1920, ibid.

[209]Draper, 206-208; also, Weinstein, *Decline of American Socialism*, 249-250; Murray, 220, 276-277; Whitehead, 52.

the nation, in which people were urged to "study, understand, and appreciate the so-called 'Red' movement." The message went on to describe the Communists as "a distinctly criminal and dishonest movement" and called their sympathizers in the US "criminals, mistaken idealists, social bigots, and many unfortunate men and women suffering with varying forms of hyperaesthesia." According to the official message, the Communists were "enemies of the Government, of the Church and of the home," and it described in details how people would be robbed of their property and possessions and how religion would be abolished if the Bolsheviks should triumph. Having thus presented the menace the Justice Department promised to defend the nation: "This department, as far as existing laws allow, intends during the forthcoming year to keep up an unflinching, persistent, aggressive warfare against any movement, no matter how cloaked or dissembled, having for its purpose either the promulgation of these ideas or the excitation of sympathy for those who spread them."[210] Thus, the public opinion was prepared for the necessity of the raids two days after.

The raids themselves were exploited to the limit to construct a public image of the dangerous revolutionaries. In Boston the aliens were handcuffed, chained together and marched through the streets while exposed to the press. A journalist in Detroit reported on a similar experience: "Six days' imprisonment without opportunity to shave, six nights of sleeping in their clothing on a stone floor, had prepared them well for the enforced role of 'Bolshevik terrorists' with which the public is regaled." He added that news reel films of these carefully orchestrated scenes were probably doing "their vicious work of rousing hate and intolerance all over the country."[211] At the same time, the press was informed by Bureau officials that a large number of weapons and bombs had been discovered during the raids, supporting the thesis about a violent revolutionary movement. Unnamed federal officials informed the *New York Times* that Communist documents seized during the raids "tended to prove that the nationwide raids had blasted the most menacing revolutionary ploy yet unearthed."[212] In fact, the number of weapons found was small and hardly more than would be expected in any nation-wide raid, taking

[210]"Palmer Pledges War on Radicals," *The New York Times,* January 1, 1920.
[211]Frederick R. Barkley, "Jailing Radicals in Detroit," *The Nation,* January 31, 1920, reprinted in *Charges of Illegal Practices,* 722; for the Boston incident, see ibid., 59.
[212]"Let Radicals Out Under $1,000 Bail, Is Official Order," *The New York World,* January 4, 1920, clipping in box 1, J. Edgar Hoover Memoriabilia Collection, RG65, NA. The claim was repeated in *AG Report 1920,* 176; quote from Levin, 131.

into account the large number of private firearms in circulation in the US at that time; as Assistant Secretary of Labor Louis F. Post remarked, "if you were to search the suit cases in the hotels of Washington, you would find in many of them deadly pistols."[213]

The Justice Department also began systematically to plant appropriate anti-radical news stories in the press. One of the articles sent to the nation's news media consisted of Palmer's New Year message under the headline "Warns Nation of Red Peril – U.S. Department of Justice Urges Americans to Guard Against Bolshevism Menace – Calls Red Plans Criminal – Press, Church, Schools, Labor Unions and Civic Bodies Called Upon to Teach True Purpose of Bolshevist Propaganda." Other articles contained extracts of the manifesto and program of the CP under the headlines "To 'Conquer and Destroy State,' U.S. Communists Call for Labor Revolt – Revolutionary Pamphlet, Found in U.S. Department of Justice Investigation, Gives Message of Communists in Chicago to Russian Headquarters" and "'Overthrow World Order!' Cry Communists – Manifesto of Communist International, Seized in U.S. Department of Justice Raids, Tells 'Reds' Own Story of Their Plans for World Wide Plunder." The Justice Department also furnished the press with the words of revolutionary songs to be reprinted under the headline "What Reds Would Have Us Sing – From I.W.W. Songs – Seized in Red Raids of U.S. Department of Justice." In addition, the pictures of a number of particularly sinister-looking alien radicals, taken after they had been imprisoned for some days without opportunity to wash or shave, were distributed under the caption "Men Like These Would Rule You." The Justice Department also provided the press with copies of anti-radical cartoons free of charge.[214]

Palmer furthermore wrote to magazine editors, conservative groups and other "leaders of the thought of this country" about the nature of the radical menace and his department's counter-measures, enclosing photostatic copies of Communist documents and articles, of which "Striking passages" were "marked for convenience." Palmer pointed out that his only motive was "the furtherance of a more realizing popular appreciation of the menace involved in the unrestrained spread of criminal Communism unspeakable social treason." He added that the department had "a vast amount of other information regarding the radical movement in this country" which was at the disposal of the proper opinion leaders: "My one desire is to acquaint men like you

---

[213]*Investigation of Post,* 71; see also, *AG Palmer on Charges,* 47-48.
[214]Propaganda page of Department of Justice, reprinted in *NPGL Report,* 66-67.

with the real menace of evil thinking which is the foundation of the red movement." The central argument of the letter was that the Communist movement was a criminal one. Its sympathizers were mainly criminals, the entire movement was "a dishonest and criminal one," aiming at acquiring all wealth and power, and political radicalism in the form as Bolshevism and syndicalism "are only names for old theories of violence and criminality."[215]

The portrayal of Communism as simply a criminal movement was elaborated on by the Attorney General in an article in the February issue of *Forum* magazine. Again, Palmer urged the necessity of educating and mobilizing the public opinion, noting that the Justice Department had endeavoured "in attracting the attention of our optimistic citizens to the issue of internal revolution in this country." He referred to the need for a sedition law when he argued that the administration had acted "almost unaided by any virile legislation." According to Palmer, the department's "confidential information" had shown beyond any doubt that the "Government was in jeopardy" in 1919 and that "the blaze of revolution was sweeping over every American institution of law and order." He painted a hair-raising scenario of how radicalism "was eating its way into the homes of the American workman, its sharp tongues of revolutionary heat were licking the altars of the churches, leaping into the belfry of the school bell, crawling into the sacred corners of American homes, seeking to replace marriage vows with libertine laws, burning up the foundations of society." Thus, the radicals were not only guided by criminal but also immoral and degenerate intentions; Communism was "the creed of any criminal mind," driven by "motives impossible to clean thought" and by the "misshapen caste of mind and indecencies of character...."[216]

The Justice Department also published several pamphlets in order to enlighten the public on the radical menace and the need to support the authorities' efforts to suppress it. *The Revolution in Action* was a "popular survey" of the history of the international and domestic radical movement. Its thesis was that the various radical groups and factions, such as the Communists, the IWW, the anarchists, unaffiliated reds and "parlor Bolsheviks," despite their differences, had united in 1919 in their enthusiasm for the Russian revolution and had begun

[215]Letters, A. Mitchell Palmer to Lyman Abbott, editor, The Outlook, January 27, 1920, JD 205492-338.5, RG60, NA (microfilm); Palmer to City Club of Chicago, February 17, 1920, OG 341761, RG65, NA.
[216]A. Mitchell Palmer, "The Case Against the Reds", *Forum*, February 1920, 173-176, reprinted in Davis (ed.), 226-227.

to work "for an actual revolutionary uprising in the United States." The Justice Department warned in conclusion: "Civilization faces its most terrible menace of danger since the barbarian hords overran West Europe and opened the dark ages."[217] Another official publication was *Red Radicalism as Described by Its Own Leaders,* an 83 page collection of extracts of the more extreme Communist documents and literature captured during the raids, which was distributed to members of Congress and the public.[218] The Justice Department also distributed a State Department pamphlet with the telling title *The Photographic History of the Bolshevik Atrocities.*[219] Finally, the department disseminated various "anti-Bolshevik propaganda material" to a number of organizations and individuals who were promised: "There will be more available later on."[220]

The reason for this anti-radical propaganda campaign was most likely to influence the political debate on the sedition bill, which had been proposed by the Attorney General following the November raids and recommended to Congress by the president in December. Most accounts of the congressional sedition debate in early 1920 have seen it as a bipartisan expression of the anti-radical hysteria then sweeping the nation; for example, Murray noted that just by debating the idea of restricting freedom of opinion "Congress betrayed the hysterical condition of many congressional minds in the winter of 1919-20."[221] However, these authors have failed to realize that the sedition debate was primarily a continuation of the partisan fight from 1919, during which the Democratic Wilson administration had tried to obtain a peacetime sedition law, while the Republicans led by Senator Poindexter had ignored the administration's proposals and instead accused it of being "soft on radicalism" while submitting its own, more drastic proposals.

---

[217]*The Revolution in Action. Part II of a popular survey prepared in the Department of Justice,* reprinted in *AG Palmer on Charges,* 215-244.

[218]US Department of Justice, *Red Radicalism as Described by Its Own Leaders. Exhibits collected by A. Mitchell Palmer, Attorney General, including various Communist manifestoes, constitutions, plans, and purposes of the proletariat revolution, and its seditious propaganda* (Washington, DC, 1920). This publication has disappeared from the Library of Congress. For the distribution to members of Congress, see letters, Hoover to Hon. William H. King, January 22, 1920; Hoover to Hon. Albert Johnson, January 22, 1920; Hoover to William S. Kenyon, January 22, 1920; Hoover to William N. Vaille, January 22, 1920, all in JD 205492, RG60, NA (microfilm); for the distribution to the public, see for example, letter, Palmer to Hon. S. Y. Grovitch, April 30, 1920, JD 202600-51-1, ibid.

[219]Mentioned in, letter, Hoover to W. L. Hurley, June 2, 1920, JD 209264-23, ibid.; see also, Powers, *Secrecy and Power,* 121.

[220]Letter, Palmer to K. L. Buell, February 17, 1920, JD 202600-33-39, RG60, NA (microfilm).

[221]Murray, 231; see also, Coben, *A. Mitchell Palmer,* 241-242.

A letter from Senator Poindexter indicates that this was still the strategy of leading Republicans in 1920. He brushed aside Palmer's sedition bill as "perfectly worthless" and went on to accuse the Wilson administration of "supporting and favoring and coming to the defense of anarchists and Bolshevists" and of "the affiliation existing between the Administration and sedition...." Perhaps the best indication that the GOP was using the issue for partisan purposes was Poindexter's criticism of Palmer for not using the existing laws to suppress radicalism while at the same time proposing his own sedition bill; clearly, if the existing laws were sufficient to repress radical activities, no further legislation was needed.[222] In line with this strategy, the Republican controlled House of Representatives pointedly ignored Palmer's sedition bill and instead agreed to consider a Republican sedition bill, the Graham bill. On January 10, the Senate passed the Sterling bill, another Republican bill which prohibited advocacy of violence against private property or the government, forbade the display of red flags and authorized the postmaster general to prohibit the mailing of seditious matter. On January 14, the two measures were amalgamated into the Graham-Sterling bill by the House Judiciary Committee and hearings on the proposal began.[223] If the Republicans intended to paint the administration as sympathetic to the radicals or even as infiltrated by subversives, they could hardly afford to pass the Democratic Attorney General's sedition bill and thus give away their own issue. The Republicans' obstructionism brought forth criticism from Palmer's allies; for example, Poindexter was accused of "playing with politics" instead of enacting the necessary laws against the reds.[224] The *Washington Post* described how the Republican Congress had ignored Palmer's sedition bill while debating its own and asked, "why should partisanship be permitted to intervene and obstruct the Department of Justice in carrying out its work?"[225] Democratic Representative Martin Davey criticized the Republicans for attacking Palmer for not doing enough while at the same time not acting on his proposals: "You ask him to protect America in a crisis; you ask him to do the difficult thing, the thing that takes courage to do; and then you

---

[222]Letter, Miles Poindexter to Arthur W. Large, February 28, 1920, box 384, Poindexter Papers, UWL.
[223]Coben, *A. Mitchell Palmer,* 241-242; Murray, 220, 230-231.
[224]Letter, Edson Johnson to Miles Poindexter, November 4, 1919, box 384, Poindexter Papers, UWL.
[225]"For the National Defense," *The Washington Post,* January 27, 1920, clipping in box 1, J. Edgar Hoover Memoriabilia Collection, RG65, NA.

stab him in the back with petty politics."[226] The Justice Department's public relations campaign following the January raids must be seen as an effort to mobilize support behind the Attorney General's sedition bill against the Republicans. Thus, on January 21, 1920, while the public and the politicians were being bombarded with official accounts of the radical menace and of the Justice Department's success in combating it, Palmer made clear that he opposed the Graham-Sterling bill and proceeded to reintroduce his sedition bill from November.[227]

In summary, the initiative to the raids was taken by aggressive and ambitious officials in the Justice Department and the Bureau of Investigation, who were able to capture control of most functions of the deportation process from the Labor Department. The preparations for the deportations of radical aliens had been going on since 1917, when Goldman and Berkman were marked for expulsion, and 1918, when the URW was identified as a target. The officials needed no outside pressure to intervene but had developed their own motivations and interests in launching a repressive campaign. Their primary concern, of course, was to put an effective end to the anarchists' agitation and to prevent the infant Communist movement in gaining adherents. A secondary purpose was to whip up political and popular support for the Attorney General's sedition bill, which would legally institutionalize the Bureau's political surveillance and thereby increase the influence of the Justice Department. Finally, the management of the operation suggests that the raids were not a spontaneous and hysterical response, organized by panicked officials. Rather, they were carefully and rationally planned and the extensive use of mass arrests, forced confessions and searches was dictated by the necessity of maintaining the confidentiality of the informers and of completing as many cases as possible.

---

[226]*Congressional Record*, April 14, 1920, 6106, clipping in Scrapbook: Impeachment Attempt, box 9, Louis F. Post Papers, LC.
[227]Letter, Palmer to Hon. Philip P. Campbell, January 21, 1920, reprinted in ibid., 6105.

Chapter 7

The Decline and Fall of the Red Scare

The January raids were by no means meant by the Bureau to be the
end of its campaign against alien radicals. On February 14, special
agents under the personal command of J. Edgar Hoover raided the
Italian anarchist group L'Era Nuova in Paterson, New Jersey, and held
29 of its members for deportation.[1] A week later, Hoover suggested in
an internal memorandum that alien members of the Industrial Workers
of the World should be arrested and deported in waves of 500 until the
organization was broken up.[2] Yet within a few months during the
spring of 1920 the Red Scare suddenly subsided, the public excitement
and political rhetoric died down, and the Bureau of Investigation was
forced to abandon all plans for further raids and had to defend its
recent actions instead. Whereas the Bureau had successfully taken
advantage of the anarchist bombs in June 1919 to obtain congressional
funding for its anti-radical campaign, its attempt to whip up an anticommunist hysteria after the Wall St. bomb on September 16, 1920,
which killed 33 and wounded more than 200, made no headway. At
the same time, while the radical issue had been used to great effect to
discredit social unrest and had advanced the careers of Palmer and
Poindexter in 1919, they both failed to gain their parties' nominations
and the Republican President-elect, Warren G. Harding, declared that
"too much has been said about Bolshevism in America."[3] Most
historians agree that the Bureau's anti-radical campaign was brought
to an end when the public hysteria died down because the Bolshevik
threat did not seem so imminent when the revolution was contained in
Russia, the social unrest and radical activities subsided in the US, and
because of public indignation against the political repression and
injustices. Especially the mistreatment of aliens during the Palmer
raids, the New York State Legislature's exclusion of five socialist

---

[1]Letter, Strictly Confidential, J. E. Hoover to Hon. Anthony Caminetti, February 11, 1920,
OG 341761, RG65, NA; J. E. Hoover, Memorandum Upon Activities of the Radical Division,
Department of Justice, May 1, 1920, OG 374217, ibid. On the Bureau's view of the group,
see *AG Palmer on Charges*, 535-545. The cases were later dismissed by the Labor Department,
see, letters, Frank R. Stone to Frank Burke, May 15 and June 11, 1920, OG 341761, RG65,
NA.
[2]Preston, 226; Powers, *Secrecy and Power*, 112.
[3]Murray, 252-253, 257-261.

assemblymen, and the proposals to restrict free speech gave many second thoughts about the anti-radical crusade. According to Murray, the change in the public opinion "unquestionably was the real key to the rapid decline in Red Scare hysteria."[4] Powers found that by staging the Palmer raids the Bureau "may have exceeded the mandate granted it by public opinion" and its campaign collapsed because "the public had grown perceptively tired of the Red Scare."[5] Seen in this way, the Red Scare was an isolated incident, a deviation from the normal political process.

The significant fact about the initiatives which brought an end to the Bureau's deportation crusade is, however, that they came from within the federal bureaucracy while the public opinion seems to have played a somewhat peripheral role. Even Murray has admitted that during the political debate and congressional hearings on the Palmer raids in 1920-21, "once again public opinion was apathetic."[6] Instead, it was the Labor Department, determined to regain its authority over the deportation process and to put an end to the Bureau's "guilt by membership" policy, which took four effective steps to stop the whole process: First, by re-establishing the former process of deciding each case according to principles of personal guilt and due process; second, by bringing a test case before a sympathetic judge on the validity of deporting alien members of the CP; third, by the secretary of labor personally reasserting his authority; and fourth, by taking part in the preparation of a public report, critical of the Justice Department's actions and signed by 12 prominent lawyers.

The Labor Department Insurrection
The reason why the Labor Department now suddenly, after seeing its authority being usurped during the latter half of 1919, decided to stand up to the Bureau of Investigation was due to one single courageous official, Assistant Secretary of Labor Louis F. Post. At the age of 71, Post was still an idealistic and tough progressive reformer, who had been a crusader for Henry George's single-tax movement and in his weekly the *Public* had supported unrestricted immigration and free speech, and opposed imperialism, the trusts and racial discrimination.

---

[4]Ibid., 240, 242-257, 261.

[5]Powers, *Secrecy and Power*, 113, 124. Even those authors who have acknowledged the importance of the bureaucratic struggle between the Justice and Labor Departments have claimed that the change in the public opinion was the decisive factor (see Higham, 232; Coben, *A. Mitchell Palmer*, 236; Blum, "Nativism, Anti-Radicalism and the Foreign Scare," 52-53; Coben, "A Study in Nativism," 74-75).

[6]Murray, 256.

In March 1920, Secretary of Labor William B. Wilson, who had taken little direct interest in the deportations and had only voiced weak protests to the Justice Department about its actions, went on a personal leave of absence. When Acting Secretary John W. Abercrombie resigned, Post was left in command of the department from March 6 to April 14 and in a position to re-establish control of the deportation process.[7]

Post immediately made three important decisions. First of all, even though the duties of Commisioner General of Immigration Anthony Caminetti consisted only of administering the Immigration Bureau and transmitting deportation cases to the secretary of labor or his representative for his final decision, over time he had arrogated to himself the power of recommending the cases and, in effect, deciding them. From his experience, Post knew that Caminetti's summaries and recommendations often were unreliable and prejudiced against alien radicals. Moreover, by early March, the process had resulted in long delays in the processing of the January cases, as the files were piling up in the Immigration Bureau. Post therefore ordered that all the files be sent to his office for his personal decision. During the following weeks, Post and his assistants decided some 1,600 cases, often as many as 100 a day.[8]

Since most of the cases were based on accusations of "guilt by membership," Post also made a decision as to what precisely constituted membership and thus necessitated deportation. According to Post's decision, deportation required proof of "conscious membership," which he defined as cases in which the alien knowingly had joined the Communist Party and subsequently had acted as a member. This entailed that the substantial number of so-called "automatic members," that is, those who had been tranferred from the Socialist Party to the CP without their knowledge when the CP was formed in September 1919, together with those who did sign up but did so either before the establishment of the party or were unaware of its doctrines, and those who were simply listed in membership lists, were not deportable. Since most aliens were good workers with families and

[7]On Post, see, Dominic Candeloro, "Louis F. Post and the Red Scare of 1920," *Prologue*, Vol. 11, No. 1 (Spring 1979), 42-44; Gengarelly, 324-325; for Wilson's leave of absence, see also letter, William B. Wilson to James Duncan, April 22, 1920, Corresp. 1920, Wilson Papers, Historical Society of Pennsylvania.

[8]*Investigation of Administration of Louis F. Post*, 61-65, 227-229; Candeloro, 44; Gengarelly, 325. The Commissioner of Immigration at Ellis Island, Frederic C. Howe, has described Caminetti's reluctance against making decisions: "His table was piled mountains high with undispatched business, with records of men and women held in immigration stations awaiting his decision" (Howe, 255).

sometimes American-born children, Post gave them the benefit of the doubt in cases of weak evidence.[9]

In his final major decision, Post broke with the Immigration Bureau and the BI's doctrine that aliens in the deportation process were not entitled to constitutional safeguards. Basing his view on the decision by the Federal Circuit Court of Appeals in *Whitfield v. Hanges* that deportation hearings were required to conform with basic principles of due process of law, Post determined that the aliens were in fact entitled to a fair hearing. Referring to recent court decisions (*Silverthorn v. the United States* by the Supreme Court and *re Jackson* by the US District Court for Montana), which held that illegally seized material could not be used to convict or deport, he disregarded confessions made by aliens without access to counsel and evidence obtained without proper search warrant.[10] By his actions, Post had reasserted the Labor Department's authority over the process and restored its role as the decision-making body. The result was that in the period from January 1 to April 28, out of a total of 2,435 cases against alien members of the Communist parties transmitted by the Bureau to the immigration authorities, 481 CP members were ordered deported by Post, 45 cases were deferred, 5 were reopened, 418 were pending, and 1,486 were cancelled by the assistant secretary of labor, thus effectively putting an end to the Bureau's deportation campaign.[11]

The Bureau strongly objected to Post's decisions but to no avail. Hoover argued that the courts had held that aliens did not have the right "to invoke the Constitutional guarantees generally in such administrative proceedings." He found that the claim that members of the Communist parties were unaware of or did not personally subscribe to the parties' doctrines was "frivolous" since all members had signed an application stating that they were aware of and would work to carry out the parties' program. In addition, the Immigration Act of 1918 required only proof of membership and not of individual guilt.[12] When it became clear to Hoover that he was unable to induce the Labor Department to change its policy, he tried to minimize the conse-

---

[9]The phrase "conscious membership" is used in, letters, Louis F. Post to Ernest Angell, October 20, 1920, box 1, Louis F. Post Papers, LC; Louis F. Post to Hon. Thomas J. Walsh, March 12, 1922, box 278, Thomas J. Walsh Papers, LC. See also, *Investigation of Post,* 74-79, 261-263; Candeloro, 44-46.

[10]*Investigation of Post,* 78, 221-227; Post summarized his decisions in, Louis F. Post, Report of Principal Activities of the Assistant Secretary During the Absence of the Secretary, April 14, 1920, Series 19/24, Wilson Papers, Historical Society of Pennsylvania.

[11]*Investigation of Post,* 72-73. See also, letter, Louis F. Post to J. E. Hoover, April 26, 1920; note, Cancellations of deportation warrants by Mr. Post and others, n.d., OG 341761, RG65, NA.

[12]Letters, J. E. Hoover to Hon. Anthony Caminetti, March 20, 1920, ibid.; J. E. Hoover to Hon. Anthony Caminetti, March 16, 1920, JD 205492-582 (DJ Invest. Files II).

quences of the cancellations. Thus, he suggested that an alien should only be released "on his own recognizance for a fixed period of time," even though there was no provision for such a procedure in the deportation rules. He argued that "as the sole purpose of the present deportation policy is to curb the activities of aliens advocating the overthrow of the Government of the United States by force or violence, I feel that by holding them upon a parole, so to speak, that they will be less inclined to actively engage in pernicious activities."[13] Hoover also requested that the Bureau be informed by the immigration authorities before the release of an alien so that it might find additional evidence against him. Referring to the situation in Detroit, where "the release of these noted agitators will result in impetus for renewed radical activities," Hoover insisted on being given another opportunity to find incriminating evidence "in order that the interests of the Government might be properly conserved and justice extended to all."[14] This time, however, the Labor Department was not about to be pushed over by the Bureau.

It is a little known fact that the Labor Department, simultaneously with Post's cancellations, was the moving force behind the second major attack on the Bureau's deportation campaign, the so-called *Colyer* case. On January 24, following a hearing before the secretary of labor, Wilson held in the case against Englebrert Preis, an Austrian immigrant who was accused of being a member of the CP, that the CP was "an organization that believes in, teaches, and advocates the overthrow by force or violence of the Government of the United States" and that consequently its alien members were deportable.[15] The decision was apparently made while the secretary was under tremendous pressure from the Justice Department and his own Immigration Bureau; thus, it was Palmer's intention to distribute Wilson's opinion to all unions in order to educate the workers about "the doctrines and teachings of Bolshevism and how inimical they are to the cause of liberty and to the safety and preservation of our institutions...."[16] In any case, in March a Labor Department official got in contact with Lawrence G. Brooks, a lawyer from Boston, and

[13]Letter, J. E. Hoover to Hon. Anthony Caminetti, March 16, 1920, OG 341761, RG65, NA.
[14]Letters, J. E. Hoover to Hon. Anthony Caminetti, March 16, 1920, ibid.; J. E. Hoover to Hon. Anthony Caminetti, April 6, 1920, JD 205492-612, RG60, NA (microfilm).
[15]The decision *in re Preis* is printed in *Investigation of Post*, 150-152. See also, "Washington Opens Hearing on 'Reds'," *The New York Times*, January 22, 1920, and, "Finds Communist Membership Reason for Deportation," *The New York Times*, January 25, 1920, box 1, J. Edgar Hoover Memoriabilia Collection, RG65, NA; Gengarelly, 322.
[16]Letter, Palmer to William Wilson, January 27, 1920, Series 16/60, Wilson Papers, Historical Society of Pennsylvania; Wilson, however, rejected the idea as it would question the loyalty of all of organized labor (letter, Wilson to Palmer, February 2, 1920, ibid.).

informed him that the department "very greatly desired" that a test case on the validity of deporting alien members of the CP be brought before a "friendly judge." In other words, the intention of the Labor Department was to have a judge reverse Wilson's *Preis* decision and thereby wreck the whole Bureau operation. The official mentioned the English couple, William and Amy Colyer, who had both been detained in the January raids, as suitable clients and that it was "very important" that Federal Judge George W. Anderson of Boston should preside over the case. Furthermore, the official suggested that Felix Frankfurter and Zechariah Chafee, Jr., two prominent liberal lawyers, be brought into the case.[17]

When Judge Anderson in April held hearings on petitions for release on habeas corpus for 18 aliens, Frankfurter and Chafee were appointed as amici curiae and assisted in preparing the lenghty written decision, thus ensuring that the Labor Department's interests were represented. The court took upon itself to investigate and expose the Bureau's operations in New England, calling federal agents, immigration inspectors and aliens to testify and compelling the Boston field office to make public the confidential instructions from Washington on the execution of the raids. Following Post's cancellations, the hearings did much to discredit the Bureau's methods by revealing its widespread use of arrests and searches without warrants, interrogations without counsel, the use of high bail, instances of brutality and the reliance on informers.[18] In his decision on June 23, 1920, Judge Anderson concluded that the CP did not seek the overthrow of the government by force or violence but was aiming at the radical change of government by the use of the general strike. Consequently, the CP had not violated the Immigration Act of 1918 and the secretary of labor had erred in his decision in the *Preis* case. Referring to the methods employed by the special agents, the court noted that "a mob is a mob, whether made up of government officials acting under instructions from the Department of Justice, or of criminals, loafers, and the vicious classes," and he characterized the proceedings as "unfair" and "lacking in due process of law" and the evidence as "not reliable." In view of these findings, Judge Anderson ordered the aliens released by

---

[17]Peter H. Irons, "'Fighting Fair': Zechariah Chafee, Jr., the Department of Justice, and the 'Trial at the Harvard Club'," *Harvard Law Review*, Vol. 94, No. 6 (April 1981), 1219-1220.
[18]Extracts from the *Colyer* hearings are printed in, National Popular Government League, *To the American People. Report Upon the Illegal Practices of the United States Department of Justice* (Washington, DC, 1920), 42-56. See also, "Colyer Trial Goes On," *The Boston Transcript*, April 7, 1920, and "Stimulated Reds to Meet on Jan 2," *The Boston Globe*, April 8, 1920, box 1, J. Edgar Hoover Memoriabilia Collection, RG65, NA. On the roles of Frankfurter and Chafee, see Irons, 1221-1222, 1226.

the immigration authorities.[19] It should be noted that in January 1922 the US Circuit of Appeals reversed Anderson's opinion on the CP, holding that the party did advocate the overthrow of government by force and violence, but by that time the issue was moot.[20]

The third initiative against the Bureau was taken by the secretary of labor when he returned from his leave. Wilson had already taken initial steps to introduce due process to the proceedings when he on January 26 reinstated the original Rule 22 which had provided that aliens should have access to counsel from the beginning of the hearing and ordered that bail should not exceed $1,000.[21] Upon his return, the secretary fully supported Post's decisions, stating that "I am responsible for the policies which he has carried out, and I shall willingly bear the brunt of any fight that may come."[22] On April 24, Wilson held a hearing on whether membership in the Communist Labor Party was a deportable offence. Since Wilson had authorized the arrests of alien members of the CP in December 1919, it would be awkward for him to overrule himself; therefore, as described earlier, he had yielded to the Justice Department's demands in the *Preis* case and had thereafter arranged for Judge Anderson to invalidate his decision in the *Colyer* trial. Wilson, however, was under no such constraints in regard to the CLP since, as previously argued, Hoover and Caminetti had neglected to consult him concerning the party before the January raids, claiming simply that the two Communist parties were similar in nature. Thus, Wilson was free to reopen the case on the CLP. On May 5, he held in *re Carl Miller,* concerning a German alien, that there were in fact "very substantial differences" between the two parties. According to Wilson, the CLP, although extremely radical in nature, did not advocate the overthrow of government by force or violence and was therefore not in violation of the 1918 Immigration Act.[23] This decision freed an additional 144 aliens.[24] That it was primarily a political decision as opposed to one of fact is indicated by the fact that the platforms and

[19]*Colyer et al. v. Skeffington,* June 23, 1920, is reprinted in, *Charges of Illegal Practices,* 38-82; the conclusions are on 63-82.

[20]*Skeffington v. Katzeff,* January 11, 1922, box 278, Walsh Papers, LC. See also, letters, A. Mitchell Palmer to Hon. Thomas J. Walsh, January 26, 1922; Walsh to Palmer, January 27, 1922; George W. Anderson to Walsh, April 26, 1922, ibid.

[21]Instruction to all Commissioners of Immigration, January 27, 1920, att. to, letter, Anthony Caminetti to J. E. Hoover, February 6, 1920, OG 341761, RG65, NA; William B. Wilson, Memorandum for the Commissioner-General of Immigration (through the Acting Secretary), February 21, 1920, Series 16/20, Wilson Papers, Historical Society of Pennsylvania.

[22]Letter, Wilson to James Duncan, April 22, 1920, Corresp. 1920, ibid.

[23]*In re Carl Miller* is printed in *Investigation of Post,* 152-155. On the hearing, see, "Palmer Denies Use of Provocateurs," *The New York Times,* April 25, 1920, box 1, J. Edgar Hoover Memorabilia Collection, RG65, NA.

[24]*Investigation of Post,* 73.

programs of the two Communist parties, despite differences in language, were, in the words of W. Anthony Gengarelly, "virtually identical." Both called for the conquest of the state, both viewed parliamentary elections as "secondary," and both envisioned the attainment of their goal with "mass action," i. e. the general strike. Furthermore, in the spring of 1920 Communist leaders were themselves denying that there were any differences and were working for a the unification of the CP and the CLP.[25]

The fourth and final major assault on the Bureau's deportation campaign, although not the direct product of the Labor Department, was an offshoot of its former initiatives. In mid-April, several liberal lawyers and members of Congress met with representatives of the National Popular Government League, a political and social reform organization, and agreed to prepare a report on the Palmer raids. Among those involved were Jackson H. Ralston, who was Post's lawyer and who hoped to use the report to gain support for the assistant secretary against the Justice Department, and Frankfurter and Chafee, who intended to publicize the disclosures from the *Colyer* case.[26] On May 28, the NPGL issued *To the American People. Report Upon the Illegal Practices of the United States Department of Justice,* which was particularly damaging to the Bureau because of its restrained, factual presentation and because it was signed by 12 prominent and respected lawyers. The report was mainly a collection of affidavits by aliens, testifying to their brutal treatment, extracts from the *Colyer* hearings, and relevant court decisions. It accused the Justice Department of conducting arrests and searches without warrants, of holding aliens incommunicado, forcing them to confess and even forging evidence, of using agents provocateurs, and of misusing the office of the Attorney General to distribute political propaganda. In short, the report claimed that the department, which was charged with upholding the law, had violated the Constitution and committed "utterly illegal acts ... which have caused widespread suffering and unrest, have struck at the foundation of American free institutions, and have brought the name of our country into disrepute."[27]

---

[25]Gengarelly, 329. Extracts of the Communist programs and platforms are printed in *Investigation of Post,* 150-155; *AG Palmer on Charges,* 122-126. For the Bureau's view that the CP and the CLP were identical, see ibid., 116-154. For the move to unify the parties, see ibid., 139-140, 150-154; Whitehead, 45, 51, 331n4. The Communists were finally unified in May 1921 in the Communist Party of America (Draper, 267-274).

[26]Candeloro, 51; Irons, 1223-1224; Coben, *A. Mitchell Palmer,* 238; *Charges of Illegal Practices,* 452-453.

[27]*NPGL Report,* 3-8; the exhibits are at 11-67.

The Bureau, then, was stopped, not from the outside by a broad public outcry against its aims and methods, but from inside the administration, by the Labor Department. Just as the federal government had played the perhaps most important role in the construction of the Red Scare, opposing forces within the federal bureaucracy put an end to the campaign. It should be noted that at the same time, several of the Bureau's most influental allies abandoned the Red Scare because it became a threat to their own interests. The conservative press, which had done so much to circulate the bureau's allegations and leaks, feared that a sedition law might be used to suppress its own freedom of speech, and the AFL, which had informed on radical labor activists, feared it might be used to combat strikes, while industrialists foresaw a shortage of cheap immigrant labor if the deportations were continued.[28] The Labor Department, reasserting its authority within the administration, and conservative groups, abandoning ideology for narrow self-interest, in combination killed the Red Scare.

The Bureau Strikes Back

Not surprisingly, Palmer and the Bureau fought hard to counter the criticism and keep the Red Scare alive. They employed three strategies: discrediting their opponents, warning of the imminent revolutionary danger, and denying all specific accusations. According to the thinking among the Justice Department and Bureau hierarchy in Washington, since the authorities were only doing their duty and purging society of its undesirable elements, any criticism must necessarily come from misinformed or radically inclined individuals. Thus, the 12 lawyers, who had signed the NPGL report, Judge Anderson, and two Protestant reform organizations, the Interchurch World Movement, which had sponsored Constantine Panunzio's critical study of the raids, and the Federal Council of Churches of Christ in America, were all investigated for radical sympathies.[29] Even ordinary citizens who had the nerve to criticize the Bureau came under scrutiny. When one Parker H. Sercombe of Chicago wrote to the Justice Department, protesting against the January raids, the local field office was instructed "to make inquiries relative to the present activities of this party."[30] Attorney General Palmer also tried to question the credibility of his detractors. He called the signers of the NPGL report "12 gentlemen said to be

---

[28]Coben, *A. Mitchell Palmer*, 239, 242-243; Murray, 245-246; Higham, 232-233.
[29]David Williams, "The Bureau of Investigation and Its Critics, 1919-21: The Origins of Federal Political Surveillance," *The Journal of American History*, Vol. 68, No. 3 (December 1983), 560-579; Irons, 1225-1226, 1228-1236.
[30]Letter, Frank Burke to E. J. Brennan, January 9, 1920, OG 341761, RG65, NA.

lawyers," adding that "I do not know all of these gentlemen. Such of them as I do know I am not much impressed by, but I am entirely satisfied that if they be reputable lawyers they have either been woefully deceived or have deliberately declared their political convictions rather than their judgement as reasoning men upon the facts presented." He tried to smear them as Communists since they had represented Communists at deportation hearings, "which indicates pretty clearly that they were there because they believed in the Communist ideas and desired to defend them everywhere."[31] When Frankfurter and Chafee protested against this accusation, Palmer answered that their willingness to take seriously the aliens' claims of mistreatment "indicates some other desire on your part than just administration of the law."[32]

The most serious effort to discredit, however, was reserved for the Bureau's nemesis, Louis Post. As early as January 1920, the Bureau launched an extensive probe into Post's political leanings, eventually collecting a file of 350 pages, but failed to come up with any definitive proof of radical connections.[33] Instead, the Bureau's conservative allies in Congress, possibly supplied with the information dug up by the agents, made an attempt to impeach the assistant secretary. On April 12, Congressman Albert Johnson of Washington and chairman of the Committee on Immigration, a strong foe of all radicals in general and the IWW in particular, accused Post of usurping the power of Caminetti. Martin L. Davey of Ohio, who was Palmer's man on the Hill and had introduced his sedition bill in the House, called Post "a man whose sympathies evidently are with the enemies of our Government."[34] On April 15, Homer Hock of Kansas introduced a resolution calling for the impeachment of Post and accused him of having "flagrantly abused his power." According to Hock, Post had pursued "a policy subversive of the welfare, the peace, and the dignity of the United States," had "in an unwarranted manner submitted to the demands" of opponents of the deportations, and had "hindered, delayed, and prevented" the deportation of "alien enemies."[35] During the ensuing hearings before the House Committee on Rules in late April,

---

[31]*AG Palmer on Charges*, 73-75. See also, *Charges of Illegal Practices*, 6, 83-86, 452-453.

[32]Letter, A. Mitchell Palmer to Felix Frankfurter, June 4, 1920, JD 205492-666, RG60, NA (microfilm); Irons, 1225.

[33]Candeloro, 48-49; Preston, 225; letter, M. F. Burger to Edward J. Brennan, May 7, 1920, JD 209264, RG60, NA (microfilm).

[34]Candeloro, 49; on Davey and his link to Palmer, see *Congressional Record*, April 14, 1920, 6104-6107, Scrapbook: Impeachment Attempt 1920, box 9, Post Papers, LC; for Palmer's view that Post was "a Bolshevik himself" and should be removed, see, Robert Lansing, April 14, 1920 entry in Private Memoranda, Lansing Papers, LC.

[35]H. Res. 522, 66th. Cong., 2d. Sess., House of Representatives, April 15, 1920, ibid.

Post was accused of having illegally usurped the power of the commissioner general of immigration, having cancelled cases in which membership in the CP had been clearly proven, and having illegally released aliens without bail. According to Representative Johnson, the Labor Department was suffering from "boring from within" and Congress should "clean out" the radical elements, meaning in particular Post, from the department.[36] The impeachment attempt, however, quickly collapsed after Post had testified before the committee on May 7-8 and explained the reasons for his actions. Post informed the committee that Caminetti had no authority to recommend or decide cases but only to transmit them for final decision by the secretary or his representative. Post explained how he had carefully laid down the requirements for "conscious" membership because of the many instances of "automatic membership," and that his establishment of due process was in accordance with the Constitution and decisions by the courts. Finally, he emphatically denied the accusations of being a radical sympathizer.[37] Not content to let the issue die, Palmer went before Congress and in a statement prepared by the Radical Division charged that Post had subverted the administration of the deportation laws because of his "self-willed and autocratic substitution of his mistaken personal viewpoint for the obligation of public law" and because of "his habitually tender solicitude for social revolutionists and perverted sympathy for the criminal anarchists of the country." In an attempt to bolster his charges, Palmer filled the record with Post's writings from as far back as 1905, which he claimed proved Post's anarchistic sympathies.[38] However, Post's effective defense had ended any possibility of unseating him.

At the same time the Justice Department tried to keep the Red Scare alive by warning that the national emergency was by no means over and the nation must not let its guards down. During the latter half of April, the Radical Division issued almost daily warnings of a nationwide plot on May 1. Citing a few Communist pamphlets, the division claimed that an attempt to kill federal officials and organize a general strike would be made. As a result the press again carried hysterical headlines and in many cities the local police went on full alert, public buildings and officials were put under protection, state militias were called up, and in Chicago 360 suspected radicals were taken into

[36]*Investigation of Post*, 5; on the accusations in general, see ibid., 3-60.
[37]Ibid., 61-65, 74-79, 221-229, 230, 232-233, 261-263; Candeloro, 50-51. See also, letters, Jackson H. Ralston et al. to Committee on Rules, May 10, 1920, box 1, Post Papers, LC; Jackson H. Ralston et al. to Committee on Rules, May 13, 1920, box 9, ibid.
[38]*AG Palmer on Charges*, 6-10.

preventive custody. In actuality, nothing happened and May 1, 1920, was even quieter than usual and the Radical Division and the Attorney General's credibility was seriously undermined.[39] Palmer also insisted that the railroad strike during the spring of 1920 was an example of the Third International's "revolutionary intrigue" and added that reports from his agents had convinced him "that the outlaw railroad strike was, and is, chiefly financed through the Communist Party organizations."[40] It seems clear that the Bureau and Palmer, in a cynical attempt to keep the Red Scare alive, tried to create an image of a monolithic Red menace, which only a powerful and expanded Bureau would be able to control.

Finally, Palmer and the Bureau emphatically denied all specific accusations of having acted illegally or committed any injustices. Palmer denied that the aliens' rights had been violated since the courts had decided that the deportation process was an administrative procedure in which aliens were not protected by the constitutional right of due process. Furthermore, the Bureau had simply followed the rules and practices of the immigration authorities and had not usurped the authority of the Labor Department. Palmer also argued that Post's principle of "conscious" membership was, in fact, unlawful since the Immigration Act of 1918 simply provided that technical affiliation with or membership in a proscribed organization be proved to necessitate deportation. Also, all special agents accused of brutality submitted sworn affidavits, denying that any form of violence or coercion had been used to force confessions from the aliens.[41] This mixture of warnings of the impending red menace, accusations that all opponents of the Bureau and the Attorney General were Communist dupes, and flat denials that any mistreatments had occurred seems to have been received mainly with apathy or at the most with distrust.[42] Clearly, the Radical Division and Palmer had failed to spark off another round of public fear and their own activities came under scrutiny instead.

[39]Murray, 252-253; Coben, *A. Mitchell Palmer,* 234-236.
[40]*AG Palmer on Charges,* 30-32; also, Robert Lansing, Private Memorandum April 14, 1920, Lansing Papers, LC.
[41]On the legal justification, see *AG Palmer on Charges,* 54-57, 68-73, 200-208, and *Charges of Illegal Practices,* 8-31, 94-95, 539-540, 560-562, 564-565, 635-642, 649; on "technical" membership, see *AG Palmer on Charges,* 46-47, 196-199, and *Charges of Illegal Practices,* 572, 574; on brutality, see *AG Palmer on Charges,* 60-63, 75-87, 100-115, 241-243, and *Charges of Illegal Practices,* 6, 93-94, 96, 134-155, 421-431, 447-448, 450-451, 458-464, 468-469, 573.
[42]Murray, 255-257; Coben, *A. Mitchell Palmer,* 241; Candeloro, 52.

The Justice Department's excesses during the Red Scare did have un-intended long term consequences for the view on civil liberties in America. Traditionally, the idea that in a democracy the minority should follow the decisions of the majority had held sway over judicial thinking, and the Supreme Court had done little to defend the right to free speech by unpopular minorities. However, the extent of the repression during World War I and the Red Scare made people aware of the dangers inherent in the centralized state and the need to defend free speech.

One institution that began expressing concern about civil liberties was the Supreme Court. During the war, an estimated 2,000 people were convicted for criticizing the war in accordance with the Espionage Act of 1917 and the Sedition Act of 1918. The courts used the doc-trines of "constructive intent" and "bad tendency" to deduce that the accused intended to violate the law and that the likely effect of the expressions was the committing of unlawful acts. In January 1919, the Supreme Court reviewed the first Espionage Act case in *Schenck v. United States.* Charles T. Schenck, a Socialist Party official, had been found guilty of distributing leaflets calling for resistance to the draft. Writing for a unanimous court, Justice Oliver Wendell Holmes upheld the conviction and asserted, in a famous phrase, that free speech was not protected by the First Amendment when it posed "a clear and pre-sent danger." One example was the man who cried "Fire!" in a crowded theatre. According to Holmes, it was a question of intent as well as "proximity and degree," and words that were normally per-mitted might pose a danger to a nation at war. However, in a dissent in the case of *Abrams v. United States,* reviewed later that year, Holmes used a more narrowly defined version of "a clear and present danger" to argue that the accused had neither intended to interfere with the war effort nor did his expressions pose any imminent danger. Although the Court's majority upheld the conviction, Holmes' argument that the best way to arrive at the truth was a free market of ideas laid the basis for future decisions in favor of free speech. The Supreme Court continued to be dominated by conservatives during the 1920s and to prefer economic rights to civil liberties, but it did begin the slow march toward federal protection of free speech. It held in *Gitlow v. New York* (1925) that the Supreme Court could use the 14th Amendment to protect civil liberties against state laws. In *Fiske v. Kansas* (1927) it overturned a conviction according to the state criminal syndicalism law because there was no evidence that the accused intended to accomplish his aims (recruitments to the IWW) with force or violence.[43]

Another institution which began campaigning for civil liberties was the American Civil Liberties Union. In 1917, the National Civil Liberties Bureau, an offshoot of the American Union Against Militarism, was organized to protect free speech and the rights of conscientious objectors during the war. The NCLB was reorganized as the ACLU in January 1920 as a reaction to the Red Scare and with the aim of influencing the opinion to protect civil liberties. The ACLU espoused the philosophy that dissent was vital for the survival of democracy even in war time, and it crusaded for the right of free speech for even the most unpopular and intolerant minorities, such as the Ku Klux Klan and the Communists. The Union's leading spirit was the social reformer Roger Baldwin and it consisted of a small number of social reformers, Protestant clergy and conservative lawyers. The ACLU used direct action and litigation in support of organized labor's free speech campaigns, to free political prisoners from the war, to overturn state criminal syndicalism laws and end the BI's political surveillance.[44] The following section will describe the third group which was aroused by the Palmer raids to protect civil liberties: the small band of progressive members of the Senate, and the obstructions they encountered in their attempt to bring the Bureau of Investigation under congressional control.

Congress Investigates

It is striking in view of the apparent injustices perpetrated during the Palmer raids and revealed by Post, the NPGL report and the *Colyer* trial and the extensive publicity concerning the Bureau's various other political activities during the Red Scare that the Congress, despite several inquiries and hearings, never passed a charter or law defining the reponsibilities of the Bureau and banning the surveillance of legal political activities. An analysis and comparison of the two congressional investigations in 1921 and 1924 might give an indication of the reasons for Congress not to intervene directly and abolish the Bureau's political role.

[43]Zechariah Chafee, Jr., *Free Speech in the United States* (New York (1941), 1969), 3-140, 318-325, 343-352; Paul L. Murphy, *The Constitution in Crisis Times 1918-1969* (New York, 1972), 21-36, 41-67, 83-93; Fred D. Ragan, "Justice Oliver Wendell Holmes, Jr., Zechariah Chafee, Jr., and the Clear and Present Danger Test for Free Speech: The First Year, 1919," *The Journal of American History*, Vol. 58, No. 1 (June 1971), 24-45; for the texts of the relevant court cases, see, Kermit L. Hall, ed., *Major Problems in American Constitutional History. Volume II: From 1870 to the Present* (Lexington, Mass., & Toronto, 1992), 142-163.
[44]Samuel Walker, *In Defense of American Liberties. A History of the ACLU* (New York & Oxford, 1990), 16-26, 37-66; Murphy, *Constitution in Crisis Times*, 68-71.

From January 19 to March 3, 1921, a subcommittee of the Senate Judiciary Committee, on the initiative of the progressive Democrat Thomas J. Walsh of Montana, held hearings into the NPGL report's accusations of illegal activities by the Department of Justice. Both supporters and opponents of the department's anti-radical policies expressed their hope that the subcommittee would issue a report and not simply fade away, such as the earlier Post impeachment investigation by the House Rules Committee had done. Palmer wanted a report so that the case could be closed once and for all and the Justice Department would have a guide for its future conduct. The NPGL lawyers warned that by remaining silent Congress would condone the actions of the Justice Department and create the impression among government officials that they were above the law.[45] Following the hearings, Senator Walsh prepared a strongly worded report on the Palmer raids in which he accused the Bureau of having conducted the arrests and searches without any legal authority whatsoever and having violated the aliens' constitutional rights when they were arrested either without any warrants or with warrants based only on Bureau agents' unsworn affidavits. He also argued that the simultaneous mass arrests had resulted in the apprehension of countless innocent and harmless immigrants as well as American citizens, overcrowded jails, and widespread suffering among their families. Walsh also criticized the imposition of excessive bail and the interrogations without counsel. According to Walsh, the raids were "an unmitigated outrage" and "the lawless acts of a mob."[46] Despite his criticism, however, Walsh did not propose to curb the power of the Bureau of Investigation. Although he did note that the raids justified the fears of the nation's founders of "a highly centralized government," he put the blame on Palmer, who, according to Walsh, "was in no ordinary frame of mind" because of the bomb attempt upon his life on June 2, 1919. Walsh's proposals were limited to a reform of the immigration laws, especially a repeal of the "guilt by membership" provision of the Immigration Act of 1918, and the establishment of constitutional protection and due process in the deportation process.[47] Even Walsh's proposals would have allowed the Bureau to continue its political surveillance.

Conservative members of the Judiciary Committee, among them Thomas Sterling of South Dakota, chairman of the subcommittee and

---

[45]*Charges of Illegal Activities*, 582, 106.

[46]US Senate, Committee on the Judiciary, *Charges of Illegal Practices of the Department of Justice*, 67th. Cong., 2d. Sess. (Senate Committee Print, n.d. (1921)), 3-34, box 106, George W. Norris Papers, LC.

[47]Ibid., 37-38.

the sponsor of the Draconian sedition bill in 1919-20, Lee S. Overman of North Carolina and Knute Nelson of Minnesota, all three of whom had been on the Overman Committee investigating Bolshevik propaganda in early 1919 and all of whom were warm supporters of the Bureau's anti-radical policies, effectively protected the Bureau. They succeeded in shelving Walsh's report for two years by evading committee meetings and postponing consideration of the report, arguing that "it were better the affair were forgotten and no report made by the Committee."[48] When finally, in January 1923, Walsh forced a vote on his report, a majority supported a motion by Overman which proposed "that under the conditions now existing it is inadvisable to make a report at this time."[49] On February 5, more than three years after the raids and two years after the hearings, the Senate approved Walsh's request to dissolve the subcommittee and print its reports in the *Congressional Record*.

There seems to have been several reasons why the majority of the committee chose not to intervene against the Bureau's political activities. First and foremost, many members seem to have justified the Red Scare as a reaction to an impending radical threat. According to a report prepared by Senator Sterling, the Palmer raids and the methods employed had to be seen in context with the violent social upheaval in 1919, in particular the major industrial strikes, in which alien agitators, paid by Russian money, had attempted to stir up revolutionary violence, and the anarchist bomb attacks against government officials. The Bureau campaign was made with the approval of the general public and "in the interests of national self-preservation" – a forerunner of the term "national security" – and Sterling could "not say but that the policy thus adopted and carried out was an effectual one."[50] In other words, Sterling and his conserva-

---

[48]Letters, Thomas J. Walsh to Hon. Thomas Sterling, January 27, 1922; Walsh to D. H. Dickason, March 21, 1922; Walsh to Hon. H. Lowndes Maury, April 28, 1922, box 278, Thomas J. Walsh Papers, LC.

[49]Committee on the Judiciary, United States Senate, Committee Minutes Relating to "Charges of Illegal Practices of the Department of Justice", n.d. (1923), ibid.

[50]US Senate, Committee on the Judiciary, *Charges of Illegal Practices of the Department of Justice*, 67th. Cong., 2d. Sess. (Senate Committee Print, n.d. (1921)), 9-12, 14, 33, box 107, Norris Papers, LC. There are indications that the BI might have assisted Sterling in preparing his report. The Bureau kept a watchful eye on the committee hearings and searched its files for information on witnesses (W. E. Grimes, Memorandum for Mr. Hoover, February 26, 1921, BS 197009-1-10X, RG65, NA; Irons, 1228), and a draft of Sterling's report in the BI files with handwritten corrections and notes by Warren W. Grimes suggests that the Bureau was given the report in advance for comments (Draft of Sterling Report, n.d., in 61-1340, RG65, NA). The Bureau was very satisfied with the final report and distributed it to people asking for information on the raids (Letters, George E. Kelleher to J. E. Hoover, April 6, 1922, 61-1340-1; Edgar R. Kiess to Chief Clerk, Department of Justice, April 4, 1922, 61-1340-2; William Burns to Edgar Kiess, April 14, 1922, 61-1340-2; Edgar Kiess to William Burns, April 17, 1922, 61-1340-3, ibid.).

tive colleagues accepted uncritically the assertion that a radical threat had existed in 1919. As a consequence, Sterling found that the Bureau had not acted illegally, it had simply followed the rules of the immigration authorities, aliens were not protected by constitutional rights in the deportation process, and the Bureau's cooperation with the Labor Department had been necessitated by that department's lack of funds. Sterling even propounded an expansive view of the powers of the Justice Department, according to which it did not need legal authority for all of its actions but that it was "permitted to exercise some administrative discretion."[51] Since Sterling accepted that the aliens taken into custody during the raids were, in fact, dangerous revolutionaries, he chose to believe the Bureau agents' denials that they had beaten them.[52] He explained away the whole row over the raids with the 12 NPGL lawyers' alleged "special interests and affiliations," especially their connections with the ACLU, which he characterized as "a supporter of all subversive movements.... It attempts not only to protect crime, but to encourage attacks upon our institutions in every form."[53] Sterling and his conservative allies not only opposed any limitation of the Bureau's ability to effectively combat any form of radicalism, they even proposed to expand its authority in deportation matters by allowing it to make arrests and to cross-examine witnesses at the hearing.[54]

Congress might have had other motives for not intervening. During the debate about the raids in 1920 and 1921, various bills were introduced in the House and Senate by Representative Walter Huddleston of Alabama and Senator William Borah of Idaho with the aim of punishing officials for interfering with people's constitutional rights. According to both bills, federal officials who willfully deprived people of their rights to free speech, spied upon their legal activities, or entered their premises or opened their mail without proper legal authority, could face a sentence of 5 to 10 years in prison and a $10,000 fine. None of these proposals, which would have checked administrative power by holding bureaucrats personally liable for their official actions and made possible legal suits by the Bureau's victims,

---

[51]*Sterling Report*, 3-9, 12-14, 24-27, 30, box 107, Norris Papers, LC.

[52]Ibid., 14-22.

[53]Ibid., 30-32.

[54]Ibid., 33-34. For Walsh's reply to the Sterling Report, see, US Senate, Committee on the Judiciary, *Charges of Illegal Practices of the Department of Justice. Reply by Senator Walsh of Montana to the report heretofore submitted by Senator Sterling touching charges of illegal practices of the Department of Justice*, 67th. Cong., 2d. Sess. (Senate Committee Print, n.d.), box 107, Norris Papers, LC; letters, Thomas Walsh to George Foster Peabody, March 20, 1922, and to Hon. Warren S. Blauvelt, March 22, 1922, box 278, Walsh Papers, LC.

were adopted by Congress. This was partly because many saw the aftermath to the raids as proof that the political system and its institutions were fundamentally sound and well-functioning, since the bureaucracy had itself put an end to the Bureau's excesses. Partly it was because many liberals, as Senator Walsh, seem to have blamed the Palmer raids on the Attorney General personally, and since he left office in March 1921 there was no need for drastic reforms or changes.[55]

Actually, Congress was more concerned about the specter of alien radicals than with official suppression. In June 1920, Congress stiffened the immigration legislation and made it a deportable offense to simply possess radical literature and to contribute to organizations that advocated the violent overthrow of government. In 1921 it enacted the Emergency Quota Act, which later became permanent as the National Origins Act of 1924. It restricted immigration and discriminated against Eastern and Southern Europe, from where most radical aliens were believed to come. At the same time, the Bureau of Immigration was allowed to resume its old habits with the result that by 1930 95% of all cases led to recommendations for deportation.[56] In other words, a majority in Congress seemed to accept the Bureau's political investigations as long as they were aimed at groups and persons outside the political consensus, such as anarchists, Communists and black radicals. As a result, Congress took no steps to curb the activities of the Bureau, which continued its surveillance of radical activities until 1924.[57]

The Bureau Oversteps the Line

The background to the controversy surrounding the Bureau in 1924, which finally brought an end to the unrestrained political surveillance, was the rampant corruption of the Harding administration and the willingness of high officials to sell their positions for personal gain. Charles Forbes of the Veterans' Bureau had sold government supplies at artificially low prices and given out hospital construction contracts for bribes. Alien Property Custodian Thomas W. Miller sold confiscated German property in return for payment in the form of Liberty

---

[55]Williams, *"Without Understanding,"* 210-212, 215-216. Because there was no law holding government officials liable for violating people's rights, the courts were reluctant to find them personally responsible. As a consequence, three private suits brought by victims or families of victims of the Red Scare against Justice Department and Bureau officials were dismissed (ibid., 199-209).

[56]Preston, 227-229, 235-237; Higham, 308-324; Leuchtenburg, *The Perils of Prosperity*, 204-208.

[57]Williams, *"Without Understanding,"* 217-235; the Bureau's continued surveillance 1921-24 is also indicated by the numerous political investigative case files in Classification 61, RG65, NA (for a comprehensive listing see the list of FBI files in the bibliography).

Bonds. In the biggest scandal, which broke shortly after Harding's death in August 1923, Secretary of the Interior Albert Fall had secretly leased Navy oil reserves, known as Teapot Dome in Wyoming, to private oil companies in return for $400,000. Attorney General Harry Daugherty who was a close friend of the president and had been rewarded with his position because of his successful management of the campaign in 1920, and his close associate, Jess Smith, were also accused of, among other things, having accepted bribes in return for dropping antitrust and war fraud cases, illegally selling liquor permits and paroles, and participating in shady stock market deals, as well as having failed to vigorously prosecute the Teapot Dome case.[58]

In December 1922, the first attempt to investigate the Department of Justice was made when Representative Oscar Keller of Minnesota, supported by labor leaders who were bitterly opposed to Daugherty's anti-union policies, filed 14 charges of impeachment against the Attorney General. One of the accusations was that the Justice Department had been shadowing and investigating the administration's opponents on Capitol Hill. Daugherty denied all charges and refused the House Judiciary Committee access to the department's files, and in his written reply to Congress claimed that the whole affair was masterminded by radical leaders and war profiteers who wanted to get rid of him.[59] However, without access to the files Keller and his allies had no firm proof against Daugherty and the matter was allowed to die.

A more serious threat against the Attorney General emerged in February 1924, when Democratic Senator Burton K. Wheeler of Montana introduced a resolution calling for an investigation into the alleged failure of the Justice Department to prosecute antitrust cases and the Teapot Dome case as well as Daugherty's other alleged illegal activities. Thanks to the recent revelations of the scandals within the Harding administration, the Senate on March 1 voted to appoint a committee to look into the allegations, chaired by Republican Smith W. Brookhart of Iowa and with Wheeler as prosecutor. From March 12, the committee held high-profile and often sensational hearings,

---

[58]On the Harding scandals, see, Burl Noggle, *Teapot Dome. Oil and Politics in the 1920's* (New York (1962), 1965); Robert K. Murray, *The Harding Era. Warren G. Harding and His Administration* (Minneapolis, 1969), 429-436, 459-473, 479-482; John D. Hicks, *Republican Ascendancy 1921-1933* (New York (1960), 1963), 74-78; Leuchtenburg, *The Perils of Prosperity*, 91-94. On the charges against Daugherty, see, Burton K. Wheeler with Paul F. Healy, *Yankee from the West* (New York, 1962), 217-218, 223-225, 229.

[59]Murray, *The Harding Era*, 426-428; US Congress, House, Committee on the Judiciary, *Reply by the Attorney General of the United States Hon. Harry M. Daugherty to Charges Filled with the Committee on the Judiciary of the House of Representatives, December 1, 1922, by Hon. Oscar E. Keller, Representative from Minnesota*, 45-46, File 10 (JD), Warren G. Harding Papers, LC.

listening to a parade of bootleggers, grafters, crooks and government officials telling sordid tales of corruption, bribery and petty crimes.[60]

On April 8, 1924, in the middle of the Brookhart Committee's hearings, Senator Wheeler was indicted by a federal grand jury in Montana for having received $2,000 from a local oil man, Gordon Campbell, shortly after his election to the Senate in 1923, in return for obtaining oil and gas permits from the Interior Department. If true, the activity would be in violation of Section 113 of the Criminal Code, according to which it was unlawful for any elected representative to receive compensation for any services rendered before a federal department. The evidence indicates, however, that it was a political indictment. As noted by Felix Frankfurter, "the circumstances under which the indictment was brought are suspicious beyond peradventure, and raise a prima facie case that the instruments of justice were resorted to for personal and partisan reasons, to obstruct or break the efforts of one who was performing a great and needed public service."[61] According to Assistant Attorney General Mabel Willebrandt's later recollections, when Daugherty got wind of Wheeler's planned attack, he summoned Bureau Director Burns and other political appointees of the department and "worked feverishly" to bring an indictment against Wheeler in order to discredit him.[62] The involvement of the Bureau in the Attorney General's counter-attack is illustrated by a memorandum to the Bureau director on March 10, just two days before the start of the hearings. In it Daugherty named several of the committee's witnesses and noted that it "is quite essential and may be necessary to act promptly in connection with persons who are making attacks upon the government and the department of justice from behind the scenes in order to help those who are being prosecuted and against whom suits will be filed. We will indict anybody we can in this connection if proved to be guilty.... Put two or three good men on this at once and see what can be developed. We will show this thing up."[63]

The political nature of the indictment is furthermore underlined by the fact that a Senate committee appointed to investigate the case and

[60]Wheeler with Healy, 213-216; Murray, *The Harding Era*, 475-479; Wheeler's resolution is printed in *Investigation of Daugherty*, Vol. I, 1. For Daugherty's answer to the accusations, see letter, Harry Daugherty to Calvin Coolidge, February 25, 1924, with att. letter, Harry Daugherty to Hon. Frank B. Willis, February 22, 1924, File 10 (JD), Serie 1, Calvin Coolidge Papers, LC.
[61]Letter, Felix Frankfurter to Harlan F. Stone, May 21, 1924, box 104, Felix Frankfurter Papers, LC.
[62]Letter, Mabel Willebrandt to Alpheus Thomas Mason, January 31, 1951, box 83, Harlan Fiske Stone Papers, LC.
[63]H. M. Daugherty, Memorandum for Mr. Burns, March 10, 1924, 62-7824-70, FBI/FOIA.

chaired by William E. Borah concluded that it "wholly exonerates" Wheeler and found that he had been paid by Campbell only for services rendered in Montana and not in Washington, DC.[64] Moreover, Wheeler was aquitted at the trial in Montana in 1925 and when the Justice Department tried to bring a second indictment in Washington, DC, the case was so weak that it was thrown out by the judge.[65] On the other hand, some authors have claimed that since Harlan F. Stone, the new Attorney General who took over following Daugherty's resignation on March 28, not only continued with the case and brought it to trial in Montana and sought the further indictment in Washington, there must have been some basis for the charges, even though the Justice Department initially had been politically motivated in its actions.[66] Stone himself repeatedly explained that his only interest was that justice be done and that it was an important principle that neither he nor anyone else should interfere in a case of such widespread public interest but that it "should be left to the decision of the courts who alone have the authority and power to determine the question of guilt and innocence...."[67] However, there were other and less noble reasons why the department went ahead with the case even after Daugherty's resignation. First, except for Director Burns, Stone did not replace the politically appointed Justice Department officials from the Daugherty regime with his own trusted advisers. According to Assistant Attorney General Willebrandt, Stone "was seriously hampered by not cleaning out his own Department more fully and more promptly."[68] The *New York World* noted in an editorial in January 1925 that the department was "still manned at critical points by Daugherty appointees" and suggested that the new Attorney Gen-

---

[64]US Congress, Senate, Special Committee on Charges Against Senator Burton K. Wheeler, *Report. Senator Burton K. Wheeler*, (Washington, DC, 1924), 1-3. The Justice Department provided confidential information on its case against Wheeler to one of its conservative allies on the Borah Committee, Thomas Sterling, and advised him how to interrogate witnesses, noting that "the source through which you received them should not be disclosed" (John S. Pratt, Memorandum for Senator Sterling, April 24, 1924, 62-7903-64, box 1, series 4, FBI Records, MU).

[65]Wheeler with Healy, 241-242. It is impossible to judge the validity of the case against Wheeler since the files are incomplete. The BI's file on its investigation on Wheeler was made public in 1985 through the Freedom of Information Act but much of the file is still classified; for example, in a 6-page report by an BI accountant on the evidence against Wheeler, 1 page is withheld in its entirety and 2 pages are almost totally blacked out (Memorandum Prepared by R. M. Houston for Mr. Davis, n.d. (before May 10, 1924), 62-7903-40, box 1, series 4, FBI Records, MU). Furthermore, following the aquittal, the records of the case were turned over to Col. William Donovan, who was in charge of the prosecution, and are therefore not in the BI files (W. W. Spain, Memo to Mr. Hoover, n.d. (c. June 19, 1925), 62-7903-457, ibid.).

[66]Alpheus Thomas Mason, *Harlan Fiske Stone: Pillar of the Law* (New York, 1956), 188-195; Powers, *Secrecy and Power*, 520-521n4.

[67]Letter, Harlan F. Stone to Felix Frankfurter, May 29, 1924, box 104, Frankfurter Papers, LC; see also, letters, Stone to Frankfurter, May 19, 22, and June 6, 1924, ibid.

[68]Letter, Willebrandt to Mason, January 31, 1951, box 83, Stone Papers, LC.

eral had been "used by a bureaucracy which hates Senator Wheeler, not for his alleged crimes but for his proven virtues."[69] Secondly, even though Stone personally appreciated the political nature of the case, according to Willebrandt, he was under tremendous pressure by the new Coolidge administration and Republican leaders in Congress "to 'do something' about the Wheeler prosecution": "I am sure the pressure on him was *very* great, and I have reason to believe that some of it also came from the White House."[70]

The Bureau's involvement in the Wheeler case began well before the Brookhart Committee hearings. From as early as December 17, 1923, until Daugherty's resignation, the Bureau kept its congressional adversaries under surveillance. Bureau agents or informants talked to senators and their staff about their contemplated strategies against the administration. After the Brookhart Committee began its investigation, Director Burns received a stream of reports on Wheeler's activities, visitors to his Senate office and the committee's hearings.[71] The field office in Los Angeles also notified Burns of information furnished by the ACLU to Wheeler on Burns' alleged use of the Bureau for his own personal gain.[72]

In a desperate search for something which could be used to smear Wheeler, the Bureau looked for evidence of "any irregularity or improper conduct" during Wheeler's tenure as US attorney in Montana during the war. It also investigated his trip to Russia in 1923, and his alleged connection with stolen bonds, and reported on rumors of his participation in "a wild party ... with two girls in a room at the Hotel."[73] Burns also instructed an agent to visit an acquaintance of Wheeler and inquire about the senator's "morals."[74] The Bureau also looked into allegations that Senator Walsh, the Bureau's critic in

[69]"Wheeler and Stone," *The New York World*, January 30, 1925, clipping in 62-7903, box 1, series 4, FBI records, MU. See also, Mason, 192, 196-197.

[70]Letter, Willebrandt to Mason, January 31, 1951, box 83, Stone Papers, LC.

[71]Reports, T. M. Smith, December 17 and 21, 1923, February 8 and 13, 1924; J. E. Hoover, Memorandum for Mr. Burns, Feburary 19, 1924; reports, March 18, 20, 26, 27, 28, and 29, 1924; R. J. Mahrer, Memorandum to Mr. E. J. Breenan, March 27, 1924, 62-7824, FBI/FOIA. On the surveillance of Congress, see also Wheeler with Healy, 227-228.

[72]Telegrams, Wheeler to Burns, February 25, 1924, 62-7824-13X, and March 1, 1924, 62-7824-15X, FBI/FOIA.

[73]On the war record, see, W. W. Grimes, Memorandum for the Director, February 27, 1924, 62-7903, box 1, series 4, FBI records, MU; on the trip to Russia, see, report, E. B. Hazlett, August 23, 1924, 62-7903-117, ibid., and, W. W. Grimes, Memorandum for Mr. Hoover, September 18, 1924, 62-7903-137, ibid.; on the stolen bonds, see, J. E. Hoover, Memorandum for Mr. William J. Donovan, October 23, 1924, 62-7903-154, ibid.; on the party, see, telegram, Wheeler to Burns, date deleted, 62-7903-15, ibid.

[74]Report, March 7, 1924, 62-7824-23, FBI/FOIA; *Investigation of Daugherty*, Vol. II, 1744-1746.

1921-23 and now Wheeler's attorney, had used his position to illegally obtain an irrigation permit from the Agricultural Department.[75]

It was the revelations during the Brookhart Committee hearings that the Bureau since 1921 had begun to operate within the political system itself that caused the bureau to lose its broad political support and subsequently led to the Attorney General's ban against political surveillance. It is revealing that during the committee hearings on the activities of the Justice Department, the transcript of which fills more than 3,000 pages, hardly any mention was made of the Bureau's recent strike-breaking activities or the raids against alleged Communists or radicals. In other words, no questions were posed by members of the committee on the propriety and legality of keeping unpopular political minorities under surveillance. On the other hand, when the committee was informed about the Bureau's snooping on Capitol Hill, it immediately launched a special investigation,[76] and the allegations provoked strong condemnations on the Senate floor.[77]

Particularly damaging to the Bureau was the admission of Gaston B. Means, an investigator on the Bureau payroll and a close friend of Director Burns, that he had been instructed by the Attorney General in connection with the impeachment attempt in 1922 to find any incriminating evidence which could be used to silence his critics. He claimed that he subsequently had broken into the offices of Representatives Keller and Roy Woodruff and Senators Thaddeus Caraway and Robert M. La Follette. Although Means was a colorful personality and of doubtful reliability, his main claims were supported by a reluctant witness, Burns' confidential secretary Mrs. Jessie B. Duckstein.[78] Moreover, during the hearings it was revealed that the Republican National Committee (RNC) had sent out a special investigator, Blair Coan, to Montana to look for incriminating information on Senators Wheeler and Walsh, and that Special Assistant to the Attorney General Hiram Todd had detailed two investigators for the same purpose.[79]

[75]William J. Burns, Memorandum for the Attorney General, April 16, 1924, 62-7903-106; J. E. Hoover, Memorandum for Colonel Donovan, February 17, 1925, 62-7903-255, box 1, series 4, FBI records, MU. On the investigation of Walsh, see also, letter, James H. Stroman to Hon. C. Bascom Slemp, n.d. (c. March 31, 1924), File 10-B (BI), series 1, Coolidge Papers, LC; Theoharis & Cox, 130.

[76]*Investigation of Daugherty,* Vol. I, 609.

[77]Wheeler with Healy, 228; Lowenthal, 291-292.

[78]Means' statements are in *Investigation of Daugherty,* Vol. I, 88-97, Vol. II, 1557-1559, Vol. III, 2850-2851, 2864-2865, and Mrs. Duckstein's in ibid., Vol. III, 2543 (as a result of her admission, she was dismissed from the Bureau the following day, ibid., Vol. III, 2897); for Means' background, see Murray, *The Harding Era,* 477-478; Hunt, *Front-Page Detective,* 142-147, 179-181; Whitehead, 57-58, 65, 94-96.

[79]*Investigation of Daugherty,* Vol. I, 117; Vol. II, 2193-2197; Vol. III, 2502-2507, 2510-2513, 2523; Wheeler with Healy, 235, 237-238.

Under questioning, Burns was forced to admit that he had discussed the Wheeler case with Daugherty, Coan and George Lockwood, the secretary of the RNC.[80] As a result of these revelations, calls were heard from as different quarters as Special Assistant to the Attorney General John W. H. Crim and the ACLU for drastic reductions of the activities and personnel of the Bureau or even its complete abolition.[81]

It is apparent that while a majority of the members of Congress in 1921-23 was willing to let the matter of the Bureau's political surveillance rest because it had been directed against radicals and others outside the political mainstream, Congress in 1924 was in uproar when it was disclosed that the Bureau had been used for partisan purposes against its critics in Congress. Despite its anger, however, Congress did not pass any laws restricting the Bureau's political activities but left the matter to the discretion of the executive branch. In a deeper sense, this reflected the shift of power during the Progressive Era from the legislative to the executive branch. It might therefore be argued that the congressional hearings in 1921 and 1924 functioned, in Morton H. Halperin's term, as "revelation as reform," meaning that by uncovering the abuses the hearings gave the impression that the democratic system was working, although Congress did not go beyond the disclosures and make any deeper structural reforms of the surveillance state.[82]

---

[80]*Investigation of Daugherty*, Vol. II, 2149-2153. An internal Bureau memo shows that Burns had instructed his assistant, J. Edgar Hoover, to furnish all information on Wheeler to the RNC (Hoover, Memorandum for Mr. Burns, March 27, 1924, 62-7903-20, box 1, series 4, FBI Records, MU).

[81]*Investigation of Daugherty*, Vol. III, 2570; Lowenthal, 299-300; letters, Harlan F. Stone to Felix Frankfurter, September 26, 1924; Frankfurter to Stone, September 29, 1924; Stone to Frankfurter, October 1, 1924; Frankfurter to Stone, October 3, 1924, box 104, Frankfurter Papers, LC.

[82]Morton H. Halperin, *The Lawless State. The Crimes of the US Intelligence Agencies* (Harmondsworth, 1977), 245.

Chapter 8

Aftermath: The FBI and Presidential Politics

The End of Political Surveillance

The Bureau's political role had become institutionalized and an integrated part of the political system during the Red Scare. Although its political activities fluctuated in response to the changing strength of American radicalism during the inter-war period, they never completely stopped and the apparatus remained in place for use in times of social and political crisis. Moreover, from the early twenties the Bureau became increasingly integrated with the center of political power, the presidency.

However, the immediate effect of the revelations of the Brookhart Committee was a reform of the Bureau and a drastic reduction of its political surveillance. On March 28, 1924, Attorney General Daugherty was forced to resign by President Coolidge and was replaced by Harlan Fiske Stone, a lawyer and former dean of the Columbia University Law School, who had a reputation of uncompromising integrity and respect for civil liberties.[1] Stone soon set out to clean up the Bureau. On May 9, Director Burns was asked to resign, and Assistant Director Hoover was promoted to acting director (his appointment was made permanent the following year). He was instructed by Stone to professionalize the Bureau, purge it of the incompetent and politically appointed agents from the Burns regime, and stiffen the requirements of new applicants.[2] Most importantly, Stone banned the Bureau's political activities. It was the Attorney General's belief that "I have always regarded any secret police system at its best as a necessary evil, and one to be kept strictly within control and to be limited in its

---

[1] For Stone in general see, Alpheus Thomas Mason, *Harlan Fiske Stone: Pillar of the Law* (New York, 1956), *passim*; Belknap, "Mechanics of Repression," 54-55.

[2] For Burns' resignation, Mason, 150; for earlier calls for his resignation, see letters, Geo. Garner et al to Warren Harding, February 18, 1922, file 10-B, Series 4, Warren G. Harding Papers, LC; Chas. W. Smith to Calvin Coolidge, March 7, 1924, file 10-B, Series 1, Calvin Coolidge Papers, LC; for Burns' defense, letter, William J. Burns to Adolph S. Ochs, April 22, 1924, 62-7824-72X, FBI/FOIA; for Hoover's appointment, letter, Stone to Hoover, May 10, 1924, 67-561-1, ibid.; for the reforms in general, Mason, 151; Whitehead, 68-74; *Investigation of Daugherty*, Vol. III, 2451, 3252-3256; US Congress, House, Subcommittee of Committee on Appropriations, *Appropriations, Department of Justice, 1925*, 68th. Cong., 2nd. Sess. (Washington, DC, 1925), 57-59; Stone to Felix Frankfurter, February 9, 1925, box 104, Felix Frankfurter Papers, LC.

activities to the support of the legitimate purposes of a Government law office."[3] In a statement issued on May 10, he warned against the potential menace posed by a secret police to the free institutions and declared that it was the official policy of the Justice Department that "the Bureau of Investigation is not concerned with political or other opinions of individuals. It is concerned only with their conduct and then only with such conduct as is forbidden by the laws of the United States."[4] Hoover was subsequently instructed by Stone that the "activities of the Bureau are to be limited strictly to investigations of violations of the law."[5] Following a Justice Department study in June 1924, which found that the existing federal laws were inapplicable to agitation or propaganda in favor of the violent overthrow of the government, the department abandoned any idea of prosecuting Communist or ultra-radical activities.[6] During the following years it was the policy of the Justice Department to refuse outside requests for the investigation or prosecution of radical activities.[7]

On the surface, at least, Hoover supported the department's policy; in a letter prepared for Stone's signature he declared: "I could conceive of nothing more despicable nor demoralizing than to have public funds of this country used for the purpose of shadowing people who are engaged in legitimate practices in accordance with the constitution of this country and in accordance with the laws of the country."[8] However, several historians have claimed that Hoover misled Stone and without the knowledge of his superiors continued to collect information on political activities. According to Theoharis and Cox, "Hoover shrewdly contrived a way to circumvent Stone's explicit ban" by accepting information from outside sources such as police informers, covering-up agents' surveillance reports as information from "confidential sources" and evading effective political control by constructing an elaborate system of parallel files.[9] According to this view, the

---

[3]Letter, Stone to Frankfurter, May 19, 1924, ibid.

[4]The statement is reprinted in Lowenthal, 298.

[5]Mason, 151.

[6]Earl J. Davis, Memorandum for the Attorney General, June 10, 1924, JD 202600-2734, RG60, NA (microfilm); also, Preston, 241-242.

[7]See letter, J. Edgar Hoover to Lawrence Richey, July 20, 1932, box 223, PPSF, HHL; also, Brien McMahon, Memorandum for Mr. Hoover, June 14, 1937, JD 202600-2265, RG60, NA (microfilm); letter, Joseph P. Keenan to Archibald Stevenson, July 19, 1934, JD 202600-59-2, ibid. Such Bureau files as 100-3-14/60 (box 1, Series 10, FBI Records, MU); 61-714 (box 4, ibid.); and Justice Department files JD 202600-6/9/40 (RG60, NA (microfilm)), contain numerous rejections of such outside requests.

[8]Letter, Stone to Frankfurter, February 9, 1925, box 104, Frankfurter Papers, LC; see also, Donner, *Age of Surveillance*, 46-47.

[9]Theoharis & Cox, 105-108; for similar accounts, Theoharis, *Spying on Americans*, 255-256n8, 260n6; Theoharis, *From the Secret Files*, 3; Williams, *"Without Understanding,"* 255, 259, 280;

Bureau's continuing political surveillance after the Red Scare was a result of the Bureau's autonomy and the lack of effective political control.

However, the available evidence indicates that most of the Bureau's political activities were, in fact, curtailed as a result of Stone's ban and that only a bare minimum of surveillance was maintained with the Justice Department's knowledge. For example, the main evidence used for the contention that the surveillance continued, the Bureau's file on the American Civil Liberties Union, shows that the surveillance ceased between 1925 and 1940 and was only interrupted by two minor inquiries in 1929 and 1931.[10] Other major political investigations, such as those into the United Mine Workers, the NAACP, the Women's International League for Peace and Freedom, the Sacco and Vanzetti Defense Committee, the Federated Farmer-Labor Party, the World War Veterans, the Cooperative League of America and the *Nation*, were all likewise stopped following Stone's ban.[11]

On the other hand, by 1924 the Bureau network of outside sources, established during the war and the Red Scare, had become so institutionalized that it continued to furnish the Bureau with hundreds of reports each month.[12] It was the policy of the Bureau, even when the reports contained no evidence of violations of the law, "that we obtain the information in order that it may be placed in our files for intelligence purposes."[13] It was known to the Justice Department that the Bureau maintained this "passive" intelligence activity of keeping its political files up to date. In 1925, Hoover advised the department explicitly that "when information concerning Communist activities in the United States is voluntarily furnished to field offices of the Bureau by parties not connected therewith, the information is forwarded to

Williams, "The Bureau of Investigation and its Critics," 578; Kornweibel, *"Seeing Red,"* 174-178.

[10]For the argument that the ACLU files prove the existence of a continuing surveillance, see Westin, "They Never Stopped Watching Us," 25; Theoharis, *Spying on Americans*, 255-256n8; Theoharis & Cox, 105-108; Williams, "The Bureau of Investigation and its Critics," 578n47; O'Reilly, *Hoover and the Un-Americans*, 18-19; Gentry, 141, 208. For the two inquiries, letter, C. D. McKean to Hoover, February 27, 1929, 61-190-170, box 1, Series 10, FBI Records, MU; C. G. Schenken, Memorandum for the Director, March 19, 1931, 61-190-174, ibid.; see further, Walker, "The Boss as Bureaucrat," 462.

[11]UMW file (61-1241) in box 2, Series 10, FBI Records, MU; WILPF file (61-1538) in box 1, Series 7, ibid.; NAACP file (61-3176) in FBI/FOIA; Sacco and Vanzetti file (61-126) in ibid.; Federated Farmer-Labor Party file (61-4203) in RG65, NA; WWV files (61-1078/1162/3516/4545/5113) in ibid.; Cooperative League of America file (61-1092) in ibid.; the *Nation* file is decribed in, Penn Kimball, "The History of the Nation According to the FBI," *The Nation*, March 22, 1986, 399-429.

[12]*Appropriations, Department of Justice, 1926*, 74-75.

[13]Hoover, Memorandum for Mr. Clegg, March 29, 1934, 100-3-60-18, box 1, Series 10, FBI Records, MU; also, E. A. Tamm, Memorandum for the File, May 26, 1939, 61-7582-118, box 1, Series 3, ibid.

this office."[14] The portions of the Bureau files from this period, which have been released, show that the Bureau received a substantial amount of information concerning radical and Communist activities after 1924 from other federal departments. The most important sources were the State Department's Division of Eastern European Affairs, which kept an eye on the political activities of Americans abroad and intercepted letters to and from foreign radical organizations, MID, which continued to monitor radical activities, and the Post Office Department, which watched radical matters in the mail.[15] It also received information from patriotic organizations, especially the American Legion, the American Vigilant Intelligence Federation, the NCF, and the ADS;[16] as well as from the business community;[17] local authorities;[18] and private citizens.[19]

Another source of information was the Bureau's informers, although their number was drastically reduced. In 1926, Hoover informed Special Agent in Charge of the Boston office John A. Dowd that since 1924 he had "discarded practically all the informants with the exception of two and these two are by no means within the inner groups."[20] According to the Bureau files, one informer had infiltrated

---

[14]Hoover, Memorandum for Mr. Ridgely, May 14, 1925, JD 202600-2728, RG60, NA (microfilm).

[15]For the State Department, letters, Robert F. Kelley to Hoover, October 4, 1929, 61-6666-1, box 5, Series 10, FBI Records, MU; Kelley to Hoover, July 7, 1931, 61-714-190, ibid.; Hoover to Arthur Bliss Lane, April 20, 1925, 61-1136-7, RG65, NA; Louis Sussdorf Jr. to the Sec. of State, March 20, 1930, 61-2571-3, ibid.; NN to the Sec. of State, July 14, 1930, 61-6728-2, FBI/FOIA; Acting Chief to Hoover, September 5, 1930, 61-6728-4, ibid.; for the military, letter, Lieut. Col. W. K. Wilson to Hoover, June 30, 1926, 61-6013-6, RG65, NA; for the Post Office, Hoover, Memorandum for Mr. Ridgely, July 23, 1924, JD 202600-2728, RG60, NA (microfilm); letters, T. M. Milligan to Hoover, March 25, 1932 and Hoover to Milligan, April 1, 1932, 61-6965-3, box 4, Series 10, FBI Records, MU.

[16]For the American Legion, letters, name deleted to Department of Justice, January 26, 1928, and Hoover to name deleted, January 30, 1928, 100-3-60-8, box 1, ibid.; name deleted to Bureau of Investigation, February 3, 1928, and Hoover to name deleted, February 10, 1928, 100-3-60-9, ibid.; Wm. Larson to Hoover, March 7, 1933, 100-3-12-17, ibid.; for the American Vigilant Intelligence Federation see its "Items of Interest," April 9, 1929 and October 15, 1929, in 62-12299-147/176, box 2, ibid.; for the NCF, letters, Ralph Easley to E. T. Clark, April 2, 1925, file 431, Series 1, Coolidge Papers, LC; name deleted to Hoover, September 16, 1925, 61-190-166, box 2, Series 10, FBI Records, MU; for the ADS, letter, Elon Hooker to Hoover, September 18, 1929, 62-4711-37, ibid.; Hoover, Memorandum for Assistant Attorney General Luhring, March 6, 1930, JD 202600-6, RG60, NA (microfilm).

[17]Letters, T. C. Wilcox to Hoover, May 3, 1927, 100-3-12-11, box 1, Series 10, FBI Records, MU; name deleted to Hoover, January 20, 1930, and Hoover to name deleted, January 23, 1930, 61-6666-2, box 2, ibid.; W. A. McSwain to Hoover, April 27, 1931, 61-714-188, ibid.; L. C. Schilder to Hoover, May 31, 1928, with att., H. G. Dohrman to Benson W. Hough, May 29, 1928, 61-6521-1, RG65, NA.

[18]Report, G. D. Gallagher, April 14, 1927, 61-1162-10, ibid.; Hoover, Memorandum for Assistant Attorney General Keenan, January 9, 1935, JD 202600-34, RG60, NA (microfilm).

[19]For example, letters, name deleted to Hoover, May 29, 1925, and Hoover to name deleted, June 24, 1925, 61-714-153, box 2, Series 10, FBI Records, MU; name deleted to Hoover, June 26, 1925, and Hoover to name deleted, July 8, 1925, 61-714-154, ibid.; name deleted, Memorandum for the Director, March 20, 1930, and Hoover, Memorandum for Assistant Attorney General Luhring, March 25, 1930, 100-3-60-12, box 1, ibid.

[20]"Strictly Confidential" letter, Hoover to J. A. Dowd, June 9, 1926, 61-126-687, FBI/FOIA.

the Communist Trade Union Educational League in New York during 1926-28 and another reported on Communist activities in Chicago 1924-27.[21] Although it is unclear whether the Justice Department was informed explicitly on the continued use of political informers, the Bureau several times submitted reports to department officials which referred openly to the informers. For example, in 1930 Hoover transmitted a letter from the New York office which contained an account of a meeting with "our confidential informant" in the Communist Party, and the following year he submitted a report from "a confidential informant" concerning Communist activities.[22] Thus, the Bureau's continued use of a few informers was known within the Justice Department.

One final source of information consisted of the Bureau's own active investigations. Although these had been strictly forbidden by Stone's order, there are a few examples that the Bureau engaged in such activity on its own initiative. For example, between June and October 1924 the Bureau investigated members of the Russian Federation of Workers Party of America, in 1926 the Pittsburgh office collected information on a coal miners strike, and the following year the Butte, Montana, office monitored IWW activities.[23] On other occasions, however, the investigations were initiated on the instructions of US attorneys or Justice Department officials. In 1926, the San Francisco office was directed to investigate two pacifist organizations, the Fellowship of Youth for Peace and the National Council for the Prevention of War, and in 1934 the Bureau obtained information on a Communist demonstration in Los Angeles on behalf of an assistant Attorney General.[24] It is still unclear to what extent the Republican

---

[21]For the TUEL informer, reports, John L. Haas, September 13, 1926, 61-714-157, box 5, Series 10, FBI Records, MU; September 29, 1927, 61-714-167, ibid.; November 10, 1927, 61-714-169, ibid.; January 31, 1928, 61-714-171, ibid.; March 16, 1928, 61-714-173, ibid.; for the Chicago informer, reports, James P. Rooney, June 6, 1924, 61-1136-6, RG65, NA; Max F. Burger, April 1, 1925, 61-1136-7, ibid.; James O. Peyronnin, February 3, 1927, 61-714-161, and February 21, 1927, 61-714-160, box 5, Series 10, FBI Records, MU.

[22]Hoover, Memorandum for Assistant Attorney General Luhring, June 10, 1930, with att. letter, C. D. McKean to Hoover, May 28, 1930, 61-6723-2, ibid.; Hoover, Memorandum for Assistant Attorney General Dodds, September 15, 1931, JD 202600-12, RG60, NA (microfilm).

[23]For the Russian Federation investigation, reports, Harry Katz, June 24, 1924, 61-5418-1, RG65, NA; Charles M. Hoyt, June 26, 1924, 61-5418, ibid.; Katz, June 27, 1924, 61-5430-1, ibid.; John A. Dowd, July 12, 1924, 61-5474-1, ibid.; J. Cirone, July 15, 1924, 61-5486-1, ibid.; Geo. J. Starr, July 31, 1924, 61-5477-2, ibid.; Katz, September 25, 1924, 61-5474-2, ibid.; Dowd, October 22, 1924, 61-5474-3, ib.; letter, Hoover to Dowd, August 16, 1924, 61-5477-2, ibid.; for the coal strike, letter, George J. Starr to Hoover, July 3, 1926, 61-6128-2, box 5, Series 10, FBI Records, MU; for the IWW, reports, D. H. Dickason, January 26, 1927, 61-2388-5, and March 29, 1927, 61-2388-26, RG65, NA.

[24]For the pacifists, reports, E. B. Montgomery, March 3, 1926, 61-6013-4, RG65, NA; A. A. Hopkins, June 7, 1926, 61-6013-5, ibid.; A. P. Harris, April 12, 1926, 61-3210-12, ibid.; for the demonstration, Hoover, Memorandum for Assistant Attorney General Keenan, May 5,

Attorney Generals between 1924 and 1933, Harlan Stone, John G. Sargent and William B. Mitchell, were informed about these activities.[25]

J. Edgar Hoover also continued to lobby for a sedition law which would enable the Bureau to investigate and the department to prosecute radical activities. Privately, Hoover complained about the "exasperating situation" of the federal government since 1924 and that it was "more or less powerless" to act against the radicals. He expressed his hope that "I would like to be able to find some theory of law and some statement of facts to fit it that would enable the federal authorities to deal vigorously with the ultra-radical elements that are engaged in propaganda and acts inimical to the institutions of our country."[26] In 1931, the House Special Committee to Investigate Communist Activities, the so-called Fish Committee, proposed to stop the spread of Communism during the depression by legalizing the Bureau's surveillance of "the revolutionary propaganda and activities of the Communists in the United States."[27] Hoover opposed the proposal since it would only authorize political surveillance but would not make Communist activities in themselves unlawful, thus the Bureau "would be in the position of having a mass of material with which nothing could be done, because there is no legislation to take care of it." Moreover, if the Bureau were authorized to investigate lawful political activities it would be vulnerable to charges of engaging in secret and illegal activities.[28] Instead, when Hoover appeared before the committee in executive session, he elaborated on the theory that the war had shown that propaganda might be more dangerous than the use of arms by undermining the soldiers' morale, and he therefore urged the committee to criminalize Communistic propaganda by making it an unlawful act to advocate the overthrow of government by force or

1934, JD 202600-29, RG60, NA (microfilm).

[25]The papers of Stone (1924-25), deposited in the Manuscript Division of the LC, and those of John G. Sargent (1925-29) and William B. Mitchell (1929-33) apparently contain no references to the Bureau's political activities after 1924 (for the contents of the Sargent and Mitchell papers, letters from Karen S. Campbell, Guy W. Bailey/David W. Howe Library, the University of Vermont, February 27, 1995, and Ruth Anderson, Minnesota Historical Society, March 24, 1995).

[26]Letter, Hoover to J. A. Dowd, June 9, 1926, 61-126-687, FBI/FOIA.

[27]US Congress, House, Special Committee on Communist Activities in the United States, *Investigation of Communist Propaganda. Report*, 71st. Cong., 3rd. Sess. (Washington, DC, 1931), 63.

[28]*Select Committee to Study Governmental Operations*, Vol. 6, 556; Book III, 391. Bureau and Justice Department officials refused to assist Fish in his investigation, see, Hoover, Memorandum for Mr. Nugent Dodds, November 26, 1930; A. R. Cozier (?), Memorandum for Assistant Attorney General Sisson, December 2, 1930; Hoover, Memorandum for Mr. Caldwell, December 22, 1930, JD 202600-9, RG60, NA (microfilm); William Mitchell, Memorandum for Mr. Dodds, December 2, 1931, JD 202600-51-1, ibid.

violence.[29] As Hoover explained to Fish, "it would be better to make it a crime to participate in such activities" since "the Bureau operates under an appropriation act, 'Detection and Prosecution of crime', and all the Bureau would need would be legislation making it a crime to participate in certain activities."[30] Hoover finally got the desired sedition law, for which he and the Justice Department had agitated so vigorously during the Red Scare, with the enactment of the so-called Smith Act in 1940.

The basic reason why the surveillance was reduced significantly after 1924 was undoubtedly due to the decline of social unrest and radicalism during this period. For example, the membership of the strongest radical force, the Socialist Party, fell from some 40,000 after the split with the Communists in 1919 to 12,597 in 1921 and 8,477 in 1926; at the election in 1928, the party's presidential candidate Norman Thomas received 267,835 votes, down from Eugene Debs' 919,799 in 1920.[31] Similarily, the membership of the Communist Party declined from an estimated total of 37,000 in 1919 to about 8,000 to 10,000 in 1923 and only 6,000 in 1930; at the election in 1924, William Z. Foster received a grand national total of 36,386 votes.[32] The calmer domestic scene was also reflected in the labor market, where the number of organized workers fell from 5 million in 1920 to 3.6 million by the end of the decade as a result of the defeat of the strikes in 1919, the open shop campaign, and economic growth. Significantly, the leading radical force in organized labor, the IWW, experienced a steep decline in its membership, from an estimated 58,000 to 100,000 in 1920 to just 7,000 to 8,000 members in 1930.[33] Consequently, the number of strikes and lock outs fell from a high of 3,630, participated in by 22.5% of the work force, in 1919, to 1,301 in 1925 and participated in by only 2.1% of the workers.[34] Finally, no major race riots took place between the riots in Tulsa, Oklahoma, in 1921 and the disturbances in Harlem in 1935, and the frequency of lynchings declined from 83 in 1919 to 16 in 1924 and 10 in 1929.[35] Thus, there was simply no need for the federal government to maintain

---

[29]The hearing is described in Donner, *Age of Surveillance*, 48-50. According to the Library of Congress the transcript is still classified (letter, Benjamin J. Guthrie to Donald F. Wisdom, February 24, 1984, Rare Books and Special Collections, LC).

[30]*Senate Select Committee to Study Governmental Operations*, Vol. 6, 556.

[31]Weinstein, *Decline of Socialism*, 239, 327; *Historical Statistics of the US*, Pt. 2, 1073.

[32]Ibid.; Draper, 207, 272, 391; Schlesinger Jr., *Crisis of the Old Order*, 222.

[33]*Historical Statistics of the US*, Pt. 1, 177; Dubofsky, 473-474.

[34]Montgomery, 97.

[35]Waskow, 219-220; *Historical Statistics of the US*, Pt. 1, 422.

an extensive and active political surveillance during the latter half of the twenties.

The Bureau and the Origins of White House Intelligence, 1921-33
According to most accounts, the Bureau either had no direct connections with the White House before about 1940 or its assistance before that was limited and of no greater consequences, thus underlining the general impression that the Bureau after the Red Scare was free of effective political control.[36] In fact, beginning as early as 1921 the Bureau was progressively brought closer to the center of federal power and entrusted with increasingly important and sensitive assignments. Thus, the major reason for the expansion of the Bureau's political role after the Red Scare was the centralization of power in the executive and his growing need for political intelligence. The modern, strong presidency was a result of the drive toward efficiency of the political process during the Progressive Era. Social reformers and others, who distrusted the legislatures and the courts as being corrupt and being influenced by special interests, saw the executive as the only genuine expression of the people's will, and corporate leaders saw the strong executive as the most efficient instrument for the regulation and stabilization of the corporate order and for the protection of American investments abroad.[37] Both Theodore Roosevelt and Wilson dramatically expanded the role of the president. Wilson, for example, declared that a president "is at liberty, both in law and conscience, to be as big a man as he can." By the end of the Progressive Era the president was expected to initiate national political debate and propose solutions, while the role of Congress was reduced to that of either approving or vetoing them.[38] The presidents after the Red Scare relied increasingly on the resources of the Bureau of Investigation to keep them informed about social unrest, radical movements, domestic critics, and subversion from abroad.

---

[36]For example, Williams, *"Without Understanding,"* 281; Theoharis, *Spying on Americans*, 157-159; Donner, *Age of Surveillance*, 241-244; Theoharis (ed.), *From the Secret Files*, 199; Theoharis & Cox, 124-125; Powers, *Secrecy and Power*, 162, 523n44.

[37]Peter N. Carroll & David W. Noble, *The Free and the Unfree. A New History of the United States*, 2nd. ed. (Harmondsworth (1977), 1988), 333; also, 302-307, 339-342; for similar views of the "corporate presidency," see Wiebe, 194, 242-255; Weinstein, *The Corporate Ideal, passim*; Otis L. Graham (ed.), *The New Deal. The Critical Issues* (Boston, 1971), 68-69, 151-158, 165-169; Kim McQuaid, "Corporate Liberalism in the American Business Community, 1920-1940," *Business History Review*, Vol. LII, No. 3 (Autumn 1978), 356-368; Sklar, 114-141.

[38]Wiebe, 189-193, 221-222; Quote from Godfrey Hodgson, *In Our Time. America from World War II to Nixon* (London, 1976), 105-106.

The Bureau began furnishing intelligence to the White House in response to two episodes of severe social unrest during 1921-22. In August 1921, when an attempt by the United Mine Workers to organize the miners in Logan and Mingo Counties in West Virginia erupted into open violence as 6,000 armed union members clashed with 2,000 private detectives and county deputies, the Bureau through the Attorney General kept President Harding informed about the situation so that he was in a position to decide if federal troops should be deployed.[39] The Bureau clearly shared the anti-labor views of the Harding administration, which refused to prosecute the coal mine operators and local authorities for their systematic campaign of suppression against union activists. When the UMW asked the president to intervene and protect union members, the White House responded that it had been assured "by agents of the Government that there is no occasion for anxiety in the matter ... (The president) is hopeful that your apprehensions are utterly unfounded."[40] In its reports to the president, the Bureau ignored the widespread violence against the unions and instead accused the miners of "preparing for another and more successful insurrection...."[41]

The second incident of social unrest was the 1922 railroad shopmen's strike, against which the administration mobilized all the resources of the federal government. Federal courts issued drastic court injunctions which outlawed any form of strike activity, 2,200 new US marshalls were deployed by the Justice Department to protect strikebreakers and federal troops were sent to union strongholds.[42] During the strike, Harding received from the strongly anti-labor Attorney General a number of reports by US marshalls and Bureau agents on the progress of the strike, highlighting incidents of the strikers' use of violence. At the same time Daugherty kept insisting that the strike was a revolutionary attempt directed from Moscow.[43] Possibly, the Bureau's information contributed to Harding's decision to break the strike. According to one historian, influenced "by daily

[39]William Burns, Memorandum for the Attorney General, August 8, 1921, BS 205194-50-215X, RG65, NA; letters, Harry M. Daugherty to Warren G. Harding, September 6, 1921, with att. telegram, Nathan to Director, September 5, 1921, file 400, Series 4, Harding Papers, LC; Harding to Daugherty, October 10, 1921, file 934, ibid.; Secretary to the President to Daugherty, October 13, 1921, ibid.; for the conflict, Dubofsky & van Tine, 77-78.
[40]Letter, Secretary to the President to Local Union No. 1938, United Mine Workers, October 13, 1921, file 934, Series 4, Harding Papers, LC.
[41]Burns, Memorandum for the Attorney General, October 12, 1921, ibid.
[42]Colin J. Davis, "Bitter Conflict: The 1922 Railroad Shopmen's Strike," *Labor History*, Vol. 33, No. 4 (Fall 1992), 443-447.
[43]Letters, Daugherty to Harding, August 19, 1922, with att. telegrams; Daugherty to Harding, August 21, 1922, with att. report, file 31a, Series 4, Harding Papers, LC; on Harding and the strike, Murray, *The Harding Era*, 238-242, 244-245, 248-251.

reports from his fanatical Attorney General, Harding became convinced that the shopmen were employing illegal and violent means to win the strike," and he authorized Daugherty to obtain the perhaps most sweeping federal injunction in US history in order to break the strike. Subsequently, the Bureau was directed to investigate violations of the injunction, and eventually 2,000 persons were investigated and 1,200 charged with having violated the court order, thereby, in effect, breaking the strike.[44]

It was also during the Harding administration, when there still was some radical activity immediately following the Red Scare, that the Bureau began submitting political information to the White House. For example, when the World War Veterans, whom the Bureau was fighting together with the American Legion, in 1921 demanded the release of all political prisoners, Director Burns informed Harding about the WWV's "extreme radicalism" and subsequently warned the president that he would be presented with a petition for the prisoners' release.[45] The Bureau was also requested to inform Harding about the activities of the American Committee for Russian Famine Relief and the Russian Red Cross and whether they were conducting Communist propaganda.[46]

The Bureau only provided few services for the Coolidge administration and this was undoubtedly a consequence of the general tranquil domestic scene and the decline of radicalism. In addition, Coolidge and his second Attorney General, John G. Sargent, narrowly defined the power of the presidency, and they both feared, in the words of Sargent, "the constantly growing danger to liberty of the assumption and exercise by Federal bureaus and agencies of the power to make rules and regulations...."[47] However, during his first year in office Coolidge did receive reports on such topics as the waiter, who had served the president's first meal in Washington and who was thought to be "a dangerous man," and on the political situation in California. The White House also instructed the Bureau to investigate the New

[44]Davis, 450-451; *AG Report 1923*, 70; *Appropriations, Department of Justice, 1924*, Pt. 2, 71.

[45]Letters, William J. Burns to George Chistian, December 20, 1921 and May 6, 1922, file 10-B, Harding Papers, LC.

[46]Letters, Harding to Daugherty, February 15, 1922; Daugherty to Harding, February 18, 1922; Burns, Memorandum for the Attorney General, February 17, 1922; Burns, Memorandum for Mr. Martin, February 17, 1922; report, "The American Committee for Russian Famine Relief" and "Memorandum Upon the Russian Red Cross," n.d., file 156-B, ibid.

[47]For Sargent's opposition to a strong federal state, see "Address by John G. Sargent at Annual Bench and Bar Dinner of the Bar Association of the City of Boston," March 15, 1935, John G. Sargent Papers, Special Collections, University of Vermont; for Coolidge's view of the presidency, Donald J. McCoy, *Calvin Coolidge. The Quiet President* (New York, 1967), 124, 139-140, 156, 315, 417.

York Coolidge League.[48] The White House used the Bureau to investigate and in some instances put an end to the use of the president's name for commercial purposes.[49] Although the Coolidge White House's use of the Bureau was limited and often non-political, it did set a precedent and increased the Bureau's prestige by its direct dealings with the Bureau director.

The role of the Bureau as political intelligence agency for the White House expanded again during the Herbert Hoover administration as a consequence of the often bitter social discontent and political criticism of the president in response to the deepening depression after the stock market crash in 1929. In addition, despite his later reputation, Herbert Hoover exhibited a greater willingness than his Republican predecessors to use the powers of the federal government.[50] At the same time, the president's confidential secretary, Lawrence Richey, was a former Secret Service employee with intelligence connections who investigated press leaks, collected derogatory information on political opponents and was more than eager to use the Bureau's resources.[51] Consequently, in 1929 the Bureau's connections to the White House were formally recognized for the first time. In the internal description of the Bureau director's responsibilities it was noted that, among other things, he received "instructions and requests from the White House with regard to the initiation of certain investigations of a confidential, delicate and important character desired there, and personally directs and supervises all investigative steps and inquiries taken in connection therewith in all parts of the country."[52] The Bureau's confidential assistance to the White House, then, was a

---

[48]Letters, Burns to Hon. Edward T. Clark, August 8, 1923, file 10-B, Series 1, Coolidge Papers, LC; Burns to Clark, October 23, 1923, file 96, ibid.; Burns to Clark, May 3, 1924, file 10-B, ibid.; Clark to Burns, May 5, 1924, ibid.

[49]Letters, Clark to J. Edgar Hoover, December 23, 1925, with att. letter; Hoover to Clark, December 24, 1925, January 7 and 26, 1926; Hoover, Memorandum for the Attorney General, December 2, 1926; letter, Clark to Hoover, December 10, 1926; Hoover, Memorandum for the Attorney General, January 10, 1927, all in file 101, ibid.

[50]Joan Hoff-Wilson, *Herbert Hoover. Forgotten Progressive* (Boston, 1975), 144-159; David Burner, *Herbert Hoover. A Public Life* (New York, 1979), 212-283; according to Ellis W. Hawley, recent scholarship has shown that while expounding the traditional conservative ideology of "rugged individualism," Herbert Hoover "was at the same time closely associated with expanding governmental agencies, bureaucratic growth, and new forms of collective action" (Ellis W. Hawley, "Neo-Institutional History and the Understanding of Herbert Hoover," in, Lee Nash (ed.), *Understanding Herbert Hoover: Ten Perspectives* (Stanford, Calif., 1987), 67); for Herbert Hoover's attempts to shape the public opinion, Craig Lloyd, *Aggressive Introvert. A Study of Herbert Hoover and Public Relations Management 1912-1932* (Columbus, Ohio, 1972).

[51]For Richey, Kenneth O'Reilly, "Herbert Hoover and the FBI," *Annals of Iowa*, Summer 1983, 49n4; memorandum, Mr. McGrath to Lawrence Richey, October 20, 1947, box 2, Lawrence Richey Papers, HHL. Richey was one of those who had recommended J. Edgar Hoover for the position of Bureau director in 1924.

[52]J. Edgar Hoover, Memorandum for the Attorney General, October 31, 1929, 67-561-35, FBI/FOIA.

334

firmly established practice at the beginning of the Hoover administration.

The Bureau continued to investigate and stop commercial uses of the president's name,[53] but more significantly the Hoover White House used the Bureau to investigate various organizations which for one reason or another came to its attention. Thus, the Bureau under "a suitable pretext" visited the Lincoln League, because the White House had been informed that it had attacked the Boy Scouts, and conducted "a very discreet investigation" of the American Citizen's Political Awakening Association, an Italian-American anti-prohibition group. It also looked into the activities of another Italian-American organization, the Federation of Lictor, because it had expressed its support for the president, and it investigated one J. G. Bey, who had invited the president to attend the convention of the Moorish Science Temple in Chicago; it discovered that Bey was a black barber and that his organization was unknown in the black community.[54] At the same time, the Bureau revived the former practice of submitting unsolicited political information to the White House; thus, Hoover passed on a Communist leaflet entitled "Hoover Declares War on Workers" to Richey, informed him about anti-Hoover rumors, and provided him with a copy of a critical magazine article entitled "Hoover's flip flop."[55]

A more serious matter was the White House's use of the Bureau against political opponents and demonstrations as the depression worsened. In November 1929 the Bureau was asked by Richey to investigate the Senteniels of the Republic, a patriotic organization which opposed the growth of the federal government and which had criticized the establishment of the Child Health Commission. The Bureau likewise furnished information to the White House about the leadership and finances of the Navy League, which lobbied for a big

---

[53]For example, letters, Harold J. Potter to J. Edgar Hoover, April 18, 1929; Lawrence Richey to William B. Mitchell, April 20, 1929; Hoover, Memorandum for the Attorney General, May 16, 1929; letters, Hoover to Richey, November 26, 1929; Richey to Hoover, November 27, 1929; Hoover to Richey, December 23, 1929, all in box 225, PPSF, HHL.

[54]For the Lincoln League, Mrs. Dwight B. Heard to the President, February 13, 1930; Richey to Mrs. Heard, February 18, 1930; Hoover, Memorandum for Mr. Chase, February 18, 1930, all in box 194, ibid.; for the ACPAA, letters, P. S. Williams to William H. Newton, February 11, 1930; Newton to Hoover, February 15, 1930; Hoover to Newton, February 18, 1930; Newton to Williams, February 20, 1930; Hoover to Newton, February 26, 1930, box 58, ibid.; for the Federation of Lictor, telegram to Herbert Hoover, May 18, 1930; Hoover, Memorandum to Mr. Carusi, May 23, 1930, with att. report, box 990, PPFA, ibid.; for Bey, letters, Bey to Herbert Hoover, September 8, 1931; Richey to William Mitchell, September 10, 1931; Hoover, Memorandum to the Attorney General, September 12, 1931, box 745, PPSecF, ibid.

[55]Letters, Hoover to Richey, January 7, 1930, box 108, PPSF, ibid.; Hoover to Richey, December 17, 1930, 62-24622-2 and Richey to Hoover, December 19, 1930, 62-24622-3, box 1, Federal Agency Records, FBI, Herbert Hoover File, ibid.; Hoover to Richey, May 25, 1932, 62-26663-3, ibid.

US Navy and opposed the Hoover administration's commitment to arms reductions.[56] At the request of Richey, the Bureau also looked into the activities of the Foreign Policy Association, which in 1929 had issued a critical report on the US occupation of Haiti, and the Bureau on at least two occasions submitted reports on the history and activities of the civil rights organization the NAACP.[57] The Bureau was also instructed by the White House to ascertain the facts concerning an extremely critical Hoover biography, John Hamill's *The Strange Career of Mr. Hoover*, which was about to be published in January 1932.[58] In at least one instance the Bureau was used to actively suppress criticism of the administration. In October 1931, J. R. Nutt of the Union Trust Company brought a financial news letter, the *Wall Street Forecast*, which contained predictions of bank failures, to the attention of the White House and suggested that its publisher, George Menhinick, "be reached." The Bureau responded by dispatching five agents, who interviewed Menhinick and examined his papers and records. According to Hoover's report to Attorney General Mitchell, the publisher "was considerably upset over the visit of the agents" and was "thoroughly scared and I do not believe that he will resume the dissemination of any information concerning the banks or other financial institutions."[59]

The depression was noteworthy for its lack of organized opposition to the existing political or economic system: the mood in 1932 has been described as "less one of revolt than of apathy" and the poor as being "sullen rather than bitter, despairing rather than violent,"[60] who

[56]For the Senteniels of the Republic, letters, Alexander Lincoln to Herbert Hoover, November 16, 1929; Hoover to Richey, November 21, 1929; R. E. Vitterli to Hoover, November 21, 1929, box 278, PPSF, ibid.; for the Navy League, Memorandum for the Director, September 7, 1929; letter, Hoover to Richey, September 10, 1929, with att.; memorandum, Re Shearer – National Security League, September 14, 1929; Hoover to Richey, September 18, 19 and 20, 1929; John Lord O'Brian to Herbert Hoover, October 10, 1929; Memorandum for the Director, September 30, 1929, all in box 1062, PPINF, ibid.; Hoover to Richey, October 30, 1931, box 231, PPSF, ibid.; O'Reilly, "Herbert Hoover and the FBI," 53-57; Burner, 291-292.

[57]For the Foreign Policy Association, letters, William T. Stone to Herbert Hoover, December 7, 1929; Hoover to Richey, December 11, 1929, box 1016, PPFA, HHL; for the NAACP, Hoover, Memorandum for Assistant Attorney General Sisson, April 19, 1930, box 105, PPSF, ibid.; Hoover to Walter Newton, September 5, 1930; Newton, File Memo, September 23, 1930, box 755, PPSecF, ibid.; T. F. Baughman, Memoranda for the Director, April 19, 1930, and September 5, 1930, FBI/FOIA.

[58]Memorandum of Telephone Call from deleted, White House, January 12, 1932, 62-65153-X2; Hoover to name deleted, January 15, 1932, with att., 62-65153-X3, box 1, Federal Agency Records, FBI, Herbert Hoover file, HHL; according to one account, the Bureau investigation forced Hamill in 1933 to publicly repudiate his book, see Richard Norton Smith, *An Uncommon Man. The Triumph of Herbert Hoover* (New York, 1984), 27-28.

[59]Letter, J. R. Nutt to Thomas G. Joslin, October 6, 1931; Hoover, Memorandum for the Attorney General, October 10, 1931; letter, Joslin to Nutt, October 13, 1931, box 731, PPSecF, HHL.

[60]Schlesinger Jr., *Crisis of the Old Order*, 252.

without any effective leadership or organization "crowded into homes of more fortunate relatives, tramped the country looking for work, or drifted into Hoovervilles."[61] Only on two occasions, the Bonus March on Washington, DC, and the Farmers' Strike in the Midwest in 1932, did the Hoover administration come under serious pressure and in both instances did the White House use the Bureau to keep it informed and to discredit the opposition.

The Bonus Riot took place on July 28, 1932, when police clashed with the remaining members of the Bonus Expeditionary Force (BEF), veterans who had been in Washington, DC, since May demanding the immediate payment of their soldiers' bonus, which was not due until 1945. At the request of the District of Columbia Commissioners the president called in the Army to restore order and under the enthusiastic command of General Douglas MacArthur a force equipped with tanks and cavalry drove the veterans out and proceeded to attack and burn down the veterans' camp on the Anacostia Flats.[62] The use of bayonets and tear gas against the destitute heroes of the World War was clearly a political disaster at the beginning of Hoover's reelection campaign, and in order to justify the use of force the administration sought to discredit the BEF as criminal and Communistic. In a statement issued on the day of the riot the president claimed that many of the veterans were "Communists and persons with criminal records" and the secretary of war claimed that only one third of the BEF were genuine veterans.[63]

In order to substantiate these accusations, the administration on August 1 called a conference at the Justice Department, attended by representatives of the federal intelligence agencies, including the Bureau, the Secret Service, the MID, the Immigration Bureau, the Veterans Administration and the DC Police. When Director J. Edgar Hoover informed the conference that the Bureau had made no investigation of the BEF and consequently had no information to offer,

---

[61]Donald J. Lisio, *The President and Protest. Hoover, Conspiracy, and the Bonus Riot* (Columbia, Missouri, 1974), 317.

[62]Burner, 309-312; Hoff-Wilson, *Herbert Hoover*, 161-165; Schlesinger Jr., *Crisis of the Old Order*, 256-265. Several authors have claimed that Herbert Hoover acted on the basis of information supplied by the Bureau on Communist activity within the BEF (see Cook, 149-159; Ungar, 59; Williams, *"Without Understanding,"* 270; O'Reilly, "Herbert Hoover and the FBI," 57); however, it is apparent from the administration's records that the president acted on the request of the DC Commissioners to restore order (letters, L. H. Reichelderfer to Herbert Hoover, July 28, 1932; Reichelderfer to William B. Mitchell, August 2, 1932, box 376, PPSF, HHL).

[63]William Starr Myers & Walter H. Newton, *The Hoover Administration. A Documented Narrative* (New York, 1936), 449; William Manchester, *The Glory and the Dream. A Narrative History of America, 1932-72* (New York, 1973), 17; also, letter, Herbert Hoover to Reichelderfer, July 29, 1932, box 376, PPSF, HHL.

the Bureau was instructed to check its fingerprint collection to determine how many of the veterans had criminal records.[64]

The Bureau used some very questionable statistics to support the administration's charges.[65] First of all, it concluded that 31.5% of the marchers had not served in the armed forces. However, this finding was based on the fingerprints of only 51 of the marchers, who had been arrested on or about July 28, hardly a representative sample of the perhaps several thousand remaining protesters.[66] Moreover, according to a much more comprehensive study by the Veterans Administration, there simply did not exist any reliable information on the number of non-veterans.[67] Secondly, the Bureau found that 22.6% of the marchers had criminal records;[68] however, although based on an impressive sample of 4,723 fingerprints, these had been taken from marchers who had received federal aid to return home before the July 28 riot, thus it is unclear if the result would have been similar for those remaining. Furthermore, the figure included "charges dismissed" and an additional third of the number of criminal records consisted of such minor offenses as disorderly conduct and vagrancy, drunkenness, violation of liquor laws and military offenses. It could be argued that when poor people and others on the margins of society protested during the depression, they could easily be discredited as criminals on the basis of the Bureau files.[69] In addition to its fingerprint analysis, the Bureau also compiled detailed biographies of the alleged radical leaders of the BEF, informed the administration of rumors to the effect that the BEF had planned to resist the police on July 28 with force, continued to investigate the conditions in the BEF camps and monitored protest meetings against the administration.[70]

---

[64]Memorandum, Bonus March Conditions, n.d., ibid.

[65]Powers, in contrast, has claimed that the Bureau was reluctant to participate in the smear campaign against the BEF and only "provided the minimum required" (Powers, *Secrecy and Power,* 168).

[66]Memorandum, Bonus March Conditions, n.d.; letter, Hoover to Richey, September 1, 1932, with att. memorandum, September 1, 1932, box 376, PPSF, HHL.

[67]Letter, Frank T. Hines to Herbert Hoover, June 15, 1932, ibid.

[68]Same as note 66.

[69]For a critique of the Bureau analysis, see also, Lisio, 250-251. During the depression it was common practice for local authorities to charge homeless people with vagrancy, thus providing them with a criminal record as 107 of the marchers had (see Manchester, 19-20, 22).

[70]For the radical biographies, Reports, Criminal Records, Exhibit A, September 6, 1932, box 375, PPSF, HHL; for the rumors, Hoover, Memorandum for Assistant Attorney General Dodds, September 10, 1932, box 376, ibid.; for the BEF camps, letters, R. L. Nalls to Hoover, August 5, 1932, 62-27038-200, box 5, Series 10, FBI Records, MU; Everett Sanders to Richey, October 8, 1932; Richey to Hoover, October 12, 1932; Hoover to Richey, October 14, 1932, all in box 376, PPSF, HHL; for the protest meetings, C. A. Appel, Memorandum for the Director, July 31, 1932, 62-27038-2138; J. E. P. Dunn to Hoover, August 8, 1932, 62-27038-223, both in box 5, Series 10, FBI Records, MU.

The Bureau study was used as the corner-stone of the Hoover administration's official version of the events. Assistant Attorney General Nugent Dodds told Director Hoover that he was under pressure from the White House to produce a report on the BEF and on September 1 directed him to turn over all of the Bureau's information. In his report Dodds claimed that "there were many hundreds" of criminals and non-veterans among the marchers and that "they were in the forefront of the serious rioting."[71] In the final Justice Department report to the president, Attorney General Mitchell concluded on the basis of the Bureau figures that the BEF "brought into the city of Washington the largest aggregation of criminals that had ever been assembled in the city at any one time" and claimed with reference to the Bureau's radical biographies that "a very large body of Communists and radicals ... were in the city as part of the Bonus Army, circulating among them and working diligently to incite them to disorder."[72] Although the discrediting of the BEF in the longer run did President Hoover little good, it did set a precedent for the White House to use the Bureau to derail any serious debate on social questions by smearing the opposition as criminals or subversives.

The second major organized protest against the depression followed immediately upon the Bonus Riot when farmers in Iowa, Nebraska and South Dakota under the leadership of Milo Reno, protested against the declining farm prices, and organized a "farm holiday" movement. The angry farmers went on strike, blocked roads, dumped milk and halted foreclosure proceedings. The Bureau was directed by the White House to keep the movement under surveillance and between August 31 and September 22 Hoover furnished daily reports to Richey on the results of the "strictly confidential inquiries." The reports in general reflected the administration and the Bureau's view of social unrest as the work of a few troublemakers. Thus, the strikers were described as "apparently hoodlums," "outsiders and drifters" and "unemployed ... (who) receive free meals" and who were "encouraged by Reds" and "agi-

---

[71]Nugent Dodds, Memorandum in re: Bonus Expeditionary Force, September 2, 1932, box 376, PPSF, HHL; also, letter, Dodds to Richey, August 19, 1932, ibid.; Dodds, Memorandum for Mr. Hoover, September 1, 1932, ibid.

[72]Letter, William B. Mitchell to Herbert Hoover, September 9, 1932, ibid. Herbert Hoover continued to claim that the BEF consisted of "about 5,000 mixed hoodlums, ex-convicts, Communists, and a minority of veterans ..." (Herbert Hoover, *The Memoirs of Herbert Hoover. The Great Depression* (New York, 1952), 226). In fact, there were no evidence that the Communists had instigated the riot (see, Transcript, Before the Grand Jurors for the July, 1932, Term, August 1, 1932, box 376, PPSF, HHL; Lisio, 310). J. Edgar Hoover continued to support the administration's line, see letter, J. Edgar Hoover to Herbert Hoover, July 16, 1951, 62-65153-70, box 1, Federal Agency Records, FBI, Herbert Hoover file, HHL.

tators," whereas the "real farmers (were) staying home attending to farm...."[73]

Thus, the Bureau's political role after the Red Scare changed its character. The general intelligence function was maintained at a bare minimum and primarily limited to the filing of reports from outside sources and a few informers. As a result of the growing responsibilities and power of the modern presidency, and in particular its acknowledged role as the protector of the existing order against domestic and foreign enemies, the Bureau was increasingly used by the White House to provide intelligence on strikes, protest movements, and critics.

FDR, the New Deal and the FBI: The Threat From the Right
While noting that the political position and power of the FBI (as it was renamed in 1935) expanded dramatically during the Roosevelt administration, historians have disagreed sharply about the causes. Several authors have contended that the Bureau stretched and misused limited presidential authorizations to conduct political surveillance and that the Bureau increasingly acted independently of the Roosevelt administration. Athan Theoharis has argued that "Hoover independently defined the scope of the Bureau's authority,"[74] while Kenneth O'Reilly has noted that the FBI's role as "an independent political force" was the last thing FDR wanted and was a result of his "inability to control resourceful and highly motivated FBI officials who sought far different and more conservative political objectives."[75] In contrast, other historians such as Richard Gid Powers have argued that "Roosevelt knew exactly what Hoover was doing" and that the extensive program of political surveillance established during the thirties "was precisely what Roosevelt intended."[76] In fact, not only was Roosevelt

[73]Letters, Hoover to Richey, August 31, September 1, 2, 3, 6, 8, 9, 10, 15, 19 and 22, 1932, with att. telegrams, box 25, PPOF, ibid. Following his retirement from the presidency in 1933 Herbert Hoover maintained close contacts with the Bureau, which assisted him during his travels and vacations and provided him with confidential information on persons suspected of Communist sympathies (see the numerous communications in Federal Agency Records, FBI, Herbert Hoover and Lawrence Richey Files, ibid.; O'Reilly, "Herbert Hoover and the FBI," 58-62).

[74]Athan Theoharis, "The FBI's Stretching of Presidential Directives, 1936-1953," *Political Science Quarterly*, Vol. 91, No. 4 (Winter 1976-77), 649; also, Theoharis, *Spying on Americans*, 65-93; Theoharis (ed.), *From the Secret Files*, 179-180; Theoharis & Cox, 172-179, 198-199, 201, 221-224n.

[75]Kenneth O'Reilly, "A New Deal for the FBI: The Roosevelt Administration, Crime Control, and National Security," *The Journal of American History*, Vol. 69, No. 3 (December 1982), 639; also, Kenneth O'Reilly, "The Roosevelt Administration and Black America: Federal Surveillance Policy and Civil Rights During the New Deal and World War II Years," *Phylon*, Vol. XLVIII, No. 1 (March 1987), 20; O'Reilly, *"Racial Matters"*, 18-19.

[76]Powers, *Secrecy and Power*, 230; also, Williams, *"Without Understanding,"* 342-344, 349; Charles F. Croog, "FBI Political Surveillance and the Isolationist-Interventionist Debate, 1939-1941," *The Historian*, Vol. 54, No. 3 (Spring 1992), 441-451.

well-informed about the FBI's political activities but the expansion of the Bureau's political role was a result of the continuing centralization of power in the executive and of Roosevelt's response to three challenges: the opposition from the extreme right and the isolationists, the conservatives' attack on the New Deal in the form of the Dies Committee, and the threat posed by foreign spies and saboteurs.

There is every reason to believe that President Roosevelt approved of the FBI's broad political surveillance program. In 1934, the president authorized Hoover to investigate Nazi activities in the US.[77] During two meetings on August 24 and 25, 1936, according to the only surviving accounts, two contemporary memoranda by Hoover, the president expressed his concern "about the movements of the Communists and of Fascism in the United States" and indicated that he was interested in "obtaining a broad picture of the general movement and its activities as may affect the economic and political life of the country as a whole."[78] These were broad authorizations and during the final meeting FDR directed Hoover to make "a survey ... on a much broader field" than previous specific inquiries of "Communist activities in this country, as well as Fascist activities."[79]

The FBI, therefore, did not stretch FDR's instructions, as it has been claimed, when it subsequently established a broad surveillance program of "subversive activities" in all areas of society. This included, according to an early FBI list, the maritime industry, government affairs, the steel and coal industry, newspaper field, clothing, garment and fur industry, general strike activities, armed forces, educational institutions, Communist and affiliated organizations, Fascist activities, anti-Fascists, and organized labor. In September 1936, having obtained the approval of the Attorney General, Hoover issued instructions to the field "to obtain from all possible sources information concerning subversive activities being conducted in the United States by Communists, Fascisti, and representatives or advocates of other organizations or groups advocating the overthrow or replacement of the Government of the United States by illegal methods."[80] Although Roosevelt both internally and publicly stressed that "we need in the United States no O.G.P.U.... We do not need any secret police

---

[77] *Senate Select Committee to Investigate Governmental Operations*, Hearings, Vol. 6, 558-559; in 1935 the White House requested an investigation of Communist and Japanese activities in Alaska (letter, Hoover to Stephen Early, July 18, 1935, OF 1779, FDRL).

[78] Hoover, Confidential Memorandum, August 24, 1936, O/C 136, FBI/FOIA; for a more unclassified copy, see, Theoharis (ed.), *From the Secret Files*, 180-181.

[79] Hoover, Confidential Memorandum, August 25, 1936, O/C 136, FBI/FOIA; Theoharis (ed.), *From the Secret Files*, 182.

[80] *Senate Select Committee to Investigate Governmental Operations*, Book III, 396-397.

in the United States to watch American people, to watch our own people" and specified at a cabinet meeting that the intelligence program "should be confined to investigation of espionage on the part of foreigners,"[81] he was well-informed about the FBI's broad political surveillance. In connection with the appropriation request for the program in 1938, Hoover furnished a memorandum to Attorney General Homer S. Cummings and FDR, which described in detail the Bureau's investigation of "activities of either a subversive or a so-called intelligence type." It listed all the categories which had been established in 1936 from government, industry and educational institutions to blacks, youths and strikes, and it described how the information was filed for instant retrieval. Finally, Hoover stressed the sensitiveness of the surveillance and the need to keep it secret in order to avoid "criticism or objections which might be raised to such an expansion by either ill-informed persons or individuals having some ulterior motive."[82] On November 2, 1938, Roosevelt notified Hoover that "he had approved the plan which I had prepared and which had been sent to him by the Attorney General...."[83] This was not the only time that Hoover informed his superiors about the existence of the broad surveillance program; for example, on two occasions in 1940 the Attorney General was informed about the FBI's surveillance of radical organizations and the establishment of a list of several thousand suspected subversives, who were to be interned in case of a national emergency.[84]

That Roosevelt was fully aware of the FBI's political activities is underlined by his close personal relationship to Hoover, an arrangement which was in accordance with the president's usual practice of maintaining control of the vast, sprawling executive branch by direct contact with subordinate bureau heads. According to Attorney General Francis Biddle, Roosevelt "cared little for administrative niceties" and would frequently by-pass the Attorney General and go directly to Hoover "about something that he wanted done quietly, usually in a hurry."[85] The president's secretary later remembered the FBI director's

---

[81]*Complete Press Conferences of Franklin D. Roosevelt* (New York, 1972), Vol. 12, 289; Homer S. Cummings, Memorandum, October 14, 1938, box 100, Homer S. Cummings Papers, Alderman Library, University of Virginia; also, statement, German Spy Ring, n.d., box 55, PSF, FDRL.

[82]Letter, Cummings to Roosevelt, October 20, 1938, with att. memorandum, box 100, Cummings Papers, AL.

[83]Hoover, Memorandum, November 7, 1938, O/C 136, FBI/FOIA.

[84]Hoover, Memoranda for the Attorney General, June 3 and October 25, 1940, with att. memoranda, box 93, Robert Jackson Papers, LC.

[85]Francis Biddle, *In Brief Authority* (New York, 1962), 182; for FDR's administrative practice in general, see James MacGregor Burns, *Roosevelt: The Lion and the Fox* (London, 1956), 373.

frequent visits to the White House.[86] In 1940, FDR told Harold Ickes that "J. Edgar Hoover was devoted to him personally,"[87] and at one point the president directed an aide to prepare "a nice letter" to Hoover "thanking him for all the reports on investigations he has made and tell him I appreciate the fine job he is doing."[88] Leading members of the administration had conflicting opinions of the close relationship; Biddle noted that it was clear that the "two men liked and understood each other,"[89] while Secretary of War Henry Stimson complained that Hoover "poisons the mind of the president...."[90] More fundamentally, Hoover's close relationship with Roosevelt might be seen as the culmination of the process which had been going on since the beginning of the Harding administration in 1921, during which the FBI's political base shifted from the Justice Department to the White House. What has often been seen as FBI autonomy or insubordination was, in fact, the result of the fact that the FBI was now carrying out political instructions directly from the president, often by-passing the nominal superior, the Attorney General. As noted by Ickes, "Hoover continued in his job and added to his power because about this time he managed to worm himself into the complete confidence of the president."[91] In short, the FBI was not out of control but was only accountable to the president and encouraged by him to investigate a wide spectrum of subversive activities.

The question is, then, what were President Roosevelt's motives for authorizing and supporting the expansion of the FBI's political role? One reason was his response to the often hateful domestic criticism, much of it from the extreme right, and the opposition from the isolationist movement to his interventionist foreign policy from 1940 to 1941. One study of Roosevelt's critics noted that no previous president was villified as FDR, who, when "moved by great resentment and exasperation ... could take direct action...."[92] Moreover, FDR was not a staunch defender of civil liberties and, for example, approved the internment of 110,000 Japanese-Americans on the West Coast in

---

[86]Grace Tully, *F.D.R. My Boss* (New York, 1949), 289.
[87]Harold L. Ickes Diaries, 4738, August 22, 1940, LC.
[88]FDR, Memorandum for General Watson, June 12, 1940, box 10, OF 10-B, FDRL; also, letters, Roosevelt to Hoover, June 14, 1940 and Hoover to Roosevelt, June 18, 1940, ibid.
[89]Biddle, 166.
[90]Diaries of Henry L. Stimson, February 12, 1941, LC.
[91]Ickes Diaries, 5660, June 28, 1941, ibid.; also, Donner, *Age of Surveillance*, 98.
[92]George Wolfskill & John A. Hudson, *All But the People. Franklin D. Roosevelt and His Critics 1933-39* (London, 1969), 297-298; also, Ted Morgan, *FDR. A Biography* (London (1985), 1986), 554, 772-773; Richard W. Steele, "Franklin D. Roosevelt and His Foreign Policy Critics," *Political Science Quarterly*, Vol. 94, No. 1 (Spring 1979), 15-32.

1942, a move that has been described as "the worst single wholesale violation of civil rights of American citizens in our history."[93]

In a few isolated instances the White House instructed the FBI to investigate strikes and Communist activities. In August 1933, FDR received a report on a milk strike in New York,[94] and in September 1934 he instructed the Bureau to monitor a violent textile strike in Rhode Island in anticipation of a request from the governor to deploy federal troops.[95] In November that same year presidential aide Harry Hopkins furnished confidential reports to the FBI on planned nationwide demonstrations by organizations of unemployed, and in September 1936 Roosevelt asked Attorney General Cummings to ascertain the positions of CPUSA presidential candidate Earl Browder.[96] Likewise, in 1940 the president requested an investigation into the financing of the publication *In Fact,* which was described by the Bureau as being backed by the Communists and its editor, George Seldes, as being regarded as sympathetic to the Communists.[97]

These were exceptions, however, and the White House seemed to be much more concerned about the often vicious personal attacks upon the president from extreme right wing elements and Fascist sympathizers. In September 1934, the White House asked for "a confidential inquiry" concerning James True, publisher of the violent anti-New Deal *Industrial Control Report,* which among other thing accused the administration of being part of a worldwide Jewish-Communist conspiracy, and the Bureau also inquired into rumors circulated by conservative stock-brokers to the effect that Roosevelt was going insane.[98] Other right-wing extremists who were investigated on the orders of the Roosevelt White House were Robert Edmunson, a publisher who claimed that the New Deal was run by a "Jewish-Communist-Alien"

[93]Robert Dallek, *Franklin D. Roosevelt and American Foreign Policy, 1932-1945* (New York, 1979), 334-336.

[94]Hoover, Memorandum for the Attorney General, August 19, 1933, with att. Memorandum re milk strike in New York, August 18, 1933, box 191, Cummings Papers, AL; Stephen Early, Memorandum for Governor Morgenthau, August 19, 1933, OF 568, FDRL.

[95]See the numerous memoranda and reports in file 61-7313, box 5, Series 10, FBI Records, MU.

[96]For the demonstrations, letters, Harry Hopkins to Hoover, November 12 and 15, 1934, box 90, Harry Hopkins Papers, FDRL; for Browder, Cummings Personal and Political Diary, September 18, 1936, box 235, Cummings Papers, AL.

[97]Letter, Hoover to Early, December 11, 1940, with att. memoranda, December 11, 1940; Early, Memorandum for the President, February 18, 1941, with att. letter, Hoover to Early, February 15, 1941, OF 4185, FDRL.

[98]For True, Note, Louis McH. Howe, September 21, 1934; letters, Early to William Stanley, September 26, 1934; Stanley to Early, September 28, 1934 with att.; Stanley to Early, October 4, 1934 with att.; Stanley to Howe, August 17, 1934; FDR, Memorandum for Hon. J. Edgar Hoover, December 3, 1940, all in OF 1200, ibid.; for True also, Wolfskill & Hudson, 69-70, 94-95; for the rumors, Hoover, Memorandum for the Attorny General, October 18, 1934, box 191, Cummings Papers, AL.

cabale, Louis T. McFadden, a former congressman with strong anti-semitic views, and William Dudley Pelley, the leader of "The Silver Shirts", an outfit inspired by the SA.[99] Sometimes Roosevelt himself ordered the investigations. When the anti-communist and anti-semitic Industrial Defense Association issued a leaflet claiming that "Roosevelt is a Socialist, pure and simple," FDR asked his Attorney General: "Try to find out who is paying for this." When officers of the Protestant War Veterans called on Roosevelt to purge his administration of "the alien parasite and economic influences," the president directed Hoover to "Check up on this" and the Bureau responded by reviewing its files, ascertaining that at least one of the officers was a known anti-semite.[100]

A much more serious threat to the administration was posed by Democratic Senator Huey P. Long, who had established a powerful political machine in Louisiana and in 1934 launched a national political organization, "Share Our Wealth." It called for the redistribution of wealth, a potentially popular proposal should the New Deal fail to restore prosperity. Long had supported Roosevelt in 1932 but soon after the inauguration the two had split, and by 1934 the president was not only worried about Long as a challenger in 1936 but also that the senator might become a Fascist leader. In a clear political attempt to discredit Long, the Treasury Department in January 1934 reopened an Internal Revenue Service investigation into Long and his associates' income taxes. The political motivation behind the move was indicated by Elmer Iry of the IRS, who noted that the intention was to "destroy Huey's image as a champion of the common people."[101] According to

---

[99]For Edmunson, letter, Chester H. McCall to Miss Marguerite Le Hand, February 3, 1936; M. H. McIntyre, Memorandum for the Attorney General, February 7, 1936; Harold Nathan, Memorandum for the Attorney General, February 18, 1936; note, FDR to Early, March 20, 1939; Early, Memorandum for J. Edgar Hoover, March 20, 1939; letter, Hoover to Early, March 23, 1939, with att., all in PPF 1632, FDRL; for Edmunson in general, Wolfskill & Hudson, 67-68, 71, 75; for McFadden, letters, Hoover to Howe, February 28, 1935; Howe to Hoover, March 5, 1935; Hoover to Howe, March 16, 1935, all in OF 1486, FDRL; for McFadden in general, Wolfskill & Hudson, 65-66; for Pelley, letters, Cummings to Roosevelt, May 25, 1938, with att., box 57, PSF, FDRL; for Pelley in general, Wolfskill & Hudson, 70-72, 96, 113.

[100]For the leaflet, FDR, Memorandum for the Attorney General, August 7, 1935; letter, Cummings to Roosevelt, August 26, 1935, with att., OF 1701, FDRL; for the veterans, Rudolph Forster, Memorandum for the Attorney General, April 16, 1938 with att.; Hoover, Memorandum for the Attorney General, April 18, 1938, box 57, PSF, ibid.

[101]T. Harry Williams, *Huey Long* (New York (1969) 1981), 826-827; in general 794-798; for FDR and Long see also, Leuchtenburg, *Franklin Roosevelt and the New Deal*, 96-100; Schlesinger Jr., *Years of Upheaval*, 43-68, 242-252; Alan Brinkley, *Voices of Protest. Huey Long, Father Coughlin and the Great Depression* (New York (1982), 1983), 57-65. The IRS investigation had initially been started by the Hoover administration in 1932 when Long was the foremost Senate critic of Hoover and it was intended to be used during the election campaign to "emphasize the bad company Mr. Roosevelt is keeping" (Col. H., File Memorandum, Huey Long, November 2, 1932, box 697, PSF, HHL).

Long's most recent biographer, "There is no doubt that the 1934-35 Internal Revenue Service investigation of Long and his cohorts was ordered by the White House for political reasons."[102]

It is in this political context that the FBI's surveillance of Huey Long must be seen. Coinciding with the Hoover administration's probe of Long in 1932 the Bureau had opened a file on the senator, filling it with newspaper clippings and speeches of Long, although apparently no active investigation was undertaken.[103] In the summer of 1934, the power struggle between the Long machine and its opponents in Louisiana turned into a near civil war situation when Long dispatched National Guard troops to occupy the registrar's office in New Orleans, declaring that he simply wanted to ensure a fair election in September, while the city authorities deployed 400 armed special deputies. At first, the FBI was requested by the Justice Department only to look into the possibility that the conflict might turn into actual violence and thereby damage federal property or interfere with the mail, but on August 17 the New Orleans office was instructed to report daily to Washington on "the Huey Long situation." The local Bureau agents were directed not to limit the surveillance to the situation in New Orleans but also to include Long's political activities "as this is for a confidential source and we want everything we can get on it – legislation, tactics, developments and the whole thing."[104] For the next month, until September 17, the FBI reported daily to the White House on such political matters as Long's legislative proposals, his continuing power struggle with the opposition, and the state of the public opinion in Louisiana.[105] Roosevelt, then, was perfectly willing to use the FBI to keep an eye on the political activities of his potential opponents in 1936.

Roosevelt's second major worry was the isolationists and other opponents of his increasingly interventionist foreign policy. As noted by one historian, FDR had a disposition to see opposition to his foreign policy "as disloyalty and the proper subject of government

---

[102]William Ivy Hair, *The Kingfish and His Realm. The Life and Times of Huey P. Long* (Baton Rouge, La., 1991), 287; also, 284-287.

[103]Files 62-27030 and 62-28479, FBI/FOIA.

[104]E. A. Tamm, Memorandum for the Director, August 17, 1934, 62-32509-10, ibid.

[105]Letters, Hoover to McIntyre, August 18, 19, 21, 24, 27, 30, September 1, 4, 5, 6, 7, 8, 10 and 17, 1934, all in file 62-32509, ibid. It has been claimed that the investigation was a proper and legitimate inquiry into possible criminal violations (Gentry, 225), but both the FBI and the Justice Department found that the FBI had no jurisdiction since the September election in New Orleans was a state primary and therefore not covered by federal statutes (see T. D. Quinn, Memorandum for Mr. William Stanley, August 29, 1934, 62-32509-28, FBI/FOIA; Tamm, Memorandum for the Director, August 30, 1934, 62-32509-38, ibid.; Harold Stephens, Memorandum to the Attorney General, September 7, 1934, box 125, Cummings Papers, AL).

action" and he set out to discredit his critics as "appeaser fifth columnists" or agents of foreign subversion.[106] This suspicion toward legitimate political dissent very much guided Roosevelt's response to the criticism of his request on May 16, 1940, to Congress for $1.18 million in additional defense spending. On May 18, the White House turned over 38 telegrams, which were addressed to the president and described as being "more or less in opposition to national defense," to the FBI with the remark that "it was the President's idea that you might like to go over these, noting the names and addresses of the senders."[107] It was Roosevelt's intention, then, that his foreign policy critics should be recorded in the FBI files. The following days numerous telegrams opposing Roosevelt's rearmament program were delivered to the FBI, which obliged by searching its files for information on the critics and prepared extensive reports for the White House, in some instances going as far back as World War I.[108] When the White House received 36 telegrams expressing support for a speech by Charles Lindbergh, these were referred to the FBI as well, and the Bureau was also requested to investigate a peace demonstration in Los Angeles arranged by the Communistic American Peace Crusade.[109]

The leading isolationist organization was the America First Committee, which was established in September 1940 by a group of Midwestern businessmen and by the time of America's entry into the war the following year it had some 850,000 members and 450 chapters nationwide. The Roosevelt administration became concerned about the Committee's influence when it led the opposition to the lend-lease proposals in January 1941. On February 21, the president referred a circular issued by the Committee to his secretary Stephen Early with the request, "Will you find out from someone – perhaps FBI – who is paying for this?"[110] Hoover responded by furnishing the president with a summary memorandum on the Committee's activities and reports on

[106]Steele, 17-20; also, Wayne S. Cole, *Roosevelt and the Isolationists 1932-45* (Lincoln, Nebraska, 1983), 12-13, 484-487.

[107]Early, Memorandum to Hoover, May 18, 1940, box 10, OF 10-B, FDRL; for the May 16 message, see Dallek, 221.

[108]FDR, Memorandum for S.T.E., May 21, 1940; Early, Memorandum for Hoover, May 21, 1940; note, FDR to RF, May 22, 1940; Rudolph Forster, Memorandum for Honorable J. Edgar Hoover, May 23, 1940; Early, Memorandum to J. Edgar Hoover, May 27, 1940; memorandum, Early to Hoover, May 29, 1940, all in box 10, OF 10-B, FDRL; letters, Hoover to Early, June 8, 1940 with att. reports, box 12, ibid.; Hoover to Early, June 26, 1940, with att. reports, box 10, ibid.; Hoover to Early, August 2, 1940, with att. telegrams, ibid.

[109]For Lindbergh, Early, Memorandum for J. Edgar Hoover, June 17, 1940, ibid.; for the demonstration, Edwin M. Watson, Memorandum for: Hon. J. Edgar Hoover, June 12, 1940; letters, Hoover to Watson, June 15 and 25, 1940 with. att., box 12, ibid.

[110]FDR, Memorandum for S.T.E., February 21, 1941, att. to Early, memorandum, February 21, 1941, 100-4712-18, FBI/FOIA; for the America First Committee, Cole, especially, 379-382, 414-415.

alleged anti-British remarks by the wife of the chairman of the Committee's California chapter, "strictly confidential" information on the Committee's plans for a national speaking tour by isolationist politicians, and a report on a speech by the leading isolationist senator, Burton K. Wheeler, in Los Angeles.[111] However, Roosevelt was not satisfied with being kept informed about the Committee's activities and he wanted to discredit and hamper their agitation. On November 17, he asked Attorney General Biddle "about the possibility of a Grand Jury investigation of the money sources behind the America First Committee? It certainly ought to be looked into and I cannot get any action out of Congress."[112] The FBI immediately went to work combing through its files and looking into the question whether the Committee had been financed by German sources, but the questions became academic when Pearl Harbor was attacked a few weeks later and the Committee ceased its activities and disbanded.[113]

Following the entry of the US into the war, Roosevelt became even more suspicious of the motives of those politicians who continued to espouse an isolationist line. In January 1942, the White House requested an FBI investigation into the authenticity of some highly critical "off the record" remarks reportedly made by Senator Wheeler to a *Milwaukee Journal* journalist concerning the damages inflicted by the attack against Pearl Harbor and that the administration was under British influence. Roosevelt also instructed the FBI to investigate whether another isolationist, Republican Representative Hamilton Fish, had received several hundred thousand dollars as payment for "subversive activities."[114] As Roosevelt explained his view in a reference to a press report about the alleged connection between a German propagandist and a US senator, "I think very definitely that

[111]Letters, Hoover to Early, March 1, 1941, 100-4712-18, FBI/FOIA; Hoover to Edwin M. Watson, February 26, 1941 with att.; Hoover to Watson, March 19, 1941, with att.; Hoover to Watson, September 22, 1941, all in box 13, OF 10-B, FDRL; Hoover to Watson, October 13, 1941, 100-4712-148, FBI/FOIA; the surveillance is also described in Cole, 486-487, 530-532; Croog, 451-458.

[112]Roosevelt, Memorandum for the Attorney General, November 17, 1941, box 56, PSF, FDRL.

[113]Hoover, Memoranda for Mr. Tolson and Mr. Tamm, November 21, 1941, 100-4712-219/220; E. A. Tamm, Memorandum, November 21, 1941, 100-4712-230, all FBI/FOIA; the America First Committee was investigated again in 1942 when the FBI received information to the effect that the Committee had not ceased to exist but was only laying low (letter, Hoover to Watson, February 13, 1942, 100-4712-290, ibid.; Hoover, Memorandum, March 16, 1942, 100-4712-320, ibid.).

[114]For Wheeler, Early, Memorandum for Hon. J. Edgar Hoover, January 26, 1942, with att., 62-55261-40; JKM, Memorandum, January 28, 1942, 62-55261-43; D. M. Ladd, Memorandum for the Director, January 31, 1942, 62-55261-41; letters, H. T. O'Connor to Hoover, January 31, 1942, 62-55261-4?; Hoover to Early, February 3, 1942, with att., 62-55261-40, all in box 1, Series 4, FBI Records, MU; for Fish, FDR, Memorandum for Edgar Hoover, May 4, 1942, OF 1661-A, FDRL.

the FBI can run down things like this. Senators and members of Congress are, of course, protected in a sense by the Constitution, but this must be strictly construed. There is absolutely no valid reason why any suspected subversive activities on their part should not be investigated by the Dept. of Justice or any other duly constituted agency."[115]

At the same time the FBI continued its practice from the Hoover administration of furnishing unsolicited political information to the White House; between 1939 and 1945 the Bureau submitted some 2,600 reports to the president. Most of the reports on domestic political activities dealt with Communist activities, especially alleged Communist attempts to infiltrate relief and youth organizations, the peace movement and organized labor, particularly the Congress of Industrial Organizations (CIO). The impression one gets is that ambitious Bureau officials were taking advantage of their close relationship with the president and attempted to educate him on the Communist threat. Apparently, this one-sided focus on Communism annoyed Roosevelt, who was more concerned about the threat from the right. As Attorney General Biddle later informed Hoover, the president had told him "that in his opinion the Federal Bureau of Investigation was spending too much time investigating suspected Communists in the Government and out, but particularly in the Government, and ignoring the Fascist minded groups both in the Government and out."[116] However, as far as can be determined, Roosevelt never took any steps to limit or curtail the FBI's broad political surveillance. Thus, one reason for Roosevelt's use of the FBI's political resources was his strong reaction to domestic political criticism, especially from the extreme right and the isolationist movement.

The Dies Committee, 1938-43

The other main reason was the Roosevelt administration's response to the attempt by the alliance of Republicans and Southern Democrats to portray the New Deal as weak and infiltrated by Communists. Following the break-down of the New Deal coalition in 1937 and the Republican midterm election victory in 1938, the new conservative majority in Congress was determined to use its influence to halt and

---

[115]FDR, Memorandum for the Attorney General, May 11, 1942, ibid. Roosevelt's concern about the domestic security made him instruct Hoover, "Have you pretty well cleaned out the alien waiters in the principal Washington hotels. Altogether too much conversation in the dining rooms!" (FDR, Memorandum for Edgar Hoover, April 3, 1942, box 57, PSF, ibid.).
[116]Francis Biddle, Memorandum for Mr. Hoover, May 29, 1942, O/C 136, FBI/FOIA; most of the unsolicited FBI reports to Roosevelt can be found in the numerical series reports in OF 10-B, FDRL.

roll back the liberal domestic reforms since 1933. Central to this strategy was the House Special Committee to Investigate Un-American Activities and Propaganda, which was established in May 1938 on the initiative of Representative Martin Dies of Texas. Dies was named chairman and the committee was dominated by conservatives, who used its public hearings as a platform for accusing the administration of being infiltrated and influenced by Communists. The committee's ranking Republican, J. Parnell Thomas, claimed at one point, "it seems as though the New Deal was hand in glove with the Communist Party."[117]

While Roosevelt appreciated the Dies Committee's not so hidden agenda and on a few occasions criticized its methods, most of the time he tried to avoid an open confrontation. This strategy was dictated by the belief that the committee like its predecessors would be short-lived, the popularity of Dies in 1938, Roosevelt's fear of antagonizing Congress, and the administration's concern about fifth-column activities.[118] The FBI fully supported the administration against the committee, not least because it perceived the committee to be a potential rival in the field of internal security and because it viewed its free-wheeling style and lust for publicity as a threat to its own investigations. In particular, Hoover feared that the committee's attacks on the administration would also hurt the Bureau's image.[119]

Consequently, the administration and the FBI cooperated closely on a strategy of containing the committee without provoking an open confrontation by giving it carefully controlled and limited assistance and thereby, it was hoped, silencing or toning down its attacks. In this way, the FBI became even more important to the administration and its political influence and prestige was increased. Thus, on the one hand the administration and the Bureau refused a request from the committee for the assistance of FBI agents to conduct its investigations, while on the other hand the committee was granted access to a

[117]Goodman, 65; also, 19-24, 28-35, 42-51, 71; for the political background, Leuchtenburg, *Franklin Roosevelt and the New Deal*, 252-254, 266-274; Burns, *The Lion and the Fox*, 369; Kenneth O'Reilly, "The Roosevelt Administration and Legislative-Executive Conflict: The FBI vs. the Dies Committee," *Congress and the Presidency*, Vol. 10, No. 1 (Spring 1983), 80-81; O'Reilly, *Hoover and the Un-Americans*, 53-54.

[118]Richard Polenberg, "Franklin Roosevelt and Civil Liberties: The Case of the Dies Committee," *The Historian*, Vol. XXX, No. 2 (February 1968), 169-173; also, *Complete Presidential Press Conferences*, Vol. 12, 202, and Vol. 14, 260; *The Secret Diary of Harold L. Ickes*, Vol. II, 529, 546-547, 573-547; letters, Roosevelt to Right Rev. Francis J. McConnell, February 17, 1942 and to Vito Marcantonio, February 24, 1942, OF 320, FDRL.

[119]For example, Hoover, Memoranda for the Attorney General, May 24, 1940, 61-7582-425; May 27, 1940, 61-7582-419X; February 27, 1941, 61-7582-931; November 29, 1940, 61-7582-640; July 5, 1940, 61-7582-449; July 10, 1940, 61-7582-459, all in box 1, Series 3, FBI Records, MU; Hoover, Memoranda for the Attorney General, August 26, September 11, November 22 and 25, 1940 and April 7, 1941, box 89, Jackson Papers, LC.

few, selected Bureau files, such as the one on the German-American Bund.[120]

This strategy only lasted until 1940, when Dies stepped up his attacks on the administration, warning of a fifth-column in the United States consisting of "approximately two million Communists, Fascists, and Nazis, and their sympathizers and dupes" and accusing the Department of Justice of incompetence in the war against spies and saboteurs. In November 1940, Dies unveiled a 7-point program aimed at combating Communist activities by, among other things, the outlawing of the Communist Party USA (CPUSA), and he proposed the establishment of a Home Defense Council, including his committee, to coordinate the work of all investigative forces.[121] These attacks forced the administration on the defense and in December 1940 it cut a deal with the committee. The committee would turn over any evidence of criminal violations in its possession to the Justice Department while the FBI would furnish the committee with information in its possession concerning subversive activities, which could not be used to prosecute; this was a one-sided victory for Dies as "it established him as a recognized force in the anti-subversive campaign, an authorized co-worker of J. Edgar Hoover."[122]

To counter the Dies Committee's attacks the administration used the FBI to argue that it was adequately prepared against fifth-column activities and that the FBI's surveillance was a responsible alternative to the Dies Committee's use of publicity and exposure. The idea was, according to Attorney General Robert Jackson, to "have a sufficiently zealous and vigorous staff engaged in law enforcement" in order to maintain the public's confidence and take the edge off vigilantes and demagogues like Dies, while at the same time protecting civil liberties.[123] Thus, the Justice Department opposed the use of the Smith Act to prosecute "subversive" individuals because of the vagueness of the term and instead called for the "steady surveillance over individuals

---

[120]Letter, Martin Dies to Hoover, June 17, 1938, 61-7582-3; Hoover, Memoranda for the Attorney General, June 11, 1938, 62-7582-2, and June 21, 1938, 61-7582-3, and October 12, 1938, 61-7582-29X, box 1, Series 3, FBI Records, MU; letters, Thurman Arnold to Dies, June 27, 1938; Dies to Roosevelt, August 24, 1938; Roosevelt to Dies, August 27, 1938 and October 1, 1938; K, Memorandum for General Watson, May 11, 1939, all in OF 320, FDRL; P. E. Foxworth, Memorandum for the Director, April 18, 1941, 61-7582-983X, box 2, Series 3, FBI Records, MU.

[121]Letter, Dies to Roosevelt, June 1, 1940, OF 1661-A, FDRL; telegram, Dies to Roosevelt, November 25, 1940, OF 320, ibid.; "A Program of Requirements and Considerations in Dealing with the Communists", att. to letter, Morris Ernest to Robert Jackson, November 28, 1940, box 89, Jackson Papers, LC; Goodman, 104-107.

[122]Ibid., 114; for the agreement, letters, Jerry Voorhis to Robert Jackson, and Jackson to Voorhis, December 10, 1940, box 89, Jackson Papers, LC; also, Dies to Jackson, December 3, 1940, ibid.; Dies to Roosevelt, December 4, 1940, OF 320, FDRL.

[123]Letter, Robert Jackson to Eleanor Roosevelt, April 29, 1941, box 89, Jackson Papers, LC.

and groups within the United States who are so sympathetic with the system or designs of foreign dictators as to make them a likely source of federal law violation."[124] During a meeting between Roosevelt and Dies at the White House on November 29, 1940, the president criticized the committee's practice of naming names and suggested that suspected subversives should be kept under "close surveillance" by the proper government agencies, thereby protecting both the national security and civil liberties.[125] Thus, as a result of the administration's defense the FBI's political surveillance was elevated to, in fact, a rational protection of civil liberties. Roosevelt expressed his support for the FBI's political investigations because they, in contrast to Dies, were conducted "without exciting undue alarm,"[126] and Jackson stressed that the FBI worked "in an efficient and workmanlike manner without alarmist tactics and without sensationalism."[127] In a deeper sense, it might be argued that the Roosevelt administration used the bureaucratic ideals of the Progressive Era, the notions of rationality, objectivity and efficiency, to legitimize the FBI's political activities.

At the same time the administration also used the FBI's resources to actively combat and discredit the Dies Committee after 1940. From July 1940, the FBI informed the Justice Department and the White House on Dies' activities and in February 1941 a number of field offices were instructed to monitor the committee's activities. At one point the FBI was asked to investigate rumors to the effect that Dies' father had been pro-German during the previous war and that the committee was infiltrated by Communists.[128] The FBI also used its extensive media contacts to influence the public opinion. For example, the field offices were instructed to give a Justice Department press

---

[124]*Senate Select Committee to Investigate Governmental Operations*, Book III, 411; similarly, Donner, *Age of Surveillance*, 61-64.

[125]Transcript, The President's Conference with Representative Martin Dies, Friday, November 29, 1940, OF 320, FDRL.

[126]Letter, Roosevelt to Dies, June 10, 1940, OF 1661-A, ibid.

[127]Department of Justice press release, November 23, 1940, 61-7582-525, box 1, Series 3, FBI Records, MU. This strategy helps to explain why a number of former liberal critics of the FBI began supporting it now; for example, the ACLU established close contacts with FBI officials and praised the FBI's regard for civil liberties (see letters, Hoover to Morris L. Ernest, November 6, 1941; Hoover to Roger G. Baldwin, November 24, 1941; Ernest to Miss Freda Kirchway, August 26, 1943, Morris Ernest folder, Nochols O/C (microfilm)).

[128]Letter, Hoover to General Watson, July 3, 1940, 61-7582-446; Hoover, Memorandum for the Attorney General, October 21, 1940, 61-7582-497, box 1, Series 3, FBI Records, MU; Hoover, Memorandum for the Attorney General, October 23, 1940, box 89, Jackson Papers, LC; Hoover, Memorandum for the Attorney General, December 18, 1940, 61-7582-864, box 2, Series 3, FBI Records, MU; S. S. Alden, Memorandum for Mr. Rosen, February 27, 1941, 61-7582-935, ibid.; Jackson, Memorandum for Mr. Hoover and Mr. Allen, November 29, 1941, 61-7582-819X, box 1, ibid.; Hoover, Memorandum for the Attorney General, December 4, 1940, 61-7582-885, box 2, ibid.; S. J. Tracy, Memorandum for the Director, November 28, 1940, 61-7582-673, box 1, ibid.

release, which criticized Dies, "to all friendly newspaper contacts in your district to insure that the release will receive the widest possible coverage."[129] A number of field offices arranged to have editorials favorable to the FBI placed in the newspapers.[130] Thus, the FBI's political role was increased and secured as a result of the Roosevelt administration's struggle with the Dies Committee.

In 1941, as part of the conservative campaign to dismantle the New Deal, Dies accused a number of New Deal agencies of being infiltrated by Communists, and he claimed, without any evidence, of being in possession of a list containing the names of 1,800 Communists working for the government.[131] Again the administration relied on the FBI as the rational alternative to take the wind out of Dies' sails. On June 28, 1941, Congress earmarked $100,000 of the FBI's appropriations to be used for the investigation of federal employees "who are members of subversive organizations or advocate the overthrow of the Federal Government" and to report its findings to Congress. As Attorney General Biddle informed Roosevelt, the step was taken by those opposing Dies with the intention that "if the investigation were competently done by the Federal Bureau of Investigation, it would make it more difficult for Dies to obtain another appropriation when the time came."[132]

Not surprisingly, Hoover supported a policy which would increase the FBI's political activities. He proposed that the FBI should be authorized to establish "a program of progressive intelligence," that "some arrangement" be established whereby the FBI could obtain information directly from the files of the Dies Committee, and that all federal loyalty investigations be centralized within the FBI.[133] Consequently, the FBI's responsibilities in the field of loyalty investigations were expanded significantly. All loyalty investigations were centralized within the FBI and the decision for initiating investigations was shifted from the department heads to the FBI. In addition, the FBI was given access to the Dies Committee's files, which consisted of 1 million

[129]Telegram, Hoover to all SACs, November 23, 1940, 61-7582-536, ibid.

[130]Letter, V. W. Peterson to Hoover, November 26, 1940, 61-7582-691, ibid.; for numerous letters from Hoover to editors see file 61-7582, ibid.

[131]Letter, Dies to Roosevelt, September 6, 1941, OF 263, FDRL; Goodman, 125-128, 131-134; for an early use of the non-existing list, James Rowe Jr., Memorandum for: Mr. Early, January 4, 1940, OF 320, FDRL. The FBI kept the administration informed about Dies' charges, Hoover, Memorandum for the Attorney General, February 28, 1941, box 89, Jackson Papers, LC; letter, Hoover to Watson, February 27, 1941, box 13, OF 10-B, FDRL.

[132]Biddle, Memorandum for the President, October 8, 1941, box 56, PSF, ibid.

[133]Hoover, Memorandum for the Attorney General, April 5, 1941, box 89, Jackson Papers, LC; Hoover, Memorandum for the Assistant to the Attorney General Mr. Matthew F. McGuire, May 31, 1941, box 93, ibid.

index cards and 135 file cabinets of confiscated radical literature and records, and the Justice Department established a list of subversive organizations, the membership of which was sufficient cause for opening an investigation; from an initial 9 organizations the list soon grew to 47 in 1942.[134]

The FBI had been charged by Congress to report on the results of its loyalty investigations and while the Bureau wanted to submit a detailed four volume report, the administration intended to use the opportunity to discredit Dies. According to Assistant to the Attorney General James Rowe, Jr., the small number of actual cases of disloyalty showed that the accusations were primarily politically motivated. He therefore suggested that the report should stress the administration's determination to "ruthlessly stamp out ... subversive activities wherever found" and "affirmatively attack the membership lists of the Dies Committee as being ridiculous...."[135] Thus, the report transmitted to the Congress by the Attorney General presented the FBI as the rational alternative to the Dies Committee, and it was pointed out that the Bureau had taken care "to not permit its instrumentalities to be used for any witch hunt or for arousing hysteria." The Bureau had shown "proper respect and consideration for the civil liberties," and it had conducted the investigation in an objective and professional manner with the sole aim of "accurately and impartially report available data and statements...."[136] Just as Palmer during the Red Scare had promoted the Bureau as the foremost expert in the anti-radical campaign due to its monopoly of information and its supposed objectivity and professionalism, the Roosevelt administration now attempted to take over the hunt for Communists in the government with the help of the responsible FBI.

---

[134]Biddle, Memorandum for the President, October 8, 1941, box 56, PSF, FDRL; US Congress, House, Committee on Appropriations, *Report of the Federal Bureau of Investigation. Letter from the Attorney General Transmitting a Report of the Federal Bureau of Investigation Made Pursuant to the Appropriation Act of June 28, 1941 (Public No. 135, 77th, Cong.)*, 77th. Cong., 2nd. Sess., Doc. No. 833 (Washington, DC, 1942), 2, 8-10, 12-13; letter, Ugo Carusi to Edwin M. Watson, October 7, 1941, OF 320, FDRL; L. B. Nichols, Memorandum for Mr. Tolson, October 14, 1941, Dies Committee folder, Nichols O/C (microfilm); letter, Dies to Biddle, October 17, 1941, 61-7582-1021, box 3, Series 3, FBI Records, MU; D. M. Ladd, Memorandum for the Director, October 22, 1941, 61-7582-1021, ibid.

[135]James Rowe Jr., Memorandum for the Attorney General. Report to the Congress on Subversive Activities, July 1, 1942, box 2, Biddle Papers, FDRL; for the FBI's wishes, see O'Reilly, "A New Deal for the FBI," 655.

[136]*Report of the Federal Bureau of Investigation*, 10-11. Not everybody applauded the "responsible" way the FBI had conducted the inquiry; Ickes noted in his diary that an employee under investigation would "be scared out of his wits if he had to go after hours and be quizzed by FBI agents," that he would be brought in "an uncomfortable position in the department" and that "people always could be found to cast reflections upon other under suspicion" (*The Secret Diary of Harold L. Ickes*, Vol. III, 637).

The report went on to present the Bureau's findings, according to which of the 4,600 government employees accused by Dies and others of belonging to subversive organizations, 2,581 had been investigated, and 2,095 cases completed with the result that only 36 had been dismissed and 13 had been the objects of disciplinary action. Consequently, the administration's Interdepartmental Committee in charge of loyalty investigations concluded that "the sweeping charges of disloyalty in the federal service have not been substantiated" and stressed that the majority of complaints were "clearly unfounded" and that "this is conspicuously true of the list submitted by Congressman Dies...."[137] While the Roosevelt administration's strategy of using the FBI to discredit Dies must eventually be judged a failure since the congressman continued with his attacks on the New Deal and the committee was given permanent status in 1945 as the House Un-American Activities Committee,[138] one consequence was the expansion of the political role of the FBI. In 1943, Roosevelt made the FBI's responsibility for conducting loyalty investigations of federal employees permanent.[139] Thus, the FBI's loyalty program was firmly established well before the Cold War and was more a product of a domestic political fight than of any genuine fear of foreign subversion.[140]

A "Suicide Squad" Against the Fifth Column

The third major reason for the Roosevelt administration's expansion of the political activities of the FBI was the growing concern within the administration during the late thirties about German espionage and sabotage activities in the US. It was well-known at the time that German agents were trying to influence the American public to oppose aid to Britain and France and were attempting to steal military secrets and sabotage military production, although historians later have characterized the efforts as "insubstantial."[141] Roosevelt's determination to stamp out these activities is indicated by his support of "quick

[137]*Report of the Federal Bureau of Investigation*, 3-5, 14-18, 26-28. The initial FBI appraisal of the information provided by Dies was that it was "without any value whatsoever" (D. M. Ladd, Memorandum for Mr. E. A. Tamm, November 12, 1941, 61-7582-1032, box 3, Series 3, FBI Records, MU).

[138]Goodman, 138-152, 167-169; letter, Harold L. Ickes to Roosevelt, June 3, 1943, OF 1661-A, FDRL.

[139]Biddle, Memorandum for the President, January 9, 1943, ibid.

[140]The irony was, of course, that while the issue of Communists-in-government was exploited for partisan purposes and innocent employees were hounded out of government service, some 350 real Soviet spies quietly infiltrated federal agencies and private institutions (Robert Louis Benson & Michael Warner, eds., *Venona. Soviet Espionage and the American Response 1939-1957* (Washington, DC, 1996), vii-xxxiii; John Earl Haynes & Harvey Klehr, *Venona. Decoding Soviet Espionage in America* (New Haven & London, 1999); Allen Weinstein & Alexander Vassiliev, *The Haunted Wood. Soviet Espionage in America – The Stalin Era* (New York, 1999)).

[141]Dallek, 226-227.

drumhead courts in wartime" against captured spies and by his regret that six Nazi saboteurs, who were executed in 1942, had not been hanged but electrocuted.[142] During 1938, FDR several times warned against the danger posed by foreign spies and called for an increased funding of the intelligence services.[143] On June 26, 1939, the president signed a secret presidential directive which specified that all investigations concerning "espionage, counter-espionage, and sabotage matters" should be conducted by the FBI, the MID and the ONI.[144] When the European war broke out in September, the White House issued a statement which declared that the FBI had been authorized "to take charge of investigative work in matters relating to espionage, sabotage, and violations of the neutrality regulations" and all law enforcement officers were requested to turn over any information on these as well as subversive activities.[145] At the same time, Roosevelt expressed the need for the expansion of the intelligence services in order to combat espionage and the spread of "subversive" propaganda. In a series of agreements between the FBI and the military intelligence services, the FBI was given prime responsibility for the investigation of "espionage, sabotage, counter-espionage, subversive activities and violations of the neutrality act" within the US.[146] The following expansion of the Bureau's counter-espionage resources, particularly its authority to use wiretapping and illegal methods, increased the FBI's potential for conducting surveillance of domestic political activities as well.

Since 1931, the Bureau had been authorized by the Justice Department to use wiretapping in cases "involving the safety of victims of kidnappers, the location and apprehension of desperate criminals, and in espionage and sabotage and other cases considered to be of major law enforcement importance." Despite the ban by the Federal Communication Act of 1934 against the interception and divulging of wire and radio communications, subsequently upheld by the Supreme Court, the Department had continued to allow wiretapping. Its rather

[142]Burns, *Roosevelt. The Soldier of Freedom*, 217, 255.

[143]*Complete Presidential Press Conferences of Franklin D. Roosevelt*, Vol. 11, 489-490; Vol. 12, 145-147, 289; Statement, German Spy Ring, n.d., box 55, PSF, FDRL; Homer S. Cummings, Memorandum, October 14, 1938, box 100, Cummings Papers, AL.

[144]Roosevelt, Confidential Memorandum for the Secretary of State et al, June 26, 1939, box 10, OF 10-B, FDRL; also, letter, Frank Murphy to Roosevelt, June 17, 1939, ibid.

[145]Samuel I. Rosenman (ed.), *The Public Papers and Addresses of Franklin D. Roosevelt*, Vol. 8: *1939. War – and Neutrality* (New York, 1941), 478-479; letter, Hoover to All Law Enforcement Officers, September 6, 1939, O/C 60, FBI/FOIA.

[146]Copies of the agreements can be found in Memorandum, May 15, 1941, att. to Hoover, Memorandum for the Attorney General, May 22, 1941; Confidential Memorandum, June 5, 1940, att. to Hoover, Memorandum for the Attorney General, June 11, 1940; Jackson, Memorandum for Mr. Hoover, June 22, 1940; Hoover, Memoranda for the Attorney General, February 5 and 10, March 12 and April 4, 1941, all in box 93, Jackson Papers, LC; see also, *Public Papers and Addresses of Franklin D. Roosevelt*, Vol. 8, 485-486.

far-fetched argument was that since the Court had only explicitly prohibited the interception *and* divulging, then "the interception of telephone or telegraph messages by telephone tap or otherwise is not in itself a violation...."[147] Clearly, the Justice Department was determined, despite the opinions of Congress and the Supreme Court, to have access to wiretapping. However, Attorney General Robert Jackson, who took office in early 1940, was apparently uncomfortable with the dubious legality of the decision and on March 15, 1940, he publicly prohibited all wiretapping by the FBI.[148]

It has been the topic of much speculation what made President Roosevelt rescind Jackson's order a few months later.[149] A recently discovered memorandum shows that the idea came from Hoover. On April 13, the FBI director complained to Jackson that the ban had made it "virtually impossible" to solve kidnapping and espionage cases and he pointed out that the Bureau's surveillance of "what appears definitely to be the real center of organized German espionage in the United States" had been "materially retarded." According to Hoover, the monitoring of the activities of a German official traveling in the US was likewise "most unsatisfactory and not particularly productive" without the aid of wiretapping. Hoover ended by stressing that the FBI was able to prevent sabotage only with the use of wiretaps, and he warned that the situation might result in "a national catastrophe" and the outbreak of "public indignation upon the Department because of its failure to prevent some serious occurrence."[150]

Faced with this grave warning, and already concerned about German activities, Roosevelt responded by addressing a confidential memorandum to the Attorney General. He noted that while wiretapping should not be conducted by federal agents "under ordinary and normal circumstances," he took it upon himself to interpret the Supreme Court's decision: "I am convinced that the Supreme Court never intended any dictum in the particular case which it decided to apply to grave matters involving the defense of the nation." He added that it was "too late to do anything about it after sabotage, assassinations

---

[147]The Justice Department opinion is reprinted in Theoharis (ed.), *From the Secret Files*, 133; for the 1931 authorization, Senate Select Committee to Study Governmental Operations, *Book III*, 277-278; for the internal Justice Department debate, letter, Cummings to Hoover, February 24, 1938, box 192, Cummings Papers, AL; Gordon Dean, Memorandum re Wiretapping, March 22, 1940, box 94, Jackson Papers, LC.

[148]Department of Justice Press Release, March 15, 1940, ibid.

[149]For example, Theoharis, *Spying on Americans*, 98; Theoharis & Cox, 198; Watters & Gillers, 290.

[150]Hoover, Memorandum for the Attorney General, April 13, 1940, box 94, Jackson Papers, LC. Hoover reportedly also took his complaints to the Secretary of the Treasury, Henry Morgenthau (Dallek, 225). The memorandum disproves Powers' assertion that Hoover "really did not care much about" the use of wiretapping (Powers, *Secrecy and Power*, 237).

and 'fifth column' activities are completed." Consequently, Roosevelt "authorized and directed" the Attorney General to approve the use of "listening devices direct to the conversation or other communications," although he stipulated that such methods should be kept "to a minimum" and limited to "persons suspected of subversive activities against the Government of the United States, including suspected spies" and "insofar as possible to aliens."[151] The authorization was a direct violation of the expressed wishes of Congress and the Supreme Court and a result of the administration's view of the presidency as the primary protector of the national security. As one internal Justice Department memorandum formulated the department's position, the president was not bound by the Supreme Court's ban against wiretapping since it was his duty as Commander-in-Chief to protect "the security of the nation."[152] Moreover, Roosevelt's vague formulation of "persons suspected of subversive activities ... including suspected spies" gave the FBI wide discretion and, in the words of Attorney General Biddle, "opened the door pretty wide to wiretapping of anyone *suspected* of *subversive activities*."[153]

The second expansion of FBI surveillance capabilities concerned the use of illegal activities. Normally, historians have assumed that the FBI's use of such techniques as mail openings, break-ins and burglaries, the so-called "black bag jobs," was done on its own initiative and without the knowledge of its political superiors. Thus, the FBI on the eve of World War II had become a truly autonomous secret police, acting outside the law.[154] However, the FBI's systematic use of illegal activities must be seen as a response to the administration's policies. For example, on May 20, 1940, Roosevelt asked Attorney General Jackson if there were "any law or executive order under which it would be possible for us to open and inspect outgoing ... or incoming mail to and from certain foreign nations" in connection with "'fifth column' activities – sabotage, anti-government propaganda, military secrets,

---

[151]Roosevelt, Memorandum for the Attorney General, May 21, 1940, box 94, Jackson Papers, LC.
[152]Charles Fahy, Memorandum for the Attorney General re: Wiretapping, October 6, 1941, att. to Francis Biddle, Memorandum for Mr. Hoover, October 9, 1941, O/C 129, FBI/FOIA.
[153]Biddle, 167.
[154]According to Theoharis & Cox, 201, "Hoover's genius in anticipating problems of external oversight prevented higher authorities from discovering his ambitious political agenda and use of illegal investigative activities." For the argument that the FBI's mail opening program between 1940-66 was never known to the Justice Department or the White House, Theoharis, *Spying on Americans*, 130; Donner, *Age of Surveillance*, 276; for the argument that "black bag jobs" were conducted on the FBI's own initiative, Theoharis, *Spying on Americans*, 125-127; Theoharis & Cox, 201-203; these accounts are primarily based on an internal FBI memo on "black bag jobs" from 1966, reprinted in *Senate Select Committee to Investigate Governmental Operations*, vol. 6, 357-359.

etc." Shortly after, apparently in response to Roosevelt's enquiry, the FBI began its mail opening program.[155]

Moreover, according to a collection of confidential Justice Department documents, the president apparently also authorized the use of "black bag jobs". During a conversation on April 26, 1941, between Hoover and Assistant Secretary of War J. J. McCloy concerning possible foreign influences behind labor disturbances in the war industry, Hoover noted that information concerning such foreign connections "could not be obtained through strict observance of the full ethics of all situations that might arise." He added that the FBI was restrained by the Justice Department against using such admittedly "unethical if not actually illegal" methods.[156] McCloy promised to take the matter up with higher authorities and two days later he informed a clearly startled Attorney General Jackson that Roosevelt had given a "green light" to the establishment of a so-called "suicide squad," consisting of FBI agents and authorized to operate "outside the law." It was supposed to use such methods as "wire tapping, in stealing of evidence, breaking in to obtain evidence, in conducting unlimited search and seizures, use of dictaphones, etc., etc." in the investigation of labor distubances.[157] Possibly, Roosevelt himself had come up with the idea when informed about the restrictions placed on the Bureau by the Justice Department; as McCloy later reminded Jackson, the plan was "a makeshift of very doubtful efficiacy" which "did not arise with us."[158]

However, the plan, which would have authorized the establishment of a predecessor to the "plumbers" of the Watergate era, came to naught because of strong opposition from Jackson, who feared it would lead to a return to the bad, old days under Palmer and constitute a political catastrophe for the administration if it were discovered. Hoover, too, objected to the idea of an independent "suicide squad" of agents outside his control.[159] It is likely that Roosevelt later authorized the FBI to use illegal methods. In May 1941, the secretaries of war and the navy again informed the president that there were strong indications that "strikes and slow-downs are in many cases

---

[155]Dallek, 225. That the administration was aware of the FBI program is indicated by a letter from Jackson to the Assistant Secretary of War, J. J. McCloy, in which he pointed out that he had "made every effort to broaden our power to do effective work concerning the interception of mail" (letter, Jackson to J. J. McCloy, May 16, 1941, box 94, Jackson Papers, LC).

[156]Hoover, Memorandum for the Attorney General, April 26, 1941, ibid.

[157]Jackson, Memorandum for the President, April 29, 1941, ibid.

[158]Letter, McCloy to Jackson, May 6, 1941, ibid.

[159]Jackson, Memorandum for the President, April 29, 1941, ibid.; Jackson, Memorandum for Under Secretary of War Patterson and Assistant Secretary of War McCloy, April 30, 1941, ibid.

instigated by Communists and other subversive elements acting in the interest of foreign enemies" and they recommended "a broadening of the investigative responsibility" of the FBI concerning "subversive control of labor."[160] On June 4, Roosevelt approved an expansion of the FBI's investigative responsibilities.[161] Possibly, it was in response to these initiatives that the Bureau began its use of illegal activities; in any case, such activity was in accordance with the president's thinking and, moreover, well-known to and sanctioned by the Justice Department.[162] Thus, the Roosevelt administration's response to the threat of foreign-directed espionage and sabotage led it to expand the intelligence functions of the FBI and to authorize the use of wiretapping, mail opening and "black bag jobs," which could then be employed by the Bureau against radicals and opponents of the administration as well.

It can be concluded that the single most important factor behind the continuation and expansion of the FBI's political activities after the Red Scare was that it was an integrated part of the political system. In particular, its political role was a function of the need of the modern presidency for political intelligence dealing with domestic unrest as well as foreign subversive threats. The Bureau's political power base might be said to have gradually shifted after 1921 from the Justice Department to the White House as it increasingly became directly connected to the president and was given more sensitive assignments. Fundamentally, however, the explanation for the continuation of the FBI's political role since 1924 must be found in the centralization of power in the modern presidency since the Progressive Era and the executive's need for political intelligence as well as the suppression and containment of domestic opposition and foreign threats.

---

[160]Letter, Henry L. Stimson and Frank Knox to Roosevelt, May 29, 1941, with att. memo, box 93, ibid.

[161]Roosevelt, Memorandum for the Secretary of War and the Secretary of the Navy, June 4, 1941, att. to Roosevelt, Memorandum for the Attorney General, June 4, 1941, OF 1661-A, FDRL; also, James Rowe, Memorandum for the President: Subversive Employees, June 26, 1941, box 56, PSF, ibid.

[162]At least one Justice Department official was informed about the results of FBI break-ins against radical organizations (Edward A. Tamm, Memorandum for the Director, May 31, 1941, Department of Justice folder, Nichols O/C (microfilm)), and in July 1944 Assistant Attorney General Alexander Holtzoff approved FBI break-ins in connection with the planting of bugging equipment as legal (Theoharis, *From the Secret Files*, 106).

Conclusion

The FBI and Political Surveillance:
From the Red Scare to the Cold War

The FBI's political surveillance began long before the establishment of the national security state during the Cold War, and the reasons for the Bureau's power must be found on a deeper level than in the machinations of its legendary director. The FBI's political role stretched back to World War I and the Red Scare and it did not originate because of a popular anticommunist hysteria or because it was out of control, as most historians have argued.

The Question About the Nature of the Communist Threat
Since the end of the Cold War, some of the archives of the American and Soviet intelligence agencies have been made available to historians. The Comintern archives have shown that the American Communists slavishly followed the directives from Moscow, that they from the very beginning to a large extent were financed by the Russians, and that the Communist Party maintained an underground apparatus for illegal activities.[1] The archives of the KGB and the National Security Agency have revealed that American Communists were recruited on a massive scale by the Soviets from the middle of the 1930s to infiltrate the government and the defense industry, influence the policy-making process, and provide information for Soviet intelligence services. Not a few of those who were persecuted during the McCarthy era were, in fact, Soviet spies.[2]

This has prompted some historians to reassess the activities of the anticommunists. Richard Gid Powers, for example, has argued that the American anticommunist movement was, on the whole, responsible, pluralistic and idealistic; it was, in short, "America at its best."[3] John Earl Haynes has likewise described how anticommunism, despite its

---

[1]Klehr, Haynes & Firsov, *The Secret World of American Communism*; Klehr, Haynes & Anderson, *The Soviet World of American Communism*.
[2]Benson & Warner, eds., *Venona. Soviet Espionage and the American Response 1939-1957*, vii-xxxiii; Haynes & Klehr, *Venona. Decoding Soviet Espionage in America* ; Weinstein & Vassiliev, *The Haunted Wood. Soviet Espionage in America – The Stalin Era*.
[3]Richard Gid Powers, *Not Without Honor. The History of American Anticommunism* (New York, 1995), especially 423-429; the quote is from p. 503.

occasional excesses, was "an understandable and rational response to a real danger to American democracy."[4] And Arthur Herman has argued that Senator Joseph McCarthy used the same methods as his liberal opponents and that he "was often more right than wrong" when he accused government officials of being Communists.[5] However, the present study has shown that at least as far as the FBI and the federal state were concerned the roots of their anticommunism went back long before the Soviet Union became a real threat to the security of the United States during the Cold War. During the inter-war period, the motives and reasons of federal officials had more to do with the emerging state's search for order and stability, a conservative ideology and bureaucratic interests, than with a realistic assessment of the Communist threat. This indicates that the motives of the anticommunists, including the FBI, during the Cold War were more complex than described by Powers, Haynes and Herman.

The FBI and the Federalization of Political Surveillance, 1919-43

The Bureau's supervision and regulation of political activities might be seen as a parallel to the increasing federal regulation of the economy during the Progressive Era, caused by the need to stabilize the emerging corporate order and protect it from wasteful and "irresponsible" competition and avoid organized popular opposition. In line with this general trend toward centralization and bureaucratization, local elites and authorities were increasingly unable to contain social unrest and radicalism. Consequently, a number of social and political control functions shifted gradually from such private and decentralized groups as business associations, patriotic societies and detective agencies to such centralized and bureaucratic state agencies as investigating committees, Red Squads and federal intelligence agencies. In response to the social problems caused by the industrialization, urbanization and immigration and the potential political threats to the existing order posed by the Socialist Party, the IWW and, in 1919, the Communist parties, industrial and political leaders began to look to the federal government, with its growing and powerful bureaucratic organizations, to monitor and control the political opposition. Thus, the Bureau's intervention against black radicalism, labor unrest and the Communist and anarchistic movements during the Red Scare was, at bottom, not an aberration from normal government policies, caused

---

[4]John Earl Haynes, *Red Scare or Red Menace? American Communism and Anticommunism During the Cold War* (Chicago, 1996), 200.
[5]Arthur Herman, *Joseph McCarthy. Reexamining the Life and Legacy of America's Most Hated Senator* (New York, 2000).

by a temporary public hysteria, but rather the logical consequence of decades of growing federal control and regulation. This was indicated by the imposition of federal segregation and suppression of black discontent, the breaking of strikes and the support of conservative labor against its radical opposition, and the organized Americanization of immigrants and the increasingly efficient process of expulsion of radical aliens. In short, the Bureau's political role during the Red Scare was the culmination of a wider process toward the federalization of social and political control, pushed by those in command of the new corporate order.

Federal officials had their own independent interests in an anti-radical crusade in 1919. President Wilson used scare tactics to gain support for the League of Nations, and some cabinet members genuinely feared the popularity of Bolshevism in the wake of the war and warned against its perils. The State Department used Communist activities in the US as an argument against the recognition of Soviet Russia. The federal intelligence services, especially the Bureau of Investigation and the MID, had expanded dramatically during the war and justified their large appropriations by calling attention to the radical threat.

The Bureau of Investigation played a larger and more aggressive role during the Red Scare than it has previously been believed. The Bureau used its network of patriotic organizations, local authorities, congressional committees, business interests and organized labor to collect information, spread anti-radical propaganda and act as the Bureau's operative arm on a local level. Thereby, it increased its influence beyond its own limited resources just as the federal government used the "associative state" to assist in the regulation of the economy. The Bureau sought repeatedly to create an anti-radical opinion and participated in the construction of the Red Scare during the first half of 1919. For example, the Bureau assisted the Overman Committee in portraying the Soviet regime as a menace to Western civilization and its sympathizers in America as being a threat to the nation's internal security. It also took advantage of the anarchist bomb attacks in May and June to warn against an imminent revolutionary attempt at overthrowing the government and to scare Congress into financing its anti-radical campaign. The Bureau's fundamental function was to contain and suppress threats to the existing social, economic and political order. The Bureau responded to the increasing black demands for equal rights since they threatened the racial hierarchy, and it responded to the labor unrest, especially the national steel and coal strikes, because they threatened the stability of the economy and the corporate order. By personifying these movements for social change and discrediting them as being caused by subversive elements, the Bureau drew attention away from a serious political debate on the reasons for the unrest and undermined attempts to introduce fundamental structural changes. The methods employed by the Bureau were visible and intimidating, something that was most dramatically shown by the Palmer raids, which were planned independently of the public opinion and carried out by an aggressive Bureau. The raids were used to destroy the anarchist and Communist movements in the US, intimidate radicals in general and create public support for the Justice Department's sedition bill, which would have increased the political power of the Bureau and the Justice Department significantly.

Following the Red Scare, the political role of the Bureau changed somewhat as it began to function as the domestic intelligence agency of the White House. Expanded significantly during the Progressive Era as head of the administrative state, the modern presidency had become the center of power in the political system and was expected to provide vigorous and effective leadership, to initiate debate and formulate solutions as well as preserve internal order and protect the national security from foreign threats. As such, the administrations from Harding to Roosevelt increasingly used the growing security resources of the FBI to be informed about, and in some cases to contain, social unrest, such as the strike wave in 1921-22 and the demonstrations in 1932. The FBI was also employed to investigate and in some cases to harass domestic critics, as during the embattled Hoover presidency and later when Roosevelt was attacked by the extreme right, isolationists and the Dies Committee. Finally, the Bureau's surveillance capabilities were expanded considerably in response to the activities of German agents and Communists during the period leading to World War II.

The growth of federal social control, combined with the short-term policies of the government and the ideological and bureaucratic interests of Justice Department and Bureau officials might be said to have constituted the driving force behind the institutionalizing of political surveillance. However, the Bureau did not operate in a vacuum and in particular three external factors aided the development of the Bureau's political role. The open shop campaign, which began in 1919-20 and continued well into the thirties, pushed by the business community and its conservative allies in the patriotic societies, the press and the states, used red-baiting to discredit organized labor and reform movements and cooperated closely with the Bureau. Congress did not interfere with the Bureau's activities, partly because it accepted political surveillance as long as it was used against marginal groups, and partly because, as a result of the centralization of power in the executive branch, it deferred to the president and the Attorney General. And, finally, the Republicans' efforts to use the radical issue to discredit both the Wilson and the Roosevelt administrations, while on occasions obstructing the administrations' activities, helped to legitimize anti-radical politics and place it on the national agenda.

FBI and the Second Red Scare

The First Red Scare was aborted primarily because the extent of the threat simply did not justify the repressive measures. Communism in 1919 did not pose a "clear and present danger" to America, and the accusations that Communists had instigated the labor unrest and the race riots were just not credible. This changed dramatically after 1945 as the Soviet Union increasingly seemed to pose a threat to American interests around the world. To American leaders, the Soviet domination of Eastern Europe, the Communst coup in Prague, the blocade against Berlin in 1948-49, the fall of China, the Soviet nuclear bomb in 1949 and the Korean War in 1950, all seemed ominous signs of Soviet expansionism.

More importantly, a number of sensational spy cases showed that the Communists posed a genuine threat to the internal security of the United States. In 1945, it was revealed that a small, scholarly journal, *Amerasia,* had obtained a mass of classified official documents on the military situation in Asia, though it was unclear if espionage was involved and none of the accused were ever convicted of any crime.[6] In 1948, Whittaker Chambers, a former Communist and Soviet courier, accused the former State Department official Alger Hiss of having spied for the Russians. Hiss denied the allegations but was convicted in 1950 for having perjured himself.[7] And, as a climax, in 1953, Ethel and Julius Rosenberg were executed for having revealed the secrets of the atomic bomb to the Soviets.[8]

We now know that the FBI, apart from its conservative ideology and bureaucratic interests, had additional reasons for its post-war anticommunist campaign. In 1948, the Bureau was informed that the Army Security Agency had partially broken 2,900 coded Soviet intelligence messages. In time, the messages, known as the Venona documents, showed that the Soviets had mounted an extensive espionage operation against the United States. Among the 349 spies mentioned in the

[6]Harvey Klehr and Ronald Radosh, *The Amerasia Spy Case. Prelude to McCarthyism* (Chapel Hill & London, 1996).
[7]Weinstein, *Perjury* ; Sam Tannenhaus, *Whittaker Chambers, A Biography* (New York, 1997).
[8]Radosh and Milton, *The Rosenberg File.*

material were such high-ranking government officials as Assistant Secretary of the Treasury Harry Dexter White and Special Assistant to President Roosevelt, Lauchlin Currie.[9] In the minds of FBI officials, this knowledge, which was not made public until 1995 in order not to reveal the methods of the intelligence services, justified their view that the Communist Party was a fifth column and spurred them on to destroy the party once and for all.

The FBI used two new weapons in its attack on the Communists, the loyalty program and the sedition act. In 1947, pressed by the Republicans, President Harry Truman established a loyalty program for all federal employees. The FBI dominated the administration of the program, and five years later it had conducted name checks on two million employees and 20,000 full-scale investigations. In 1948, the Bureau delivered a brief of 1,850 pages against the Communist Party to the Justice Department. The FBI argued in the brief, which basically was an updated edition of Hoover's briefs against the Communist parties in preparation for the Palmer raids, that the party advocated the violent overthrow of the government and, thus, violated the Smith Act of 1940. Having taken the initiative, collected the evidence and pressured the Justice Department, the FBI won the conviction of the national leadership of the Communist Party in 1949. In effect, the FBI had succeeded where Palmer had failed in 1920.

It is remarkable, however, the extent to which the FBI's structure, role and methods during the 1940s and 1950s were repetitions, although on a greater scale, of the Bureau's activities during the Red Scare. The FBI's influence was to a large extent based on its image as a professional, efficient and nonpartisan institution; these were all values of the Progressive Era that Palmer and Roosevelt had used to promote the Bureau. As it had done since the time of Harding, the Bureau continued to maintain close links to the White House and to provide sensitive political intelligence to the president. The FBI used its Crime Records Division to educate the public about the Communist menace, just as it had done in connection with the Palmer raids. The Bureau maintained its network, established during the Red Scare, consisting of local authorities, Red Squads, congressional committees, patriotic groups, the American Legion, the business community, and organized labor, and used it to gather information and distribute anticommunist propaganda. When the FBI established the Counterintelligence Program (COINTELPRO) with the aim of using intelli-

---

[9]Benson and Warner, eds., vii-xxxiii; Haynes & Klehr, *Venona* ; Weinstein & Vassiliev, *The Haunted Wood.*

gence to harass radicals, it was simply formalizing efforts that the field agents had been doing on an ad hoc basis since the Red Scare. The Bureau's automatic response to its critics during the Cold War was to investigate and discredit them, something it had done since the campaign against Louis Post and the critics of the Palmer raids. The basic pattern of the FBI's political role had been established and institutionalized during the first Red Scare.

In one important way did the Cold War era FBI differ from the Red Scare era BI. The Cold War, the Imperial Presidency and the prestige of the FBI all contributed to its growing autonomy. Hoover kept aspects of the Custodial Detention Program secret from his superiors, he was not always completely frank about the use of "black bag jobs," he used his files to blackmail politicians, and he fought with the Department of Justice about the prosecution of Communists. However, it must be emphasized that much about the political surveillance was known by Hoover's superiors, and that he was accorded so much freedom of action because it was believed by officials to be in the interest of the state.[10]

The FBI had grown in size and authority to such an extent that it was the single most important component of the McCarthy era. According to the most comprehensive account of the era, the FBI dominated the internal security debate and ran much of the machinery of repression; the Bureau was, in the words of Ellen Schrecker, the "bureaucratic heart" of McCarthyism.[11] As during the Red Scare, the Bureau's surveillance was not limited to Communists, but included civil rights advocates, radical unionists, pacifists, anti-Vietnam protesters, liberals, and so on. The extent of the FBI's reach is indicated by the number of investigative cases: From 1955 to 1978, the FBI ran 930,000 surveillance cases, between 1940 and 1970 it employed 37,000 informants, used 13,500 illegal buggings, conducted 7,500 illegal break-ins, and it ran 2,340 aggressive COINTELPRO operations between 1956 and 1971.[12]

---

[10]For the FBI in general during the Cold War, see for example, Powers, *Secrecy and Power*, 275-485; Theoharis & Cox, 230-485; Donner, *The Age of Surveillance*, 52-240; Theoharis, *Spying on Americans*; Theoharis, ed., *From the Secret Files of J. Edgar Hoover*; Whitehead, 265-320; Schrecker, *Many Are the Crimes*, 190-239; David Caute, *The Great Fear. The Anti-Communist Purge Under Truman and Eisenhower* (New York, 1978), 111-138; Nelson Blackstock, *COINTELPRO. The FBI's Secret War on Political Freedom* (New York (1975), 1976); O'Reilly, *Hoover and the Un-Americans*.

[11]Schrecker, 203.

[12]Donner, *The Age of Surveillance*, 127, 131, 137, 181; Theoharis & Cox, 10.

"The Most Dangerous Agency in the Country"

The FBI's political surveillance had become so institutionalized that it continued despite the death of Hoover in 1972, congressional hearings into the Bureau's illegal activities in 1975-76, and the winding down of the Cold War. In 1988, it was revealed that the FBI had been watching opponents of the Reagan administration's Latin America policy, peace groups and black militants.[13] Later revelations have raised the disturbing question whether Bureau officials, as Flynn, Garvan, Burns and Hoover did during the Red Scare, have deliberately exaggerated the threat of terrorism in order to increase the Bureau's appropriations, authority, and, ultimately, its control over the American people. A 1997 analysis of Justice Department records showed that the Bureau continued to use intrusive techniques to collect information. For example, in 1993, it conducted 300 break-ins, federal agents listened to 1.3 million conversations, and in 1996 the government obtained 839 warrants for taps, bugs and break-ins in national security investigations. The analysis described the FBI as "the most powerful and secretive agency in the United States today" and claimed that its political power was "greater than at any time in its eighty-nine-year history...."[14]

The internal security bureaucracy of today, with its inherent dangers to civil liberties and free speech, had its roots in the search for order and stability during the Progressive Era at the beginning of the century. When Attorney General Harlan Stone in 1924 banned the Bureau's political surveillance, he declared that "There is always the possibility that a secret police may become a menace to free government and free institutions because it carries with it the possibility of abuses of power which are not always quickly apprehended or understood."[15] In 1997, FBI Director Louis Freeh told Congress: "We are potentially the most dangerous agency in the country."[16]

---

[13]Sanford J. Ungar, "The F.B.I. on the Defensive Again," *The New York Times Magazine*, May 15, 1988, 46-47, 73-80.
[14]David Burnham, "The FBI," *The Nation*, August 11/18, 1997, 11-24.
[15]Lowenthal, 298.
[16]Burnham, 24.

Abbreviations

AL		Alderman Library, University of Virginia
CL		Clemson University Libraries, Clemson, South Carolina
FBI/FOIA		FOIA Reading Room, J. Edgar Hoover FBI Building, Washington, DC
FDRL		Franklin D. Roosevelt Library, Hyde Park, New York
	OF	President's Official File
	PPF	President's Personal File
	PSF	President's Secretary's File
HHL		Herbert Hoover Library, West Branch, Iowa
	PP	Presidential Papers
	CO	Cabinet Offices
	FA	Foreign Affairs, General Subjects & Countries
	INF	Individual Name File
	SecF	Secretary's File
	SF	Subject File
	TG	Taylor-Gates Collection
LC		Library of Congress, Manuscript Division, Washington, DC
MU		Marquette University Archives, Milwaukee, Wisconsin
NA		National Archives, Washington, DC
	RG65	Record Group 65, Records of the Federal Bureau of Investigation
	BS	Bureau Section Files
	JEH	J. Edgar Hoover Memoriabilia Collection
	Misc	Miscellaneous Files
	OG	Old German Files
UWL		University of Washington Libraries, Seattle, Washington

Bibliography

I. Unpublished material

1. FBI files

National Archives, Washington, DC
Record Group 65. Federal Bureau of Investigation
Investigative Case Files of the Bureau of Investigation, 1908-22
Jane Addams, 1919-20 (OG 382224)
African Blood Brotherhood/Cyril Briggs/*The Crusader* (OG185161/
208369/OG387162/BS202600-203/667/2031/1628/1728)
Brent Dow Allison/AFSC, 1921 (BS 202600-1383)
American Civil Liberties Union, 1920-21 (OG 303695/380868/ 383537/
BS202600-39/823/1768/51/108/144/39/22/33/391/ 49/
36/37/418/586/1290/1613/1628/1768/1775/2126)
American Defense Society, 1917-20 (OG 93248/208369/344415/
367403)
American Friends Services Committee, 1917 (OG 52661)
American Legion, 1919-21 (OG 21746/371688/BS 216034/202600-
9/33/1613/1693/1943/2334)
American Union Against Militarism/National Civil Liberties Bureau,
1917-21 (OG 382224/253184/285940/3666/183857/184123/ 158172/
206746/BS 202600-1689/9/823/1768)
Amnesty for Political Prisoners, 1918-20 (OG 180980)
Black Agitation, 1917-20 (OG 3057)
Black Press, 1917-1919 (OG 17011)
Black Press, 1919 (OG 3056)
Black Press, Nashville, Tenn., 1919 (OG 267600)
Boston Police Strike, 1919 (OG 372926)
Centralia Massacre, Nov. 11, 1919 (OG 376413)
The Chicago Defender, 1916-18 (Misc 9969/ OG 5911)
Chicago Riot, 1919 (OG 369914)
Coal Strike, 1919 (OG 303770)
Coal Strike, Scranton, Penn., 1920 (BS 205194-66)
Coal Strike, Mingo, W. Vir., 1921 (BS 205194-50)
Communist Party and Communist Labor Party Raids, Jan. 2, 1920 (OG
341761)
Consumers League, 1919 (OG 347188)
Criminal Syndicalist Laws, 1919-21 (OG 345429/BS 202-
600-2105)
W. E. B. Du Bois, 1918-21 (BS 198940-269/202600-667/1768/2260)
James Duncan/Seattle Central Labor Council, 1918-20 (OG339091)
Max Eastman/*The Masses,* 1917-20 (OG 9814)
Max Eastman/*The Liberator /The Revolutionary Age,* 1918-24 (OG
136944)
East St. Louis Riot, 1917 (OG 28469)
Elaine, Arkansas, Riot, 1919 (OG 373159)
Election Fraud, Southern Missouri, 1916 (Misc 8024)
The Fellowship of Reconciliation, 1917-20 (OG 29452)
Finances of Radicals, 1919-21 (BS 202600-1451/2126)

Emma Goldman/Alexander Berkman, 1916-20 (OG 15446)
The Great Migration/Fraudulent Voting, 1916 (Misc 10015)
Labor Conditions Northeast/Seattle General Strike, 1915-20 (OG 91928)
John L. Lewis/UMW, 1919-21 (OG 377229/BS 202600-113)
Lusk Committee, 1919-20 (OG 185161/147169/350625/208369/BS 212293-2)
The Nation, 1920 (OG 208369/368200/370279/384378/386663/BS 202600-33/591)
National Association for the Advancement of Colored People, 1917-21 (OG 185161/132476/258421/306451/309855/370678/198940/ 198900/ BS 213-410-2/202600-1689)
National Brotherhood Workers of America, 1919 (OG185161/ 370467)
National Civic Federation (OG 388447/BS 202600-33/51)
National Equal Rights League/Monroe Trotter, 1918-19 (OG 185161/258421/369936)
National Negro Press Association, 1920 (OG 384671)
National Security League, 1917-20 (OG 24621/208369)
The New Republic, 1918-20 (OG 182249)
The New York Call, 1917-20 (OG 27151)
Lee S. Overman, 1917-19 (OG 94701/108999/115940/ 175392/ 201641/363726)
Overman Committee, 1919 (OG 341494)
Race Agitation, Texas, 1919 (OG 369955)
Race Agitation, Dallas, Texas, 1919 (OG 382422)
Race Agitation, Houston, Texas, 1919 (OG 382476)
Radical Division, 1919-20 (OG 374217)
Radical Press, 1918-21 (OG 96282/359940/BS 202600-282)
Railroad Strike, 1920 (OG 370556)
A. Philip Randolph/Chandler Owens/*The Messenger,* 1919-21 (OG 258421/215915/265716/258694/369936/387162/387519/BS 202600-33/667/1628/1717/1754/2126)
John Reed, 1917-20 (OG 182787)
Reorganization, 1920 (OG 390982)
Sabotage Act 1918 (OG 175019)
Servant's Union/National Colored Soldiers Comfort Committee, 1917-18 (OG 369936)
"Silent Parade", 1917 (OG 67118)
Sisson Documents, 1921 (BS 202600-1998)
Steel Strike, 1919 (OG 352037)
Archibald Stevenson, 1921 (BS 202653-2)
Strikes, In General, 1919 (OG 290720)
Union of Russian Workers, 1919-21 (BS 202600-184)
Urban League, 1919-21 (OG 381410/BS 198940-164/202600-14)
Oswald Garrison Villard, 1918-21 (OG 82811/58778/180980/ 206399/ 33042/286634/353815/368200/BS 202600-33/36/282/ 823/1449/1453/1617/2126)
Washington, DC, Riot, 1919 (OG 369936)
Women's International League for Peace and Freedom, 1917-21 (OG 82811)
World War Veterans, 1929-21 (BS 207238)

Class 61 – Treason or Misprision of Treason, 1921-31
Alleged Radicals at Renton, Pa./Miners Strike, 1923 (61-4326)
American Birth Control League/Anna Inglis, 1922 (61-1095)

Bomb Explosions, June 2, 1919, 1922-24 (61-1003)
Communist Activities, Chicago, 1924-25 (61-1136)
Communist General Strike, May Day 1922 (61-1176)
Cooperative League of America, 1922-24 (61-1092)
CPUSA, 1921-22 (61-606)
CPUSA (Unified), Baltimore, 1922-23 (61-2571)
Criminal Syndicalism Law of Calif., 1923-25 (61-3741)
Max Eastman, 1922-26 (61-783)
"Elements of Political Education", 1927 (61-6201)
Federated Farmer-Labor Party, 1923-24 (61-4203)
Fellowship of Youth for Peace, 1926 (61-6013)
International Steel Workers of the World/Steel Strike/William Z. Foster
    (61-4080)
IWW Activities, Montana, 1922-27 (61-2388)
IWW Situation, Salt Lake City, 1921-23 (61-147)
IWW/Syndicalist Activities, Calif., 1923-24 (61-3675)
William Ross Knudsen/TUEL, 1922 (61-920)
Jacques Roberto Libario, 1919-23 (61-454)
National Association for the Advancement of Colored
    People, 1921 (61-308)
National Civic Federation, 1927 (61-6230)
National Council for the Prevention of War, 1923-26, 1934
    (61-3210/7338)
National Popular Government League, 1920-22 (61-1340)
Oil Industry/IWW Activity, Calif., 1922-24 (61-997)
Radical Propaganda in Churches, 1923 (61-4216)
Radical Propaganda Through Theaters, 1922 (61-792)
A. Philip Randolph/Executive Committee of 3rd. Int., 1929-31 (61-
    6657)
Riot, Sarasota, Fla., 1934 (61-7281)
Riot, Wabash, Ind., 1933 (61-7108)
Russian Federation of Workers Party of America, 1924 (61-5486)
Strike, Gastonia, North Carolina, 1929 (61-6626)
Strike, Indiana Harbor, Ind., 1933 (61-7189)
Strike, Jacksonville, Fla., 1935 (61-7376)
Strike, Lexington, Ky., 1933 (61-7190)
Strike, New York and New Jersey, 1928 (61-6521)
United Mine Workers, 1926-27 (61-6128)
United Mine Workers, 1933 (61-7212)
Workers Council of the US, 1921 (61-557)
Workers' Party of America, Seattle, 1923 (61-3275)
World War Veterans/Association of Disabled Veterans of the World War,
    1923-24 (61-3516)
World War Veterans/Jack Bradon, 1922-23 (61-1078)
World War Veterans/Edwin B. Neal, 1923 (61-4545)
World War Veterans/Edgar Owens, 1922-27 (61-1162)
World War Veterans Political Union, 1924 (61-5113)

Investigative Reports, box 1
  Mexican Matters, 1920 (61-01)
  Japanese Matters, 1920 (61-1X)
  Radical Matters, 1920 (61-01)

J. Edgar Hoover Memoriabilia Collection
  Scrapbooks, 1913-24

Freedom of Information and Privacy Act Reading Room, J. Edgar Hoover FBI Building, Washington, DC
  Jane Addams (61-1538)
  America First Committee (100-4712)
  W. E. B. Du Bois (100-99729)
  Warren G. Harding (62-7824)
  Adolph Hitler (65-53615)
  J. Edgar Hoover (67-561)
  J. Edgar Hoover Official and Confidential Files
  Huey Long (62-27030/28479/32509)
  Vito Marcantonio (100-28126)
  Moorish Science Temple (62-25889)
  National Association for the Advancement of Colored People (61-3176)
  National Negro Congress (61-6728)
  A. Philip Randolph (100-55616)
  Sacco and Vanzetti (61-126)

Marquette University Archive, Milwaukee, Wisconsin
FBI Records
  Series 3: Dies Committee/HUAC Investigative Files, 1938-75 (61-7582)
  Series 4: Burton K. Wheeler, 1924-33, 1937-60 (61-7903)
  Series 7: Women's International League for Peace and Freedom, 1922-78 (61-1538)
  Series 10: David J. Williams Papers
    American Civil Liberties Union, 1922-40 (61-190)
    Senator William Borah/World War Veterans, 1923-30 (61-3546/62-22968)
    Communist Labor Party, 1925-35 (61-1136/4390)
    CPUSA, 1923-36 (100-3)
    Information Volunteered from Outside Agencies, 1925-31 (61-190/714/6666/11933/62-4711/12299)
    International Labor Defense, 1932-43 (61-7347)
    Postal Department/Radical, 1932 (61-6965/62-27038)
    Trade Union Education League, 1921-45 (61-714)
    Trade Union Unity League (61-6128/6666/6723)
    Unemployed Citizens' League, 1932 (61-6699)
    United Mine Workers, 1924 (61-1241)
    United Textile Workers, 1934 (61-7313)
    Workers Ex-Service Men's League, 1931-35 (61-6723/62-27038)

2. Manuscript Collections

Herbert Hoover Presidential Library, West Branch, Iowa
  Herbert Hoover Presidential Papers
    Cabinet Offices
    Foreign Affairs, General Subjects
    Individual Name File
    Secretary's File
    Subject File
    Taylor-Gates Collection
  Federal Agency Records. FBI
    Hebert Hoover File, 1921-70
    Lawrence Richey File, 1930-58

Westbrook Pegler Papers
  Subject File
Lawrence Richey Papers

Franklin D. Roosevelt Library, Hyde Park, New York
  Franklin D. Roosevelt Presidential Papers
    President's Official Files
    President's Personal File
    President's Secretary's File
      Departmental File
      Confidential File
  Francis Biddle Papers
  Stephen T. Early Papers
  Harry Hopkins Papers
    Special Assistant to the President
    General Correspondance
  Henry A. Wallace Papers
    Vice Presidential Papers

Manuscript Division, Library of Congress, Washington, DC
  William E. Borah Papers
    General Office Correspondance
  Calvin Coolidge Papers
    Series 1: President's Executive Files
  Felix Frankfurter Papers
    General Correspondance
  Warren G. Harding Papers
    Series 4: Presidential Executive Files
  Harold L. Ickes Diaries
  Robert H. Jackson Papers
    Legal File
    General Correspondance
  Robert Lansing Papers
    Private Memoranda, 1919-20
    Desks Diaries, 1919
  George W. Norris Papers
  Louis F. Post Papers
    Correspondance, 1900-39
    Miscellaneous, 1864-1939
  Henry L. Stimson Diaries
  Harlan Fiske Stone Papers
    General Correspondance
    Miscellaneous
  Thomas J. Walsh Papers
    Legislative File, 1913-33

Special Collections/Manuscripts, Alderman Library, University of Virginia,
Charlottesville, Virginia
  Homer S. Cummings Papers
    Attorney General's Personal File
      Correspondance of the Attorney General
    Personal and Political Diary

374

Special Collections, Clemson University Libraries, Clemson, South Carolina
Robert A. Bowen Papers

Manuscript & University Archives Division, University of Washington Libraries, Seattle, Washington
Miles Poindexter Papers
Correspondance on Public Affairs, 1917-20

Historical Society of Pennsylvania, Philadelphia, Pennsylvania
William B. Wilson Papers
Correspondance 1919-20
Labor Department Series 19/24 and 16/60

Rare Books and Manuscripts Division, The New York Public Library, New York City
National Civic Federation Papers
General Correspondance

Special Collections, Guy W. Bailey/David W. Howe Library, University of Vermont, Burlington, Vermont
John G. Sargent Papers

3. Microfilm Releases

Kornweibel, Jr., Theodore (ed.), *Federal Surveillance of Afro-Americans (1917-1925): The First World War, the Red Scare, and the Garvey Movement.* University Publications of America, Frederick, Md., n.d.

Naison, Mark (ed.), *Department of Justice Investigative Files. Part II: The Communist Party.* University Publications of America, Frederick, Md., 1989.

Theoharis, Athan (ed.), *Federal Bureau of Investigation. Confidential Files. FBI Wiretaps, Bugs, and Break-ins: The National Security Electronic Surveillance Card File and the Surreptitious Entries File.* University Publications of America, Frederick, Md., 1988.

Theoharis, Athan (ed.), *Federal Bureau of Investigation Confidential Files. The "Do Not File" File.* University Publications of America, Frederick, Md., 1989.

Theoharis, Athan (ed.), *Federal Bureau of Investigation Confidential Files. The Louis Nichols Official and Confidential File and the Clyde Tolson Personal File.* University Publications of America, Frederick, Md., 1990.

US Military Intelligence Reports: Surveillance of Radicals in the United States, 1917-41. University Publications of America, Frederick, Md., 1984.

II. Published Material

1. Government publications

New York State Legislature, Joint Legislative Committee Investigating Seditious Activities, *Revolutionary Radicalism. Its History, Purpose and Tactics with an Exposition and Discussion of the Steps Being Taken and Required to Curb It Being the Report of the Joint Legislative Committee Investigating*

Seditious Activities, Filed April 24, 1920, in the Senate of the State of New York, Vols. 1-4. Albany, N.Y., 1920.

US Bureau of the Census, Department of Commerce, *Historical Statistics of the United States, From Colonial Times to the Present,* Parts 1-2. Washington, DC, 1975.

US Committee on Public Information, *The German-Bolshevik Conspiracy.* Washington, DC, 1918.

US Congress, House, Committee on Appropriations, *Report of the Federal Bureau of Investigations. Letter From the Attorney General Transmitting a Report of the Federal Bureau of Investigation Made Pursuant to the Appropriation Act of June 28, 1941 (Public No. 135, 77th. Cong.),* 77th. Cong., 2nd. Sess., Doc. No. 833. Washington, DC, 1942.

US Congress, House, Committee on the Judiciary, *Reply by the Attorney General of the United States Hon. Harry M. Daugherty to Charges Filed with the Committee on the Judiciary of the House of Representatives, December 1, 1922, by Hon. Oscar E. Keller, Rep. from Minnesota.* Washington, DC, 1922.

US Congress, House, Committee on Rules, *Attorney General Palmer on Charges Made Against the Department of Justice by Louis F. Post and Others. Hearings,* 66th. Cong., 2nd. Sess., Parts 1-3. Washington, DC, 1920.

—, *Investigation of Administration of Louis F. Post, Assistant Secretarty of Labor, in the Matter of Deportation of Aliens. Hearings,* 66th. Cong., 2nd. Sess. Washington, DC, 1920.

US Congress, House, Special Committee to Investigate Communist Activities in the United States, *Investigation of Communist Propaganda. Hearings,* 71st. Cong., 2nd. Sess., Pt. 1. Washington, DC, 1930.

—, *Investigation of Communist Propaganda. Report,* 71st. Cong., 3rd. Sess. Washington, DC, 1931.

US Congress, House, Subcommittee of Committee on Appropriations, *Appropriations, Department of Justice, 1923. Hearings,* Pt.2, 67th. Cong., 2nd. Sess. Washington, DC, 1922.

—, *Appropriations, Department of Justice, 1924. Hearings,* Pt. 2, 67th. Cong., 4th. Sess. Washington, DC, 1922.

—, *Appropriations, Department of Justice, 1925. Hearings,* 68th. Cong, 1st. Sess. Washington, DC, 1924.

—, *Appropriations, Department of Justice, 1926. Hearings,* 68th. Cong., 2nd. Sess. Washington, DC, 1925.

—, *Department of Justice Appropriation Bill for 1940. Hearings,* 76th. Cong., 1st. Sess. Washington, DC, 1939.

—, *First Deficiency Appropriation Bill Fiscal Year 1920. Hearings,* 66th. Cong., 1st. Sess. Washington, DC, 1919.

—, *Sundry Civil Appropriation Bill, 1921. Hearings,* Pt. 2, 66th. Cong., 2nd. Sess. Washington, DC, 1920.

—, *Sundry Civil Appropriation Bill, 1922. Hearings,* Pt. 2, 66th. Cong., 3rd. Sess. Washington, DC, 1920.

—, *Sundry Civil Bill, 1919. Hearings,* Pt. 2, 65th. Cong., 2nd. Sess. Washington, DC, 1918.

—, *Sundry Civil Bill, 1920. Second Hearing,* 66th. Cong., 1st. Sess. Washington, DC, 1919.

US Congress, Senate, Select Committee on Investigation of the Attorney General, *Investigation of Hon. Harry M. Daugherty Formerly Attorney General of the United States. Hearings Pursuant to S. Res. 157, Directing a Committee to Investigate the Failure of the Attorney General to Prosecute or Defend Certain Criminal and Civil Actions, Wherein the Government is Interested,* 66th. Cong., 1st. Sess., Vols. I-III. Washington, DC, 1924.

US Congress, Senate, Select Committee to Study Governmental Operations with Respect to Intelligence Activities, *Hearings*. Vol. 6. *Federal Bureau of Investigation*, 94th. Cong., 1st. Sess. Washington, DC, 1976.

—, *Supplementary Detailed Staff Reports on Intelligence Activities and the Rights of Americans*. Book III. *Final Report*, 94th. Cong., 2nd. Sess. Washington, DC, 1976.

—, *Supplementary Reports on Intelligence Activities*. Book VI. *Final Report*, 94th. Cong., 2nd. Sess. Washington, DC, 1976.

US Congress, Senate, Special Committee on Charges Against Senator Burton K. Wheeler, *Report. May 14, 1924*. Washington, DC, 1924.

US Congress, Senate, Subcommittee of the Committee on Appropriations, *General Deficiency Bill, 1917. Hearings*, 65th. Cong., 1st. Sess. Washington, DC, 1917.

—, *Sundry Civil Appropriation Bill, 1920. Hearings*, 66th. Cong., 1st. Sess. Washington, DC, 1919.

US Congress, Senate, Subcommittee of the Committee on Foreign Relations, *Recognition of Russia. Hearings. Letter From the Secretary of State Transmitting Information Relative to Propaganda Carried on in the United States, Directed From Russia*, Pt. 2, 68th. Cong., 1st. Sess. Washington, DC, 1924.

US Congress, Senate, Subcommittee of the Committee on the Judiciary, *Charges of Illegal Practices of the Department of Justice. Hearings on "Report upon the Illegal Practices of the United States Department of Justice", Made by a Committee of Lawyers on Behalf of the National Popular Government League, and a Memorandum Describing the Personnel of the Committee. Referred "for such Action as the Committee on the Judiciary May Care to Take with Reference to the Same." January 19 to March 3, 1921*, 66th. Cong., 3rd. Sess. Washington, DC, 1921.

US Congress, Senate, Subcommittee on the Judiciary, *Brewing and Liquor Interests and German and Bolshevik Propaganda. Report and Hearings Submitted Pursuant to S. Res. 307 and 439, Relating to Charges Msde Against the United States Brewers' Association and Allied Interests*, 66th. Cong., 1st. Sess. Washington, DC, 1919.

US Department of Justice, *Annual Reports of the Attorney General of the United States, 1917-1941*. Washington, DC, 1917-41.

—, *Bureau of Investigation. A Booklet Concerning the Work of the Bureau of Investigation. Published for the Information of Law Enforcement Officials and Agencies*. Washington, DC, 1930.

—, *Investigation Activities of the Department of Justice. Letter From the Attorney General Transmitting in Response to a Senate Resolution of October 17, 1919, a Report on the Activities of the Bureau of Investigation of the Department of Justice Against Persons Advising Anarchy, Sedition, and the Forcible Overthrow of the Government. November 17, 1919. Senate Doc. No. 153*, 66th. Cong., 1st. Sess. Washington, DC, 1919.

US Department of State, *Papers Relating to the Foreign Relations of the United States. 1918. Russia*, Vol. I. Washington, DC, 1931.

—,—*1919. Russia*. Washington, DC, 1937.

—,—*1920*, Vol. II. Washington, DC, 1936.

—,—*Lansing Papers 1914-1920*, Vol. II. Washington, DC, 1940.

US Federal Bureau of Investigation, *Abridged History of the Federal Bureau of Investigation*. Washington, DC, n.d. (1991).

—, *Significant Dates in FBI History, 1789-1936*. Washington, DC, n.d.

—, *Significant Dates in FBI History (Abridged)*. Washington, DC, n.d. (1991).

2. Private reports

American Civil Liberties Union, *Thumbs Down! The Fingerprint Menace to Civil Liberties*. New York, 1938.

Civil Rights Federation, *FBI Detroit. The Facts Concerning the FBI Raids in Detroit*. Detroit, Michigan, 1940.

Federal Council of the Churches of Christ in America, The Department of Research and Education, et al, *The Centralia Case. A Joint Report on the Armistice Day Tragedy at Centralia, November 11, 1919*. New York, Washington, DC & Baltimore, October 1930.

National Civil Liberties Bureau, *The Truth about the I.W.W. Facts in relation to the trial at Chicago by competent industrialist investigators and noted economists*. New York, April 1918.

National Popular Government League, *To the American People. Report Upon the Illegal Practices of the United States Department of Justice*. Washington, DC, 1920.

3. Published Sources

Coben, Stanley (ed.), *Reform, War, and Reaction: 1912-1932*. New York, 1972.

Complete Presidential Press Conferences of Franklin D. Roosevelt, Vols. 1-25. New York, 1972.

Cronon, E. David (ed.), *The Cabinet Diaries of Josephus Daniels 1913-1921*. Lincoln, Nebraska, 1963.

Davis, David Brion (ed.), *The Fear of Conspiracy. Images of Un-American Subversion From the Revolution to the Present*. Ithaca, N.Y., 1971.

Hall, Kermit, L. (ed.), *Major Problems in American Constitutional History. Volume II: From 1870 to the Present*. Lexington, Mass., & Toronto, 1992.

Hill, Robert A. (ed.), *The Marcus Garvey and Universal Negro Improvement Papers*, Vols. I-V. Berkeley, Ca., 1983-86.

Ickes, Harold L., *The Secret Diary of Harold L. Ickes*, Vols. II-III. New York, 1954.

Lane, Anne Wintermute and Louise Herrick Lane (eds.), *The Letters of Franklin Lane. Personal and Political*. Boston, 1922.

Lilienthal, David E., *The Journals of David E. Lilienthal*, Vol. I. New York, 1964.

Link, Arthur S. (ed.), *The Papers of Woodrow Wilson*, Vols. 1-69. Princeton, N.J., 1966-94.

Rosenman, Samuel I. (ed.), *Public Papers and Addresses of Franklin D. Roosevelt*, Vols. 1-8. New York, 1938-41.

Theoharis, Athan (ed.), *From the Secret Files of J. Edgar Hoover*. Chicago, 1991.

4. Books

Allen, Howard, W., *Poindexter of Washington. A Study in Progressive Politics*. Carbondale and Edwardsville, Ill., 1981.

Auerbach, Jerold, *Unequal Justice*. New York, 1976.

Avrich, Paul, *Sacco and Vanzetti. The Anarchist Background*. Princeton, N.J., 1991.

Belknap, Michal R., *Cold War Political Justice. The Smith Act, the Communist Party, and the American Civil Liberties*. Westport, Conn., 1977.

Bell, Daniel, ed., *The Radical Right*. New York (1955), 1979.

Bennett, David H., *The Party of Fear. The American Far Right from Nativism to the Militia Movement.* New York (1988), 1995.

Benson, Robert Louis & Michael Warner, eds., *Venona. Soviet Espionage and the American Response 1939-1957.* Washington, DC, 1996.

Bernstein, Irving, *The Lean Years. A History of the American Worker 1920-1933.* Boston, 1960.

Biddle, Francis, *In Brief Authority.* New York, 1962.

Blackstock, Nelson, *COINTELPRO. The FBI's Secret War on Political Freedom.* New York (1975), 1976.

Brinkley, Alan, *Voices of Protest. Huey Long, Father Coughlin and the Great Depression.* New York (1981), 1982.

Brody, David, *Labor in Crisis. The Steel Strike of 1919.* Philadelphia and New York, 1965.

—, *Workers in Industrial America. Essays on the 20th. Century Struggle.* New York, 1980.

Buitrago, Ann Mari and Leon Andrew Immerman, *Are You Now or Have You Ever Been in the FBI Files?* New York, 1981.

Burner, David, *Herbert Hoover. A Public Life.* New York, 1979.

Burns, James MacGregor, *Roosevelt: The Lion and the Fox.* London, 1956.

—, *Roosevelt: Soldier of Freedom.* New York, 1970.

Caro, Robert, *The Years of Lyndon Johnson. The Path to Power.* New York (1982), 1983.

Carroll, Peter N. and David W. Noble, *The Free and the Unfree. A New History of the United States. 2nd. ed.* New York (1977), 1988.

Caute, David, *The Great Fear. The Anti-Communist Purge Under Truman and Eisenhower.* New York, 1978.

Chafee, Zechariah, Jr., *Free Speech in the United States.* New York (1941), 1969.

Chamberlain, Lawrence H., *Loyalty and Legislative Action. A Survey of Activity by the New York State Legislature 1919-1949.* Ithaca, N.Y., 1951.

Cline, Majorie W., Carla E. Christensen and Judith M. Fontaine (eds.), *Scholar's Guide to Intelligence Litterature: Bibliography of the Russell J. Bowen Collection in the Joseph M. Lauinger Memorial Library, Georgetown University.* Frederick, Md., 1983.

Coben, Stanley, *A. Mitchell Palmer: Politician.* New York, 1963.

Cole, Wayne S., *Roosevelt and the Isolationists, 1932-45.* Lincoln, Nebraska, 1983.

Cook, Fred, *The FBI Nobody Knows.* New York, 1964.

Cooper, John Milton, Jr., *Pivotal Decades. The United States 1900-1920.* New York & London, 1990.

Cooper, Wayne F., *Claude McKay. Rebel Sojourner in the Harlem Renaissance.* Baton Rouge, La., 1987.

Copeland, Tom, *The Centralia Tragedy of 1919. Elmer Smith and the Wobblies.* Seattle & London, 1993.

Dallek, Robert, *Franklin D. Roosevelt and American Foreign Policy, 1932-45.* New York, 1979.

Davis, Daniel S., *Mr. Black Labor. The Story of A. Philip Randolph, Father of the Civil Rights Movement.* New York, 1972.

Davis, Kenneth S., *FDR: The Beckoning of Destiny, 1882-1928. A History.* New York (1972), 1975.

de Toledano, Ralph, *J. Edgar Hoover. The Man in His Time.* New York (1973), 1974.

Dictionary of American Biography: Supplement 4. New York, 1974.

Donner, Frank J., *The Age of Surveillance. The Aims and Methods of America's Political Intelligence System.* New York, 1980.

—, *Protectors of Privilege. Red Squads and Police Repression in Urban America.* Berkeley, Ca., 1990.

Dowell, Eldridge Foster, *A History of Criminal Syndicalism Legislation in the United States.* Baltimore, 1939.

Draper, Theodore, *The Roots of American Communism.* New York, 1957.

Dubofsky, Melvyn, *We Shall Be All. A History of the Industrial Workers of the World.* Chicago, 1969.

— and Warren van Tine, *John L. Lewis. A Biography.* New York, 1977.

Dulles, Foster Rhea, *The Road to Teheran. The Story of Russia and America, 1781-1943.* New York, 1944.

Edwards, John Carver, *Patriots in Pinstripe. Men of the National Security League.* Washington, DC, 1982.

Ekirch, Jr., Arthur A., *Progressivism in America. A Study of the Era from Theodore Roosevelt to Woodrow Wilson.* New York, 1974.

Etzioni-Halevy, Eva, *Bureaucracy and Democracy. A Political Dilemma.* London (1983), 1985.

la Feber, Walter and Richard Polenberg, *The American Century. A History of the United States Since the 1890s.* New York, 1975.

Fogelsong, David S., *America's Secret War Against Bolshevism. U.S. Intervention in the Russian Civil War, 1917-1920.* Chapel Hill & London, 1995.

Fried, Richard M., *Nightmare in Red. The McCarthy Era in Perspective.* New York, 1990.

Friedheim, Robert L., *The Seattle General Strike.* Seattle, 1964.

Gaddis, John Lewis, *Russia, the Soviet Union and the United States. An Interpretive History.* 2nd. ed. New York (1978), 1990.

Garrow, David J., *The FBI and Martin Luther King, Jr. From "Solo" to Memphis.* New York, 1981.

Gentry, Curt, *J. Edgar Hoover. The Man and the Secrets.* New York, 1991.

Goldman, Emma, *Living My Life,* Vols. I-II. New York (1931), 1970.

Goldstein, Robert J., *Political Repression in Modern America. From 1870 to the Present.* Cambridge/New York, 1978.

Goodman, Walter, *The Committee. The Extraordinary Career of the House Committee on Un-American Activities.* New York, 1968.

Green, Marguerite, *The National Civic Federation and the American Labor Movement 1900-1925.* Washington, DC, 1956.

Griffith, Robert, *The Politics of Fear: Joseph R. McCarthy and the Senate.* Lexington, Ky., 1970.

— and Athan Theoharis, eds., *The Specter. Original Essays on the Cold War and the Origins of McCarthyism.* New York, 1974.

Grubbs, Frank L., Jr., *The Struggle for Labor Loyalty: Gompers, the A. F. of L., and the Pacisists, 1917-1920.* Durham, N.C., 1968.

Haber, Samuel, *Efficiency and Uplift. Scientific Management in the Progressive Era 1890-1920.* Chicago, 1964.

Haines, Gerald K. and David A. Langbart, *Unlocking the Files of the FBI. A Guide to Its Records and Classification System.* Wilmington, Delaware, 1993.

Hair, William Ivy, *The Kingfish and His Realm. The Life and Times of Huey P. Long.* Baton Rouge, La., 1991.

Halberstam, David, *The Powers That Be.* New York, 1979.

Halperin, Morton, *The Lawless State. The Crimes of the US Intelligence Agencies.* New York, 1976.

Hapgood, Norman, ed., *Professional Patriots. An Exposure of the Personalities, Methods and Objectives Involved in the Organized Effort to Exploit Patriotic Impulses in These United States During and After the Late War.* New York, 1927.

Haynes, John Earl, *Red Scare or Red Menace? American Communism and Anticommunism in the Cold War Era*. Chicago, 1996.

- & Harvey Klehr, *Venona. Decoding Soviet Espionage in America*. New Haven & London, 1999.

Hays, Samuel P., *American Political History as Social Analysis. Essays by Samuel P. Hays*. Knoxville, Tenn., 1980.

Heale, M.J., *American Anticommunism. Combatting the Enemy Within, 1830-1970*. Baltimore, 1990.

Herman, Arthur, *Joseph McCarthy. Reexamining the Life and Legacy of America's Most Hated Senator*. New York, 2000.

Hicks, John D., *Republican Ascendancy 1921-1933*. New York (1960), 1963.

Higham, John, *Strangers in the Land. Patterns of American Nativism, 1860-1925*. New Brunswick, N.J., 1955.

Hoff-Wilson, Joan, *Herbert Hoover. Forgotten Progressive*. Boston, 1975.

—, *Ideology and Economics. U.S. Relations with the Soviet Union, 1918-1933*. Columbia, Missouri, 1974.

Hofstadter, Richard, *The Paranoid Style in American Politics and Other Essays*. Chicago (1965), 1979.

Hoover, Herbert, *The Memoirs of Herbert Hoover. The Great Depression*. New York, 1952.

Hoover, J. Edgar, *Masters of Deceit. The Story of Communism in America and How to Fight It*. New York, 1958.

—, *A Study of Communism*. New York, 1962.

Howe, Frederic C., *The Confessions of a Reformer*. New York (1925), 1967.

Hunt, William J., *Front-Page Detective: William J. Burns and the Detective Profession 1880-1930*. Bowling Green, Ohio, 1990.

Jaffe, Julian F., *Crusade Against Radicalism. New York During the Red Scare, 1914-1924*. Port Washington, N.Y., 1972.

Jensen, Joan, *Army Surveillance in America, 1775-1980*. New Haven, 1991.

—, *The Price of Vigilance*. Chicago, 1968.

Johanningsmeier, Edward P., *Forging American Communism. The Life of William Z. Foster*. Princeton, N.J., 1994.

Karl, Barry Dean, *Executive Reorganization and Reform in the New Deal. The Genesis of Administrative Management, 1900-1939*. Cambridge, Mass., 1963.

Keller, William W., *The Liberals and J. Edgar Hoover. Rise and Fall of a Domestic Intelligence State*. Princeton, N.J., 1989.

Kellogg, Charles Flint, *NAACP. A History of the National Association for the Advancement of Colored People*, Vol. I. Baltimore (1967), 1968.

Kennan, George F., *Soviet-American Relations, 1917-1920*, Vols. I-II. London, 1956.

Kessler, Ronald, *The FBI*. New York (1993), 1994.

Klehr, Harvey, John Earl Haynes & Fridrikh Igorevich Firsov, *The Secret World of American Communism*. New Haven & London, 1995.

—, John Earl Haynes & Kyrill M. Anderson, *The Soviet World of American Communism*. New Haven & London, 1998.

— & Ronald Radosh, *The Amerasia Spy Case. A Prelude to McCarthyism*. Chapel Hill & London, 1996.

Knock, Thomas J, *To End All Wars. Woodrow Wilson and the Quest for a New World Order*. New York, 1992.

Kolko, Gabriel, *Main Currents in Modern History*. New York, 1976.

Kornweibel, Theodore, Jr., *No Crystal Stair. Black Life and the Messenger, 1917-1928*. Westport, Conn., 1975.

—, *"Seeing Red." Federal Campaigns Against Black Militancy, 1919-1925*. Bloomington & Indianapolis, 1998.

Larson, Simeon, *Labor and Foreign Policy. Gompers, the AFL, and the First World War, 1914-1918*. Rutherford & London, 1975.

Latham, Earl, *The Communist Controversy in Washington. From the New Deal to McCarthyism*. Cambridge, Mass., 1966.

Leuchtenburg, William E., *Franklin D. Roosevelt and the New Deal 1932-1940*. New York, 1963.

—, *The Perils of Prosperity 1914-32*. Chicago, 1958.

Levin, Murray B., *Political Hysteria in America. The Democratic Capacity for Repression*. New York, 1971.

Lewis, Eugene, *Public Entrepreneurship. Toward a Theory of Bureaucratic Political Power. The Organizational Lives of Hyman Rickover, J. Edgar Hoover, and Robert Moses*. Bloomington, 1980.

Lloyd, Craig, *Aggressive Introvert. A Study of Herbert Hoover and Public Relations Management 1912-1932*. Columbus, Ohio, 1972.

Link, Arthur S., *Woodrow Wilson and the Progressive Era, 1910-1917*. New York (1954), 1963.

Lipset, Seymour M. and Earl Raab, *The Politics of Unreason. Right-wing Extremism in America, 1790-1970*. London (1970), 1971.

Lisio, Donald, J., *The President and Protest. Hoover, Conspiracy, and the Bonus Riot*. Columbia, Missouri, 1974.

Logan, Rayford W., *The Betrayal of the Negro, From Rutherford B. Hayes to Woodrow Wilson*. New York, 1965.

Lowenthal, Max, *The Federal Bureau of Investigation*. New York, 1950.

Manchester, William, *The Glory and the Dream. A Narrative History of America 1932-72*. New York, 1973.

Marx, Gary, *Undercover. Police Surveillance in America*. Berkeley, Ca., 1990.

Mason, Alpheus Thomas, *Harlan Fiske Stone. Pillar of the Law*. New York, 1956.

McClelland, John M., Jr., *Wobbly War. The Centralia Story*. Tacoma, Washington, 1987.

McCormick, Charles H., *Seeing Reds. Federal Surveillance of Radicals in the Pittsburgh Mill District, 1917-1921*. Pittsburgh, 1997.

McCoy, Donald R., *Calvin Coolidge. The Quiet President*. New York, 1967.

McKay, David, *Politics and Power in the USA*. Harmondsworth, 1987.

Metz, Harold W., *Labor Policy of the Federal Government*. Washington, DC, 1945.

Montgomery, David, *Workers' Control in America*. Cambridge, 1979.

Morgan, Ted, *FDR. A Biography*. London (1985), 1986.

Morn, Frank, *"The Eye That Never Sleeps". A History of the Pinkerton National Detective Agency*. Bloomington, 1982.

Morton, Marian J., *"Nowhere at Home". Emma Goldman and the American Left*. New York, 1992.

Murphy, Paul L., *The Constitution in Crisis Times 1918-1969*. New York, 1972.

—, *World War I and the Origin of Civil Liberties*. New York, 1979.

Murray, Robert K., *The Harding Era. Warren G. Harding and His Administration*. Minneapolis, Minnesota, 1969.

—, *Red Scare. A Study of National Hysteria, 1919-1920*. New York (1955), 1964.

Myers, William Starr and Walter H. Newton, *The Hoover Administration. A Documented Narrative*. New York, 1936.

Nash, Lee, ed., *Understanding Herbert Hoover: Ten Perspectives*. Stanford, Ca., 1987.

The New York Times Index 1919. New York, 1920.

Noggle, Burl, *Teapot Dome. Oil and Politics in the 1920's*. New York (1962), 1965.

O'Reilly, Kenneth, *Hoover and the Un-Americans. The FBI, HUAC, and the Red Menace.* Philadelphia, 1983.
—, *"Racial Matters". The FBI's Secret File on Black America, 1960-1972.* New York (1989), 1991.
—, *Nixon's Piano. Presidents and Racial Politics from Washington to Clinton.* New York, 1995.
Pencak, William, *For God and Country. The American Legion 1919-1941.* Boston, 1989.
Perkus, Kathy (ed.), *COINTELPRO. The FBI's Secret War on Political Freedom.* New York, 1976.
Peterson, H.C. and Gilbert C. Fite, *Opponents of War, 1917-1918.* Madison, Wis., 1957.
Powers, Richard Gid, *G-Men. Hoover's FBI in American Popular Culture.* Carbondale, 1983.
—, *Secrecy and Power. The Life of J. Edgar Hoover.* New York, 1987.
—, *Not Without Honor. The History of American Anticommunism.* New York, 1995.
Preston Jr., William, *Aliens and Dissenters. Federal Suppression of Radicals, 1903-1933.* Cambridge, Mass., 1963.
Radosh, Ronald and Joyce Milton, *The Rosenberg File. A Search for the Truth.* London, 1983.
Robins, Natalie, *Alien Ink. The FBI's War on Freedom of Expression.* New York, 1992.
Rogin, Michael Paul, *The Intellectuals and McCarthy: The Radical Specter.* Cambridge, Mass., & London, 1967.
Russell, Francis, *Sacco & Vanzetti. The Case Resolved.* New York, 1986.
Salter, J. T. (ed.), *Public Men in and out of Office.* Chapel Hill, 1946.
Schlesinger Jr., Arthur M. (ed.), *The Almanac of American History.* New York, 1983.
—, *Crisis of the Old Order, 1919-1933.* Boston, 1957.
—, *The Politics of Upheaval.* Cambridge, Mass., 1960.
Schrecker, Ellen, *Many Are the Crimes. McCarthyism in America.* Boston & New York, 1998.
Sklar, Martin J., *The United States as a Developing Country. Studies in US History in the Progressive Era and the 1920s.* Cambridge, 1992.
Small, Martin (ed.), *Public Opinion and Historians. Interdisciplinary Perspectives.* Detroit, 1970.
Smith, James Morton, *Freedom's Fetters. The Alien and Sedition Laws and American Civil Liberties.* Ithaca, N.Y., 1956.
Smith, Richard Norton, *An Uncommon Man. The Triumph of Herbert Hoover.* New York, 1984.
Stein, Judith, *The World of Marcus Garvey. Race and Class in Modern Society.* Baton Rouge, La., 1986.
Smith, Walker C., *Was It Murder? The Truth About Centralia.* Seattle, 1922.
Summers, Anthony, *Official and Confidential. The Secret Life of J. Edgar Hoover.* New York, 1993.
Tanenhaus, Sam, *Whittaker Chambers. A Biography.* New York, 1997.
Theoharis, Athan, *Seeds of Repression: Harry S. Truman and the Origins of McCarthyism.* Chicago, 1969.
— (ed.), *Beyond the Hiss Case: The FBI, Congress, and the Cold War.* Philadelphia, 1982.
—, *Spying on Americans. Political Surveillance From Hoover to the Huston Plan.* Philadelphia, 1978.
—and John Stuart Cox, *The Boss. J. Edgar Hoover and the Great American Inquisition.* New York (1988), 1990.

Thorsen, Niels Aage, *The Political Thought of Woodrow Wilson 1875-1910.* Princeton, N.J., 1988.

Tomlins, Christopher L, *The State and the Unions. Labor Relations, the Law, and the Organized Labor Movement in America, 1880-1960.* Cambridge (1985), 1989.

Tully, Grace, *F.D.R. My Boss.* New York, 1949.

Tuttle, William M., *Race Riot. Chicago in the Red Summer of 1919.* New York, 1975.

Tyler, Robert L., *Rebels of the Wood: The I.W.W. in the Pacific Northwest.* Eugene, Oregon, 1967.

Ungar, Sanford, *FBI.* Boston, 1976.

Vaughn, Stephen L., *Holding Fast the Inner Lines. Democracy, Nationalism, and the Committee on Public Information.* Chapel Hill, 1980.

Vile, M. J. C., *Politics in the USA.* 3rd. ed. London (1970), 1983.

Wade, Wyn Craig, *The Fiery Cross. The Ku Klux Klan in America.* New York (1987), 1988.

Walker, Samuel, *In Defense of American Liberties. A History of the ACLU.* New York & Oxford, 1990.

—, *The American Civil Liberties Union. An Annotated Bibliography.* New York, 1992.

Washburn, Patrick S., *A Question of Sedition. The Federal Government's Investigation of the Black Press During World War II.* New York, 1986.

Waskow, Arthur I., *From Race Riot to Sit-in, 1919 and the 1960s. A Study in the Connections Between Conflict and Violence.* New York, 1967.

Watters, Pat and Stephen Gillers (ed.), *Investigating the FBI.* New York (1973), 1974.

Weinstein, Allen, *Perjury. The Hiss-Chambers Case.* New York (1978), 1979.

— & Alexander Vassiliev, *The Haunted Wood. Soviet Espionage in America – The Stalin Era.* New York, 1999.

Weinstein, James, *The Corporate Ideal in the Liberal State: 1900-1918.* Boston, 1968.

—, *The Decline of Socialism in America 1912-1925.* New York, 1967.

Weiss, Nancy J., *The National Urban League 1910-1940.* New York, 1974.

Wheeler, Burton K. with Paul F. Healy, *Yankee From the West.* New York, 1962.

Whitehead, Don, *The FBI Story. A Report to the People.* New York, 1956.

Whitney, R. M., *Reds in America.* Belmont, Mass. (1924), 1970.

Who Was Who in America, Vols., I-IV. Chicago, 1968.

Wiebe, Robert H., *The Search for Order 1877-1920.* New York, 1967.

Williams, David J., *"Without Understanding": The FBI and Political Surveillance, 1908-1941.* Ph.D. Dissertation, University of New Hampshire, 1981.

Williams, T. Harry, *Huey Long.* New York (1969), 1981.

Wolfe, Alan, *The Seamy Side of Democracy. Repression in America.* New York, 1973.

Wolfskill, George and John A. Hudson, *All But the People. Franklin D. Roosevelt and His Critics 1933-39.* London, 1969.

Woodward, C. Vann, *The Strange Career of Jim Crow,* 3rd. ed. New York (1955), 1974.

Young, William and David E. Kaiser, *Postmortem. New Evidence in the Case of Sacco and Vanzetti.* Amherst, 1985.

Zangrando, Robert L, *The NAACP Crusade Against Lynching, 1909-1950.* Philadelphia, 1980.

4. Articles

Alexander, Jack, "Profiles: The Director," I-III, *The New Yorker,* September 25, 1937, 20-25; October 2, 1937, 21-26; October 9, 1937, 22-27.

Ambrose, Stephen E., "The Case Against Hoover," *The Washington Post Book World,* February 21, 1993, 4-5.

Auerback, Jerold S., "The La Follette Committee: Labor and Civil Liberties in the New Deal," *The Journal of American History,* Vol. Li, No. 3 (December 1964), 435-459.

Belknap, Michal R., "The Mechanics of Repression: J. Edgar Hoover, The Bureau of Investigation and the Radicals 1917-1925," *Crime and Social Justice,* Vol. 7 (Spring-Summer 1977), 49-58.

Blum, John M., "Nativism, Anti-Communism, and the Foreign Scare, 1917-1929," *The Midwest Journal,* Vol. III, No. 1 (Winter 1950-51), 46-53.

Boskin, Joseph, "The Rite of Purification: The FBI and the Black Historical Possibility," *Reviews in American History,* Vol. 11, No. 3 (September 1983), 472-478.

Bradsher, James Gregory, "The FBI Records Appraisal," *The Midwestern Archivist,* Vol. XIII, No. 2, 1988, 51-66.

Brands Jr., Henry William, "Unpremediated Lansing: His 'Scraps'," *Diplomatic History,* Vol. 9, No. 1 (Winter 1985), 25-33.

Brendon, Piers, "Our Own Big Brother," *Columbia Journalism Review,* Vol. 31 (March/April 1992), 50-51.

Burnham, James, "The FBI," *The Nation,* August 11/18, 1997, 11-24.

Candeloro, Dominic, "Louis F. Post and the Red Scare of 1920," *Prologue,* Vol. 11, No. 1 (Spring 1979), 40-55.

Cary, Lorin Lee, "The Bureau of Investigation and Radicalism in Toledo, Ohio: 1918-1920," *Labor History,* Vol. 21, No. 3 (Summer 1980), 430-440.

Coben, Stanley, "A Study in Nativism: The American Red Scare of 1919-20," *Political Science Quarterly,* Vol. LXXIX, No. 1 (March 1964), 52-75.

Cobb-Reiley, Linda, "Aliens and Alien Ideas: The Suppression of Anarchists and the Anarchist Press in America, 1901-1914," *Journalism History,* Vol. 15, Nos. 2-3 (Summer/Autumn 1988), 50-59.

Cohen, William, "Riots, Racism, and Hysteria: The Response of Federal Investigative Officials to the Race Riots of 1919," *The Massachusetts Review,* Vol. XIII, No. 3 (Summer 1972), 373-400.

Cooper, Jerry M., "The Army as Strikebreaker – The Railroad Strikes of 1877 and 1894," *Labor History,* Vol. 18, No. 2 (Spring 1977), 179-196.

Croog, Charles F., "FBI Political Surveillance and the Isolationist-Interventionist Debate, 1939-1941," *The Historian,* Vol. 54, No. 3 (Spring 1992), 441-458.

Davis, Colin J., "Bitter Conflict: The 1922 Railroad Shopmen's Strike," *Labor History,* Vol. 33, No. 4 (Fall 1992), 433-455.

Ellis, Mark, "J. Edgar Hoover and the 'Red Summer' of 1919," *Journal of American Studies,* Vol. 28, No. 1 (April 1994), 39-59.

Fine, Sidney, "Anarchism and the Assassination of McKinley," *The American Historical Review,* Vol. XL, No. 4 (July 1955), 777-779.

Fishbein, Leslie, "Federal Suppression of Leftwing Dissidence in World War I," *Potomac Review,* Vol. 6, No. 3 (Summer 1974), 47-68.

Foner, Philip S., "United States of America Vs. Wm. D. Haywood, et al.: The I.W.W. Indictment," *Labor History,* Vol. 11, No. 4 (Fall 1970), 500-530.

Forbath, William E., "The Shaping of the American Labor Movement," *Harvard Law Review,* Vol. 102, No. 6 (April 1989), 1111-1256.

Friedheim, Robert L., "The Seattle General Strike of 1919," *Pacific Northwest Quarterly,* Vol. 52, No. 3 (July 1961), 81-98.

—, "Prologue to a General Strike: The Seattle Shipyard Strike of 1919," *Labor History*, Vol. 6, No. 2 (Spring 1965), 121-142.

— and Robin Friedheim, "The Seattle Labor Movement, 1919-20," *Pacific Northwest Quarterly*, Vol. 55, No. 4 (October 1964), 146-156.

Galambos, Louis, "The Emerging Organizational Synthesis in Modern American History," *Business History Review*, Vol. XLIV, No. 3 (Autumn 1970), 279-290.

Gengarelly, W. Anthony, "Secretary of Labor William B. Wilson and the Red Scare, 1919-1920," *Pennsylvania History*, Vol. XLVI, No. 4 (October 1980), 311-330.

Gibson, James L., "The Policy Consequences of Political Intolerance: Political Repression During the Vietnam War Era," *The Journal of Politics*, Vol. 51, No. 1 (February 1989), 13-35.

—, "The Political Consequences of Intolerance: Cultural Conformity and Political Freedom," *American Political Science Review*, Vol. 86, No. 2 (June 1992), 338-356.

—, "Political Intolerance and Political Repression During the McCarthy Red Scare," *American Political Science Review*, Vol. 82, No. 2 (June 1988), 511-529.

Goldstein, Robert J., "The Anarchist Scare of 1908. A Sign of Tensions in the Progressive Era," *American Studies*, Vol. XV, No. 2 (Fall 1974), 55-78.

—, "Political Repression in Modern American History (1870-Present): A Selective Bibliography," *Labor History*, Vol. 32, No. 4 (Fall 1991), 526-550.

Gutfeld, Arnon, "The Ves Hall Case, Judge Bourquin, and the Sedition Act of 1918," *The Pacific Historical Review*, Vol. XXXVII, No. 2 (May 1968), 163-178.

Hacker, Barton C., "The United States Army as a National Police Force: The Federal Policing of Labor Disputes, 1877-1898," *Military Affairs*, Vol. 33, No. 1 (April 1969), 255-264.

Hawley, Ellis, "The Discovery and Study of 'Corporate Liberalism'," *Business History Review*, Vol. LII, No. 3 (Autumn 1978), 309-320.

—, "Herbert Hoover, the Commerce Secretariat, and the Vision of an 'Associative State', 1921-1928," *The Journal of American History*, Vol. LXI, No. 1 (June 1974), 116-140.

Hays, Samuel P., "The Social Analysis of American Political History, 1880-1920," *Political Science Quarterly*, Vol. LXXX, No. 3 (September 1965), 373-394.

Heale, M. J., "Red Scare Politics: California's Campaign Against Un-American Activities, 1940-1970," *Journal of American Studies*, Vol. 20 (1986), 5-32.

Hill, Robert A., "'The Foremost Radical Among His Race:' Marcus Garvey and the Black Scare, 1918-1921," *Prologue*, Vol. 16, No. 4 (Winter 1984), 215-231.

Hong, Nathaniel, "The Origin of American Legislation to Exclude and Deport Aliens for Their Political Beliefs, and Its Initial Review by the Courts," *The Journal of Ethnic Studies*, Vol. 18, No. 2 (Summer 1990), 1-36.

Irons, Peter H., "'Fighting Fair': Zechariah Chafee, Jr., the Department of Justice, and the 'Trial at the Harvard Club'," *Harvard Law Review*, Vol. 94, No. 6 (April 1981), 1205-1236.

Kennan, George F., "The Sisson Documents," *The Journal of Modern History*, Vol. XXVIII, No. 2 (June 1956), 130-154.

Kimball, Penn, "The History of The Nation According to the FBI," *The Nation*, March 22, 1986, 399-429.

Layton, Edwin, "The Better America Federation: A Case Study of Super-patriotism," *Pacific Historical Review,* Vol. XXX, No. 2 (May 1961), 137-147.

Leiren, Terje I., "Ole and the Reds: The 'Americanism' of Seattle Mayor Ole Hanson," *Norweigan-American Studies,* Vol. 30 (1985), 75-95.

Leuchtenburg, William E., "The Pertinence of Political History: Reflections on the Significance of the State in America," *The Journal of American History,* Vol. 73, No. 3 (December 1986), 585-600.

Maas, Peter, "Setting the Record Straight," *Esquire,* May 1993, 56-59.

McClelland, John M., Jr., "Terror on Tower Avenue," *Pacific Northwest Quarterly,* Vol. 57 (April 1966), 65-72.

McClymer, John F., "The Federal Government and the Americanization Movement, 1915-24," *Prologue,* Vol. 10, No. 1 (Spring 1978), 23-41.

McKelway, St. Clair, "A Reporter at Large: Some Fun with the F.B.I.," *The New Yorker,* October 11, 1941, 59-65.

Meier, August and Elliot Rudwick, "The Rise of Segregation in the Federal Bureaucracy, 1900-1930," *Phylon,* Vol. XXVIII, No. 2 (Summer 1967), 178-184.

Muraskin, William A., "The Social-Control Theory in American History: A Critique," *Journal of Social History,* Vol. 9, No. 4 (June 1976), 559-569.

Murphy, Paul L., "Sources and Nature of Intolerance in the 1920s," *The Journal of American History,* Vol. LI, No. 1 (June 1964), 60-76.

Murray, Robert K, "Communism and the Great Steel Strike of 1919," *The Mississippi Valley Historical Review,* Vol. XXXVIII, No. 3 (December 1951), 445-466.

—, "Centralia: An Unfinished American Tragedy," *Northwest Review,* Vol. 6, No. 2 (Spring 1963), 7-18.

New York Times, The, Articles 1919-20.

O'Reilly, Kenneth, "Herbert Hoover and the FBI," *Annals of Iowa,* Summer 1983, 46-63.

—, "A New Deal for the FBI: The Roosevelt Administration, Crime Control and National Security," *The Journal of American History,* Vol. 69, No. 3 (December 1982), 638-658.

—, "The Roosevelt Administration and Black America: Federal Surveillance Policy and Civil Rights During the New Deal and World War II Years," *Phylon,* Vol. XLVIII, No. 1 (March 1987), 12-25.

—, "The Roosevelt Administration and Legislative-Executive Conflict: The FBI vs. the Dies Committee," *Congress and the Presidency,* Vol. 10, No. 1 (Spring 1983), 79-93.

Overman, Lee S., "Reactionary Policies of Our Social Revolution," *The Forum,* Vol. LXII, No. 1 (July 1919), 41-47.

Palmer, Dewey H., "Moving North: Migration of Negroes During World War I," *Phylon,* Vol. XXVIII, No. 1 (Spring 1967), 52-62.

Pawa, J. M., "Black Radicals and White Spies: Harlem, 1919," *Negro History Bulletin,* Vol. 35, No. 2 (October 1972), 129-133.

Pinkerton, Robert A., "Detective Surveillance of Anarchists," *The North American Review,* Vol. 173, No. 5 (November 1901), 609-617.

Polenberg, Richard, "Franklin Roosevelt and Civil Liberties: The Case of the Dies Committee," *The Historian,* Vol. XXX, No. 2 (February 1968), 165-178.

Polsby, Nelson W., "Towards an Explanation of McCarthyism," *Political Studies,* Vol. 8, No. 3 (1960), 250-271.

Powers, Richard Gid, "Taking Hoover Out of Context," *The New Leader,* Vol. LXXV, No. 2 (February 10-24, 1992), 19-20.

Pratt, William C., "Using FBI Records in Writing Regional Labor History," *Labor History,* Vol. 33, No. 4 (Fall 1992), 470-482.

Propas, Frederick L., "Creating a Hard Line Toward Russia: The Training of State Department Soviet Experts, 1927-1937," *Diplomatic History,* Vol. 8, No. 3 (Summer 1984), 209-226.

Ragan, Fred D., "Justice Oliver Wendell Holmes, Jr., Zechariah Chafee, Jr., and the Clear and Present Danger Test for Free Speech: The First Year, 1919," *The Journal of American History,* Vol. 58, No. 1 (June 1971), 24-45.

Rosenfeld, Seth, "Keeping Secrets. The FBI's Information Bottleneck," *Columbia Journalism Review,* Vol. 31 (March/April 1992), 14-15.

Rosswurm, Steven and Toni Gilpin, "The FBI and the Farm Equipment Workers: FBI Surveillance Records as a Source for CIO Union History," *Labor History,* Vol. 27, No. 4 (Fall 1986), 485-505.

Scheiner, Seth M., "President Theodore Roosevelt and the Negro, 1901-1908," *The Journal of Negro History,* Vol. XLVII, No. 3 (July 1962), 169-182.

Seagle, William, "The American National Police," *Harper's Monthly Magazine,* November 1934, 751-761.

Seltzer, Alan L., "Woodrow Wilson as 'Corporate Liberal': Toward a Reconsideration of Left Revisionist Historiography," *The Western Political Quarterly,* Vol. XXX, No. 2 (June 1977), 183-212.

Sims, Robert C., "Idaho's Criminal Syndicalism Act: One State's Response to Radical Labor," *Labor History,* Vol. 15, No. 4 (Fall 1974), 511-527.

Small, Robert T., "A New Kind of Government Sleuth in Washington," *The Literary Digest,* Vol. 84, No. 4 (January 24, 1925), 44-46.

Steele, Richard W., "Franklin D. Roosevelt and His Foreign Policy Critics," *Political Science Quarterly,* Vol. 94, No. 1 (Spring 1979), 15-32.

Taft, Philip, "The Federal Trials of the IWW," *Labor History,* Vol. 3, No. 1 (Winter 1962), 57-91.

Theoharis, Athan, "The FBI and the American Legion Contact Program, 1940-1966," *Political Science Quarterly,* Vol. 100, No. 2 (Summer 1985), 271-286.

—, "The FBI's Stretching of Presidential Directives, 1936-1953," *Political Science Quarterly,* Vol. 91, No. 4 (Winter 1976-77), 649-672.

"'They Never Stopped Watching US'. A Conversation Between Roger Baldwin and Alan F. Westin," *The Civil Liberties Review,* November/December 1977, 18-25.

Ungar, Sanford J., "The F.B.I. on the Defensive Again," *The New York Times Magazine,* May 15, 1988, 46-47, 73-80.

Wakstein, Allen M., "The Origins of the Open-Shop Movement, 1919-1920," *The Journal of American History,* Vol. LI, No. 3 (December 1964), 460-475.

Walker, Samuel, "The Boss as Bureaucrat," *Reviews in American History,* Vol. 16, No. 3 (September 1988), 460-465.

Werking, Richard Hume, "Bureaucrats, Businessmen, and Foreign Trade: The Origins of the United States Chamber of Commerce," *Business History Review,* Vol. LII, No. 3 (Autumn 1978), 321-341.

Williams, David, "The Bureau of Investigation and Its Critics, 1919-1921: The Origins of Federal Political Surveillance," *The Journal of American History,* Vol. 68, No. 3 (December 1983), 560-579.

Wolgemuth, Kathleen L., "Woodrow Wilson and Federal Segregation," *The Journal of Negro History,* Vol. XLIV, No. 2 (April 1959), 158-173.

Wreszin, Michael, "'Gee But I'd Like to Be a G-Man'," *Reviews in American History,* Vol. 20 (June 1992), 258-263.

Index of Names

5/03 2 6/02